I0483508

PROCEEDINGS

POETICS AND PRAGMATISM

Building Technology Educators' Society
2017 National Meeting
Des Moines, IA

8-10 June, 2017

Editors

Shelby Doyle
Thomas Leslie
Robert Whitehead
Iowa State University

Scientific Committee

Diane Armpriest, University of Idaho
Caryn Brause, University of Massachusetts
Erin Carraher, University of Utah
Robert Dermody, Roger Williams University
Shelby Doyle, Iowa State University
Dana Gulling, North Carolina State University
John Kerner, University of Pennsylvania
Thomas Leslie, Iowa State University
Erin Moore, University of Oregon
Rashida Ng, Temple University
Deborah Oakley, University of Nevada, Las Vegas
Kate Simonen, University of Washington
Patrick Tripeny, University of Utah
Marci Uihlein, University of Illinois at Urbana-Champaign
Rob Whitehead, Iowa State University
Andrzej Zarzycki, New Jersey Institute of Technology

Proceedings: Poetics and Pragmatism, BTES 2017 Meeting, Des Moines, IA

©2017, Building Technology Educators' Society.
ISBN: 978-0-9895980-2-6

CONTENTS

SESSION 01: MAKING

Session Chair: Shelby Doyle
Iowa State University

SESSION 02: POETICS

Session Chair: Deborah Oakley
University of Nevada-Las Vegas

SESSION 03: CASE STUDIES

Session Chair: Robert Dermody
Roger Williams University

SESSION 04: MATERIALS

Session Chair: Marci Uihlein
University of Illinois at Urbana-Champaign

SESSION 05: STUDIO

Session Chair: Dana Gulling
North Carolina State University

SESSION 06: DIGITAL TOOLS I

Session Chair: Andrzej Zarzycki
New Jersey Institute of Technology

SESSION 07: TECTONICS

Session Chair: Diane Armpriest
University of Idaho

SESSION 08: HISTORY

Session Chair: Thomas Leslie
Iowa State University

SESSION 09: ATMOSPHERES

Session Chair: Naomi Darling
Five Colleges—Hampshire, Mt. Holyoke, UMass Amherst

SESSION 01: MAKING

Session Chair: Shelby Doyle
Iowa State University

Chad Schwartz, Southern Illinois University: "Examining Strategies For Delivering Design/Build Content In High-Enrollment Architecture Courses."

Margaret Kirk, California Polytechnic State University, San Luis Obispo: "Qualitative Collaboration."

Nathan Fash, Roger Williams University: "Widening The Field: Technology and the Developing World."

Examining Strategies for Delivering Design/Build Content in High-Enrollment Architecture Courses

Chad Schwartz
Southern Illinois University - Carbondale

Abstract

Design/build is a classification of practice in the architecture and construction fields in which the same entity both designs and builds a project. Starting in the 1960s, this practice has gradually made its way into the academic environment. Here, students generate a design and actively participate in transforming that design into a real structure or space. Over the past two decades, this pedagogical construct has become increasingly popular in schools of architecture for its ability to deliver a number of critical lessons to students through the first-hand experience of the integration of the poetics of design with the practicalities of assembly and construction.

Most academic design/build projects have a similar set of core objectives. These courses commonly "remove design projects from the studio vacuum and push students to reconcile their drawings with real structures they can build, weld, wire, and plumb. They encourage students to work as part of collaborative teams, resolving conflicts, managing finances, and communicating with clients."[1] Despite the success of many design/build programs, however, its pedagogy has been critiqued in recent studies, most notably in 2011 by W. Geoff Gjertson.[2] In a survey of design/build programs across the United States, Gjertson found that less than 15% of the programs responding *required* students to engage with the practice of design/build. This statistic is not surprising given that 93% of the respondents stated that their design/build courses operate in a studio-based model. Typically, a design/build studio is one of several studios offered in a semester to students in a given year of a program. This construct offers only a percentage of the student population the opportunity to engage in this academic forum. The ideal number of students for a design/build studio is also between seven and ten to allow for appropriate division of labor, student focus, and efficiency within the group,[3] again limiting the number of students impacted.

This paper presents efforts to expand the influence of the design/build experience within a school of architecture. It examines the strategies utilized over a three-year period to translate the learning experience of a design/build studio into a building technology course serving between 40 and 60 students each semester it is offered. Through five iterations of the class, several variables have been identified – including project complexity, group size, and partnerships – that have a significant impact on not only the success of the project, but also the learning experience of the students involved. The conclusion presents a series of best strategies for implementing design/build in a high(er)-enrollment architectural course.

Introduction[4]

Academic design/build is a pedagogical construct used to provide students an opportunity to actively participate in transforming their designs into real structures. This practice is not new, originating in 1960's, but over the past twenty years or so, its popularity in schools of architecture has significantly increased due to its ability to deliver critical lessons through first-hand experience. According to researcher W. Geoff Gjertson, in 2011 there were approximately 100 design/build programs underway in United States universities.[5] It is likely that in 2017 this number has increased. The projects undertaken by these groups vary greatly. "In some cases, design/build involves small structures built in and around the school; in others, the students spend weeks or even semesters living and building in places very remote from and very culturally different than their university classroom."[6] In other situations, design/build involves the creation of objects, furniture, and other full-scale endeavors in lieu of a building. In all cases, however, these courses involve the hands-on making of some portion of our built environment.

Design/build courses commonly "remove design projects from the studio vacuum and push students to reconcile their drawings with real structures they can build, weld, wire, and plumb. They encourage students to work as part of collaborative teams, resolving conflicts, managing finances, and communicating with clients."[7] The construct of the design/build curriculum, however, can impact the experience and absorption of learning objectives by the students. Gjertson found that less than 15% of the programs responding to his survey request *required* students to learn in a design/build environment. This result is not surprising given that 93% of the respondents indicated that their design/build programs operated in a design studio model. In a given semester, most schools offer multiple design studios at each level; when design/build is offered in a studio, it can be assumed in most cases (certainly not in all cases) to be one of several options for students. The design/build studio ideally operates with a small number of students, perhaps in the ten to twelve range. As such, only a portion of the students in a typical program will have the opportunity to participate in this type of design/build experience.

Technical courses typically operate in a lecture or lecture/lab construct where all of the students in a given year of the program attend the same class. As such, the technical course has the potential to reach a much larger audience (potentially the entire audience) than the design studio in delivering design/build content in a school of architecture. This paper reflects on the use of design/build in a foundation level building technology course over the past five years. Over this timespan, around 260 second year architecture and interior design students have engaged in two distinctly different types of design/build activities. The first involved the building of residential wall sections, while the second involved building a variety of project types at a regional environmental education center. This study serves as an attempt to quantify and qualify the experience for the students in relationship to how well the projects fulfill the learning objectives of the course. It also seeks to understand the level of success in the effort to translate the potency of the design/build studio into this distinctly different course construct serving an average of fifty students each semester.

The study builds on two previous works published after year three in the program. The first, "Constructing Experience: Exploring Design/Build Strategies within a Technology Course," was delivered at the Fall ACSA Conference in 2014 and highlighted the relative success of the two different project types to meet the course learning objectives. The second paper, "Debating the Merits of Design/Build: Assessing Pedagogical Strategies in an Architectural Technology Course," expanded the discussion to include a range of other issues confronted with the process of transitioning design/build to a building technology course. In the past two years, the design/build projects offered to the students have been configured to respond to the results of the initial research. This paper offers insights and reflections on the continued trajectory of this endeavor.

Course and Project Structure

This introductory technology course is a core offering in the architecture and interior design programs and centers on developing an understanding of wood construction. Taken in the spring semester, the primary course content is delivered through (2) one-hour lectures each week while (2) two-hour labs provide a forum for instruction in construction documents and Building Information Modeling [BIM]. The lab sessions also provide an arena for the exploration of the course's projects. Each year the students complete three projects. The first project is a short introductory exercise and has varied from year to year. The second project is the design/build component and the subject of this paper. Finally, the third project is centered on the generation of a small set of BIM manufactured construction documents for a wood light frame building.

Design/Build 2012: Courtyard Build I

Design/build was introduced to this technology course in 2012. In the initial iteration, groups of six or seven students were presented with a sectional drawing of a single-story, wood light frame residence. The students were required to study the drawing and develop a strategy for building a 4'-0" wide mock-up of the wall.

The working process for the project emphasized translation. Each group completed the design of the wall, generated a parts list from their design, created a cost estimate from the parts list, and, finally, developed a storyboard detailing the construction sequencing and scheduling. After all submittals were approved by the faculty, the student groups built their wall sections at full scale in the courtyard of the architecture building. The build was accomplished in a single day, with demolition coming the following week (Figure 1). After completion of the project, each group was required to submit a photo narrative of their process.

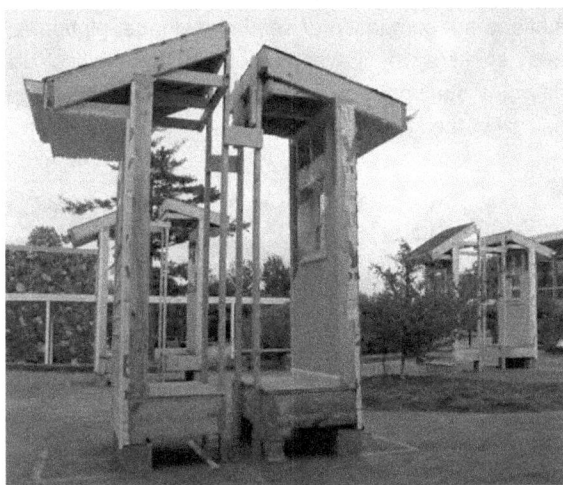

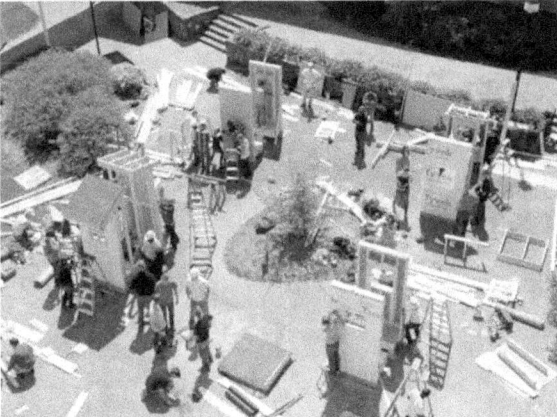

Fig. 1. Images of 2012 Courtyard Build. Photos by Author.

Design/Build 2013: Courtyard Build II

The 2013 design/build project was identical in process to that in 2012. This year, however, the student groups were asked to build a corner of the building instead of a simple wall span. The students were also responsible for designing and building a custom opening in their wall in lieu of the traditional window used the previous year.

Design/Build 2014: Hillside Build

In 2014, the course was awarded a grant from the University to initiate a design/build project at a regional environmental education center. The center is located within a 3100 acre forest preserve that serves a wide variety of University and non-University programs. After a survey of the property and discussion with staff, the faculty decided to focus the efforts of the students on the rebuilding of a hillside amphitheater. The structure was in poor condition, but utilized frequently by the campers and other visitors to the center. In addition to reaching the center's primary users, the project required no electrical, mechanical, or plumbing work; simplified engineering limited the necessary interaction with the local unions. The rigorous working process established with the 2012 build was adapted to the complexity of this community based design/build. As the class is divided into three lab sections, each was assigned one facet of the project to complete: the stage, the primary seating area, or the threshold and rest stop. The three components comprise a total footprint of 1400 gsf.

The amphitheater project began with a site visit. After this trip, the students worked in pairs to generate schematic designs for their facet of the project – coordinating with students in the other labs to create cohesive design strategies for the overall project – which were presented to the center staff for final selection. After receiving a decision, each lab was divided into four task groups for project development. The timeframe and project scope necessitated each group to focus on specific tasks: material list and cost analysis, storyboard and construction sequence, site analysis and construction documentation, or mockups and models. This process required significant coordination between task groups and between lab sections. The creation of the task groups also alleviated the majority of the student disengagement that could have occurred from not having ownership in the chosen design, replacing potential disappointment with new responsibilities. At the conclusion of design and documentation, the project moved to the site (Figure 2). Students were required to attend three build days and were rewarded with extra credit for attending additional days. As with the previous builds, the project ended with the creation of a summary document of the project's process along with a set of redline or as-built drawings.

Design/Build 2015: ELOO Build

Following the amphitheater project and the initial reflections on the process of integrating design/build into the course, the design/build program continued its work at the environmental education center. The process and general working construct remained very similar to that of the previous year, but instead of one large project, the students were divided into smaller groups (as they were in 2012 and 2013) with each group working on its own project. This semester, the focus was the development of a series of six enclosures for new composting toilets to be located in the remote areas of the center's property.

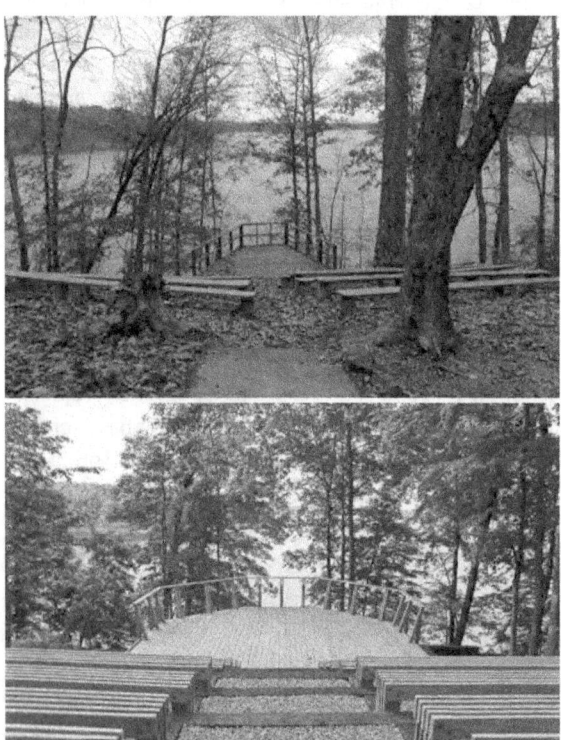

Fig. 2. Before (top) and After (bottom) images of 2014 Hillside Build. Photos by Author.

It should be noted that this project was the only one in the five year timespan to remain uncompleted at the end of the semester. Due to circumstances involving the campus labor force and the installation of the plumbing fixtures along with the limited timeframe available for another training operation to pour the concrete slabs-on-grade, the project was halted towards the end of the semester with the enclosures partially prefabricated and ready for installation in

place. Half of the enclosures have since been fully installed by the center's staff and a volunteer labor force.

Design/Build 2016: Trail Build

The most recent iteration of the design/build project parallels the structure of the 2015 build of the composting toilet enclosures. The project for this semester asked the student groups to design and build a series of educational stations along a new trail system being developed for the center (Figure 3). The stations are composed of seating, signage, platforms, and shelters in a variety of configurations. Six different stations were built by the class over the course of the semester.

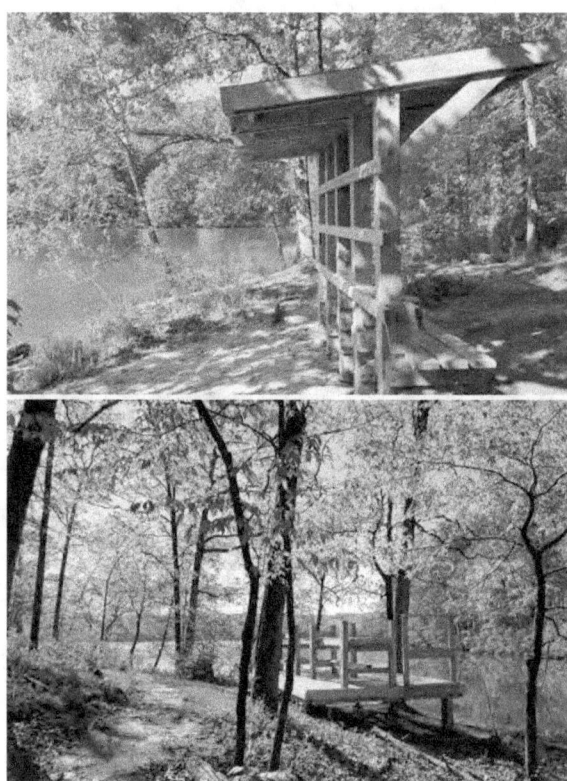

Fig. 3. Images of 2016 Trail Build. Photos by Author.

Project Analysis

Timeframe

No single component has a more significant impact on an academic design/build project than *time*. Large, complex design/build endeavors frequently span multiple semesters, but as that is not a possibility in this building technology course that is only offered once per academic year, the discussion must stay within the bounds of a single semester design/build project. First, a comparison must be made between the available time for design/build in this technology course and a typical upper division design studio. A typical studio has around twelve contact hours per week (will vary per university) and we will assume eight weeks of design and eight weeks of build in a single semester effort. This building technology course has six contact hours per week. Given the fact that students are concurrently enrolled in design studio and that there are other requirements to satisfy for this course, three scheduled class days were all that could be dedicated to the build process. Therefore, while a design studio will have around 96 class hours dedicated to construction, this building technology course has 9 class hours dedicated as such (or less than 10% of those available in studio). With so few dedicated hours, a design/build project in this environment needs to be efficient and certainly far less complex than those undertaken in the studio.

The initial Courtyard Build projects excelled with the limited timeframe. Most groups were able to build their projects in a single day, with a handful requiring part of a second build day in 2013. The third day is then saved for demolition and recycling of materials. When participating in community-based design/build however, time became much more of an issue. The Hillside Build, in particular, was substantially more complex. In addition to the three required build days, eighteen additional days were necessary to complete the project. About 70% of the class participated in one or more of the additional build days.

The two final builds attempted to mitigate the significant need for additional time by limiting the scope and complexity of the projects. In particular, the Trail Build project was able to limit the need for additional build days to five, a much more reasonable number. Additionally, as the groups worked on their own projects, those that operated more efficiently and finished faster were able to wrap up their projects even earlier. Although the available timeframe works well for the on-campus builds (which were designed to work within the timeframe), the latter constructs also proved to be fairly optimal for delivering design/build education while retaining the ability to serve the community through service learning.

Scope

Second in importance only to time, and significantly intertwined with it, is the *scope* of the design/build project undertaken. While certainly having an impact on the ability to get the project done by the end of the semester (as explained above), project scope is important for other reasons as well. In the first two years, the students worked in small groups on individual projects, resulting in eight or nine built pieces each of the semesters. The projects were relatively simple, but, more critically, they were virtually identical to each other. The variations between the constructions were limited as most of the design work was not completed by the students. As such, although there were a high number of student projects to oversee by one faculty member, their similarity allowed for a manageable process.

This was not the case in the past two years with the ELOO and Trail Builds. Although there were fewer groups in each of these two years than there were with the Courtyard Builds, each group had a distinctly different design, leading to more work to coordinate and monitor the overall process. Each group's project had its own set of unique details, materials, and challenges that could not be addressed to the class as a whole. Resultantly, the process was much more cumbersome and required significantly more effort from the faculty than in previous years given the previously mentioned limit on weekly contact hours.

Contrasting the multi-project approach is the single-project approach that was utilized in the Hillside Build. Although certainly easier to manage with a single design scheme and focus, it presented a series of unique challenges as well. One primary challenge is that of division of labor, which will be discussed in the following section on Learning Objectives. Another of those challenges is the notion of ownership. With a single project and fifty students, the sense of ownership can become diluted for those students who have not had a direct contribution to the design or technical concepts being utilized in the project. This was most certainly the case with the Hillside Build and was evident in the extra build days. Although 70% of the students participated in the extra days, only about 25% were there for more than one or two of the extra days. These were the students who had established ownership. In the multi-project model, fewer students are responsible for a single designed work and, as such, there is a far greater possibility of the majority of the students believing the work is in some way their own. The larger the group becomes, the more likely there will be students who can become divested from that ownership role. This past year with the Trail Build, the number of consistent participants in the extra build days was substantially higher than that of the Hillside Build.

Place

The site and context of a project is of prime importance in any design/build course. In a high(er) enrollment building technology course, however, place plays a role in the ability to supervise the students and their work. In the first two years of the project, the course had its highest enrollments of 69 and 61 students respectively. However, because all of the construction occurred in a very limited and contained area in the courtyard lab-space, it was relatively easy for a single faculty member along with one graduate assistant to effectively monitor the projects, assist with questions, problem solve challenges, and maintain a safe working environment. Additionally, as the construction happened literally in the middle of the school of architecture, other faculty and staff assisted throughout the build day as they were close at hand and drawn out by the activity.

The community-based projects were significantly more difficult to monitor. The Hillside Build involved a project site that was a quarter-mile from the material drop site. It also consisted of three separate areas, which sat remote from each other: the main amphitheater site, the rest stop bench site, and an open air pavilion that was utilized as our project wood shop and closest source of electricity. This arrangement of space made the site more difficult to monitor as it could not all be seen from one vantage point. Time was wasted in transit between the locations that was not used in the Courtyard Builds. Two additional graduate assistants were utilized to help combat this issue, which helped considerably, but each was generally assisting with the build itself due to the complexity of the project instead of monitoring the overall safety and status of the jobsite.

The Trail Build was the most complex due to the nature of the place. Components of all of the

structures were pre-manufactured in a common shop facility set up at the environmental center. This provided a single location for monitoring much of the initial construction. When site elements were built and the prefabricated components were installed at their permanent locations, however, the situation changed drastically. The educational stations were spread out along a 3/4 mile hiking trail. The only way to monitor the construction was to walk the trail back and forth and then drive to the shop facility to check in on the fabrication process. The entire circuit could take an hour or more, leaving a great deal of time for each group to be without both supervision and an outlet to ask questions. In order to ease these issues, six graduate students were enlisted – one to assist each of the groups as mentors. This system worked fairly well, but required much more coordination than earlier models. While the decentralization of the project into individual groups was beneficial in some ways, with this particular point, it increased the complexity of the process and decreased the ability for the faculty to properly evaluate the ongoing status of the project.

Learning Objectives

As is true of all university courses, this building technology course is responsible for delivering a series of learning objectives to the students it serves. In this particular case, those objectives are derived from four separate sources: the School's master syllabi, the accreditation boards for architecture and interior design "The National Architectural Accrediting Board [NAAB] and the Council for Interior Design Accreditation [CIDA]), and the specific curricular imperatives of the course's faculty. Figure 4 outlines all of the course objectives and rates the five iterations of the design/build project on their ability to deliver those objectives to the student body via a three point scale of meets, partially meets, and does not meet. There are 26 total objectives for the course, although there are a handful that have near duplicates cross-category. Fifteen of those objectives are assigned to be at least partially satisfied by this project (in bold text) while the other eleven are primarily delivered through other course components. The percentage score attributed to each iteration of the design/build project is based on a 2/1/0 points sum divided by the total number of points available. In the final calculation, more weight was given to the objectives specifically assigned to this project.

Fig. 4. Comparative chart of course learning objectives.

The level of fulfillment of each objective was derived from a careful analysis of the project process from each semester. For each objective, a chart was developed that listed primary traits of a given project that either created a case for or against it meeting the assigned objective (Figure 5). Taken in to consideration were not only the lessons and the experiences available to the students, but the ability for the majority of the class to attain those experiences. The project takes place in a group learning/working environment. As such, a division of labor is a necessary component of navigating and completing the assignments. Group size plays a significant role in this process. In larger groups, the division of labor is typically greater and the ability to disseminate critical information throughout the entire group lessens. The same is true with an increase in complexity. As such, although the Hillside Build was the single most impressive undertaking in the course, its reality as a single, large-scale build worked on by three larger groups created a situation in which many students in the class only experienced a small part of the entire set of learning objectives. The specialization was too great and the transfer of knowledge too difficult given the timespan of the project and the complexity of the process needed to complete it. This project has a relatively low score compared to the other projects for just this reason.

Conclusion

This paper outlines just a small portion of the study currently underway in reflecting on the potential for and the future use of design/build pedagogy in this context. Two years ago, the initial version of this study led to significant changes in project, engagement, and group structures for the design/build project. In the last two iterations, this latest study has revealed that those changes were successful in increasing the learning potential for the students going through the program.

It is very difficult to assess relative individual success in this type of group working environment as individual performance can be skewed for a number of reasons. This course uses group evaluation surveys at three points during the semester (along with faculty observation during construction) to ensure that all participants are contributing relatively equally. The project assessment, however, is done for the group (not individually) except in special situations revealed through the surveys. As such, this reflective study has also tracked the performance of the students on their major individual project, which runs concurrent to the design/build project for the last twelve weeks of the semester. The thought behind this strategy is that too much of an increase in complexity of the design/build project could result in a negative impact on each student's performance in the rest of the course. The data backed up this assumption as there was a drop in performance of about six percent on the individual project between 2013 and 2014 when the design/build complexity was significantly increased (overall scores in the class only dropped about 1% over this same span). They bounced back in 2016 with the optimization of the Trail Build project. Other points of analysis concur with this finding.

Fig. 5. Sample objective comparison study.

A great deal has been learned over the past five years about how best to utilize design/build within an entry level technology course. The lessons provided through this means of studying architecture and design are invaluable for students moving through the design fields, allowing them to engage more thoroughly with the practice, their own design work, the community, and their classmates and faculty. Focusing on small-group scale projects located in the community and requiring relatively simple

construction procedures has been the focus of the past two years of work since the initial study. Moving forward, especially in a time of university of cost-cutting, projects will continue this trend while also striving to stay more compact in their distribution to ease the substantial amount of graduate assistant participation required to properly monitor, for example, all of the stations of the Trail Build simultaneously. The development of projects that can be fabricated efficiently and with minimal additional oversight will be essential in this environment. In addition, projects need to be sought out that can be at least partially funded and supported by external sources.

It is imperative that through this process of design/build, each student in the class is given ample opportunity to not just end up with a successful project, but to engage with their group mates in a rigorous and thorough working process that delivers as many required learning objectives as possible. In this type of environment, no two students are going to have the same experience, but they all should have one that is equal in quality and one that will be impactful on their future career trajectory.

Notes:

[1] Joseph Bilello, "Learning from Construction," *Architecture* 85, no. 8 (1996): 145

[2] W. Geoff Gjertson, "House Divided: Challenges to Design/Build from Within," in *2011 ACSA Fall Conference* (Houston, Texas, October 6, 2011).

[3] William Carpenter, *Learning by Building: Design and Construction in Architectural Education* (New York: Van Nostrand Reinhold, 1997). and Gjertson, "House Divided."

[4] The Introduction and Course and Project Structure sections of this paper are derived from those of the earlier study: Chad Schwartz, "Debating the Merits of Design/Build: Assessing Pedagogical Strategies in and Architectural Technology Course," *Journal of Applied Sciences and Arts*, 1, no. 1 (2015): 1-14.

[5] Gjertson, "House Divided," 23.

[6] Chad Schwartz, Laura Morthland, and Shannon McDonald, "Building a Social Framework: Utilising Design/Build to Provide Social Learning Experiences for Architecture Students," *Architectural Theory Review* 19, no. 1 (2014): 78.

[7] Bilello, "Learning from Construction," 145.

Qualitative Collaboration

Margaret Kirk
California Polytechnic State University, San Luis Obispo

Abstract

Building, as a practice, occupies an interesting and complex paradigm in seeking to reconcile the poetics of design with the technicalities (pragmatics) of construction. What is sought- the collaboration of a team that is to envelop both through a design project- is itself a paradox.

Although they are to work seamlessly on the same project, the partnership between architects, engineers and other disciplines that could add value to the design process are often separated from each other- thus partitioning system design which should evolve towards integration with the use of advanced fabrication techniques and access to technology. This paper shall explore the roles collaboration (in multiple forms) should take if the design process is to evolve in regards to integrative system design as it relates to *technological architecture*.

The content of this paper examines the common ground, through process, in which design teams comprised of multiple disciplines partner and face the shared problem of designing a building to be symbiotic with the environment in challenging scale and network. This project- starting with the conception of architecture as an organism- seeks to abstract the design process in order to divorce discipline (in function as well as in task) from expected and assumed roles. Through this abstraction, the problem opens itself to a larger field, breaks down rank and thus, the network of collaboration is blurred. This, in turn, spawns a new level of creativity through innovation to take architecture out of its proverbial box- both literally and figuratively- via the auspice of connection- that of a broad and encompassing definition.

The abstraction of the project is the first part of the process in seeking to question form, structure and materiality to harvest bioclimatic flows for the initial project. This process then shifts to building design in recognizing the feedback loops from the abstraction for translation to integrative building systems in design. The model of the abstraction is the manifestation of the process steeped in a network in which no singular aspect has greater hierarchy than others. It itself must function as a field.

This process is not limited to integrated system design but is a more expansive and enveloping model for the team involved. The development of the project relates the technicalities of systemic, ecological design based in the abstraction to building construction and is shared by multiple disciplines in creating architecture. The project serves as the investigation of the means and a question of process.

The means, in the end, essentially becomes one of connection- connection to the system, connection to the site and the program but also connection to the vast definition of 'team'. This addresses the crux at which the poetics and pragmatics of the project and process meet, keeping in mind that it may not be manifest as physical form.

A Model for the Role of Technology in Design

The Manimal

In UNStudio's article *Hybridization*[1], we are introduced to the *Manimal*- the output of a man, lion and snake as the result of technology (software). The unique identity of the product, *Manimal*, is the seamlessly amalgamated parts, in which it is challenging, if not impossible, to find the boundary/ limits between the component parts and in turn a new being is created. At the core of the *Manimal* investigation is the question of design as a technological and computational derivative- a tool that is fundamentally evolving the practice of architecture and the roles of those involved. The *Manimal*, as an analogy, demonstrates a new credo in regards to technology that exposes a process that is not rooted in a traditional lineage of design but one that must

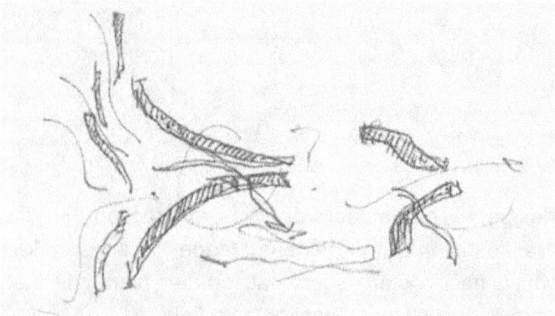

Fig. 1. Investigation of form through sketch. Margaret Kirk.

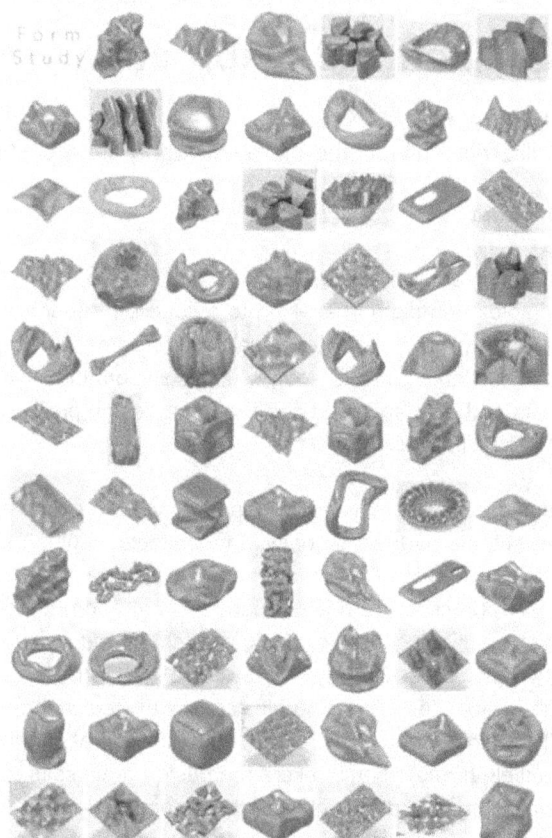

Fig. 2. Formal studies. Aleksa Salve, Caroline Dunn

evolve to be more open and collaborative and like the *Manimal*, the parts of the whole cannot be distinguishable from each other. Instead the *Manimal*, through its development in technology, has spawned its own independence and thus cannot be categorized any longer- it is its own being with its own traits (performance).

Technological Architecture in Redefinition

Architecture and building technology (technological architecture) are increasingly questioned for authorship, especially in regards to parametric and computational design. Through this process, design is often perceived as being devoid of authenticity in its lack of authorship- much like the *Manimal*. However, in order to examine technological architecture, we must displace it from traditional understandings of architecture. The *Manimal* is difficult to categorize as it does not favor any lineage. Its origins are ambiguous. Technological architecture faces the same criticisms. Just as the *Manimal* is the indefinable product of technology, architecture in this light is *also* the indefinable product of technology. However, what may seem to be devoid of meaning (according to this definition) is the opposite. On the contrary, technology and the *Manimal* are steeped in historicity and meaning though performance. What is important to note is that this is not a singular function but one that is fluid as a relationship. The relationships through this methodology are indistinguishable from the whole and present a fluctuating and constant reading and re-reading of being.

Performative Architecture as Site

The ontological relationship of technology and architecture is becoming ever more paramount specifically as architecture is becoming more performative. Architecture, in seeking to become increasingly symbiotic as an ecological organism, is the coalescence of material, geometry and bioclimatic information[2] as an interface (site) in which the role of material and structure is indivisible from ecology. This approach is the technical evolution of design through the manifestation of the *Fourth Industrial Revolution*[3]- the purported technological era in which we are enraptured. It is the era of confrontation with new modes and methodologies of digital design, computational analysis and fabrication and as such, it is fundamentally changing the way we design and build and is opening architecture to truly

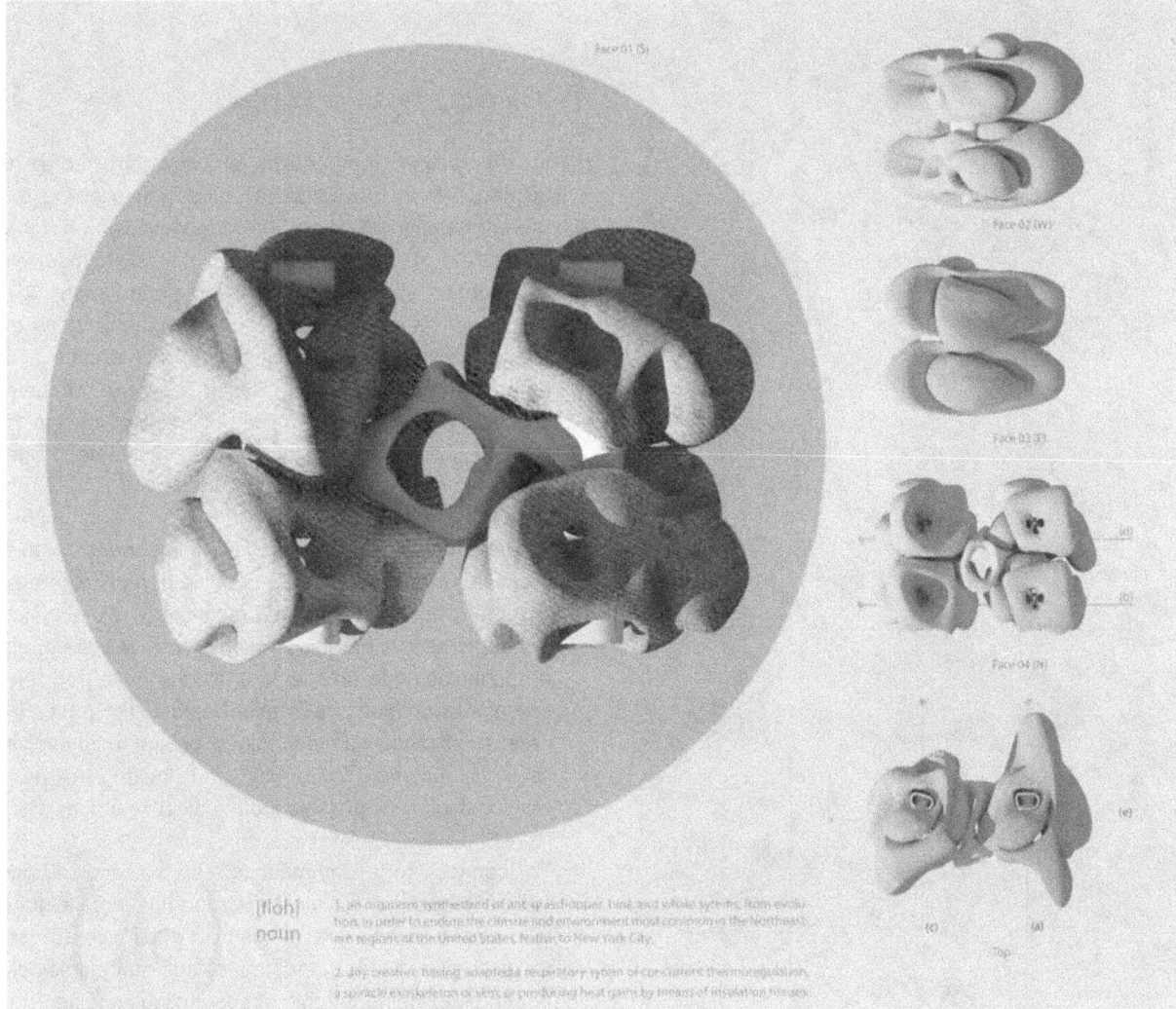

Fig. 3. Flu. Architecture as organism. Nathanael Ramos, Tess Radisch.

transformative investigations. The hallmark of this new industrial revolution is marked by the fusion of the biological, digital and physical- leading to the dissolution of traditional order, category and compartment because at its core is a seamless and interconnected matrix that extends beyond architecture into the technium[5]- the synthesis of technology and culture.

In architecture, we are witnessing its influence in ecologically integrated design- an emerging platform based in biomimicry through which architecture is burgeoning an independence via feedback loops-dependent upon behavior-based design. This behavior-based design differs from traditional, 'sustainable' architecture in that it is purely performative. By virtue of this ethos, behavior-based design allows architecture to become more ecologically integrated while granting the designer greater freedom to analyze more perceptively and

thus foster a greater level of creativity with the ability to examine a problem multi-dimensionally via the inspired development of form, intentional materiality and investigation of intuitive structural systems- those based on modeling in their conception and development as opposed to strict calculation. These ideals may not necessarily be new to architecture but are now readily possible in their manifestation through advancements in computational design and fabrication and thus, the required cross-pollination with disciplines not traditionally associated with architecture. Because of this new industrial revolution, architecture has the potential to connect to a much larger matrix of technology and culture. It is amid the joints and connections where architecture meets this matrix.

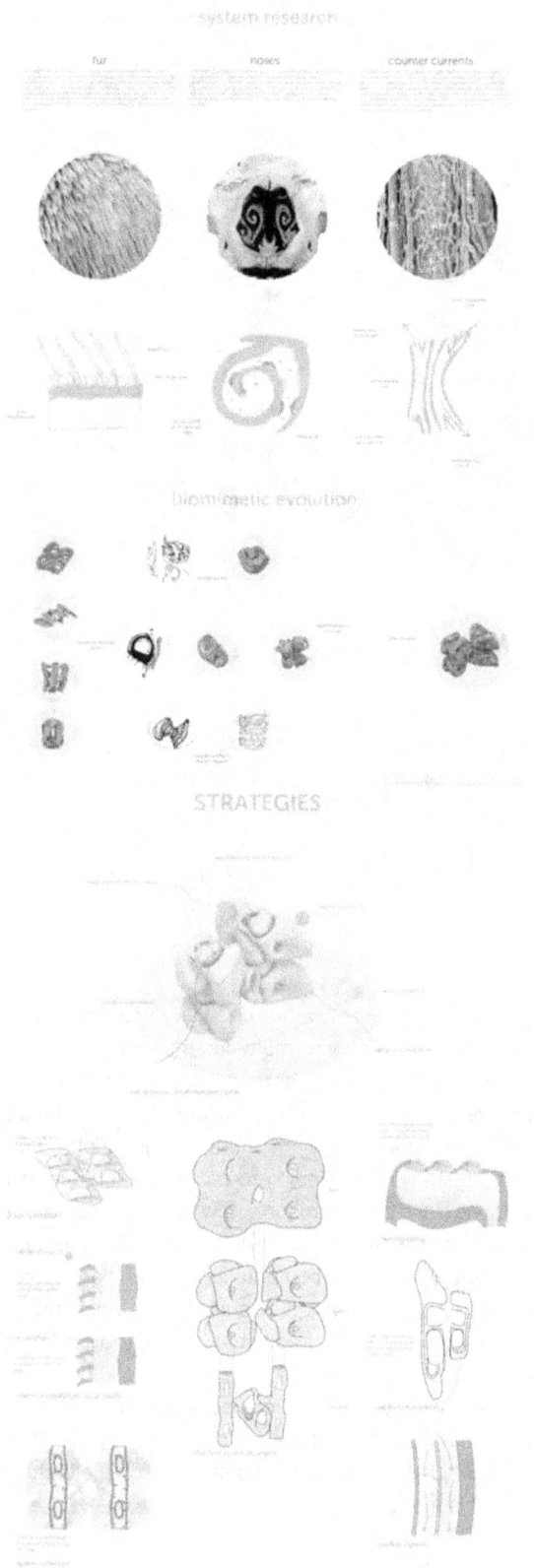

Fig. 4,5. Strategies. Nathanael Ramos, Tess Radisch.

Abstracting the Design Process

In abstracting the design process, the core is displaced from the sensibility of design allowing for the interrelation of points and connections within the larger field of site to clarify and manifest themselves as opposed to following a predetermined path- one that could be rooted in design strategies or rules of thumb. Program placement based on narrative and ethereal experience as design drivers become secondary where the real embodiment of design is through the investigation of systems and performance.

The abstraction of design is of base importance in this process simply because the practice of architecture is not changing at the rate that technology is changing. Although there is progressively a greater envelopment of technology into architecture, for the most part, the process of architecture is still rooted in the past. In order to advance with technology, design must evolve itself in flattening hierarchy and looking to new relationships through which to manifest its process.

To connect to an immediate site as ecologically integrated design, we must question how architecture is to evolve in the wake of this new order with access to innovative design and fabrication methodologies and thus, examine the role of abstraction in design.

Biological organisms have evolved with utmost efficiency and economy. Highly engineered and efficient beings, they're a model for architecture to come into its own through function as defined as the sum of the fusion of its constituents. In abstracting our preconceived notions about architecture, we are better able to analyze the role of technology in building design.

Through this process of design, architecture seeks the fittest forms and definition of system design that evolves as it grows more complex. Systemic design incurs a complexity with the integration found in nature in recycling everything, fitting form to function, awarding cooperation, banking on diversity, utilizing local expertise, curbing excess from within, tapping the power of limits and being beautiful[6]. The more architecture recognizes this, the more architecture truly becomes performative and ecologically integrated without the need for applied technologies.

Performance, then, is not evaluated through *additive* technologies but *integrated* technologies.

This word, *integration*, stands at the heart of this investigation and is crucial to the performance of technological architecture in redefining the relationship between form and function. New questions of aesthetics in regards to form *is* function have the potential to profoundly change the way we value architecture. Value as a performance metric thus re-defines the aesthetic based on how well it executes function versus in composition, proportion, etc. In such, the role of the designer may envelop the process of defining (or creating as may be possible in this new technological era) new materials as required by design. However, this necessitates that the designer look beyond their discipline in order to truly examine the limits of design. What we may find in the future are *Manimals* in their own right- the redefinition of the design role and/or designer. In this process, the design team must seek to wear many hats as well as fusing seamlessly with other disciplines to further the exploration of form, material and structure (among a field of possibilities) in order to push design- and thus the meaning of design- to and past its limits.

Meaning Through Performance

The evolution of materiality is not based in the capacity of the material itself but the actualization of a material. In focusing on performance in materiality, materials have evolved with purpose. However, this interaction is not without constraint. The states of these systems are essentially infinite where their actuality is not[7]. For example, materials on their own could potentially perform multiple functions; however, they gain meaning and constraint through purpose. It is in that vein that performative architecture and the generation of form through function is very specific under the limits of this exploration. Where form and space are potentially infinite, they are constrained through performative design. This becomes a question of definition. The role of form and function and the consequence of either has been historically an architectural conundrum. This process sees performance as the form and the form is resultant of the performance. That is the new definition of aesthetics in the age of technological architecture. This connection to aesthetics extends

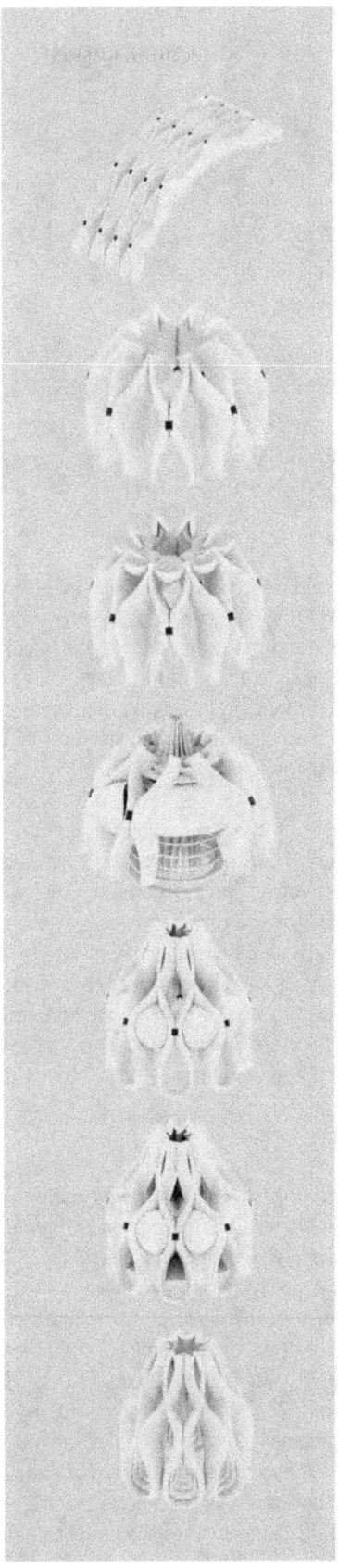

Fig. 6. Evolution of form. Nico Unverzagt, Lewei Wang.

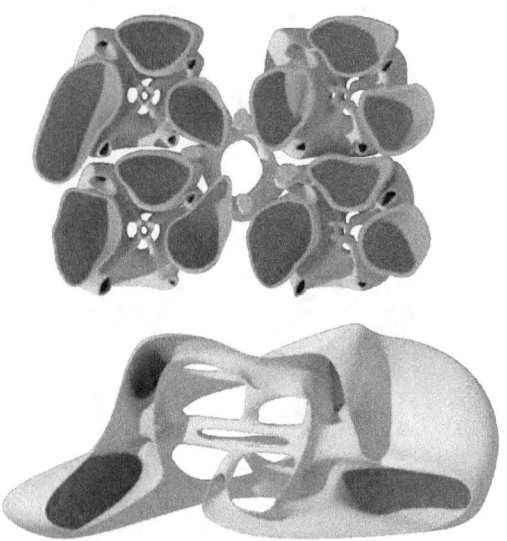
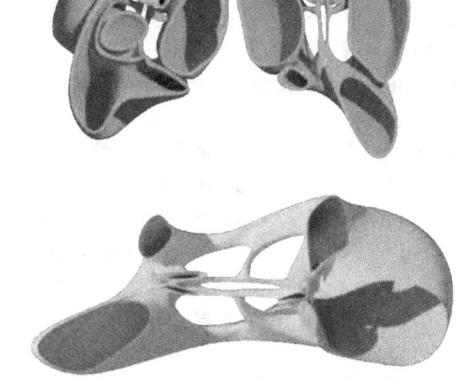

Fig. 7. Organism sections. Nathanael Ramos.

technology and performance into the realm of culture. Technological architecture thus gains new, heightened meaning in placing architecture within the *technium* in connecting architecture to technology and technology to culture.

The space of the technological culture is that of information. This space of reception is the abstraction and has evolved with precision. The value in the abstraction of this model lies in the space of interaction and discovery that is at its core. The assessment of value is not through the end result but through the process to evolve architecture in this new space- for architecture to be seamless with information and technology.

In Project

In practice, this investigation was performed through the architecture studio, *Pragmatic Geometry*, held at California Polytechnic State University. The studio began by creating an organism- an exercise in generating a *Manimal* of sorts- which served as the abstraction. It was the examination and incorporation of systems into the abstraction that were truly integrative. These systems, rooted in biomimicry, could combine both plant and animal traits as required. These traits were not in attitude but in how unique characteristics of an organism allowed the organism to evolve to its home climate through

material and form. The key to the development of the organism as abstraction was questioning the purpose through which it was designed and activated in its role as part of a network or feedback loop connecting its survival to the climate in which it 'lives'. It was imperative through this process to recognize that this feedback loop is not at one scale and hence, requires the exercise to work at multiple scales simultaneously- not only on the macro scale but the micro, or even nano, scale.

This investigation eventually translated itself to building form but with the studio gaining new insight into the role of materials and assemblies in integrated building system design and how geometry and materiality evolve with new meaning as networked systems of performance.

This process questions the scale at which system design operates in recognizing that buildings should be designed to *also* be symbiotic with the climate in which they 'live'. Because of this, it forces the designer and team to re-examine and truly scrutinize design based on performance. This also questions the scale of the design- often forcing the designer to explore roles outside their own and expanding their knowledge in the possibilities that networked systems may encompass.

The abstraction of the design process tested architecture as a post-orthogonal investigation- feasible in construction ascribable to the continued advancements in fabrication offered by the technological revolution and the race for better fabrication processes and modularity. Building systems were not inserted into a box structure as they so often are. Instead, the form the building is the performance and the building systems support the formal and material logic to the point that they cannot be distinguished from each other and are a performative whole (a *Manimal* in its own right). This requires a break (hence the abstraction of the organism) from the understanding of traditional buildings systems in incorporating passive systems that rely heavily on the bioclimatic flows and climate resources from the site- either extending the definition of 'site' well beyond property lines and formal boundaries or the reverse and defining site as a material condition. That is a point of exploration. As such, the architectural problem presents itself as a field condition- that of feedback loops and information as ecologically integrated architecture. This also includes the incorporation of program within the building.

Material and structural engineers were matriculated into the studio to foster an informed and intuitive approach to design. This collaboration may not be common in a traditional architectural academic setting (especially with material engineers); however these are the relationships that need to be fostered in order to inject meaning into technological architecture- the crux of performance, process and innovation. These relationships encourage a level of design that extends beyond implementation and allows the designer to investigate a deeper level of design, thus being more innovative and worldly in their practice.

Lessons of Qualitative Collaboration

The space of reception- the space of interaction and discovery- is the space of lesson of this investigation. Traditional roles that were once distinctly separate find themselves with blurred boundaries. Through the abstraction of this investigation, the process is shifted from a linear process to a network. The result is a greater understanding and integration into the project which has evolved to one of problem solving in performative design. Process changes with intuitive knowledge, not regurgitation, and relationships are positioned to be truly collaborative through the flattening of hierarchies and the exploration of subjects that are exposed through defining performance and site as a feedback loop (among others). In some cases, roles are blurred so as to create multi-hyphenates. Qualitative collaboration seeks to re-discover and re-evaluate building with intuitive outcomes that fundamentally change interaction.

The definition of qualitative collaboration is open. It is not defined by the collaboration of teams, the collaboration of building to site or the site to the climate. Nor is it the collaboration of materials, the collaboration of systems or technologies of fabrication, algorithms or the tools by which design happens or is tested. The collaboration is the process and as such, the real value of qualitative collaboration is the evolution of the collaboration through discovery.

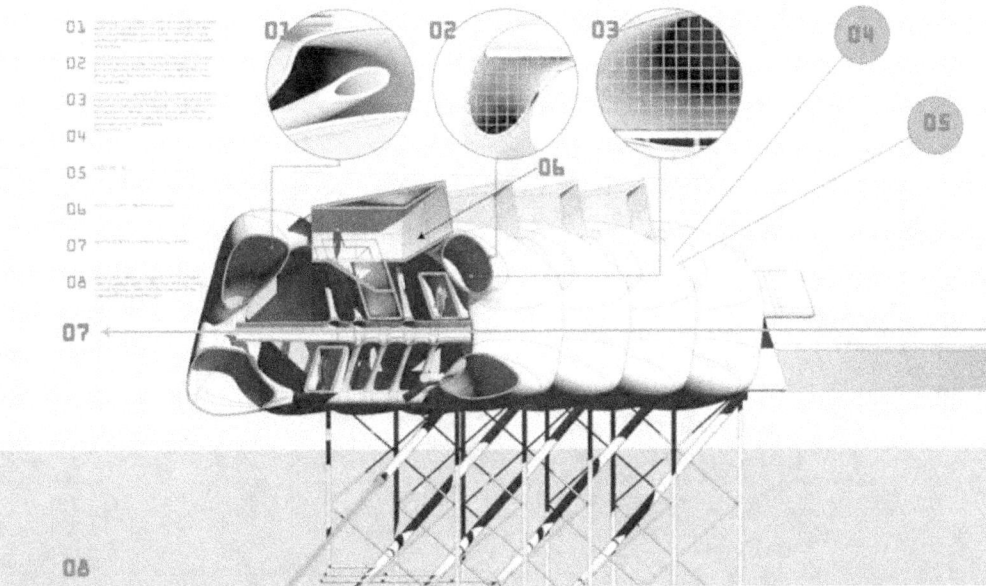

Fig. 8. Pavilion section. Nathanael Ramos.

Notes:

1 Berkel, Ben van, and Caroline Bos. "*Hybridization*." In *Move*. Amsterdam: UN Studio & Goose Press, 1999.

2 This was the central theme of the studio, *Pragmatic Geometry*, held at California Polytechnic State University, 2017

3 Schwab, K. (2017). *Fourth Industrial Revolution*. The Crown Publishing Group.

4 Schwab, Klaus (January 11, 2016). *The Fourth Industrial Revolution*. World Economic Forum. ISBN 1944835008.

5 Kelly, K. (2014). *What technology Wants*. New York: Penguin Books.

6 These tenets of biomimicry were taken from:
Benyus, Janine M. *Biomimicry: Innovation Inspired by Nature*, 291-292. Pymble, NSW: HarperCollins e-books, 2009.

7 DeLanda, M. (2015). The New Materiality. *ArchitecturalDesign*, *85*(5), 16-21. doi:10.1002/ad.1948

Widening the Field: Technology in the Developing World

Nathan Fash
Roger Williams University

Abstract

This paper asks whether we as building technology educators are doing enough in our teaching and research to consider the practices, delivery systems, and impacts of construction in regions beyond the typical sphere of interest (North America and Europe). Population forecasts show that the majority of growth—and therefore construction associated with that growth—will be in less developed and warmer countries in Africa, Asia, and Latin America. Anticipating a continued need for environmentally sensitive buildings in the developing world as part of a global effort to reduce carbon emissions, I suggest that our understanding of construction in these parts of the world should include multiple strands of context, and be well grounded in climate. When we teach about climates other than our own, we often turn to the concept of the vernacular, which is a good tool for distilling climate sensitive thinking, but falls short of describing the reality on the ground today, which is globalized, industrialized, and less climate sensitive, as evidenced by the indiscriminate spread of air conditioned glass boxes. Thermal envelope, which we often think of as the locus of innovation in building technology aimed at energy use reduction, is only rarely even considered in these parts of the world, where more often than not, simple concrete structure with infill is dominant.

Rather than focus on tighter enclosure and thermal isolation with its subsequent reliance on mechanical cooling, I instead point out that with simple means of construction also come lowered expectations for comfort held by the many of people who live in these parts of the world. And that those culturally embedded expectations have the potential to be a passive means to keep energy demand for cooling in buildings low. As such there is architectural potential in finding ways to derive buildings that are connected to their exterior environment while taking advantage of passive strategies to stay cool. Further I point out that there are inherent advantages and opportunities for architectural expression (the realm of poetics) in this simplified construction reality.

Finally, I describe some of the experiences of a design studio I recently led in the Dominican Republic which sought to bridge across cultures and across climates to make an immersive learning experience for students that merged architectural design and building technology with several interconnected layers of context.

Developing Mindset

The most recent projections from the United Nations show that population growth over the next 35 years is expected to be especially high in developing nations. Predictions indicate that Europe's population will shrink, while Africa is expected to account for more than half of the world's population growth in the same period. By 2050, Nigeria will be more populous than the United States, becoming the third largest country behind, respectively, India and China.[1]

While irreversible global climate change may be inevitable at this point, the goal of reducing greenhouse gas emissions originating in the built environment will likely remain a pressing challenge in the near term, and perhaps most so where population is growing fastest.

We, as building technology educators, should be asking ourselves how much we are teaching about practice in these parts of the world. We should consider how we might equip our students to leverage climate sensitive architectural thinking for positive change. Some of our students may return home to practice with new knowledge, others may become educators or practitioners in other parts of the world, and others still could become enmeshed in the delivery of buildings in yet unimagined ways. At the very least, we should be sending them forth with an increased cross-cultural understanding of the world and a conviction that smart architecture has a decisive role to play in the era of climate change.

Strength and Weakness in Vernacular

In developing an understanding of building technology in the developing world, we should be helping students recognize how technology fits within a non-homogenous cultural, historical, and climatological context. For the purposes of this paper, much of the discussion will revolve around the Latin American context.

Often when teaching outside our home climate, we rely on a generalized framework of vernacular construction, which we characterize simply as architecture without architects. We conjure images of time-proven and climate appropriate indigenous (or otherwise "local") constructions built by anonymous craftspeople using local techniques and materials. One such example might be the houses of Caledonia being dressed in white and built with low thermal mass cladding as a way to reject solar heat.[2]

While this has the benefits of distilling some basic concepts about how to adapt buildings to different combinations of temperature and humidity found throughout the world, vernacular architecture is also a problematic concept, in part because we often fail to recognize that the category is a shifting one. In other words, the architecture-without-architects being built today is not the same as it was a century ago. The reality today is that much of the simplest construction around the world (including in the tropics) has shifted away from the what we nostalgically imagine when we think of the vernacular and towards a present that is characterized by industrialized construction systems, and most often concrete frame with CMU infill. Considering the contemporary condition in the tropics, much of the wisdom of light, open, and well-shaded construction has been subsumed by the desire for permanence and economy.

Another problem with the generalized concept of vernacular construction is that it typically revolves around simple single story construction, with techniques or construction systems that may not always be applicable at larger scales present in the denser urban conditions of cities where we expect concentrated population growth. Perhaps the more approach should be a cross comparative one, demonstrating on the one hand the logic inherent in passive construction prior to globalization, and on the other hand the reckless disregard for it since then.

Globalizing Influences

In the rush to modernize cities in the tropics, such as those in Latin America, the aesthetic characteristics of buildings representing the emergent modernism often were (and continue to be) taken at face value and without regard for the climate in which they were (and are) being transposed. Since the United States has controlled the majority of the world's manufacturing following World War II, North American architectural symbols of postwar efficiency and organization were the architectural model of choice. The ease with which glass box high-rises, in the direct lineage of SOM's Lever House, could be constructed provided an irresistibly simple way to achieve the visual illusion of technological advancement.[3]

Despite continued investments in developing countries directed towards infrastructure including transportation, housing, urban planning, and administration, only a small minority of buildings since the post-war era reflect a sensible architectural response to the special conditions of the tropical climate.[4] The result of this global trend is a homogenized landscape with a preponderance of energy intensive buildings.

The taught glazed envelope, especially when used to clad tall buildings, makes very little sense from a thermal and energy use perspective in the tropics, but is nonetheless still pervasive in urban centers worldwide (think of Singapore). This is a testament to the strength of association in architecture, for better or worse, wherein the perception of modern advancement is embodied in the exterior disposition of a building. As a result, not only is energy demand inevitably higher, but the potential for poetic evolution in the façade of tall buildings is sadly diminished.

Climate Driven Envelopes

The imported tall building in glass and concrete is less concerned with climate, and more with the image of progress, an open flexible plan, and profitable fast construction. Now, as ever, there is a strong case to be made for contemporary design that accounts for climate conditions while still allowing flexibility and originality in its exterior disposition. In short, there is a need for buildings which provide shade to keep surfaces and people cool, and allow an open relationship to the outdoors, taking advantage of natural cooling through ventilation, and making a pleasurable experience.[5] In pursuing appropriate climate driven envelope design, we need to understand the relevance of passive strategies against a cultural backdrop. I will briefly unpack this idea before touching on some context sensitive examples.

Passive Principles

Designers of building envelopes in much of the cooler portions of the United States and Europe are concerned with slowing heat transfer between exterior and interior environments through strategies of thermal insulation, avoiding thermal bridging in the envelope, reducing air infiltration, and finding efficiencies in sophisticated heating systems. Meanwhile a tropical climate in the developing world demands an altogether different design response. The heat equation is reversed, and the goal is to keep cool despite intense levels of solar radiation, and high humidity. Given these conditions, the human body relies on evaporation to stay cool, and the primary way to promote evaporation is through air movement. This leads logically to open structures that shade thermal mass with architecture designed to reject heat. This is simple enough in concept, but the complication arises when we consider the role of mechanical cooling.

Thermal Isolation

Thermal envelope, which is a primary preoccupation of ours in North America and in Europe, especially in relation to energy efficiency, receives very little attention in much of the developing world. Contemporary construction in the tropics favors speed, economy, and durability. This most commonly leads to reinforced concrete structure with CMU or other infill, and little or no consideration for thermal isolation.

In the United States, the building code has power to influence construction, whereas building codes in the developing world, where they exist, are often unenforced. The popularity of a certain product, method of construction, material, or a style depends on cultural, economic, and other factors, more than on a top-down code-driven logic, and even less on an environmentally-driven agenda.

With air conditioning systems, however, the building envelope benefits from thermal isolation, and therefore insulation of the thermal envelope and minimal

exchange with the outdoors. Because thermal insulation is not part of the construction lexicon in so much of the tropics, I propose that we may do well to pursue alternative means of staying cool, and on the way potentially reduce the amount of mechanical cooling in the big picture.

In some climates, comfort is unachievable without mechanical cooling. The dividing line between who gets air conditioned interiors and who does not is an economic one. This is so much so that the convenience and comfort of air conditioned interiors are often associated with socio-economic status and accepted as a luxury for wealthier. So, while it is possible to achieve comfort through mechanical means with the advent of air conditioning in nearly any construction, the socio-economic context of much of the developing world compels the designer to find other ways to create comfort while avoiding reliance upon mechanical cooling systems and their inherent financial and environmental costs.[6] As one steers away from air conditioning, thermal isolation of the interior environment becomes a lower priority than avoiding head in the first place.

Comfort and Culture

While passive strategies for keeping buildings cool and naturally ventilated have much to recommend them, good intentions can be negated when imported cultural expectations for comfort are overlaid, as is the case with the Sheraton Hotel in Rio de Janeiro. That building is oriented to take advantage of the directionality of offshore winds in the evening and morning to create comfortable living conditions, but all of the hotel bedrooms are outfitted with air conditioning systems to meet the expectations of international tourists.[7]

While architects hold a number of cards in the design of the building envelope, creating comfortable environments has a strong cultural component. People living in tropical climates have adapted their own clothing habits in response to the need to stay cool. Thin, light colored, and loosely woven fabrics are often popular. It is also culturally acceptable for males to be shirtless in public. Furthermore, the relatively constant temperature throughout the year leads to activity cycles that are largely diurnal rather than seasonal. In tropical societies where the industrialized nine to five workday expectation has not taken over, working habits tend to take place earlier in the day when the sun is low, or late in the evening soon after sunset. This adjustment in cultural expectations and behavior allows tropical inhabitants to tolerate the excessive heat present in the middle of the day by avoiding exertion.[8] These low cost and highly effective passive strategies leverage culture and behavior rather than building technology to stay cool and represent the latent potential in coupling architecture that does not absolutely need mechanical cooling with people who already do without it in many ways.

Contextual Sensitivity

Modern architecture as an ideology has a built-in universal quality which disregards the importance of designing for specific geographic conditions. The common narrative holds that with globalization comes a flattening of construction technology. What we think of as good climate-sensitive vernacular architecture, with its time-tested means and methods, is squeezed out by pragmatic valuation of durability, low cost, and easy availability of industrial materials. And yet, we do see certain architectural precedents that make use of the formal vocabulary and material traditions of modernism with deference to climate sensitive logic.

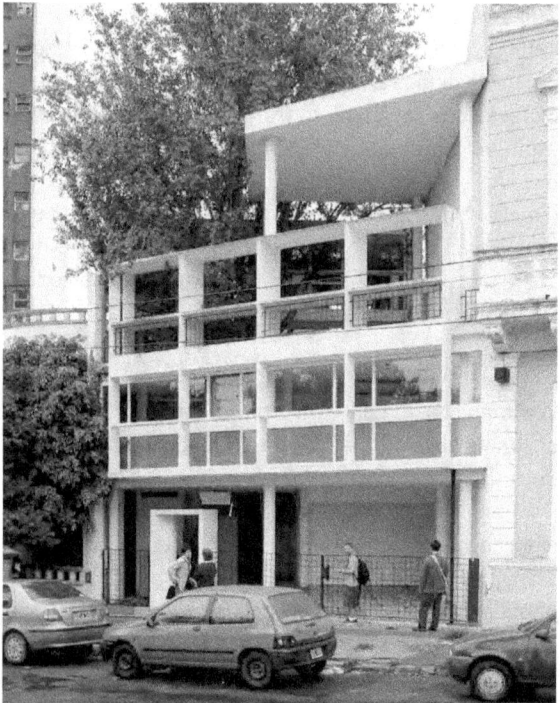

Fig. 1. Curuchet House, designed by Le Corbusier.

One such example is Le Corbusier's Curuchet House in Argentina (Fig. 1). Whereas monolithic concrete construction is anathema to thermal isolation strategies, it is much less problematic when applied as a shading strategy in a climate like that of Buenos Aires. The simplified reinforced concrete structure and the fruitful interplay between interior and exterior, revolving around a tree that exists in the center of the project beyond the porous depth of the appropriately oriented north-facing *bris-soleil* actually make sense in this context. Another interesting precedent is Alfonso Reidy's Museum of Modern Art in Rio de Janeiro, completed in 1953. It is a building designed with an external trapezoidal concrete skeleton which creates flexible interiors for display while simultaneously hosting a robust exterior shading structure soaring above the building mass and oriented appropriately to protect the north facing glazed façade. The occupiable levels are raised above and free the ground plane in a monumental but rigorous expressive structure.[9]

Still another example of well-tuned shading strategies can be seen in the Ministry of Education and Public Health building in Rio de Janeiro, one of the first modernist high-rise buildings ever built. Both of its fully glazed facades are treated differently depending on orientation. Facing the direct sunlight of the north is an array of horizontal moveable sunscreens, giving the façade an ever-changing appearance. Meanwhile the south facing glazing offers an unobstructed oblique view of the ocean.[10]

I have highlighted here just a few examples of modern architecture which have been suitably adapted to their climate through passive strategies to demonstrate that the presence of a particular formal vocabulary need not be an obstacle to accounting for the local economic, social, and climatic conditions of a place in a multi-layered design effort.

Poetics via Pragmatism

The ubiquity of simple construction and a wider comfort range in the tropics arguably translate to a less oppositional relationship between pragmatism and poetics in architectural design. In other words, the thing that makes most sense from a climate perspective, namely to aspire to make more with less through passive strategies, also leans towards an architecture of greater visual and experiential pleasure.

Passive strategies that rely on shading and natural ventilation without mechanical cooling tend toward an envelope that is non-isolating. The goal of creating inherently open envelopes allows opportunities for a fluid relationship between outside and inside and a sensation of intimacy with nature.[11] Internal core spaces are commonly surrounded by shaded open spaces allowing cross-ventilation of living spaces as seen in Fig. 2 below.

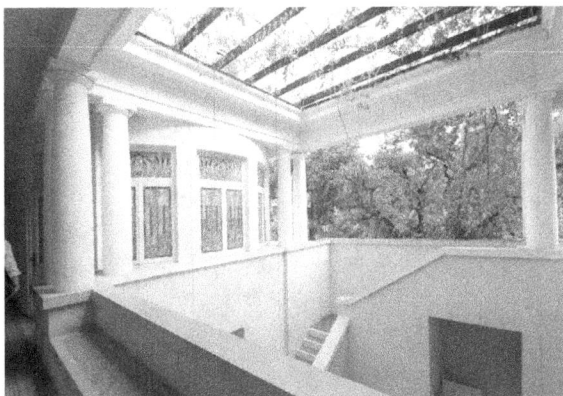

Fig. 2. Shaded Courtyard, Santo Domingo.

Materials performing a structural role are allowed to bridge from inside to outside, circumventing the challenges faced by thermally isolating exterior envelopes that often create redundancies and mediated appearances in insulated envelope assemblies. The work of Felix Candela in Mexico stands out for its exemplary experimentation with the potential of concrete as a structural material. And while the flexibility to pursue structural expression may not be the most important priority in all cases, it nonetheless represents a definite advantage for architectural design.

Immersive Experience

In a recent graduate level design studio that I taught at Roger Williams, students spent the first half of the semester studying the context before beginning their design work. Their research touched on cultural, geographical, historical, and climatological aspects of the Colonial City of Santo Domingo in the Dominican Republic where the studio was sited.

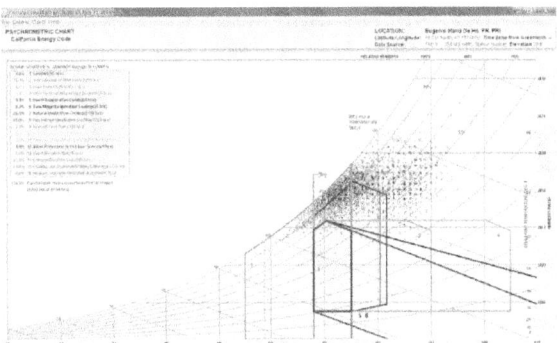

Fig. 3. Psychrometric Chart, Puerto Rico.

Students used tools like Climate Consultant to engage the empirical realities of temperature and humidity in the tropical climate, as seen in the psychrometric chart (Fig. 3). The research portion culminated in a studio trip to Santo Domingo which helped tremendously in bringing the place, the people, and the climate to life in their minds. Interesting discussions with our local partners in Santo Domingo, for instance, revealed the line between necessity and expectation when it comes to conditioning spaces, and students saw that the decision-making process is a complex one, but that they nonetheless have influence over how much the building envelope and selection of materials contribute to the performance of a building in this part of the world.

Students studied devices for buffering the interior core of buildings from the sun like the arcades, vegetated screens, verandas, balconies, or lightweight louvers on operable shutters. All of these enriching architectural devices originate from the same sensible climate-oriented goal: shading. We recognized the benefits of light colors on the exterior surfaces of walls and roofs designed to reject solar heat, which creates as a side benefit a cohesive and often visually pleasing urban disposition. We identified examples of both Colonial (Fig. 4) and Modern (Fig. 5) architecture that responded sensibly to the problem of shading the façade.

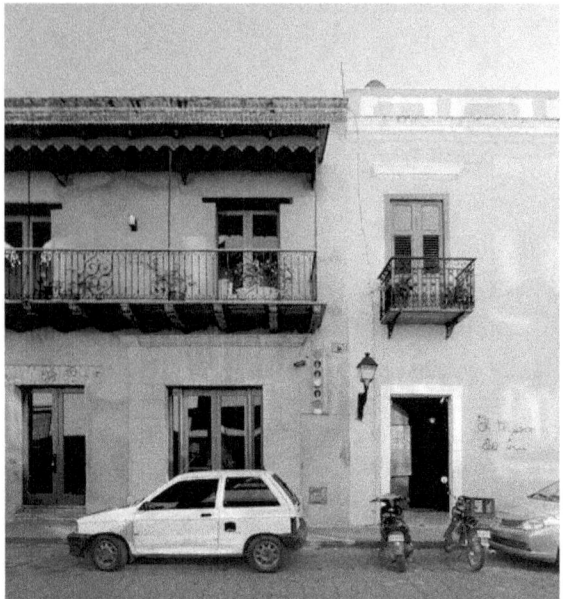

Fig. 4. Colonial Shaded Facade, Santo Domingo.

The potential loss of these elements in favor of the sealed and mechanically controlled box with little or no connection to its surroundings is problematic for energy consumption, for experiential reasons, and because of the impoverished architectural vocabulary and diminished versatility that it entails.

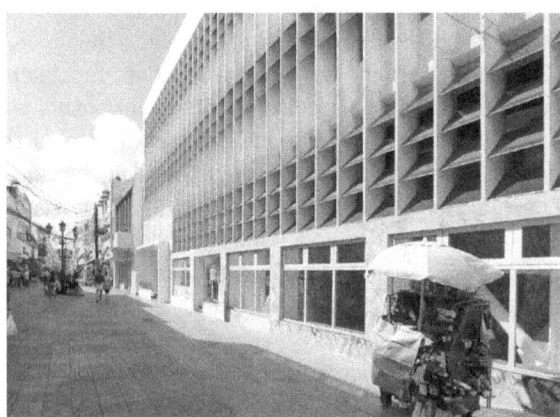

Fig. 5. Modern Shaded Facade, Santo Domingo.

Still, we witnessed how the urban arcade (Fig. 6), intended to attract pedestrians to commercial offerings is losing out to the air-conditioned shopping mall.[12] This is a transformation that comes with social consequences for public space.

While the challenge of designing climate-conscious tropical architecture can be simplified to the

simultaneous drive to stay cool during the day through shading of thermally massive surfaces while encouraging convective cooling at night, these goals could also be imagined at the urban scale, and in relation to public space beyond the individual building project.[13] The potential to organize urban form with climate in mind, setting up pathways for breezes, and providing mutualistic shading between constituent parts remains a fruitful if unexplored avenue in contemporary architectural and urban design practice.

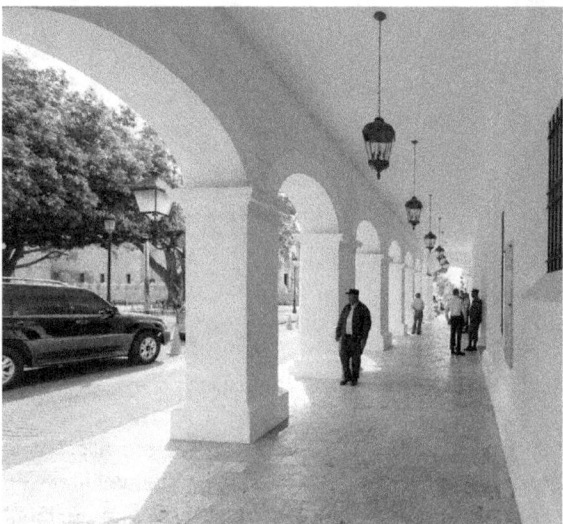

Fig. 6. Urban Oriented Portico, Santo Domingo.

We should be looking for opportunities like this to bridge across cultures and across climates to make meaningful connections with areas outside our own. Doing so not only pushes our students to design more context-sensitive architecture but also arms them for the challenges of a world being altered by climate change. In a historical moment when countries are turning politically inward, it is ever more important to realize and act upon the value of looking outward. My recent experience with students in Santo Domingo shows that students both appreciate and are energized by being engaged in a world beyond their immediate surroundings while working on problems that are global in nature yet highly contextual. Viewed in this light, cross-cultural teaching is moral imperative.

Notes:

[1] United Nations Department of Economic and Social Affairs, *World Population Prospects: The 2015 Revision* (New York: United Nations, 2015), 1-4.

[2] Bruno Stagno. "Tropicality," in *Tropical Architecture: Critical Regionalism in the Age of Globalization,* ed. Alexander Tzonis et al. (London: Wiley-Academic, 2001), 68.

[3] Luis E. Carranza and Fernando Luiz Lara, *Modern Architecture in Latin America: Art, Technology, and Utopia,* (Austin: University of Texas Press, 2014), 140-141.

[4] Wolfgang Lauber, *Tropical Architecture: Sustainable and Humane Building in Africa, Latin America and South-East Asia,* (Munich: Prestel, 2005), 29.

[5] Rahul Mehrotra, "Architectural Responses in Tropical India," in *Tropical Architecture: Critical Regionalism in the Age of Globalization,* ed. Alexander Tzonis et al. (London: Wiley-Academic, 2001), 213.

[6] Lauber, *Tropical Architecture*, 9.

[7] Lauber, *Tropical Architecture*, 33.

[8] M Rohinton Emanuel, *An Urban Approach to Climate-Sensitive Design: Strategies for the Tropics*, (New York: Spon Press, 2005), 66.

[9] Carranza, *Modern Architecture in Latin America*, 175.

[10] Carranza, *Modern Architecture in Latin America*, 79.

[11] Bruno Stagno, "Designing and Building in the Tropics," in *Tropical Architecture: Critical Regionalism in the Age of Globalization,* ed. Alexander Tzonis et al. (London: Wiley-Academic, 2001), 178.

[12] Rahul Mehrotra, "Architectural Responses in Tropical India," 195.

[13] Emanuel, *An Urban Approach to Climate-Sensitive Design*, 100.

SESSION 02: POETICS

Session Chair: Deborah Oakley
University of Nevada-Las Vegas

Randy Deutsch, University of Illinois Urbana-Champaign: "The Practical And Ineffable In Architecture: On The Convergence Of The Pragmatics And The Poetics Of Building."

Patrick Doan, Virginia Tech: "What Lies Beneath the Surface."

Bruce Wrightsman, Kansas State University: "Operation: Lightness."

Judy O'Buck Gordon, Kansas State University: "The Metrics Of Poetics: Poetic Detailing And The Study Of Daylight Quality At The Gipsoteca Canoviana Addition By Carlo Scarpa."

The Practical and Ineffable in Architecture: On the Convergence of the Pragmatics and the Poetics of Building

Randy Deutsch
University of Illinois Urbana-Champaign

The word "practical" is trending in the AEC industry. For example, the 2016 USC BIM Symposium was entitled, *Effective, Productive, Profitable Workflows*. Many of the sold out Autodesk University 2015 classes featured the word "Practical" in their title.[1] And yet, the 2016 AIA Convention in Philadelphia Day Two keynote was delivered by the American-Israeli designer, architect and professor Neri Oxman. Described as "using computational algorithms, 3D printing, robotics, and cutting edge fields such as synthetic biology, Neri Oxman's work is nothing short of breathtaking and inspiring."[2] While Oxman's research is "at the intersection of computation design, additive manufacturing, materials engineering and synthetic biology,"[3] she nonetheless told a crowd estimated at 8,000 architects that she was not interested in giving practical advice to professionals. Her research and designs landed squarely on the side of the poetic and ineffable. More typically, a recent symposium at the University of Minnesota explored the convergence of the three fields of architecture, art and biology that result in works for the built environment. Points of intersection between the speakers and panelists included "the measurable benefits that such work can deliver, despite its inherent difficulties."[4] Their solutions – applied research – were largely practical. This paper looks at the convergence of the practical and ineffable in the creative work of two representative Toronto architecture firms. PARTISANS' robotics and technology-driven design work captures the range of mastering the practical and ineffable in architecture: "What impressed me most [about PARTISANS] – beyond the material palette and use of advanced technology – is how they make me *feel*."[5] And Philip Beesley Architect: Beesley is a practicing visual artist, architect, and professor in Architecture at the University of Waterloo who leads an interdisciplinary design collective in Toronto, Canada. His Living Architecture Systems Group undertakes collaborations with architects, engineers, artists, scientists. Beesley himself is a convergence of architect, artist, and professor. Together, these firms' work mediates between pragmatics and poetics; craft and manufacturing; meaning and behavior; physicality and psychology. It is almost that, in their creative work, these firms were thinking in terms of convergence of these opposite poles, and their inevitable impact on the education of a new generation of architects.

The practical and ineffable

It's not just the element of place, but also each moment in time presents a convergence of potentials and challenges, and these specifics are translated through concepts and tectonics into a unique architecture. – Chris McVoy, Senior Partner at Steven Holl Architects on their design approach.[6]

Starting with divergence and convergence, divergent thinking is associated with evolution, ideating and creativity, whereas convergent thinking comes into play when required to make a decision, or go with a course of action. In the world of creativity, "convergence is most important during the stage when ideas are being ironed out and made tenable."[7] Convergence takes the novel and impractical and makes it practical and useful. According to the authors of *Wired to Create*, "convergence refers to the ability to conform, put in the hard effort necessary to exercise practicality, and make ideas tenable. Convergence consists of high conscientiousness, precision, persistence, critical sense, and sensitivity to the audience."[8]

To converge is practical; to diverge, ineffable. The two seldom overlap. When we first learn to brainstorm, we're told to hold back our judgment (convergence) until we're done ideating (divergence.) For example, Autodesk's structured brainstorming methodology for innovating, the Innovation Genome, helps illustrate both divergent and convergent thinking in the creative process to generate multiple ideas in a short period of time.[9] And yet, the same thinking that believes the right brain is associated with creativity, misses the nuanced reality that creative thinking requires both, the right and left, sides of the brain. Even with these seemingly polar opposites, we're increasingly seeing a melding, a blurring, a *convergence*.

Ideation is almost antithetical to automation

Today, humans and robots are learning how to collaborate together so that they don't have to be an either/or, but rather a both/and proposition.[10] In the digital age, especially for architects and postdigital artisans, the notion of craftsmanship is still very much evolving.[11] Recent books have attempted to close the robot/human, and algorithm/gut instinct divide. Author Brian Christian not only holds degrees in, but also works at the intersection of, science, philosophy, and poetry. In his co-authored book, *Algorithms to Live By,* he explained "how simple, precise algorithms used by computers can also untangle very human questions."[12] On navigating the robot/human spectrum, there's a recent entry to the literature, *Machines of Loving Grace: The Quest for Common Ground Between Humans and Robots* that looks for "common ground between humans and robots," at a time when "we have seen some impressive demonstrations of artificial intelligence, including Watson, IBM's 'Jeopardy' champion; Siri, Apple's personal assistant; and Google's self-driving car."[13] Another recent book, *Art and Science* covers the ongoing convergence of – as opposed to the more expected opposition of – art and technology in the digital age.[14]

Markku Allison got his start in architecture as a building designer. "Within our profession we have all the different breeds: project manager, project architect, project designer. Because I'm at the designer end of that spectrum, I'm really interested in the data and intuition and the practical and ineffable. That is where my passion is." Allison continued, "You can go to Louis Kahn, the difference between the architecture of the little 'a' and the architecture of the capital 'A,' or beauty with a little b or capital B. If it didn't have the *ineffable,* we would lose the heart and soul of what architecture is. That ineffable piece is the life-giving spark that really makes the building sing."[15] Many architects have a similar sentiment, that the aesthetic component – Vitruvius's *delight* – distinguishes architecture from mere building, and that architecture wouldn't be worth the trouble to practice without that distinguishing element.

Toru Hasegawa sides with the thinking that computers cannot replicate creativity. "As everyday goes by, I'm less inclined to make this statement: Design is the last thing that technology will roll over," said Hasegawa.[16] "Let's throw out all of the possible behaviors humans have. Throw out the garbage. Do our own laundry. Wash the dishes. Clean the house. You can classify these tasks as functions. If you list all of these functions, and compare what has been replaced by machines, the majority has or will be. There's a world in which a lot of this can be automated. The stuff that doesn't resonate well with automation is ideation. Ideation is almost antithetical to automation. If you don't have functions to automate, there is no automation. Or machine inquiry. Creation comes before automation can possibly happen. Machines have not been well-crafted to make things up. If an alien were to come down to earth and saw what humans could be consolidated to – it would be creation or creativity. We create stuff. Instead of repeatedly doing some task. That's where we are in terms of human-machine relationship. If a machine has no drive or necessity to create, there is no intent. Machines will always be in support of the creator."

Falling squarely on the side of creativity being something that has evolved for millennia, and will continue to evolve in the age of computers, algorithms and robots, works are appearing that explore Assisted Creation and Generative Creation, and the role AI plays in replicating, approximating, or replacing human creativity.[17] Recent research argues that beauty is *not* in eye of beholder (personal preference,) but instead is part of our biology (neurological.)[18] The field of neuroaesthetics uses neurology to understand human response to art.[19]

Between firmness, commodity, and delight

It can be said that *architecture is nothing more than the masterly, correct & magnificent convergence of firmness, commodity and delight.* Architecture throughout history has always mediated between the practical (commodity) and ineffable (delight.) Recent attempts at architecture serve to make this tendency more explicit. It's too late for architects to turn their backs on technology. As Norman Foster has stated, "Since Stonehenge, architects have always been at the cutting edge of technology. And you can't separate technology from the humanistic and spiritual content of a building."[20] One example, AADRL Spyropoulos Design Lab explores an architecture that is self-aware, self-structured, and self-assembles. "The research explores high population of mobility agents that evolve an architecture that moves beyond the fixed and finite towards a behavioural model of interactive human and machine ecologies."[21]

Recent industry literature, such as *The Death of Drawing: Architecture in the Age of Simulation*[22], bemoans the loss of meaning in architecture due to the rise of such technologies as BIM. While others, such as MIT Architecture's Design and Computation Group, don't let the rise of technology curtail their pursuit of meaning in architecture, as it exists to inquire "into the varied nature and practice of computation in architectural design, and the ways in which design meaning, intentions, and knowledge are constructed through computational thinking, representing, sensing, and making."[23] The practical and ineffable, and the technological and mystical, can not only coexist, but must do so in order for a complete work of architecture to be realized.

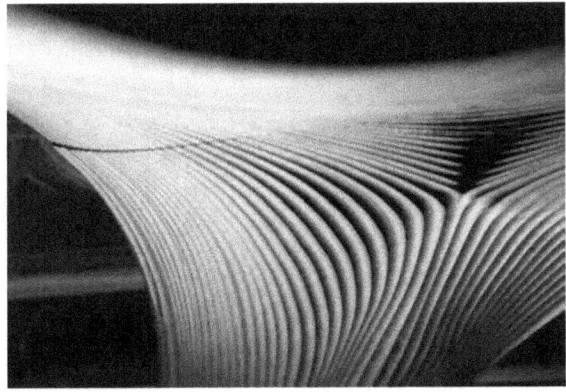

Fig. 1. PARTISANS worked closely with their fabrication partner, MCM Inc., and the software engineers at Mastercam on Bar Raval to innovate the milling process.

The work of PARTISANS

Design and fabrication are converging. Today, we are seeing the maturing and scaling of digital design-to-fabrication tools. Until now, in piecemeal fashion design professionals output digital designs for laser cutting, 3D printing, or CNC production by combining 2D-to-3D workflows. The historical separation of design and construction means and methods — for liability,

legal, and insurance reasons — is starting to blur, and the industry is moving closer to a unified workflow, moving one big step away from the limitations of 2D CAD.[24] Design and fabrication convergence puts the power of making in the hands of design professionals.

One firm that is creating what can only be considered Total Architecture is PARTISANS. "It sounds like exactly what is going on in our office at PARTISANS," said Alex Josephson.[25] "I like this word 'convergence.' It definitely describes our practice and our ethos. Architecture for us is a surprise. Only through a willingness to engage in a problem or technology or subject you're not necessarily familiar with can you discover something. We believe that 'beauty emerges when design misbehaves.' By misbehaving we mean using processes and design thinking that hack conventional methods to produce something unexpected."

PARTISANS started as fabricators, then ventured into R&D, and has found that the type of convergence found in their projects scales. "We work on everything from smaller projects and objects to others the scale of Toronto's Union Station, which occupies an entire city block, and the Hearn Generating Station, which sprawls over several acres," explained PARTISANS partner Jonathan Freidman. What does that convergence actually look like? "That's exactly what we're exploring and figuring out," said Freidman. "The smaller projects, like the Grotto Sauna and Bar Raval, have taught us strategies we are now employing on residential and office projects, like the value of 3D laser scanning, for example. All of our projects influence and inform one another. Convergence is ultimately about deepening the learning process and forging partnerships with people in other disciplines to help you continue to learn."

PARTISANS has been of late working on the largest of scales. "I started school right after September 11, 2001," explained Josephson. "Like everyone, it had an impact on me, as did the ensuing war between secular culture and radical religion, and Islam in particular. I became interested in how architecture could be deployed as an intervention in the Abrahamic religions. Pooya and I met while we were doing our Masters degrees. I was working on a project about Islam and Mecca, and Pooya was working on one about Los Angeles. We realized that we were working on inverse projects: whereas Mecca is the city of God, LA is the city of the self! From the beginning we've been intrigued by the possibility of designing for cultures, religions, cities, and questioning what architects can aspire to design. In other words, we didn't start with buildings. Buildings are just one of the ways that cultures manifest themselves. But basically before we even started our practice, we were asking ourselves: Why are architects just building museums and airports? Why did architects stop redefining the very foundations of civilization?"

"But one of the things we are very conscious of is not letting the technology drive the design," added Freidman. "You see that now in a lot of buildings. You can tell whether it is a SketchUp building or a Revit building. We have made a very conscious decision to treat technology as a toolkit and not be bound by any one particular kind of software. If we have an idea for something, we will research which technology best allows us to visualize, implement or fabricate it. Or in some cases maybe we work with the software developer to develop software patches that allow us to fabricate what we imagine. Even though we prioritize technologies, drawing and hand-sketching are fundamental techniques in our office. There's a convergence between manual craft and technology. One summer we had an artist come in once a week and work with the staff on their hand-sketching. So we go back and forth between technology and hand drawing, keeping freedom and organic-ness fundamental in our design. We don't want the technology alone to be pulling us along. We like to think that we're bringing back the role of the architect, not as a master builder, but as a visionary and as a doer. Someone who can facilitate things. Most of the time architects are relegated to being permit pushers, where owners go to architects to get a permit. We resist that and fight that daily."

In reference to the work of PARTISANS, perhaps no assessment of the work of a design firm captures the range of mastering the practical and ineffable in architecture than this assessment of their work: "What impressed me most – beyond the material palette and use of advanced technology – is how they make me *feel*."[26] While recent advances in robot art may raise questions concerning the monopoly humans hold on creativity, it is in the collaboration between robots or machines and humans where the greatest opportuni-

ties reside for advances in the fields of architecture, engineering, and construction.[27] The consensus so far is that robots can't achieve the creative solutions normally expected of humans, and that their function ought to be to supplement by taking-over automated tasks. "If there's any comfort offered during the current debate around robots, automation and the future of work, it's that robots can't do creativity. Machines are great for automated, precise, repetitive work; not so great for creative, expressive work, robots can't do creativity."[28]

Projects need experts as well as generalists – who serve as glue for the project team, and who are able to see the big picture. "Without the Architect the specialists are lost, fragmented, caught in their reductive view. The Architect brings to the activity that which the specialists cannot, sees the whole, and looks towards costs, utility, as well as aesthetics."[29] A firm such as the Turner Prize-winning interdisciplinary London-based Assemble collective, working across the disciplines of art, architecture and design, is able in their work to bridge the divide between the practical and ineffable. One architectural critic has found similar affinities between Assemble and other individuals or firms with similar goals, including Theaster Gates in Chicago, and Alejandro Aravena's Elemental in Chile.[30] Neri Oxman, mentioned in the abstract, combines four disciplines – art, science, engineering, and design – in the *Age of Entanglement*.[31] "The role of Science is to explain and predict the world around us; it 'converts' information into knowledge. The role of Engineering is to apply scientific knowledge to the development of solutions for empirical problems; it 'converts' knowledge into utility. The role of Design is to produce embodiments of solutions that maximize function and augment human experience; it 'converts' utility into behavior. The role of Art is to…create awareness of the world around us."[32]

The work of Philip Beesley

Philip Beesley is a practicing visual artist, architect, and professor in Architecture at the University of Waterloo who leads an interdisciplinary design collective in Toronto, Canada. His Living Architecture Systems Group undertakes collaborations with architects, engineers, artists, scientists. Beesley himself is a convergence of architect, artist, and professor. What does the resulting work process look like? "Thinking of how we need to work in our unstable, constantly shifting environment, it is interesting to think about the way agile, flexible approaches are needed. I realize I'm working in a rather curious hybrid practice," offered Beesley.[33] "Through the generations of this past century, we've moved through an extraordinary turbulence with massive apprehension about the scale of nations and institutions. My own world has tended to gravitate to increments, with small group conversations and neighborhood-level organization. My parents were deeply affected by the Second World War and responded with an activism rooted in local ethics and in immersion in nature. I have tended to respond with urban scales and with strong interest in artificial technologies." Beesley continued:

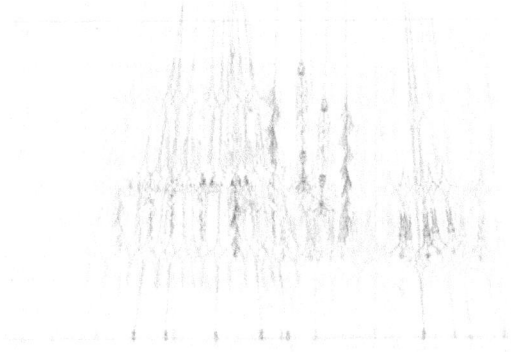

Fig 2. Philip Beesley/LASG/PBAI Epiphyte Chamber, Museum of Contemporary and Modern Art, Seoul, 2014. Elevation illustration of an immersive environment mounted for the inauguration of the Museum of Contemporary and Modern Art

"Seen as multiple cycles, perhaps this makes a personal narrative of overlapping, stuttering movements, in which wholes are progressively sought. One can think of more systematically engineered living systems and other examples of movements that have a tremendous optimism about unification. Conversely, there are some fertile examples that resist whole-systems thinking and insist on decoupled, granular divisions. A good example might be our recent focus on emergence in computational design. This might resonate with a social model of agency rooted in individual action. In a hopeful sense it results in highly resilient, complex, extremely interesting assemblies. I savor the kind of churn that happens from the intersection of those different scales. That leads me to think optimistically about the kind of fertility that can come from classical disciplines working strongly,

while at the same time alteric hybrids work experimentally, creating productive annoyance and friction."

Beesley sees the aforementioned impatience in the current generation that might lead to some of the solutions brought about by convergence. "I do see impatience, and we could have an interesting debate about whether that quality is an affliction or a virtue. Both would be true in their ways. It's very hard and challenging to find oneself in conversation with such distraction and short attention span. It's hard to have confidence in working with deeply complex and nuanced things when things are raised to the level of the paragraph at best. That doesn't seem compatible with the kind of integrated viability of whole systems my studio is dedicated to. On the other hand, to bring it home, I accuse my daughter of being completely obsessed with texting, turning herself into the most superficial machine. That was a cruel judgment of what she was doing to herself. Looking again, and treating her with respect, one could detect a radical poly-consciousness of multiple literacies, of being able to weave together 50 different conversations simultaneously. It's worth not being so quick to erect a moral judgment, before the radical facilities and agility of that way of approaching things, is also grasped. It would be true to say that the radical fragmentation and fluidity of individual increments of conception, is not simply decay, but it does create some different scales which have a pretty ferocious liability in their own right. Moreover, if this symptom is not simply apocalyptic, from one thing falling apart to the other, but rather is one of cyclical churn in which that kind of sensibility radiates itself intact back into a monolithic kind of consciousness that is dedicated long term into the deep whole. Then it is possible for it to have a refreshing kind of affect. Whether those things crash and cancel each other out is a very fraught question indeed, and depends on the emotions of the day as well. I'm becoming rather optimistic about it. I'm finding that kind of cycling is renewing. It makes it way more intense to navigate. But it can offer a tremendous contribution to resilience."

"The ingredients do need to have a certain richness to them," continued Beesley. "If you only drink Coke exclusively, it's going to get pretty thin. But the profound mixture of small increments can have a certain viability. Personally, I enjoy some periods that are almost monastic in their longevity. A long arc of just dwelling rather quietly, allowing multiple ingredients to rest and to be present. To wait for them to somehow condense into something that's much subtler and finer. That would be a model of something like a petri dish in which solutions are present and given enough peace and sanctuary to crystalize, for formation to occur. That's something that is very dependent upon boundaries. What are those ingredients? And how does that boundary work? There's great liability in it as well. Because that kind of model of creating sanctuary with a vital life inside it in unfortunate hands could be one of fascism, where the boundary is total. Where homogenization happens as opposed to fertility. It is no guarantee, but some periods of contemplative or quieter practice does seem to be important in thinking about how disciplines can work together."

Start with utter practicality

To achieve both the practical and ineffable, where does one begin? "If one were to stand amidst a very large forest, and for imagining strategies for building something of that complexity, it would be easy to be utterly swamped with the challenge," said Beesley. "A cruel question would be to be asked to clean a battleship with a toothbrush. However, a satisfying involvement is of course possible. Our work tends to begin with utter practicality. Each joint is fashioned so that it fits in the next, and is developed to have a satisfying click—and if the forces for each component are worked on thoroughly so that they are balanced, they become capable of interlinking, and making a highly competent matrix where all the forces can be dynamically shed effectively, to create well-performing, resilient structures. If the assembly of these things is tuned to that your hands can push these elements together, using tools and jigs, out of that initial harmonization which exists at a highly incremental scale, it becomes possible to orchestrate collective assembly systems and design systems, where things are not only done efficiently and expedited, it becomes possible to put them together and to work cooperatively in small tribes. The systems at that point start to get really interesting. A cadence can emerge, handing things off and assembling them. A stride emerges which tends to be amplified in a really extraordinary way, when you experience the rhythms of those assembled systems. That kind of meta-organization becomes a very significant thing. You might be helped by some enabling technologies. Digi-

tal fabrication in my case is a very significant tool. The significance of the cadences that combine at scale into rhythms that emerge are the most significant thing of all. Rather than simply making a complex environment by blowing your way through it, or having the money to make it happen, it's much more an experience of collective agency, of a deeply organized group of people. Not working individually but in multiple tribal clusters. A lot of energy gets generated with those interactions. Also in the agency of those quite small groups working together, there's a sense of stewardship that emerges that tends to flow outwards. This is very much a kind of a collective activity that produces the rather satisfying emergence that result. It couldn't possibly be achieved as a frozen music model."

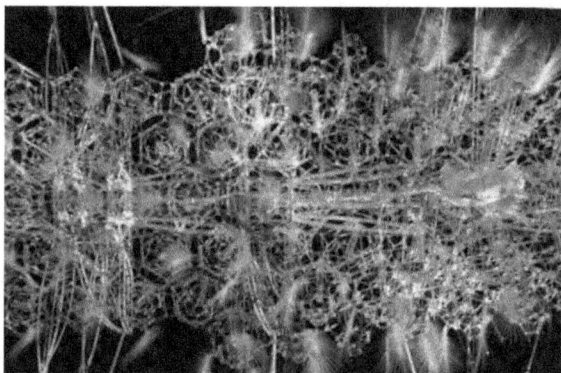

Fig 3. Philip Beesley/LASG/PBAI Detail of Grove, Waterloo Architecture Nest Studio, Waterloo, 2014. Laser-cut wood and polymer sheets are combined with thermally expanded acrylic skeletons.

On their way to the ineffable, Beesley's installations are described in almost human terms. "Lightweight interlinking systems are interwoven with next-generation chemistry that supports exchanges within the environment, in pursuit of an environment that 'cares.'" How important in the end is it that there is a practical side to the work that has been described as *an environment that cares*? "If I imagined being part of a community in the 13th century in a European town, coming up to the cathedral that would deeply guide my life," explained Beesley. "The hall and the framing of the space would be a religious act requiring the utmost of organization. The collective imagination of where the world is going in that kind of operation would be a central quality of a thing. In terms of my own practice, both utterly pragmatic function and unapologetic fiction and poetics are inevitably intermixed, and serve as reflections for each other. This sense of how very productive it is, inhabited fictions, is something I find entirely tantalizing. And is a very helpful way to understand architecture. I've tried to emphasize utter practicality as a kind of grounding. Looking locally, and having very deliberate conversations how much it weighs, how much waste, and how much is costs, and will it break as it ages? And yet at the same time the accompanying qualities are ones of consciousness, and the emotion that comes by imagining possibility. I simply don't know how to separate those things. Nor do I want to. Rather than seeing those as a polarity, where you have to choose between form and function, they work in multiple cycles. Stuttering, hiccupping cycles. Where you absolutely ground yourself. The consequences, as soon as you look at the impact of anything, you see it having ripples and objects around it. Those ripple out into the future as well. This to me almost qualifies as an internal question about how architecture works. As intermixing fact and fiction."

In conclusion, Beesley sees the convergence of the practical and ineffable in the opportunity to work collectively with living systems. "Looking to the future, on a practical level the achievements of The Human Genome Project (HGP) and the apparent completion of The General Theory of Relativity, the more recent work in gravitational waves, coupled to the wholesale agency that comes with this current generation in the widening and deepening of design tools, and enabling of fabrication methods, makes it possible to speak quite assertively about the possibility of working with life. Life as a genetic quality. A living system. Moving beyond analogies of a previous generation. Speaking quite literally about living systems. That calls on a harmonization of multiple disciplines. It invites a vision of convergence that is far from homogenizing or totalizing, but rather involves weed-like hybrids. Mongrels. Which produce tremendous vitality. So it is a stuttering, hiccupping, compulsive kind of convergence that I'm feasting on. Which has turned into a sense of commitment to a collective project."

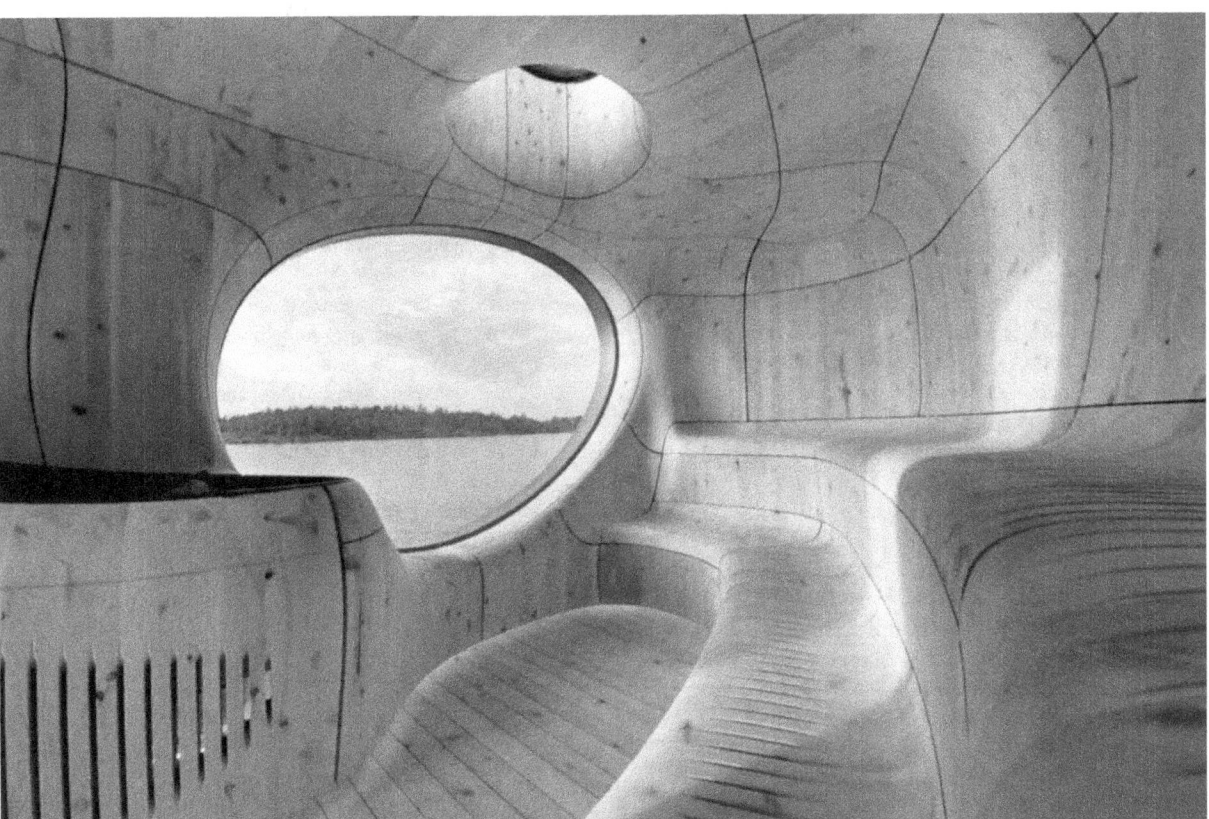

Fig. 4. PARTISANS, Grotto Sauna, 2016. The curved interior emulates Lake Huron's waves and mirrors the Precambrian shield—a soft, undulating rock surface that has been worn over billions of years. PARTISANS collaborated directly with our fabrication partners to develop new prototyping and milling methods.

Notes:

[1] Zach Kron, Dynamo at Autodesk University 2015, http://dynamobim.org/dynamo-at-autodesk-university-2015/ December 8, 2015.

[2] Anthony Frausto-Robledo, In Brief: Highlights from AIA 2016 Philly, http://architosh.com/2016/05/in-brief-highlights-from-aia-2016-philly/, May 21, 2016.

[3] Pete Evans, Perspectives on BEST of SHOW 2016: From Edge of Market to Maturing BIM, Framing a New Lens, http://architosh.com/2016/06/perspectives-on-best-of-show-2016-from-edge-of-market-to-maturing-bim-framing-a-new-lens/, June 3, 2016.

[4] Blaine Brownell, When Architecture, Art, and Biology Collide, http://www.architectmagazine.com/technology/when-architecture-art-and-biology-collide_o?utm_source=newsletter&utm_content=Opinion&utm_medium=email&utm_campaign=AN_052516%20, may 24, 2016.

[5] David Dick-Agnew, Toronto's Partisans is on a Winning Streak, http://www.azuremagazine.com/article/update-on-partisans/, November 23, 2015.

[6] http://www.archdaily.com/775210/breaking-ground-steven-holl-architects-celebrates-8-projects-currently-under-construction

[7] Scott Barry Kaufman, Carolyn Gregoire (2015-12-29). Wired to Create: Unraveling the Mysteries of the Creative Mind (p. xxv). Penguin Publishing Group. Kindle Edition.

[8] ibid.

[9] Scott Sheppard, Autodesk Innovation Genome Example: How to Make Visualization Obsolete, http://labs.blogs.com/its_alive_in_the_lab/2016/02/autodesk-innovation-genome-example-how-to-make-visualization-obsolete.html, February 19, 2016.

[10] Madeline Gannon, Madeline the Robot Tamer, https://vimeo.com/148982525, January, 2016.

[11] Jeff Link, Ways Architects and Postdigital Artisans Are Modernizing Craftsmanship, https://lineshapespace.com/postdigital-artisans/, January 18 2016.

[12] Brian Christian, Tom Griffiths, Algorithms to Live By: The Computer Science of Human Decisions, April 5, 2016

[13] David Alan Grier, 'Machines of Loving Grace,' by John Markoff, http://www.nytimes.com/2015/08/23/books/review/machines-of-loving-grace-by-john-markoff.html, August 21, 2015.

[14] http://www.abbeville.com/bookpage.asp?isbn=9780789212191

[15] From author interview with Markku Allison, May 11, 2016

[16] From author interview with Toru Hasegawa, April 19, 2016

[17] Samim Winiger & Roelof Pieters, CreativeAI: On the Democratisation & Escalation of Creativity, https://medium.com/@ArtificialExperience/creativeai-9d4b2346faf3#.gun5063a8, March 7, 2016

[18] Klaus Philipsen, Beauty- Not in the Eye of the Beholder, http://archplanbaltimore.blogspot.com/2016/03/beauty-not-in-eye-of-beholder.html, March 25, 2016.

[19] Stephanie Hughes, Beauty and the Brain: Understanding Our Responses to Art, http://www.sciencefriday.com/articles/beauty-and-the-brain-understanding-our-responses-to-art/, March 6, 2015

[20] Norman Foster: Building the future, http://news.bbc.co.uk/2/hi/uk_news/330624.stm, April 29, 1999.

[21] Theodore Spyropoulos, AADRL Spyropoulos Design Lab, https://vimeo.com/131823232, 2015.

[22] http://deathofdrawing.com

[23] https://architecture.mit.edu/computation/program/overview

[24] Randy Deutsch, in Wanda Lau, The Tech to Expect in 2016, http://www.architectmagazine.com/technology/the-tech-to-expect-in-architecture-in-2016_o, January 12, 2016.

[25] From author interview with PARTISANS, April 29, 2016

[26] David Dick-Agnew, Toronto's Partisans is on a Winning Streak, http://www.azuremagazine.com/article/update-on-partisans/, November 23, 2015.

[27] Robot Art Raises Questions about Human Creativity, https://www.technologyreview.com/s/600762/robot-art-raises-https://www.technologyreview.com/s/600762/robot-art-raises-questions-about-human-creativity/#/set/id/600857/

[28] Alexandra Spring, Can machines come up with more creative solutions to our problems than we can?, http://www.theguardian.com/sustainable-business/2016/mar/29/can-machines-come-up-with-more-creative-solutions-to-our-problems-than-we-can?linkId=23041602, March 29, 2016.

[29] Journal of Design and Science, Discussion: Age of Entanglement, http://jods.mitpress.mit.edu/pub/AgeOfEntanglement/discussions, January 20, 2016.

[30] Christopher Hawthorne, Assemble might have a Turner Prize, but the London collective continues to defy categorization, http://www.latimes.com/entertainment/arts/la-ca-cm-assemble-architecture-20160501-column.html, April 28, 2016.

[31] Neri Oxman, Age of Entanglement, Journal of Design and Science, http://jods.mitpress.mit.edu/pub/AgeOfEntanglement?version=2, January 20, 2016.

[32] ibid.

[33] From author interview with Philip Beesley, March 18, 2016

What Lies Beneath the Surface

Patrick Doan
Virginia Tech

"The cosmetic is the new cosmic..."

Rem Koolhaas - *Junkspace*

Abstract

In 2002, the Modern Art Museum of Ft. Worth (or the Modern as it is called in Ft. Worth) located in the museum district of Ft. Worth, Texas, opened to the public. Designed by the Japanese Architect and Pritzker Laureate, Tadao Ando, the new museum was conceived and built to serve as the Modern's new home; replacing the existing museum building which had become too small to hold the museum's vast and growing collection.

Situated across the street from the Kimbell Art Museum designed by Louis Kahn, immediate similarities and nods to the Kimbell can be read in the Modern: a relationship of garden to building, galleries planned and articulated in bays, and emphasis placed on the integration of natural light introduced into the gallery spaces through the ceiling and roof structure. Ando's use of exposed cast-in-place concrete walls are featured prominently within both the conceptual development and the physical realization of the museum, drawing immediate comparisons to the care taken in the design and construction of the Kimbell concrete walls.

However, appearances can be deceiving. A deeper examination into the constructive tale of the Modern reveals that over fifty percent of the form tie holes that articulate the finished face of the exposed concrete walls are cosmetic. They are present only to maintain the visual articulation and continuity of the finished concrete surface and pattern Ando desired, playing no active role in the physical construction of these walls.

In light of this revelation, would Ando's use of the cosmetic form tie be considered a case of architectural blasphemy, where the form tie's constructive nature is reduced to visual imagery, especially in the face of Kahn, whose presence casts a large and influential shadow on questions surrounding a building's making? Or could this be a situation where the use of the cosmetic form tie is not about a disregard for 'constructive honesty' on Ando's part, but rather suggests a different sensibility in the consideration of the wall, where surface expression governs.

This paper will address Ando's use of the cosmetic form tie at the Modern examining the significance of the constructive, formal, spatial, and experiential conditions and questions that emerge from its application.

In Situ

The Modern is situated within the museum district of Ft. Worth, Texas, nestled within a dense and rich architectural array of museums and civic institutions that include The Amon Carter Museum of American Art designed by Philip Johnson, the Kimbell Art Museum designed by Louis Kahn with a just recently completed addition designed by Renzo Piano, and the Will Rogers Memorial Center that includes a 2,800 seat auditorium and a contiguous series of exhibit halls that total 94,000 square feet. The Modern is the oldest established museum in Texas chartered in 1892 as the Fort Worth Public Library and Art Gallery. Prior to the commissioning and completion of the museum's new building by Ando, the Modern's home was located one block to the southwest of the Kimbell. It's first permanent facility was completed in 1954 and offered 12,000 square feet of exhibition space. Because of its growing and extensive collection, a new museum was needed.[1]

In 1996 the Modern held an invited competition asking six architects to provide design proposals for a new 150,000 square foot museum. The six invited architects were Tadao Ando, Arata Isozaki, Ricardo Legoretta, Richard Gluckman, Carlos Jimenez, and David Schwarz. Of the six submissions, the jury unanimously selected Ando's in May of 1997.

Construction began in 2000 and in 2002 the new Modern opened its doors to the public. The Modern sits on an eleven-acre site across the street from the Kimbell Art Museum and provides 53,000 square feet of exhibition space.[2]

Exposed

On March 2, 2004 a symposium entitled *Architectural Concrete - Pursuit of Perfection* was held at the University of Texas at Arlington in Arlington, Texas. Organized and moderated by W. Mark Gunderson, AIA - an architect practicing in Fort Worth, Texas - a panel comprised of Fred Langford, consultant to Louis I. Kahn on the Salk Institute in La Jolla, California, the Kimbell Art Museum in Fort Worth and the Capital complex at Dacca; Tom Seymour, past president of Thos. S. Byrne, Inc., responsible for the construction of the Kimbell Art Museum from 1969-72; and Paul Sipes, Vice President of Linbeck and Senior Project Manager for the construction of the Modern Art Museum of Fort Worth, discussed how Ando and Kahn considered and used concrete in these two museums.[3]

It was from this symposium that the use of the cosmetic form tie in the Modern was revealed. Typically, the form tie is considered a constructive necessity to the making of a cast-in-place concrete wall. They work in combination with the formwork system to secure the forming panels in place during the placement and curing of the concrete. The formed holes left in the finish face of the concrete wall is the constructive mark left by the form tie.

The reduction of required form ties was enabled by the use of a wood girder wall formwork system developed by PERI, a provider and manufacturer of concrete formwork and scaffolding systems. The PERI – VARIO GT 24 was the specific system used in forming the concrete walls at the Modern. The strength offered by this formwork system to resist the hydrostatic loads generated during the placement of the concrete allowed for a reduction in the number of form ties necessary to secure and hold the formwork in place.[4] To compensate for the reduction of required form ties, and maintain the ordered expression of the wall that Ando desired, the cosmetic form tie, or 'blind plug' as the PERI website described them, was introduced - secured to the face of the formwork and designed to match the diameter and depth of the 'active' form tie

holes.[5] Starting from the finish floor every even row of form tie holes is cosmetic in the Modern.[6]

The 'active' form tie openings as well as the cosmetic form tie depressions were sealed and finished with a cementitious grout. The face of the grout was held back from the finish face of the concrete wall one quarter of an inch to provide depth and shadow; bringing emphasis to the pattern the form ties created on the walls surface. Once the wall was completed, it became virtually impossible to distinguish between the two (Figure 1).

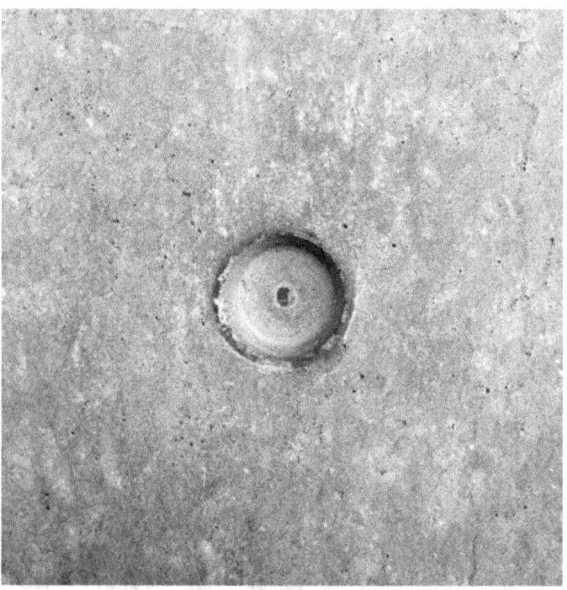

Fig. 1. Form tie hole: 'necessary' or 'cosmetic?' – the Modern

In discussing the use of the cosmetic form ties at the Modern, Paul Sipes explained that the primary reason they were considered was to,

"…eliminate a major item that could create a form leak problem and therefore produce a less than desirable concrete. Keeping the ties sealed in order to prevent concrete leakage at the tie hole location of the formwork is more difficult than keeping the formed corners from leaking. The eliminating of a process not needed to produce the result and increase the quality of the concrete was readily accepted by the project team. It did cost less to install the dummies and the formwork was assembled in less time."[7]

Sipes noted that in conversations regarding the concrete walls, Ando's primary focus was on the finish of the concrete. He wanted to achieve and maintain a continuity of surface that minimized both pour and form panel lines left by the formwork. Ando was not concerned over the type of 'active' form ties specified or the use of the cosmetic form tie, only that what was used would provide the diameter of the form tie hole he desired and that their spacing and arrangement was in keeping with his design intentions.

It was during the initial construction phase of the Modern that the use of the cosmetic form tie was discussed as a viable option. During this time, Sipes was in consultation with PERI in the design and development of the shop drawings for the formwork system. Ando was aware of and approved the use of cosmetic form ties.[8]

It should also be noted that the use of the cosmetic form tie is not unique to the Modern or Ando's work. The Pulitzer Arts Foundation in St. Louis, Missouri completed in 2001 and the Langen Foundation in Neuss-Hombroich, Germany completed in 2004 are two examples of other buildings of his that have integrated the use of the cosmetic form tie in the casting of the concrete walls. The PERI system was used in the forming of the concrete walls for these museums as well.[9]

Commenting on Ando's use of the cosmetic form tie at the Modern, Fred Langford mused at how Kahn may have reacted to its consideration:

"One afternoon we were walking with Dr. Salk and his son through the courtyard and talking about this very subject. "Well, we've got to plug these things with something unusual," and so the kid said, "How about gold?" We used to repeat that story. To continue with what I learned today at the Modern, I didn't know that every other row was a dummy set. We never used any dummies. Kahn would do back flips if you put a dummy in. He would say, "We'll find another way. Find another expression." If you don't need the tie in there, then don't use it."[10]

Kahn and the Kimbell

Across the street at the Kimbell, a similar constructive tale pertaining to the expression of structural verse formal expression was played out during the design of the north and south exterior elevations (Figure 2). In recounting the development of these elevations, Marshall Meyers, Kahn's project architect for the Kimbell, explained that Kahn called for a piece of glass, called a lunette, to be placed between the concrete cycloid shaped diaphragm (the thickened end of the concrete cycloid vault) and the travertine infill wall to make a clear separation and distinction between the building's structure and the non-bearing walls. According to Komendant's initial design, the diaphragm was to maintain a uniform depth of twelve inches. The glass lunette Kahn proposed was to maintain a uniform depth of six inches.

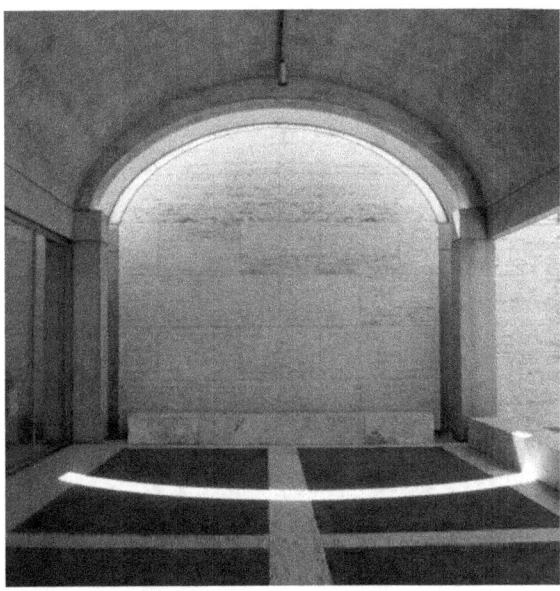

Fig. 2. Exterior Elevation – tapering lunette – Kimbell Art Museum

As the project developed a structural revision to the diaphragm made by Komendant changed its depth so that only at the apex of the cycloid vault did the diaphragm need to be thickened to twelve inches. The remainder of the diaphragm could taper in depth. Komendant took the position that this was the correct visual expression of these structural forces. Kahn saw this issue differently and was insistent that the diaphragm maintain its uniform depth of twelve inches. As Meyers points out,

"...to Kahn, this absolute expression of a minor structural condition was not his inclination. He preferred to express the more general aspect of a structural member rather than every nuance. As an example he would design cantilevered concrete beams with a constant height for the full length rather than reduce the beam's section the farther it cantilevered."[11]

While Kahn was determined on changing Komendant's mind, it was Komendant who prevailed in the end. Responding to this new structural condition Kahn kept the glass lunette in place and allowed it to follow the tapering profile of the diaphragm. The lunette became the mediator between the formal expression of the non-bearing walls and the structural expression of the diaphragm (Figure 3). Meyers noted that this type of detailing, which was so unlike Kahn, "generated great attention in the completed building and was a superb demonstration of his artistry."[12]

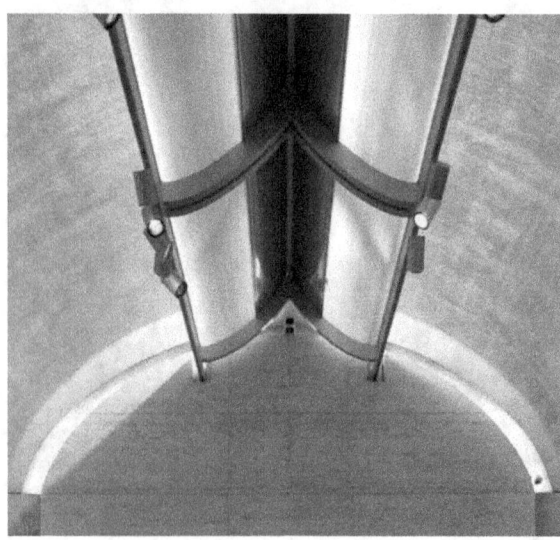

Fig. 3. Interior Elevation – tapering lunette – Kimbell Art Museum

What this tale from the Kimbell helps to illustrate is that Ando is not alone in trying to manage and balance the challenges of technological and constructive demands with structural and formal expression - a line that is (literally and metaphorically) not always so clearly or easily defined and asking the questions: at what point in the architect's decision making are certain architectural conditions selected to be expressed, concealed, or even engaged cosmetically? To what scale are these decisions scrutinized and acted upon?

Mistaken Identity

On the surface, the revelation of Ando's use of the cosmetic form tie appears to be at odds with a body of work that seems to favor tectonic expression demonstrated through the masterful use of exposed cast-in-place concrete. By allowing the form tie to become a 'negotiable' condition within the making of the wall brings this perceived tectonic position into question. Underlying Ando's work might be an inherent preference for the (a)tectonic – a position that may have always been present, yet overshadowed by his use of exposed concrete. The concession of the form tie becomes a silent admittance to the desire of maintaining and favoring surface over the 'honesty' of constructive expression or technological advancements.

In writing about architecture's constructive nature, Ando is careful to point out that it is the architect who must control how technology is considered and folded into their work. A point he articulates in the following passage from his essay, *The Traces of Architectural Intentions*:

"I believe it is important to be sensitive to the weight, hardness, and texture of materials and to have an intuitive grasp on the technical limits in their fabrication. Above all, the architect must define his own vision with respect to technology. Without precise individual aims, the architect will become subject to the economic logic and banal conventions that dominate technology. Technology is nothing more than knowledge. The architect's intentions and ideas control knowledge; these are more essential."[13]

Ando's use and deep understanding of a select material palate, comprised primarily of concrete and glass, helps to bring an acute awareness and focus to his crafting of spatial conditions and building details. The ordering and rhythm of the panel impressions and form tie holes left in the concrete wall establish a measured order and a scaled relationship of the formed spaces to the human body. The dense opaque boundaries that define the exterior walls provides a backdrop for an inward focused orchestration of spatial relationships, sequences, and encounters. Walls of concrete and glass frame, bound, and filter, bringing into focus and intensifying the experience of place through the lens of architectural space. The surface and order of the wall establishes a continuity of architectural thought Ando iteratively maintains from one building to the next. It could be speculated that the opportunity to change both the formal and constructive composition of the wall through a technological advancement in formwork would compromise his larger vision (Figure 4).

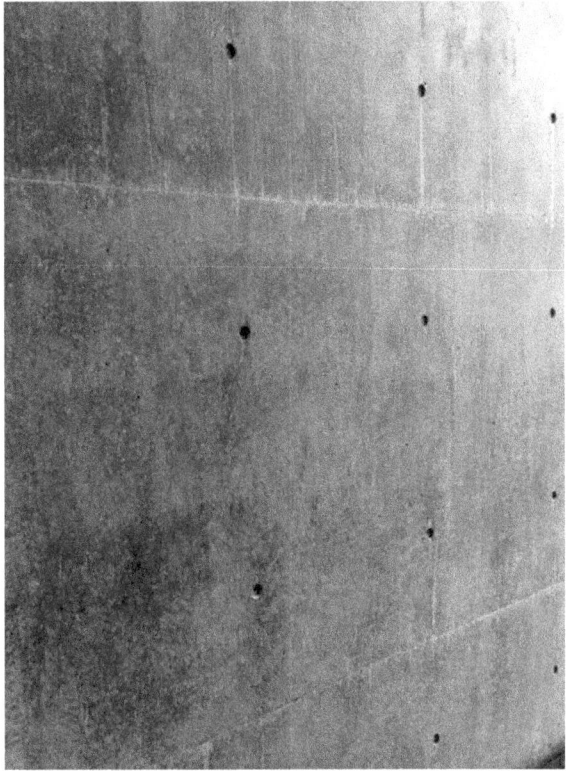

Fig. 4. Interior concrete wall – the Modern

"I attempt to use a modern material – concrete and, specifically, concrete walls – in simplified forms to realize a kind of space that is possible because I am Japanese. This rests on a simple aesthetic awareness cultivated in me as a Japanese person. It seems to me that at present, concrete is the most suitable material for realizing spaces created by rays of sunlight. But the concrete I employ does not have plastic rigidity or weight. Instead, it must be homogeneous and light and must create surfaces. When they agree with my aesthetic image, walls become abstract, are negated, and only the space they enclose gives a sense of really existing. Under these conditions, volume and projected light alone float into prominence as hints of the spatial composition."[14]

Seen in this light, the word cosmetic seems an apt way of describing Ando's walls. While cosmetic deals with surface, its etymological roots are found in *cosmos* – "an ordered and harmonious system of ideas, existences, etc., e.g. that which constitutes the sum-

total of 'experience.'"[15] His treatment of the wall surface begins to suggest a painterly sensibility where surface depth, color, geometry, and order define and govern the walls physical and formal presence and attributes. Ando's sensibilities could be compared to those of the American artist, Donald Judd:

"There is also, of course wholeness and unity of Judd's art itself, both in individual pieces and in the entirety of the work. For Judd, art was a totality, and to be this it had to be clear, with things resolved, and put together in a clear and exact way. (He would be compulsive about detail, and I remember trying to persuade him, to no avail, that it was probably impossible to join one-ton slabs of concrete in the Marfa field without a seam showing.)"[16]

Detailed Consideration

Edward Ford writes in his book, *The Architectural Detail*, that,

"The good detail is not consistent, but non-conforming; not typical, but exceptional; not doctrinaire, but heretical; not the continuation of an idea, but its termination, and the beginning of another."[17]

What could be taken away from Ford's words is that a condition such as the cosmetic form tie can stand as a detailed counter point within an architectural work; running contrary to building conventions and at times not bringing about a desired harmonic resolution. A dissonance emerges in the play between the formal, constructive, and performative forces coupled with architectural desires and intent. It is in these detailed struggles where the architect's true position is revealed.

If Ando had not built next door to Kahn, perhaps this question surrounding his use of the cosmetic form tie would not resonant so deeply (at least with this author) and might have otherwise been seen more as a construction anomaly in his other buildings. The initial knee-jerk reaction to blasphemy and deception especially in the presence of Kahn gives way to a surprisingly more empathic reading and consideration of its use. The cosmetic form tie is not a technicality, technological residue, or a victim of value engineering or indifference. Rather its use is intentional and controlled; asserting a position rooted within an (a)tectonic expression of an enveloping spatial totality. For Ando the cosmetic form tie's presence resonates at all scales; revealing that it does matter and is consequential - offering another lens in which to view and consider Ando's work.

"Details express what the basic idea of the design requires at the relevant point in the object: belonging or separation, tension or lightness, friction, solidity, fragility…. Details, when they are successful, are not mere decoration. They do not distract or entertain. They lead to an understanding of the whole of which they are an inherent part."[18]

Notes:

[1] *Making the Modern*, directed by Harry Lynch (a TRINITY FILMS production, 2003), DVD.

[2] *Making the Modern*, Lynch, DVD.

[3] W. Mark Gunderson, "Architectural Concrete: The Pursuit of Perfection," in *TEX FILES: Issue 01: Toward Architecture 2 The University of Texas at Arlington,* ed. Karen Bullis (Arlington, Texas: University of Texas, School of Architecture, 2004), p.

[4] Paul Sipes, e-mail message to author, August 14, 2012.

[5] "Langen Foundation," PERI-USA, accessed March 14, 2017. https://www.peri-usa.com/projects/cultural-buildings/langen-foundation.html

[6] Gunderson, "Architectural Concrete," 69.

[7] Sipes, e-mail message to author, August 14, 2012.

[8] Ibid.

[9] "Langen Foundation," PERI-USA, accessed March 14, 2017.

[10] Gunderson, "Architectural Concrete," 70.

[11] Marshall Meyers, "Making the Kimbell: A Brief Memoir," in *Louis I. Kahn: The Construction of the Kimbell Art Museum,* ed. Luca Bellinelli (Milano: Italy Skira, 1999), 11.

[12] Ibid.

[13] Tadao Ando, "The Traces of Architectural Intentions," in *Tadao Ando: Complete Works,* ed. Francesco Dal Co (London: Phaidon, 1995), 461.

[14] Tadao Ando, "From Self-Enclosed Modern Architecture towards Universality," 448.

[15] *Oxford English Dictionary Online*, s.v. "cosmos," accessed February 10, 2017, http://www.oed.com.ezproxy.lib.vt.edu/.

[16] William Agee, "Donald Judd in Retrospect: An Appreciation," in *Donald Judd: Sculpture : September 16 - October 15, 1994, The Pace Gallery 32 East 57th Street NYC* (New York: PaceWildenstein, 1994), p 9.

[17] Edward Ford, *The Architectural Detail* (New York: Princeton Architectural Press, 2011), 312.

[18] Peter Zumthor, *Thinking Architecture / Peter Zumthor*, 2nd, expanded ed., tran. Maureen Oberlin-Turner (essays 1988-1996) and Cahterine Schlebert (essays 1998-2004) (Boston: Birkhäuser, 2006), 15.

Images:

All images taken by author.

Operation: Lightness

Bruce Wrightsman
Kansas State University

Abstract

"Eighty percent of the environmental impacts of the products, services, and infrastructures around us is determined at the design stage."

John Thackara – *In the Bubble - Designing in a Complex World*

This quote by John Thackara holds especially true in the building industry. The cost and energy expended during the process significantly increases the closer you approach the material reality of construction. In normative architectural practice there is little opportunity to experiment and test building performance during a building's conception. This is when the designer can profoundly influence its long-term performance. However, with a few exceptions, construction methodologies and material application have not changed significantly over the past several generations. Buildings are heavy, often material inefficient, and reliant on wasteful, site-intensive fabrication methods. In contrast, for other design industries outside the architectural milieu, the building process has significantly transformed the relationship between design and fabrication. The development of new material synergies and lightweight building systems has lightened material assemblies, fabrication techniques and the design of form.

What is 'lightness'? Lightness is more than an associative quality of weight. Architecturally speaking, it is an ideal that reaches beyond the physical domain of material substance. It is a holistic framework for design that fundamentally questions how to responsibly construct the built and natural environments. My research into this architectonic philosophy I term 'lightness' investigates alternative material systems and design methodologies that value lightness and tread lightly on the earth. This paper will present the design methodologies of architects and industry leaders whose work embodies these same ideals. The research has evolved and transformed my teaching of design and architectural structures at the grassroots level of the classroom.

LEAN systems

Nowhere is this ideal of 'lightness' as a design system more apparent than through the LEAN production system at Boeing Airlines. *Kaizen* is a Japanese term for a continuous cycle of incremental process improvement. The identification of waste within a system starts with the process of continuous improvement or *kaizen*.[1] The Boeing LEAN system focuses on the entire value stream of the Boeing operation from raw material to finished product. It covers areas of space, labor, energy, material, time, transportation and safety. What has developed is a guide of nine tactics to a Lean System. Included is an understanding of the flows of values, which comes through mapping the entire production flow from raw material to finish project, identifying values in the system and how they develop. Strategies include documenting and balancing the distribution of work; even re-designing the manufacturing process and the tools to improve efficiency and performance. The most profound change at Boeing came from redesigning the mode of production from a stationary line to a 'pulsing line'.[2] In a pulsing line, the movement of the system is not constant, but it will stop if a detected problem is not fixed in a designated period of time. Production will not restart until the problem has been resolved. While production time is affected; quality, performance and safety issues are not impacted in the process. The idea is for each tactic to provide immediate improvement to the current production system. Boeing engineers report that the LEAN system has proven a resounding success.

The act of building should be a reflective act, one that recognizes its repercussions. It should reinforce the need for lighter, less wasteful design approaches for architects and designers. Architects and educators should lead the charge through rigorous research and introspective practice to understand and discover an architectural paradigm that treads lightly. In my research, the focus on lightness is investigated through design methods and buildings systems that challenge traditional paradigms and discover inventive solutions, which improve construction efficiency and tread lighter on the landscape.

Neil Astle

One architect whose methodology epitomizes this critical exploration of the design process is Neil Astle. He opened his first practice, Astle/Ericson, in Omaha, Nebraska in 1965. Initially Astle began exploring wood as a building material, testing its structural limits and potential as a craft. During his career, spanning over thirty years, he incorporated multiple iterations of wood assemblies into his practice.

Neil Astle was a proponent of modern systems theory, which consists of a set of elements intrinsically linked together. It is important to understand Astle's underlying philosophical approach to the design process. The relationship between elements is such that all actions and activities are interrelated, and a change in one part will cause an integral change in all parts, as well as the system as a whole. In systems design, the designer is guided by the understanding of contextual systems where a design response emerges from the relationships between multiple contexts. Design is about economy and efficient construction, based on understanding specific limitations, which may vary greatly for the prospective project. For Astle, this approach informs and directs his investigation on material performance and on-site building strategies. It is most evident in the design of his own house in 1968, when Astle faced numerous limitations that would ultimately direct his decision to abandon traditional wood frame construction methods and invent an innovative approach to structure, material and space.

A range of factors influenced Astle to abandon traditional stick frame construction and find new construction logic from which to build. Traditional wood framing is based on dimensional members nailed together and given rigidity through the application of interior and exterior sheathing that resist lateral forces. These assemblies form walls, floors and roofs that are then conventionally nailed together through simple plate surfaces. These connections are not considered rigid and must be supplemented with specialized connection components. In contrast, the Astle house incorporates an interconnected rationale: a wood system based upon the lap joint, utilizing overlapping 2x2 cedar scantling (collection of small wood pieces), which form an interlocking bearing wall structure. Similar to a weaving process, the alternating layers of 2x2's are rotated in the opposite directions, forming interlocking vertical and horizontal planes. [Figure 1].

Thinness is a fundamental principle of the Astle house. Under normal beam loads, a pair of 2x4s nailed together could structurally span about 12'-0". However, Astle was able to increase the span capabilities of the 2x4 assembly through fixed wall to floor and wall to ceiling connections. The interlocking joint created a rigid connection, which reduced critical moment stresses by allowing some of the bending stress of the floor or ceiling to be taken by the walls [Figure 2]. Staggering alternate members increased the span at the ceiling and floor structure vertically, thus increasing the effective depth and stiffness of the assembly. At the roof, the vertical stagger is increased to work with the slope of the roof. This increases the effective depth of the section, allowing 2x4's to span greater distances as long as 17-0".

The exterior wall assembly in contrast is quite thin, utilizing a sandwich assembly of 2x2 nailed cedar wood for the outer layers. The inner layer of 2x2's were oriented horizontally and became an integral part of the structure as it interlocked with the floor and ceiling. In this way, it eliminated the need for plates, which are typically required in conventional wood framing, giving the house a striking lightness revealed through its thin exposed edges. [Figure 2]. The lengths of each wood member are left random to allow walls, floors and roof planes to engage one another. The overlapping ends were then trimmed and creatively used in other parts of the construction, thereby minimizing material waste. The waste of wood was limited to below three percent, far less than traditional wood frame construction practices.

The Astle house is built on a severely sloping site with a basement in the middle section of the house. The outside walls, which are supported by concrete piers, overhang the basement walls. Pushing the piers inward from the outside bearing wall allows the main floor to overhang effectively. Weaving together the external forces within the floor to wall connection reduces the moment at the center of the floor span to almost zero. This is typically where moment forces would normally be the greatest [Figure 2]. This allows the floor assembly to use smaller 2x4's and retain a thinner sectional depth from that of a standard framed house. The interconnected methodology generates significant increases in spanning ability of the scantling. This allows greater volumetric space through shallow floor depth, making the house feel much larger.

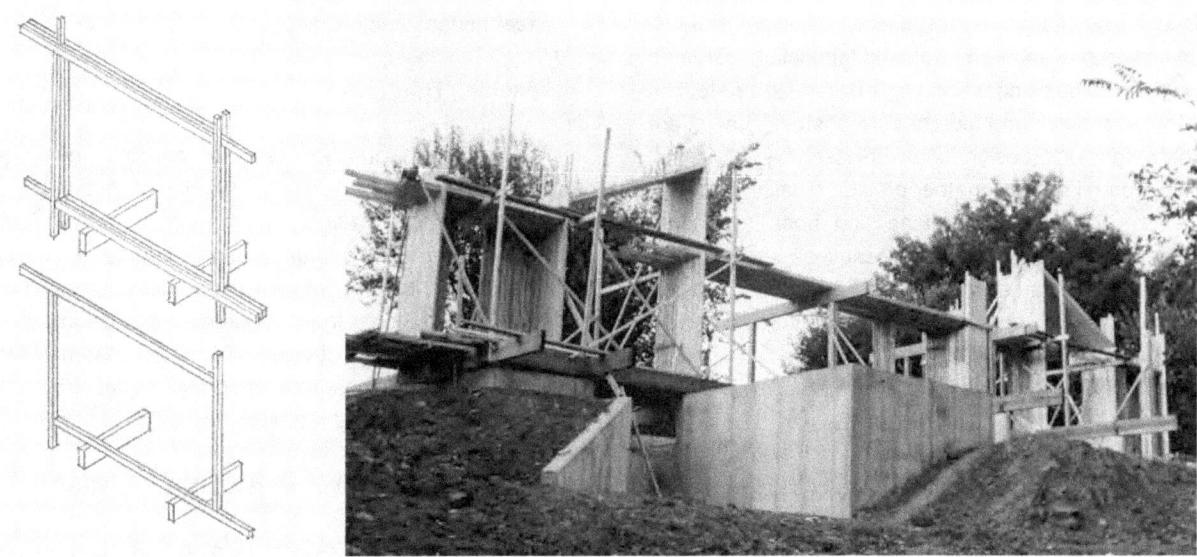

Figure 1: Interlocking wood scantling system: single row showing rotational placement (bottom left). Three consecutive rows showing alternating clockwise and counter-clockwise rotations nailed to each other (top left). House during construction (right). Images courtesy of Kari Astle.

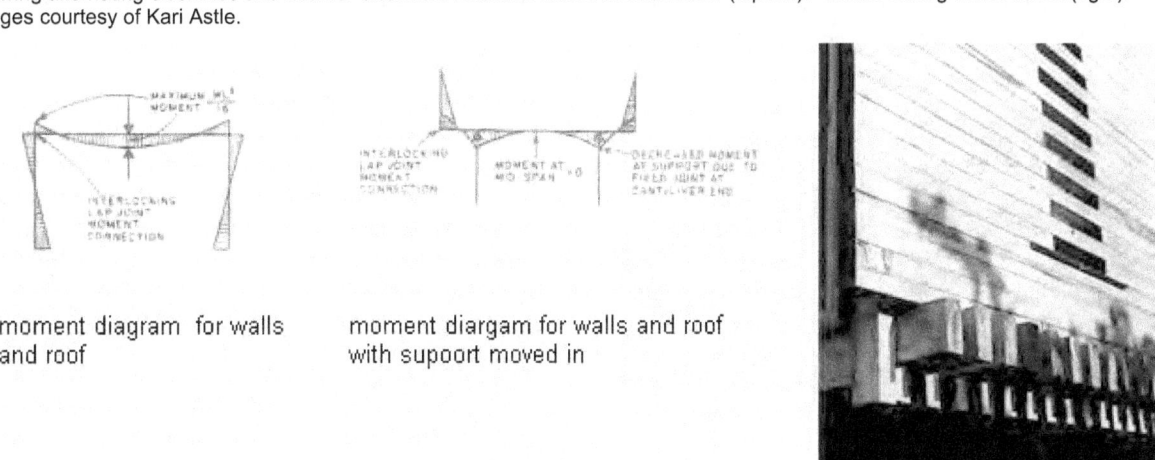

moment diagram for walls and roof

moment diargam for walls and roof with supoort moved in

Figure 2: Moment diagrams for Astle house (left). Floor wall detail (right). Images courtesy of Kari Astle.

Hiroaki Kimura

Architecture is a synthesis of structure and material, merged through method (practice) and crafted by technique (tools). The work of Japanese architect Hiroaki Kimura employs this principle through a deep understanding of the physical properties of large sheet steel and its ease to be factory-produced. Kimura's residential work employs a monocoque steel sheets facade which constitutes both structure and surface, [Figure 3]. Monocoque (French term for single shell), is a structural approach whereby loads are supported through an object's external skin. This type of system is predominantly lighter than its site built counterparts and for architecture could play a key role in shortening the assembly process on the building site.

Like Astle, Kimura is interested in developing simpler methods, which reduce labor intensiveness of on-site construction. The large dense population in Japan has resulted in very small building sites from which to build on. Because they have little or no area for on-site storage for materials and equipment, Kimura focuses on the factory production of sheet steel to develop a new method of on-site fabrication. Created with a rigorous understanding of material production and its architectural potential, the steel sheets are lightweight and designed for disassembly into units, shipped and bolted together on-site, creating a unitary facade[3]. Similar to airplane and boat fabrication, joints are welded, forming a seamless surface. The steel sheet exterior walls arrive at the site and are quickly fixed at upper and lower beams like a curtain wall. This significantly reduces the amount of components needed to structure and enclose the building.

Kimura uses technology already practiced in the steel industry to roll, shape, and cut steel panels. The sizes of the steel sheets are determined by the structural design and transportation limitations of the material. After the sheets are bolted together on site, the joints are welded forming a unitary façade of sheet steel.

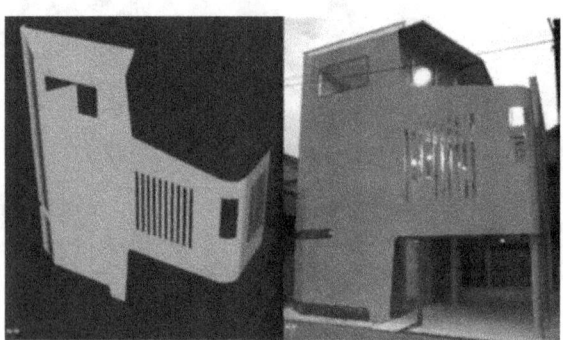

Figure 3: Digital model for steel sheet pattern (left). A-House by Hiroaki Kimura (right). Photograph by Ueda Miyoji

Kimura progresses a structural and material comprehension that transcends aesthetic criteria, offering an alternative practice based upon the expression of lightness and performance within the design and fabrication process. His research of a normative material process such as steel critically illustrates its high-strength properties, capabilities,

and manufacturing flexibility. Through design and manufacturing, the steel sheets could be digitally modeled then cut and rolled into various shapes assembled into more complex forms. The design flexibility within the sheet steel manufacturing process has opened the design opportunity for numerous steel sheet houses and buildings.

Teaching lightness

Architectural education should critically evaluate building design as a holistic system of material and technique (assemblage), integrating materials, form and structure as a fundamental principal. My research focus on lightweight building approaches has filtered into the Structures curriculum and graduate seminars. Projects focus on material and structural investigation strategies to inspire and explore lightness and material inventiveness.

Exploring tension: Innovators Lounge

Founded in 2004, HATCH is a 4-day, semi-annual innovation summit for creative professionals and thought leaders who are serious about transforming their ideas and talent into bold action, while being inspired by others who are doing the same. Topics in the summit cover areas from film to music to architecture.

The Innovators Lounge space is a community design/build project for HATCH. The 2011 project brought together the students from a graduate seminar and a local design firm to transform the ballroom space of a local Cultural Center into the Innovators Lounge space, serving as a multi-function social space, which hosts numerous events for the HATCH summit.

The Innovator's lounge is an experiential space of surface, light, and sound. The project challenged students to think about materials, fabrication details, and assemblies. Material assemblies had to be easily broken down into basic components for reuse in future installations, or recycled. This goal drove students to find a highly innovative yet fully sustainable design approach for the 2011 Innovators Lounge project.

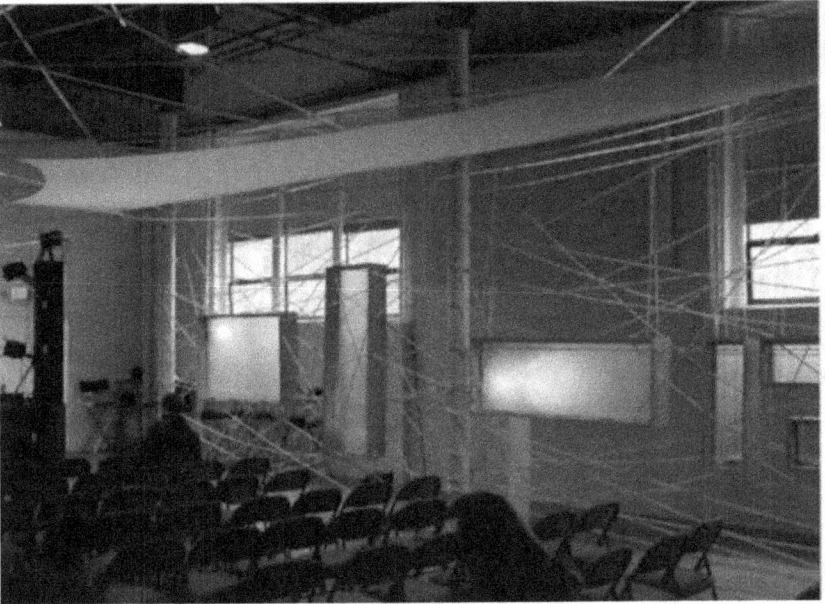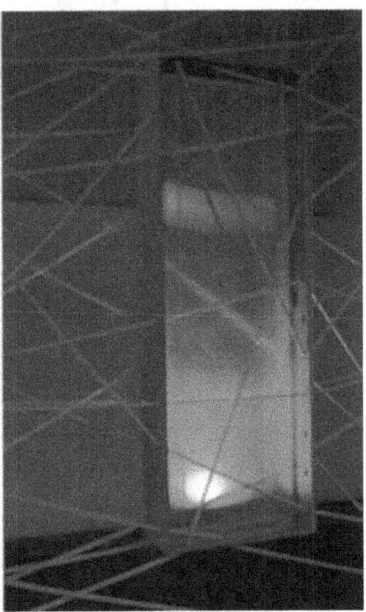

Figure 4: Innovators Lounge installation, 2011. Photographs by author

"The simplest representation of a structural element is the line…" Cecil Blamond

The class investigated the design opportunities of nylon rope as a supplement to large fabric sheets used in previous installations. The tensile properties of nylon rope were explored as a strong yet flexible material system that could be easily manipulated. Students learned through the experimentation that the rope needed constant stretching to apply the required tension as they weaved the perimeter of the space together. Suspended through the tension system were translucent panels where guests were able to write and exchange their ideas, which then became part of the installation. The Innovator's Lounge is a uniquely dynamic social space celebrating inventiveness and creativity through physical engagement with materials and light.

Engaging elasticity and the theory of strength

Materials are structurally passive; they can only resist eternal forces when subjected to stress (deformation). This exploration into material properties continued in my Advanced Structures seminar, which investigated elasticity and the theory of strength. A critical area of this class investigated the science of the material world and how it functions, to develop an understanding of the micro-scale of material performance and what gives materials their strength. The class completed design projects that tested lightweight macroscopic material and structure systems.

One group project explored the elastic properties of plastic and its associative tensile strength. The students tested common plastic wrap, renowned for its stretching properties and typically used for sealing food items. The stickiness of the material allowed the students to use the single material as surface, structure and connection.

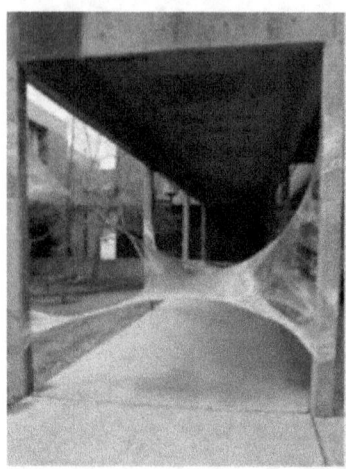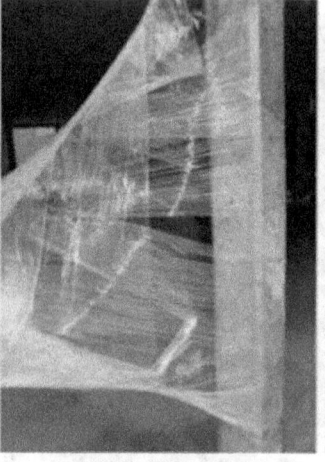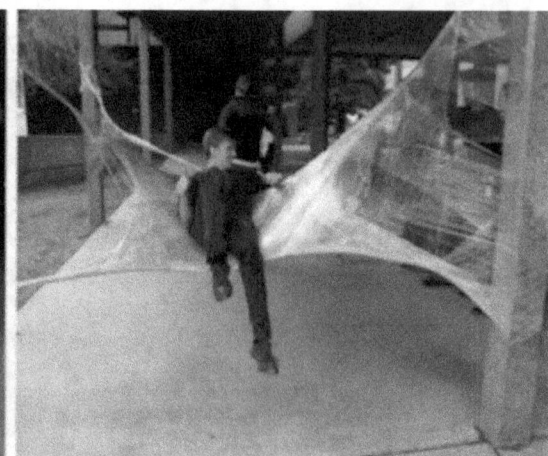

Figure 5: Plastic-wrap tensile structure installation. Photographs by author.

Using rolls of plastic wrap and multiple prototypes, they wrapped a series of columns together at a busy covered entryway to a campus building. The material process formed a flexible spatial object that could support the weight of multiple people. This elastic object activated the space, allowing curious students and faculty to physically engage its strength through manipulation of its elastic properties.

Operation: Lightness

Architects and educators must become leaders for the charge toward new ideas on lightness, material efficiency, and building performance through rigorous research and introspective practice. These innovations help uncover architectural paradigms that value lightness and tread more lightly on the earth.

The role of lightness in architecture does not solely lie in invention; it should question current material practices and seek to modernize those practices, transcending into fields in and outside the architectural milieu. Innovation in architecture is better understood as real outcomes, such as new

.

design methods and construction practices. In my classroom, exploring lightness has led to the re-envisioning of material systems. It has expanded structural expression and emboldened the learning of architectural education on materials, structure and assembly.

Notes:

[1] Boeing, LEAN A Pocket Guide

[2] Boeing, LEAN A Pocket Guide

[3] Kimura, Hiroaki, "Steel Sheet House", Armus Press, 2001.

The Metrics of Poetics: Poetic Detailing and the Study of Daylight in the Gipsoteca Canoviana Addition by Carlo Scarpa

Judy O'Buck Gordon
Kansas State University

Abstract

The juncture of poetics, the act of making/revealing with materials and tectonics in play, is the area of my interest. Through architectonic poetics - the intersection of architectural materials, textures, light and space with human sight, touch, sound and scent - the spaces of the Gipsoteca Canoviana Addition focus on the immediacy of the experience by awakening our bodily senses. In this project, the inherent programmatic relationships were overlaid with the subjective experience and the physical structured space was enriched with detailing that enhances the experience.

Architecture is participatory and objective, it is the spatial artifact that shapes us. By using architectural detailing and phenomenology, the spaces of the Gipsoteca Canoviana Addition, Possagno, Italy, Carlo Scarpa created a tangible, but uncanny, spatial realm.

The intent of this paper is to investigate the spatial realm through the "joining" of the phenomenological detailing with spatial experiential properties through the evaluation and analyzation of daylight.

The performance of the Scarpa's detailing will be evaluated through the programs, Radiance[1] and DI-VA,[2] simulating the lighting conditions at the solstices and equinoxes. The simulated daylighting conditions of the Gipsoteca will be compared to current illuminance recommendations for a sculpture gallery as well as contemporary metrics for luminance-based contrast. It may be that contrast and glare contribute to the poetics of the space. The question to be answered is this - does the poetic daylighting created by Scarpa's detailing align with contemporary metrics?

The three spaces that will be analysed and evaluated are: the double height gallery with two types of skylights that "capture the blue of the sky" ("Volevo ritagliare l'azzurro del cielo"[3]), a room without corners; the spatial transition as defined by the four translucent sky vitrines at the first level change near the statue *Dirce;* and the southern gallery that houses the *Three Graces.* It is intended that this research will establish the impact of the detailing on these three spaces and the contribution, or interference/intervention, of the detailing with respect to daylight performance.

Museo Canoviana di Possagno Addition: The Gipsoteca[4]

Poetics

The Canova Museum addition, the Giposteca, was commissioned in 1955, by the Superintendent of Fine Arts, Soperintendenza alle Gallerie e alle Opera d'Arte of Venice to Carlo Scarpa. The superintendent, Moschini, had worked with Scarpa on the Accademia Gallery in Venice.[5] The Gipsoteca was planned to house the plaster casts and terracotta modelli[6] from Antonio Canova's Rome studio, which could not be housed in the Canova Museum due to lack of space Also 1957, was the bicentennial year of Canova's birth and the desire was to reveal the casts to the public

Moschini entrusted Scarpa to re-envision the museum as Scarpa thought necessary.[7] Scarpa's response was to leave the original 1836 museum untouched and to site the addition to the west of the museum.[8] The gently north to south sloping site was bounded tightly by the existing property lines, within a grove of trees and a small lane. The footprint of the addition worked with the constraints and the Gipsoteca was primarily designed as an interior experience.[9] The roof of the gallery can be seen from the stables courtyard, but more importantly the form of the Gipsoteca is revealed as one is leaving the museum grounds along the lane. It is the first time that the Gipsoteca is seen and is the last building of the complex to be seen.[10] The addition seems to furtively appear as not to disturb its surroundings, in particular not to detract from the significant Canova Museum; but its interior is a radical departure from the interior of the museum.

The 1836 Canova Museum was one of the first buildings to be designed specifically as a museum[11]. The original gallery had light grey walls with focused light,[12] with a red and white patterned floor. The casts lined the walls bounding the central axis of the basilica plan. Scarpa used a monochromatic color scheme that was in direct opposition to the idea of display of sculpture in the 1950s[13]. The selection of the wall color was one of deduction, analyzation and intuition.

...not because I wanted to argue with traditional reason, but out of a sudden intuition, I thought it would be better to have a white background, because in the other gallery, the larger one (museum), they had chosen ash-grey colors...to make the statues stand out. What sort of color would I have? Black? Impossible, it doesn't reflect at all...[14]

Scarpa understood that the color scheme and layout of the original museum served an illustrative purpose, however Scarpa realized the spaces of the addition required a certain reflectance and that "white was best."[15] The white-on-white - floor, celling, and walls - at the Gipsoteca, while a critical response to the exhibition conventions[16], enabled Scarpa to challenge the visitor's perception of light, dark and shadow.[17]

The interior walls and ceilings of the Scarpa's addition are exceptionally smooth, slightly reflective as a result from Scarpa's particular mix of the Venetian plaster, *stucco lucido,*[18] - slaked lime (lime and water)with finely powdered marble.[19] The floor is composed of eleven[20] distinct patterns with nine interior patterns and two exterior patterns. The patterned interior floors are composed of slabs of highly reflected "seamless" Clauzetto white marble, with some patterns clearly delineating a specific space and others indicating that there is an intentional overlapping of space.
The approach to the Museum is direct from the street entrance. One passes through the dark archway that is the depth of the building that lines the street, passing marble statues to the ones right and finding relief, from the light filled courtyard, to the left. The smooth walkway directs one to the pair of doors ahead. When opened a small statuette indicates one is to enter. Immediately upon entering the visitor is shifted right

around the restored sculpture[21] and is confronted with a choice. Should one move to the west toward the lighted room with plaster casts in silhouette and direct light in unusual positions - the Gipsoteca? Or should one move into the "basilica" - the Canova Museum, toward *Hercules and Lichas* located in the apse[22]?

As one moves toward the galleries of the addition from the museum, Scarpa evokes a "speculative tension" which induces anticipation and goes beyond memory. [23] The body leaves the floor of patterned red and white marble tiles set on a 45 degree angle in the museum and negotiates the level change by climbing three floating treads composed of a highly reflected "seamless" Clauzetto white marble.[24] The floating treads defy gravity and mark the waterline of the imagined canal. The beckoning of the plaster cast male torso, located at the threshold of the addition and the museum, not quite in one place or the other, with his partial body , slightly twisted, gesturing with his head and body and shoulder and implied (missing) arm, pointing the way into the 1957 Scarpa addition, creating a moment of desire filled with uncertainty. What lies beyond? It is the starkness of the white galleries that signals the uncanny, otherworldliness of the addition - a world that is disconnected and contained.

One enters the rectangular gallery which serves as a juncture; at this point there is a choice to move toward the light of the double height gallery, as first seen from the 18th original museum, or around the corner into the unknown. For Scarpa this moment was clear, for him a sense of "uneasiness" and "anxiety" is in the dominion of architecture[25] and must be made manifest.

This rectangular dimly light gallery, receiving little direct light, is positioned between particular architectural moments: double height, light filled gallery that contains the two sets of corner skylights; the elongated gallery which is delineated by the threshold skylight at the first descending level change and reinforced by the position of plaster cast of the headless *Dirce* and the compressed elongated wedge gallery, displaying the *Three Graces,* that continues beyond to the reflecting pool and bucolic world[26] through the wall of glass that begins at the floor and wraps upward to become the ceiling. (Fig. 1)

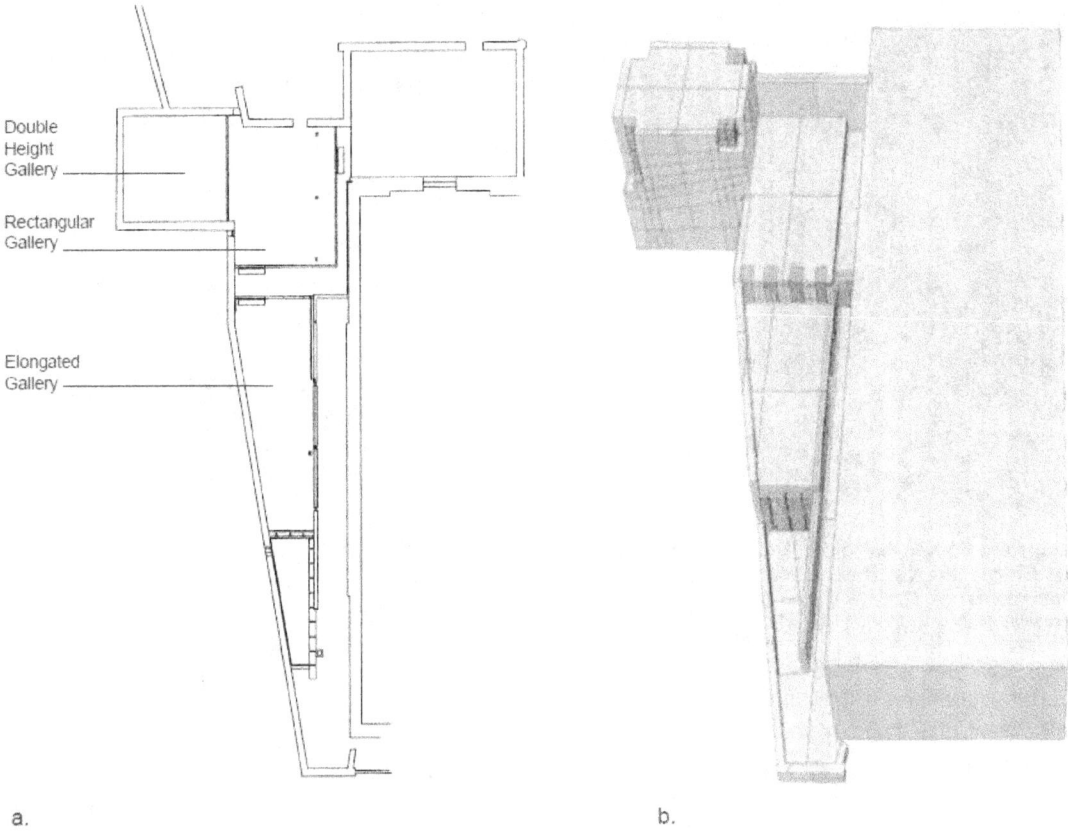

Double
Height
Gallery

Rectangular
Gallery

Elongated
Gallery

a.

b.

N▲
Fig. 1. Plan (redrawn) and Axonometric. (source: redrawn plan: Author; axonometric W. Al Mutawa)

The double height gallery is volumetrically reminiscent of Canova's studio and plaster cast storeroom, which is located diagonally opposite in Canova Museum compound.[27] This reminiscence is Scarpa's way of connecting to history by a presencing of the past.[28] Spatially it is the studio rotated ninety degrees; experientially it is an ethereal world. It is disconnected from the rectangular juncture gallery by an upward level change and two reveals - a glass reveal in the west wall allowing light to spill across the floor and a recess in the north wall. This disconnection clarifies spatial independence of the double height gallery and allows Scarpa to change the atmosphere. It is this room that transforms to become the realm of the sky, through two types of corner skylights, that are in matching pairs on the west and east walls.[29] These skylights are made of the same black iron and glass as the vitrines holding the terracotta modelli[30] - the grounded vitrines have been transformed to capture light and the sky. It is this light from the first pair of elongated vitrines on the west wall that reveal themselves immediately and draws one into the space. (Fig. 2) The light fills the room in a particular way.

The south corner of the western wall is bright. *Cupid and Psyche with Butterfly* are illuminated and caressed by the sun. The cast of *George Washington* with its back to the entry, calls one to face him. He seems to be in conversation with the bust of *Napoleon*, but *Napoleon* seems uninterested, he is casting his gaze toward the bust of *Canova*. Below this datum of the line of gazing, the *Sleeping Nymph* rests, while *Naiads* looks over her shoulder away from the moving, living body - the visitor. At the eye level

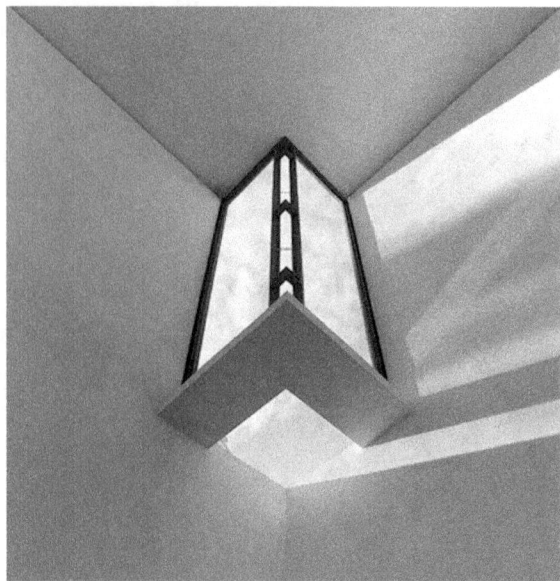

Fig. 2. Southwest Corner Skylight in Double Height Gallery from Entry (source: Seier+Seier [photographer]. (2012.) *detail: corner skylight, type one.* [Photograph]. Retrieved from www.flickr.com/photos/seier/9023203200/)

of the visitor, the butterfly of *Cupid and Psyche* comes into view. Upon turning the moving body is face-to-face with the cast of *George Washington* only to be ignored as he is still gazing at *Napoleon*. The live eye is then drawn to upward to the east to the two cubic outward light vitrines that dissolve into the sky. The corners of the room have been dematerialized. One then turns to the west to depart to find that the sky is framed at the bottom of the two inward elongated light vitrines. *Volevo ritagliare l'azzurro del* cielo,[31] Scarpa truly "cut out the blue of the sky."[32] The double height gallery is a room without corners, a room where the intangible (light) becomes tangible. An uncanny architectural condition.

As one progresses through the rectangular gallery and proceeds south toward the elongated gallery, the spatial transition is defined by the dissolution of the ceiling by the glare of the four translucent sky vitrines at the threshold of the first level change. (Fig. 3) The threshold is marked by the plaster cast of the reclining headless *Dirce*.[33] She is facing the *Three Graces*, with her back toward the visitor, ever staring at toward the *Three Grace*, encouraging us to place our head where hers is not. The space is guarded by the glass vitrines, filled with terracotta models on thin iron stands, resembling impaled heads on stakes, which present their broad side (face) for viewing, reminding us of the headless *Dirce* at the threshold.

As the space compresses, with the glass east wall transforms into a solid mass with small openings, providing a "twinkling" surface for the *Three Graces*. Details such as the last level change and new paving pattern disconnects the space of the *Three Graces* from the interior of the Gipsoteca to form a theatrical stage. The *Three Graces,* intertwined to form one, are off-center of this stage, yet are centered with the reclining *Dirce*, in a continuing reciprocity. This off-centered position allows the visitor to occupy the stage with the *Three Graces*. The stage of the *Three Graces* is detailed to disconnect from the interior gallery to join the (captured) pastoral world. Here Scarpa, the Venetian,[34] places water contained by exterior walls, which "dissolve" the floor to a reflective transparency; that reflective transparency is the found again on the glass walls and ceiling. Scarpa removes the entire end of the space - the ceiling and walls are transparent - the sky is revealed; the space of the water and sky is presented to the visitor. At this boundary a presencing begins.[35] The pool of water creates a caustic network that can be seen on and above the *Three Graces,* placing them in an uncanny scene. The lead pins that pierce the "skin" of the delicate *Graces,* that transformed them into a marble sculpture, transforms them into other "beings."

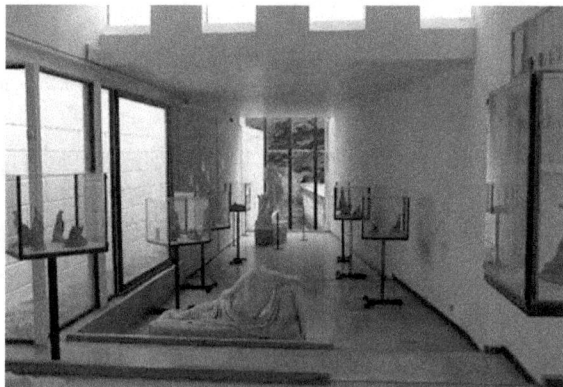

Fig. 3. Elongated Wedge Shaped Gallery from Rectangular Gallery (source: Mathew Roberts [photographer]. (2013.) *Canova Museum Wing by Scarpa.* [Photograph]. Retrieved from https://www.flickr.com/photos/btx91/8806025473/)

Thus the experience of the visitor through the three discrete volumes at the Gipsoteca,[36] the rectangular space gallery, the double height gallery and the elongated, wedge shaped gallery, the interaction with the plaster casts and clay modelli are arranged by Scarpa.[37] The movement from space to space is choreographed by commissioning light[38] via Scarpa's phenomenological architectural detailing. It is this intersection of architectural materials, light and space with human presence that reveal his intentions. This interaction puts the visitor in a place "in which one does not know where one is"[39] and blurs the distinction between imagination and reality.[40]

Metrics

The use of light by Scarpa is unintentionally, but accurately described by the architect Louis I. Kahn as he writes of his use of natural light at the Kimbell Museum, *"...light, this great maker of presences...has all the moods of the time of the day, the seasons of the year, (which) year for year and day for day are different from the day preceding."*[41] This is true for Scarpa's use of light. For Scarpa, is not the marking of the passing light that is of importance, but it is the way that the light creates "moods," unexpected encounters with light as found in the double height gallery with its four corner skylights; the lighted threshold of space in the elongated wedge gallery and the release of the gallery to the light at the *Three Graces*.

The two concepts used in the basic metrics of daylighting studies are illuminance and luminance. Illuminance is the amount of light falling on a surface and spreading, directly calculated as 1meter² and measured in the SI unit lux, *lx* or foot-candle, which is "the illuminance on a surface by a candela source one foot away." Luminance is the light reflected from the surface and perceptible to the human eye; the SI unit is *cd/m²*, candela/meter².[42] Luminance often referred to as the "brightness of the light reflected off of a surface."[43] Glare, the "condition of vision where there is discomfort or a reduction in the ability to see details or objects, caused by unsuitable distribution or range of luminance or extreme contrasts"[44] will be noted, as well as, contrast which is the ability to perceive luminance difference on adjacent surfaces.[45]

The analytics considered when reviewing the galleries of the Gipsoteca were the horizontal and vertical luminance, horizontal and vertical illuminance from fixed locations at two points in the gallery. Both locations are in the rectangular gallery that joins the double height and the elongated wedge gallery. The first location was facing west, toward the double height gallery. The second location was just north of the threshold of the elongated wedge gallery. Looking

toward the south and the *Three Graces*. When using the program DIVA-for-Rhino a reflectance percentage is assigned to the surfaces, for the Giposteca it is known that Scarpa used reflective white marble for the floor and *stucco lucido*, a mixture of plaster, with equal amounts of powdered marble and *grassello* (slaked lime – lime and water that has been aged) for the walls and ceiling. The surface of this material is said to be "shiny."[46] The reflectance percentage used in the simulation was 75%, with the understanding that this would accurately illustrate the described surfaces.

Vicenza is the city closest to Possagno and was used for the Sky Cover Range was generated from the software Climate Consultant 3.0 as seen in Figure 4. This chart indicates that for approximately 45% of the year Possagno has cloud cover. Therefore in the Radiance simulations, Intermediate Sky Conditions were used for this study.

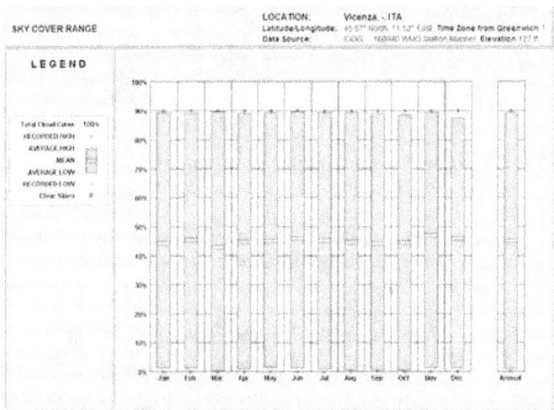

Fig. 4. The "Sky Cover Range" Chart for Vicenza. Climate Consultant 3.0 (source: M. Gibson)

The recommended lux levels issued by the Illuminating Engineering Society (IES) for "Room Illumination Level for Museums and Art Galleries General" is 300lx for "Exhibits Insensitive to Light."[47] The plaster casts and clay models fall under this category and do not deteriorate at these levels. Also the luminance-based contrast or luminance ratio for museums is 3:1 between the object being displayed and the surrounding area.[48] While these are the contemporary metrics for museum design and are the parameters used in this paper to evaluate the conditions at the Gipsoteca, it is not being supposed that Scarpa used such data.

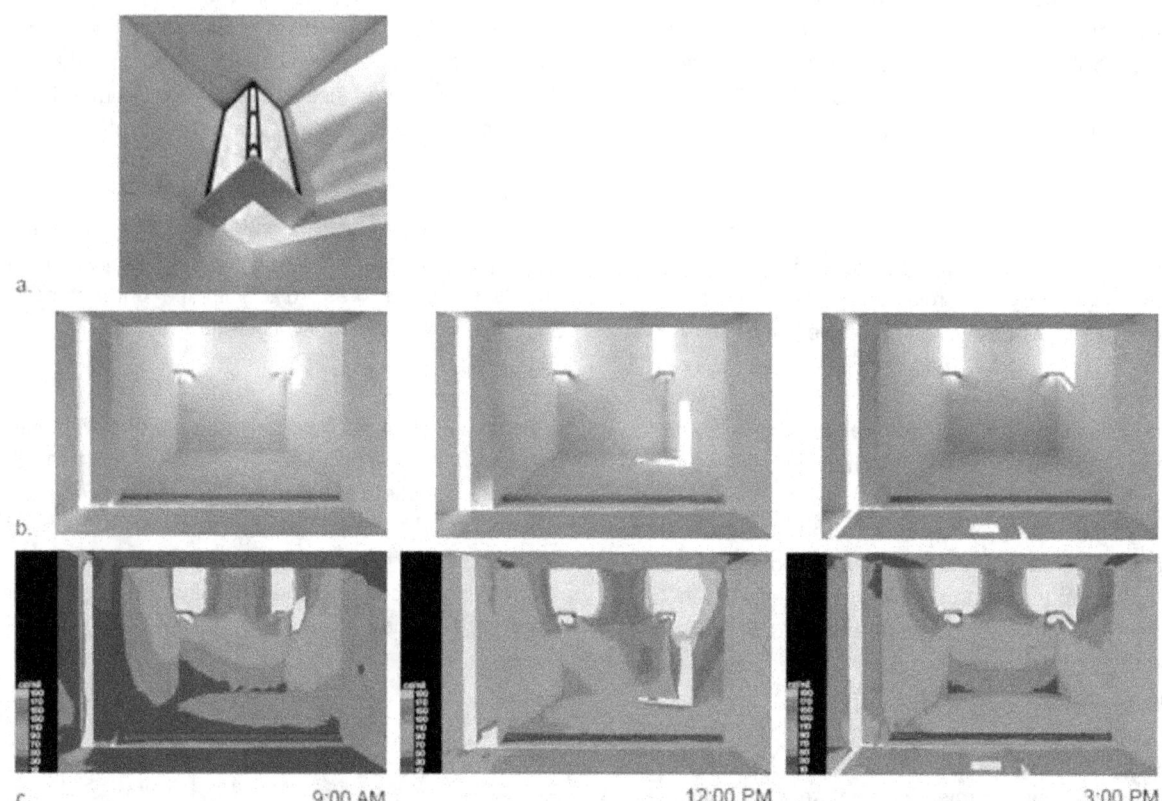

Fig. 5. Double Height Gallery: Luminance, Intermediate Sky
a. Photograph of southwest corner skylight (source: Seier+Seier [photographer]. (2012.) detail: corner skylight, type one. [Photograph]. Retrieved from https://www.flickr.com/photos/94852245@N00/9023203200/)
b. DIVA-for-Rhino Daylight Visualizations (source: M. Gibson)
c. DIVA-for-Rhino Daylight, Falsecolor Rendering (source: M. Gibson)

In Figure 5, the double height gallery is being analyzed on the Autumnal Equinox, September 21[49], at 9:00 AM, 12:00 PM and 3:00 PM. The long corner skylights are located on the west (far) wall. From the Falsecolor Renderings the vertical luminance at noon has the highest reading 150 - 190cd/m² at the face of the west wall and the western part of the north wall. The northwest corner of the double height gallery, near the bust of Canova, is bathed in light. This places bright light behind the cast of *Cupid and Psyche with Butterfly*, causing a contrast and the cast is seen in silhouette. From the 9:00 AM reading, the daylight of the double height gallery at the level of the plaster casts is low with readings in the 30-90cd/m², but high at the level of the skylights, 150-170cd/m². At 3:00 PM, a high reading of 150-190cd/m² takes place on the west wall above the plaster casts while at the level of the plaster cats, at the lower walls, it is 50-90cd/m². The Daylight Visualizations reinforce this daylight analysis.

The Daylight Visualizations and Falsecolor Renderings in Figure 6 represents two areas of the elongated gallery. The first is the threshold marked by four skylights and the headless statue of *Dirce* as is seen in the photograph. The second area is at the far end of the gallery, with the glass wall that wraps the roof creating a skylight; this is where the *Three Graces* reside. The lighted threshold has a presence throughout the day as seen in the three visualizations rendered at 9:00 AM, 12:00 PM and 3:00 PM. In the first simulation at 9:00 AM, the range of luminance is approximately 130-150 cd/m² and is primarily lit at the upper half of the skylights and along the skylight at the west wall. At 12:00 PM, because of the building's orientation, the threshold is now elongated with the daylight reaching into the dim rectangular gallery. The range of luminance is at the highest levels of 250-290 cd/m² and glare is evident. The threshold is filling the space of the rectangular gallery. At 3:00 PM, the levels drop to 70-90 cd/m² and the threshold recedes.

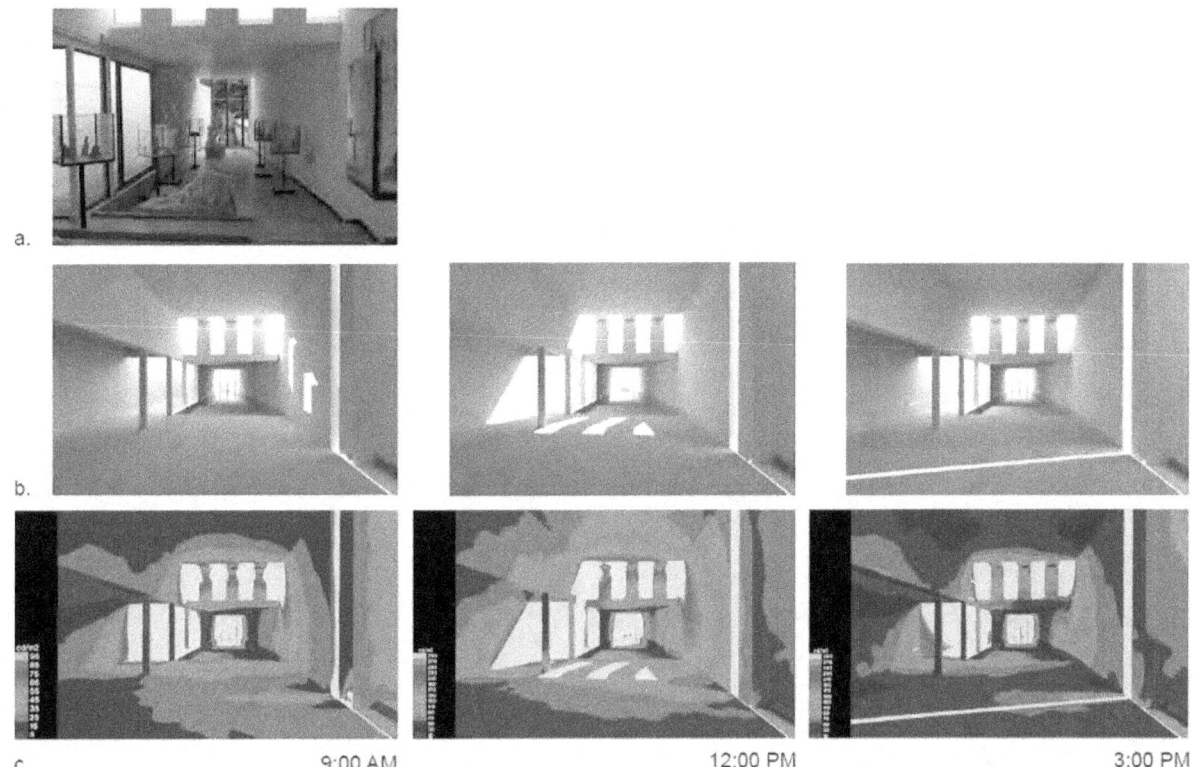

Fig. 6. Elongated Gallery: Luminance, Intermediate Sky
a. Photograph of Threshold at Dirce and Area of Three Graces (source: Mathew Roberts [photographer]. (2013.) Canova Museum Wing by Scarpa. [Photograph]. Retrieved from https://www.flickr.com/photos/btx91/8806025473/in/album-72157633627675255/
b. DIVA-for-Rhino Daylight Visualizations (source: M. Gibson)
c. DIVA-for-Rhino Daylight, Falsecolor Rendering (source: M. Gibson)

The Daylight Visualizations and Falsecolor Renderings in Figure 6 represents two areas of the elongated gallery. The first is the threshold marked by four skylights and the headless statue of *Dirce* as is seen in the photograph. The second area is at the far end of the gallery, with the glass wall that wraps the roof creating a skylight; this is where the *Three Graces* reside. The lighted threshold has a presence throughout the day as seen in the three visualizations rendered at 9:00 AM, 12:00 PM and 3:00 PM. In the first simulation at 9:00 AM, the range of luminance is approximately 130-150 cd/m² and is primarily lit at the upper half of the skylights and along the skylight at the west wall. At 12:00 PM, because of the building's orientation, the threshold is now elongated with the daylight reaching into the dim rectangular gallery. The range of luminance is at the highest levels of 250-290 cd/m² and glare is evident. The threshold is filling the space of the rectangular gallery. At 3:00 PM, the levels drop to 70-90 cd/m² and the threshold recedes.

At 3:00 PM at the space of the *Three Graces* seems to be in constant contrast with glare, but this occurs in the space immediately in front of the *Three Graces* at 30-50 cd/m² and at the full window 190 cd/m².

Scarpa allows the glare to exist just above the line of vision in both the Double Height Gallery and the Elongated Gallery. The foveal area of the eye cannot accept high levels of brightness, however above the line of vision ranging from 5 degrees (580 cd/m²) to 45 degrees (2500 cd/m²)[50] and at the peripheral vision, the eye can perceive if not accept the glare. It is this type of awareness of the limitations of the human body and the richness of working in this area that speaks to Scarpa's phenomenological detailing.

Fig. 7. Plan: Diva-for-Rhino Illuminance Analysis, Intermediate Sky (source: M. Gibson)
a. 9:00 AM
b. 12:00 PM
c. 3:00 PM

The DIVA-for-Rhino Illuminance Analysis at 9:00 AM, Figure 7a, indicates that the Mean Illuminance is 100.37 lux and 5.2% of the area of the Gipsoteca is greater than 300 lux. The IES standards for a sculpture gallery is 300lux is an acceptable level. The area in the Gipsoteca at 9:00 AM at this high light level is the area at the full window at the end of the elongated gallery housing the *Three Graces*. The general gallery has a much lower level of light.

The Mean Illuminance level at 12:00 PM, Figure 7b, is 348.38 lux over the acceptable level of light. This happens in three places, the Double Height Gallery, the Elongated Gallery at the Threshold at *Dirce* and at the end of the Elongated Gallery at the *Three Graces*. Almost one third of the Gipsoteca, 30.3% of the floor area, is greater than 300lux. The Gipsoteca is flooded with light at noon.

In Figure 7c, 3:00 PM, the illuminance level 204.75 lux. This afternoon reading is very is similar to Figure 7a, 9:00 AM with the exception of the rectangular gallery. The light from the two elongated western sky-lights in the Double Height Gallery are lighting the floor of the Rectangular Gallery. Two constants are the area just prior to the *Three Graces* which has a level of 50-100 lux throughout the day and the area of the *Three Graces*, which is highly illuminated above 300 lux. This is a purposeful by Scarpa as one is drawn through the darkness to the *Three Graces*, coerced by the high level of illumination. Also the large window dissolves the barrier between inside and out, allowing nature to enter the gallery and envelop the *Three Graces*.

Conclusion

It has been said that Carlo Scarpa was for his "gazing".[51] In his contemplative state, he is reviewed his past work and anticipated new situations for his ideas to be replayed and renewed. Scarpa was not in dialogue with the past, "but with the presence of the past in the present."[52] Scarpa did this at the Gipsoteca in two ways. As mentioned, he referenced Canova's plaster cast storage room and studio found in the complex, in the spatial disposition of the Double Height Gallery and its corner skylights and he also referenced the Venezuela Pavilion where he first used the four wrapping wall-to-ceiling skylights; he re-examined and refined these light innovations at the threshold at *Dirce* and at the *Three Graces*.

It could be said that Scarp's use of light was intuitive, however at the Giposteca, it was a studied element, in concert with the spatial volumetric of each gallery; the human eye; the positioning of each plaster cast, vitrine, opening and skylight; their patterns of the flooring; reflectance of the finished surface, the *stucco lucida* and the dematerialization of the interior to the exterior. Scarpa understood how to use glare as a tool of awareness, not as a detriment.

This use of light by Scarpa is accurately described by the architect Louis I. Kahn in his writing of his use of natural light at the Kimball Museum, *"...light, this great maker of presences...has all the moods of the time of the day, the seasons of the year, (which) year for year and day for day are different from the day preceding."*[53] This is true for Scarpa's use of light, however it is not the *marking* of the passing light that is of importance - it is the way that the light creates lighted thresholds of space and interacts with the plaster casts individually. Scarpa needed light to give depth to the casts, as he said *"plaster is an 'amorphous material,' it has no luster and can gain life only by being 'placed in the sun.'"*[54] It is the interplay between the light of the sun and the plaster casts, the gently touching of the plaster casts by the light, which allows the casts to "live."

The disposition of light and space at the Gipsoteca results in an experience that grounds and focuses one in the immediacy of the interaction of space and light while phenomenally time is suspended. It is uncanny. Perhaps this is Henri Bergson's "la durée réelle"[55] - elastic time - the time of experience as opposed to measured time. As said by Carlo Scarpa's contemporary, Louis I. Kahn:

A great building must begin with the immeasurable, must go through measurable means, and in the end must be unmeasured.[56]

Acknowledgements

I would like to thank my colleague at Kansas State University, Michael D. Gibson, Associate Professor, for his help, guidance and enthusiastic support for this paper. Michael generated the DIVA-for-Rhino perspectives and contour images, as well, as the Illuminance Analysis. He also helped me in understand the results of these images and their impact upon my study. I would also like to thank Wadha Al Mutawa, a Master of Architecture student at Kansas State University, who drew the Rhino model, while under pressure of her own studio deadlines. I am indebted to Michael Gibson and Wadha Al Mutawa for their contributions. Their support allowed this paper to reach its fruition.

Notes:

[1] "Radiance was written (primarily) by Greg Ward at Lawrence Berkeley National Laboratories," accessed September 15, 2016, http://sustainabilityworkshop.autodesk.com/buildings/radiance-accurate-daylighting

[2] "DIVA-for-Rhino is a highly optimized daylighting and energy modeling plug-in for the Rhinoceros, first developed at the Graduate School of Design at Harvard University and is now distributed and developed by Solemma LLC. DIVA-for-Rhino allows users to carry out a series of environmental performance evaluations of individual buildings." accessed September 15, 2016, diva4rhino.com

[3] "I wanted to cut the blue sky" (reduced transcription from a recording of lectures by Carlo Scarpa), in Review, 7, year III, in July 1981, special issue: "Carlo Scarpa, 1926/1978 Fragments", p .82. accessed March 28, 2016, http://www.carloscarpa.it/attivita_scheda.php?id=108

[4] Parts of this paper originally appeared online in the proceedings of the 3rd Annual Global Conference: Time Space & the Body, "Other Worldly Spaces", 2014, first published by Inter-Disciplinary Press, 2014. The paper was then published as a chapter, Simon Dwyer, Rachel Franks and Reina Green, eds., *With(out) Trace: inter-disciplinary investigations into time, space and the body*. (Oxford: Inter-Disciplinary Press, 2016), 135 – 147. http://www.interdisciplinarypress.net/product/without-trace-interdisciplinary-investigations-into-time-space-and-the-body/

[5] Robert McCarter. *Carlo Scarpa*. (London: Phaidon Press Limited, 2013), 98.

[6] Axel Menges, *Four Museums*. (Edition Axel Menges, Stuttgart/Londom,2004) 6.

[7] Judith Carmel-Arthur and Stefan Buzas.

 Carlo Scarpa Museo Canoviano, Possagno. (Stuttgart/London: Edition Axel Menges, 2002), 13.

[8] McCarter, *Carlos Scarpa*, 98.

[9] Ibid., 109.

[10] Ibid.

[11] Sergio Los. *Carlo Scarpa 1906-1978*. (Köln: Benedikt Taschen, 1993), 58.

[12] Maria Antonietta Crippa. *Carlo Scarpa: Theory Design Project*. (Cambridge, Massachusetts, London England: The MIT Press, 1986), 129.

[13] Carmel-Arthur and Buzas. *Carlo Scarpa Museo Canoviano,* 14.

[14] McCarter, *Carlos Scarpa*, 109

[15] Ibid.

[16] Crippa, *Carlo Scarpa: Theory*, 129.

[17] Carmel-Arthur and Buzas. *Carlo Scarpa Museo Canoviano,* 14.

[18] Guido Beltramini and Italo Zannier. *Carlo Scarpa: Architecture and Design*. (New York: Rizzoli, 2007), 22.

[19] Los, *Carlo Scarpa 1906-1978*, 64

[20] Nexus Network Journal, Architecture and Mathematics, "Volume 1 Numbers 1-2, June 1999." Marco Frascari, "Architectural Traces of an Admirable Cipher: Eleven in the Opus of Carlo Scarpa." 11. Accessed March 27, 2016, http://www.nexusjournal.com/volume-1/numbers-1-2-june-1999.html

[21] La gipsoteca ottocentesca," *The Plaster Cast Gallery*, Museo Canova, accessed March 29, 2016, http://www.museocanova.it/index.php?option=com_content&view=article&id=50&Itemid=34&lang=en. Microsoft Translator, March 29, 2016, https://www.microsoft.com/en-us/translator/default.aspx, translated file:///C:/Users/judygordon/AppData/Local/Microsoft/Windows/Temporary%20Internet%20Files/Content.MSO/DA3F1572.html

[22] Ibid. Note: This statue was partially destroyed in WW2.

[23] Nicholas Olsberg, et al., *Carlo Scarpa Architect Intervening with History*. (Montréal, New York: Canadian Centre for Architecture The Monacelli Press, 1999) 14.

[24] McCarter. *Carlo Scarpa*, 100.

[25] Olsberg, et al., *Carlo Scarpa Architect,* 14.

[26] McCarter, *Carlo Scarpa,* 103.

[27] Ibid., 100.

[28] Olsberg, et al.,*Carlo Scarpa Architect,* 15

[29] Carmel-Arthur, *Carlo Scarpa Museo Canoviano*, 14.

[30] Ibid., 15.

[31] "I wanted to cut the blue sky" (reduced transcription from a recording of lectures by Carlo Scarpa), in Review, 7, year III, in July 1981, special issue: "Carlo Scarpa, 1926/1978 Fragments", p .82. accessed March 28, 2016, http://www.carloscarpa.it/attivita_scheda.php?id=108

[32] Beltramini and Zannier, *Carlo Scarpa: Architecture and Design,* 114.

[33] McCarter, *Carlos Scarpa*, 104.

[34] Dean Hawkes. *The Environmental Imagination: Technics and poetics of the architectural environment*. (London and New York: Routledge Taylor and Francis Group, 2008), 111.

[35] Martin Heidegger. *Poetry, Language, Thought*. Translated by Albert Hofstadter. (New York: Harper & Row, Publishers, 1971), 154.

[36] Carmel-Arthur, *Carlo Scarpa Museo Canoviano*, 13.

[37] Los, *Carlo Scarpa 1906-1978*, 64

[38] Ibid.

[39] Sigmund Freud, 'The Uncanny,' last modified October 21, 2004, accessed July 5, 2014, web.mit.edu/allanmc/www/freud1.pdf, 2.

[40] Ibid., 14.

[41] Louis I. Kahn, *Light is the Theme* (Fort Worth, Texas: Kimball Art Foundation, 2002), 16. This holds true for Scarp's use of light as well.

[42] Sensing, Konica Minolta. "Luminance vs. Illuminance." Konica Minolta Color, Light, and Display Measuring Instruments. Accessed February 28, 2017. http://sensing.konicaminolta.us/2015/08/luminance-vs-illuminance/.

[43] Ibid.

[44] Baker, Nick, A. Fanchiotti, and Koen Steemers. *Daylighting in architecture: a European reference book.* (London: James & James (Science Publishers) Ltd., 1993), 2.15.

[45] Ibid., 2.14

[46] "Glossary." Stucco Italiano. Accessed February 28, 2017. http://www.stuccoitalianoinc.com/glossary/.

[47] Hefferan, Steven. *"Working with Daylight in the Museum Environment".* , WAAC Newsletter Volume 30 Number 1 January 2008, February 23, 2017. Http://cool.conservation-us.org/waac/wn/wn30/wn30-1/wn30-107.pdf

[48] Ibid.

[49] "September equinox." Wikipedia. Accessed February 28, 2017. https://en.wikipedia.org/wiki/September_equinox. Note: The Autumnal Equinox occurs between September 21st and 24rd.

[50] N. Baker, A. Fanchiotti, K. Streemers, *Daylighting in Architecture*, 2.15.

[51] Francesco Dal Co, "The Architecture of Carlo Scarpa.' In *Carlo Scarpa The Complete Works.* eds. Francesco Dal Co and Giuseppe Mazzario (New York: Electa/Rizzoli New York, 1985), 28.

[52] Ibid., 28.

[53] Louis I. Kahn, *Light is the Theme* (Fort Worth, Texas: Kimball Art Foundation, 2002), 16. This holds true for Scarpa's use of light as well.

[54] Friedman, *Carlo Scarpa Architect Intervening with History,* 210-211.

[55] Henry Plummer, *Cosmos of Light The Sacred Architecture of Le Corbusier.* (Bloomington and Indianapolis: Indiana University Press, 2013), 12.

[56] "Louis I. Kahn Quotes." Accessed February 23, 2017.http://www.goodreads.com/author/quotes/210887.Louis_I_Kahn.

SESSION 03: CASE STUDIES

Session Chair: Robert Dermody
Roger Williams University

Naomi Darling, Five Colleges - Hampshire, Mt. Holyoke, UMass Amherst: "The Kern Center at Hampshire College – Beauty and Spirit in a Living Building."

Liane Hancock, Louisiana Tech University: "Jobsite As Laboratory."

Clifton Fordham, Temple University: "Communicating the Technological, Functional, and Aesthetic Virtues of a Comprehensive Row House Renovation."

The R.W. Kern Center at Hampshire College: Beauty and Spirit in a Living Building

Naomi Darling
Hampshire College / Mt. Holyoke College / University of Massachusetts, Amherst

Abstract

This paper will look at Beauty and Spirit in architecture using the newly completed Kern Center at Hampshire College as a case study. The Kern Center is a 17,000 sf building pursuing Living Building Challenge 3.0 certification. Living Building Challenge is currently the most rigorous building performance standard requiring that projects meet ambitious performance requirements over a minimum of one year of continuous occupancy. Unique among certification assessment tools, LBC requires projects to fulfill criteria for "beauty", "culture" and "spirit".

The Beauty Petal documentation requires distribution of a survey to a randomized sampling of 10% of project occupants and asks respondents whether they think the project has succeeded based upon the designer's narrative of the project. The paper will report on the results of the survey with lessons learned for both Hampshire College and the requirements of the beauty petal.

Introduction

In an age of rapid climate change such as we are now experiencing with the past three years setting a new record for being the hottest year on record[1] and with accompanying effects such as increasing incidents of extreme weather events, a global refugee crisis brought on by drought and food shortages and the 6th mass extinction of life forms on earth underway, the time has never been more urgent for drastically rethinking the way that we shape our built environment.

Living Building Challenge

The Living Building Challenge, first launched in 2006, has established an aspirational metric for green building that has reframed the question from "how can we be less bad" to "what does good look like"? While others have asked this question, notably William McDonough, in Cradle to Cradle,[2] the LBC is the first metric with a certification process that does so in a holistic way. Characteristics that distinguish LBC from other green building metrics such as LEED (Leadership in Energy and Environmental Design), the industry standard, is that all requirements must be fulfilled and certification is only awarded after demonstrating that the project has fulfilled all criteria for twelve consecutive months of occupancy. This differs from LEED, which allows projects to be certified based on modeled performance.

The Living Building Challenge uses a biomimicry[3] model with a flower as a metaphor for what a building can aspire to be. On website of the International Living Futures Institute, the organization that administers LBC, it states that Living Buildings should be as simple and efficient as a flower.[4] Like a flower, living buildings give more than they take, they are healthy, and beautiful. LBC strives for a "symbiotic relationship between people and all aspects of the built environment."[5] To achieve certification, the project must satisfy all seven petals as set forth by the International Living Future Institute: Place, Water, Energy, Health and Happiness, Materials, Equity, and Beauty. Each petal has one or more imperatives that must be fulfilled for a total of twenty imperatives. For energy and water, this is simply stated as net positive energy and net positive water. For the other petals, the imperatives expand on the petal as can be seen in Figure 1. As LBC is aspirational, it is rigorous, and since its inception, only 12 projects have achieved full certification while an additional 33 projects have achieved petal and/or net zero certification.[6]

Although the first five petals are familiar and track to categories in other sustainability metrics, Living Building Challenge is unique among certification assessment tools in requiring an evaluation of "Equity" and "Beauty." The Equity petal promotes

SUMMARY MATRIX

The 20 Imperatives of the Living Building Challenge: Follow down the column associated with each Typology to see which Imperatives apply.

Imperative omitted from Typology   Solutions beyond project footprint are permissible

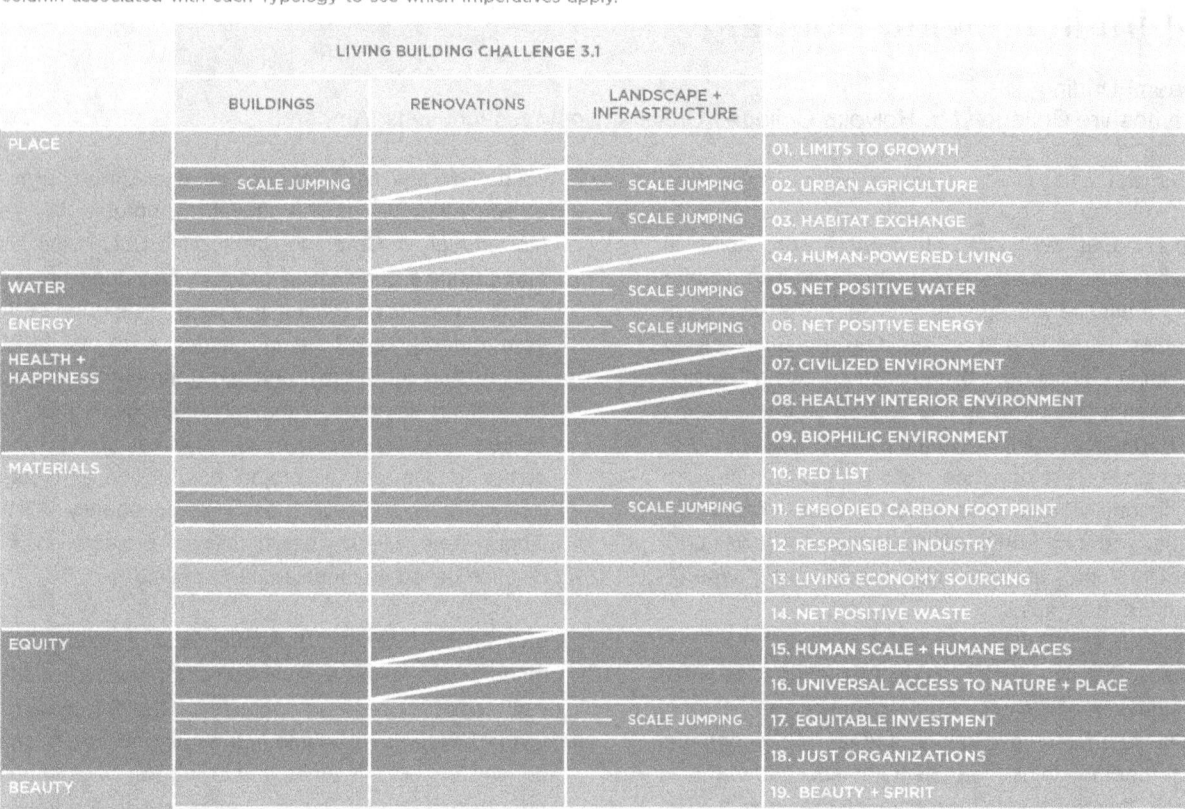

Fig. 1. Living Building Challenge Summary Matrix (https://living-future.org/lbc/basics/#buildings-around-the-world)

social justice and elevates the concept of "citizen" above that of "consumer".[7] While as architects, aesthetics is central to our profession, how beauty can be evaluated in a sustainable building metric seems much more subjective. The Beauty Petal is the focus of this paper.

Beauty in Architecture

Ironically, the term "beauty" is rarely part of the discourse in schools of architectural education to the extent that even an overview of a symposium on Aesthetic Activism held at Yale's School of Architecture in the fall of 2016 noted that "the word *beauty* seems to derail the conversation."[8] Elizabeth Meyer's Manifesto, *Sustaining Beauty: the Performance of Appearance,* makes many points that can be equally applied to architecture. She notes, "Beauty is rarely discussed in the discourse of landscape design sustainability, and if it is, it is

dismissed as a superficial concern. What is the value of the visual and formal when human, regional, and global health are at stake? Doesn't the discussion of beauty trivialize (landscape) architecture as ornamentation..."[9]

Meyer makes an argument for the performative aspect of aesthetics and indeed that beauty and aesthetics are a prerequisite for a project to have a significant cultural impact.[10] I agree that beauty is perhaps the *most important* aspect of a sustainable building and the long-term use of a project over time. If a building is beautiful, it is loved. If a building is loved, it is maintained, upgraded and adapted as the needs of society change so that it remains a vibrant center for human life and activity. The initial investments of time, energy and resources continue to pay-back over an extended period of time. The initial construction becomes proportionally smaller relative to the lifecycle environmental footprint of the project and the operations and maintenance begin to account for a bigger proportion of the total impact of a project. With this in mind, the upfront investments required for a high-performance building envelope and environmental control systems can be justified.

This allows me to return to the question, how is beauty measured or evaluated and are there any ways that the beauty petal documentation and certification process in LBC can be improved?

The R.W. Kern Center at Hampshire College

"The R.W. Kern Center is a living symbol of Hampshire's values in practice and ideas in action."[11]

Hampshire College is a small liberal arts college in Amherst, Massachusetts that was formed as an experiment in alternative education conceived by the presidents of Amherst College, Mt. Holyoke College, Smith College and the University of Massachusetts, Amherst. With the founding of Hampshire, these schools became the Five Colleges Consortium with aligned academic schedules enabling students to take courses on all campuses and a bus network that operates regularly between them. Hampshire College matriculated its first class in 1970. The R.W. Kern Center was the first major building project for the college in nearly three decades. The symbolism of this new project is significant.

The R.W. Kern Center, dedicated in the fall of 2016 and currently pursuing LBC certification, is a project that was spear-headed by Hampshire College's President Jonathan Lash, who came to the school in 2011 from the World Resources Institute, an environmental think tank in Washington D.C.[12] President Lash brought to Hampshire a deep commitment to sustainability and from the beginning, the vision for the Kern Center was to aim for the highest possible environmental standard.

After an internal call for architects and a RFQ that solicited responses from more than 40 firms, the Cambridge firm of Bruner/Cott & Associates was hired by Hampshire to be the architects for the new building. The Bruner/Cott team, lead by principles Jason Forney and Jason Jewhurst (affectionately known as the Jasons), fully embraced the LBC challenge and developed a close collaborative working relationship with the Hampshire College team

led by director of facilities Carl Weber and the construction manager for the project, Wright Builders, founded by alumni Jonathan Wright.

The R.W. Kern Center (Figure 2) is a 17,000 sf building completed at $420/sf not including soft costs. Programmatically, the project is home to the admissions office, financial aid, several classroom spaces, an exhibition space and a central coffee shop and public lobby space. As a college with a very small endowment and an operating budget that relies almost entirely on tuition, it was clear that all costs associated with any construction project would need to be specifically fundraised. Fortunately, Hampshire alumni were excited by the idea of a Living Building and the environmental goals of the project helped in the fund-raising efforts.[13] At the dedication ceremony, the principal donor to the project, William Kern, Hampshire College 75F (Hampshire students are grouped by incoming semester), spoke about his father, Ralph W. Kern for whom the building is named. R.W. Kern was an avid sailor and Bill Kern spoke poetically about the correlations between the systems of the new building to the systems on a sailboat. As on a sailboat out at sea, the occupants of the Kern Center must be vigilant about energy and water use, and learn how all of the interconnected systems within the building work together. Bill Kern expressed his desire that the R.W. Kern Center become a prototype for many more living buildings.[14] The fact that the new building was being designed with aspirational environmental goals excited Bill Kern and other donors who could see their values, and Hampshire's values, materialized in this project.

The Beauty Petal

The Living Building Challenge Beauty Petal is composed of two imperatives – Imperative 19 for Beauty and Spirit, and Imperative 20 for Inspiration and Education. In the introduction to the Beauty Petal, LBC states that the intent of the petal is indeed to recognize that beauty is a precursor to caring about our environment. The LBC challenge skillfully excuses itself from defining beauty and transfers that responsibility to each project team by stating: "Mandating beauty is, by definition, an impossible task. And yet, the level of discussion and ultimately the results are elevated through attempting difficult but critical tasks. In this Petal, the Imperatives are

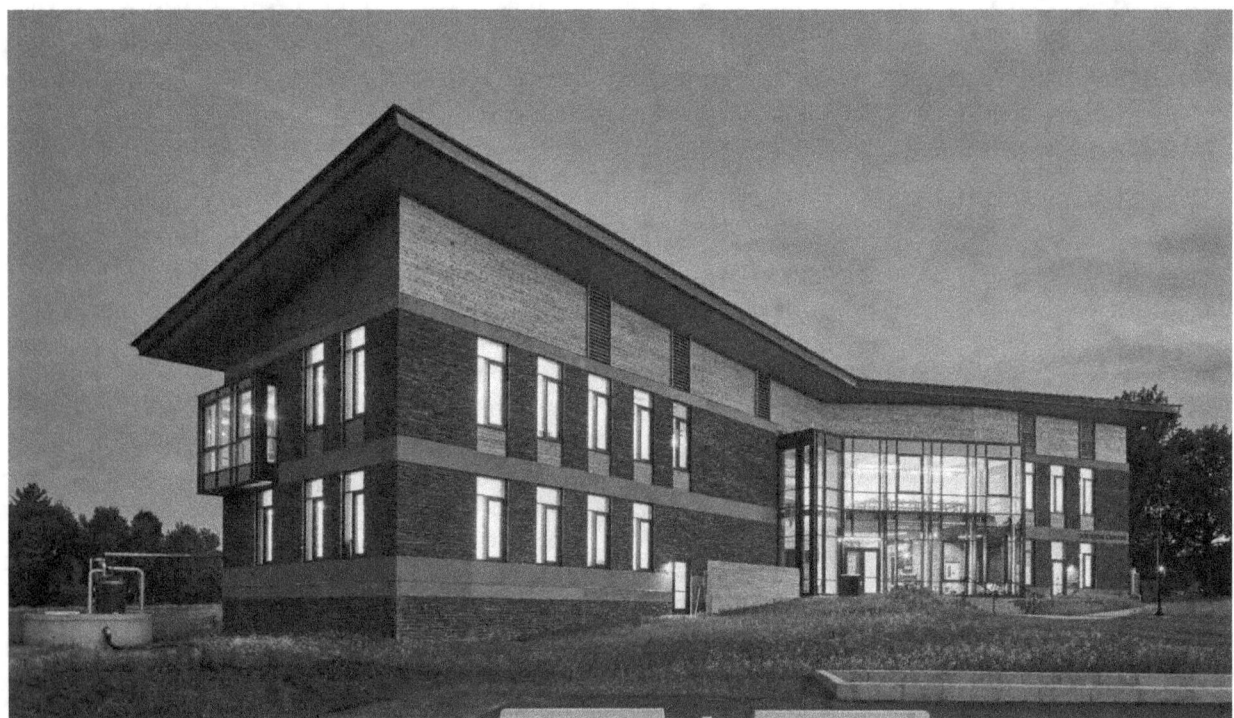

Fig. 2. The R.W. Kern Center - photo by Robert Benson (http://www.brunercott.com/projects/kern-center/)

based on genuine efforts, thoughtfully applied. We do not begin to assume that we can judge beauty and project our own aesthetic values on others. But we do want to understand people's objectives and know that an effort was made to enrich people's lives with each square meter of construction, on each project."[15]

The requirements state: "The project must contain design features intended solely for human delight and the celebration of culture, spirit and place appropriate to its function and meaningfully integrate public art." The documentation requirements are for a 2-4 page beauty narrative written by the project designer or owner describing how this intent was met as well as submitting a survey and results from the projects' users. LBC does not provide the survey or even samples of previous surveys – rather the petal requires that project teams write surveys tailored to the specific project in question to assess whether the project team has succeeded in creating a building that is considered beautiful "by at least a portion of those who occupy it."[16]

R.W. Kern Center Beauty Petal

The project team from Bruner/Cott & Associates, Jason Forney, Jason Jewhurst and Chris Nielson,

cited several design features as being elements that were intended to make the project beautiful. The soaring and aspirational roof line, the abundance of filtered and diffuse light, the use of a local stone, Ashfield Schist, in its various states of polish, the exposed timber frame structure, the patterns within the curtainwall and stone, and the visual contrast between the stone, wood and glass. In addition, the design team mentioned the planters that also filter gray water and the puzzles, by Ira Fay, Assistant Professor of Computer Science and Game Design, that are hidden throughout the building.[17] Immediately, it is apparent that the beauty of the project, as conceptualized by the architects, lies in how the various components of the project come together to create a whole that is greater than the sum of its parts: the design of *the pattern* within the curtainwall, *the shape* of the structure, *the contrast* of materials. In addition the filtered and diffuse light that flood the space and the aspirational form of the roof. But all of these features serve multiple purposes – the natural daylight is beautiful but is necessary to achieve net zero energy and occupant comfort as defined by the health and happiness petal. The shape of the roof reflects the aspirations and optimism of Hampshire College, but it also provides a south facing surface to mount solar panels to meet the energy requirements of LBC. The local schist fulfills the local material radius requirement but utilizing the stone with various levels of finish adds a layer of education/interest/beauty about the stone for the attentive observer. In all of these cases, those elements that the design team cited as being the special and beautiful parts of the building all served multiple roles. In pin-pointing design features *intended solely for human delight and the celebration of culture, spirit and place*, the design team several times cited the hidden puzzles by Prof. Fay and the gallery space which currently showcases a exhibition of faculty work.

R.W. Kern Center Beauty Survey

The R.W. Kern Center Beauty Survey was developed with a combination of questions with a sliding scale response (0-100) followed by questions where respondents could provide more substantive feedback. (Figure 3) The questionnaire was administered using SurveyMonkey, an online interactive survey software. In addition to being used to satisfy the requirements of the beauty petal, the survey results will also be used for building commissioning and research and awards applications.

After a first welcome screen, participants were asked basic personal information about their role at Hampshire (i.e. student, faculty, staff, visitor), how the participant uses the Kern Center (classes, meetings, work, etc.) and how they access the building (bus, bike, walk, etc.) Following are three screens – one for building comfort, a second for delight and culture, and a third for impact of the project and LBC. On each of these screens there are a series of questions framed positively such as "12. The RW Kern Center has elements dedicated solely for human delight." Below is a sliding scale from one to one hundred where you can disagree (0) or agree (100). Below the questions, there is room for elaboration on each question asked. (Figure 3) The final screen defined the Beauty Petal imperative and asked participants if they felt that the R.W. Kern Center successfully meets the Beauty Imperative. The survey was structured in this way with a key question about the beauty imperative at the end, because the design team felt that responses would be more honest if participants didn't know that

the survey was required documentation for the Beauty Petal.

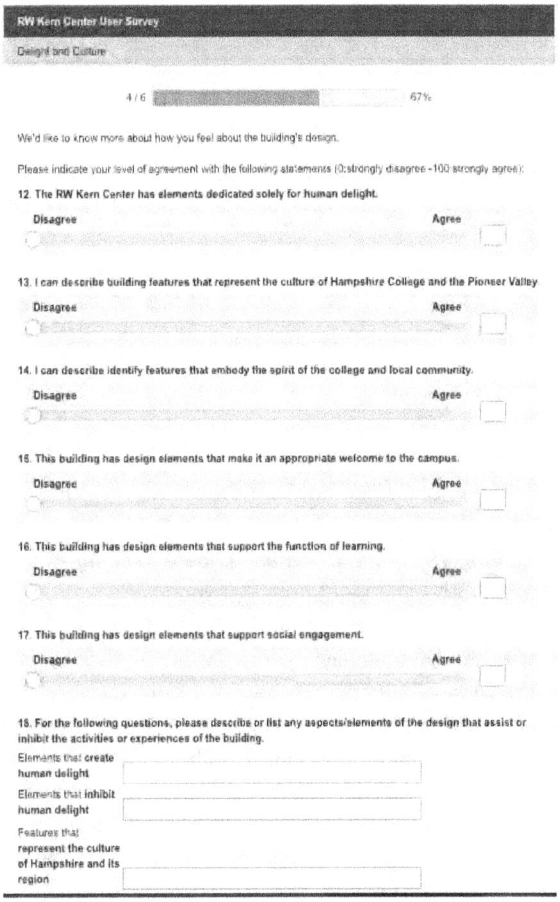

Fig. 3. Beauty Survey for the R.W. Kern Center

R.W. Kern Center Beauty Survey Results

A total of 136 people responded to the survey which was distributed on campus between February 9 to15, 2017. The survey was specifically e-mailed to staff who work in the building as well as announced in the daily news e-mail sent to the Hampshire community. The breakdown of respondents was: students – 74 (54.8%), Faculty – 9 (6.7%), Staff – 52 (38.5%). Results are downloaded from Survey Monkey as excel spreadsheets and summaries with average responses for each question.

In answer to the final survey question, *Q24 Do you think the Kern Center is successfully meeting the requirements of the LBC Beauty + Spirit Imperative, as follows? "The project must contain design features*

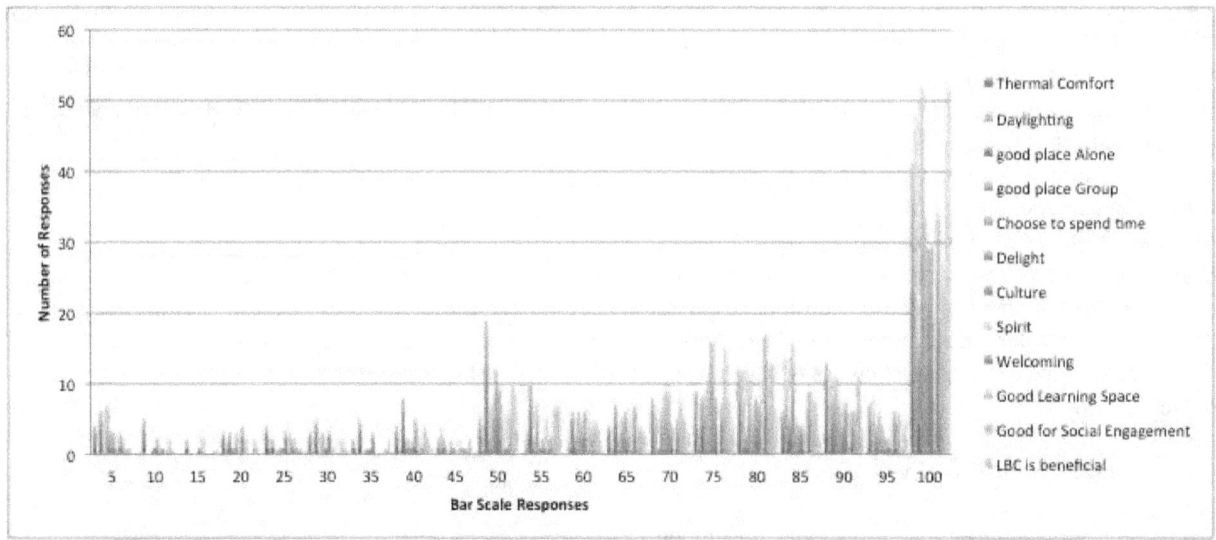

Fig. 4. Final Survey Results for all 12 Questions with Numerical Responses

intended solely for human delight and the celebration of culture, spirit, and place appropriate to its function." One hundred and eight people responded with 90.7% responding positively and 9.3% (10 people) responding negatively. This was a resounding expression of support for the R.W. Kern Center. To analyze this further, in all there were 12 questions that the design team assembled with a sliding scale response. The total results of these questions are shown in Figure 4. As can be seen, respondents answered favorably with the most responses, for all questions, coming in between 95 and 100.

Students versus Staff and Faculty

First, I was curious to see if there were substantial differences in the way that students responded to a few representative questions compared to faculty and staff. The questions I chose for comparison were "Q4 The Kern Center is thermally comfortable", "Q12 The RW Kern Center has elements dedicated solely for human delight", "Q16 This building has elements that support the function of learning", and "Q20 Do you think the LBC is a valuable pursuit for Hampshire?"

The thermal comfort question was chosen because in a quick overview of the comments, I noticed that many staff members who work in the building commented specifically about the temperature control issues. The comparisons for these four questions can be seen in Figures 5 and 6. While there is general agreement about the "delight" (or beauty) of the Kern

Center (the student average rating was 72.5% while that of faculty and staff was 74.2%) and the value of pursuing LBC (student average rating at 79.4% vrs 82.8% for staff and faculty), there was greater disagreement over thermal comfort and whether the

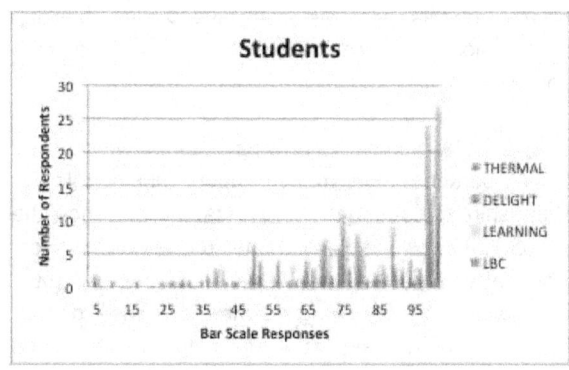

Fig. 5. Survey Results for Student Respondents

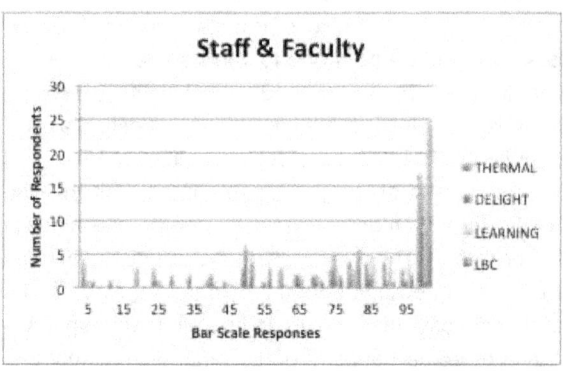

Fig. 6. Survey Results for Staff & Faculty Respondents

space supports learning. In general, the staff who work in the building daily were less satisfied with the thermal comfort of the R.W. Kern with a positive rating of 68% while students and faculty who use the building more occasionally gave it a positive rating of 82%. Written responses included multiple suggestions about improved acoustic quality and more personalized heating control. The most common complaint among staff was that the space is too cold and raw. Among all respondents, the most common response to "What could make the Kern Center feel more comfortable" was the suggestion of more tables and chairs and some soft seating including couches (see Figure 7).

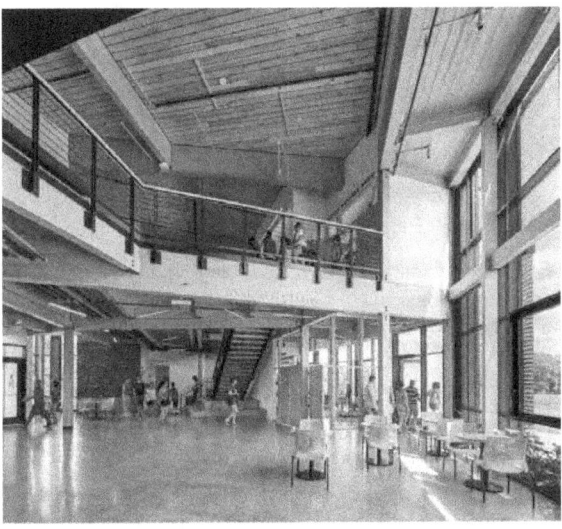

Fig. 7. Public Lobby Space - photo by Robert Benson (http://www.brunercott.com/projects/kern-center/)

Delight, Culture and Spirit

The three survey questions that correlate most closely to the intents of the beauty petal as defined by the LBC are those that ask specifically about Delight, Culture and Spirit. As the responses from all participants correlated quite well for "Delight" (Figures 5 & 6), these results are shown with all respondents in Figure 8.

Looking at the written responses, those features most often cited as creating human delight are the ample daylight (30+ responses) and the Kern Kafé with the availability of food and coffee (30+ responses). The openness and plants came in at ~20 responses followed by the design of the project and the hidden

puzzles which each garnered ~15 responses each. Other responses included the use of materials and comfortable seating (~10 responses each), and the artwork in the gallery space. Most often cited for inhibiting delight were the lack of seating, especially comfortable seating (~15 responses), the loud acoustics and odors (from the gray water system) receiving 10+ responses, the lack of temperature control and the space feeling cold and raw (the survey was distributed in the middle of winter) receiving 5+ responses, and a few comments about the glare, the cost of food at the Kern Kafé, and a few people who really dislike the composting toilets even though they understanding their value. Almost everyone who responded to those "elements that represent the culture of Hampshire and the region" cited the sustainability of the project (50+ responses) while a few specifically cited the sourcing of local materials. Although there were very few write in responses to those elements that are counter to the culture of Hampshire, the most frequent was the expense of building the project (5+). There were fewer responses for the "spirit of the community" and in general echoed the responses for both delight and culture.

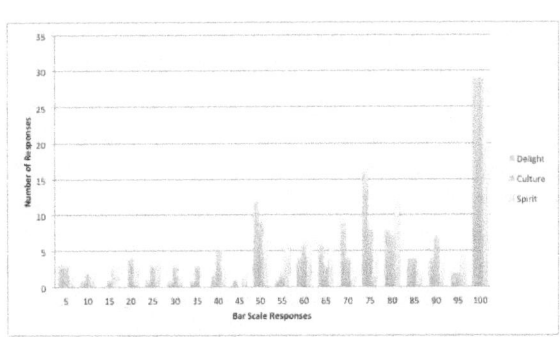

Fig. 8. Delight, Culture & Spirit Survey Responses

Discussion and Recommendations

Suggestions for RW Kern Center

Having reviewed the survey results and write-in responses, perhaps the easiest way for Hampshire to incorporate the feedback would be to provide more seating, including some soft seating, for the main atrium space where the Kern Kafé is located. This would address the most frequent responses of lack of seating, and comfortable seating, as well as make the space feel visually warmer and improve the acoustics. To address the odor issue, Carl Weber, the director of facilities, said that the operation of the gray water system is being refined and an early issue created by milk from the Kafé caused some of the early problems which has been resolved. Increased building hours and more public programming were additional suggestions that could further engage the Hampshire community in the R.W. Kern Center.

To address the comments about the expense of the Kern, Hampshire College needs to make it known more widely that the money used to built the Kern Center was fundraised specifically for a new admissions building and was not taken from tuition or other services on campus. Finally, if at all possible, Hampshire College could subsidize cost of the Kern Kafé for students or allow students to use their meal plan at the Kafé. This would address a recurring comment that while the Kern Kafé is a great amenity on campus, it is prohibitively expensive for students.

Conclusions

Including a Beauty Petal is an important recognition of the aesthetics and delight of a project for its long-term sustainability. However, I believe the beauty petal as laid out by the LBC is too narrow. As can be seen from the many responses, building users recognized that the quality of daylight, the overall openness of a space, the choice of materials, are all things that contribute to one's delight in a building. Indeed, an essential part of what makes any project beautiful is how all of the disparate components come together to satisfy the all of the requirements of a project. In the case of a living building, these requirements are environmental as well as programmatic. In a successful project, everything is working together to contribute to the general feeling of delight. In the LBC wording, *"The project must contain design features intended solely for human delight and the celebration of culture, spirit and place appropriate to its function and meaningfully integrate public art,"* the word "solely" trivializes the beautiful to the non-functional or ornamental. Although the pendulum has swung and digital fabrication has helped to usher in a new appreciation for the decorative and ornamental, they alone are not what makes a project beautiful.

Returning to the R.W. Kern Center, when pressed to describe features "intended solely for human delight," the design team mentioned the hidden puzzles and

gallery space, knowing that these features alone are not what makes the project beautiful. Rather, they, along with numerous aforementioned large-scale design moves, such as the inspirational form of the roof, are what bring delight, culture and spirit to the project. The phrasing of the beauty petal may be broadened to have design teams describe in their narratives how the various components and petal requirements come together with additional features to foster delight, culture, and spirit

Notes:

[1] Jugal K. Patel. "How 2016 Became Earth's Hottest Year on Record," *The New York Times*, Jan 18, 2017. Accessed at: https://www.nytimes.com/interactive/2017/01/18/science/earth/2016-hottest-year-on-record.html

[2] William McDonough & M. Braungart. "Why Being "Less Bad" is No Good" in *Cradle to Cradle, Remaking the Way We Make Things.* North Point Press: New York, NY. 2002.

[3] Janine M. Benyus. *Biomimicry – Innovation Inspired by Nature.* Harper Perennial: New York, NY. 1997.

[4] For more information see: https://living-future.org/lbc/basics/

[5] https://living-future.org/lbc/

[6] https://living-future.org/lbc/case-studies/

[7] Living Building Challenge Standard 3.1, p 51.

[8] Matt Shaw. "Aesthetic Activism" in Constructs, Spring 2017, pp 10-12, p 12.

[9] Elizabeth Meyer. "Sustaining Beauty: the Performance of Appearance" in *Landscape Architecture*, v 98, issue 10, 2008, pp 92-131, p 92.

[10] Meyer, ibid, p 98.

[11] https://www.hampshire.edu/discover-hampshire/rw-kern-center

[12] https://www.hampshire.edu/presidents-office/jonathan-lash

[13] Conversation with Clay Ballentine, Chief Advancement officer for Hampshire College, March 6, 2017.

[14] Bill Kern. "A Remembrance" in *Non Satis Scire – the Hampshire Magazine*, summer 2016, pp 28-33, p 32.

[15] Living Building Challenge Standard 3.1, p 59.

[16] Living Building Challenge 3.0, Documentation Requirements, August 2014, p 25.

[17] Kenneth Chang. "Can you Solve this Building?" The New York Times, Nov 4, 2016.

Jobsite as Laboratory

Liane Hancock
Louisiana Tech University

Steve Morby
Former Project Superintendent, Pulitzer Arts Foundation

Introduction

This paper presents the method by which a Pritzker prize winner, a Midwestern architecture firm and a union contractor achieved what was widely considered the world's best quality concrete in 2001. The building was the Pulitzer Arts Foundation; the Pritzker Prize winner was Tadao Ando.

Ando's work relies upon the expression of material behavior in relation to carefully defined geometry. In order to achieve this, the organic variation in material, and as a result its expression of beauty, must be attributable to the behavior and character of the material rather than due to anomalies in craft or precision. The Pulitzer is constructed of simple concrete – which was very precisely mixed and poured. To achieve quality, the project did not heavily rely upon technology to solve problems. Instead Ando established a laboratory-like environment across the design and construction teams to promote problem-solving through innovation, creativity, and trust.

My aim is not to dwell solely on the abstract; instead, it is to explore abstract concepts by expressing them through material phenomena... Hidden within the sensual and narrative riches of these phantom worlds are clues to architecture's physical essence. – Tadao Ando[1]

Japanese Model

Achieving an exemplary building by a renowned architect has as much to do with the process of design and construction as it has to do with the final design that is committed to paper. To understand the process that was established by Ando's office, the local architect, and the contractors, one must first understand a little about the working relationship between these teams in Japan. Fundamentally, the Japanese process is rooted in collaborative problem solving, where material expression is revealed

through precision and advances in technology often balanced with hand-made techniques.

In Japan, architects provide contractors with drawings that show the general intention of the project, but which do not dictate specificity in detailing. Instead, contractors, and fabricators through them, produce shop drawings and mockups for approval. The shop drawing and mockup process creates a laboratory-like environment where the design, construction, and fabrication team fully participate in developing the detailing for the building. With all team members involved, no one is operating in a vacuum, and the intentions of the designer are met with the construction knowledge of the contractor and fabricator. Throughout construction, the architect challenges the team to develop improved solutions, including asking contractors and fabricators to decrease tolerances beyond those stated in the original documents. Fabricators are encouraged to develop new technological advances, which are then incorporated into product lines after the completion of the project. These advances at the jobsite improve a fabricator's capability for future projects.

The design and construction team often employ a "just-in-time" method for solutions, allowing fabrication of building components to occur directly prior to installation. Instead of ordering many of the same components months earlier, the just-in-time delivery provides the opportunity for a high level of specificity, modifying individual component dimensions to respond directly to field dimensions and achieving zero tolerance for installation.

To accomplish this, the Japanese architect-contractor relationship fundamentally differs from its counterpart in the United States. There are no artificial contractual separations between architect, contractor, and manufacturer, or phases of design and construction. The architect leads, but because of the communal emphasis on quality and problem solving, a level of reliance spans across the entire team. Initial pricing by the contractor includes flexibility and change in the design. Change orders are not used, and since there are no cost repercussions clients are not involved in modifications. The architect exercises fluidity in de-emphasizing or deleting design features if emphasis moves to other parts of the projects, or cost overruns occur. When there are substantial errors, liability is solved through arbitration, with little reliance upon initial contracts. Instead the course of the project is taken into consideration when arbitration is required. This fundamentally differs from United States contract law, where initial conditions and agreements outweigh changes in situation as the project progresses, and clear lines are drawn between the architect's role and that of the contractor.

I think it is important that the architect should hear each opinion carefully and try to improve the design without any compromise. It is necessary for us as architect to have a positive attitude to think it is a great chance to reconsider the architecture and improve the design furthermore. The architect should be always pliable and flexible. – Masataka Yano, Associate Tadao Ando Architect & Associates[2]

Creating a Working Relationship

Ando's initial experience with U.S. construction began with Eychaner house, which was built during the span of time between when the Pulitzers' initially contacted Mr. Ando regarding the original design of the building, and when the Pulitzer Arts Foundation began construction. It was during that time that Ando, Fred Eychaner, and the owner's representative, Peter Clarkson, came to understand that a cost plus contract, rather than a fixed cost contract, was more suitable to achieve Ando's requirements for flexibility, testing, and precision. As owner's representative for Emily Rauh Pulitzer, Peter Clarkson then helped to determine which portions of the contract at Pulitzer would be cost plus and which could remain fixed bid. This bidding arrangement produced a structure of flexibility that paralleled the Japanese model.

Next, it was necessary for Ando's office and the architect of record, Christner Inc. to forge a working relationship. Adopting a method similar to the way details were developed in Japan, Mr. Ando's office encouraged the architects at Christner Inc. to develop

details, and then Mr. Ando's office would suggest improvements and alterations. Using this method, the local architect was intimately involved with the design process. At the same time, Ando's office maintained complete control over the design.

Throughout the process Ando and his office continued to design and make modifications. Concrete seems set in stone – and yet the team learned to build a flexibility into the process, providing both "just in time" construction options and by incorporating redundancy throughout the building for MEP infrastructure. This method of working delivered the ability to adapt to changes in the field, and changes from Mr. Ando's office. When construction began, there were some basics instructions, but not a full set of construction drawings. Normally the drawings should be three months, maybe longer, ahead of the construction crews. But in this case not knowing what the next step actually made everyone more involved. The initial drawings only went to the first floor because Ando had not yet completed his thoughts on what was going to happen on the second floor. The final completed building had the same roots as the first sketches, but Ando, himself, evolved with everyone else as they moved through the process.

With regard to specifics, Jim Cartwright, the project architect from the local firm, Christner Inc. worked directly with Steve Morby and his team to develop the refined character of many of the details. Drawing the construction details was not enough: the two worked together on how those details could be accomplished in the field. Often the method of construction informed the way that it was drawn. Such a blur between means and methods and design is unusual in the United States: clarity of liability rests upon demarcation between design professionals and tradesmen. But in this case, the designers and the tradesmen had to forge a relationship of trust and reliance in order to deliver the highest quality of work.

We would ask for clarification on a detail and what returned was a meditation and new design for that entire part of the building. - Jim Cartwright, AIA. [3]

The Client

In Japan, an architect typically designs an art museum with little idea of the specific works that will be housed. The client rarely gives this information, and mostly remains removed from the process of design. Not so at the Pulitzer: Emily Rauh Pulitzer worked professionally as curator at the Fogg Art Museum, and for nine years at the St. Louis Art Museum. Initially, the Pulitzer Arts Foundation was conceived to house the family's art collection. She lived with the art and knew how best it might be exhibited. When it came time to make decisions about the design she asked for certain configurations of walls, in particular a prevalence of corners, and specific directional sourcing for light. Besides attending meetings with Ando and his associates, she also was present at nearly every weekly construction meeting and regularly visited the construction site. In addition to Emily Rauh Pulitzer, Richard Serra and Ellsworth Kelly also participated in key design meetings, as they had been commissioned to complete permanently installed sculptures for the building. In response, Ando's design creatively adapted and responded to this input, tailoring the building to the specific needs of the artwork.

She could talk to Tadao Ando, and yet, she could come and talk to Tom Betts. Tom Betts was the labor foreman for quite a while in the building. And there was no difference, none whatsoever. She made both feel quite at home, quite relaxed, and they never were on edge talking with her. That's the grounded, down-to-earth character she has. It's a very rare trait, very rare. – Steve Morby[4]

The Jobsite as Laboratory

What is most important is that all related people at the job site should have strong will and wish to accomplish their best and perfect work, as good and perfect as was never done before. We often make the effort to enhance their awareness and consciousness. – Masataka Yano, Associate Tadao Ando Architect & Associates[5]

Following the Japanese model, Ando asked the construction team to constantly better their work. If they attained a goal, he asked for more. This resulted in the questions: is personal best static? Does an individual's talent have bounds? When the team tried something, failed at it, and then figured it out, tried again, and succeeded or failed, the team learned. As a result personal best advanced one step further, and in a way the tradesmen were always chasing it. Ando

encouraged the chase, because he understood that was how to achieve true excellence.

Ando also gave an individual the opportunity to advance in his own personal creativity. On a typical construction project no one encourages creativity. A skilled craftsman has his tools and his skill. The challenges are the schedule, and the dollars, not the quality. The boss has a price that he promised he could do the work for; beyond that is the profit; there is not any other incentive to work differently or to achieve better quality. However, on Pulitzer, everything was different; the contract supported Ando's concept of the work.

Problem solving as a team created a special atmosphere. Normally, tradesmen draw upon their past experience. But at Pulitzer, it was new territory. The better an individual problem solved and the better the team problem solved, the more everyone wanted it. Especially, since it was something everyone loved.

You can say that you're at the end of your abilities but the thing is, is that really true? Because at a point like that, you could just stop, and that's the level where you will work from then on. Or you can just simply go back to work the next day, and find a solution through another person or let enough time pass to think about the problem in a systematic way. It became part of the job. – Steve Morby[6]

The kind of input the construction team wanted on Pulitzer is rarely, if ever accepted on a jobsite. The team drastically changed the way that labor was treated; people were given respect and asked to think. Some tradesmen responded very well to the idea of involvement, some did not. On a broader scale, involving each individual allowed the group to learn collectively. However if there was not order within that involvement, then there could be chaos. The key was to break all the rules but not to cause a job site that was so confusing and unproductive that nothing got done. To understand the rules it is important to understand a little about the jobsite. The individual trades run separately along contract lines; while coordination must occur, each trade works on separate parts of the job, and there is a clear order of command across the jobsite. For instance, a laborer would never be asked their opinion on how the carpenter's part of the project should be done. But at Pulitzer, across trade lines, everyone could suggest different working methods or ways to solve problems. The leadership created an environment where these suggestions could be heard without causing offense; the key was respect across the team.

Sometimes this method backfired. An experienced carpenter in St. Louis with 15 to 18 years of experience in the field might arrive on the jobsite. He was respected; a good hand, he knew what he was doing; he could follow directions; and he could make money for his boss. He considered himself productive and secure in his job. Now, a superintendent from out-of-town was changing all of the rules. He wanted the carpenter to think along those traditional lines, yes, but there were some things that the new boss asked the carpenter to do that he did not feel not comfortable doing. Should the carpenter follow along and risk failing with the new superintendent when he failed? The superintendent would leave town, and now, having failed, would the carpenter need to do that too to find a job? The carpenter would think of his future, and worry about his reputation. It takes a while to get a reputation established in a town, and that reputation can be lost very quickly. – Steve Morby[7]

For the most part a carpenter who was less experienced, who was a blank slate was more comfortable at the Pulitzer. Some first and second year carpenter apprentices picked up the way the team was working a lot faster than people with 10 to 15 years of experience, simply because the young tradesmen did not know any other way.

We saw countless times when somebody got it. They actually got what we were here for. It was amazing. It was wonderful! Because we knew from that moment on we had another pair of eyes. Now they had a direction. Now they understood what the rest of us have been trying to do for so long. – Steve Morby[8]

Failure

At the Pulitzer, the construction team was told they were to pour perfect concrete, with no tolerances, no variations. The notion of perfect concrete came from Tadao Ando, it came from Peter Clarkson, but it also came from Emily Rauh Pulitzer, too. It was to be the most perfect poured in place concrete building in the world; that was the standard; something like a 1/16th of an inch of deflection in 24 feet though that was never written on a piece of paper.

But what is perfect concrete? The word "perfect" assumes the inference of flawlessness in the tradesman himself. Humans have limits that they have no control over. So on the jobsite, the team navigated away from the word "perfect," and instead strove for "trade excellence" or "personal best."

The work itself was a study in how to achieve this excellence; but the target could not be hit every time, it was just not humanly possible. When things turned out well, it was easy to keep everyone working; but when things failed, people began to feel they were being asked to do something they were never really going to achieve, and they began to question whether it was worth spending the time and effort. To provide motivation at that point was more about psychology. Failure could never be considered as the realm of the individual. It had to be seen as across the group; the group could deal with failure in a much broader way than an individual could.

So, when everything succeeded and the walls were good, and everybody was amazed and there were oooo's and the ahhh's, everybody took it. By the same token when the owner's representative or the architect was negative because the construction team had failed, or they could not get a wall poured, or they had a detail that failed, it was not just the person that thought of the detail or worked on that part of the project, it was the whole crew. This approach showed everybody that was involved in the hands-on construction that they were never going to be cut out or left swinging in the wind by themselves. As a result there was a lot more creativity, open thinking, and problem solving on the jobsite. The crew understood that if something went wrong, no individual was going to be the one to take the full brunt of the failure simply because he happened to ask the question. This never never is the case on a typical construction project. It is an unwritten rule. If a person challenged something or asked a question, or made a decision, and it was a wrong decision, then it costed them their job. Unfortunately construction is about schedule and dollars; even on projects of this level. And every action on a construction site, good or bad, involves money.

Our families, they paid a price for this too, because I couldn't have just a normal conversation and talk about anything else but this building. My mind was

consumed, absolutely! At some point my family just got tired of listening. At that time I still had Max. He was probably a seven year old yellow lab, and that dog saved me so many times. He listened to everything I was saying. And it was a whole lot more comfortable talking to him than sitting there talking to myself. If that dog had opposable thumbs, he could pour some fine looking concrete work! Absolutely!
– Steve Morby[9]

The Construction Industry

Now the real question is why was this way of building so different? Why has the construction industry gotten to a point where it makes something like this difficult? If an architect and an owner challenge a group of craftsman to do this quality of work it should be a welcome opportunity. If craftsmen think about a project like this correctly, it should be important to them. This is what they have chosen to be their life's work, and now, they have the challenge to do their life's work to the finest level, the highest level that they may ever be asked during in their careers. Craftsmen have changed: work ethics, where the line of quality that a craftsman accepts lies. Those changes need to be challenged, not in just a singular project, but across the building industry.

In today's world, I feel like the ordinary job, that just gets passed, is acceptable; to me, that is tragic, because I don't think that this is why any of my fellow brothers, the members in the Carpenters Union, do this. It's not why we got into it. We don't do this just so that we can do an average job. It should be too important to us to do just an average job.

Not too long ago, I sat in on an interview for a general contractor who was going to do some work in Chicago. It was an example of a rare moment, an important moment. We went around the room introducing ourselves. This older man stopped the conversation and he looked at me and he said, "You built the Ando building, the one in Chicago, the Eychaner job? And you built the Pulitzer? I want you to know that we've done projects here in Chicago and we have used your work as a benchmark in what we are defining as excellence, as quality." There's no bigger compliment that I had ever received in my life. He was a perfect stranger, someone I had never met before. It wasn't so much that my name was there,

but what my guys had accomplished; that was what he was referring to; and he was legitimizing our work. That was an amazing feeling, it really was.
– Steve Morby[10]

Conclusion

With each pour, Ando asked the team to better their work, to advance their personal best. In turn, the construction team used the Pulitzer Arts Foundation to develop procedures as "trade excellence" for pouring methods, mix design, and formwork design. While the building is constructed of simple concrete – to achieve the quality Tadao Ando sought, the design and construction team had to establish a unique laboratory-like environment to promote problem-solving, innovation, and creativity. As a result, the construction of the Pulitzer Arts Foundation serves as a model of how the building industries' traditional ways of working can be toppled to achieve a project of this superiority.

Notes:

[1] Isozaki, Arata. *The Contemporary Tea House: Japan's top architects redefine a tradition*, Kodansha International: Tokyo. 2007. P. 60.

[2] Yano, Masataka. "Pulitzer Building and challenges in the projects outside Japan," keynote lecture, *Building Pulitzer Colloquium*, St. Louis, MO. 2013.

[3] Cartwright, James. Interview, Pulitzer Arts Foundation, St. Louis, MO. 2011.

[4] Morby, Steve. Interview, Pulitzer Arts Foundation, St. Louis, MO. 2011.

[5] Yano, Masataka. "Pulitzer Building and challenges in the projects outside Japan," keynote lecture, *Building Pulitzer Colloquium*, St. Louis, MO. 2013.

[6 – 10] Morby, Steve. Interview, Pulitzer Arts Foundation, St. Louis, MO. 2011.

Communicating the Technological, Functional and Aesthetic Virtues of a Comprehensive Row House Renovation

Clifton Fordham
Temple University

Abstract

Most of Philadelphia's residents live in narrow row houses constructed between 1880 and 1920. Post-industrial flight, neglect, and aging of the row house infrastructure means that majority of houses are in need of substantial updating often approaching the scope of new construction. Opportunities to build in open lots are limited, and the feasibility of demolishing existing structures tempered by the aesthetic appeal of older facades and limits of financial resources. Arguments for revitalizing Philadelphia's row houses instead of abandoning or demolishing them are buffered by David Owen and Vishaan Chakrabarti in their respective books *Green Metropolis* and *A Country of Cities*. A dense urban grid, the compact nature of row houses, existing public transportation infrastructure, and walkable amenities make Philadelphia row house living one of the least carbon intensive realities in the nation. Advantages of urban density can be extended beyond environmental impacts to include social and health benefits from weaving exercise into everyday life.[1]

Although green by virtue of size and location, row houses are difficult to adapt to contemporary living expectations due to restrictive foot prints, existing floor plans that reflect historic living patterns, and lack of contemporary technology infrastructure. Because opportunities for big expressive gestures are limited within a standardized building volume, and many necessary improvements suppressed from view, row houses designs are difficult candidates for recognition in forums that are heavily weighted toward attractive imaging and which tend to glance over technical issues. This raises a challenge regarding our ability to appreciate the results of design particularly if they involve building systems, and expression is not overly gestural. When function and performance are tightly meshed with aesthetics, can the manner in which they underpin each other be appreciated? This paper surveys the design and construction of a comprehensive Philadelphia row house renovation

where standards for residential functionality, comfort, and carbon use were exceeded. In this case, design strategies meshed comfort objectives achieved through passive and active systems, planning, detailing, and material choices that optimized the potentials of the existing fabric. The results are different, yet quiet, making it difficult for occupants to put their finger on why spaces feel better than normal. This study unpacks pragmatic and poetic qualities of the project providing a model by which architectural performance can be better appreciated.

Introduction

The chief characteristic of the row house typology is compactness and common walls shared with neighboring structures. Typically built three or four units at a time by non-architect builders, row house designs were generally copied so entire neighborhoods gained a common aesthetic. Regularity of form contributed to ease of construction and street-scape uniformity, and to the primary critique of row houses which is that they resist personalization. Another criticism of row structures is that they are difficult to expand, hemmed in on three sides since the front facade typically abuts the public right of way.

Interest in the row house as a building typology has coincided with increased awareness of the virtues of older cities which includes compactness and proximity to amenities. In their respective books *Green Metropolis* by David Owen and *A Country of Cities* by Vishaan Chakrabarti, an ecological argument for the virtues of cities and dense housing are established. According to Owen, the compactness of row houses prevents excess acquisition of material goods, minimizes energy-use, and preserves rural lands by consolidating development. Energy efficacy is baked into the DNA of the row houses because of their compactness and low exterior surface area relative to interior volume.[2] The primary vertical structure and enclosures of row houses are typically made of brick which is resistant to decay unless neglected. Small exterior surface areas ease maintenance costs, and short structural spans allow for open plans.

Architecture within limits imposed by narrow lots, and existing fabric, contrasts with visibility and expressiveness achievable with open sites. Older industrial structures such as loft buildings lend themselves to large open interior expanses, but the compactness of row house structures means that modifications are less likely to be experienced in totality, or captured in photographs. Considering the virtues and limits of row structures, understanding how contemporary row house design can be understood on ground comparable to new construction, which is celebrated, is a worthwhile endeavor. To counter this perceptual challenge, this paper features a renovation of Philadelphia row structure undertaken with the benefit of an architect owner, and without funding that typically accompanies celebrated works. A goal is to foster better comprehension and appreciation of architecture that is not overtly expressive.

Questioning Evaluation Scope

Like most single family housing in the United States, row house design and construction falls outside the central concern of architects except for a small number of expensive prototypes. Causes for lack of participation in single family housing is attributable to domination of new development by large commercial development firms catering to popular whims, and renovation work in built-up areas by builders who are able work without architects. Ramifications include an environmental aesthetic which has been subject of extensive criticism from the architectural community, and arguably lower quality construction.

Effective responses require diligence on the part of critics and designers with respect to educating consumers and demonstrating better alternatives. It also involves accepting that results gained in the single family residential market will not directly correlate with current design culture expectations primarily due to budget limitations. Because demonstration projects are typically not accessible in person, project accounts in journals and lectures rely heavily on imaging and tilt evaluation toward visual impact. However, when acknowledgement of the ramifications of building extends beyond the

aesthetic, the absence of architects from residential work takes on more significance. Increased interests in higher performing buildings that respond to user needs and ecological concerns are shifting the responsibilities of building and architecture.

Tension between subjective criticism that favors aesthetics, and building performance evaluation using objective measures, is the central theme of the book *Architecture Beyond Criticism: Expert Judgement and Performance Evaluation*. In the introductory essay by the editors, they note that efforts over the last fifty years to measure functionality and user satisfaction have largely failed to gain traction within the culture of architectural criticism which the discipline relies on for analysis. Practice oriented journalists have made inroads merging performance and aesthetic evaluation, but a schism remains in the discipline where creativity and performance are largely perceived as distinct.[3]

Criticism and Performance

Later in *Architecture Beyond Criticism*, Thomas Fisher offers a paradigm in which to frame the performance of architecture by celebrating the different roles of the designer, evaluator, a critic. Before introducing his model, Fisher highlights the notion of architecture as a static art versus performance art as dynamic and fluid. Static art privileges singular authors and is closely tied to modern traditions in the visual arts where media are assumed to be well understood by the artist and thus beneath criticism. Performance on the other hand, which offers a better analogy to building production, is a group activity contributing to an experience. With a more dynamic process in mind, building evaluators, foster understanding of what building do across time, increasing knowledge and performing a comparably valuable role to that of critics who define meaning.[4]

In her book the *Allure of the Incomplete, Imperfect, and Impermanent*, Rumiko Handa identifies aspects of architectural criticism that prevents it from being more inclusive of building performance. She identifies the works and writings of Leon Bartista Alberti as a turning point where perfection displaces incompleteness as an objective of design. In order for architecture to elude perfection, it has to be judged primarily on its intent as framed by the designer as opposed to its reality which unfolds over time. A perspective on architecture existing in a reality framed by the designer's vision was solidified as the discipline appropriated a culture of criticism from the visual arts where the authority of the artist was cemented with the original concept of the author.[5] Within a culture that freezes buildings in time, a work of architecture like the National Gallery of Art Addition is celebrated at its opening, and continues to be celebrated after technical failures undermine its merit. In the case of the East Wing Gallery, design flaws cost the federal government over $80 million dollars.[6]

Temporal Considerations

In light of the technical complexity and numerous participants in the building realization process, the primary practical responsibility of architects lies with the conveyance of design intent thought the effective management of design documents. Architects assume liability with space planning, structural and systems integration, weatherproofing, and assembly stability. They also are expected to design within budget expectations and schedules. Because of the numerous risks involved in design, and the execution of design is dependent on others, architects carry insurance against design errors and rely on conventions and standard specifications designed to mitigate risks inherent in building operation. Equipped with defenses against undesirable future events, the architectural profession can privilege the immediate.

It is not surprising that medium utilized by architects to convey design intent, with the exception of specifications, skews heavily toward the visual. Predicting building performance is difficult, and architects have steadily lost influence over cost related components of building design and construction. Future performance flies in the face of a design culture that privileges perfection of complete works over works that age, and that are modified by users over time. Post construction photography exemplifies a recognition system that granted the architect of the National Gallery of Art Addition an AIA National Honor Award, one of the highest honors bestowed by the profession. Handa also correlates a culture that privileges perfection the does not factor performance over time with shortcomings of photography used to represent building that privileges perspectives seldom experienced by occupants.[7]

Designing for Time

Liability and modest compensation are not the only reasons why architects privilege results that limit performance projections. Factoring the future life of buildings into building design beyond traditional strategies utilizing conventions, works contrary to the specific contextual conditions of a project. Responding to particular program requirements and site conditions highlights a central value of designers which is their ability to cut through ill-defined and seemingly contradictory conditions to consolidate a vision. Static drawings do not capture environmental conditions that are dynamic and represent flows of forces across time. As Fisher notes, understanding architecture as more than the resultant of a static vision requires an expansion of the prevailing framework.

In *Whole Life Costing: A New Approach*, Peter Caplehorn outlines an argument for conceiving of the building life over time resisting the temptation to make poor material choices based on low cost. Cost should not be the primary driver of design decisions with whole life costing - rather the benefits of decisions should be weighed. A result of whole life thinking is making predictions and introducing risk assessment.[8] Designing for whole life requires expanding notions by which design decisions are assessed and their future implications. Drawings, models, and photographs under this paradigm are tools for evaluating decisions and tradeoffs, performance is privileged above perfection, and the rewards for design extended over the life of buildings.

Recognizing Cost and Design Performance

Decisions by the author during the design and construction of the case-study project were made with value across time in mind. Value considerations included durability of assemblies, energy use, environmental comfort, daylight harvesting, and finish quality. With an intention to live in the home indefinitely, long-term yields allowed for investments that would be difficult to capture in a real-estate market where details, especially hidden ones, are not well described. Control of outcomes were enhanced since the architect shared general contracting responsibilities with two carpenters who did not desire to take on risks normally expected of general contractors. Shared contracting responsibilities allowed the architect to procure building materials and products heightening opportunities to evaluate and weight options.

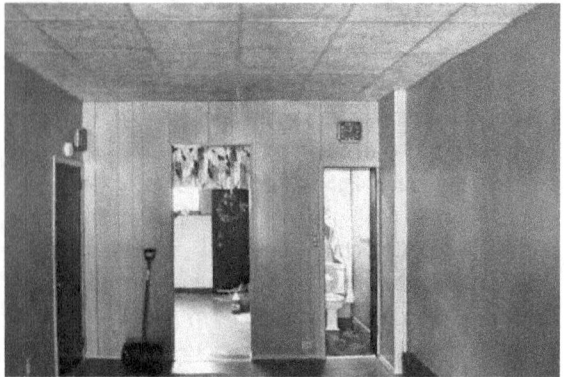

Fig. 1. Existing condition at first floor looking north.

Project goals included reconfiguring an aged row house to accommodate a growing family, replacing inadequate building systems, minimizing energy-use, and investing in high quality materials and building products when feasible. By applying architectural talents to a project type that seldom captures it, the author sought to demonstrate the value of forward looking design services by increasing both the short-term and long-term return on investment beyond what a developer-builder would normally deliver within the locality. An alternate goal was to exceed the aesthetic standards by which most row houses are renovated in Philadelphia, raising expectations that architects should be involved in such projects.

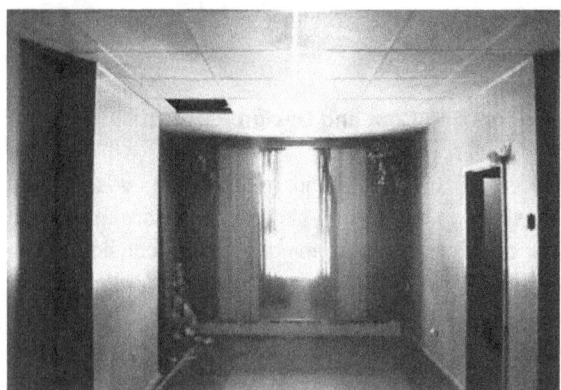

Fig. 2. Existing condition at first floor looking south.

Existing Condition of Structure

The case project is a three story row house in South Philadelphia constructed in the last decade of the nineteenth century[9]. It had been incrementally

modified to introduce additional plumbing, a powder room addition, and electricity, modifications that compromised the floor joists. The brick façade, which was in good shape, included vinyl windows and metal front door which was incompatible with traditional row house aesthetics. Siding on the second floor rear bay was noticeably deteriorated, and numerous penetrations had been made in the rear brick walls to accommodate air-conditioning, windows, and a door.

Interior finishes were in poor condition [Figs. 1 & 2] with the exiting plaster walls showing deflection, textured paint in some locations, and faux wood paneling and ceiling tile in others. There was also sagging in the floor around the top stair landings. To learn more about the structure and gain a head-start on construction while design plans were formulating, the interior of the structure was gutted so that the exterior envelope, floors structure, sub-floor and stairs remained. A benefit of early demolition was that a dormant window at the kitchen was discovered and comprehensive inspection with a structural engineer possible before solidifying plans.

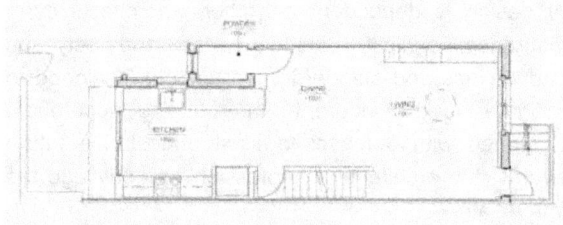

Fig 3. First floor plan.

Planning Moves

Major design actions aimed at increasing the size and feel of spaces, and increasing accommodations including storage space. The ground floor was opened up so that the former entry foyer, stair passage, living and kitchen were no longer isolated spaces. The gallery kitchen design included an oversized slider to maximize daylight. [Fig. 3] The next move was a response to lack of closet space, an undersized bathroom on the second floor, and a laundry machine location in the basement. This entailed creating a larger bathroom, a walk-in closet, and a laundry niche where a middle bedroom once existed. [Fig. 4] The third floor was converted to a master suit with a larger bathroom and closet niches. A new slider at the third floor rear wall provides light to the front space via a central hallway and over a guardrail at the open stairway to the second floor.

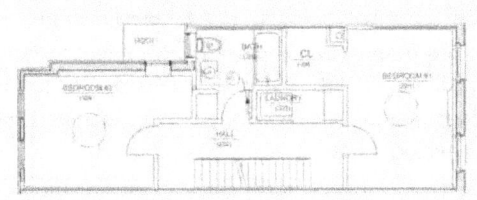

Fig. 4. Second floor plan.

At fourteen-hundred square feet, the house is well below the average for new American homes of almost twenty-seven hundred square feet. Also working against a feeling of openness is the low-amount of exterior surface area at the front and rear of the house. This oriented the design toward strategies of maximizing the impact of light brought into the house which included specifying lighter colored finishes, selecting simple trim profiles, and using products and fixtures that could fade into the background. Key to a minimalist effect was eliminating duct soffits from rooms, something that clutters older homes in the area, and keeping partition surfaces as close to structure as possible gaining extra inches and maximizing open area.

Since the historic fabric of the front façade is maintained, increasing daylight from the front of the building was accomplished with thinner window profiles and removing old frames.[10] Fiberglass clad double hung windows were chosen at the front to respect historic character, and a wood-clad awing transom window was placed above the front door where a fixed window would normally be.[11] This allows for secure ventilation at of the house when no one is home since the living room window is double hung and can be breached. During the demolition a dormant window was found at the location of the future kitchen sink and a new awning window was located there. The slider at the kitchen was oversized to maximize natural light at the expense of some extra heat transfer.

Achieving Minimalism with Building Systems

With fixed outside building dimensions, achieving a clean effect impacted decisions made about building systems, materials, and details. Some of the

decisions had a small impact on overall cost as in the choice of low VOC paint at a premium over less expensive paint. The health benefits of such a decision and the durability of the paint cannot be captured in a photograph. Other decisions had a more direct impact on the experience of the space on top of planning moves to open up the floor plates. In many cases options involved spending more than expected to achieve desired results. Decisions regarding heating and cooling had a major impact on visual results, and also illustrate the intersection of non-visible performance and costs.

The primary heating system in the building is zoned hot water supplied to wall mounted radiators with a thin profile. Radiators were deliberately undersized despite warnings from a local plumbing contractor who bid on the package and who like most contractors bases assumptions on typical insulation scenarios. Radiant heading is supplemented on the first floor by a gas fireplace which allowed for further under-sizing the radiators at the first floor. Air-conditioning was installed primarily to account for the short period during the summer when temperatures rise above 90 degrees rendering cross-ventilation and fans less effective.

The heating system is complemented by air-conditioning available only on the upper two floors via three recessed mini-spit fan units. This allowed for elimination of duct soffits, and lowering of ceilings in most spaces. Soffits for blowers were hidden in niches above the second floor bedrooms and closet niche on the third floor. As a contingency, space was reserved at the side of the fireplace bump-out for supply from another mini-split, although at this time the first floor has remained cool enough during the summer season that there is no immediate plan to install air-conditioning at the first floor. Four ceiling fans with a minimal profile were installed as the primary means of conditioning spaces in the warmer months along with cross breezes.

At almost $38,000, a complex HVAC solution represented the largest cost premium over what would normally be expected with a combined forced air system. Of all the components, the $5,800 gas fireplace system (minus extra carpentry) would on initial appearances seem frivolous if heat can be delivered another way. However, by including a fireplace in the heat load calculations, a radiator was eliminated from the project. The fireplace is able to heat the living space much quicker than the radiators permitting the radiator control at the ground floor to be set at a low temperature during heating days. A fireplace also creates a visual anchor the living room and integrated relief from plane wall surfaces. [Fig. 5]

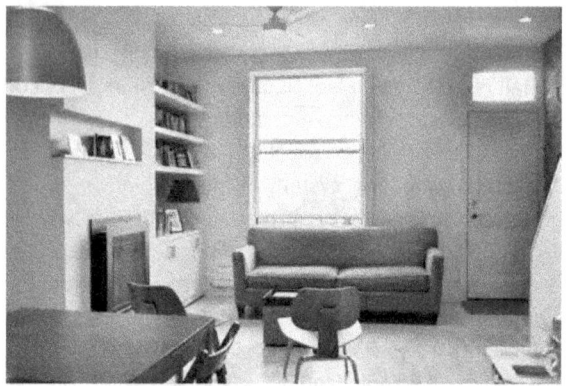

Fig. 5. Photo looking south toward living room.

At $21,800, the radiator system alone was more expensive that a forced-air system. Comfort gained from radiant heating system was an initial driver of the system choice as well as use of small diameter pipes vs. ducts. The $11,000 mini-spit system also entailed small diameter pipe conveyance to interior fans units. Because the house is fourteen foot-four inches from common wall brick to common wall brick, adding four inch studs and drywall at two sides would result in an eight inch encroachment if air distribution is in the walls without bump-outs. Even full furring at one side would result in approximately twenty-five square feet less floor space.

The cost of purchasing extra space, and estimated difference in value of a higher ceiling have to be considered against the HVAC system premium to help justify its cost. With approximately fifty square feet of floor space saved at an estimated market value of $350 a square foot, the offset for not furring is $17,500. This number would be significantly less if only vertical chases are used, but chases bump-outs would upset the minimalist continuity of walls.

Materials and Details

Maple hardwood floors with a clear finish were installed at the lower levels against the recommendation of the supplier who was concerned

about temperature and humidity shifts in spaces not continually conditioned. Installation of a clear finish floor with wood harvested in the United States and finished on site reflected a cost premium of over double similarly categorized pre-finished wood imported from Asia. This was a good test for a value proposition as the Asian Maple was in terms of hardness, color, finish, beauty, and continuity since it had beveled edges.

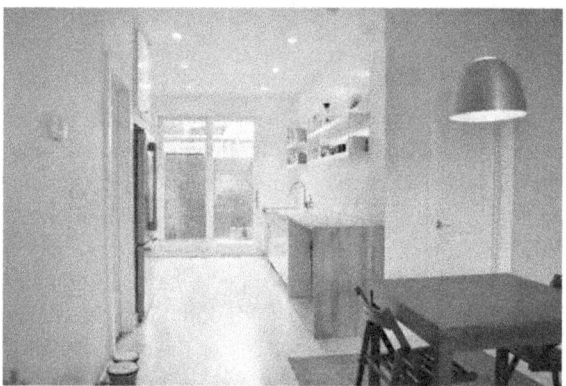

Fig. 6. Photo looking north toward kitchen.

Custom millwork added cost to the project that local builders would typically not consider. In the kitchen open shelving was built over a counter creating a more open alternative than cabinets which are deeper. [Fig. 6] In the living room the fireplace assembly was integrated with cabinets and shelving above. Along with the fireplace, the cabinets and shelving provide visual relief, and on all levels, reduces the need for supplemental shelving which would clutter the spaces. [Fig. 7] At $10,000, the premium of the millwork has to be weight against the cost of furniture, cabinets, and visual detraction from less openness.

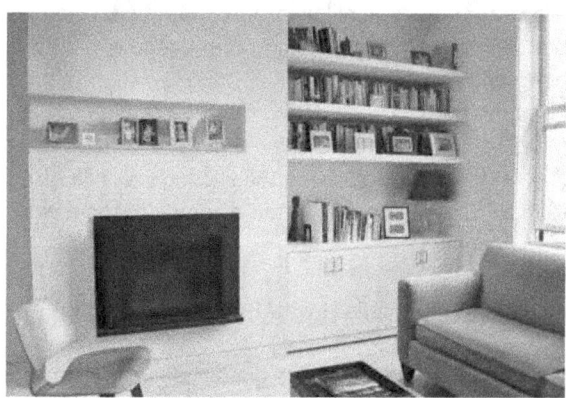

Fig. 7. Fireplace and built-ins.

Within an overall minimalist pallet, the stair details became a moment of expressiveness and color. The first floor to the second floor stairs are lined with maple plywood paneling which carries to the second floor railing system. The guard system for the second to third floor stairway integrate wood slats running from the top of the second floor guard rail to the underside of the third floor allowing light to dissipate down from the slider on the third floor. [Fig. 8] At the kitchen a wood counter extension was included as an alternative to the white quartz countertops. The wood wraps the end the counter reaching the floor and conceals a recessed cabinet and radiator.

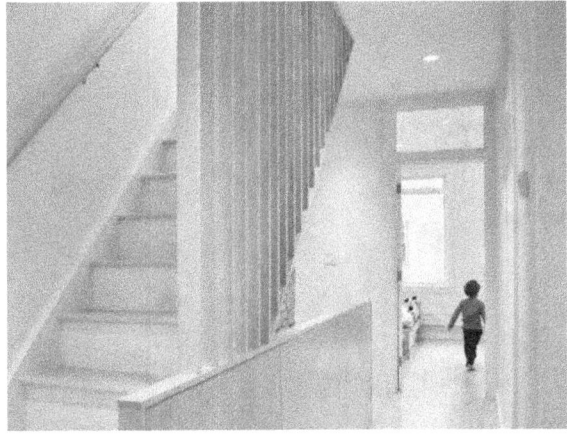

Fig. 8. Stair guard at second floor hal.

Some details introduced extra cost into the project which in isolation are difficult to understand. Plaster was removed from brick walls along one side of the living room and at the top floor bedroom gaining an inch in each location. Both walls were originally going to be painted white but were left unfinished to add another touch of color to offset the white walls. Subtle details that builders would not likely introduce included Shaker styled doors, and matt finish light-switches cover plates that do not have visible screw heads.

Other decisions made included removing existing roofing to accommodate installing a new roof system that included a moisture barrier, and foam board insulation on the deck.[12] Sheathing was replaced throughout the house when the original sub-floor was deemed inadequate. A liquid applied membrane was installed at the rear of the house and the roof. Rigid insulation was added on top of the roof decking and under the new rubber roof. This was supplemented with batt insulation between the existing roof rafters.

At the rear building faces ridged insulation was installed as part of a synthetic stucco system. The interior face of the front brick wall was faced with closed-cell spray-on insulation and studs are set off of the front brick to prevent thermal bridging.

Conclusion

Decisions that architects make are tempered by overall budget parameters established by owners who ultimately own the project. Owners also own most of the risks although major construction deficiencies are enclosed by insurance policies carried by designers and the builders. Designing for the future life of buildings also entails risk due to forecasts that must be made in order to predict future viability of immediate decisions. If architects embrace more risks of future performance, they can play a greater role in supporting owner interests and demonstrating greater value for design services.

Evaluating the value of complex decisions requires greater factoring of financial ramifications with design decisions extending beyond defensive strategies to navigate the construction process. It also means moving significantly beyond limited perspectives captured in photographs. A performance centered approach also entails expanding the methods in which design is appreciated to include time dependent perspectives. Designs for older building of limited dimension which are not contusive to broad expressiveness, can be better appreciated too.

Notes:

[1] Chakrabarti, Vishaan. *A Country of Cities: A Manifesto for Urban America.* Metropolis Books. NY. 2013. pp 75-97, 103–110.

[2] Owen, David. *Green Metropolis: Why Living Smaller, Closer, and Driving Less are Keys to Sustainability.* Riverhead Books, New York, NY. 2009. pp 1- 17, 210-220 .

[3] Preiser, Wolfgang F. E. et al. "Introduction "in *Architecture Beyond Criticism: Expert Judgement and Performance Evaluation.* New York, NY. Routledge. 2015. pp 3–4.

[4] Fisher, Thomas. "The Performance of Buildings, Architects and Critics" in *Architecture Beyond Criticism: Expert Judgement and Performance Evaluation.* Routledge. New York, NY. 2015. pp 74–79.

[5] Handa, Rumiko. *Allure of the Incomplete, Imperfect, and Impermanent: Designing and Appreciating Architecture as Nature*. Routledge. New York, NY. 2015. pp 58–62.

[6] Handa. pp 19–22

[7] Handa. pp 180–191.

[8] Caplehorn, Peter. *Whole Life Costing; A New Approach*. Routledge. London, UK. 2012. Pp 1–4.

[9] Most building permit records prior to 1914 in the City of Philadelphia were lost to fire.

[10] Existing vinyl windows were set into the original frames reducing the area available for glazing.

[11] Wood cladding was chosen to allow for painting to match the door and casing.

[12] Most roofs in the area are added on top of existing roof reducing construction costs and passing costs into the future. In this project and estimated building life of roofing layers were removed.

SESSION 04: MATERIALS

Session Chair: Marci Uihlein
University of Illinois at Urbana-Champaign

Chad Schwartz, Southern Illinois University: "A Detail(Ed) Analysis: Unpacking The Latent Meanings Of "God Lies In The Details.""

Ane Gonzalez Lara, University of New Mexico: "Concrete And Latin American Architects: A Love Affair."

Lisa Huang, University of Florida: "Fearless: Confronting Weight And Gravity In Manipulating Matter."

A Detail(ed) Analysis: Unpacking the Latent Meanings of "God Lies in the Details"

Chad Schwartz
Southern Illinois University - Carbondale

Abstract

In "The Tell-the-Tale Detail," Marco Frascari discusses the history of the architectural mantra, "God lies [or is] in the details." This quip, identified in most architectural circles to be professed by Mies van der Rohe, has a lineage that extends earlier to Aby Warburg and Gustave Flaubert working in the realms of art history and literary production respectively.[1] This paper, however, sidesteps this history and instead investigates the possible interpretations of this quote for the contemporary student of architecture. Central to this examination is the notion of ownership of the architectural detail. Who is responsible for the actualization of these critical components of our built environment? Is it the architect who dreams them up, the draftsman who draws the lines, the engineer who makes them sound, the foreman who oversees their construction, the craftsman who tightens their bolts, or the visitor who experiences them first hand?

In this discussion, a number of interpretations of this expression (with respect to architecture) are offered. The first understanding centers on the notion of **respect** for the architect and his or her command of the nuances of the development of our built environment. The second reading of the quote focuses on the **responsibility** endowed upon the architect through licensure and the profession. A third interpretation of Mies' quote pulls from Frascari's work above and examines the **understanding** embedded in the building blocks of architecture, for they are, as Frascari has described, "the minimal units of signification" in the architectural production of meaning.[2] The final elucidation on this quote engages the topic of **intimacy** and architecture, posing that the detail is the nexus of our first-hand connection to architecture. These four interpretations of "God lies in the details" create a framework of understanding for the implicit complexity that lies latent in the architectural detail – the intersection of the poetic and pragmatic possibilities of architecture.

Introduction

Each day, we inhabit a world which exists because of the infinite set of relationships developed between our environment's discrete parts. We experience thousands of these connections each day, most of which are rarely acknowledged or noticed. These are the details of the built environment, the architectural details that make our buildings stand up and stand out, make them habitable and safe, make them memorable or easily forgotten. But, what is a detail?

At its simplest, perhaps, a detail is "a small part in relation to a larger whole."[3] As the late architect and educator Marco Frascari points out, however, this definition is all but useless in helping us understand architecture. Virtually everything we create is both a whole containing smaller elements as well as part of a larger construct. As such, everything is a detail of something larger.

A more architecturally significant definition for the detail is "the joining of materials, elements, components, and building parts in a functional and aesthetic manner."[4] With this understanding, Frascari paints the detail specifically as a joint in our architectural fabric. He further defines two specific types of joints at work in our built environment: material joints such as the bolt connecting a wood slat to its support or the connection of the capital of a column to a beam above (Figure 1) and formal joints such as the entry porch that connects the exterior and interior environments of a home or the bridge that connects the farmland on the east side of the river to the city on the west (Figure 2).[5]

In his paper "Re:constructing Detail," Eric Bellin provides a thorough examination of the joint.[6] Bellin states that although the architectural detail may be classified as a joint, in utilizing a more elemental approach to examining architecture, a wide range of relationships in our architectural environment are

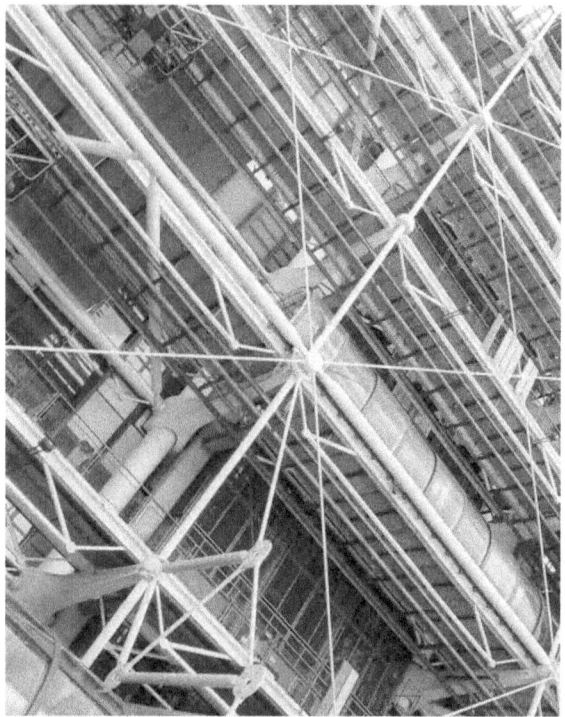

Fig. 1. Material Joints of the Centre Pompidou by Richard Rodgers and Renzo Piano, Paris, France. Photo by Author.

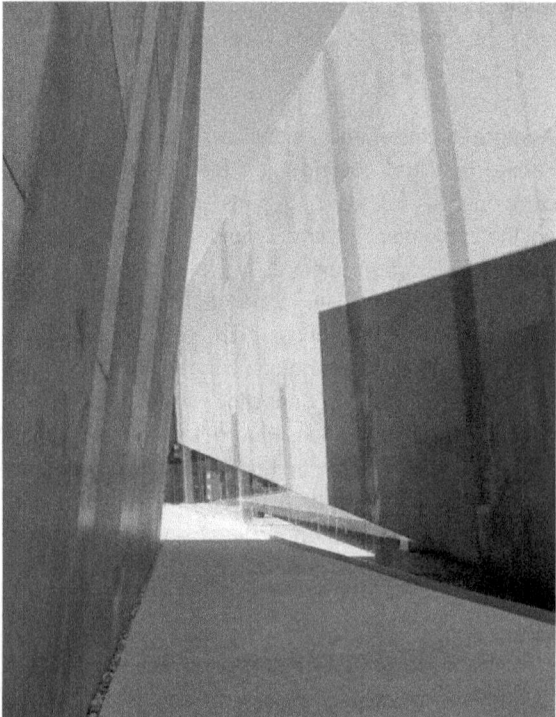

Fig. 2. Formal entry joint of the Arabian Library by Richärd + Bauer, Scottsdale, Arizona. Photo by Author.

revealed in which the joining of elements occurs. Material joints serve a particular purpose and are responsive to the specific conditions of that particular moment in the construction and the material qualities of the elements being joined. Spatial joints (akin to Frascari's formal joints) are utilized as nodes or intersections between the primary spaces we occupy and the programmatic areas of our projects. Phenomenological joints utilize elements of the natural environment to articulate material, space, or experience in a building, whereas corporeal joints are created between our physical bodies and the building as we interact in space.

In his book *The Architectural Detail*, Edward Ford expands the palate and offers a series of five alternative readings of the detail,[7] the first of which proposes that the detail is an abstraction. In this typology of the architectural detail, the visible presence of the detail is often subdued, hidden, or masked whether by intently concealing all means of assembly or through the careful creation of consistency in which no particular condition stands out from the rest. Ford's second category is that of the detail as a motif (Figure 3). In the most ambitions efforts of this type, detail is created "using a repetitive geometric device at every scale and in every material to solve every problem."[8] The third category of the architectural detail centers on its creation of order and the development of a relationship, whether actual or symbolic, between the expression of the building and its structural reality. The fourth category parallels those outlined above by Frascari and Bellin – the detail as a joint. In this type, it is the articulation of the intersection of elements, or often the accentuation of specific intersections, that helps develop our understanding of space. Finally, Ford's last category is the detail as a subversive activity, which he believes to be of particular importance. In this strategy, the detail is used to create a counterpoint to the design of the building; it purposely stands out in order to create a moment of experience. This type of detail does not try to hide. It is designed to engage and provoke.

Peggy Deamer shifts the focus of detailing from the object to the subject – or maker – in her essay "Detail: The Subject of the Object."[9] Here, Deamer insists that when discussing the architectural detail and its role in the assembly of space, we cannot focus on the built work, but on the variety of entities and individuals who are not only responsible for its creation, but who have significantly impacted how, why, and where this assembly was accomplished. For her, the detail is as much a political and social subject as it is one of construction and assembly. This definition or way of thinking is a significant departure from the phenomenologically centered thoughts on the subject presented by other noted scholars.

It is in this variety of perspectives regarding the architectural detail that this paper is rooted. This discrete element of our built world is associated with the fabrication of architecture, with the character of the spaces we inhabit, and with the means and methodologies of our product manufacturing. Its effect is implicit in every built structure that has ever existed on the planet. Noted architect and anthropologist Gottfried Semper, writing in 1860 in his book *Style in the Technical and Tectonic Arts: Or Practical Aesthetics*, notes that the origins of building and assembly may very well be tied directly to what he describes as the first architectural detail: the knot.[10]

Over a century later, in a 1964 article in *Architectural Record*, architect Philip Johnson makes mention of a quote from Mies van der Rohe that has since become one of the most often repeated phrases in architecture.[11] Although possessing an extended lineage outside of architecture, "God lies [or is] in the details" has a resonance in architecture that speaks to the varied definitions and means discussed above. Mies believed that "[a]rchitecture begins when two bricks are put carefully together."[12] He always designed with respect to clear and logical construction. For him theory involved the solution of the practical problem of working out each individual moment of the building's construction in detail.[13]

This paper, however, sidesteps the lineage of this quote and all but ignores what Mies meant when he utilized it with respect to his work. Instead, it focuses on how these five words can be interpreted by the contemporary student or practitioner of architecture. The following discussion offers four different perspectives to consider (of what is certainly a far larger number), each with a distinctly different take on the relationship of the detail to our built environment. The first understanding centers on the notion of *respect* for the architect and his or her command of

the nuances of the development of the world we inhabit. The second reading of the quote focuses on the *responsibility* endowed upon the architect through licensure and the profession. A third interpretation of Mies' quote pulls from Frascari's work and examines the *understanding* embedded in the building blocks of architecture. The final elucidation on this quote engages the topic of *intimacy* and architecture, posing that the detail is the nexus of our first-hand connection to the space we inhabit. These four interpretations of "God lies in the details" create a framework of understanding for the implicit complexity that lies latent in the architectural detail – the intersection of the poetic and pragmatic possibilities of architecture.

Fig. 3. Motific details of Thorncrown Chapel by E. Fay Jones, Eureka Springs, Arkansas. Drawing by Author.

Respect

The first meaning of the phrase "God lies in the details" involves our innate respect for someone with a command of the practice of design and construction. Architect and educator Jean Labatut stated, "Whatever the air spaces, areas, and dimensions involved, it is the precise study and good execution of details which confirm architectural greatness."[14] It begins with study. First, one must learn to command the tools of his or her profession. An architect goes through a rigorous training process to develop this command, to understand the intricacies of the practice and of the design of our built environment. Those who develop the best grasp of this knowledge then are granted the privilege to execute that knowledge in the development of architecture. The breadth and depth of this knowledge is often not demonstrated or felt in the broad strokes, but in the fine grained detail of the work. The knowledge is seen when the architect is careful to address each and every issue with the same level of consideration and craft. It is in the best of this practice, as Labatut has suggested, that we find the potential for our greatest work. As such, our quote finds itself linked to a respect for those who have command of the process of creation.

Techne is the "willful working or reworking of matter until it becomes not only what it was not but also what it was our intention that it should become."[15] We have immense respect for the designer and the craftsman who can look at a tree and see a house. That respect is only increased as the individual is able to oversee, design, guide, lead, and complete the transformation of a tree, to a log, to lumber, and to a precise element systemically interwoven with thousands of others in the development of space. "To suggest that there is 'excellent detailing' in a building is to imply that someone understood the responsibility of construction. The maker/subject of the building is always implicated."[16]

In addition to having a command of the creation of architecture, the architect also must understand the relationships between distinct components and the relationships between those components and the larger systems of a building. Leon Battista Alberti describes beauty as the skillful joining of parts in a way in which nothing should be added, subtracted, or altered. In this definition, architectural greatness is achieved when each detail, each joint, is specifically chosen and placed correctly with respect to a larger system. These details, according to Alberti, must all work in unity for beauty to be present. Again, the command of the details of architecture is a measure for the respect of the profession and those who practice it with the utmost care. "God lies in the details" can be understood, then, as a reflection of this respect for the practice of design and construction.

Responsibility

Another interpretation of "God lies in the details" may be tied to the responsibility imparted on the architect through licensure and professionalism. As a licensed professional, an architect is legally and ethically bound to create works that fulfill his or her obligations to the client and to the public. The architect's work does not end with a compelling site plan or an intriguing elevation, but in the conception of a complete work where even the smallest details are not just aesthetically pleasing but also working together to provide an environment that is safe, healthy, and accessible for those that call it home, work, school, etc.

More critical to this discussion, however, may be determining *who* is responsible for the development of the architectural detail. Who is responsible for the actualization of these critical components of our built environment? Is it the architect who dreams them up, the draftsman who draws the lines, the engineer who makes them sound, the foreman who oversees their construction, the craftsman who tightens their bolts, or the visitor who experiences them first hand? It is apparent that this notion of responsibility and ownership is indeed quite complex.

In his introduction to Stephen Caldwell's book *Strange Details*, Nader Tehrani states that the roles of architect and builder became autonomous during the Renaissance when the work of the architect first became separated from the builder's guild.[17] Over time, this separation has become far more distinct and defined, and eventually the work of realizing the architectural detail shifted from the responsibility of the craftsman in the field to the draftsman in the architect's office. It is here that the definition of detail becomes particularly cloudy. Is the detail a built assembly or a drawn set of instructions for someone else to use as a blueprint? According to Frascari, more contemporary definitions of details often position them as "verbal and graphic means for controlling the work of variable crews of vocationless workers who are unprepared for their own jobs and possibly even financially dishonest."[18] Although this position may be hyper-critical, it adds to the question of ownership and responsibility. Should the architect not venture beyond the page and should the builder just blindly follow the instructions given?

In *Five Houses, Ten Details*, Edward Ford also acknowledges the increasing complexity involved in coordinating the construction of a building.[19] Here, Ford discusses his time in practice in the 1960s, an era of growing specialization in the construction industry. Instead of a single contractor taking on most of the responsibility for building, construction had become dependent on specialized sub-contractors who desired to work independently of one another. As a result, primary joints and intersections in the building were less about assembly and more about coordination of labor, the filling of the resulting gaps with caulk, and dealing with the "legislated inaccuracy of the American building industry."[20]

Tehrani points out that current legal regulation of the building industry also plays a key role in muddying the ownership of the architectural detail. The architect is charged with design, while the contractor is responsible for selecting the means and methods of constructing that design, providing assurances that end product will reflect the intent of the architect. This construct effectively limits the ability of the architect to develop a meaningful relationship between the construction documentation and the resulting construction. The system is effectively setup to ensure that the architect's investment is in the image of the work, not the makeup of the assembly.[21] The development of the actual detail then becomes a negotiation, a passing of specifications, requests-for-information, and substitutions or alternatives. Tehrani believes that the act of "severing the architect from the means and methods of construction is somewhat like permitting the writer to use a certain vocabulary, but disassociating it from the very alphabet from which the text emerges."[22]

Deamer extends the conversation about the diversity by including modes of production in her analysis of the architectural detail:

The subject is likewise determined by a parallel dispersal. Neither chopping wood alone in the forest, nor designing at a drafting board, nor milling in the shop, nor standing in an assembly line, nor sitting alone at the computer, the subject is all and none of these, distributed throughout the points of production, at all points of the globe.[23]

She asserts that unlike the fine arts, architecture is not created by one person or one entity. In production, this list includes not only the contractor but the myriad of manufacturers that produce the vast majority of the components that reside in our buildings. Most contemporary buildings are not constructed per the process of architects such as Carlo Scarpa (the subject of Frascari's "The Tell-the-Tale Detail"), who worked diligently in the field with master craftsmen to create unique custom detail work throughout his projects. A great majority of our "details" are not a result of genius design by the architect or exquisite craftsmanship by the contractor; instead they are the product of efficient manufacturing strategies by global entities that churn out our building components on assembly lines in factories halfway around the world. Many buildings built today are less about design and more about choosing details out of a catalog of pre-programmed choices. Is this truly an architectural detail? Who is responsible for its relationship to the building, to the place, to the space, to the greater whole?

If "God lies in the details," then whose details are they? This quote can certainly be linked to an understanding of the responsibility tied to the profession of architecture. Perhaps, however, it is linked more closely to the responsibility of coordination of this network of stakeholders than it is in the development of a conscientious joint. For a project to be truly successful, each partner in the fabrication process must be working with the same care and poise as the next. Today, many architects are beginning to understand the role manufacturing processes in our industry and are either trying to make use of them or reclaim them as their own. We see practices like KieranTimberlake working to develop progressive working strategies with industry partners, while others have embraced digital fabrication as a means to reconnect the designer and maker in the fabrication of space. As we move forward, these collaborative practices may truly help us realize why "God lies in the details" both physically and socially.

Understanding

In "The Tell-the-Tale Detail," Frascari states that "the 'construction' and the 'construing' of architecture are both in the detail. Elusive in a traditional dimensional definition, the architectural detail can be defined as the union of construction, the result of the *logos of techne*, with construing, the result of the *techne of logos*."[24] With this statement, Frascari illuminates a duality latent in this smallest scale of our built environment. The *logos of techne* can be translated as the logic of making or the locus of assembly and fabrication. The *techne of logos*, on the other hand, is the making of logic or the creation of understanding of space. For it is the sum total of the expressed details of a space from which we derive our understanding and experience of said space. Change the set of details and you potentially change how the same environment is read by those occupying it or moving through it.

It is in this realm that the next interpretation of "God lies in the details" resides; that of understanding. Details are not just subordinate parts of a larger whole. They are primary contributors to the development of spatial experience. Just as words give character and meaning to a sentence, the details of architectural space provide the language and character of the aesthetic expression of the architecture.

Architect Peter Zumthor has built his practice around consideration for each expressed detail in the work. He believes that architects must work to ensure the perception of the whole cannot be distracted by inessential details; each joint should be utilized to reinforce the overall presence of the work. As such, details establish the formal rhythm of a building.[25] In his designs, Zumthor looks for rational constructions and forms for edges and joints, for the points where surfaces intersect and different materials meet, as a way of combating the constant challenge in

architecture of developing a comprehensive whole out of innumerable details, various functions and forms, and a multitude of materials. Within this theory, details express what the basic idea of the design requires at each relevant point in the building whether it is "belonging or separation, tension or lightness, friction, solidity, fragility..."[26]

Ford also sees the detail as a conveyor of understanding in a building. He believes that we can hardly design a building without a large number of consistent, abstract, and motific details. As such, it is critical that we recognize the necessity of autonomous ones. For example:

- the materially expressive detail that speaks of an inner force in an architecture of surface
- the structurally expressive detail that speaks of weight in a structure that resists the impact of gravity
- the joint that speaks of dynamic movement in a structure that is static [27]

The autonomous detail occurs in the context of a series of details that are consistent and generally oppose its expression. The counterpoint of difference has an effect of enhancing the understanding of place while also allowing for a particular experience with the autonomous condition. The understanding of the whole is facilitated by an experience of contrast. This configuration, for Ford, provides a significant opportunity to develop a relationship between a space and those inhabiting it.

Regardless of the strategy of detailing, there is a distinct relationship between those details we choose to use or express and the character and experience of the space in which they reside. For each connection or joint, there are a virtually unlimited number of design options. The same is true for material selection, textural qualities, and environmental stimuli, all of which can be classified as architectural details. It is the details of a space that turn it from a simple volume to an experiential space, from a neutral palate to an articulated environment. In interpreting "God lives in the details," we must consider the layers of meaning conveyed through the specific set of details chosen for a project.

Intimacy

The final reading of "God lies in the details" that will be discussed in this paper involves not only the architecture, but those who inhabit it as well. This concluding interpretation proposes that the details of architecture are also the generators of intimacy between the built world and those who occupy it. In *Thinking Architecture*, Zumthor wrote:

> Our attention is caught, perhaps for the first time, by a detail such as two nails in the floor that hold the steel plates by the work-out doorstep. Emotions well up. Something moves us.[28]

Zumthor believes that work must start with notions of material and detail. Architecture needs to be touched, to be seen, heard, and smelled. We live in a world that we experience through our senses and although vision dominates our daily experience, things like our memories can be triggered much more emphatically at times through our other senses. The details of architecture are critical to engaging the senses of those who inhabit it. From the selection of the correct wood to provide an aroma, to the cool touch or shifting materiality of the railing at the stair, to the sound of the heavy, oversize door closing at the end of the long, echo-y hallway, it is the details that can engage us, arouse us, and elicit a response from us.

Through a combination of *Einfühlung* (empathy) and architectural tectonics, we also have the ability to physically relate to the inanimate structure of a building, providing another opportunity for an intimate connection. The idea of empathy in relation to architecture originated in the late 1800s with philosopher Robert Vischer. The theory proposes that we have an innate understanding of gravity and other acting forces because we also possess a body dealing with the same forces.[29]

The theory of empathy can be combined with the understanding of architectural tectonics as the configuration of a building to express its underlying forces to create a strong connection between the detailing of the architecture and the emotive, empathetic response latent in its expression. The detailing of Thorncrown Chapel, for instance, with its finely articulated, lattice-like truss structure, allows the

eye of the visitor to be drawn upward, through the "canopy" to the skylight and the heavens above.

Additionally, Frascari discusses the work of physician Hermann von Helmholtz, who proposed the idea of indirect vision:

> In architecture, feeling a handrail, walking up steps or between walls, turning a corner, and noting the sitting of a beam in a wall, are coordinated elements of visual and tactile sensations. The location of those details gives birth to the conventions that tie a meaning to a perception. The conception of the architectural space achieved in this way is the result of the association of the visual images of details, gained through the phenomenon of indirect vision, with the geometrical proposition embodied in forms, dimensions, and location, developed by touching and by walking through buildings.[30]

Vision and tactility play a significant role in this theory and both can be controlled by the architect to create the opportunity for experience in space. If the perception of space is the reading of a series of signs, then meaning is generated only through experience. Again, this theory places the detail at the crossroads of us and our understanding of space. As such, details are the catalyst for intimacy; they are the places where we begin to understand space through our own bodies and our own sensory engagement with place.

Concluding Thought

This analysis of "God lies in the details" proposes no answer as correct or best. These four interpretations are but a starting point for investigating the role of the detail in the production of the architectural space we occupy each day. The detail is a complex element, playing a role in the technical realization of structures, in the social and political realities of the process of design and construction, and in the phenomenological experience of space. Each of us may align our particular views more closely with one or more of these interpretations, but we cannot deny that they *all* have merit (as surely do a slew of other interpretations not mentioned in this text). Perhaps the greatest takeaway from this discussion is that the complexity of the architectural detail is why "God lies in the details." For these building blocks of our built environment are far more than ornamentation or the hammering of a few nails. They are the basis for both constructing and understanding the world around us.

Notes:

[1] Marco Frascari, "The Tell-the-Tale Detail," in *Theorizing a New Agenda for Architecture: An Anthology of Architectural Theory 1965-1995*, ed. Kate Nesbitt (New York: Princeton Architectural Press, 1996), 500.

[2] ibid, 511.

[3] ibid, 501.

[4] ibid, 501.

[5] ibid, 500.

[6] Eric Bellin, "Re:constructing Detail," in *98th ACSA Annual Meeting Proceedings: Rebuilding*, eds. Bruce Goodwin & Judith Kinnard (New York: ACSA Press, 2010), 114-120.

[7] Edward Ford, *The Architectural Detail* (New York: Princeton Architectural Press, 2011).

[8] ibid, 27.

[9] Peggy Deamer, "Detail: The Subject of the Object," *Praxis: Journal of Writing + Building* 1, no. 1 (2000): 108-115.

[10] Gottfried Semper, *Style in the Technical and Tectonic Arts: Or Practical Aesthetics*, trans. Harry Francis Mallgrave and Michael Robinson (Los Angeles: Getty Research Institute, 2004), 219. (Originally published as Semper, Gotfried. *Der Stil in den technischen und tektonischen Kunsten; oder, Praktische Aesthetik: Ein Handbuch fur Techniker, Kunstler und Kunstfreunde*, 2 vols. Frankfurt am Main: Verlag fur Kunst & Wissenschaft, 1860.)

[11] Philip Johnson, "Architectural Details," *Architectural Record* (1964): 137-147.

[12] Walter Wagner, "Ludwig Mies van der Rohe: 1886-1969," *Architectural Record* 146 (1969): 9.

[13] Werner Blaser, *Mies van der Rohe: Continuing the Chicago School of Architecture* (Boston: Birkhauser Verlag, 1981), 10.

[14] Jean Labatut, "An Approach to Architectural Composition," *Modulus* 9 (1964): 55-63. As cited in Frascari, "The Tell-the-Tale Detail," 501.

[15] Robert Meagher, "Techne," *Perspecta* 24 (1988): 160.

[16] Deamer, "Detail: The Subject of the Object," 108.

[17] Nader Tehrani, "Forward: A Murder in the Court," in *Strange Details*, written by Michael Cadwell (Cambridge: The MIT Press, 2007), vii-xii.

[18] Frascari, "The Tell-the-Tale Detail," 503.

[19] Edward Ford, *Five Houses, Ten Details* (New York: Princeton Architectural Press, 2009).

[20] ibid, 145.

[21] Tehrani, "Forward: A Murder in the Court."

[22] ibid, ix.

[23] Deamer, "Detail: The Subject of the Object," 115..

[24] Frascari, "The Tell-the-Tale Detail," 500.

[25] Peter Zumthor, *Thinking Architecture*, 2nd ed. (Boston: Birkhauser, 2006), 15.

[26] ibid.

[27] Ford, *The Architectural Detail*.

[28] Zumthor, *Thinking Architecture*, 16.

[29] Heinrich Wölfflin, "Prolegomena to a Psychology of Architecture," in *Empathy, Form, and Space: Problems in German Aesthetics, 1873-1893*, ed. Harry Francis Mallgrave (Santa Monica: The Getty Center for the History of Art and the Humanities, 1994). Originally published as Heinrich Wölfflin, *Prolegomena zu einer Psychologie der Architektur*, Inaugural-Dissertation der hohen philosophischen Fakultat der Universitat Muchen zur Erlangung der hochsten akademischen Wurden (Munich: Kgl. Hof- & Universitats-Buchdruckerei, 1886).

[30] Frascari, "The Tell-the-Tale Detail," 506.

Figure Citations:

3: Chad Schwartz, *Introducing Architectural Tectonics: Exploring the Intersection of Design and Construction* (New York: Routledge, 2016), 43.

The Use of Materials in Latin American Architecture, comparing concepts of 1979 Versus Contemporary Architecture's approach

Ane Gonzalez Lara
University of New Mexico School of Architecture and Planning

Abstract

This paper analyses the concepts of materials in 1979 in Latin America in comparison to contemporary architecture, focusing primarily in the use of brick and concrete in the region. The paper takes the interviews that Damian Bayon made to different Latin American architects in the book *The Changing Shape of Latin American Architecture: Conversations with Ten Leading Architects* written in 1979, as a baseline to compare the current situation of architecture in the selected countries.

Introduction

In 1979, Damian Bayon wrote the book *The Changing Shape of Latin American Architecture: Conversations with Ten Leading Architects*. The book was written following a meeting UNESCO organized in Buenos Aires in 1969 in which different experts on architecture and urban planning gathered "to decide on how to implement the resolution to study the literary and artistic expressions of Latin American culture."[1] This meeting recommended conducting a series of interviews with ten leading architects from Latin America in which they would give their points of view on Latin American architecture.

The Argentine art critic Damian Bayon asked the ten architects somewhat similar questions covering an array of topics from urban planning and architecture to building materials and techniques. The responses to the questions on materials and techniques were fairly different and broad; although, to some extent, the majority of the interviewed architects saw industrialization and prefabrication as the future of Latin American architecture.

Almost forty years later, it is surprising to see that an evolution in the techniques and materials used by the

current leading architects in Latin America hasn't been the driver of the design and development of the architecture in the region. On the contrary, we can see how the dominant contemporary architects from Latin America today still use traditional materials instead of more avant-garde ones.

Following the structure of the aforementioned book, the current use of different materials in the region will be analyzed to then compare it to the opinions that the interviewed architects held in 1979 regarding this same issue.

In the book, the interviewed architects are Clorindo Testa (Argentina), Roberto Burle Marx (Brazil), Rogelio Salmona (Colombia), Fernando Salinas (Cuba), Emilio Duhart (Chile), Pedro Ramirez Vazquez (Mexico), Carlos Colombino (Paraguay), Jose Garcia Bryce (Peru), Eladio Dieste (Uruguay), and Carlos Raul Villanueva (Venezuela).

Due to the political situations in Cuba and Venezuela, their architectural production has paused or even stopped. Therefore, it is hard to define and evaluate the development of the architecture in these regions, and their analysis has been omitted from this paper. Additionally, Bayon's interview with the Peruvian architect José Garcia Bryce doesn't deal with tectonics, materials, or prefabrication, so, consequently, the comparison of this country's architecture has been omitted as well.

The tectonics of modernism in Latin America: An overview

The science of construction in Latin America around 1979 was highly divided in two: On one side, major technological advances were being made, but on the other, a large majority of the region's new buildings were still being built with rough materials and primitive means. The majority of the houses outside the main capitals were built with adobe or mud over reeds. The main challenge in bringing new materials like plastic composites or steel to the area wasn't the complexity of the technology, but the economic situation in all the Latin American countries.[2]

Regarding the various technological advancements of the period, a lot of improvements were done around concrete and its finishing techniques, which reached a high degree of perfection. Some examples of the refined use of concrete are the Banco de Londres (Bank of London and South America) in Buenos Aires, where concrete was used as a finish for both the interiors and exteriors, and Oscar Niemeyer's work in Brazilia. Additionally, Felix Candela approached the use of concrete from its structural capabilities, exploring its use in roofs and undulating surfaces as seen in the Los Manantiales restaurant in Mexico City, creating light and thin structures.[3]

In Uruguay, Eladio Dieste conducted a lot of research around the use of brick. Atlantida Church is a great example of how far he stretched the techniques and craftsmanship of the material to achieve the striking undulating walls. At the same time, steel was a commonly imported material and was used primarily in industrial buildings and only occasionally in smaller-scale buildings. In Chile, steel was used to build the National Polytechnic Institute and also in the construction of some middle schools across the country. [4]

The tectonics of contemporary architecture in Latin America: An overview

The duality that the region was suffering in 1981 in terms of building materials and techniques is still present today in all the countries in Latin America.

As previously described, in the twentieth century, Latin American architects tried to challenge gravity by designing very light and thin structures. We can see this approach in Felix Candela's buildings in Mexico, Oscar Niemeyer's Pampulha, and Eladio Dieste's brick vaults. On the other hand, and contradicting the predictions of the interviewed architects, twenty-first century's architects are still using brick and concrete as the main materials in their buildings. However, the way they used these materials and techniques is clearly

different than how modernist architects approached them.

Contemporary architects express heaviness and weight both in the proportions and materials they use.[5] It is as if gravity and its conditions are one of the main drivers of these architects' projects. We can see this approach in Jose Maria Saez Vaquero's Casa Pentimento in Quito, Ecuador. The project is resolved with a single concrete block that can be connected in four different positions. These pieces serve as structure, enclosure, furniture, stairs, and even a vertical garden, which was the original idea for the project.

Comparing the use of materials and building techniques in seven countries from 1981 to the present time

Argentina

In the conversation that Damian Bayon had with Clorindo Testa, the writer asked the architect, among other questions, what is the "defect" of architecture, if any. Testa answered that he would like to be practicing a somewhat different type of architecture, an architecture that is more advanced technically. He also added that "an architect does what he does but he is hoping all the while to be able to accomplish other things which as yet can't be done because the technique or the difficulties it would bring, or the cost, still can't be absorbed by the market." [6]

Far from being restricted by the availability of materials in Argentina, Rafael Iglesia has been one of the most acclaimed contemporary architects in the country. Having built a wide range of project types and explored the use of different materials, Iglesia wrote numerous times that his work isn't inspired by the materials or techniques, but that the inspiration comes to him from literature, not necessarily from architecture. [7] In his buildings, he usually uses materials in a pure manner, always focusing his experimentations on the essential components of the design process. The structure is always one of the main drivers behind the conceptualization of his work. On the Casa Cruz, the weight of the house becomes the solution to its structure and proportions. The house was designed in sections to work from and with the gravity. The elements that form the structure were stacked to counterbalance their moments and weight, creating an harmonious structural and proportional balance.

In Argentina, the "School of Rosario," a group Iglesias was part of, has influenced younger architects' work. This is the case with Diego Arraigada, a young Argentinian architect. On his buildings, he is not restricted to any material in particular, making the material selection according to the project type, location, budget, etc. The availability of materials has grown exponentially since 1981, but still on the Casa de Ladrillos, Arraigada uses brick as the main material, creating an elegant and delicate pattern. (Fig. 1) The geometry of this pattern is then translated into the interior openings and spaces resulting in a very interesting use of the brick as a lattice.

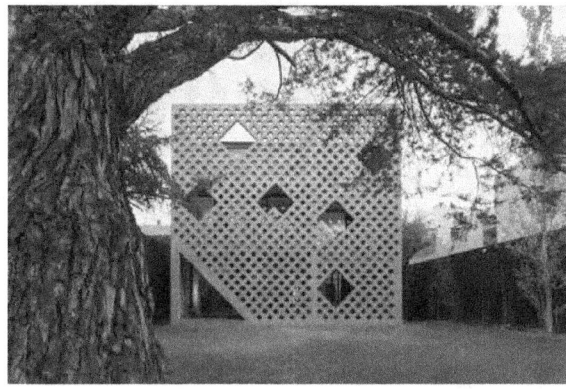

Fig. 1. Casa de Ladrillos, Diego Arraigada.

Brazil

In the book that we are taking as a baseline, the person interviewed in Brazil was the landscape architect and painter Roberto Burle Marx. The conversation that Bayon and Burle Marx had didn't address the technical and material aspects of built projects. Instead, the conversation is about Burle Marx's work as a landscape architect and his point of view on landscape architecture at the time.

On the other hand, leaving Brazil out of this research would seem a bit inappropriate given all the documentation around Oscar Niemeyer's work and the influence of both Paulista and Carioca schools in the region. Therefore, the focus of this section will be on the broad work of the Brazilian architect Oscar Niemeyer.

Niemeyer learned the technological advancements with concrete that were occurring at the time and used them in almost all his projects. Niemeyer wanted to "reinvent the school building, to design something that made no reference to old schools."[5]

Pampulha Church was one of his most controversial buildings. With this building, he set his work apart from the influence of Le Corbusier's mandates. His work was nonetheless heavily tied to the use of concrete, and Niemeyer kept using the material for his entire career. The buildings Niemeyer designed, in most cases, tried to defy the gravity and heaviness of the concrete through the use of light columns or slabs. His passion for structures was even manifested in the book *Conversa de arquiteto* published in 2002 that documented the conversations that Niemeyer had with his structural engineer José Carlos Sussekind.[9]

Continuing the use of concrete, but with a different approach, contemporary Brazilian architect Paulo Mendes da Rocha also experiments with the material. Mendes da Rocha has continued the brutalist movement in his buildings. One of his masterpieces is the Brazilian Museum of Sculpture in Sao Paulo in which he makes the program disappear under a public park. A generous canopy covers the museum's entrance and serves as a datum for visitors.

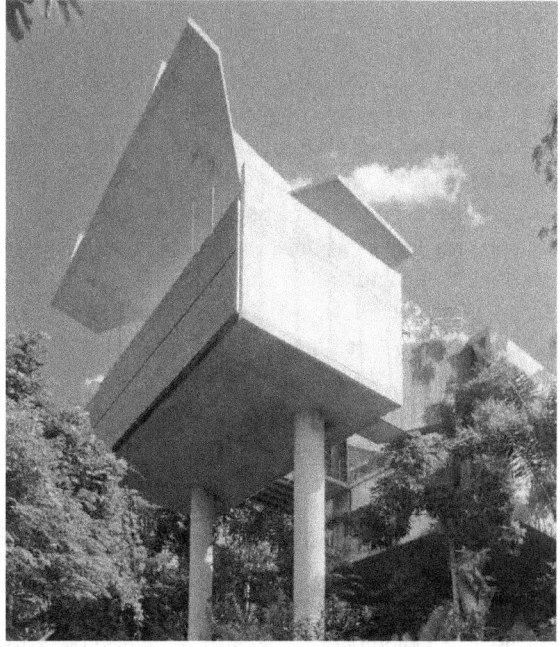

Fig. 2. House in Ubatuba, Angelo Bucci.

From a contemporary perspective, Angelo Bucci has been able to merge the designs of Joao Alvaro Rocha's and Vilanova Artigas's work. Bucci also approaches some of his projects from their structural challenges, making the heaviness of his buildings somewhat visible. In his House in Ubatuba project, he pushes overhangs and cantilevers to their limits. Due to the steep site and existing trees, the house rests on three columns. (Fig. 2) The structure is counterbalanced by its cantilevers, so the house was not stable until it was complete. Bucci has said of the project, "In the beginning, I thought of Alexander Calder. Considering this structure could be balanced almost as a mobile, I thought the slabs could be arranged to counterweigh each other in suspension over the site." [10]

Bucci's use of materials is more idiosyncratic than his predecessors'. Even though the majority of his built work in Brazil is made with concrete, he has used other materials when building abroad, like his Student Housing project in Ourcq-Jaurès, Paris, where he uses wood to clad the exterior façade and the Housing Building in Lugano, Switzerland, where he uses a similar finish for the façade. What seems to be clear is that Bucci hasn't taken the experimentation of new materials as the leitmotif of his projects, he has used the structural challenges and proportions to create a very strong and bold body of work.

Colombia

In Colombia, Rogelio Salmona thought that the lack of prefabrication was Colombia's biggest problem when he was interviewed by Bayon. At the same time, he thought that Latin America, and Colombia specifically, couldn't use the same systems that were being used in Europe. He believed that "the design should be invented in Colombia, and we should also invent the systems of construction and adapt the systems of prefabrication to those needs."[11]

Salmona worked with Le Corbusier in his Parisian office for seven years. While there, the Colombian architect started to become critical about Le Corbusier's dogmas and decided to quit to go back to Colombia and start his own practice. In 1963, the architect was selected to build the Torres del Parque complex, a project that made Salmona a well-known architect in Colombia. Salmona used this project to apply his ideas about an "organic architecture made

with the bricks that were, at the time, becoming a trademark for Colombian architecture" [12]

Years later, Daniel Bonilla would continue the use of traditional Colombian brick on the Anglo Colombiano Primary School Building in Bogota. (Fig. 3) Although Bonilla uses a wide array of materials on his buildings, from wood to glass to concrete, in his work he always uses traditional materials.

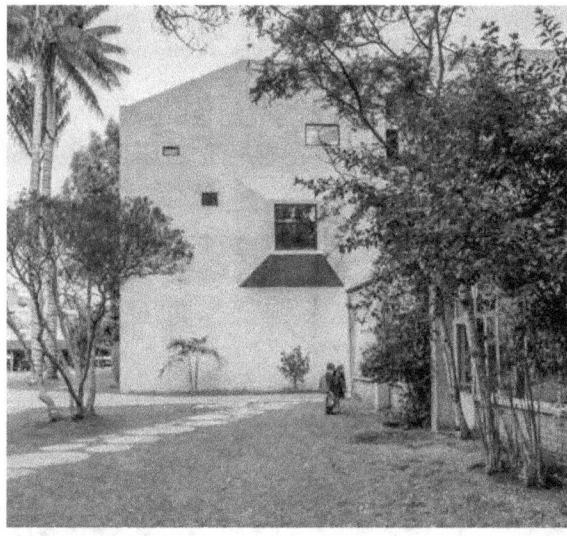

Fig. 3. Anglo Colombiano Primary School Building, Daniel Bonilla.

Chile

Emilio Duhart was a Chilean architect who was one of the main representatives of modernism in the country. His most famous work was the building for United Nations Economic Commission for Latin America and the Caribbean, known by its Spanish acronym CEPAL. Like Rogelio Salmona, Duhart also worded for Le Corbusier on some of his most iconic buildings. Years later, Duhart studied for his master's degree under the guidance of Walter Gropius at Harvard. Despite the influence these two architects had on Duhart's work, he had a deep sensibility for local materials and references as well as a great control of the scale of his buildings.

Duhart was chosen as the representative of Chilean architecture for *The Changing Shape of Latin American Architecture*. In his interview, he gave a sensible and accurate response to the issue of prefabrication. He believed that prefabrication was one of the ways to solve the problems they faced at the time, but that it is not the panacea. He added that compared to other continents, Latin America has a great amount of hand labor and not so many economic resources. Therefore, prefabrication in Latin America can't be approached the same way it is approached in Europe or North America.

The twenty-first century, apart from bringing new concerns in terms of the tectonics and structures of the buildings in Latin America, also brought social awareness to architecture. This is the case with Alejandro Aravena's work. The architect and his firm, Elemental, worked on several housing projects after the 2010 earthquake and tsunami that hit Chile.[13] The houses Aravena designed don't require a high upfront cost, and the design allows the houses to be expanded once the owners can afford it.

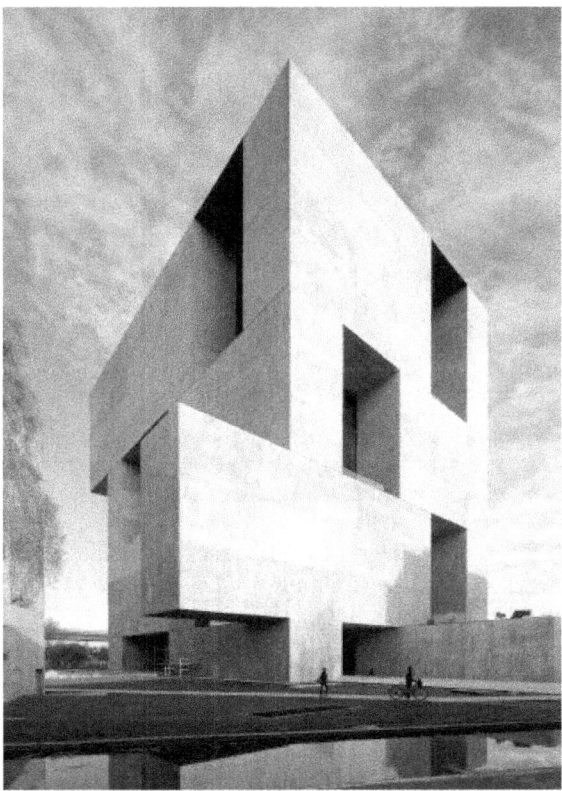

Fig. 4. Innovation Center of Santiago, Alejandro Aravena.

Apart from the socially engaged work Aravena does, his firm also focuses in other building types. With the Innovation Center of Santiago, one of the biggest challenges Aravena faces with such an avant-garde

program was obsolescence. (Fig. 4) The architect said, "A clean, direct and even tough form is, in the end, the most flexible way to allow for continuous change and renewal. From a stylistic point of view, we thought of using a rather strong monolithic materiality as a way to replace trendiness by timelessness."[14] He achieved a strong, monolithic look by using exposed concrete on the exterior. The combination of the solid and empty spaces is also an answer to the need for timelessness, which is also expressed in the interior spaces. While navigating the project, the continuous sequences of spaces and views accompany the people who work and gather in the Innovation Center.

The material selection on all Aravena's projects comes from an answer to a problem or necessity. He approaches each project as a new question or problem that he has to identify and solve by understanding and observing the people and society that will use the building. He uses the materiality of the projects as a tool to connect the people and the buildings he creates.

In some manner, Duhart's answer to prefabrication was connected to the people, and so is Aravena's work. Nonetheless, we see in Aravena's work that prefabrication and industrialization are far away from Chile's architectonic reality.

Mexico

Pedro Ramirez Vazquez is a Mexican architect mostly recognized for the large scale of his projects. One of his most famous projects is the Anthropology Museum in Mexico City, built in 1964. This project proved Ramirez Vazquez's ability to work at a large scale, and therefore, years later he was named the organizer of the 1968 Mexican Olympics.

In his interview with Bayon, he was of the most radical architects regarding his ideas about prefabrication. He told Bayon, "It's my firm conviction that prefabrication or, better, mass production with designs having a very elastic, very versatile application, is the future not only in Latin America, but in the entire world. The problem of housing can't be solved in any other way."[15]

Mexico has since gone through a huge revolution in terms of design and architecture. The country has position itself as one of the main capitals of design, but the reality is that prefabrication is far from being a tool of the main Mexican architects.

Choosing between contemporary productive and creative architects of Mexico is a hard task, but Alberto Kalach has proven himself to be one of the most successful architects. Kalach's work ranges in scale and material. One of his most acclaimed works is the Casa GGG. (Fig. 5) The project plays with the use of concrete in a very raw and elemental manner, comprising and expanding the different spaces within the house. The house is designed as a massive concrete piece that is fragmented, creating different cracks that allow light to penetrate the geometry in a magical and diverse manner.

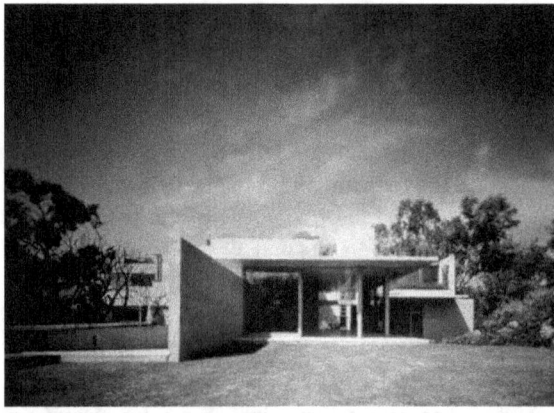

Fig. 5. Casa GGG, Alberto Kalach.

Even if experimentation with the technical limits of concrete still continues, and is the main focus of research for some architects, a new movement is now occurring among contemporary Latin American architects where the exploration is no longer with the techniques of the materials nor with the same ideas that the brutalists pursued, but in the quality of the spaces created with concrete. Casa GGG is a great example of this approach. We could also add to this list Tatiana Bilbao's sactuary along the Ruta del Peregrino in Jalisco, Mexico, or in Pezo von Ellrichshausen's Poli House in Concepcion, Chile. This reality is far away from the prefabricated architecture that Ramirez Vazquez envisioned for the future.

Paraguay

In Paraguay, Bayon interviewed architect and artist Carlos Colombino. Colombino expressed his frustration with the lack of technical possibilities available in Paraguay compared to Europe: "I feel a great frustration because I think that an architect, as a creator, needs the new materials such as, for example, plastics, aluminum, glass and steel." [16]

Years later, and with much more refined techniques available in Paraguay, Solano Benitez, a principal of Gabinete de Arquitectura, one of the most prominent firms in Paraguay, uses brick as the main material in all his buildings. According to *Modern Architecture in Latin America*, "Using mostly a very uneven artisanal brick as his main material, Benítez is able to create various types of surfaces: from the most heavy load-bearing walls to the most transparent screen-like envelopes." [17] (353) The brick lattice at the Unilever Headquarters is made with bricks positioned in alternating diagonal directions working almost like a truss system. (Fig. 6) Benitez's experimentation with bricks resulted in him and his firm winning the Golden Lion at the 2016 Venice Biennale for "harnessing simple materials, structural ingenuity and unskilled labor to bring architecture to underserved communities." [18]

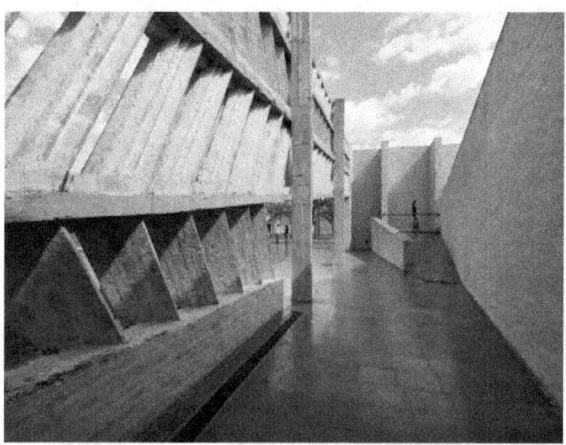

Fig. 6. Unilever Headquarters, Gabinete de Arquitectura.

Uruguay

Eladio Dieste received his degree in engineering from the School of Engineering of Montevideo in the 1930s. He wasn't trained as an architect, but from the beginning of his career he showed great interest in brick structures. By 1955 he had already built a total of over 15 million square feet of large buildings in Uruguay, Argentina, and Brazil. Dieste's work was a continuous search for "an economical use of materials and that could be assembled by poorly educated construction workers." [19] In 1952, Dieste was commissioned to build a church in the community of Atlantida. The church has some unique and elegant undulating brick walls that support a undulating brick roof, creating a magical interior space.

In the interview with Bayon, Dieste said that even if prefabrication is important for Latin America, he didn't think that prefabrication should be the answer to all the building elements, explaining that "the prefabrication for floor structures, of roofs, is very logical. But I don't think total prefabrication is the most economic technical solution." [20]

Marcelo and Martin Guluano, of Gualano + Gualano Arquitectos, are two of the most prominent architects in Uruguay today. Their Calera del Rey House is a great example of what Dieste envisioned for the future of materials in the county. (Fig. 7) The house's public spaces are covered by a metal vaulted ceiling that is supported by two stone walls. The walls are made in a very rustic and traditional manner, while the roof is made with metal and contradicts the roughness and heaviness of the walls.

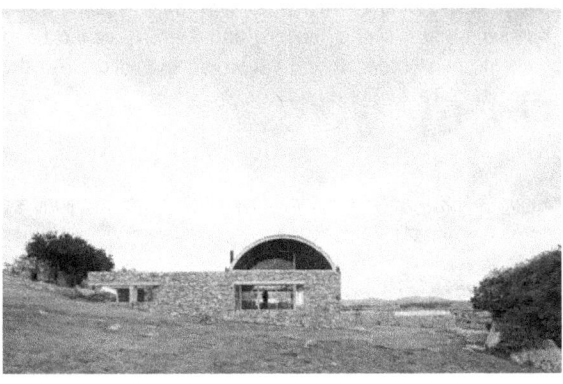

Fig. 7. Calera del Rey, Gulano + Gulano.

Conclusion

After understanding the evolution of the materiality of architecture throughout Latin America, we can see that the approach contemporary architects take with building tectonics hasn't changed much since 1981. Latin American architects have proven to be creating an architecture that attracts critics, scholars, and architects from all over the world.

It is a complex task to understand what makes Latin American buildings so bold and cohesive. There might

actually be more than one answer to this question, but the approach architects take to the materials is clearly one of them. In their use of brick and concrete, Latin American architects have found some faithful allies to help them fulfill their dreams and aesthetic desires. These materials—in some cases, used to express roughness, and in others, applied as soft and delicate components—have been the predominant construction materials in the region for centuries.

Despite being challenged by the form, use, context, or aesthetics required for different buildings, the majority of Latin American architects who build with brick and concrete have always gone back to them, as if their marriage was unbreakable. Whenever the use of these materials was challenged, instead of looking for alternatives, they explored the capabilities of the materials until they discovered new techniques for building with them.

Contemporary architects are still enamored with these materials, and it is from this continuous exploration, and also from the study of what has already been achieved, that the majority of the projects that come out of Latin America still surprise and captivate us. The results of this approach is an architecture that is rooted to its place, an architecture that is not capricious or superficial—a mature and cohesive architecture that is born from this longstanding love affair.

Notes:

[1] Bayon, Damian., and Paolo Gasparini. 1979. *The Changing Shape of Latin American Architecture : Conversations with Ten Leading Architects.*Chichester: Wiley. p 1

[2] Segre, Roberto, and Fernando Kusnetzoff. 1981. *Latin America in Its Architecture.* New York: Holmes & Meier. p 161

[3] Carranza, Luis E., Fernando Luiz Lara, and Jorge Francisco Liernur. 2014. *Modern Architecture in Latin America : Art, Technology, and Utopia.* Joe R. and Teresa Lozano Long series in Latin American and Latino art and culture. Austin: University of Texas Press. p 352

[4] Segre, Roberto, and Fernando Kusnetzoff. 1981. *Latin America in Its Architecture.* New York: Holmes & Meier. p 161-165.

[5] Carranza, Luis E., Fernando Luiz Lara, and Jorge Francisco Liernur. 2014. *Modern Architecture in Latin America : Art, Technology, and Utopia.* Joe R. and Teresa Lozano Long

series in Latin American and Latino art and culture. Austin: University of Texas Press. p 352-353

[6] Bayon, Damian., and Paolo Gasparini. 1979. *The Changing Shape of Latin American Architecture : Conversations with Ten Leading Architects.*Chichester: Wiley. p 18

[7] Plaut, Jeannette, and Sebastián. Bianchi. 2011. *Rafael Iglesia.* 1a ed. Santiago de Chile: Universidad Andrés Bello. p 6-8

[8] Niemeyer, Oscar. *Conversa de arquiteto.* Editora Revan, 1993.

[9] Niemeyer, Oscar, and José Carlos Sussekind. *Conversa de amigos: correspondência entre Oscar Niemeyer e José Carlos Sussekind.* Editora Revan, 2002.

[10] Bucci, Angelo, Kenneth. Frampton, and Columbia University. 2015. *The Dissolution of Buildings.* GSAPP transcripts; GSAPP transcripts. New York, NY: GSAPP Transcripts. p 12

[11] Bayon, Damian., and Paolo Gasparini. 1979. *The Changing Shape of Latin American Architecture : Conversations with Ten Leading Architects.*Chichester: Wiley. p 76

[12] Carranza, Luis E., Fernando Luiz Lara, and Jorge Francisco Liernur. 2014. *Modern Architecture in Latin America : Art, Technology, and Utopia.* Joe R. and Teresa Lozano Long series in Latin American and Latino art and culture. Austin: University of Texas Press. p 225

[13] Elemental website. Elementalchile.cl http://www.elementalchile.cl/en/about/ (accessed February 21, 2017).

[14] ArchDaily. 2014 "Innovation Center UC – Anacleto Angelini / Alejandro Aravena | Elemental". Archdaily, September 22. http://www.archdaily.com/549152/innovation-center-uc-anacleto-angelini-alejandro-aravena-elemental (accessed December 11, 2016)

[15] Carranza, Luis E., Fernando Luiz Lara, and Jorge Francisco Liernur. 2014. *Modern Architecture in Latin America : Art, Technology, and Utopia.* Joe R. and Teresa Lozano Long series in Latin American and Latino art and culture. Austin: University of Texas Press. p 225

[16] Bayon, Damian., and Paolo Gasparini. 1979. *The Changing Shape of Latin American Architecture : Conversations with Ten Leading Architects.*Chichester: Wiley. p 162)

[17] Carranza, Luis E., Fernando Luiz Lara, and Jorge Francisco Liernur. 2014. *Modern Architecture in Latin America : Art, Technology, and Utopia.* Joe R. and Teresa Lozano Long series in Latin American and Latino art and culture. Austin: University of Texas Press. p 353

[18] Gabinete de Arquitectura's "Breaking the Siege" – Winner of the Golden Lion at the 2016 Venice Biennale http://www.archdaily.com/tag/solano-benitez

[19] Carranza, Luis E., Fernando Luiz Lara, and Jorge Francisco Liernur. 2014. *Modern Architecture in Latin America : Art, Technology, and Utopia.* Joe R. and Teresa Lozano Long series in Latin American and Latino art and culture. Austin: University of Texas Press. p 190

[20] (201)

* Figures 1, 2, 4 and 5 used with permission. Permissions for figures 3 and 6 still pending.

Fearless: Confronting Weight and Gravity in Manipulating Matter

Lisa Huang
University of Florida

Abstract

In architectural design education, the majority of studio time is invested in introducing students to new tools, techniques and a verbal and visual language that are the foundation for design thinking. A range of media and methods are available to formalize this visual language. In parallel to design studio, student typically learn about building technology regarding materials and construction methods through lecture-based courses. However, for most students, the capacity to apply this knowledge and transform their design ideas into a physical built form is unfamiliar and intimidating territory. Rote learning about materials and assemblies may unintentionally create a disconnect between the concept and reality - occupying an abstract realm where weight and gravity have no impact. What are the methods to narrow the space for design ideas to translate into the material realm? Is there value in developing a student's haptic understanding of building matter that materializes architectural ideas?

Since matter is the medium of the architectural field, it is essential that students engage materials in their education. Architectural design students typically use materials at a "representative" scale (paper, metal wire, wood, Plexiglas) in their design work as opposed to working directly with full-scale materials (concrete, steel, stock wood or glass). Differences in physical properties and behaviors of each material challenge a student to develop strategies to manipulate each material and methods of joining dissimilar materials. In the act of drawing and then assembling matter, students are not only contending with thinking and making but also with negotiating between representation and built reality. This struggle in grappling with weight and gravity is essential in understanding standards, potentials and the possibility of invention.

This paper will reflect on the development of a laboratory-based building materials technology course where students construe and construct through drawings and full-scale assemblies. Two lab projects will be examined: one where students join two dissimilar building materials and then another where students swap drawings to address both generating and interpreting/fabricating details. The paper will explore tactics to develop an architectural design student's haptic understanding and then reflect on how these trajectories cultivate design processes that seek meaning in material assemblies.

The Need for Developing the Haptic

Architects are not typically involved in the manual construction and fabrication of their own design work. In "Notes for a Theory of Making in a Time of Necessity," Guiseppe Zambonini raises questions, still pertinent in current times, regarding whether the architect is then limited only to the representational realm and how the architect can cultivate a more intimate link between what is drawn and what is produced. Zambonini points out that craftsmanship and quality work relies on an interdependent relationship between the processes involved in material transformations and the physical tools that are required in that transformation.[1] In most architecture educations, design students only work in the representational realm. But as Zambonini writes "[k]nowledge of the entire process…is essential so that every minute choice involving materials and methods can be bent, at the artisan's direction, so to clearly and fully address the objectives of production."[2] Architecture students not only need to intimately experience material and fabrication processes but also experience of the design process through the fabricator's perspective.

The Architecture program at the University of Florida is a 4-year undergraduate and a 2-year Masters. The projects discussed in this paper occur in the Materials and Methods of Construction 2 course – a required course for all architectural design majors. The undergraduate architectural design curriculum is intensive with students taking eight semesters of design studios. Students take building technology courses in parallel. The first course on Materials and Methods of Construction corresponds with the Architectural Design 4 Studio during the spring semester of the second year of design studios. The second course on Materials and Methods of Construction is a lecture and laboratory class with 75 to 95 students. The course also corresponds with the Architectural Design 8 Studio during the last semester of the four-year undergraduate design program. The first Materials and Methods course focuses on systems based on material types. The second Materials and Methods course focuses on systems based on assembly. It is more focused on understanding details and how materials come together in assemblies.

Most of the undergraduate students in this program go through their four-year education with an abstract and remote knowledge about building materials. The concern is that students memorize information and facts in the course when they need it for an exam, but then once exam is done, the course contents are quickly forgotten. How can the course present the content in a way that makes it hard for students to forget? The curriculum at University of Florida places heavy emphasis on making, but student seldom get to design and make things at a full-scale. For the last 3 years, the second Materials and Methods of Construction course has experimented with focusing on lab projects in lieu of exams. The course has two 8-week long projects that required students to confront the behaviors, processes and application of building materials at full-scale. The projects are not about making a beautiful object at the end, but rather it is designed to encourage struggle with and an intimate understanding of materials and methods of assembly. Failure is built into the process and it is a critical aspect to ensure that the students retain course information.

The lab projects were derived the author's own experience from architectural practice working at a firm, Office dA in Boston, that focused on innovative uses of materials. In the design process, ideas regarding unconventional materials or uses of materials required testing. Full-scale mock-ups were built to understand the limitations and possibilities. It is difficult for material ideas to live just in the

theoretical realm. Most of the design work occurs within 3d-modeling programs, but within these digital programs, design work float within a gravity-less space. These programs don't provide the opportunity to confront material characteristics, weight and gravity that essentially impact architecture. The process of building full-scale mock-ups and working directly with the materials and assemblies provided insight into potential problems and the opportunity to translate innovative design ideas into built reality.

In professional practice, the luxury of experimentation is not always possible. Architecture education is the time to explore creative possibilities in the design and building process. In combination with visual learning strategies, these Material and Methods of Construction lab projects address strategies of learning through touch: students actively participate instead of passively listening to the professor lecture, students work hands-on tactilely engaging with building materials, students experiment and learn from failure and students role-play in a process to practice through experience. Through these haptic oriented strategies, the objective with these projects is for students to link building technology knowledge with poetic meaning in their design work through the act of making and experimenting.

Project 1: Joining Two Dissimilar Materials

The project objectives are as follows:
- Work hands-on with full-scale building materials to understand material behaviors, characteristics and methods of assembly
- Understand the methods and issues associated with joining together two dissimilar materials
- Confront issues of craft when working with full-scale materials
- Recognize actual costs and labor associated with the things we design. You will address industry-relevant issues such as: material selection, comparing cost versus performance, formwork building, casting, aesthetics and material testing

The first project is simple in its premise – students collaborating in teams of two people work with full-scale building materials and figure out how to attach two building components into a sound assembly without the use of adhesives. One required component is a cast concrete slab (12 inches x 18 inches x 2 inches in dimension) that incorporates a surface texture and an aperture. The other component is a material of their choice that is approximately 12 inch by 18 inch in dimension. The two material components have to create a corner condition. In addition, each team had to keep track of their material costs and time spent on the project. The project was evaluated based on creativity, structural integrity and craft of the assembly.

The project starts with the concrete slab that could be oriented either vertically or horizontally – a parallel to casting a wall or a floor slab respectively. Based on preliminary design proposals, each team thinks through the best material and method to make the formwork. In the first pass at constructing a form, many students, surprisingly, did not think about the material characteristics and consequences of concrete in its liquid state. Many teams made forms using paper based materials like cardboard and chipboard or using thin materials like 1/16" thick sheets of Plexiglas - materials that absorb water and that lack structural integrity to resist the outward and downward pressures exerted by slurry. (Fig. 1) Students forgot fundamental information about concrete as a material that requires water in order to chemically react with cement to cure into a solid form. Teams also brought in formwork that had gaps at seams and used fasteners that were not scaled appropriately for the thickness of the form material. Each team poured concrete into these forms to see the consequence of their material and assembly choices. This misstep reinforces that the material choice and craft of the formwork is just as important as the concrete itself. Once a concrete slab was cast, there were group discussions examining the concrete surfaces in relation to the form material. (Fig.2) Wood forms that were not sealed properly would produce sandier surfaces because it absorbs water that prevents chemical reaction with the cement against that surface. While plastic and non-porous materials produced smooth surfaces since water cannot seep into the form. In this process, concrete reveals itself as an unforgiving material that shows every misstep or inconsistency in the casting process and locks onto other materials if given the opportunity. Students not only have to anticipate the designed form of the concrete and develop a negative form, but they also have to anticipate the sequence and process of removing the form from the concrete. (Fig. 3)

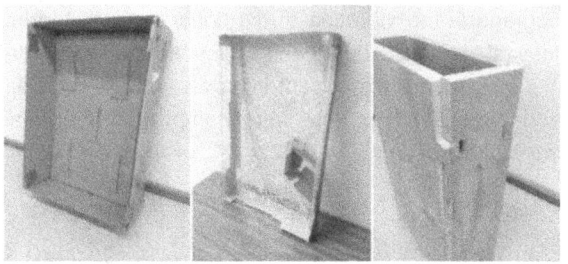

Fig. 1. Preliminary forms for casting concrete slabs consisting of cardboard, thin sheets of acrylic and large gaps in the seams. Students have forgotten that concrete starts in a liquid state (Spring 2015).

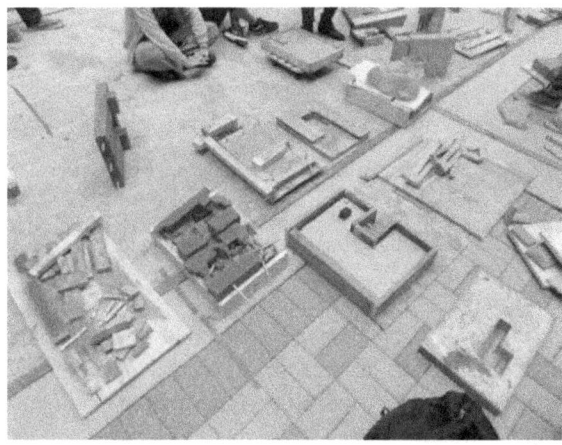

Fig. 2. Group discussions to review the first concrete cast. (Spring 2016)

The purpose of the surface texture requirement is for students to explore the possibilities of manipulating the surface of concrete and the methods to manipulate the formwork to produce texture. The objective of incorporating an aperture within slab is to struggle with strategies for making a precise opening in the slab. As a result, the formwork and the disassembly process will become more complex. That complexity also has consequences of creating dimensional inconsistencies in the concrete thus producing concrete slabs that are more prone to cracking. This then introduces issue of incorporating reinforcing materials of rebar or steel meshes and properly supporting the reinforcement within the formwork in order to strengthen the concrete slab. In the first casting, students are surprised by the irregularities in the surface of concrete. The challenge to reduce these irregularities provides a first-hand understanding of effects of the consistency of concrete mix, the percentage and size of the aggregate and vibration of the concrete in the form. Inevitably, most teams need to remake their concrete slab. There is a significant improvement of precision and craft between the first attempt and the final attempt at casting.

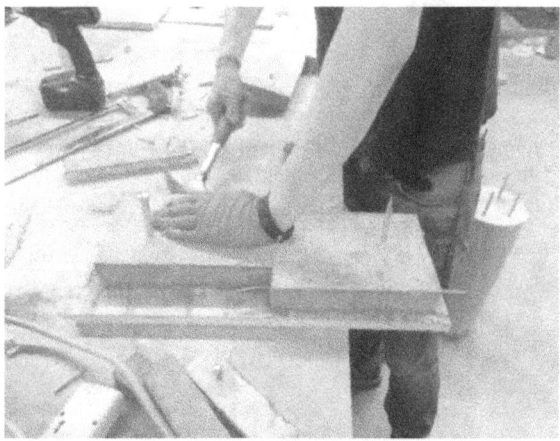

Fig. 3. Removing the formwork from the concrete slab (Spring 2016).

The second component in the assembly establishes a material contrast for students to experiment with any other material than concrete. Each material whether metal, wood, fabric, etc. has its own set of characteristics, parameters and limitations. Students are accustomed to building physical models where they can glue together materials. In this project, they have to investigate mechanical strategies for attaching two materials together. In this process, they develop an understanding that primary material components usually require mediating material components like brackets, girts and fasteners for a support structure. A material such as fabric needs to be held in tension for structural stability, so then a support framework is required to hold the flexible material. In thinking about how the two material components turn a corner together, secondary components of attachments or fasteners have to be anticipated. Teams have to consider whether the attachments are embedded in the concrete or attached after the casting. If they are cast into the concrete, students learn that fasteners need help staying straight during the casting process when the weight and force of concrete slurry takes over. With the proportions of the 12"x18"x2" slab dimensions, students also have to contend with weight of the concrete component. The second material component also contributes to resisting gravity and supporting

upright concrete slabs. The final assembly has to be structurally sound, so the joint between the two materials has to be tight and unwavering. (Fig. 4)

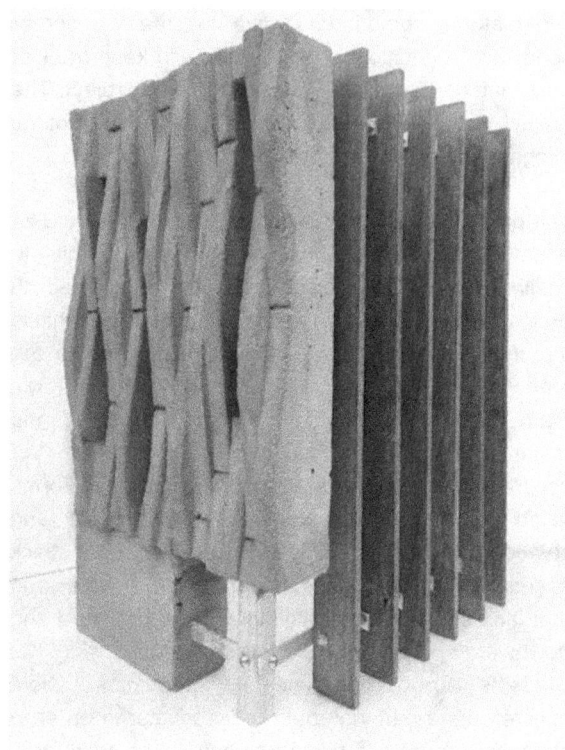

Fig. 4. Final Project 1 construction (Taylor Hayes + Alexandra Oliviera, Spring 2017)

In parallel with the project process, the weekly lecture component of the class presented case studies following the step-by-step construction of two Office dA projects: a 400,000 square foot multi-family residential building, the Macallen Building Condominiums and a private residence, the House in New England. The images of construction process from beginning to end and strategies of how materials come together draws parallels between what they are making and the construction of buildings. The act of keeping track of the construction costs and labor is a strategy to have them understand relative material costs and time required in the construction process. In lectures, the students can be told that the concrete formwork typically costs more than the concrete material itself, but in the project, they experience it first hand so they are more likely to remember implications of cost with each material and in the assembly.

Project 2: Communicating and Constructing Details

The project objectives are as follows:

- Design a stair that complies with 2014 Florida Building Code requirements
- Develop the ability to draw details of material assemblies
- Produce drawings that are notated, coordinated and technically clear
- Learn to work in a collaborative team to produce design and details
- Learn to read detail drawings to understand design intent.
- Learn the basics of value engineering and negotiations necessary in the design + construction process

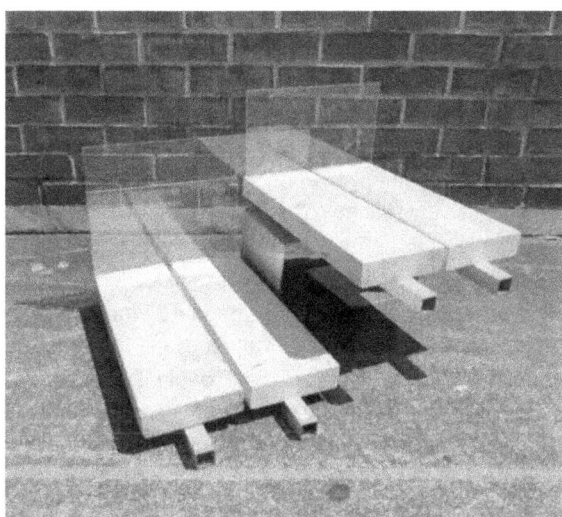

Fig. 5. Project 2 construction of a detail of a stair design (Spring 2016)

The second project in the course creates a role-playing scenario where teams of four students take on the position of both designer and fabricator. The project is divided into two phases of design and then construction. Each team designs a stair to access a library mezzanine with a ten-foot floor-to-floor height. After completing a construction drawing set that communicates their design intention, the design team swaps drawings sets with another team and they become each other's contractors/fabricators. In the construction phase, each team has to comprehend design intent in the drawings and then build a fragment of the stair at a full-scale. (Fig. 5) The construction team pays for the full-scale construction so they can negotiate with the design team on

substituting materials and methods of detailing the assembly - a parallel to the value engineering process in professional practice.

The project begins with acknowledging building code parameters. The teams have to design the stair to comply with the 2014 Florida Building Code. The stair is located in a public place, so there are more restrictions on the design in comparison to a private residence. Students are encouraged to look at the building code not as just restricting design possibilities but also as opportunities for invention. The design phase emphasizes visually oriented learning - students learn how to draw details and how to communicate design ideas through a properly coordinated drawing set. The strategy to connect visual learning to haptic thinking is through a full-scale detail drawing of the stair and handrail. The detail is studied and refined at the scale of the human body. This step is critical in process – the moment when the detail is explored as a full-scale drawing, it the helps the student to visualize the stair and the dimensions of proposed materials and assembly methods become relatable. However, the design proposal as a 1:1 scale drawing is still weightless. (Fig. 6)

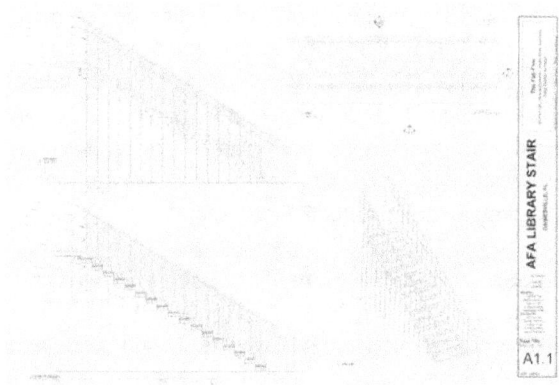

Fig. 6. Sheet from a coordinated drawing set for a stair design (Spring 2016)

Haptic learning in this project differs from previous project. Instead of direct interpretation of design ideas into a materials of a built assembly, here the design ideas must be interpreted and manipulated by others. The associated construction team visually "reads" and physically tests the design team's drawings. Based on their budget, the construction team evaluates availability of materials and the cost of constructing the detail. They then propose to the design team the design changes that are necessary in order to build the stair detail. At the end of the project, each construction team presents the adjustments, transformations and material implications are discussed in relation to how it maintained or affected the original design ideas. Then each design team presents what they would have changed in the original design after the construction of the detail.

In swapping drawing sets, each team learns to mediate between visual representation and tactile construction - making a connection between what is drawn and how to build it. Throughout project process, students investigate a range of possible solutions based on material type while still maintaining design intention. Essentially they develop skills in flexibility of design thinking through a tactile understanding of the building materials. Constructing a physical manifestation of the design at full-scale allows students to see and experience for themselves. Evaluating material implications during the design process requires intimate knowledge of the building material. The construction assembly is small in size, but it is enough to give the students an idea of what material and construction issues to keep in mind during the design process. The significance of role-playing in the project provides practice before going into processional practice and enables each student to experience the project from two different perspectives. The experience of working on a project from a fabricator's standpoint generates an understanding of and sensitivity towards efforts required in the construction process.

Poetics and its Relationship to Tactile Experience

How does haptic learning cultivate design processes that seek meaning in material assemblies? A tactile awareness adds the dimension of weight and mass to the design work. Weight and gravity are no longer abstract concepts. When we built sandcastles as young children, we learn very quickly in the process that dry sand doesn't hold together at its edges as well as wet sand. When we built forts using bed sheets, we figured out that the sheets needed to be held in tension to keep it in place. This process of trial and error requires the hands to work with the eyes in learning through experience and in creating meaningful constructions. In architectural design, the poetics in the construction of design work happens at

all scales and in the process of manipulating materials. The proportions between materials, the juxtaposition and relationships of materials and textures, the rhythmic positioning of fasteners, and the celebration of craft and precision in the building process are just a few aspects that enhance visual appeal but require a heightened sense of touch from the designer. The effort of working with full-scale materials hands-on develops an aesthetic appreciation of the detail and assembly as a composition not only in drawing but also in the final product.

The opportunity to experiment and be encouraged by failure is a strategy to increase the students' ability to design innovatively and fearlessly. Making full-scale assemblies with concrete is not about becoming an expert at casting concrete but rather empowering students to know that they can work with any material and be in control of it while also increasing their awareness of material translations from design work into full-scale. During the course, students were more engaged and involved working with projects rather than passively taking exams. Whether or not this methodology is effective in increasing a student's haptic understanding in design practice needs to be further researched as they become immersed in professional practice. At the end of the second project, students displayed their original drawing set paired with the built detail and we discussed lessons learned in the process. One student stated that it was eye-opening to see that designs continue to transform in the process between drawing phase and building phase and the need to clearly detail and communicate ideas in their drawings. Another student said they learned that flexibility in thinking of alternate solutions was key to trying to maintain their design ideas despite the budget and the fabrication team's building skill level. The most common phase heard from the students in both projects was "it didn't turn out the way I imagined it would." But through this process, they have developed fearlessness in working with materials and linking it closer to their design ideas.

Notes:

[1] Zambonini, Guiseppe."Notes on the Theory of Making in a Time of Necessity," *Perspecta*, Vol. 24, MIT Press, 1988. p. 18.

2. ibid, p. 17.

SESSION 05: STUDIO

Session Chair: Dana Gulling
North Carolina State University

Jerry Stivers, Oklahoma State University: "Reaping What You Sow: Cultivating Technology For Design."

James Leach and Kristin Nelson, University of Florida: "Overt Operations: Teaching Technology In Intensive Design Studio Workshops."

Margaret Mcmanus, Marywood University: "Old Sketch, New Meaning: An Architectural Outreach Exercise."

Brian Grieb, Morgan State University: "Comprehensive Design Studio For The Beginning Design Student."

Sowing What You Reap: Cultivating Technology for Design

Jerry Stivers
Oklahoma State University

Abstract

Most students coming into architectural / architectural engineering programs have limited experience with and understanding of building construction. This starting point presents educators with challenges when trying to help students develop a tectonic understanding of how buildings go together.

The "section" is one design tool in which students are confronted with the realities of how materials, assemblies, and details interrelate. This paper surveys the use of the section as an educational tool across a five year undergraduate A / AE curriculum. The overall objective of its use is to engage students with the design and tectonic nature of their work. Through studio iteration at multiple levels of the curriculum and additional classroom technology instruction, students begin to deepen and broaden their design understanding of how building structure, systems, and materials underpin successful design solutions.

When introduced, students typically consider a section drawing as a retrospective means for technical documentation rather than a generative tool for design thinking. Maturing beyond the abstract concepts of a single line sketch into the concrete truths of a construction document is a difficult process to learn (not to mention teach). If planted early and nurtured continually throughout the curriculum, analog and digital section explorations (both through drawing and physical making) help students to engage their work at a more magnified and intimate scale.

The poetics of Paolo Belardi's "Why Architects Still Draw" brings to light the paradox of the acorn, where he discusses how a project emerges from a drawing. "Even a sketch, rough and inchoate - just as an oak tree emerges from an acorn".[1] To further paraphrase his words, good design begins with a conceptual seed, which provides the basic yet unique characteristics of the architecture to come. Even in a single-line conceptual section, many general characteristics of the architectural design are easily imagined: its functional

uses, exterior form, and spatial relationships. Yet the other unique technical characteristics, such as its material enclosure, structural systems, and tectonic assemblies are yet to be revealed, although existent within the section's DNA from the start.

Much like plants during their development, students require different levels of "tending" and different types of "nourishment" during various stages of their design education for healthy development. This paper will discuss those different student needs and teaching challenges as well as speculate on what pedagogical strategies should be considered to help students develop a more holistic understanding of building design, technology, and construction. If considered early and often throughout a student's design education, sections can become much more than tectonic placeholders, rather they will become a vehicle for creativity, expectant with the possibilities of the architecture to come.

The Farmer and The Crop

Effective instruction requires faculty to know and at some level understand who are in their classrooms and studios. Architecture students today are composed primarily of "Millennials,"[2] i.e., the generation born between 1982 and 2002. As you might expect, Millennials (students) differ from previous generations (their faculty). Millennials grew up with technology unlike their instructors. The term "digital natives"[3] has been used to describe those who were born and grew up with technology and have a deep understanding of its concepts and the value it has to society. On the other hand, most faculty did not grow up in this virtual world. With the generational differences between faculty and students, the relationship between and appreciation of both analogue and digital teaching methodologies become an important bridge to build if effective instruction is to take place with regard to building technology and design.

The Soil

Our present curriculum has two fully accredited and integrated professional programs leading to a Bachelor of Architecture and Bachelor of Architectural Engineering. The five-year NAAB-accredited BARCH degree is designed to provide students with a well-rounded studio-based education accompanied by supporting core areas of emphasis in technology, architectural history and theory, and architectural management. [3] The five year ABET accredited BARCH Engineering degree's primary objective is to provide basic and professional education to engineering students in building-related structural engineering. The program is designed to prepare the student to contribute to society as a professional engineer dealing with analysis, design, and related activities within the construction industry. [4]

Both programs' curricula have been purposefully woven together throughout the studio sequence to develop an understanding of and empathy for the problems faced by their fellow A and AE classmates with whom they will potentially work with closely in professional practice. We are fortunate to share facilities, equipment, faculty, and many other common courses. The curricula for the design studio is team taught and focused on basic compositional and formal principles for buildings as well as various methods for their design communication. At this time, the technology courses are separated from the design studio and each other. They include statics, building systems, strengths of materials, building materials, steel structures, timbers structures, concrete structures, and two environmental systems courses.

Nutrition and Cultivation

Much like plants' need for healthy development, students require different levels of "tending" and "nourishment" during various stages of their design education. My position suggests that if considered early and often throughout a student's design education, sectional studies cultivate more than retrospective building tectonics, rather they provide essential nutrients for creativity, expectant with the possibilities of the architecture to come.

Creativity exists within a conceptual section's DNA from the start. The relationship between design and technology germinates with the student's first sketch. Many general characteristics (space, form, and relationship) of the architecture to come are easily imagined, while other unique characteristics (material, tectonics, and performance) are yet to be revealed. The conceptual section cultivates the design / technology relationship by looking forward to something else. In order to fully realize the seed's potential, students must move beyond the sketch by developing schematic drawings and development details that consider building systems and materials. Mention the word "detail" to a young student and watch their eyes glaze over as if it were something far less important than the overall. Therein lies the challenge as to how to help students embrace the evolution from conceptual section to a fully realized wall section. The following paragraphs pose several questions, which help to establish a position suggesting that the section is a relevant investigative tool which exemplifies and exposes possibilities throughout the design process from sketch to detail.

What makes the section the right pedagogical tool for design / technology integration and innovation?

The future presents architectural practice with many complex functional and performative challenges. Retrospective and underexplored in most design curriculums as a tool for design, sectional studies provide opportunities for students to consider the integration and innovation of tectonic forces with design forces becoming a fully realized architectural solution.

What is a section drawing?

Francis D.K. Ching defines a section as "an orthographic projection of an object, as it would appear if (vertical) cut through by an intersecting plane. It opens up the object to reveal its internal material, composition, or assembly." [5] Thomas Wang adds, "Section and elevation drawings are more realistic and easier to understand . . . and the viewing position is more similar to the way we experience space visually and therefore presents a more realistic picture." [6] A section drawing provides a view that is not normally seen. "Sections provide a unique form of knowledge, one that by necessity shifts the emphasis from image to performance." [7] "In cutting through walls, floors, and the roof structure of a building, as well as through window and door openings, we open up the interior of a building to reveal conditions of support, span, and enclosure, as well as the vertical arrangement of spaces." [8] Sections can show the interior elevation, as well as when combined with perspective drawing, show the depth of the interior space. Graphic conventions for the section cut can range from solid poche' (which emphasizes form and space) to construction lines and hatch (which depict materials and construction detail). Sections have the ability to emphasize image as well as performance, surface as well as structure and materiality.

How does history frame the discussion of the section as a tool for design?

From Lewis, Tsurumaki, and Lewis' book "Manual of Section", the section drawing was historically used as a retrospective drawing for analysis as evidenced by Leonardo da Vinci's famous sectional studies of human remains, as well as by documenting archeological building remains. In the fifteenth century, Italian architects used the section to investigate material and structural properties of buildings. It was further developed by Boullee (who was interested in architectural affect), Violle-Le-Duc (who explored structural profile and static force), as well as many others. Fast forwarding to today, complex section drawings can be created with great ease by simple computer commands and the click of the mouse. Which brings me to my next pedagogical question.

Should sections be studied by hand or computer?

In Jonathan Seigison's essay – "Working drawing / the tension between hand and computer drawing", he writes that, "Drawing by hand offers certain possibilities that do not exist in digital drawing. A hand drawing contains a sense of doubt and represents an attempt to work things out, that which we value highly. It contains a level of inaccuracy that is closer to the reality of building. A computer drawing has the capacity to represent a level of precision that is rarely possible in construction. With a hand drawing, every element has to be scaled. A repeated element has to be drawn again and again and, like the modules that are actually built, it is, in reality, never the same." [9] Digital programs (CAD and now BIM) have the ability to duplicate the same sections as well as produce unique complex spatial geometries that prior to the computer

would have been impossible to see, not to mention construct. This ability to cut a section through a virtual model has pushed the section from being a retrospective tool to a forward-looking tool that reveals technology as a catalyst for design. Now, with parametrics, computational aspects reinforce the section as a tool for determining building performance. Each position is compelling suggesting both hand and digital methodologies should be incorporated into the curriculum.

Should sectional studies be drawn or built?

At the beginning of the Renaissance, the medieval "master builder" stopped designing and making buildings. Rather, Alberti proposed a new design / build relationship. Alberti believed that architecture was conceived in the mind, expressed by drawings and models, and constructed by others. This new way of thinking about the design / build relationship established the definition for the modern architect. Because of this inherited knowledge / experience gap between design and construction, students must have opportunities to develop sectional studies in both drawing and model formats to develop a tactic understanding of the intrinsic relationship between design and making. Establishing the section's importance and relevance to architectural design, the question now becomes how to apply its use across an architectural and architectural engineering undergraduate curriculum.

The Growth Cycle

As it is important to know the growth stages of a plant to determine the nutrition needed to thrive, it is also important for educators to know the academic stages of students to determine their needs for healthy development. The following paragraphs track typical sectional studies within a five-year undergraduate curriculum.

Sections Before the Academy

It was never our intention to "grow" an architect. The last of three, and the only girl, Julie wasn't into organized sports like her older brothers. She chose a different childhood. Looking back, it is easier to see some of the innate and environmental characteristics that "prepared the soil" for her choosing architecture.

Julie simply enjoyed an unstructured environment, using her imagination and creating her own entertainment. With two older brothers, we had our share of Lego's which she did enjoy, but her real passion was making something from nothing by drawing on 8 ½" x 11" paper or reinventing a costume from the "dress-up" box. Living in a "fixer upper", there were always plenty of leftover building supplies to assemble when inspiration struck. It was a learning environment with little right or wrong, just possibilities. Included below is one of her drawings - a "building section" of Julie's dream house. Before formal training, she approached drawing with enthusiasm, freedom and imagination. The section cut in her drawing was represented as a single line with spaces somewhat related both horizontally and vertically based on her experience and imagination.

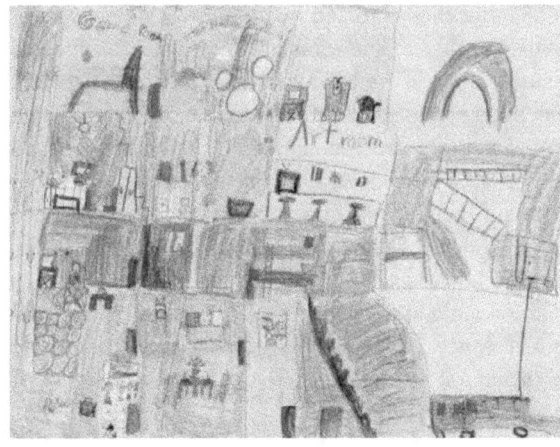

Fig. 1. Building Section – Julianna Stivers, age 8

Sections in First Year

Most students begin formal design training having little experiential or scientific knowledge rather, operating primarily from instincts. As they absorb, observe, and experience new "architectural" information, their design metabolism increases, roots take hold and the growth cycle begins. Moving beyond the freedom of a single line section as shown prior, sectional studies taken during student's early academic training establish the spatial and experiential relationship parameters of design. Sections are explored by observation, as well as produced from their own design propositions primarily by hand with limited digital communication techniques. Walls begin to have thickness, created by two profile lines with infill poche'. Drawings are created

at a small enough scale (typically 1/8" – 1/4") and with simple graphic convention (line weight and tonal values) that "establishes a clear figure-ground relationship between solid matter and spatial void – between container and contained." [10]

Students' first year in our curriculum begin with a hybrid classroom / studio, which introduces the professions of architecture and architectural engineering. "The key issues addressed are the observation / analysis of architecture along with basic design principles. Various types of drawings and design communication are introduced. . . . . By studying the work of architects and architectural engineers, students begin to recognize formal ordering systems and fundamental concepts of architectural design evident in the architecture they experience every day." [11] Section drawings are first introduced by asking students to carefully study and recreate finished precedent examples. Next, students are then asked to create plan and section drawings 'from scratch' which document a public stair on campus.

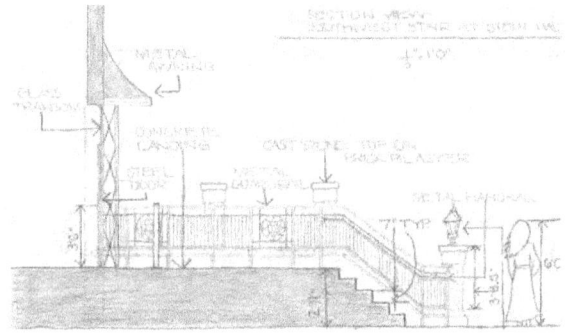

Fig. 2 Observation Section – First Year

The follow up first year studio "introduces architecture as dependent upon 2D and 3D systems of order." [12] Introduced to orthographic project in the previous studio, students are asked to draw and build their own abstract 8" planar composition (including a full-scale composition section). As the final project, students apply what they had learned on all previous abstract composition assignments to their first "Architecture" project, a showroom for the world-renowned "Vitra" furniture company. The final design was presented in both physical model and drawings, which included: a roof plan, entry floor plan, and a building/site section illustrating the most important horizontal and vertical relationships between these spaces.

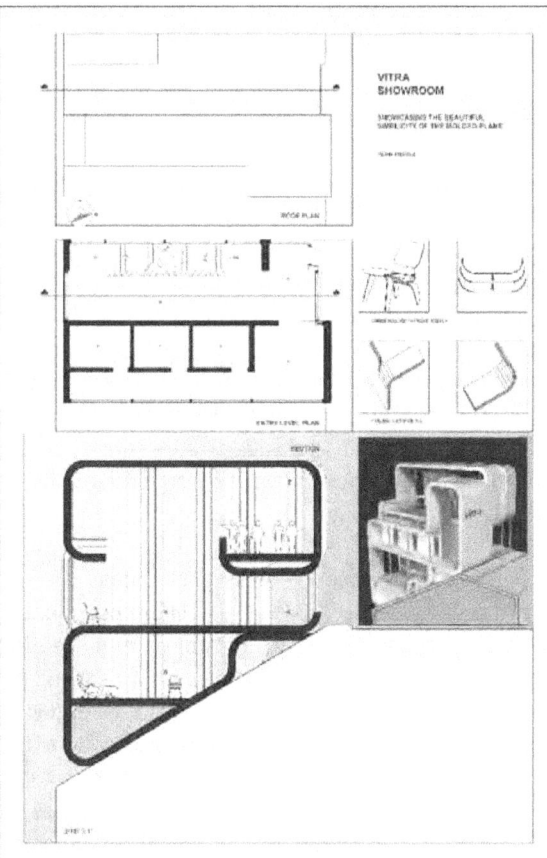

Fig. 3. Building Section – First Year

Sections in Second Year

During second year, students are introduced to many new design methods, communication techniques, and processes that initially seem mechanical and isolated in action. Supportive technology classes beginning in second year include: statics, strengths of materials and building systems. Often times this new "technical" information, even though grounded in theory and principle, makes students rigid in their design approach causing them to lose their sense of freedom and spontaneity. Design thought can freeze in calculation and analysis and become academically stifling. Necessary in a student's training, this very mechanical stage cultivates truths to be applied and harvested in future development. This awkward middle phase is student specific with large gaps of intellectual development. Although hard for students to see at times, significant learning has taken place by means of pure repetition.

Sections begin to show the connection between how a building's spatial form is created and enhanced by structural logic, environmental systems distribution, and materiality of the skin. Typically, drawings and models are developed at a larger scale (by both hand and digital techniques) considering the buildings relationship to the ground plane and sky. When doing physical section models gravity becomes a reality as students consider vertical loads in the building as well the horizontal loads on the building skin.

The first design studio in second year "continues to emphasize the fundamental design principle as well as introduces students to beginning architectural problem solving. Emphasizing both analogue / digital design communication, it is foundational in teaching students drawing fundamentals of sketching, orthographic projection, perspective and shade / shadows and physical model making. This studio also introduces the role of precedent in design helping them to develop abilities in formal analysis and concept generation." [13] Two projects specifically required section drawings and models to be cut through the students design propositions. The first a rowhouse in Amsterdam, Netherlands (seen below) and the second, a community library in Oklahoma City, OK.

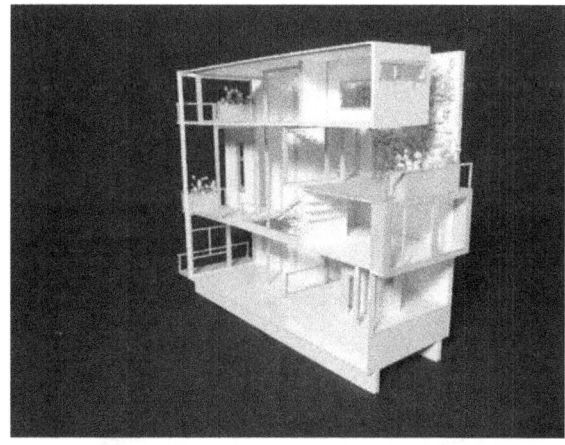

Fig. 4. Model Section – Second Year

In the final studio of second year, students are introduced to principles of site planning, building systems, parking, landscape design, vertical circulation, and the relationship of building orientation and sun control to sustainable principles. Key design projects are framed around a co-requisite building systems course, which has technical teaching modules including: site, space, structure, and skin. The collaborative teaching strategy was structured around the premise of both "isolation" and "integration" of the architectural design and technology curriculum.

Parallel to the final second year studio, an introductory building systems course establishes a foundational understanding of the following building systems: site, building, structures, envelope, mechanical / electrical / plumbing, and systems integration. The course attempts to create linkages between the "understanding" (classroom) and the "application" (studio) of how these systems inform or are informed by design. Students have a final team project (groups of 3, two architects and 1 architectural engineer) that support and explore at a deeper developmental level the integration of building systems into their previous systems precedent studies. A biography board was developed as a collage of text, drawings, and images, which engaged the viewer with the basics of the project and building systems. Students developed a wall section drawing that was large enough in scale to understand basic systems anatomy and their interrelationships. An extrusion model was then built out from the wall section drawing. The model was "systems focused" showing how the building: interacted with the site (foundation, slab, drainage), developed the qualities enclosed space (MEP, lighting, ceiling), was supported structurally (material, horizontal span, vertical support, frame), and defined the envelope between outside and inside (materials, thermal condition, wall construction type, sustainable strategies).

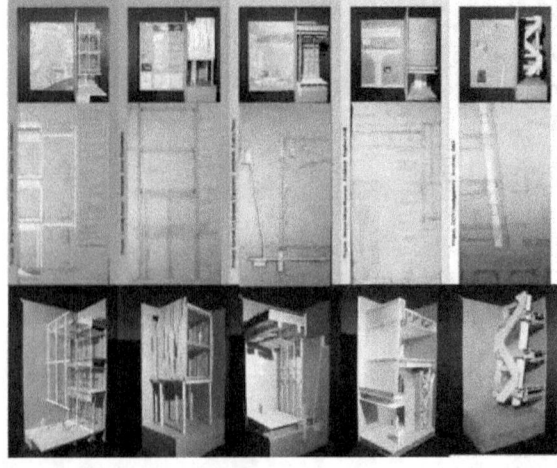

Fig. 5. Systems Precedent Project – Sectond Year

Sections in Third Year

Third year continues emphasis on basic architectural problem solving with increasingly larger and more complex projects, in parallel with integrating digital media (Rhino and Revit) into their design process. During the third year of the curriculum, students take two structures courses (timber and steel) as well as their first environmental systems course. The follow up studio in the spring, addresses increasingly sophisticated and complex architectural projects, including issues surrounding multi-storied buildings, building skin material investigations, their use and integration, and a hands-on design experience utilizing the digital fabrication shop and/or other suitable workshops on campus.

A parallel digital media class introduces Building Information Modeling (BIM). Projects are coordinated between classroom and design studio offering several opportunities to explore parametric wall sections by both physical and virtual methodologies. . Software such as Revit, facilitate the design and modeling of the students' studio work as well as communicate and test fundamental data. With an expanding design vocabulary, the orthoganal qualities from beginning design sections take a back seat as students become more profitient with digital spatial manipulation. This new spatial freedom presents educators with challenges when confronted with the student response, "I don't know, this is what the compter gave me"! Trends toward programatic and performative driven design open new and exciting opportunities and discourse between faculty and students.

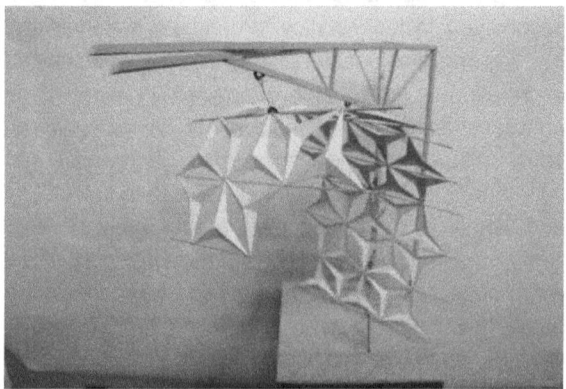

Fig. 6. Parametric Skin System Model – Third Year

Sections in Fourth and Fifth Year

During the final two years of the curriculum, students begin to rise above the mechanics and develop a more fluid, natural, response to technology integration. Students take their final series of technical courses, which include: concrete structures and a second environmental systems class. After learning the fundamentals taught during the beginning of the curriculum and through iteration and repetition of the middle, the final phase begins to produce the fruit allowing the student to create unique technologically informed design responses. Examining precedents, studying standard details give way to possibilities and potential of their own design response.

The first fourth year studio introduces students to issues of design development. Integration of materials and structural systems as well as sustainability are also emphasized. The scale of the wall section studies was enlarged to expose the materials, structural assemblies, and envelope performance. Sections are studied physically by building a large-scale bay model as well as virtually with a digital bay model. At this point, students have had parametric computer training and are well versed with the laser cutter and CNC machine. Design solutions and their craft are quite sophisticated. Projects have longer durations to allow for design development and connection detailing.

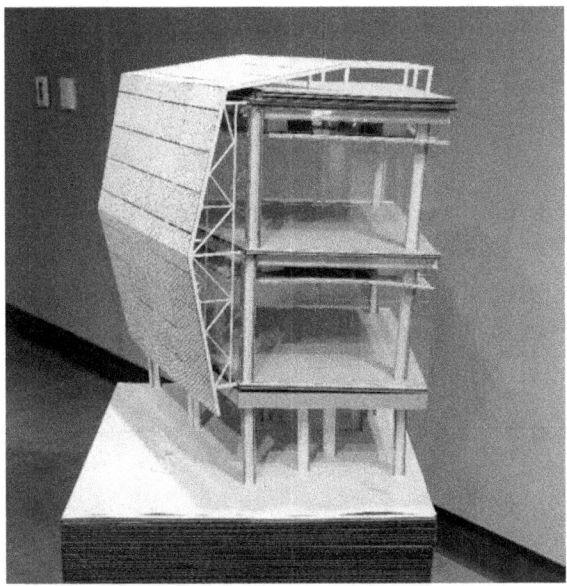

Fig. 7. Design Development Bay Model – Fourth Year

The capstone studio in the spring of the fourth year emphasizes synthesis and application of all the design and technical skills that the A / AE student has developed in the previous years of the undergraduate curriculum. The course is organized around a single 16-week project focusing on the comprehensive analysis and design of a building and its many technical and aesthetic systems. The educational objective is to help the student develop a more comprehensive and mature understanding of the interaction between the aesthetic influences and the major technical, legal, and human factors that shape the design of most professional architectural projects.

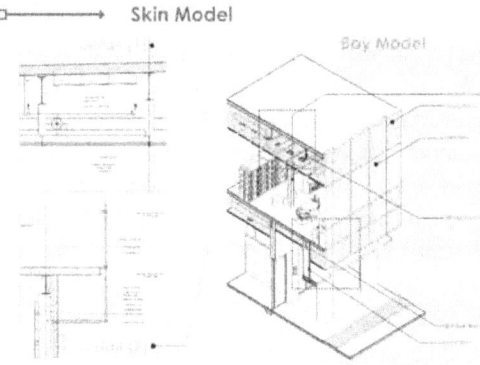

Fig. 8. Design Development Bay Model and Construction Document Wall Section – Fourth Year

The students' final design studio in fifth year is an introduction to urban planning, design, and development. As a team based studio, it builds on an entire sequence of studios wherein projects increase in size, scope, and complexity. At the same time, students are challenged to make proposals that are increasingly thoughtful, developed, and compelling. As such, this studio is directly related to the prior work in the comprehensive studio, design development studio, and design build studio. Students are asked to plan a significant multi-block development in an urban setting. It is intended that students address a number of key issues related to urban and/or master planning, including: transportation, density, community, the economy, and the environment. Because of the urban focus, sectional studies zoom back out to engage and develop an understanding of the increasingly complex layering and relationship of the site / building / urban infrastructure.

The Harvest

In retrospect, I realize my research about sections is but a beginning producing few definitive answers, rather an intrigue and attitude for further investigation in the semesters to come. One thing I do know, design thinking and technological knowledge are dependent on each other. When they are too separated in the curriculum, technology is not thought about and developed as a partner to the overall architectural expression. Curriculums should link technological knowledge and design imagination through sectional iteration and exploration of form and project issues informed by constructive realities.

When considering sectional studies for a particular project or studio, keep the overall curriculum and competence levels in mind. In doing so, a more comprehensive curriculum with holistic levels of competence can be developed. Encourage all types of sectional study methods i.e. analogue / digital and drawing / making. There is no singular way to explore sections during the design process. If considered early and often throughout a student's design education, sections can become much more than tectonic placeholders, rather they will become a vehicle for creativity, expectant with the possibilities of the architecture to come.

If sections are to become a vehicle for creativity and integration, the perception and use within the curriculum must change from simply a reductive drawing produced at the end of a project to satisfy requirements for constructability to a drawing of discovery. Because architectural learning is by nature integrative, sectional studies are the one tool that can help to bridge the gap between design and technology learning because they require the viewer to consider both aesthetics and performance.

The poetics of Pier Luigi Nervi say it best, "A good architect is someone capable of seeing the main problems of a design, capable of examining with serenity the various possible solutions, and who finally has a thorough grasp of the technical means necessary to accomplish the project."

Notes:

[1] Belardi, Paolo. "Why Architects Still Draw" The MIT Press: Cambridge, MA. 2014. p ix.

[2] Howe, Neil and Strauss, William. "Millennials Rising: The Next Great Generation" Vintage Books, a division of Random House, Inc. New York, NY.

[3] Oklahoma State University, School of Architecture, Programs, Architecture Program, http://arch-ceat.okstate.edu/content/architecture-program (accessed 28 Feb. 2017).

[4] Oklahoma State University, School of Architecture, Programs, Architectural Engineering Program, http://arch-ceat.okstate.edu/content/architectural engineering-program (accessed 28 Feb. 2017).

[5] Ching, Francis D. K. "Design Drawing" John Wiley & Sons: Hoboken, NJ. 2010. p 170.

[6] Wang, Thomas C. "Plan and Section Drawing" Second Edition. John Wiley & Sons: Hoboken, NJ. 1996. p 91.

[7] Lewis, Paul and Tsurumaki, Marc and Lewis, David J. "Manual of Section" Princeton Architectural Press, New York, NY. 2016. p 7

[8] Ching, Francis D. K. "Design Drawing" John Wiley & Sons: Hoboken, NJ. p 171.

[9] Sergison, Jonathan. "The Tension between Hand and Computer Drawing." In The Working Drawing, edited by Annette Spiro and David Ganzoni, Park Books AG: Zurich, Switzerland, 2013. p 276.

[10] Ching, Francis D. K. "Design Drawing" John Wiley & Sons: Hoboken, NJ. p 175.

[11] Bilbeisi, Suzanne, "Syllabus - ARCH 1112" Oklahoma State University, Fall 2016.

[12] Bilbeisi, Suzanne, "Syllabus - ARCH 1216" Oklahoma State University, Spring 2016.

[13] Stivers, Jerry, "Syllabus - ARCH 2116" Oklahoma State University, Fall 2016.

Overt Operations:
Teaching Technology in Intensive Design Studio Workshops

James Leach & Kristin Nelson
University of Florida

Context

In 2015, the authors left Iowa State University (ISU), an institution with a strong history of integration between design studios and technology courses, to accept jobs at the University of Florida (UF), an institution with an established design studio curriculum that was definitively segregated from the building technology coursework. Hired as part of a larger initiative to reconsider the relationship between building technology and design pedagogy, the authors each teach design studios and in the technology sequence. Efforts to revise the larger curriculum are ongoing, but as at most universities, this entails numerous faculty meetings and consensus-building, followed by contingent subsequent approval by the departmental curriculum committee, followed by administrative changes to course descriptions and the course catalog. In the near-term, the authors conducted a series of short, focused project-based workshops over their first three semesters within the limited context of their own studios. These workshops allowed them to test methods and outcomes of introducing building technology teaching to the studio without waiting for lengthy approvals or administrative changes. In addition to teaching a design studio each semester, the authors taught Environmental Technology, Materials and Methods and Structural Systems courses and used this opportunity to investigate crossover into studio for each of these disciplines.

Positioning Technology in the Design Studio

The studio teaching method, a foundational aspect and core strength of design education, has a long history, tracing back through the Basic Course at the Bauhaus, to the "design problem" structure of the Ecole des Beaux Arts, and before that, to hands-on learning in the master-apprentice relationship of the medieval guild.[1] Studio teaching is typified by active, open-ended, collaborative learning that engages different learning styles and is project-based, inquiry-based, student-directed, and hands-on. Studio teaching is recognized as an effective pedagogical structure generating superior learning outcomes and greater student engagement when compared to traditional passive teaching methods, and in recent years, has been increasingly adapted to the teaching of STEM subjects at multiple education levels under such titles as the "student-centered", "active-engagement" or "flipped" classroom.[2] Despite the efficacy of studio teaching and its history as a cornerstone of design education, in many institutions, only design courses are typically delivered in a studio format, while other topics, such as history and technology, are delivered in passive-learning lecture-based classes. Problematically, the content and sequencing of these lecture courses is usually only tenuously linked to, or completed disconnected from the issues and foci of the concurrent studio.

Walter Gropius described his vision of the integration of the design studio with other courses at the Bauhaus in the following terms:

> "...all the teaching programmes should exist only to support the studio and the design problems it is working on, reflecting the reality of professional practice, which is entirely driven by the needs of the project."[3]

This focus on the project as the center of teaching is key. There is potential to strengthen both the building technology and design studio courses by creating meaningful connections between them, using the studio project as a nexus. In this case, each course provides meaningful context for the other. The building technology course benefits from the superior teaching method, and through demonstrating the ability of technical issues to realize design ideas, fosters greater engagement and investment in building technology. This makes building technology operative, an active from-giver for design, rather than passive or an afterthought. If, as Charles Eames states "design depends largely on constraints"[4] then the design studio benefits by adding a focused suite of building technology concerns as productive and form-giving design drivers to the typical concerns of design studio.

Strategies

The initial purpose of these investigations was threefold. Firstly, the overlap would take advantage of the superior teaching model and high engagement that studio offers. Secondly, the direct application of the technology topics would increase the students' interest in building technology and demonstrate the potential to enrich, rather than impede design. Thirdly, the pilot was intended to illustrate that building technology is best taught, not as independent subject, but as part of an integrated whole.

The first step in the pilot project was to identify potential overlaps where the topics and learning goals of existing studio courses and building technology courses productively reinforce one another.

Opportunities within Existing Coursework

Design 3 is the first semester sophomore level design studio. This studio includes both architecture and interior design students, and is comprised of two projects of approximately eight weeks apiece. The overlap for this studio was centered on the Door-Window-Stair project, where students develop a 3/8" scale model of a spatial fragment to house an itinerary based on a cultural artifact. Students develop involved physical models using frame elements and skin elements to define space, and this was seen as an opportunity to focus on tectonics of assembly and structures. The overlap takes advantage of the concurrent beginning Materials and Methods course, where students learn about stereotomic and tectonic systems. In previous versions of the studio, a lack of system logic was noted. In this overlap, students were introduced to the basic concepts of structural geometries in post and beam construction – beams want to be deeper than wide in section, columns want to be symmetrical in section. Furthermore, tectonic systems have a hierarchy, with primary, secondary and tertiary elements. In the studio, these were presented as a primary structural frame comprised of columns and beams, a secondary structure of studs and minor framing, and a tertiary system of skin elements. The overlap asked students to sketch their

project using a color code to explain their system, and to use these sketches to begin to build their model in way that revealed the hierarchy and scale of constructional logic. Dimensional constraints were mandated, such as a maximum skin panel size of 5'-0" by 10'-0", and panel materials limited to thin paper that could not support itself without an associated frame.

Fig. 1. Analytical Mapping of the Maudlandia Antarctic Desert from Design 4

Design 4 is the second semester sophomore level design studio. This studio includes only architecture students and is comprised of three projects. The initial project is brief, at only three weeks, while the remaining two projects are approximately six weeks apiece. The final project in the studio, Desert, asks students to work in an open setting described as having the qualities of a desert. In the past, this has included varying degrees of specificity, with invented sites often used instead of specific locations. The pilot faculty saw an opportunity to provide an introduction to basic climatology, solar geometry, shading and mass, and a differentiation between stereotomic systems of retaining and tectonic systems.

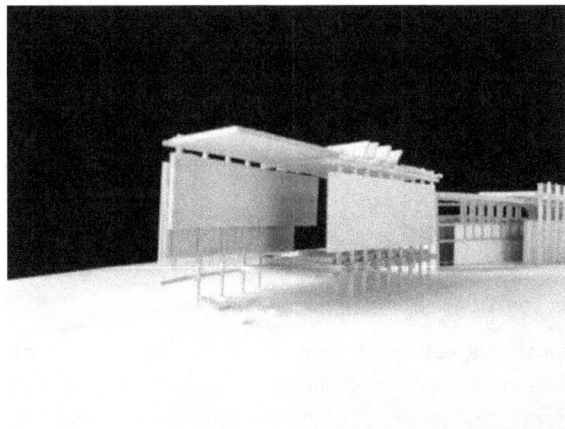

Fig. 2. Final Model based on the Black Rock Desert from Design 4

Design 5 is the first semester junior level design studio. This semester is comprised of two, often linked, projects sited in the diverse natural landscape of Florida. The program for the studio is often a small building or series of buildings linked to the site, such as a nature camp, nature center or retreat residency. The final project proposal is built through a series of investigations of surfaces that address the conditions of overhead, boundary and constructed ground. The pilot reframed this investigation, asking students to specifically view the building skin as a moderator of the surrounding environment. Overhead moderates the relationship to the elements of the sky, the rain and the heat and light of the sun. Boundary moderates the relationship to surroundings through view and visibility, how people and air are allowed to move through the space, and how daylight enters a space. The constructed ground manages the relationship of the architecture to the complex surface

and subsoil conditions of Florida. The pilot was conducted twice at this level. The initial version of the pilot took advantage of an opportunity in the structural coursework to create a specific overlap between soils, foundations and structural systems. The second version of the pilot focused on passive climatic response through the development of climatically responsive building skin systems.

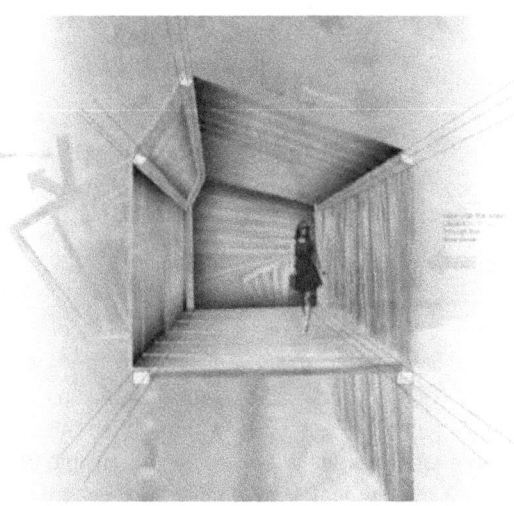

Fig. 3. Section Study of environmental strategies from Design 5

Design 6 is the second semester junior level studio. This studio focuses on pre-industrial southern cities, typically Savannah, Georgia, and Charleston, South Carolina, and features a larger, more complex building program with a public or civic function. Small museums, performing arts centers or schools, or cultural centers are frequently used. This studio is offered concurrently with the initial course in environmental technology. The environmental course is taught by one of the pilot faculty and this allows for an overlap focused on environmental control and choreography.

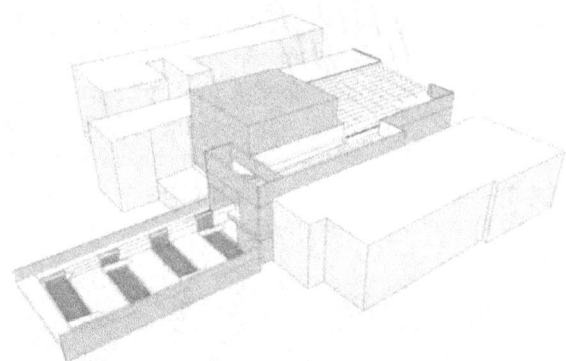 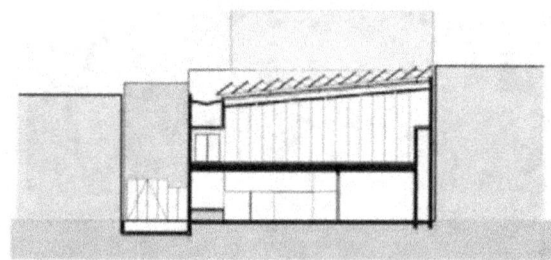

Fig. 4. Diagrams of integrated design strategies for sunlight and rainwater from Design 6.

Implementation

In the authors' first year at the University of Florida, technology courses did not include a laboratory period. As a first step, spring semester course meeting times were revised from three 45 minute lecture periods per week to two 45 minute lecture periods supplemented by a laboratory period. In the pilot program, one 45 minute lecture and one 45 minute interactive laboratory period were used to introduce the core technology concepts and perform basic simulations and calculations.

Due to the limited time available in the coordinated studio system, the instructional format limited the teaching time for the pilot program in each studio to a single three hour studio period. In the authors' studio sections, this studio period was used as a workshop to consider the students' studio projects through the lens of the content delivered earlier that week in the technology lecture and lab. Prior to the studio meeting, the students were assigned the task of proposing a schematic solution to integrate the technology content into their studio project. The technology faculty member then joined the studio faculty member during class, and they jointly critiqued and sketched through design solutions with students.

Outcomes

The extremely short exposure time for the pilot program was initially viewed as a weakness when compared to the intensive technology integration offered at ISU, but this limitation yielded some of the most interesting conclusions from the experiment. The student project outcomes and feedback resulting from this brief interaction were overwhelmingly positive. Equally, or perhaps more importantly, it was demonstrated that a large investment of time was not necessary to affect a large impact on the studio design as long as the building technology issues were relevant to and supportive of the studio design agenda and the studio faculty was willing to reinforce the importance of technology in design.

Tellingly, without such reinforcement, the integration of building technology in the design studio did not carry forward. In the semester following the above experiments, in a studio of sixteen students, eight teams, only two students, a single team, strongly integrated building technology as part of the core design drivers of their studio project.

From the perspective of technology faculty, the stronger integration of our previous institution might be considered close to ideal. However, the reality of competing priorities within most programs means that this will take many years to achieve, even at amenable institutions, and will never be a possibility at many institutions. This project offers a method of working within a transitional curriculum or a curriculum that is unable to shift towards a deep, formal integration. The project includes results from each of the three major technical areas, including successes and failures.

Notes:

[1] Elfland, Arthur D. "A History of Art Education: Intellectual and Social Currents in the Teaching of the Visual Arts" Teachers College Press: New York, NY. 1990

[2] Gropius, Walter.   "The Bauhaus" in Architectural Education no.1 1983. p 53-79

[3] Perkins, Dexter.   "The Case for a Cooperative Studio Classroom: Teaching Petrology in a Different Way" in Journal of Geoscience Education, v. 53, n. 1, February, 2005, p. 101-109

[4] Eames, Charles. "Design Q & A." Interview by L. Amic. 1972

Figures:

[1] Analytical Mapping of the Maudlandia Antarctic Desert. Design 4, Spring 2016. Samantha Janollo.

[2] Final Model based on the Black Rock Desert. Design 4, Spring 2016. Anne Morrison.

[3] Section Study of environmental strategies. Design 5, Fall 2016. Mani Karami.

[3] Diagrams of integrated design strategies for sunlight and rainwater. Design 6, Spring 2016. Nicolas DelCastillo

Old Sketch, New Meaning: An Architectural Outreach Exercise

Margaret McManus
Marywood University

Abstract

Architects, while sharing some commonalities with traditional fine artists, do not share the clean slate of a blank-canvas when embarking on a new project. On the contrary, they are given a full canvas – full of context, topography, adjacencies, environmental factors, underground conditions, above-ground conditions, etc. This paper explores a drawing exercise that was presented to 3rd grade students through a university outreach program: *Architecture In Schools*. Third-grade students were handed abstract sketch line drawings representing a 'non-blank' canvas as a way to introduce architecture in an unconventional way. They were tasked with the challenging and creative exercise of imagining scenarios in the given context of the sketch.

Unlike typical line-drawings they have encountered upon this age, i.e. the standard coloring book, these black and white line-drawings were rooted in more abstract thinking. This allowed students to envision themselves in the context of the lines and shapes of the sketch, and *to search for* meaning within the collection of markings. Discussions took place that related to how architects represent factors that are intangible like wind and direction; how architects draw lines that have innate meaning to a design; and how architects give a literal presence on the paper for "invisible" things that are underground and above ground (transit lines, roof overhangs, etc.).

Too often, in the minds of the general public and elementary students, the word *architect* conjures up ideas of blueprints, drafting, math and construction, but with little knowledge of the artistic and creative thinking involved in the design process. In addition to bringing forth a fun, imaginative exercise through outreach, the emphasis of this project was an attempt to clarify those overlooked architectural roles, and was based primarily in revealing the early creative processes that an architect must take on as part of the job description.

Introduction

In an attempt to relate the teaching of beginning design students with outreach efforts to elementary students, this paper explores an experiment that involved a common sketch and assisted each of the sectors in their further understanding of the architecture profession.

Service outreach with 3rd grade students through Northeastern Pennsylvania's Architecture in Schools (AIS) has revealed common stereotypes about the architecture profession; therefore, the effort becomes much less about teaching architecture, but more accurately about dispelling the myths about architecture. This exercise looked at sharing a common denominator- a sketch- between two realms: the discussion with collegiate architecture students and the imaginations of 3rd graders. This common sketched assisted in educating both parties on the role of an architect. The second-year design students were engaged in visual literacy exercises, and the third graders were engaged in imaginative "landscapes" within a given context.

Part 1: The University Design Students

The first part of this exercise—with a focus on understanding what a sketch *is* and what it *could be*-- had its origins with 2nd year college design students. Up until this point in their design careers, a sketch had been a drawing that replicated the literal likeness of something. This is, in fact, in line with the general public's definition of the word as expressed in Webster's dictionary: *"a quick, rough drawing that shows the main features of an object or scene."*

But what happens when you want to explore preliminary ideas of intangible or ethereal versus an object or scene? This requires a new way of thinking about the word 'sketch.' When thinking and conversing about architecture there becomes a need to relate it to its surroundings. Gestures and speech may become limiting when discussing ideas on the scale of a city, a park, or a plot of land. An alternate form of communication is necessary: a visual sketch. These "large scale" discussions beg for visual communication support along with the necessity to adjust scale via lines that we can put on paper--that we can relate to and chat about. Verbal communication is important for support at this stage as students integrate this new meaning of 'sketch' to their arsenal of communication tools.

This notion of speaking while documenting ideas through sketching, records ideas in ways that are fairly novel when associated with the word *sketch*. Sketching while talking is what I refer to in this paper as an "in-line chat" (a play on and contradiction of the term *on-line chat*). This strategy enforces the notion that-- though shifting from *replicating* to *revealing*, to collectively understand a site there needs to be a way to grasp it or capture it on a human scale that can bring forth layers and patterns which may otherwise be ethereal or non-visual.

The In-line Chat

Professor to student: chatting and sketching; lines become arrows that have meaning in order to convey a concept; cross hatch or shade is implemented to indicate something else perhaps more static in nature than the arrow. To engage in in-line chats is to collect ideas and information as a beginning step toward working out problems or finding new ones. The word 'diagram' is consciously left out at this point, because diagrams convey the delivery of information that has already been gathered and sorted, and represents more of a final product in a clear and simple manner; where sketch still pertains to the research, the brainstorm, and the messy phase that comes before the diagram. The in-line sketch is an important tool for the student to understand and it may be difficult to *teach* it without *doing* it. *Figures 1, 2, 3* and *4* have been authored by myself while speaking and collecting ideas with 2nd year university design students.

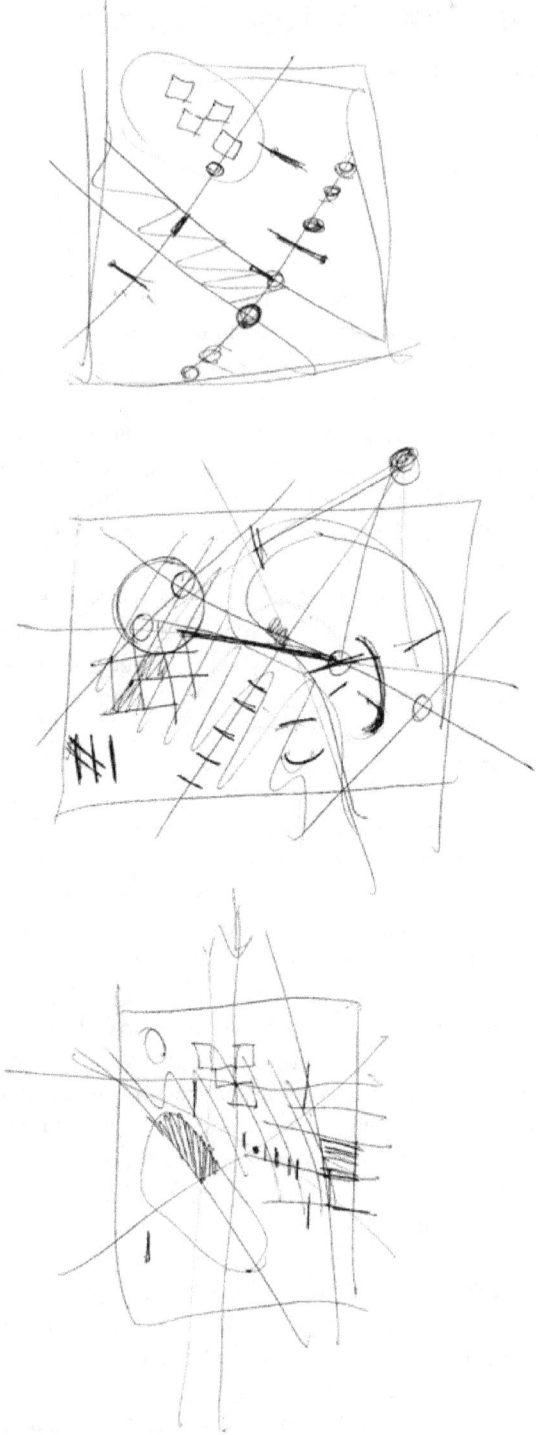

Fig. 1. The images above represent *In-line Chats*: the product of sketching while conversing and drawing as a means of communicating an architectural process.

Once manifested on paper, the 'in-line chat' has now played its role: it has served as a thought from which to advance upon or to ignore. It is—more often than not--never seen again. This is true not only in architecture education, but in the profession as well. That sketch may very well be saved; but it is most likely archived indefinitely. These messy brainstorms are so much a part of our process of an architect; countless hours and days discovering and exploring solutions to problems in these thoughtful, messy sketches, and then they are discarded or hidden.

But not this time. The in-line chats between professor and student captured relative meaning to a conversation. They grappled with notions of organizing and understanding topography, boundary, water flow, edges, site lines, air traffic, etc. When removed from the conversation the sketches retain an abstract sense of organization that can inspires abstract connections. Nonetheless, they showcase part of the art of architecture, and then essentially become solidified into abstract pieces that often record a fundamental understanding of context and surroundings.

Can this abstraction of a fundamental thought as preserved in these sketches be understood or even further abstracted by another person's thought on the organizational composition?

Part 2: The Third-graders

The exercise continued—or began an afterlife--in a creative experiment with 3rd grade elementary students. The in-line chats that were the result of once-meaningful sketch-exchanges of ideas and thoughts with 2nd year college architecture students became the context in which 3rd graders revealed their own understanding of a "landscape."

Far from a blank piece of paper, or a coloring book; they were given an opportunity to *see* things; to *search* for things; to *imagine* or *invent* things; and then to respond to them. After all, that is an important part of what the architect is doing when embarking on a project. The original in-line chat became a permanent abstraction that once had inherent meaning; the 3rd grade students were then challenged with finding new meaning within it. You can see in the upper portion of Fig. 2 the embedded in-line chat in

which the children imagined new landscapes; and the lower portion shows an effort to finalize this new landscape after remove the abstract sketch.

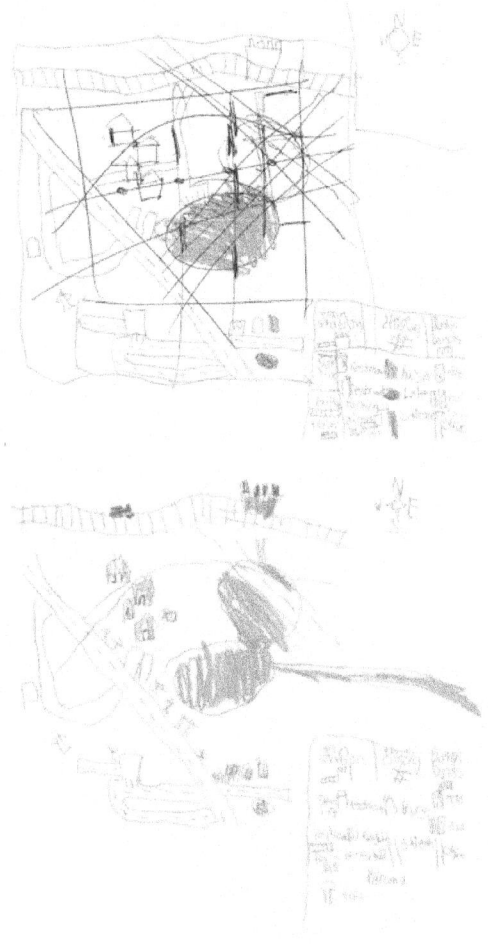

Fig. 2. A third-grade student imagines a new landscape within the in-line chat. The in-line chat base drawing can be seen in the dark marking of the upper image.

The students enthusiastically imagined their own space and place at a scale that had nothing to do with the origination of the sketch, but only after discussions of representation helped them to *see* things differently than just lines and shapes. Discussions took place that related to how architects represent factors that are intangible like wind and direction; how architects draw lines that indicate meaning to a design; and how architects give a literal presence on the paper for things that are underground and above ground (transit lines and roof overhangs). This discussion of collapsing a vast amount of information into a sketch through mark-making prompted conversations relating to building and site systems and early considerations for sustainable strategies on different scales and how these may involve collaborative solutions or they may be integral to the role of an architect. In Fig. 3 you can see the inclusion of power lines and "wind meels" and in Fig. 4 the consideration of wind and lighting systems.

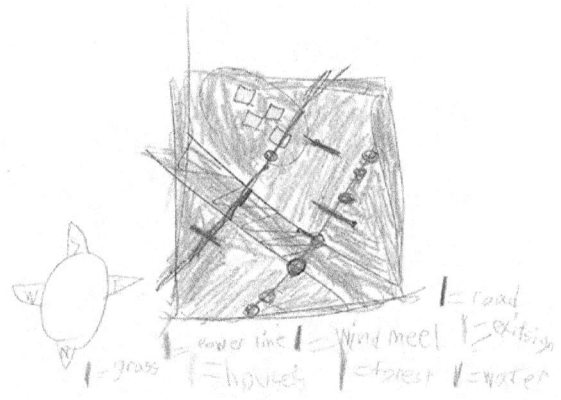

Fig. 3 This image begins to integrate strategies involving "wind meels" and power lines.

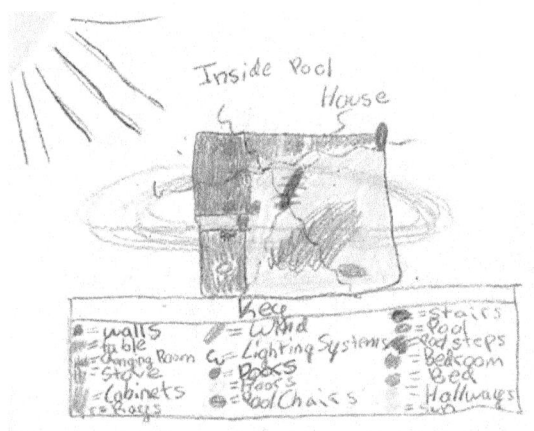

Fig. 4 Wind and Lighting Systems play a dominant role in this sketch.

The experiment, though challenging in the beginning, proved to be very engaging as the young students seemed able to envision themselves in the context of the lines and shapes of the "in-line chat." Many of the original sketch markings were reimagined in a literal sense as a valid interpretation; but also, many new

markings by the students were made to impose ideas and to respond to their given contexts.

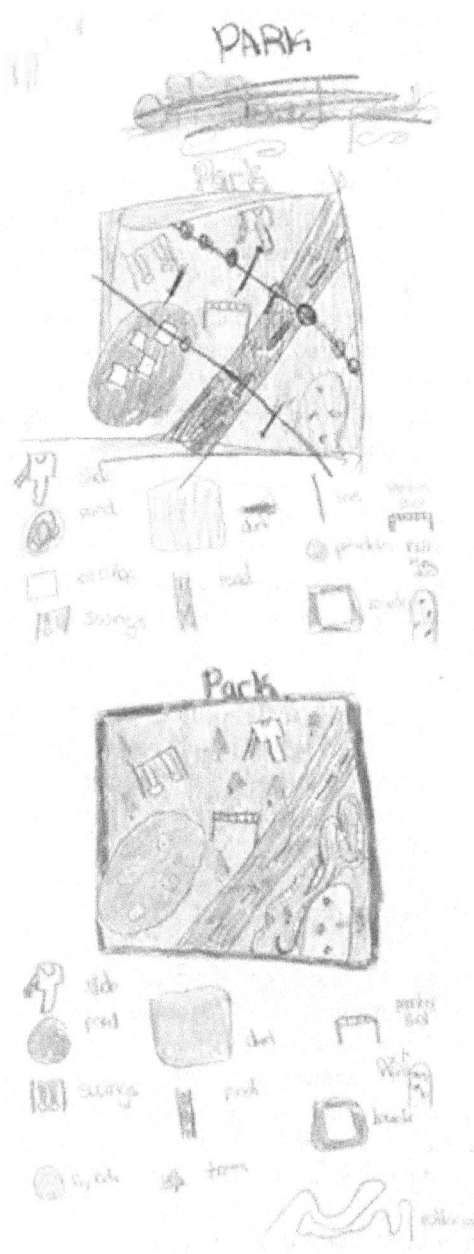

Fig. 5. This image highlights many of the revisions students made when transferring their designs onto trace paper.

This exercise also introduced many of the students to tracing paper. The implantation of this can be seen in the lower portions of both Fig. 5 where a more finalized drawing has been created. This introduction to a new medium alone provided enough excitement and motivation for them to push their designs forward (see also Fig. 6). It also gave them another opportunity to reinterpret their own designs again and to revise a number of issues, including scale and program. Figure 5 showcases such a revision: the large "ice cubes" that were a result of residual square shapes of the in-line chat, have been revised to reflect the more appropriately-scaled lily pads resting in the pond.

This exercise was an attempt to have children understand the process of the architectural profession and emphasize the architects' responsibility in the *response* to a non-blank canvas. Leaving this knowledge with them can serve as an effort to dispel the myth of the architecture profession. Although the face of the architecture profession arguably belongs to the construction documents; it is important to reveal the fun and the problem-solving aspects of the design *process* with the children. This exposure can only assist in clarifying creative aspects involved in architecture and other design professions.

Conclusion

Communicating ideas visually is paramount in the architecture profession. In-line chats reinforce this notion through pedagogical habits between professor and student within a studio setting. The complexity, organization and collection of meaningful markings inherent in these visual records of communication deserve to be expressed as part of the process and the art of architecture. Revealing these visual records by introducing them into exercises that encourage searching for problems in a given context and subsequently inventing solutions gives younger students a better understanding of the role of an architect.

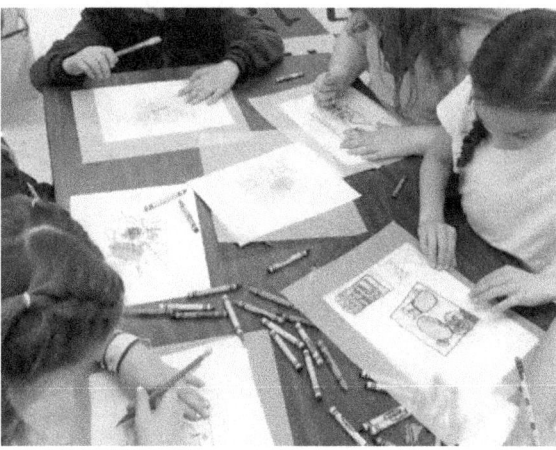

Fig. 6 Third-grade students using trace paper to re-imagine their own landscapes and environments within an abstract sketch.

Comprehensive Design and the Beginning Design Student

Adam Bridge, Brian Grieb
Morgan State University School of Architecture and Planning

Abstract

As architecture and construction become increasingly complex, the need for sophisticated building information modeling programs to assist design teams in both the creation and assembly of our built environment is becoming the norm. Our technological capabilities and computing infrastructure are providing architects with the means to visualize projects in ways like never before. What was once a profession dominated by the tactile is now evolving into a realm of virtual design and digital exploration. Through the click of a mouse or the swipe of the finger, buildings are brought to life on screen with increasing realism. We are no longer building brick by brick, but byte by byte.

Students entering into architectural design programs today are "digital natives", weaned entirely in a digital world. To them, the digital world filled with smartphones and tablets, Google and Facebook, is the only world they know. But for all that technology has afforded, it has yet to replace the direct human "touch" required to create our built environment. While many industries have evolved, physically creating things by computer, robot and machine, the realization of our homes and cities is still rooted in an intimate orchestration between material and the touch of the human hand. Yet, for many students the physical (and associated technical understanding of material and assembly) is the area that they are least familiar. In particular, the students in the early stages of the design curriculum are challenged to learn and balance the complex interrelationship of design and technical prowess. Commonly, young students differ blindly to material libraries and standard component assemblies provided within BIM software. This, unknowing and often passionate desire of the student to create realistic "designs" unfortunately results in quite the opposite. Early studio projects more often than not result in designs with little reference to the materials and design assemblies in which they might be constructed.

We surmise this dilemma is not isolated to our students and design program and believe it is imperative to find new ways to embrace the complexity of building design. By shifting methods of educational delivery and significantly increasing blended course content, we can strike a new balance between time-tested methods and student-centered techniques. To achieve this, we have developed a curriculum for early design students modeled on the ideals of comprehensive design studios typically found at the upper levels of architectural curriculums. Working across our program, the faculty team devised a pedagogical model that blends the lessons of design studio with the core content of history and building technology courses historically taught in conjunction as "co-requisites". Through the exploration of curriculum and the examination of student work this paper seeks to share the successes and failures encountered when shifting from a compartmentalized curriculum to a comprehensive beginning design studio model.

Design Disconnect: Digital Observations

We are in the midst of a new era. Students entering the university are members of the largest generation in the history of our nation. But unlike the generations that have preceded them, they are the first group to have a purely "digital bond" with the internet since birth. From cradle to grave, this generation will be the first to spend their entire lives in the digital epoch. Like no other generation has digital technology impacted daily communication as it has for Generation Z. For them, the digital ecosystem that connects daily social, civic and business activities is simply a way of life. In this new age, never has one generation been privy to so much information and knowledge.

At the forefront of this new reality is the pervasive attunement to the machine and screen. Though certainly not limited to Generation Z, our digital devices

– laptops, mobile phones and tablets are recasting our expectations of speed, convenience and flexibility at the touch of a finger. These seemingly innocuous devices are the backbone of the communication highway in our world today. However, despite the seemingly endless features and apps, providing everything from construction calculators to emergency flashlights, these digital Swiss army knives are changing the classroom and studio landscape. Preying on our insatiable appetite to be "connected," a recent study published in the Journal of Media Education, examined how students are using devices during class time for texting and social networking. Conducted by the University of Nebraska-Lincoln, the study discovered that the typical college student "plays" with their digital device during class an average of 12 times per day.[1] According to psychologist and author Daniel Goleman, these "interactions mold brain circuitry; the fewer hours spent with people – and the more staring at a digitized screen - portends deficits."[2] With this ever-increasing bond with the digital machines, the question is, are we more connected or is the minted digital world alienating our interactions with people?

Beginning with research and subsequent books authored by Howe and Strauss in the late nineties, much debate has been volleyed over the identifying personality of the digital generations. In the article, Sollohub and Sweeney suggest that the digital generation is "leading an epochal transition in human history, one from analog to digital."[3]

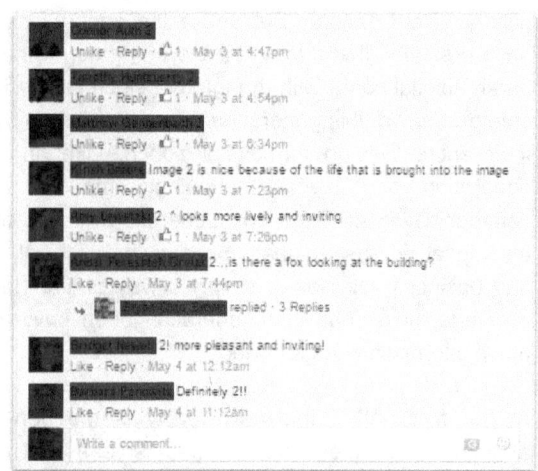

Fig. 1. *Facebook decision-making: Vote for design 1 or 2!*

The opportunities afforded by digital technologies to learn and engage with the world have never been greater. Communication occurs quickly and often in an abbreviated form. This new mode, delivered in a "140 characters or less" format, has no patience for the extraneous. Students exchange ideas and solicit feedback on social media platforms such as Facebook, Instagram and Pinterest. For Generation Z, this new medium isn't utilized simply for casual social interaction, but increasingly evolving as a collaborative space for their work. Within these mediums, peer feedback is the norm, widely accepted and made easy through the use of "like" buttons and libraries of emojis. While these tools within the digital media encourage and speed the feedback loop amongst peers, the structure promotes a simplified, non-critical dialogue. This influx of positive affirmation branded into these social media platforms, challenges critique and debate, a vital attribute in the creative process and design iteration.

Technique: Chicken and the Egg?

In the traditional pedagogical model of many undergraduate architecture programs, introductory courses in architectural history, building materials and construction technology are taught concurrently with beginning design studios. Although these courses are typically arranged in parallel and delivered within a semester by semester framework, direct connection of the material between the respective courses is often circumstantial. Historically American architectural education, with its emphasis on the design studio separated from an array of supporting classes has pretty much the same structure since the early part of the [20th century].[4] Foundational courses introduce students to architecture as a marriage of the poetic and pragmatic, both art and science. Yet, despite this, the teaching of design studio and the technical subjects generally remain a specialized and separate activity.[5] Only by manifesting this duality through a formal blending of the canon of historical precedent and construction technique can we make a foundational connection between these realms.

Design Syntax

How can one understand language, if a syntax is not provided? Can an artist create a masterpiece without a refined understanding of the materials and tools in which they craft? Just as these require a both/and approach, architecture too, is born from both the abstract and the finite. For many students, formal design education begins with an introduction of an architectural syntax based around concepts of form, space and order. These principles help ground the understanding of the abstract, providing a framework for the student to comprehend and create. In these formative stages, complex architectural ideas are simplified, fundamentally relying on points, lines and planes to communicate design intentions. Yet, with the manipulation of these elements, represented through computer modeling (digital) or cardboard and glue, the specificity of the architecture they represent is devoid of the material reality that ultimately governs architectural assemblies. Digital, and to a lesser extent the analogue, permit a suspension of constructional reality. Important factors such as material characteristics, environmental conditions and gravitational forces provide little consequence, thus stripping the work - and more importantly the practitioner of an opportunity to develop a more robust reality.

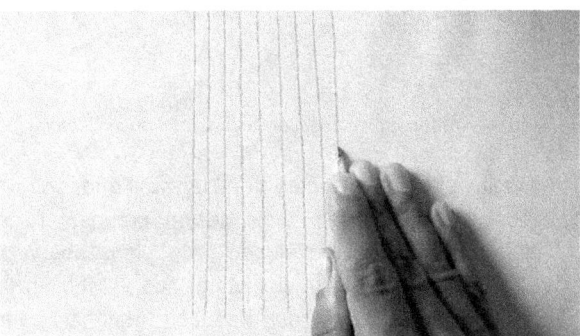

Fig. 2. *Fundamentals: know the media, know the method.*

Curricular Explorations

Over the last few years, we have created a series of projects and design exercises to address the ever-changing dynamics of our students. Over the first four semesters, students in the beginning design curriculum are taking courses that have been re-imagined to work in concert, in ways in which the material is both explicitly and implicitly aligned. The design studio remains the primary realm of content synthesis, but its projects and assignments have been structured strategically focused to deliver fundamental design knowledge through familiar mechanisms of technology blended with time-tested methodologies.

Students today want to learn what they need to know, and move on. They have little patience for the extraneous. They have a desire to make and discover solutions quickly. Just as many of the products created in today's world become obsolete the moment they come to market, our students are ever more aligned with these forces in the ways they embrace the educational process.

The Whole Truth and Nothing But the Truth

The origins of this strategy began in an observation regarding Sketch Up. As a free software, Trimble Sketch Up is often a digital gateway for students entering a design program. Unlike more sophisticated BIM programs - where models are based on pre-sized components - Sketch Up models are compositions of line and plane in the purest sense. Though we are able to create three-dimensional spaces, any articulation of three-dimensional mass is an illusion - paper-thin planes enclosing voided space. With a clear understanding of basic architectural principles and construction methods, this is not a significant issue, but without them the result is often walls and floors without thickness, construction without hierarchy. There is little understanding of structure or skin and any attempts to establish primary and secondary relationships are framed by Post-Modern allusions to hierarchy (not that there is anything wrong with that) than real construction relationships.

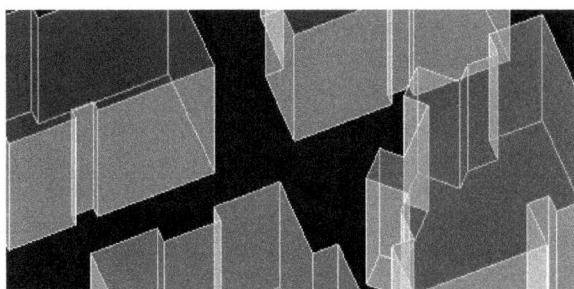

Fig. 3. *Sketch Up and non-dimensional enclosures*

3

COMPREHENSIVE DESIGN AND THE BEGINNING DESIGN STUDENT

The typical approach to resolving this has been to assign depth and dimension to each item. Often, whole numbers are given so students can focus on composition rather than dimension and "math". As a strategy to resolve the issue of 'no depth', this is effective. As a practice, however, this does little to advance a design approach, based on actual materials and methods. Alarmingly, we have seen it establish a counter standard that becomes embedded in student thinking (they have practiced with these standards after all) that lingers and confusing and slowing their adoption of actual construction technologies. The 6" riser and 12" tread takes a long time to shrug off.

Rectifying this practice can often take place within the design studio course. A lecture on basic stair and ramp design paired with proper review and enforcement (grading and evaluation) of those standards and requirements plays a critical role. And yet teaching construction techniques and standards within the studio stresses the capacity of that curriculum and may overwhelm its larger pedagogical goals. This studio overloading often has the dual side effect of diluting the overall quality of studio work and taking additional attention away from lecture courses.

Instead, we have begun to establish direct accountabilities across lecture and studio courses that evaluate student application of construction principles within their studio projects. This requires lecture course content to be immediately applied within design studio and 'tests' for accurate implementation through project evaluation conducted within the lecture course. As a result, lecture content and studio content becomes less abstract, more concrete and more integrated.

Precedent and Execution

One of the earliest application of this cross course integration was the research and documentation of architectural precedents in our foundational *History of the Built Environment II* course. Precedent research is nothing new, but in this instance it subject and goals were driven by a much simpler and prosaic goal - drawing accurate wall and roof thicknesses for studio projects.

Rather than arbitrarily assign dimensions (and just create another problem as referenced above) we had students thoroughly document the wall sections of architectural precedents utilizing a variety of structural and cladding techniques. Students were asked to use a provided Sketch Up material template and model a sample bay of their precedents' wall system highlighting structure, insulation, exterior cladding and interior finishing. Each layer of the 'material sandwich' needed to be specifically identified and its properties outlined using the textbook and lecture content of a second course - *Building Materials I*. Once the research, modeling and documentation were complete, students presented their finding within their *Design Studio I*.

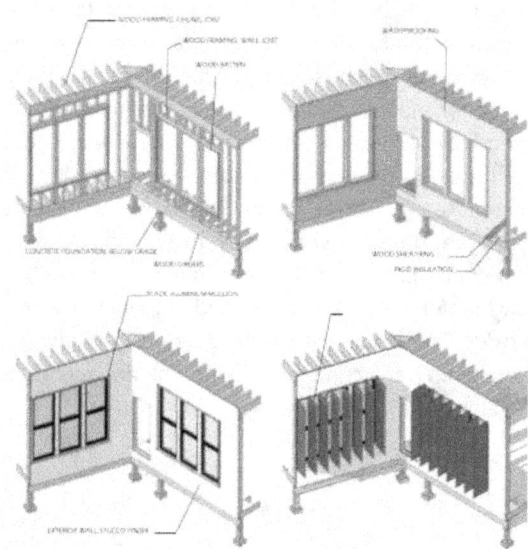

Fig. 4. *Precedent wall section reconstruction in Sketch Up.*

Finally, students selected the floor, wall and roof system most consistent with their design proposal (a small artist's retreat) and developed 1'=⅛" plans, sections and elevations accurately depicting floor, wall and roof dimensions as well as elevation material patterns. Technically the material information was far more advanced than necessary for the *Design Studio I*, but the process reinforced the importance of lecture course content and placed structure, material and dimension - a the repercussions of those decisions - within the student's initial investigative lexicon. For many students, the notion of architecture as assembly and construction entered their mind for the first time.

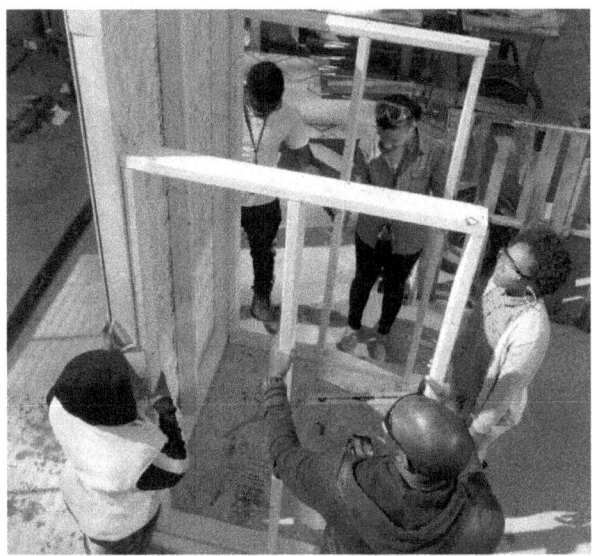

Fig. 5. *Building Materials I*: framing construction mockups.

Framing Project

Increasingly, students are looking at opportunities that lead them away from fundamental aspects of design and the traditional, narrow role of the architect. They seek opportunities to learn architecture, not merely in front of computer or over a drafting board, but in ways that are engaging, tactile and expansive in content. This redirection of curricular approach is no more evident than in the increase of programs that are providing alternative approaches to design education. In particular, studios that combine designing and building have, by some estimates, increased threefold over the past two decades and now influence architecture and design curriculum more than ever before.[5]

Design/build, arguably provides better than any other current curricular approach, a forum that promotes the exploration of the *how* and *why* we build. Within the context of the design/build model, students connect across disciplines, often blending design, materials, structures, construction technique as well as the social, environmental and political forces that act on a project. Yet, despite the intersection created though this approach that blends function, beauty and poetics, a multitude of complexities challenge the implementation of the this educational model. While these qualities evoke shared aspirations and allow disciplines to

converge, the design/build model is not without faults. First, these projects typically require a tremendous commitment of time and money to execute within the university structure. Secondly, these projects tend to attract students towards the end of their academic careers, seldom engaging the younger student. Lastly, because of this academic segregation, it deemphasizes the importance of the intersection of ideas and disciplines by delaying it to the latter part of a student's educational career.

In our earliest curricular attempts to diminish the alienation of the technical from design, our course in building materials and assemblies explored projects that provided students an opportunity to physically engage with the materials. The very first project required teams of students to construct a small shed using conventional, light wood framing techniques. Working in teams of four or five, students gained an appreciation for the complexity imposed in the assembly, even when it is at the scale of a 16 square foot structure. While the project achieved much success in introducing the concepts of technical knowledge and improvisational skill required to create a building, the project's major shortcoming was the segregation of design from the process. It was this primary factor from this initial project that guided us in the development of the *Framing Project*.

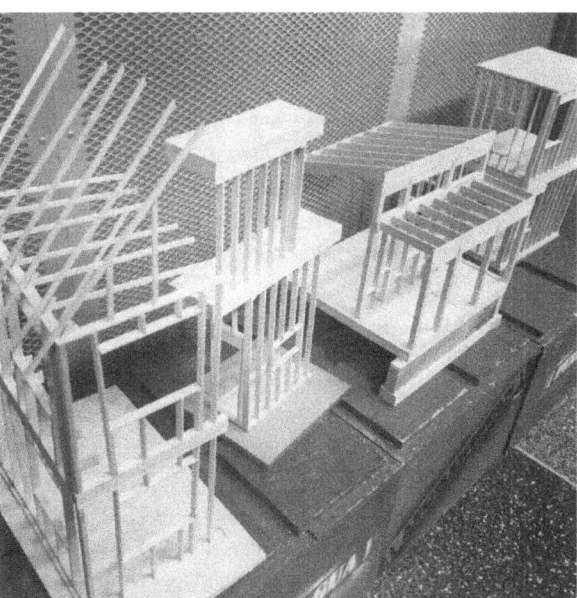

Fig. 6. *Design Studio I / Building Materials I*: framing models.

For us, the development of the *Framing Project* is a direct response to the needs and pressures of teaching students raised in an age of instant feedback. The project provides an alternative approach that seeks to harness the alluring qualities of design/build projects with the blended, informational rich content that appeals to Generation Z students.

The project, as conceived, occurs in the third undergraduate semester (first semester, sophomore year). It blends the content of three courses: *Design Studio I, Building Materials I* and *History of the Built Environment II* by challenging the student to solve a design problem (a small residence) using a comprehensive approach. The pedagogical premise of the project is to, from their very first studio, instill a process of design requires exploration of a problem from a series of both convergent and divergent issues.

Over the duration of the project, the students explore design, as almost all beginning students do, using basic ordering principles - symmetry, axis, proportion, datum, and module - to execute their project. These principles are initially discussed and conceptually reinforced by a *History of the Built Environment II* curriculum that is partially organized around compositional strategies instead of traditional chronologies. By reframing architectural history as the development and iteration of formal or programmatic typologies, students find the examples more immediately accessible and relevant to their *Design Studio I* work.

Where in earlier versions of studio this exploration would have ended, the students are given the added responsibility to implement beyond beauty and poetics, and must include lessons and principles discussed in the lecture course, *Building Materials I*. At this juncture, no longer can the simple volumes of Sketch Up or planes of chipboard suffice. Students must test the plausibility of their design ideas by incorporating real structure and material into their design.

Using large scale models (1"=1'-0), students must "build" a framing model of their respective design. While, ultimately the structure they construct is still a replica of their actual building, these large models have a tendency to mimic the tactile nature of the material, construction methodology and the unforgiving nature of

gravity. As one suspects, this particular moment in the project becomes the great equalizer, as it validates (or invalidates) the students design direction. Through the lessons they acquire through their "build," students are encouraged to reevaluate earlier decisions to enhance their final designs.

Structural Project

In the fourth semester, a similar pattern of integration has been repeated in the development of design methodologies in *Design Studio II*. Students begin with detailed research and documentation of an architectural precedent in which the structural system place a predominant spatial and aesthetic role. Using information from lectures from both the *Design Studio II* and *Building Materials II* courses, students demonstrate how force paths are handles in each structure and assign primary force resistance roles (tension, compression, etc.) for each precedent's structural elements. As in the previous semester, students present their work within *Design Studio II* and it serves as a principal influence for the development of structural conceptual models for the course's final project. These studies requires students to create specific spatial divisions using only elements necessary for the stability and support of the structure.

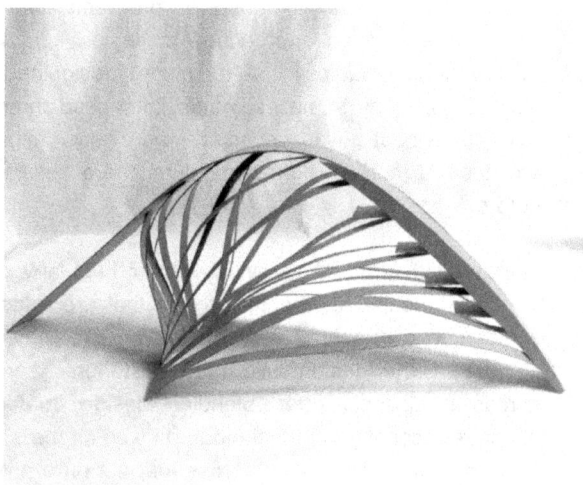

Fig. 7. Final structural concept model.

Like the *Framing Project*, student design work is executed at scale using proximate sizes and materials to those proposed for the actual project. Student's build multiple iterations of these prototypes testing them (light weights and finger pressure) to understand how the model reacts to gravitational and wind forces. Students record their observations and postulate potential solutions. Models are then modified in response. Final models are produced to highlight their inherent aesthetic characteristics. The process results in greater student understanding of basic structural principles and greater appreciation of the role structure can play in the definition of architectural character. Remarkably, student who often struggled to create 'dynamic' forms find an inner Calatrava and develop proposals of sculptural and technical sophistication.

Preliminary Observations

Our initial observations on the implementation of the curricular restructuring are being embraced positively by faculty and students alike in the program. Through this endeavor, it has challenged us to recognize and accept the impactful potential technology is placing on the professional development of students entering our program. Of equal importance to this transformation, has been the emphasis we've placed on blending with the technical the "hands-on" learning methods desired by Gen Z.[7] Most importantly, we believe the blending of these refined pedagogical methods of content delivery, we are creating a revolutionized environment for which information can be exchanged, allowing creativity to flourish.

Anecdotes

Our first feedback regarding initial course integration attempts came directly from the students. In fact, they were often ahead of us in this regard:

"My experience was a very challenging one however a way to make building materials more relevant to studio would be to integrate the topics into one another."
- *Student Exit Survey, Spring 2013*

Student feedback after the first few semesters of course alignment was also supportive:

"The cohesiveness between the three sophomore courses which influenced projects in ARCH 201 was significant. The ability to apply historical theory and

structures in ARCH 201 allowed me to properly develop a process of design."
- *Student Exit Survey, Spring 2015*

Faculty observations correlate with student comments. Cross-course projects and assignments seem to be the focus of significant cognitive leaps within the semester. Student engagement is at its highest, the work at its most creative and the connection between verbal articulation and physical design product at its most clear and succinct.

On an administrative level, course alignment and project/assignment integration has contributed to a more robust beginning design curriculum. Attempts to increase course overlaps has resulted in more frequent faculty discussion, content assessment and collegiality. Lecture faculty actively engage and support studio work and co-teaching moments allow students to benefit from specific faculty expertise. This has not only allowed faculty to teach more to their strengths, but have enable our varied teaching methods to overlap, cover gaps and reach students with different learning styles. Students have requested increase coordination of their upper level seminar and studio material.

Statistics

Initial data collection supports the observations listed above. A comparison of student performance showed 15-25% (studio) and 10-15% (lecture) increases in academic performance for the new aligned sophomore curriculum versus previous non-aligned courses. Even more encouraging, students performed better on cross-course assignments (approximately a half letter-grade) than assignments that were not coordinated.

Limitations

Implementation of this approach has three related complications that limit the degree and success of course integration - re-registration, transfer and non-major students. Whether a student is re-enrolling in the course due to a previous withdraw or failure, receipt of transfer credit, or is taking the course as an elective for another major, the task of developing content that work for both the 60-80% of the students on the standard second-year curriculum path and those who for the

7

reasons stated above are not taking the three aligned courses can be difficult. Though course overlaps help to generate significant synergy between studio and lecture courses and in many ways lesson the overall student workload, students who find themselves out of sync with the standard curriculum often find the opposite to be true. Though each assignment has a 'B-track' which does not require studio integration the discussion and content delivery within any single course is often circumscribed. Students often feel as if they are entering the conversation midstream.

Lastly, for every group of students inspired and engaged by the overlapping coursework, there are one or two students who find the synthesis of the material too much of an organizational or intellectual burden and their work suffers - late, incomplete and underdeveloped. These students often visibly struggle during class discussion and critiques of the integrated work. Overall, however, even these student are performing above (increased comprehension of dimensional standards) than struggling students of earlier cohorts who did not participate in the integrated coursework.

It's Not Perfect...But It's a Start

We consider our exploration and the reshaping of our curriculum as a work in progress. While this has helped retool our course structure to better serve the needs of our program, the pedagogical approach we believe finds success by refreshing time-tested methodologies of content delivery to meet the attributes of today's students. These directions have emerged from our realization that our curriculum was fragmented, and that a more comprehensive approach to teaching architecture to the students entering our program was a necessity. These techniques have been applied to varying extent and in multiple iterations over the last six semesters. It would be ideal if their application had been formulated and coordinated from the start, but admittedly our initial efforts were in response to 'symptoms' we observed in the learning patterns and academic performances of our students. As a small faculty (9 faculty for 250 students) we benefitted from an intimate knowledge of our entire curriculum and in particular our second-year courses for which we have taught or coordinated for much of the past six years. Though by no means scientific, we have made observations and conducted limited analysis that suggests our cross-course integration and "byte-size making" efforts are improving student outcomes.

Notes:

1 McCoy, Bernard, "Digital Distractions in the Classroom: Student Classroom Use of Digital Devices for Non-Class Related Purposes." *Journal of Media Education,* 7:1 (January, 2016): pp. 5-32

2 Goleman, Daniel. <u>Focus: The Hidden Driver of Excellence.</u> Harper (2013): p.6

3 Sollohub, Darius and Sweeney, Richard. "Millennials and Design Education", Digital Aptitudes + Other Openings: Proceedings of the 100th ACSA, Boston, MA, pp. 469-476

4 Ochshorn, Jonathan, "Separating Science from Architecture: Why Technology is Taught Outside the Design Studio," The Architecture of the In-Between: Proceedings of the 78th Annual Meeting of the ACSA, 1990, San Francisco, CA, March 17-20, 1990

5 Ochshorm, op. cit., p 2

6 Hailey, Charlie, *Design/Build with the Jersey Devil* (New York: Princeton Architectural Press, 2016), p 8

7 "Gen Z in the Classroom: Creating the Future," last modified March 1, 2017, http://www.adobeeducate.com/genz/adobe-education-genz

SESSION 06: DIGITAL TOOLS I

Session Chair: Andrzej Zarzycki
New Jersey Institute of Technology

Mahsan Mohsenin, Florida A&M University: "Application of BIM Simulation Tools in Architecture Education."

Robert Holton, Louisiana State University: "Virtual: Contruction Modeling & Material Logic."

Vincent Hui, Jennifer McArthur and Pierre-Alexandre Lelay, Ryerson University: "Digital Integration: Synthesizing Poetic Possibilities and Pragmatic Production."

Integration of Building Energy Modeling In Architecture Education

Mahsan Mohsenin
Assistant Professor, Florida A&M University

Abstract

The goal of this paper is to investigate thermal analysis results among different Building Energy Modeling (BEM) software to better select a thermal simulation tool for building analysis for the purpose of teaching Environmental Systems. Hence, this paper aims to focus on both the comparison of simulation results and the educational experiment of the simulation softwares as a means of collaboration between academia and passive design.

This research demonstrates examples of student's project in Environmental Systems course improving their original studio design using energy analysis based on the appropriate passive strategies. This research applies experiment and simulation methodology to compare the results.

The results provide a comparison chart for different energy metrics in a shoebox building using Autodesk Revit and DesignBuilder with hand calculation as the calibration. The EUI results are very close among the compared simulation software, while the difference is the features and parameters that each simulation directly provides. The results of student projects represent the significance of including energy analysis and the perception of EUI in design alternatives at early stages of projects in the curriculum.

Introduction

"Integrated design, which is the crux of sustainable building design, necessitates early involvement of all project consultants in the design process."

(Hayles and Holdsworth, 2008; p 29, quoted in Shannon and Radford, 2010)

Theories in design education call for an integrated method to merge the gap between theories, architectural design and technological aspects.

As energy saving in architecture design has turned into a challenge, the application of building simulation software has increasingly become important. For instance, targets such as AIA 2030 aim to build and renovate buildings carbon-neutral. The reduction of fossil fuel energy in the building sector can be achieved through passive design strategies, predicting energy usage of buildings and using simulation software at early stages of design. This paper focuses on the significance of including energy analysis in design curriculum to provide students with energy load feedback in their projects. There is a myriad of building simulation software such as OpenStudio in SketchUp, DesignBuilder, DIVA for Rhino, and Autodesk Revit to analyze energy usage. This paper is mainly focused on Autodesk Revit because of its prevalence in architecture practice. Most of the softwares available presently employ EnergyPlus as their analysis engine, developed by the U.S. Department of Energy. Autodesk Revit, Building Energy Modeling (BEM)-based software, employs DOE-2 as its energy calculation engine, while DesignBuilder uses EnergyPlus as its embedded engine.

This research provides a comparison between Revit and DesignBuilder simulation tools from a designer's perspective. It will then explore pedagogical results of an experiment using simulation in teaching Environmental Technology course. This paper is to compare and evaluate thermal performance of a shoebox building and a more complex design using DesignBuilder v.4.7 and Autodesk Revit 2016. The next objective of this research is to experiment the application of Revit simulation software in teaching the Environmental Technology course. As a validation, the present study compares Energy Use Intensity (EUI) and peak heating/ cooling load results of a shoebox office building using Autodesk Revit and DesignBuilder with hand calculation. EUI is the total energy per square foot per year. The students in this study become familiar with the impact of their design decisions on EUI in their projects. The current study assumes the same construction materials and weather data to compare the results using different simulation softwares.

The literature on integration of building information in architecture school curricula is limited due to the fast pace of computer technological advancements. Building Technology is taught in some schools of architecture as a separate graduate level program, while changes are not adopted for undergraduate courses. Courses such as Introduction to Technology and Environmental Systems are undergraduate level courses that provide students with the understandings of energy in buildings. Becerik-Gerber et al. (2011) investigated integration of Building Information Modeling in architecture, engineering and construction management, using survey methodology. Their findings represented the reasons for not incorporating building information modeling into curriculum, where the main cause was the lack of updated instructors. While teaching building energy modeling is not possible without grounding the basic understandings, this research investigates integration of energy modeling in upper level undergraduate course.

Research Methodology

There is an extensive body of knowledge on comparison of simulation engines such as DOE-2 and EnergyPlus (Crawley et al.), while this research focuses on comparing the results from the designer's viewpoint and experimenting in teaching architecture students. This research employs computer simulation methodology and experimental results for the pedagogical section.

"EnergyPlus is the U.S. Departments of Energy's 3rd generation building energy simulation engine for modeling heating, cooling, lighting and ventilation, which is a combination of the BLAST and DOE-2 simulation engines." (Ibarra and Reinhart, 2009) Both of these engines are validated (Sullivan et al., 1998). Crawley et al. (2004) investigated an in-depth comparison between EnergyPlus, DOE-2 and BLAST categorized under the main criteria describing general features, internal loads, building envelope and daylighting and results reporting. Table 1 reviews a

summary of EnergyPlus modeling capabilities beyond DOE-2.

Table 1 Summary of EnergyPlus Advanced Modeling Capabilities beyond DOE-2 (Hong et al., 2008; 28-29) based on architecture pedagogy

Item	EnergyPlus	DOE-2 (both 2.1E and 2.2 unless otherwise noted)
Building Loads and Systems	Building response to thermal loads is calculated simultaneously with system operation.	Building response to thermal loads is calculated independently of system operation.
Renewable Energy	Can model PV either standalone or BIPV.	DOE-2.2 can model PV.
Daylighting and Controls	EnergyPlus has detailed daylighting models.	DOE-2 tends to overestimate daylighting benefits.
Windows and Shading Controls	EnergyPlus has more shading controls for windows and skylights.	DOE-2 has limited shading controls.

DOE-2, which is used by Autodesk Revit, has some limitations compared to EnergyPlus, the engine used in DesignBuilder. But there are factors such as accessibility of the software, architect or engineer's need, ease of learning, simulation run time, etc. that play an important role in selecting the software for energy analysis.

In addition to the difference in the simulation engines, the mentioned simulation tools also differ in their user interface and file exchange systems. Autodesk Revit has two modes for energy analysis: conceptual mass mode and building element mode. For a simple design, the user may draw the project from scratch in each tool and sets the thermal properties, whereas for a more complex project, there is a need to import and export files between Revit and DesignBuilder to compare the results. DesignBuilder uses an export format of XML, which is not imported by Autodesk Revit. Conversely, Revit provides the gbXML (Green Building XML) format to export the 3D geometry along with its thermal properties. gbXML files contain building information along with energy properties. DesignBuilder also supports the IDF export option used for detailed analysis in EnergyPlus, while Revit requires another software to create the IDF file.

A simple shoebox office and a more complex design (multi-zone) are analyzed in this study using Autodesk Revit, DesignBuilder and hand calculation as calibration. Next, this research experiments using Autodesk Revit's simulation tool in the Environmental Technology course for undergraduate architecture students to practically evaluate energy savings in student's design projects. The project given to students asked for the energy analysis of one of the student's design projects. The goal of this assignment was to make them aware of the energy consequences of their design and instruct them how to practically use the energy analysis simulation tool and Energy Use Intensity (EUI), which is energy per square foot per year. The students were then asked to make changes to their project based on passive design strategies and re-evaluate their project. Students experimented two design strategies and evaluated the percentage of improvement in peak heating/ cooling loads. Students learned to work with "Climate Consultant Tool" (Energy Design Tools, 2016), passive strategies and simulation settings in this project. The building parameters that were considered to improve the building performance include building orientation, shape, window to wall ratio, envelope thermal mass, and insulation. Passive strategies that students explored include:

- Solar Direct Gain
- Solar Indirect Gain
- Minimize East-West Glazing
- North-South Orientation
- Architecture Design
- Window to wall ratio
- Night Cooling Ventilation
- Shading (Overhangs on South Side)
- Decks and Porches
- Building material properties

To test the results between Autodesk Revit and DesignBuilder, a simple shoebox office building is drawn with the following assumptions.
Dimension: 232 m2, windows are ignored

Location: Tallahassee, FL
Type: Office
By default general lighting (IECC 1998) is on and HVAC is set as Fan-coil unit. Table 2 and Table 3

provide the building and weather assumptions used in this study.

Table 2 Construction specification of the shoebox model

Component	U-values
Roofs	4 in lightweight concrete (U=1.2748 W/m^2.K)
Walls	8 in lightweight concrete block (U=0.8108 W/m^2.K)
Floors	Passive floor, no insulation, tile or vinyl (U=2.9583 W/m^2.K)
Doors	Metal (U=0.7022 W/m^2.K)

Table 1 *Weather data default settings*

	Design Builder 8.1	Revit 2014	Hand calculation
Cooling Setpoint (C)	24	23.3	23.9
Heating Setpoint (C)	22	21.1	21.1
Winter dry-bulb Temp (C)	-1.7	0	0
Summer dry-bulb Temp (C)	34.4	35.6	35.6

Heating load is calculated based on $Q = UA\Delta T$ where U-value is the material conductivity, A represents the area of the building surface and ΔT is the temperature difference between indoor and outdoor. Hand calculation weather data are based on ASHRAE, 2009. Since cooling load depends on both thermal mass and solar radiation, it is calculated based on ASHRAE's Cooling Load Temperature Difference (CLTD). This method provides engineers with corrected cooling temperature differences for each building component calculated for a specific time and day of a year.

The primary results (Table 4) indicate that the difference in results among software and hand calculation is mostly caused by the difference in temperature setpoints and modeling capabilities.

Table 4 Preliminary comparison Heating/ cooling results between Autodesk Revit, DesignBuilder and Hand Calculation

Thermal metric	DesignBuilder	Autodesk Revit	Hand Calculation
Peak cooling load (kW)	24.56	22.67	23.74
Peak heating load (kW)	11.63	10.60	12.25
EUI (kW / sm / yr)	155.82	143.25	155.82

The data represent that in a simple shoebox design, the results are reasonably close, while in a multizone space there is a need to select the simulation tool based on the case, required needs and modeling capabilities. Further research is performed to compare the results in a multi-zone design office project, using default Revit thermal properties. The comparison demonstrates a mismatch, occurred due to the way thermal properties transfer between Revit and DesignBuilder through the gbXML file.

The results indicate that for student projects and early design evaluations, Autodesk Revit is helpful for non-experts in energy modeling. It is important to mention that in addition to the difference in the simulation engine, Revit and DesignBuilder use a different interface and hierarchy of the model data. For instance, DesignBuilder dissects the design based on the Building, Block, Zone, Surface, and Openings, while Revit requires the user to manually add zoning to the building level. In other words, DesignBuilder interprets drawings as spaces and zones, while in Revit the hierarchy is based on an architect's thought process, which includes creating walls, roofs, etc. In Revit, the user then needs to define zones to get the peak heating/ cooling load results for each zone.

The energy analysis results provided reasonably similar values between Revit and DesignBuilder, while the user interface of Revit is more student-friendly. As for results, DesignBuilder provides annual and peak heating and cooling, while Revit results include EUI and peak heating/ cooling in Revit Mechanical Electrical and Plumbing (MEP). In terms of daylight analysis, DesignBuilder calculates daylight factor, visual comfort and sustainability code evaluations, while Revit is limited in providing an illumination map. Both of the tools provide data on cost and life cycle analysis. For these reasons and free student access to Revit, the author decided to use Revit in the Environmental Technology course.

Pedagogical Lessons Learned

The pedagogical approach in this experiment is based on evidence-based design, with a focus on learning from vernacular architecture for any specific region. Decades ago, architects did not use simulation tools, while many of those buildings are efficient and timeless masterpieces. What factors did they include to design sustainably and what added values can simulation bring to us? Sustainability occurs when an element has multiple functions. For instance, when designing a roof, it is the combination of aesthetic, structure, energy efficiency and daylight penetration. Including this holistic teaching combined with new methods of evaluating buildings and BEM techniques is the outcome we may expect from today's architecture pedagogy. The following projects describe the pedagogical approach taken in the Environmental Technology course:

Project 1

Project 1 asks students to evaluate a shoebox project in two different climates as a conceptual mass design. During this process students practically learn the necessity for the difference in climatic design and passive strategies in diverse climates. By reviewing design recommendations from Climate Consultant, students can apply changes to the mass design to improve building's performance. After primary considerations for building's size, shape and orientations, students will learn to explore window to wall ratio, using the "Energy Settings". In this project, students will experiment with the impact of designing aperture in different sides of the building such as south or north.

Project 2

The second project in Environmental Technology course required the students to evaluate and improve the performance of their design studio projects. The goal in this project is to have students work with energy modeling in design development phase and learn about different zones that a more complex project may require. This exercise was the first time for undergraduate architecture students working with

U-values in practice, which provided a valuable integration between theory and practice. This project asks students to provide two appropriate strategies based on their climate condition and design and then implement one in their project to re-evaluate the performance.

Generally speaking, this paper found Autodesk Revit Energy Analysis an appropriate tool for architecture students, because of the general understanding it provides and the compatibility of the software with what most architecture firms use. There is no doubt on DesignBuilder's strong capability for professionals, while for undergraduate teaching purposes using Revit simulation provided successful outcomes as a quick evaluation in mass design. DesignBuilder was a user-friendly tool for an expert in simulation, while Autodesk Revit was more accessible and easy-to-learn for architecture students for quick building energy estimates. Figure 1 illustrates a sample of student's work, comparing the improved design based on changing the wall thickness and type. The project

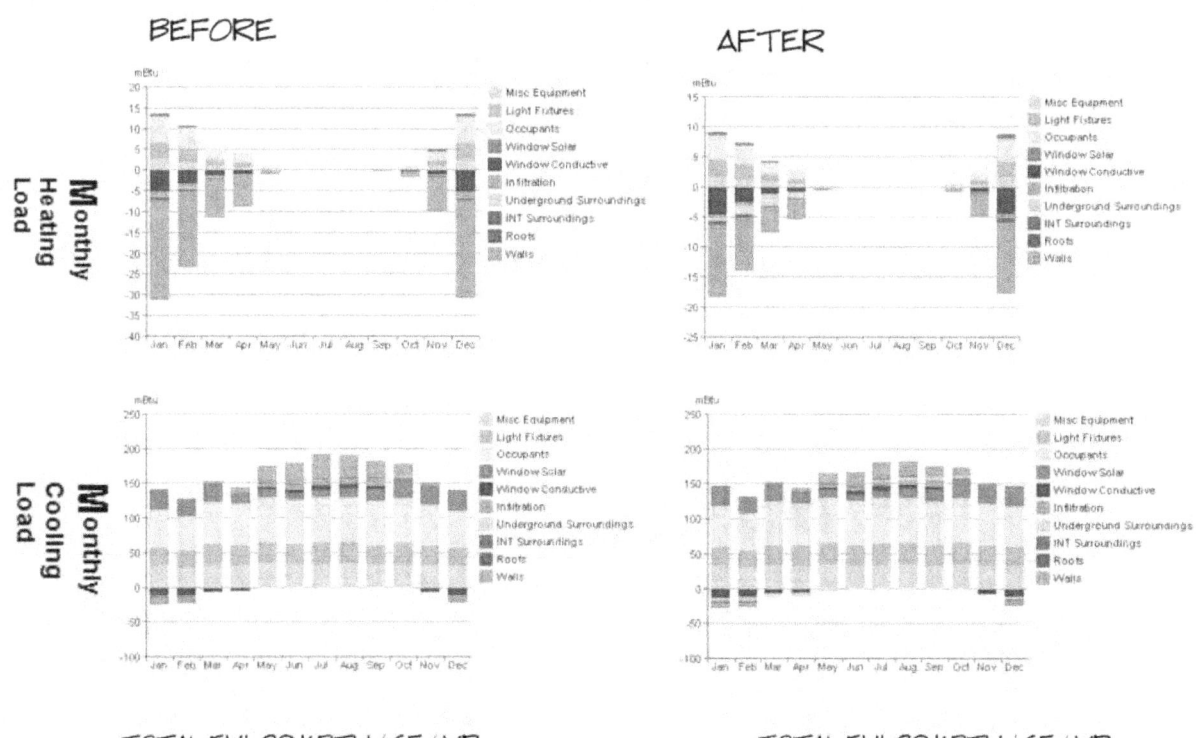

Figure 1 Student sample project representing Autodesk Revit energy analysis results

represents an understanding of monthly evaluation of heating/ cooling load for the project's base case and the improved version.

Student's success was evaluated based on the selected strategies and improvement they made to the base case design. Most of the projects demonstrated that the students understood the improvement concept, while there were challenges in implementing the selected strategies, settings and getting the correct results.

This research, in addition to thermal comparison among two softwares, focuses on pedagogical lessons learned from using Revit in the Environmental Technology class. The project intends to foster student's understanding of energy loads in practice with relation to climate, building type and size. The project given to students required them to analyze a design and edit the project based on the climate and passive strategies to improve their building's peak heating/ cooling load and EUI. Running a simulation does not necessarily mean that the students understand the results and the impact of the climate and their design on the outcomes. To address this

issue, this project aimed to educate students about design strategies based on the climate, rather than focusing only on simulation. The following is a list of significant steps in teaching students how to understand and evaluate thermal performance of their design in Autodesk Revit:

- Interpret the climate using Climate Consultant tool and follow its climate-specific recommendations

- Understand how to use weather data files

- Understand thermal zones and basics of heating/ cooling load and EUI

- Evaluate projects in conceptual mass mode

- Define thermal zones and customize the settings

- Evaluate the building performance and understand how to interpret the loads based on the building function and size

- Figure out avenues of improvement based on thermal loads per each component such as walls,

DESIGN STRAGY BEING USED: THICKEN WALLS

BEFORE   AFTER

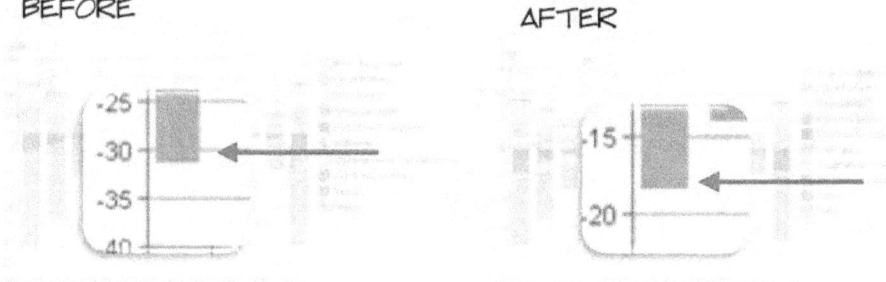

CHANGING THE WALL THICKNESS FROM 8" TO 12" BROUGHT THE MBTU DOWN ABOUT 15,000.

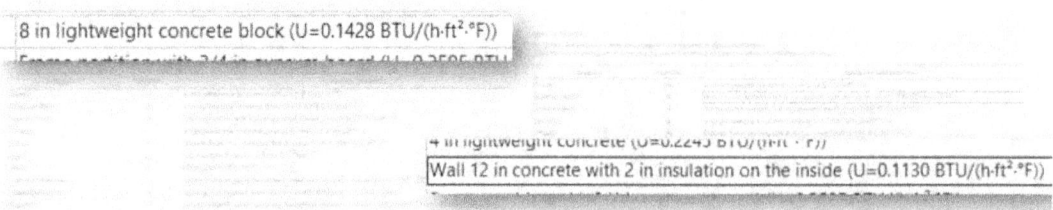

8 in lightweight concrete block (U=0.1428 BTU/(h·ft²·°F))

4 in lightweight concrete (U=0.2243 BTU/(h·ft²·°F))

Wall 12 in concrete with 2 in insulation on the inside (U=0.1130 BTU/(h·ft²·°F))

Figure 2 Student sample project representing challenges working with Revit Simulation

roofs, glazing, etc. for a specific climate

- Change material properties and track the impact on energy loads

- Simulate both heating/ cooling "Load Report" in Revit MEP and "Energy Analysis" to check the EUI

- Perform daylight analysis

- Compare the results

There were challenges using the energy analysis tool in Autodesk Revit for undergraduate students listed below:

Material properties: This experience was the first time for most of the undergraduate architecture students to use material properties and change them in Revit. For instance, there are two separate setting options for U-values through building components or overriding the construction tab of the energy analysis toolbox.

Graphical representation: The next challenge concerned the graphical representation of energy results in Autodesk Revit, where the axis units of the chart change through different results and make the charts difficult to compare. An example is represented in Figure 2.

Green Building Studio: Students faced difficulties working with a cloud-base "Green Building Studio" feature in Revit, which is an online dashboard to help with changing design features but its interface looks confusing.

Active design HVAC features: Analyzing active design strategies such as different HVAC systems was the next set of students' questions.

While Daylighting is touched in Autodesk Revit, the capacity of daylight analysis provided in Revit is not comparable with DIVA for Rhino or DesignBuilder toward meeting building codes and certificates. However, the daylight distribution map in Revit provides a comprehensible daylight analysis as an educational tool. Despite all the challenges that students faced to optimize their projects, this research finds Autodesk Revit significantly helpful in providing students with the understanding of EUI values and

conceptual mass mode evaluation in early stages of design. This research provided students with detailed deliverables to make sure the students paid attention to the technological changes in their design projects. To assist students with the passive design process, workshops and feedbacks were planned to better integrate passive design theories in practice.

Conclusion

This paper compares basic thermal results between Autodesk Revit and DesignBuilder in a shoebox building. The results demonstrate reasonably similar outputs for simple projects, while the difference is the features and parameters that each simulation tool directly provides. For instance, Autodesk Revit demonstrates peak heating/ cooling load and EUI results, whereas DesignBuilder directly provides annual and peak results. To summarize the pedagogical experiment in this paper, the current study recommends using Autodesk Revit's simulation tool for teaching architecture purposes, although the engine that Autodesk Revit employs is limited in comparison to DesignBuilder especially for complex projects. Autodesk Revit provides an evaluation in early stages of design to professionals, educators and students. In other words, Autodesk Revit analysis assists in energy-efficient design decisions, while further technical analysis is needed for complex projects using advanced simulation engines through EnergyPlus. This paper discusses the educational aspects of the explored software and pedagogical lessons learned from student's experience using Autodesk Revit energy simulation. The projects given to students aimed to practically prepare them for climatic design and 2030 net-zero energy challenge. This experience provides students with the power of design and simulation to make a difference in energy efficient practice. Finally, this paper concludes with the advantages of including simulation in advanced studio assignments to provide students with a practical understanding of energy simulation in conceptual design and developing passive design features. The goal is to educate students with the practical understanding of climatic design and 2030 challenge, rather than training them with BEM software or simulation tools. This research was an attempt to demonstrate the significance of evidence-based design to shape architecture pedagogy toward sustainable design.

Notes:

ASHRAE. *ASHRAE Handbook of Fundamentals*, Atlanta, GA: American Society of Heating, Refrigerating and Air-Conditioning Engineers. 2009.

Becerik-Gerber, B., Gerber, J., and Ku, K. "The pace of technological innovation in architecture, engineering, and construction education: integrating recent trends into the curricula" in *ITcon* (16), 2011. p. 411-432.

Crawley, D., Lawrie, L.,... and J. Glazer. "EnergyPlus: an update", *Proceedings of SimBuild*, 4-6. 2004.

Energy Design Tools. Climate Consultant, 2016. Retrieved from http://www.energy-design-tools.aud.ucla.edu/

Hayles, C.S. and Holdsworth, S.E. "Curriculum change for sustainability" in *Journal for Education in the Built Environment*, 3(1), 2008. p. 25–48.

Hong, T., Buhl, F. and P. Haves. EnergyPlus analysis capabilities for use in California building energy efficiency standards development and compliance calculations, Berkeley: Lawrence Berkeley National Laboratory. 2008.

Ibarra, D. and C. Reinhart. DesignBuilder// EnergyPlus Tutorial, Harvard Graduate School of Design. 2009.

LBNL. EnergyPlus. 2016. Retrieved from https://energyplus.net/

Shannon, S. and Radford, A. "Iteration as a strategy for teaching architectural technologies in an architecture studio" in *Architectural Science Review*, 53(2), 2010. p. 238-250.

Sullivan, R. and F Winkelmann. Validation studies of the DOE-2 Building Energy Simulation Program. Final Report, Lawrence Berkeley National Lab. 1998.

1:1 Drawing   An Architecture of Performance

Robert Holton
Louisiana State University, College of Art & Design, School of Architecture

Abstract

"How can an understanding of material attributes, assembly techniques, and environmental conditions inherent in the 'act' of 1:1 building be evidenced in the 'act' of 1:1 drawing?"

Material attributes profoundly define the experiential process of building. The human scale of a brick allows it to be placed and set by hand. The heavy weight of a beam requires mechanization for alignment and placement. The soft density of a stone necessitates a delicacy of handling. The hot temperature of asphalt defines the temporal extent of application. The sharp edge texture of glass mandates cautionary and protective measures. Can the ability to develop a *sensibility* for the application of materials, linked to their distinct properties, be revealed in 1:1 drawing?

Assembly techniques delineate the construction sequences in the performance of building. Connections are an outcome of the actions utilized in placing materials and the detail is the confluence of these histories. Joinery describes a relation between specific surface conditions and an understanding of tolerances. Fasteners elucidate material properties through the movement and resistance of securing. Can 1:1 drawing promote the ability to comprehend necessary assembly *sequences* relative to specific construction techniques?

Environmental conditions impact the routine and course of actions in the feat of building. Temperature can make unavoidable the restrictive use of additional layers that slow movement. Moisture and temperature impact soil consistency and the ease of workability. Wind can impinge precision causing hazardous conditions and increased production time. Can 1:1 drawing demonstrate an understanding of the physical *context* that guides building construction?

The objective of the building technology exercise seeks to investigate material attributes, assembly techniques, and environmental conditions intrinsic in the *'act'* of building: realized in the *'act'* of drawing. Drawing techniques are explored with an emphasis on the ability to communicate the processes inherent in the practice of making architecture: *pragmatics & poetics*. The *'act'* of 1:1 drawing is our format.

Approach

"How can an understanding of material attributes, assembly techniques, and environmental conditions inherent in the 'act' of 1:1 building be evidenced in the 'act' of 1:1 drawing?"

'Architectural Systems', an introductory course in materials and constructions, emerged around this question and is based on an understanding of specific conditions, an iterative process of application, and the resulting outcome. The pedagogical approach is grounded in the conviction that the processes by which something comes to be is critical to what it is. The method towards developing this technique of critical thought is the presentation of knowledge, *'what is something'*, and the practice of application, *'why is something'*. The approach strives to understand the potential of architectural drawing as a means to communicate physical conditions, the processes by which they are achieved, and the physical and cultural parameters in which they exist. The corresponding relevance of setting, performance, and result are expressed in a quote by Peter Gluck published in the monograph, The Modern Impulse.

"Architecture has often been likened to frozen music. If so, the construction of a building is the equivalent of a musical performance, which is in fact the only thing that makes it real. To realize a design, the architect ought to be not only the composer but also the conductor, the more so because with a building there is only one performance. The best way to maintain whatever balance the architect has managed to achieve during the design phase is to direct the architectural process from initial conception to final construction. This makes it possible for the constant

interaction among the various attributes to continue until the building is completed, so that issues of cost, technique, and construction help to inform the design and insure its integrity rather than impede its realization. The responsibility for the alignment of attributes in the completed building lies with the architect. And the goal of this complex process is the building it produces – a building that resolves the overlapping attributes in so strong and elegant a manner that experience of it is all the explanation it needs."

In the example of audible constructs, lines, signs, and characters set out the pitch, rhythm, and tempo of a composition. This notation describes a specific sequence of actions as a way to perform the resulting composition. The simultaneous existence of both the process and the result is an inherent quality of a musical score. In the example of physical constructs, lines, symbols, and annotations are conventions used to set out the shape, size, and arrangement of a composition. This notation describes a specific completed work, however the sequence of actions, as a way to perform the resulting composition, is often traditionally undefined. Through the inclusion of processes of generation and contextual parameters in conjunction with material characteristics, the act of architectural drawing has the potential to question why specific conditions are relevant in the complex union of multiple variables. This dynamic set of relations is fundamental to the practice of making and constructing architecture.

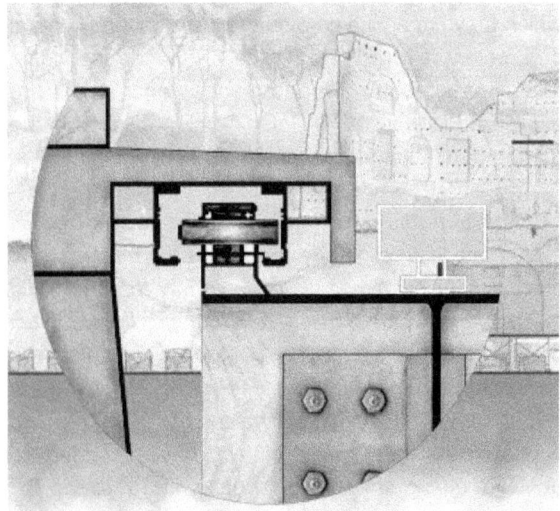

Fig. 1 Enlarged connection detail

Objectives

The course objectives of *'Architectural Systems'* seek to investigate material attributes, assembly techniques, and environmental conditions intrinsic in the construction of architecture and apply the findings through the varied processes of architectural drawing. Drawing techniques and objectives are explored with an emphasis on questioning the procedures inherent in the practice of making architecture: *pragmatics & poetics*. The following primary objectives are focused around both tangible and abstract concepts fundamental to design thinking.

• *Ability to develop a sensibility for the application of materials linked to their distinct properties.*
• *Understand and evaluate factors that influence material selection and assembly methods.*
• *Ability to comprehend necessary assembly sequences relative to specific construction techniques.*
• *Develop an understanding of fabrication processes, tools, and established communication procedures.*
• *Understand the means by which building systems and assemblies influence one another.*
• *Understand the implied possibilities implicit in transferring a material from one application to another.*
• *Demonstrate an understanding of the physical and social context that guides building construction.*
• *Understand the environmental, historical, and cultural impact on an applied tectonic language.*
• *Develop an ability to investigate the built environment through a series of detailed drawings.*

Context

Organized around the goal of developing an awareness of the built environment, *'Architectural Systems'* examines the means by which materials, assemblies, and context influence design thinking. The course initially presents topics that explore the elemental qualities of physical building components and the varying processes by which they are both manufactured and standardized. This beginning inquiry is built upon through additional topics that investigate the parameters and possibilities by which components may be combined. Contextual questions related to environment, cultural methodology, and proximity are introduced through historical case studies. Drawing on this knowledge, assignments provide an opportunity for creative synthesis based on unique design queries. The assignments intend to engage a tectonic language and seek to establish a vocabulary capable of communicating complex issues of selection, technique, fabrication, and assembly. The course utilizes the decision processes inherent in the act of drawing and aspires to address the many associations essential to developing architecture.

The material presentations offer a foundation of knowledge intrinsic to an architectural process of formulating questions and making decisions. Each presentation is structured around three categories titled 'Properties, Manufacturing, and Standards'. The objective is to develop an understanding of natural materials, the methods by which they are transformed, and then subsequently regulated.

'Properties' focuses on basic material attributes. Classifications are presented to relate material types of similar qualities as in the cases of hardwood and softwood or ferrous and non-ferrous metals. Compositions are introduced to reveal a commonality of elements across materials as evidenced in the silica, soda, and lime makeup of glass in comparison to the lime, alumina, and silica makeup of a brick. Attributes are specified to define unique material characteristics of strength, stability, and performance. Awareness of distinct aspects of strength, such as compression and tension, are vital to the selection of concrete, steel, or wood structural components. The stability of materials is important to ensure dependable enclosures and requires the separation of certain metals, especially aluminum and steel, to prevent galvanic action. Understanding the performance characteristics of a material, including expansion and contraction, is critical to proposing appropriate components in response to specific environmental conditions. Each of these aspects plays a pivotal role in the inquiry towards why a specific material is appropriate for a particular application.

'Manufacturing' highlights techniques that have been used to transform primary material elements into composite building materials. A historical evolution of fabrication technologies, from manual to mechanized processes, is presented to address advancements in quality, time, and expense. One example is the

advancement of masonry production processes from soft-mud to stiff-mud to dry-press to the highly automated contemporary brick fabrication assembly line. These modern assembly production sequences are shown to articulately describe the current practices of converting raw materials into finished building components as illustrated in the process of producing float glass or rolled steel sections. The location where materials originate and how they are extracted from specific sites is emphasized. Of significant importance to understanding the management of natural resource sites such as forests or mines are issues of sustainability. Sustainable matters in question include harvesting expenditures, renewability of resources, site resiliency, and relative locale. Understanding the processes, including energy expenditure and renewability, by which materials are brought into existence is vital to asking why a material is suitable to a certain demand.

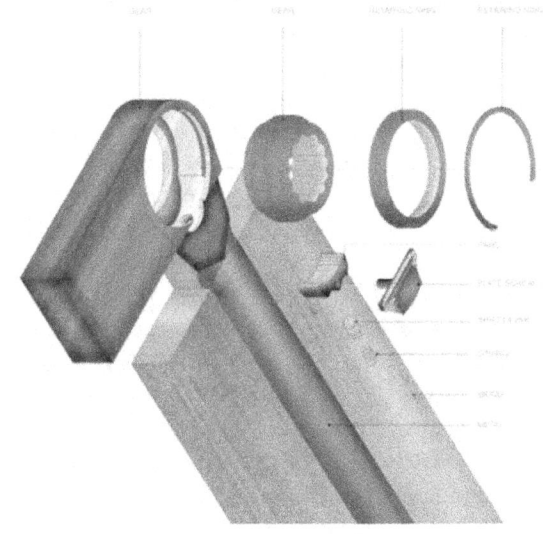

Fig. 2 Exploded connection detail

'Standards' concentrates on the norms, customs, and regulations to which building components are manufactured. Benchmark dimensions of wood, steel, concrete, masonry, and glass are considered as a set of parameters to work with in the development of architectural concepts. An awareness of nominal and dressed wood dimensions provides a relevant link between the manufacturing processes and the regulated sizing nomenclature. The intrinsic necessity of buildings to transfer loads from the structure to the ground is similarly based on an understanding of sizes. In steel construction, simple rules of thumb can be used as a way to preliminary size components and realize the dimensional impact of design goals. Steel shapes ranging from a W-section to a tube are similarly significant in the determination of structural performance. Material types are presented to realize that material properties are commonly modified and specialized to meet the demands of particular applications. The modification of annealed glass to heat strengthened or tempered exemplifies the refashioning of a material to meet specific security needs. Quality specification and determination is a critical part of the construction process as represented by the process of cylinder testing concrete samples over a series of daily intervals. Correspondingly, material grading is a method used to specify the strength or appearance of a building component and is often linked to the means by which it is distributed and sold as is in the case of timber. A cognitive understanding of the standards that articulate material properties is fundamental to inquiring why certain physical attributes are necessary to achieve unique design decisions.

The assembly presentations are of equal importance in the learning of knowledge that is essential to the processes of formulating questions and proposing techniques. The presentations are structured around categories of architectural components titled *Foundations, Floors, Walls, and Roofs'*. The aspiration is to achieve a level of knowledge that can be applied in the development of constructible building systems.

Foundations' focuses on the means by which an interface between buildings and the ground they are placed within is established. An understanding of both land composition and building characteristics is critical to how they come together. An analysis of soil classes and types is discussed to reveal that a particular site may be made up of various materials with differing characteristics. The different behavior of fine or course material is critical to the load bearing capacity of a soil. Likewise, the contrasting performances of sand and gravel to silt and clay play a vital role in soil stability. The composition of the material that supports a structure plays a key role in the transmission of live and dead loads from the building to the earth. The importance of geographic location is introduced as a factor in the determination

of a particular foundation type. The knowledge of Northern freeze and thaw cycles bares a relevant factor in the degree to which a foundation extends into the earth, necessitating foundation designs of greater depth compared to Southern regions with warmer climates. All of these attributes contribute to the formulation of questions into why a particular set of foundation specifications is needed for a specific building site.

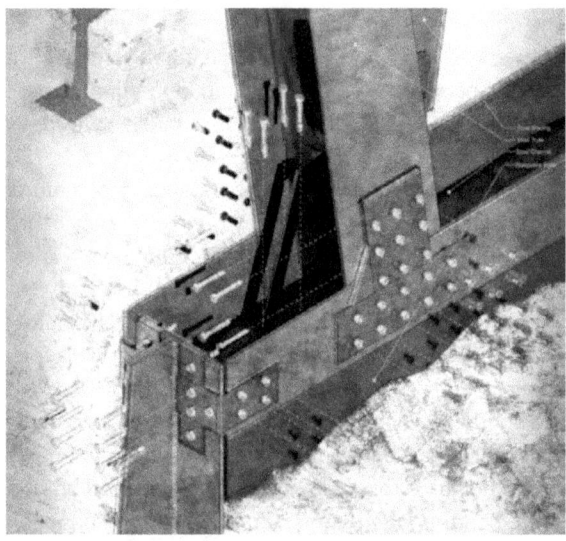

Fig. 3 Exploded foundation assembly

Floors' is centered on structural concepts and explores the spanning capacity of beams, joists, and slab compositions. Wood, metal, and concrete components are presented along with the relative merits of each material. Wood framing standards are oriented relative to individual applications to call attention to questions of performance relative to corresponding joist span and depth. An investigation of different framing types leads to questions and tradeoffs associated with considerations of schedule, economics, and aesthetics. Metal systems are similarly presented through questions of performance linked to different types of structural members as seen in the application of W-section beams to transfer heavier loads and open web joists to transfer lighter loads. The use of a moment or shear steel connection is investigated as a response to resolving structural forces of varying floor configurations as in the case of cantilevered areas. Properties of concrete elements are described to apprehend the strength and means by which forces are transferred through different slab configurations. Recognition of precise attributes of structural capacity is vital to the selection of a slab type, such as flat plate or waffle, relative to specific programmatic requirements.

'Walls' discusses assembly types oriented around the many plies that define the multiple layers of an enclosure system. Both the structural and insulating properties of wood, metal, masonry, concrete, and glass components are considered. For example, wood is a material with limited load bearing capacity compared to steel, masonry, or concrete, but it's ease of on site workability make it a common selection for small structures. Also, relative to the other materials, the cellular composition of wood acts as a thermal barrier reducing a temperature exchange from one side of a wall to the other. Metal framing has the capacity to carry great loads while having the advantages of being lightweight, noncombustible, and damp proof. The capacity of structural steel shapes to carry greater loads makes them a frequent selection for large structures, however the performance of the components under high heat requires added layers of fire protection. Load bearing masonry walls perform well in compression, but a reduced capacity to transfer tensile forces requires the inclusion of lintels to form openings. With the pairing of steel and concrete walls perform well in both compression and tension, however the process of forming and curing is often not cost effective and beyond scheduling constraints. An understanding of the structural role a component can play and how it responds to environmental conditions is key to questioning why it is applicable to a particular use.

Comparable to 'Walls', 'Roofs' are assembly types that can also be described as a series of layers in the composition of an enclosure. The oblique surface, with a minimal required slope to manage runoff, must transfer dead and live loads and protect against environmental conditions. Questions of where a wall ends and a roof begins are critical to adequately shedding water off a building and preventing inundation. The parapet is the resolution of this meeting and can result in a range of connection details from the unnoticeable to the profound. Roofs are constructed by way of both tectonic and stereotomic systems. The selection of a technique has as much to do with local culture and traditions as an economy of means. A roof can be viewed as the

culmination of a building proposal, take on many forms, be both structurally and environmentally responsive, and conceptually guide a design inquiry from formulation to constructed outcome.

Assignments

The assignments intend to link the course learning objectives and activities through the application of knowledge in a series of drawings that respond to specific architectural questions. The questions are presented as sequential investigations toward the development of drawings that begin by exploring material attributes, then incorporate assembly techniques, and culminate with the inclusion of environmental conditions. The goal is to put into practice presented knowledge, approaches, and circumstances in the formulation of unique architectural proposals.

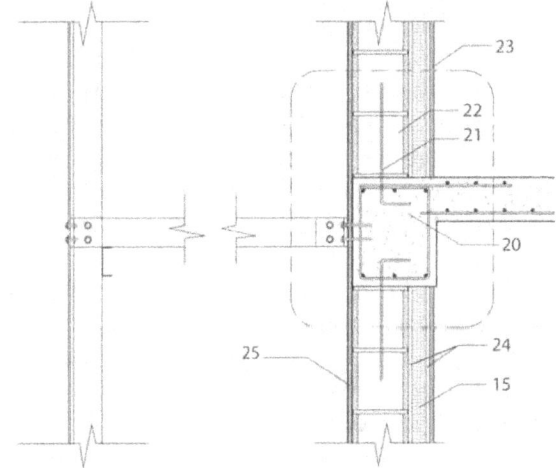

Fig. 4 Wall section

The initial inquiry is based on the development of a wall section drawing that communicates the integration of systems required to meet the specific needs of a design generated by each student in studio coursework. The wall section is intended to be holistic and include all necessary components in the composition of foundation, wall, floor, and roof assemblies. Special consideration is given to questions of materials, structure, enclosure, and construction. Drawing explorations focus on materials with unique qualities and how they are assembled to communicate a clear architectural proposal. Ideas of structure and enclosure are advanced relative to one another and take into consideration specific site conditions by way of drawn layers in each assembly composition. The processes of sequencing construction and assembling material components are researched and expressed through conventions of line styles and weights. This initial set of drawings strives to investigate the integration of and relationships between site conditions, material qualities, structural forces, and construction processes.

Continuing the focus on a unique design generated by each student, the subsequent inquiry is established on the development of a series of detail drawings that present the interface between primary building components. These details include the connections of foundation to wall, wall to floor, and roof to wall. The details aspire to show the connections between components as part of the multiple systems necessary in the articulation of a design proposal. Attention is now given to questions of materials, structure, enclosure, and construction at a finer scale. Drawings seek to emphasize the connections between materials and why certain affiliations are appropriate. A series of joints between the structure and enclosure are included in the drawings as an expression of exterior and interior environmental conditions. The process of installing connection fasteners is understood through the drawing of spaces and gaps to illustrate construction tolerances. This iteration of drawings develops enlarged detail connections in the demonstration of a tectonic language equally responsive to material logics and environmental conditions.

The culminating inquiry is positioned on the generation of a comprehensive exploded perspective drawing that includes the specific components of foundation, wall, floor, and roof along with the necessary connections to define and communicate the process of assembly. The exploded perspective continues the design exploration into the unique proposals of each student based on materials and techniques and orients the process of assembly within an exact contextual framework. The final series of drawing iterations works with the following questions that strive toward a synthesis of previous investigations and incorporates the complex set of contextual parameters deep-rooted in the practice of constructing architecture.

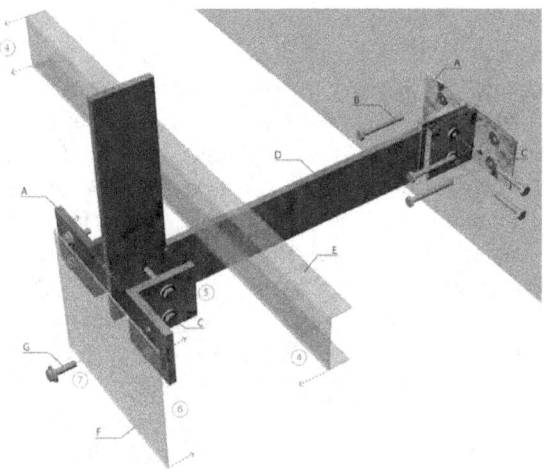

Fig. 6 Exploded wall assembly

Material attributes profoundly define the experiential process of building. The human scale of a brick allows it to be placed and set by hand. The heavy weight of a beam requires mechanization for alignment and placement. The soft density of a stone necessitates a delicacy of handling. The hot temperature of asphalt defines the temporal extent of application. The sharp edge of glass mandates cautionary and protective measures. Can the ability to develop a sensibility for the application of materials, linked to their distinct properties, be revealed in 1:1 drawing?

Assembly techniques delineate the construction sequences in the performance of building. Connections are an outcome of the actions utilized in placing materials and the detail is the confluence of

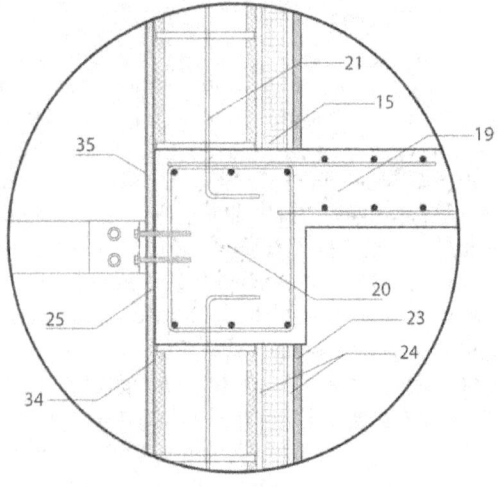

Fig. 5 Detail

these histories. Joinery describes a relation between specific surface conditions and an understanding of tolerances. Fasteners elucidate material properties through the movement and resistance of securing. Can 1:1 drawing promote the ability to comprehend necessary assembly sequences relative to specific construction techniques?

Environmental conditions impact the routine and course of actions in the feat of building. Temperature can make unavoidable the restrictive use of additional layers that slow movement. Moisture and temperature impact soil consistency and the ease of workability. Wind can impinge precision causing hazardous conditions and increased production time. Can 1:1 drawing demonstrate an understanding of the physical context that guides building construction?

Results

The opening question proposed by the course, *"How can an understanding of material attributes, assembly techniques, and environmental conditions inherent in the 'act' of 1:1 building be evidenced in the 'act' of 1:1 drawing?"*, inspired drawing investigations founded in an understanding of natural order, a system of repetitive takes, and an aspiration for conclusive results. The assignment outcomes are a materialization of the goal to simultaneously investigate materials, assemblies, and context intrinsic in the act of building through the act of drawing. Knowledge of material properties, fabrication practices, and component standards gave way to design proposals grounded in actual real world parameters. Along with illustrating the relationship between dimensioned architectural components, the drawings also represent projected interactions between adjacent materials and environmental conditions. The drawings are enriched with a myriad of surface textures, hues, and values that bring to light a series of both temporal and performance questions.

An understanding of assembly methods and precise construction sequences resulted in the development of buildable connection details with an allowable amount of room for fabricators to maneuver. The effect of drawing connection fasteners installed and then pulled apart along sequential lines of assembly brings in an understanding of the necessary

tolerances to the picture. The drawings visually illustrate the means by which an assembly goes together. Realization of contextual factors allowed for appropriate design strategies relative to specific environmental and cultural conditions. Geographic location is annotated as *'degrees North'* with probable atmospheric conditions both rendered and reflected in the materials. This approach sheds light on the individual experience of putting together components within a variety of contextual factors. The methodology of staging assignments with complimentary objectives innately reinforces a cyclical process of applying knowledge, reflecting critically, and then reapplying design strategies with a revised awareness. The series of drawings that commence with wall sections that address architectural components, then move to details that speak to connections between components, and then advance to exploded axonometric diagrams that articulate sequencing allow for a continued focus on a subject through the perspective of multiple frames. The resulting architectural drawings reveal a gradual refinement of initially proposed design and construction strategies.

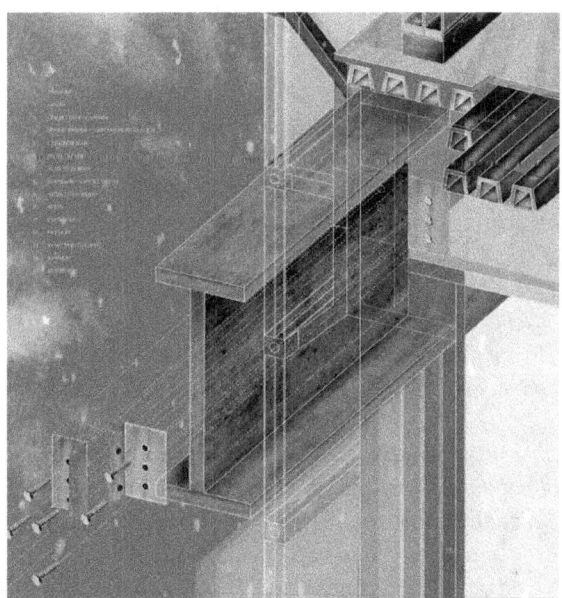

Fig. 7 Exploded floor to wall connection

Conclusion

To conclude, a personal learning assessment was developed by each student through reflecting on three considerations expressed in the following question. *In the exploded perspective drawing, qualitative characteristics of material attributes, assembly techniques, and environmental conditions were investigated as a means to further explore the quantitative attributes of size, dimension, and connections from the wall section and detail drawings. In what ways did the three considerations of sensibility, sequence, & context transform how you think about building assemblies?* The written contemplations offer an insight into the learning of each distinct individual.

Sensibility, for the application of materials:

"*My great revelation was how materials do not exist in a vacuum. Steel conducts heat from the sun. Wood expands when rained on. You can choose certain materials to work along side the environment, you don't have to fight it.*"

"*I began to understand in real life how something would be built which added to my understanding of what the limits of a building supposedly are and how I can engage and challenge that.*"

Sequence, relative to construction techniques:

"*In creating the detailed axon and wall sections, there was a lot of change in scale. The whole structure has to make sense as well as the placement of a bolt. I found it easiest to start from the bottom and work upward because it makes you think about the actual construction of your building.*"

"*Cliché as it is buildings don't appear out of thin air. Thought has to be put into what is first what is second and so on.*"

"*It was impossible while I was drawing to not think about the assembly and construction sequence of the material components. In this way I feel the exploded axon is really great in trying to understand how things would actually be constructed.*"

"*There was order in a process that didn't exist beforehand. I would begin to understand the logic of structure and visualize it somewhat like Tetris.*"

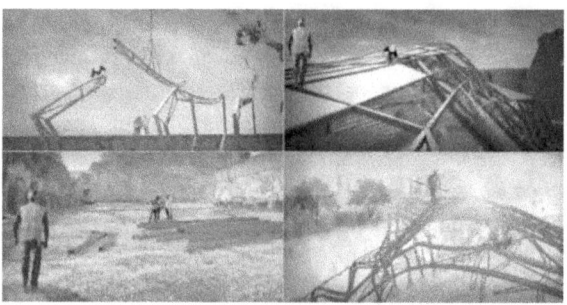

Fig. 8 Construction sequencing

Context, that guides building construction:

"*Considering the environment of Chicago helps to determine the materials used to compose the buildings, but also how they would actually be constructed. Different locations have different requirements for their buildings. Structure in many ways expresses the people within a region.*"

"*While people are out in the world constructing our beautiful creations the weather doesn't always cooperate. We need to understand the sequencing so fully that we can begin to alleviate outside variables for the people trying to assemble these buildings.*"

Through the learning outcomes and learning assessments it is evident that the systemic application of knowledge, exemplified by the process of drawing, acted as a linkage between the learning objectives and the learning outcomes. Inspired by the individual inquisitiveness of the students the investigations uncovered unique conditions relative to a specific context. The iterative process of questioning the subject and developing the drawings shifted the course focus from teaching to the eccentric learning of each individual design student.

Notes:
Fig. 1 Tina Naraghi-Pour, LSU School of Architecture.
Fig. 2 Xueru Lan, LSU School of Architecture.
Fig. 3 James Babin, LSU School of Architecture.
Fig. 4 Fernando Chavez, LSU School of Architecture.
Fig. 5 Fernando Chavez, LSU School of Architecture.
Fig. 6 Fernando Chavez, LSU School of Architecture.
Fig. 7 Madeline Luke, LSU School of Architecture.
Fig. 8 James Babin, LSU School of Architecture.

Digital Integration: Synthesizing Poetic Possibilities and Pragmatic Production

Vincent Hui, Jennifer McArthur and Pierre-Alexandre Le Lay
Department of Architectural Science, Ryerson University

Abstract

Digital workflows and emerging technologies in architectural praxis are undergoing a convergence. Virtual reality (VR), augmented reality (AR), and other immersive visualization and simulation technologies empower architecture students in literally rendering a virtual world of poetic possibilities. As if in parallel, the increased ubiquity and integration of building information modeling (BIM) and advanced digital fabrication serve as excellent tools in the pragmatic production of the built world. It behooves architectural educators to deliver curricula that empowers and acclimatizes students with the spectrum of these digital technologies in the synthesis of architecture. Unfortunately, architectural pedagogy often fails to do so. The authors of this paper contend that these tools are excellent complements to conventional architectural pedagogy rather than incompatible, esoteric supplements. Beginning with an integrated digital design tools in first year design studio to a standardized adoption of BIM and contract documents, the authors outline an extremely successful architectural curriculum that actively integrates digital technologies to ensure students are capable and comfortable with pragmatic production without compromising poetic intention. This presentation serves as a case study and provides a framework for best practices in integrating current digital technologies (including AR, VR, BIM, and embedded technologies) as a complementary component of a core architecture program. The impacts on key student performance criteria including output, design sensitivity, feasibility, documentation, and engagement highlight the potential of integrating a strong digital convergence in contemporary architectural pedagogy.

Introduction

Architecture as a discipline has always been amenable to the integration of technological advances. From the structural and construction marvels of Otto and Gaudi to the parametric feats of Schumacher and Fornes, a small vanguard of architects have drawn the poetic through to production. Ironically, architecture as a profession has been slow to do so. It is hard to imagine that even in Canada at the turn of the 21st century, design information was "still exchanged in its traditional form (i.e. hardcopy drawings and documents) while other professions had digitized the majority of their workflows.[1] The proliferation of, and accessibility to, industry-changing technologies has increased dramatically over the past decade, specifically within architectural curricula. Though some technologies were quite powerful at extending the capacities of representation or development of architectural design (such as with immersive caves and advanced packages such as CATIA), they often struggled in their integration into curricula on account of costs or capacity. More recently, the disparate technologies available to architecture students have consolidated. From industry-standard file formats and workflows (e.g. BIM and CAD/CAM formats) to consistent hardware expectations (e.g. laptops, smartphones, fabrication facilities) digital workflows and emerging technologies in architectural praxis are undergoing a convergence. The synthesis of these factors lay the framework for an exciting reformation in architectural education where a greater fidelity between the poetics of design and the pragmatics of production.

The foundations of poetics in architectural praxis are not exclusive to the ephemeral, metaphysical, or aesthetic components of design; rather it is the ability to bring these ideas to a higher level of resolution, if not reality, within real world networks that distinguishes it from simply visual art. While architectural pedagogy prioritizes the poetic demands of studio, it remains a single curricular component complemented by a range of other courses focused on the resolution of these ideas, ranging from materials and methods to sustainable practices. Accreditation and licensing have mandated a level of standardization and consistency in what is taught, however the methods, specifically with the integration of digital technologies, differ greatly from one program to another.

For centuries, the portfolio of architectural design, development, documentation, and delivery tools were constant and consistent. As digital technologies entered the workflow, students and practitioners alike gained access to entire ecosystems of products to support their creative outputs. CAD, CAM, and BIM packages grant students with the ability to generate not only high fidelity representations of a built project, but have completely created entire subsets of digital design. Accessible modeling and visualization software skills have become commodities in contemporary architectural education. To digitally reproduce and emulate a "Star"-chitect's latest icon can be done by any "digital native", let alone an architecture student, with ease if given the time and software. For contemporary architecture students, any design can be made into convincing imagery. The leap from 2D representations to immersive environments has resurfaced on account of the new baseline for software skill and dramatically diminishing hardware costs.

Contemporary Architectural Pedagogical Practice

If one were to remove the advances in technology, architectural pedagogy has remained fairly constant for generations. It is a "rinse-and-repeat" model of teaching. Whether correct or not, design studio is prioritized over other courses by faculty and students, and typically concurrently taught with a constellation of complementary courses in history/theory and materials/methods. Each subsequent term simply presents students a different, complex building typology while coursework simply further delves into the respective course materials. It is a repetitive cycle. For some programs, a model of breaking from this pedagogical monotony is simply the injection of technologies. Often these are seen as pedagogical "gimmicks" as opposed to appropriate foundational tools that aggregate over a student's academic career. In a global study on creativity catalysts in architecture design studios, researchers showcased the failings of short term technological introductions. At best it was seen as yet another medium for "motivating creativity" and at worst computing technologies were relegated as artifacts that "are not diligently applied and also not formally incorporated in the curricula".[2]

Distinguished sociologists Palfrey and Gasser, authors of the "*Born Digital*" series describe the dilemma contemporary educators face with adopting technologies into curricula, essentially the need to think beyond the "cool" factor of technology and understand their value in accomplishing pedagogical goals.[2] Though far from extensive, the following is a review of notable work and authorities on new technologies in architectural pedagogy. These all serve to underscore the fundamental issue raised by Palfrey and Gasser – these technologies are excellent supports for architectural education and synthesis yet they must support and fulfill an integrated pedagogical goal. Unfortunately, despite the best of intentions these technologies fail to do so.

Virtual & Augmented Reality

There is a great deal of exciting innovations emerging in architectural practice and pedagogy that showcase the various ways technologies can potentially change methods of design, detailing, and delivery. In many instances, these initiatives are isolated to a single course. From individual faculty members dabbling in digital electives with Google cardboards to the tech-saturated HCI (human-computer interface) prototypes utilized in the *Tecton 3D* project, architectural educators are integrating emerging technologies into their classrooms.[3] Unfortunately for various reasons, including a lack of resources, institutional inertia, and operational sustainability, widespread adoption and integration of these technologies throughout an architecture program have yet to occur.

In a recent comprehensive global survey of over 200 papers on AR/VR use in architecture, the authors conclude that the strengths of the platforms lie in the visualization and collaborative potential while cautioning the need for promotion and innovation within architectural pedagogy. "*VR and AR have been yet fully incorporated in architectural practice, despite its almost half century of existence and evolution in other technical areas. Education is an important driving force promoting technology appropriation in practice.*"[4] It is incumbent on architectural educators to reaffirm and direct the adoption of these technologies for future generations of practitioners.

There is a great deal of potential between architecture and augmented reality beyond visualization and design refinement. Similar to the early adoption and evolution of BIM in the AEC industry from a tool for efficiency between drawing, modeling, and coordination, to a system of project oversight throughout a building's lifecycle, new directions in the adoption of AR for construction, regulatory compliance, and facilities management and operations are emerging and will be critical tools in architectural practice.[5] This will be explored in future applications to further strengthen the three specializations of architecture, building science, and project management in the Architectural Science program. Though VR and AR technologies are appropriate for architectural applications and pedagogy, the landscape has been quite volatile. Only recently has platform and media convergence harmonized a once overpopulated ecosystem of VR and AR software. Hardware improvements in mobile computing and white-labeling of technologies (VR headsets and HD cameras) have also dramatically reduced costs for adoption by students and schools alike. It is imperative for educators to capitalize on this moment to integrate these technologies properly into their curricula.

Building Information Modeling

While Building Information Modeling (BIM) has been developing as early as the 1980's, it has become the definitive paradigm of the AEC industry within the past decade. Advanced modeling and parametric tools are no longer the exclusive arsenal of Foster or Gehry, but currently reside in even a modest proprietorship. Foreseeing the incredible paradigm shift that would emerge due to the transition from CAD to BIM workflows, the AEC industries were generally receptive to adopt and learn. In the early days of BIM, its adoption in architecture programs was niche with a few exceptions.

One celebrated program was run between Penn State University and Autodesk (Revit) in the integrated BIM curriculum, which effectively dispensed with BIM work throughout several undergraduate studios and even professional courses. Survey data from students and faculty indicated a great value in BIM integration in the curriculum regarding design, visualization, analysis, and collaboration.[6] Despite the program's success and availability of pedagogical assets, BIM tools remain esoteric to many studio faculty and worse still, carry the stigma of compromising students' design opportunities.

Authorities on BIM from Briscoe to Deutsch, have shattered the AEC "misconception that BIM is about production, not design" and instead integrates a network of design considerations including sustainability and operations.[7,8] Though its use is rapidly saturating the AEC industry, inexplicably the majority of architecture programs do not adequately provide a consistent BIM curriculum on account of "pedagogical issues such as assignments, tutoring methods, engagement, and assessment methods and criteria". For example, in Canada, of the twelve architecture degree programs, only one has a standardized BIM curriculum that exposes students to the design implications and execution capacities of BIM through multiple courses.[8]

Simply demanding that students execute their final capstone projects using BIM or foisting its use during industry internships is neither effective nor consistent yet those are two models many architecture programs use to validate fulfillment of accreditation criteria. As with the initial adoption of CAD before the turn of the century, merely using the tools does not engender innovation or industry leadership. BIM, as with many of the emerging technologies in this paper, facilitates more than representation of ideas; rather it holds opportunity for design innovation, simulation, and ultimately facilitation of pragmatic production.

Digital Fabrication & Embedded Technologies

The widespread adoption of digital fabrication in architectural programs emerged as a response to the existent framework of architectural pedagogy – creating scaled representations of architectural ideas. From laser cutters and 3D printers to CNC routers and robotic arms, these technologies gained traction due to their production efficacy and precision. Fortunately academics including Kolarevic and Iwamoto were able to champion the imminent ubiquity of these technologies in professional practice thereby reaffirming the relationship between translating architectural concepts to built form.[9] Their works and those of their contemporaries showcased a range of methods and materials that demonstrated the widespread use of digital fabrication on full scale projects by the largest multinational firms to proprietorships, to even small student groups.[10]

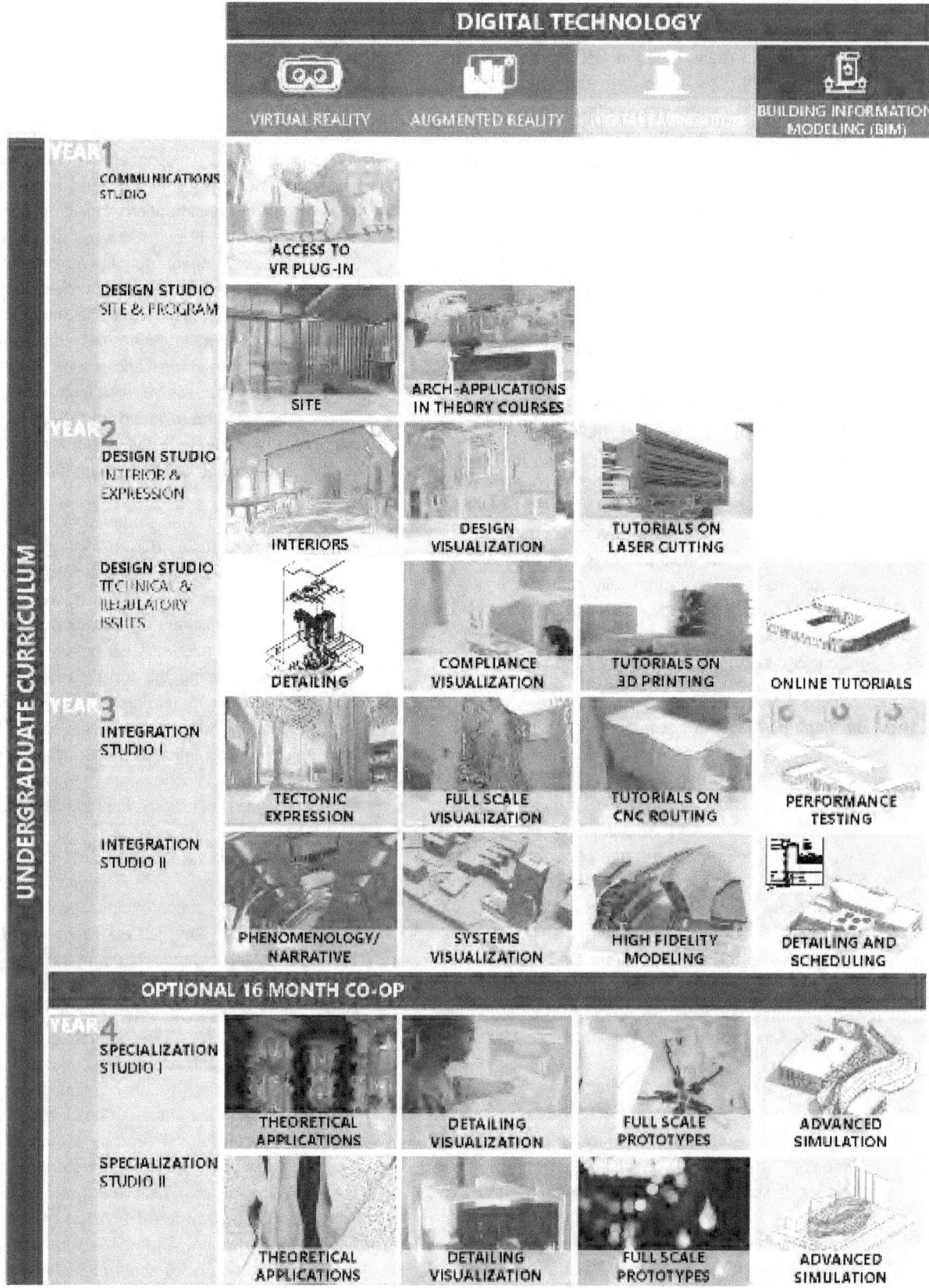

Fig. 1. Digitally-Enhanced Curriculum at Ryerson University's Department of Architectural Science.

The adoption of digital fabrication in generating scale architectural representations is now understood as the most rudimentary adoption of these tools. Instead it is in rare design-build opportunities that most students are able to successfully bring their ideas to reality. The scarcity of and resource intensity in design-build projects often mire the ability for students to bring their early design work beyond imagery. Worse still, the inconsistency in scale and scope of available projects has made program administrators question the value of these initiatives despite their growing popularity.[11]

The accessibility of digital fabrication and full scale construction has also afforded many architecture programs to facilitate not only architectural innovation and exploration in materials and methods, but also with embedded technologies. From physical computing to smart materials, a range of technologies hybridizing the conventional portfolio of architectural media has emerged over the past two decades. Whether inspired by Kieran Timberlake's *SmartWrap* or prototypes by Bob Sheil, students, educators, and practitioners have witnessed the rapid integration of embedded technologies (from the mundane array of products connected via the Internet of Things to responsive façade systems) and realize its value in contemporary architectural pedagogy.[12] Unfortunately, much like design-build initiatives, these pedagogical opportunities are often incumbent on specific faculty and isolated to their respective courses as opposed to dispensed with throughout a student's academic life. That courses engaging physical computing and smart materials often require a great deal of investment in consumables, fabrication, and equipment also proves to be a challenge many programs, despite the best of intentions and enthusiasm, fail to adequately address.

Digitally-Enhanced Architectural Curriculum

This paper presents a digitally-enhanced architecture curriculum delivered at Ryerson University. It is neither a perfect nor a complete solution. The digitally-enhanced curriculum at Ryerson University did not emerge in a vacuum. Studies on architectural adoption of digital workflows and innovations outline two key success factors: a) the engagement of internal influencers (one study referred to it as "copying behaviors"), and b) the mandates of external forces (ranging from standards from professional bodies to

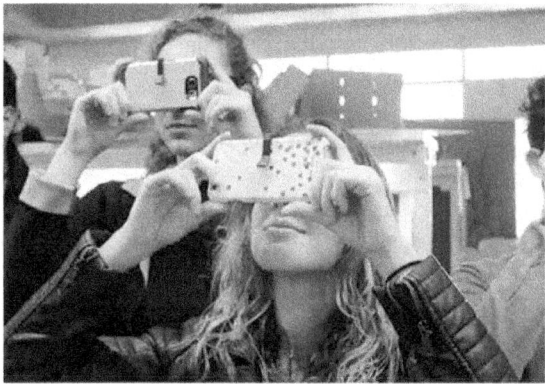
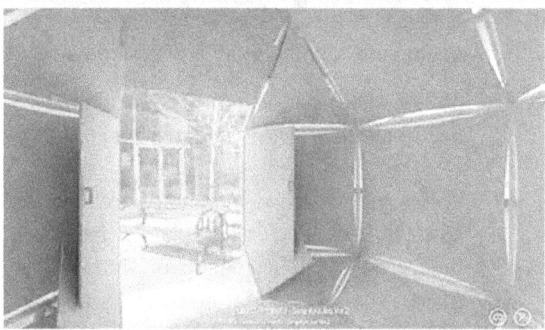
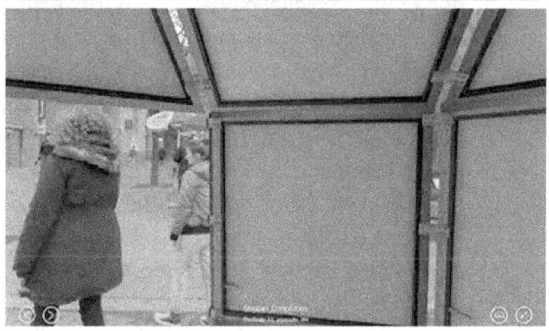

Fig. 2. Virtual Reality Use and Incremental Design Development in First Year Studio.

market demand).[13] As the largest architecture program in Canada with a robust co-op program and connections to the profession, the curriculum is a reflection of faculty initiatives, research, and foresight, as well as input from students and industry.

Ryerson University's Architectural Science program is accredited by the CACB (Canadian Architectural Certification Board) and is unique in that it fulfills all the accreditation core criteria within the first three years and is followed by a fourth year whereupon students may take courses in order to specialize in Architecture, Building Science, or Project Management. Between the three year core curriculum and the fourth year specialization there is an optional 16-month cooperative education work term where students in the top 20% of each class gain work experience in the AEC industry.

Ryerson University Architectural Science Program

As illustrated in Figure 1, the undergraduate studios and notable courses are where components of the digitally-enhanced curriculum are introduced and reinforced. Ryerson University's curriculum emulates what has already been described where each term consists of a studio and complementary courses pertaining the history/theory and materials/methods.

photoediting, and layout (the Adobe Suite) via a series of tutorials (online and in class).

Within the first three months of entering the program, students are also introduced to the workflows and theory behind the creation of virtual reality environments. Already familiar and comfortable with the fundamentals of digital modeling and rendering, students utilize a virtual reality plugin, Yulio, that creates cube maps that effectively can be viewed on any computing device, including cell phones. As nearly all students have smart phones, Yulio accounts, and the appropriate software, the method of VR production is extremely accessible. Combined with the low cost of VR goggles and displays and the installation of a headset in each studio section (supporting 15 students), barriers to visualizing and sharing VR experiences were reduced. Within the first term of their architectural education, students in the program are able to go beyond conventional methods of design development and presentation, and literally transport themselves and critics into their designs.

From student surveys, the vast majority of participants gained a "greater sense of design resolution" than their peers who did not use the technologies. The immersive ability of VR provided students an early insight on everything from the scale of space, nature of materials, illumination, details, and even functional programming that often escapes first year students usually more preoccupied with developing iconic, monumental design proposals (Figure 2).

The use of VR is reinforced in the subsequent first year studio where a focus on Site and Program man-

First Year Implementation

The first year Communications Studio course lays the foundation of architectural representation and communications via modest design proposals (ranging from variations on Hejduk's 9 square grid to the design of a small info kiosk). Sketches, physical models, and manual drafting are techniques introduced to students in order to provide an appreciation of conveying design ideas in accordance to convention with some license. The communications studio is also where students are taught computer design skills including digital modeling (Rhino), rendering (VRay

dates use of VR to explore and demonstrate an awareness of appropriate ephemeral qualities ranging from materiality, structure and tectonics to site factors such as solar orientation and views.

In addition to the use of VR in first year, the term introduces students to the use of the Arch-App whereupon students can use their mobile phones to explore building data throughout the city. By holding up a phone to a notable landmark in the city, the Arch-App allows users to view historic data, drawings, and even structural information. In tandem with their history/theory courses, instructors also mandate that students not only use the AR technology to view content but also create reports that would serve as content for future generations of students using the AR software. This AR app has been utilized by not only the architecture student population, but has gained traction in other departments and institutions as well as the general public.

Second Year Implementation

Within the second year curriculum, the first term focuses upon Intention and Expression. Concurrent with courses in building construction, envelope systems, and theory focused on the underpinnings of modernism, the studio demands a greater insight on reinforcing the poetics of space using VR models as well as the conventional methods of presenting design work. The accessibility of immersion that VR provides at this point in students' education allows them to virtually enter their peers' designs and provide feedback loops at a far finer level of articulation than what has been explored in the past.

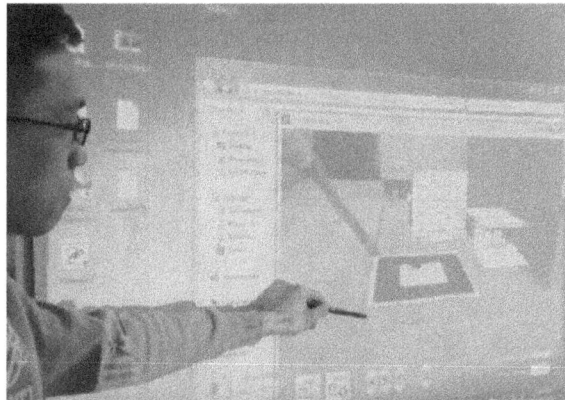

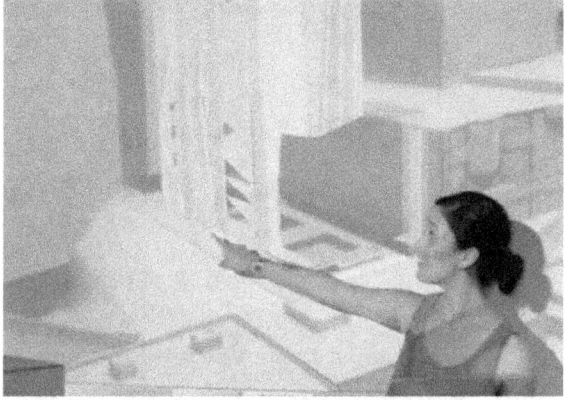

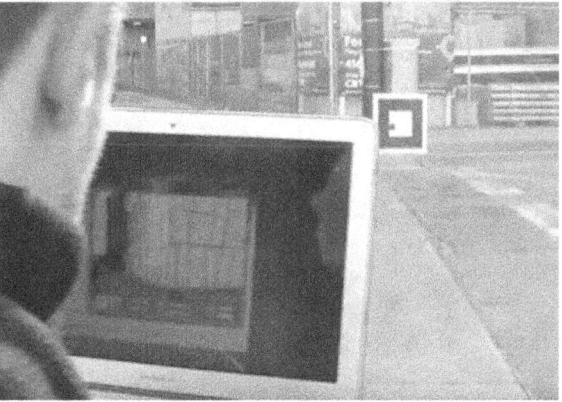

Fig. 3. Augmented Reality Use in Second Year Design Studio Validating Design and Technical/Regulatory Compliance.

Beyond the VR tools established in first year, second year is also where students are introduced to the use of AR with the Augmented Reality in Design Development (ARIDD) software. Already familiar with creation of digital models, students are able to use the AR software to visualize and superimpose their digital designs for various purposes. Whether visualizing their work relative to zoning conditions, comparing different designs against each other on a shared

physical model, or even visualizing a project on the real site, augmented reality is instrumental in allowing students to better understand and communicate their designs relative to real world constraints (Figure 3). The success of the ARIDD project has aligned with the research outcomes of other architecture programs' use of mobile and ubiquitous computing for augmented and virtual reality applications which have merited notable "improved academic achievement" by participants on a range of facets including design detail awareness, context sensitivity, and design development/refinement. [14]

Second year also marks the point in the curriculum where students are familiar with digital workflows to transition their virtual digital designs to physical representation via digital fabrication techniques. Laser cutting and 3D printing are made accessible to students in order to produce precise, scaled models. These subtractive and additive fabrication methods are taught via online video tutorials as well as sessions undertaken by the workshop staff. These low-cost fabrication tools establish a comfort with production and open channels for greater design exploration and experimentation in subsequent studios.

The second year studio also marks the standardized introduction of BIM to the students and is integrated in both the studio and mechanical systems course. Typically, this studio engages a multi-unit residential typology (e.g. student housing, mixed-use apartments, etc.), which is conducive to the platform and is of a scale that warrants BIM capacities. Once again students are provided a series of BIM software tutorials (Revit) that they go through at their own pace fully aware of the value it has on their studio and other courses. The coordination between studio and the mechanical and structures courses allowed students to integrate knowledge from courses into studio and vice versa. For example, students would have to create initial mechanical and structural layouts based upon their typical residential units. The use of BIM familiarizes students with the tool as a design, modeling, and visualization platform as well as introduces them to the robust features that bring their designs closer to a feasible reality such as detailing and systems coordination.

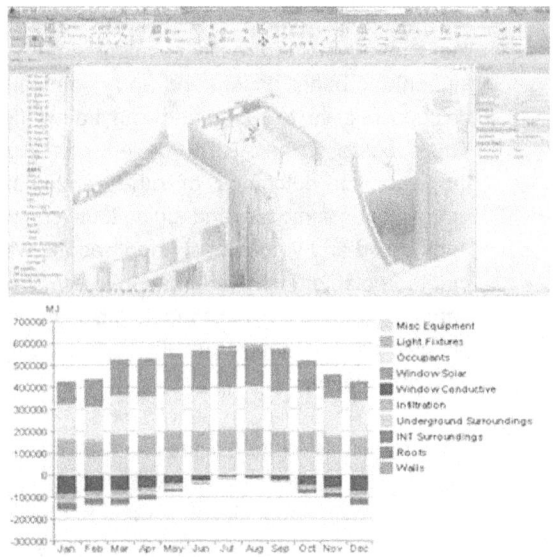

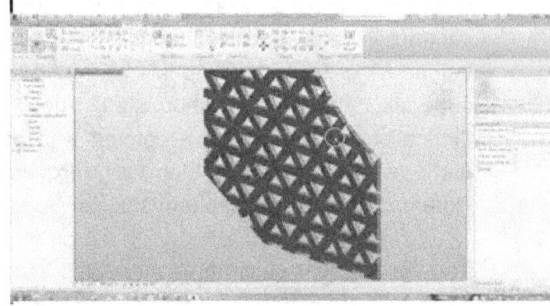

Monthly Cooling Load

Fig. 4. BIM Use in Third Year Studio Overseeing Design Exploration, Documentation, and Simulation.

Third Year Implementation

The third year of the program is a comprehensive, integration studio with a standardized adoption of BIM in the studio as well as in supporting courses such as contract documents and project management. While AR, VR, and fabrication skills developed in the previous two years are incorporated in the design and development of architectural intent in third year, due to the volume and level of resolution of the studio project, students must use BIM to thoroughly design, document, simulate, and validate the feasibility of their design work. The third year integration studio is the culmination of all the digital technologies available to the students and equips students to implement a broad spectrum of BIM uses beyond design authoring and documentation. To further root this teaching in praxis, a BIM Curriculum Development Toolkit has been developed, consisting of a series of interviews

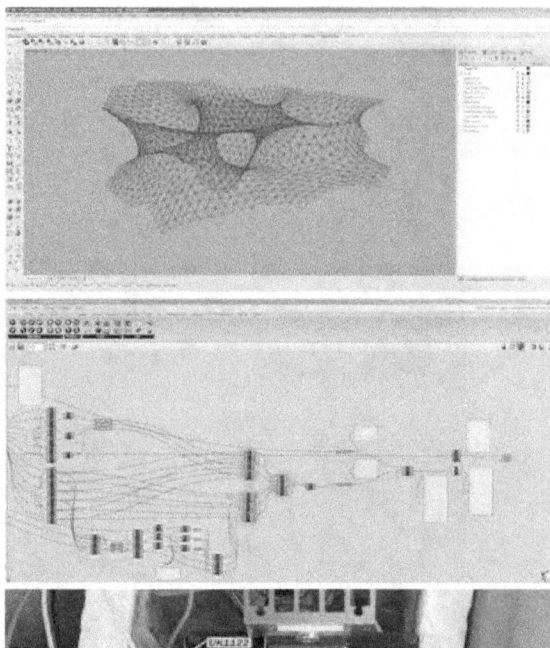

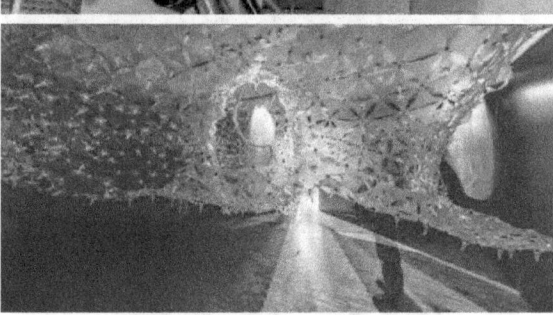

Fig. 5. An Example of Digital Design Exploration and Synthesis to Full Scale Built Projects.

with architects and contractors, case studies, and tutorials, which are used to supplement a range of 3rd year courses (Figure 1).

To introduce BIM-based building performance simulation, students investigated the effect of both massing and materiality on energy consumption and life cycle cost in a factorial study during the conceptual design stage of their studio project. Each student generated two massing options with the same nominal gross floor area in Revit, applied two envelope concepts (different materials or same material with varying glazing percentage) to each, and created energy simulations using Green Building Studio and bills of quantities for cost estimation. Fig. 4 shows a sample of this work. Building upon this learning in the following term, students performed a second energy simulation – along with a daylighting analysis - of their realized schematic design, and used the data generated to inform their next design iterations. As one student designing a church noted in response to the daylight analysis, "Daylighting proved that without more glazing or the introduction of constant artificial lighting, the main nave area would be uncomfortable." Students were encouraged to revisit these tools regularly over the term and submit their analyses and lessons learned as part of their design process for their final studio project.

Fourth Year Implementation

The fourth year is the culmination of the digital integration throughout the undergraduate program. Where a range of digital technologies and platforms are introduced and reinforced in the first three years, the fourth year is where students are expected to demonstrate critical thinking in adopting these tools to their respective specializations.

Though the fourth year of the program trifurcates into the Architecture, Building Science, and Project man agement specializations, the digital integration is maintained through the studios and elective offerings. Augmented reality is used in building science studios to simulate updating the impact of changing HVAC systems, while in architecture studios it is used to present design proposals for potential installations. Virtual reality is used in courses on the one hand to demonstrate theoretical experiments in architecture studio while simultaneously used in advanced fabrication courses to posit what prospective upcoming design-build projects will look like. Within the project management specialization students gain further experience in BIM as a project planning, construction management, coordination, and communication tool on a complex multi-disciplinary studio project, while in an advanced digital design course building data is used to develop full-scale prototypes for responsive shading arrays (Figure 5).

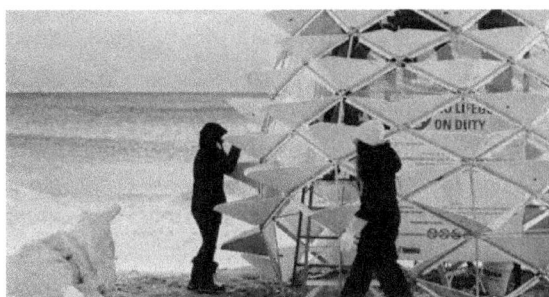
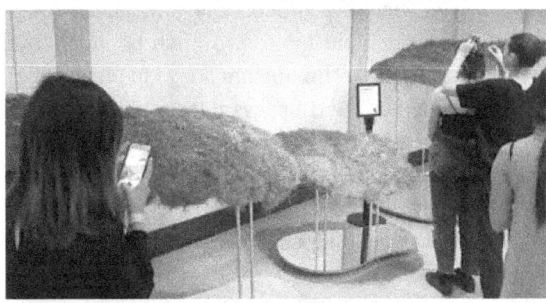
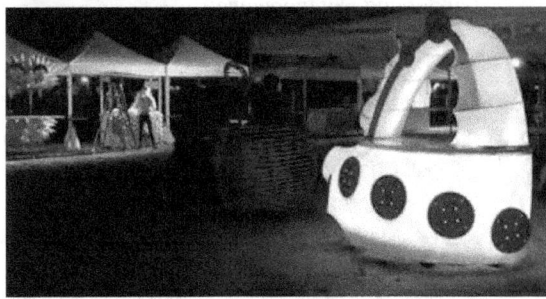

Fig. 6. Sample of Extracurricular Digital Design Work Translated into Fabricated Reality.

Extracurricular Activities

As the Department of Architectural Science is the most prolific student design-build group in Canada, its students have been able to translate poetic design intentions to pragmatic, feasible productions. These incredible volume of extracurricular activities ranging from Nuit Blanche installations and cultural events to urban furniture and space renovations, are a function of the students' confidence with digital design workflows. From visualization to fabrication, students have gained invaluable experience working with groups in the community ranging from the City of Toronto to the Art Gallery of Ontario. In vertically organized teams (first years to grad students), students within the program collaborate on approximately a dozen design-build projects each year. A quarter of the student population participates in carrying a project from digital ideation to digital fabrication (Figure 6).

Conclusion

The results of the standardized, digitally-enhanced architecture curriculum deployed at Ryerson University reinforces a growing body of pedagogical research that highlights the creative value of digital tools in not only the studio, but other courses as well. In studies on digital integration in architectural education around the world, two key themes emerge: a) digital technologies increase productivity and fidelity, and b) students adopting them also push boundaries in design exploration. The authors are in the latter phase of the deployment and assessment of the digital integration in the program however early survey and interview data from students and comparative studies indicate a general improvement in the quality of work against several key metrics summarized below.

Output and Documentation

The most immediate and visible impact of the digital curriculum is the higher quality and volume of design output. The early introduction and aggregation of digital skills has allowed students to gain confidence in efficiently creating multiple iterations, higher fidelity representations and models, and explorations of multiple design factors all with conventional and more immersive media. This familiarity removes design limitations based upon the technical skills a student has.

This comfort in creating digital design media has also extended into other courses where students do not isolate creative outputs to the studio. To find digitally fabricated models, VR environments, or BIM performance animations in technical or theory courses is quickly becoming commonplace in the program.

Engagement and Design Sensitivity

With the ability to develop multiple iterations, greater levels of design exploration allow students to pursue specific facets. This higher engagement effectively personalizes design pursuits which motivate students to pursue in the studio environment, whether it is phenomenological experience to material effects. In a similar way, the higher representational fidelity and immersion of the digital media outlined in this paper have allowed students to not only engage their in-structors during reviews but also have made for active peer-to-peer relationship when sharing design work.

With the curricular BIM integration, students appreciate the range of impacts design decisions make with real world factors such as scheduling, costs, and operations. Inculcating an awareness of architecture as creating real buildings (as opposed to speculative icons) has remarkably made students value the technical and realistic components of their curriculum in their design work.

Feasibility

Though much of the digitally-enhanced curriculum generates virtual outputs, the potency of the outcomes all mandate that students consider their work with a higher level of feasibility. Whether in a VR environment showcasing material connections or an energy performance model demonstrating optimal solar orientation, students are able to bring their design ideas one step closer to considered reality. Over the past three years that this curriculum has been developed, a common adage has been brought up by students and faculty alike: "If you design it, you have to know how to make it." This omnipresent thinking throughout the program has been made possible by the digital convergence within the program.

These digital outputs reinforce the value of both studio and complementary courses, specifically those in building technology. There is a great potential in investing in the digital convergence of these technologies in contemporary pedagogy. These tools are not exclusive to simply artistic initiatives. The challenge architectural educators face is not which technologies are appropriate, but which suit their goals and how they can be sustainably integrated. These tools are capable of not only expressing the poetics of design possibilities but are critical in executing pragmatic production.

Notes:

[1] Rivard, Hugues. "A Survey on the Impact of Information Technology in the Canadian Architecture, Engineering and Construction Industry," in *Journal of Information Technology in Construction,* vol. 5, no. 3. 2000. p 37-56.

[2] Palfrey, John and Gasser, Urs. *Born Digital: How Children Grow Up in a Digital Age.* Basic Books: New York, NY. 2016. p 211-212.

[3] Mateus, Daniel, Sousa, Mauricio, de Klerk, Rui and Duarte, Jose. "From Τέκτων to Τέχνη: Going Back to the Classical Roots of Architecture using Virtual Reality," in *eCAADe 33 Virtual Reality – Evaluation,* vol. 1. 2015.

[4] de Freitas, Marcia Regina and Ruschel, Regina Coeli. "What is Happening to Virtual and Augmented Reality Applied to Architecture," in *Open Systems: Proceedings of the 18th International Conference on Computer-Aided Architectural Design Research in Asia (CAADRIA 2013).* 2013.

[5] Chi, Hung Lin, Kang, ShihChung and Wang Xiangyu. "Research Trends and Opportunities of Augmented Reality Applications in Architecture, Engineering and Construction," in *Automation in Construction,* vol. 33, no. 12. 2013. p 116-122.

[6] Autodesk. "Penn State University – BIM Curriculum" *Autodesk.* Autodesk, 2017. Web. 17 Feb. 2017.

[7] Deutsch, Randy. *BIM and Integrated Design: Strategies for Architectural Practice.* Wiley: New York, NY. 2016.

[8] Briscoe, Danelle. *Beyond BIM: Architecture Information Modeling.* Routledge: New York, NY. 2016.

[9] Kolarevic, Branko. *Architecture in the Digital Age: Design and Manufacturing.* Taylor and Francis: New York, NY. 2005.

[10] Iwamoto, Lisa. *Digital Fabrications: Architectural and Material Techniques.* Princeton Architectural Press: New York, NY. 2009.

[11] Schwartz, Chad. "Debating the Merits of Design/Build: Pedagogical Strategies in an Architectural Technology Course" in *Journal of Applied Sciences and Arts,* vol. 1, no. 1. 2015. p 2.

[12] Stacey, Michael, Beesley, Philip and Hui, Vincent. *Digital Fabricators.* University of Waterloo School of Architecture Press: Cambridge, ON. 2004.

[13] Kale, Serdar and Arditi, "Diffusion of Computer Aided Design Technology in Architectural Design Practice," in *Journal of Construction Engineering and Management,* vol. 131, no. 10. 2005.

[14] Fonseca, David, Marti, Nuria, Redondo, Ernest, Navarro, Isidro and Sanchez, Albert. "Relationship Between Student Profile, Tool Sse, Participation, and Academic Performance with the Use of Augmented Reality Technology for Visualized Architecture Models," in *Computers in Human Behavior,* vol. 31, no. 3. 2014. p 434-445.

SESSION 07: TECTONICS

Session Chair: Diane Armpriest
University of Idaho

Chad Schwartz, Southern Illinois University: "A Taxonomy of Architectural Tectonics."

Ismael Olivares, Texas Tech University: "earth + form : experience."

Michael McGlynn, Kansas State University: "Toward a Theory of Architectural Technology: Tracing Attempts to Reconcile the Technical in Design."

A Taxonomy of Architectural Tectonics

Chad Schwartz
Southern Illinois University - Carbondale

Abstract[1]

[O]ne might argue that a building is intensified through the elaboration of its own medium – *a language of sticks and stones* – to induce a state of architecture. The "material" that underlies architecture is somehow rooted in construction and its details, and yet beguilingly, the devices that engage the building practice are most often in tension with the seemingly direct necessities of fabrication. Herein lies one of the most fertile and debated topics in architectural theory: the subject of tectonics.[2]

Architecture is often described as the intersection of art and science. These two distinct realms, however, cannot be set in opposition; they must be cooperatively utilized in the creation of the built environment. Architecture is an integrative art, one that combines the design of productive space with the tangible realities of gravity, material properties, and assembly sequences. The study of architectural tectonics can help to illuminate the partnership between these elements in the creation of the built environment. Tectonics has many definitions, but they all tend to focus on the relationships between those architectural elements we tend to hold apart: space and construction, structure and ornamentation, atmosphere and function. It seeks a relationship between the design of space and the reality of the construction that is necessary for it to exist.

This paper outlines a framework for examining the core concepts ingrained in the history and evolution of architectural tectonics. Each of the following topics examines a particular characteristic of the theory drawn from different lines of historical and contemporary thought:

- **Anatomy** | the study of the primary components and systems of a building

- **Tectonic + Stereotomic** | the study of the means and methods of construction as well as the materiality of the built environment

- **Detail + Intersection** | the study of the joints and other critical conditions that make up the smallest scale of a work of architecture

- **Place** | the study of the impact of a specific place or context on the tectonic makeup of a building.

- **Representation + Ornamentation** | the study of the relationship between the actual construction of the building that is required for stability or enclosure and the cladding or ornamentation that is used to create the aesthetic scheme.

- **Space** | the study of the relationship between the creation of space and the construction and representational qualities of a building.

- **Atectonic** | the study of conditions that run contrary to typical tectonic ideas

The tectonic theories of Karl Bötticher, Gottfried Semper, and others have evolved over time to be able to successfully integrate into contemporary society, but this "transformation, adaptation and above all the reduction of and simplification of an extremely ambitious theory of tectonics was in fact ineluctable."[3] Despite its shifting, its transforming, and its adapting, architectural tectonics remains a central tenet of both the study of architecture and the practice of its design and construction. The lessons available to all students of architecture that have arisen from this linage of architectural thought have the potential to positively influence our built environment for the foreseeable future.

Introduction

In his 1844 work *Die Tektonik der Hellenen*, architectural scholar and archaeologist Karl Bötticher wrote the following words:

> We conceive of tectonics in the more narrow sense: the activity of building or of making objects of use, as soon as this activity is *ethically suffused*, and can rise to the charges placed upon it by intellectual or physical life. At that point, this activity not only seeks to satisfy mere needs by *forming a volume* in accordance with material necessity but instead may elevate that volume to a Kunstform.

> Thus, we conceive of the tectonic activity in two groups: the group of the pure built work, or the architectonic; and that of the smaller forms, of the *tectonic of useful objects*. Both are based upon the same principles of formal constitution. The architectonic, because of the scope of its duties and the compass of its means, requires that these principles be described more broadly and drastically.[4]

This manifesto on architecture provides key insight into the origins of tectonic thought. Bötticher, along with Gottfried Semper, is widely regarded as a founding father of the theory of architectural tectonics. His ideas about architecture originate in the study of Hellenic building and the principles with which the Greeks designed their greatest works. Bötticher claimed that this era of architecture was unmatched in its ability to convey the underlying essence of an architectural work though the expressiveness of the ornamentation with which it was clad.

As an example, take the Greek column (Figure 1). The structural function of the column is relatively simple; a beam above transfers gravity load generated by the overhead structure to the top of the column, which in-turn transfers the load through its mass to the base. The base then evenly distributes the load to the ground or structure below. When the ornamentation of a Greek Order is applied, the two points of primary transfer are also the points adorned with the most intricate elements of the design, highlighting or revealing the work underway below the surface.

Fig. 1. Analysis of a Greek column.

Bötticher refers to the actual work being done below the surface of this "object of use" as the *Kernform*, which can be translated as core-form or the underlying ontological truth of the object. The ornamentation is the *Kunstform* or the art-form that both covers and reveals the *Kernform* below. This concept is one of the most essential and formative ideas of architectural tectonics, the notion that there is a distinct relationship between how a building works and how its visible components help reveal that truth to those occupying its spaces.

Although certainly stemming from a passionate study of Greek architecture, architectural tectonics was also responsive to popular sentiment among the intellectual community of the Germanic states in the early 1800s. A group of philosophers, including Immanuel Kant, were studying the fine arts and had come to the conclusion that the purpose-driven practice of architecture was inferior as an art to those with no functional intent such as painting, sculpture, or music. In Kant's terms, architecture was centered on purpose, while the remaining fine arts were associated with purposiveness, a term derived to describe an act in which the concept of an object was independent of any functional value (Figure 2). Bötticher, Semper, and others reacted to this slight to the practice of architecture by introducing architectural tectonics as a way of connecting the underlying functional aspects of a building to its ornamented, visual facades. They sought a way to elevate the architectural object to a *Kunstform*.

Fig. 2. Understanding of purpose and purposiveness.

Adaptation

About 150 years later, around the turn of the century, a resurgence, led by architectural theorist Kenneth Frampton, brought the ideas of architectural tectonics back into the spotlight. In his essay "Towards a Critical Regionalism," Frampton writes:

> [T]he primary principle of architectural autonomy resides in the *tectonic* rather than the *scenographic*: that is to say, this autonomy is embodied in the revealed ligaments of the construction and in the way in which the syntactical form of the structure explicitly resists the action of gravity.[5]

This definition is paralleled and expanded in the essay "From Techne to Tectonics" by Demetri Porphyrios:

> The concern of tectonics is threefold. First, the finite nature and formal properties of constructional materials, be those timber, brick, stone, steel, etc. Second, the procedures of jointing, which is the way that elements of construction are put together. Third, the visual statics of form, that is the way by which the eye is satisfied about stability, unity and balance and their variations or opposites.[6]

Although there are some similarities to the definition offered by Bötticher in the mid-1800s, there are also some distinct differences. Bötticher was seeking to reveal the underlying forces at work through the ornamentation of the building. He was seeking representational and referential understanding of the useful purpose of building. Frampton and Porphyrios, however, are shifting that definition. They both believe that the tectonic building must demonstrate how gravity is moving through the structure and that we must be able to perceive this reality and be satisfied through our understanding of how the building is stable. The art-form, however, is not mentioned in these later definitions, pulling back from historicist modes of representation. There is also, in both definitions, a clear call for an understanding of the joining of material, the ligaments that tie the building together and help to achieve the stability that is sought. Finally, Porphyrios urges for an understanding of materials, although much more closely tied to Gottfried Semper's studies than those of Bötticher.

What this very brief snippet of the history of tectonics illuminates is that the theory has, over the past century and a half, necessarily evolved. The "transformation, adaptation and above all the reduction of and simplification of an extremely ambitious theory of tectonics was in fact ineluctable."[7] It has transformed and shifted to adapt to changing technologies and cultural attitudes, architectural styles and environmental needs. Despite its adaptations, however, and likely because of them, it is relevant to the contemporary architect and the contemporary architecture student. Architectural tectonics "remains a central tenet of both the study of architecture and the practice of its design and construction. The lessons available to all students of architecture that have arisen from this linage of architectural thought have the potential to positively influence our built environment for the foreseeable future."[8]

Framework and Analysis

The evolutionary process of architectural tectonics has led, naturally, to the interweaving of a series of complementary lines of thought that have organically sprouted and grown over time. In order to best convey the full breadth and depth of the theory of tectonics, each of these ideas must be explored. To simplify the experience, like ideas can be classified into a taxonomical structure; this strategy also has the potential to make this involved theory easier to understand for those more novice to architectural theory in general, like architecture students. The following sections briefly outlines each point and provide examples of how each can be utilized in the development or analysis of an architectural work.

Anatomy

The first category is anatomy, which examines the primary components and systems of a building. This line of thought builds heavily on the concept of the four elements of architecture proposed by Gottfried Semper in the mid-1800s: the hearth, the earthwork, the roof and framework, and the cladding. The hearth is the social center, the call for gathering and society, and is protected by the other elements. Although certainly this classification system can be taken quite literally, Semper's elements can also be viewed as a foundational system open for significant interpretation as technological systems advance over time.

Although certainly a departure from Semper's system of classification, the Loblolly House by Kieran Timberlake demonstrates the use of a clear set of construction elements. This system, derived by the architects through their study of manufacturing processes, consists of seven primary building systems: site work, scaffold, cartridges, blocks, fixtures, furnishings, and equipment (Figure 3). While the site work is accomplished in the field, the rest of the components in this system are pre-manufactured off-site before being delivered and installed by the contractor.

Construction

The second category builds on the notion of anatomy by examining how these systems are constructed. Specifically, there are two significantly different ways in which we approach the construction of our built environment: tectonically and stereotomically. This pairing, outlined by Frampton in his work in the mid-1990s, separates tectonic construction – those elements which are assembled through the articulation of joints – from stereotomic construction – accomplished through the piling or massing of material. This category holds the opportunity to examine the means, methods, and materiality of the built environment.

Fig. 3. Partial anatomy of Loblolly House by Kieran Timberlake.

A clear example of the pairing of tectonic and stereotomic systems can be found in the Chapel of Reconciliation, which is located in the no-man's-land formerly contained by the two sides of the Berlin Wall in Germany. This small building, designed by the team of Rudolf Reitermann and Peter Sassenroth, is composed of two nested ovaloid forms (Figure 4). The inner volume is rammed earth and is quiet, contemplative, and introverted. The outer volume is defined by an open-air wooden screen, which allows for a connection to the surrounding environment while providing weather protection for the rammed earth construction within.

Fig. 4. Stereotomic and Tectonic plans of the Chapel of Reconciliation by Reitermann and Sassenroth.

Detail

The architectural detail is the subject of the third category and is divided into two parts: the joining of elements to form a detail and the joining of critical systems to form the primary intersections of a building. The joint has been of primary concern throughout the evolution of architectural tectonics. It is examined in the intersection of the Greek column discussed previously as well as in recent literature by the likes of Edward Ford and Marco Frascari who find that the architectural detail can tasked with both creating structurally sound spaces through the assembly of the construction systems and emotively strong spaces through the character they bring to our built environment.

Created through a design/build process led by architect Anna Heringer, the METI Handmade School provides a pristine example of the notion of a primary intersection in a building. This project, which was built by a local labor force in Bangladesh, consists of a lower story of earth construction and an upper story constructed primarily with bamboo. It is the interlacing of the two building systems in the upper floor construction that unites the building as a whole (Figure 5). The bamboo is used structurally to carry the weight of the floor, while also tying the tectonic system above to the stereotomic walls of the lower level.

Fig. 5. Construction detail of the METI Handmade School by Anna Heringer

Place

From Semper to modern day, the role of place in how we build has played a crucial role in the understanding of architectural tectonics. This fourth category asks us to study the impact of a specific place or context on the tectonic makeup of a building. Semper understood very well the role of environment and available resources in the development of architecture by different cultures. Zooming in, we must also carefully consider the role of the site in the development of the tectonic whole. "One cannot disregard the enormous importance of the plane separating above and below. That plane is basic to the tectonics of building...It is the beginning of our taking possession of the land."[9]

Debartolo Architects created a unique construction in the Sonoran Desert of Phoenix, Arizona that is distinctly connected to the environmental conditions of the place, albeit in an unlikely way. The Prayer Pavilion of Light utilizes multiple layers of glazing and a thermal chimney to mitigate the desert heat while allowing through the ever changing and dramatic light of this region of the country (Figure 6). By articulating the tectonics of the building, the architects were able to create a space that is conscious of the environment without removing it from the experience of the space.

divided into its two intertwined namesakes, provides the original foundation for the theory of architectural tectonics (as outlined above). It seeks "a relationship between the actual construction of the building that is required for stability or enclosure and the cladding or ornamentation that is used to create the aesthetic scheme."[10] Although historically, this was focused on the visual conveying of the utilitarian purpose of the building, in contemporary times we certainly can see these ideas playing out in other ways as well, including through environmental responsiveness of our building systems.

Outside Eureka Springs, Arkansas, E. Fay Jones built one of the most significant pieces of American architecture: Thorncrown Chapel. This small space is a glass box in the forest, surmounted by an expansive wooden roof and supported by a repetitive series of truss frames fabricated out of traditional dimensional lumber. The structure is a representation of the forest, which is enhanced by the glass which reflects and amplifies the surrounding landscape (Figure 7). "The glass veils the chapel in the forest itself, camouflaging it into the surroundings"[11] while the exposed interior structure is reflective of the structure of the surrounding tree canopy.

Fig. 6. Wall section of the Prayer Pavilion of Light by Debartolo Architects

Representation + Ornamentation

Perhaps the most robust of the categories of architectural tectonics is that of representation and ornamentation. This category, which can be further

Fig. 7. Axonometric of Thorncrown Chapel by Fay Jones

Space

The sixth category examines the relationship between the creation of space and the construction and representational qualities of a building. This idea is explored by Bötticher, who wrote about designing for human need, which defines spatial arrangement. The supporting structure of the sheltering roof is then formed based on the spatial configuration, creating a correlation between space and structure. The advancing technology of construction has played a significant role in this relationship, most clearly seen in the introduction of iron as a primary structural system for architecture. As structure dematerialized, the spatial relationships of our buildings changed dramatically as well.

This A-B-A relationship is, as Bötticher proposed, driven equally by spatial needs and the construction systems necessary to support the enclosing roof above.

Atectonic

Composing the final category of this taxonomy is the atectonic or the conditions that run contrary to typical tectonic ideas. Although certainly there is architecture that has been developed without the use of tectonic input, the primary concern here is with architecture in which tectonic expression has been purposely distorted in order to create a specific experience, feeling, or effect in a building or space. Eduard Sekler offers a few ideas of these tectonic abnormalities in his writings: the construction and structural principles could be out of alignment (i.e. building in one material with the detailing of another), the expression could be vague (i.e. a floating building), or the use of exaggerated building elements.[12]

Fig. 8. Spatial plan of the Parrish Art Museum by Herzog & de Meuron

The concept of spatial tectonics can be observed while studying the Parrish Art Museum, designed by Herzog & de Meuron for a collection in New York. The building's profile consists of an extruded double-gabled roof. While this profile creates a unique building form that relates the project to a number of contextual drivers, it also has a significant impact on the qualities and use of the interior spaces of the building (Figure 8). The low, central valley pushes the space downward along its spine, encouraging circulation, while each gable extends upwards creating move voluminous space for the collections.

Fig. 9. Section of the Chapel del Retiro by Undurraga Devés

Within the category of atectonic buildings with a vague expression can be found the Chapel del Retiro, designed by Undurraga Devés Arquitectos in Auco, Chile. The building's mass is supported by four massive concrete beams arranged in the form of a hashtag symbol and suspended over a pit excavated into the ground. Visitors travel down a ramp and under the supporting structure to enter. Once inside the small chapel, you will find the concrete structure supports a wooden box that conceals the concrete from view on the interior (Figure 9). The wooden box hovers several feet above the floor, magically suspended with no indication of support. Here, the eye is certainly at a loss for the stability and understanding of the forces at work beneath the surface.

Conclusion

This tectonic framework has the potential to be of great value to students of architecture. Architectural tectonics is a study in dualities. As such, it has the ability to help novice practitioners begin to understand and develop connections between design and construction, between systems that are assembled and those that are massed, between the architectural detail and the building of which it is a part, and between the visible surface of a structure and the substance beneath that keeps the building stable.

In addition, this taxonomy of ideas provides an excellent way to study the world around us. The close analysis of precedents is an excellent way for the novice student to learn about the built environment. By using a tectonic lens to study great works of architecture, students have the potential to draw from these case studies critical lessons about the practice of architecture that will serve them for the rest of their education and as they move out into the professional world.

Notes:

[1] The abstract draws heavily from content outlined in Chad Schwartz, *Introducing Architectural Tectonics: Exploring the Intersection of Design and Construction* (New York: Routledge, 2016), xxvii-xxviii, lxv.

[2] Nader Tehrani, "Forward: A Murder in the Court," in *Strange Details*, ed. Michael Cadwell (Cambridge: The MIT Press, 2007), xii.

[3] Werner Oechslin, *Otto Wagner, Adolf Loos, and the Road to Modern Architecture* (New York: Cambridge University Press, 2002), 50.

[4] Karl Bötticher, "Excerpts from Die Tektonik Der Hellenen," in *Otto Wagner, Adolf Loos, and the Road to Modern Architecture*, ed. Werner Oechslin (New York: Cambridge University Press, 2002), 190. Originally published as Botticher, Carl Gottlieb Wilhelm. *Die Tektonik Der Hellenen* (Potsdam, 1844).

[5] Kenneth Frampton, "Towards a Critical Regionalism: Six Points for an Architecture of Resistance," in *The Anti-Aesthetic: Essays on Postmodern Culture*, ed. Hal Foster (New York: The New Press, 1998), 30.

[6] Demetri Porphyrios, "From Techne to Tectonics," in *What is Architecture?*, ed. Andrew Ballantyne, (New York: Routledge, 2002), 135-136.

[7] Oechslin, *Otto Wagner, Adolf Loos, and the Road to Modern Architecture*, 50.

[8] Schwartz, *Introducing Architectural Tectonics*, lxv.

[9] Carles Vallhonrat, "Tectonics Considered: Between the Presence and the Absence of Artifice," *Perspecta* 24 (1988): 125-126.

[10] Schwartz, *Introducing Architectural Tectonics*, xxviii.

[11] ibid, 43.

[12] Eduard Sekler, "Structure, Construction, Tectonics," in *Structure in Art and Science*, ed. Gyorgy Kepes (New York: Braziller, 1965), 94.

Figure Citations:

1: Chad Schwartz, *Introducing Architectural Tectonics: Exploring the Intersection of Design and Construction* (New York: Routledge, 2016), I.

2: ibid, xxxv.

3: ibid, 8.

4: ibid, 146.

5: ibid, 196.

6: ibid, 91.

7: ibid, 44. Drawing inspired by Figure 25 on page 111 of Edward Ford's *The Architectural Detail*.

8: ibid, 122.

9: ibid, 227.

earth + form : experience

Ismael Olivares
Graduate Student - Texas Tech University

abstract

The broad spectrum of material options available to architects today is a result of the post-industrial revolution, both a blessing and a curse. Oftentimes opposing opinions, formed to answer the barrage of challenges contemporary design demanded, allowed for people to fall into smaller more focused directions within the field of architecture. Within these new niches, earth construction has found a renewed interest for its community centered construction process and physical benefits. These benefits are largely undocumented due to its tactile nature providing opportunities for students, faculty, and professionals alike to explore materiality through a hands-on approach.

regionalism + the industrial revolution

In the time before industrialization, regional architecture was needed to react to different climates and microclimates as well as socioeconomically driven forces. The availability, limited mobility, and understanding of materials shaped the architecture of each region or community. As the industrial revolution contested the need for regionalist architecture, Frank Lloyd Wright immortalized it as an architectural movement through his locally adapted use of modern forms and technologies through his selection of local materials and techniques that could perform and culturally integrate like the local vernacular. Throughout the 20th century regionalists strove to create an architecture that was not only locally sensible through materiality but also through craftsmanship and a deep respect for historical context.

Carlo Scarpa is the epitome craft. His precisely layered and composed designs combined local techniques with modern materials and technologies to be able to accomplish intricate detailing – combining craft with design and materiality with metaphor. His renovation projects are perfect examples of respecting local building traditions and forms while presenting new insertions in modern ways. The Castelvecchio renovation is a composition of concrete, wood, and steel insertions that pop in and out of the original stone building. The proportions of the interventions are based off the original stone; however, the insertions float and lightly land on the original building to make clear to the user that they are not of the original construction. As one moves through the spaces, one understands the level of craftsmanship required to create every small connection and joint. All his work, including that at the Olivetti store in Venice, Italy, showed how stone could not only create beautiful modern spaces but also an architecture that was born of the Italian landscape and formed with Italian hands and technology.

Tadao Ando is not traditionally seen as a regionalist architect; however, many of his sensibilities to site and culture are very much of the same ideological circles. Ando is known all over the world for his use of silky concrete in the Japanese tradition by making it a material of high quality and a reflection of careful craftsmanship[i]. His projects in Japan might have seemed more sensible had he used wood and glass; yet, his use of high craftsmanship and creative openings and spaces created a modernist alternative that was still very much in the Japanese spirit. Ando is also very observant of his surroundings. At the Modern Museum in Fort Worth, Texas there are many references to the Louis Kahn designed Kimball Art Museum across the street – from the long rectangular volumes and the open courtyards to the use of concrete and glass as the main building materials [ii]. At the same time, he distinguishes himself from the Kimball using his iconic "Y" shaped columns and through a deep connection to natural elements on the site, both reflecting Japanese sensibilities. Ando was using the same clay but making clear and unique impressions.

The advent of the Industrial Revolution in the 19th century led to many of the great accomplishments of the 20th century but also laid the ground work for many of the issues that we face in the 21st century. Architecturally this technological surge made construction more affordable and controllable epitomized by the International Style. These affordable design solutions were primarily concerned with output and efficiency just like the machines that influenced le Corbusier's design philosophies[iii]. By focusing on efficiency in space and construction, hermetically-sealed glass buildings, such as the Seagram building in New York, became more reliant on mechanical systems than on environmentally cognizant design solutions. Unfortunately, this exemplifies the hubris of man as his efficient construction methods led to buildings that seemed detached from their environments as they often disregarded the human scale and social sensibilities. A close cousin to the International Style, the Brutalist Movement produced buildings that are often at the center of polarizing opinions and sentiments as is the case with the Station at Tel Aviv and the Boston City Hall [iv]. As architectural technologies continue to push the limits of design and efficiency, the global implications of these ecologically and sociologically damaging designs required a new approach. LEED fostered a growing concern over global warming and the humanization of space taking advantage of the tools and materials available today and decreed that design and architecture be more responsible.

Through a renewed sense of responsibility combined with technological and conceptual advances, a golden age of architecture exists today. Anything can be built. Champions of every technological advancement are resources to many young designers today. Zaha Hadid's parametric designs have produced spaces and forms that sit on the fringe of architecture in computer aided design, materiality, and fabrication/construction. Foster and Partners stand at the forefront of efficiency and sustainability in design. Some firms like BIG and Elemental apply these technological advancements with socially directed and responsible designs that deliberate the needs of both communities and individuals[v]. In a recent interview with Architizer Penda talked about the creative freedom that today's professionals can now explore when he says "I think this new generation is actually a really lucky one. We are all "start architects," and not "star architects," in this generation that is coming now. The playing field of architecture is getting much wider, with these new technologies — an architect doesn't even need, necessarily, to build

buildings. He or she can focus on other things, and specialize." [vi]

As architects begin to deviate from the broad traditional design roles and into these more concentrated roles, designers have found space to look not only to the future but to the past for solutions to today's design challenges. One such direction has been to try and reimagine, repurpose, and rebrand local materials and techniques[vii]. Bamboo treated with Borax has been made into an insect resistant material so that its incredible strength and flexibility can be used in a much wider set of architectural applications[viii]. Elora Hardy and her father John Hardy have shown that new contemporary designs can be made with locally sourced materials that are easier to access and sometimes require that craftsmen take on little to no new training[ix]. These materials can also be used in infrastructural roles such as durable structural elements for water catchment systems found in Ethiopia [x].

returning to earth + building communities

Rammed earth is another such material that has garnered new attention. Buildings such as the Peter Klaus Field Chapel in Germany designed by Peter Zumthor and the compressed earth block school in Burkino Faso by KERE Architecture have shown the dexterity and poetry that contemporary design could gain from using earth construction [xi]. The beauty and intrigue of this material lies in its simplicity. It literally takes the ground and shapes it into habitable space.

Earth construction is a very labor intensive material and that involves or creates a community. D U S T are a design/build firm that have experimented and learned through first-hand experiences with rammed earth. During a recent lecture, they talked not only about their approach to their designs and the technical processes that led to their vision becoming reality but also about how they came together as a firm making their eggs together in the morning after nights out around the campfire in isolated sites. While D U S T's projects have been small and larger applications of this material can provide opportunities to engage and incorporate entire communities. In much the same way that the Romans felt proud and honored of the monuments that pushed the empire's economic and technological limits, rammed earth offers a time-tested alternative that requires commitment and responsibility but without a steep price tag.

From an educational standpoint, rammed earth offers a very intriguing topic for the field of architecture. It couples a deep history rooted in a wide array of buildings and monuments such as the Great Wall of China, and the Sun Pyramid in Teotihuacan, structurally supported by rammed earth cores and covered in stone to protect against erosion[xii]. As it is a material that is still largely based on a loose system of trial and error best learned from people who have previously worked with it before, rammed earth has yet to be quantified through rigorous material testing – crucial in the era of calculated and analyzed construction. Doing so would provide a more sustainable alternative to ecologically inefficient concrete and steel construction methods.

There are many different types of earth related construction techniques ranging from rammed earth to aerated loam construction that have strengths and weaknesses are still relatively manual processes. To try and better understand earth construction, two different projects examined the physical processes of earth construction within real projects with real clients. Each had unique goals and requirements; however, both found rammed earth to be best suited for their respective situations as a material that is durable and easily constructed. Both projects started with teams that created a design community that incorporated various colleges of the university to produce more inclusive designs.

Kenya

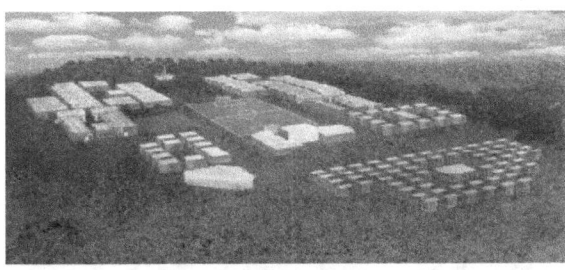

Fig. 1 Digital rendering of the Top of the Hill National High School of Art Science and Entrepreneurship for Girls

The Top of the Hill National High School of Art, Science, and Entrepreneurship for Girls aims to be at the forefront of the education of girls in Kenya. The client inherited some land from her father at the top of a hill held spiritual significance to her. What initially started as a one-building school grew to become a campus for 500 students, 150 guests, and a live-in faculty and staff team. As it was in rural Kenya, the design would not only have to provide an infrastructural base but also a material that could easily and economically be erected by the community. Rammed earth construction provided a solution that would provide a durable material made out of the wide swaths of earth that would have to be disturbed to be able to create more suitable topographical conditions and incorporate the local community to project a positive image from the start. Techniques learned during the construction of the school could then be applied by craftsmen in local projects.

To better understand what rammed earth construction entailed, a sample wall was designed and built (Fig. 2). It would measure 16 in. x 28 in. x 22 in. and would include a 4-in. concrete base and 2 in. concrete cap to simulate the construction of a complete wall system. The base of the wall would sit on a wooden moving dolly that would be reinforced and capped with a plywood top. This would allow for the wall to be mobile while providing a base that could, in theory, hold up the weight of the sample. The vertical faces of the form were made of ½" plywood that were to be braced and held up by 3 rings of 2 x 4s. To show the client how the material is unique to each site and geological composition, 5-gallon bucket sized soil samples from different locations were to be layered on top of each other. Six samples were donated from a local civil engineering firm that sourced the earth from nearby towns and two samples were collected from a local construction site. It was calculated that each layer needed 24 oz. of concrete as a binding agent to be able to meet the recommended 10% ratio [xiii]. Finally, a 1 in. square profile reveal was added between the foundation and the rammed earth to test out the difficulty of subtle detailing.

To protect the casters that allowed the wall to be mobile, a rig was made using scrap material from the woodshop on which the previously mentioned set-up was to sit. The crisscrossing members of the base were then laid out to allow for a future dismount using leverage. Pam, a product used in cooking to prevent food from sticking to cookware, was sprayed on the form as a form release. While vegetable oil and other similar products may be used, the ability to easily distribute even coats with the spray provided a more controlled and even application method.

The soil and concrete were mixed in a trough with a hoe until it looked as homogenous as possible. Water was then mixed in until a handful of the material could be squeezed and maintain its integrity without crumbling from being too dry or running from being too wet. Additionally, several compaction techniques and tools were tested to try and find which option or combination worked best. It was found that dropping a sledgehammer onto a 2 x 4 sample roughly 8 in. long produced the best results. With 4 people helping in the construction each layer took around 20 minutes. Each 5-gallon soil sample produced a 2-in. layer and was concurrent with the 8:5 compression ratio of earth that was found to be ideal [xiv]. After adding an angled concrete cap, the sample wall used base's leverage and a coordinated effort to safely guide it from the rig onto the wheels. The wall was then wheeled out and unfortunately got stuck as the casters did not support the estimated 1,483 lbs. sample. New heavy duty casters were later added with the help of 4 car jacks.

While most of the formwork was made to be able to be easily disassembled, the bottom bracing ring was found to have been bolted from below without proper clearance. The weight of the wall made it very difficult to try and raise it to be able to release the form. Fortunately, the bolts were only holding together the vertical components and a reciprocating saw could be used to cut behind the bolts. Once all the screws were removed, the wall released with ease revealing a varying degree of success between layers and a 1" wooden reveal form that could not be removed without damaging the stability of the wall. Each layer showed varying levels of success in form surface smoothness and resistance to weathering. Mixes with a higher clay and water content produced sharper and stronger layers while the least successful were dry and had bigger soil particles.

There were many lessons that were learned during the construction of this wall sample including the initial mistake of using concrete mix over Portland Cement as a binding agent. These would not be corrected in this sample, but would be addressed in later research.

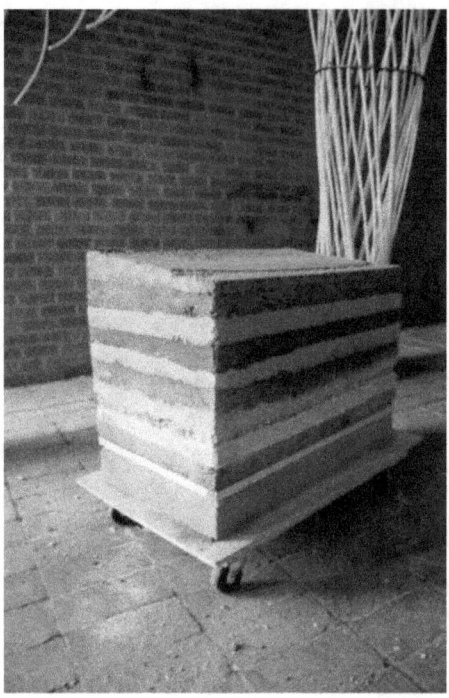

Fig. 2 Sample wall before the new casters

While there were mistakes there were also several surprises.The tapping on the angled form that would help shape the profile produced areas of smooth concrete attributed to the redistribution of air bubbles. It produced an interesting contrast the rough patches that were formed due to a missing coat of form release that caused the concrete to stick to the formwork. Most surprising of all was the striping of the formwork that formed after a thin layer of earth adhered to the form (Fig. 3). The vertical form surfaces became record of the faces of the wall sample.

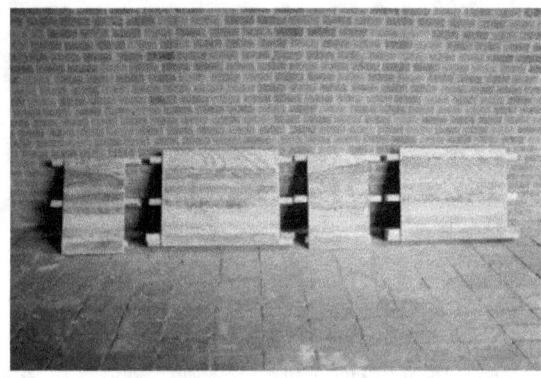

Fig. 3 Formwork stained after ramming process

Malawi

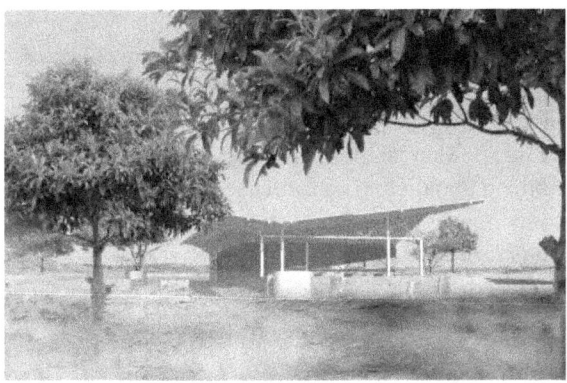

Fig. 4 Digital rendering of the new cafeteria at the Grace Center in Malawi

The Grace Center in Malawi is an existing school and orphanage that much like the Kenya project was to be built in a rural Africa. As such the need for community engagement was of top priority. In this project, the use of compressed earth blocks instead of rammed-in-place construction offered the opportunity to experiment with the composition and ratios of the constituents of rammed earth construction. A reusable form was constructed with smooth Plexiglas walls and a hinge to produce sample blocks easily and while minimizing the accumulation of material on the form's surfaces as one of two controls for the rest of the study. (Fig. 5)

By calculating the compressive factor of soil it was determined that roughly 24 oz. of cements needed to be added to be able to produce the 4 in. cubes. A piece of tracing paper was to be placed at the bottom of the mold to prevent the samples from sticking to the base of the form. The mold was then secured with a bolt and a wooden block that was wedged in place. The mix is then poured into the mold with a wooden insert used to distribute the compaction force evenly across the top surface. The force was provided by a mallet and compaction stopped when the mallet was no longer compacting the earth and bounced off the block. The mold is opened and the resulting samples are then carefully pulled out with the help of the tracing paper. The compressed cubes left some residual material that often stuck around in the corners of the mold. A toothbrush used to clean the mold helped to reduce deficiencies due to what would

have become an increasingly coarse mold and a mixing of different material compositions.

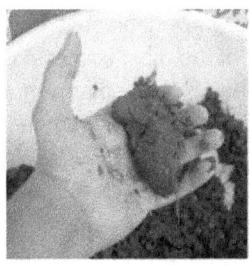
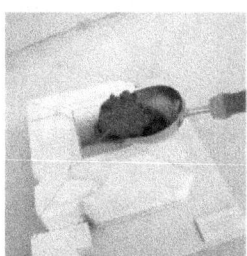
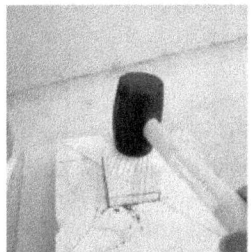
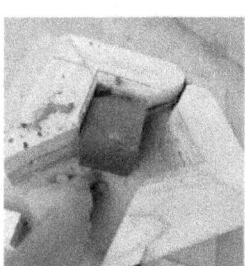

Fig. 5 (From top to bottom) Testing the soil for the right consistency. Loading the form with raw material. Ramming the block using a wooden insert and a mallet. Unveiling a finished sample.

The first block produced used 5% cement, the smallest recommended ratio, and 95% earth without any additional ingredients to serve. The second control used a 10% cement mixture and showed a great improvement in overall integrity and surface quality.

To try and study the effects of cotton as an additive two secondary controls were used. The first used 5% hand-picked and cleaned cotton that provided a very stable block even with a 5% cement ratio. The second and most predictable control used 5% unprocessed cotton. Even with the use of a 10% cotton ratio, it proved to be a very poor additive in general. The use of more than 5% crushed cotton proved to produce blocks that were not stable when freshly released from the form.

Crushed cotton, possibly benefiting from the binding traits of flexible strands as well as insulating properties that air pockets created by the seeds can help. The use of more than 5% crushed cotton proved to produce blocks that were not stable when freshly released from the form. The block with 10% cement / 5% cotton block / 85% yours was stable but had rough edges and corners. One of the most successful blocks overall, the 5% cement / 5% cotton mix produced a stable and block while reducing the need for cement.

Serving as a middle ground between raw and fully processed cotton, crushed, milled, and cut cotton was added to the loam in hopes that it would help to stabilize and enhance the block. Surprisingly the least stable crushed cotton block used a 10% cement ratio. The 5% cement / 5% cotton mix produced a stable and block while reducing the need for cement. The next step is to produce more samples to be able to use in lab and field test analyze and record the distinct properties. In doing so a quantifiable set of variables can be produced to help in construction endeavors that extend beyond the Grace Center, that is currently in design development.

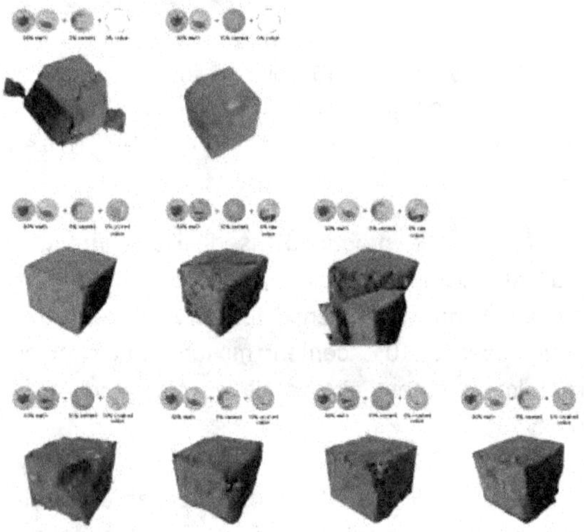

not only the land but the lives of the people that build and inhabit it.

Rammed earth presents only one of many options for a design + build + test opportunity and is concurrent with *Building With Earth* author Gernot Minke when he acknowledges the challenges of teaching and learning about earth construction. "On many accounts earth can offer an interesting alternative to industrialized building materials. No theoretical treatise, however, can substitute for the experience of actually building with earth." [xv]

Learning the reality of what the lines drawn on paper represent is a priceless lesson and will help to create specialties in architecture in an ever more diverse field. In an increasingly digital world, hands on experience with the poetics and pragmatics of real materials and real communities is vital early in the educational process of young architects.

Fig. 6 All of the different samples produced and their respective compositions

final thoughts

Striations in natural rock formations tell a story of the passage of time and the forces of change. As architecture has blossomed into a new age of design possibilities, rammed earth offers an elegant construction technique that is yet to be fully understood. This ancient material can help to shape

Notes:

[i] Tadao Ando. Produced by Michael Blackwood. Directed by Michael Blackwood. New York, NY: Michael Blackwood Productions, 1988

[ii] Dal, and Tadao Andō. Tadao Ando, 1995-2010. Munich London New York: Prestel, 2010.

[iii] Corbusier, Le, and Frederick Etchells. Towards a new architecture. United States: BN Pub, 2008.

[iv] Mars, Roman. "Hard to Love a Brute - 99% Invisible." August 11, 2015. Accessed October 4, 2016. http://99percentinvisible.org/episode/hard-to-love-a-brute/.

Mars, Roman. "The White Elephant of Tel Aviv - 99% Invisible." March 29, 2016. Accessed October 4, 2016. http://99percentinvisible.org/episode/stop-that-bus/.

[v] Aravena, Alejandro. My Architectural Philosophy? Bring the Community into the Process. November 6, 2014. Posted October 1, 2016. http://www.ted.com/talks/alejandro_aravena_my_architectural

Ingels, Bjarke. "Bjarke Ingels: 3 Warp-speed Architecture Tales." YouTube. 2009. Accessed April 20,2016.https://www.youtube.com/watch?v=4AYE3w5TWHs. (Minke n.d.)

[vi] Keskeys, Paul. "'We are start architects, not Star Architects': Penda on Staying Small and Thinking Big." June 6, 2016. Accessed October 3, 2016. http://architizer.com/blog/start-architects-penda/.

[vii] Amelar, Sarah. "Material Futures." October 2016. Accessed October 10, 2016. http://www.architecturalrecord.com/articles/11857-material-futures.

[viii] INKtalks. "Elora Hardy: Building a Sustainable (bamboo) Future." YouTube. April 18, 2012. Posted October 3, 2016. https://www.youtube.com/watch?v=XOSQksSlr9c.

[ix] Hardy, Elora. Magical Houses, Made of Bamboo. May 12, 2015. Posted October 3, 2016. https://www.ted.com/talks/elora_hardy_magical_houses_made_of_bamboo?language=en.

Hardy, John. My Green School Dream. November 18, 2010. Posted October 3, 2016. https://www.ted.com/talks/john_hardy_my_green_school_dream.

[x] Warka Water, Inc. "Design." Accessed October 1, 2016. http://www.warkawater.org/design

[xi] Sveiven, M. (2011, January 26). Bruder Klaus field chapel / Peter Zumthor. Retrieved October 3, 2016, from http://www.archdaily.com/106352/bruder-klaus-field-chapel-peter-zumthor

[xii] Minke, Gernot. Building With Earth : Design and Technology of a Sustainable Architecture. Basel, Switzerland: Birkhäuser, 2013.

[xiii] Ibid.

[xiv] Ibid.

[xv] Ibid.

*All images by author

Tracing Attempts to Reconcile Technology in Design

Michael McGlynn
Kansas State University

Abstract

To clarify and deepen our understanding of the dual role that technology plays in architectural design, I evaluate the ideas of James Marsten Fitch, Dean Hawkes, and Lance LaVine. I follow this with a synthesis of these ideas that can serve as a framework for restructuring technology teaching in both technical and design coursework. Lastly, I broadly consider the implications of this framework on course content and the degree to which particular content should be emphasized.

The Dual Role of Technology in Architecture

"...architecture is a unified discipline that, while it clearly participates in and refers to the worlds of both art and science, must be primarily understood as an unique enterprise in which these worlds find a synthesis that transcends their differences."

- Dean Hawkes[1]

The persistent disconnect between the technical and non-technical aspects of architectural design is an outgrowth and continuing reinforcement of a false dichotomy - that technology and design are synonymous with science and art, respectively. In fact, science and art commingle in design, and technology is essential to both. The *science* of design employs technology to achieve performance objectives. This is the province of the engineer who uses structural, constructional, and mechanical systems with a focus on utility and efficiency to redirect the flow of environmental forces. The *art* of design employs technology to address cultural objectives. This is the province of the architect who uses these same systems with a focus on formal, spatial, and aesthetic concerns to engage all of the senses. (Of course the architect is also concerned with performance, but this concern is always in relation to the broader humanistic context.) Methods and objectives differ, but for both engineers and architects, technology is integral to design.[2]

So technology in design must serve two masters simultaneously, one that resides in the world of empirical fact and the other in the world of interpreted value. This is essential if society is to create more than mere building. In "Symbolic and Literal Aspects of Technology", architectural critic Alan Colquhoun eloquently summarized the relationship, "The science of building, the rationalisation of construction and assembly, however vital in themselves, remain in the world of literal action. It is only when the architect, seizing this world, organises it according to the logic of symbolic forms that architecture results."[3] Given the dual role that technology must play in design, one would think that technology teaching in architecture would have much to say in regard to both. Yet, technology courses remain, at best, heavily biased toward the former to the substantial neglect of the latter. The reasons for this are many, not the least of which is the long-standing separation between the so-called "technical" courses and design courses. While some may say the situation calls for a wholesale reconsideration of the architectural curriculum, that is a tall order. However, there is still much that can be done within and across architectural courses to fuse these two worlds.

In order to frame such discussions and establish a basis for action, we must gain a better understanding of these two different uses of technology in architecture and the relationships between them. To this end, I evaluate the work of three theorists of architectural technology - James Marston Fitch, Dean Hawkes, and Lance LaVine. These three are of value as each articulates technology's architectural aspects while respecting the roles that engineering and building science play in architecture. Each, in his own way, situates the scientific aspects within the broader humanistic project of architecture.

Multi-Sensory Experience Through Scientific Understanding

Just after World War II, architectural historian and historic preservationist James Marston Fitch (1909-

2000) was the first to comprehensively address the promise and perils of modern industrial technology in architecture, giving voice to nascent environmental design approaches. At a fundamental level, Fitch viewed architecture as a type of environmental technology analogous to a biological organism. Mediating between the natural and human environments, what he termed the "third environment"[4] exists to optimize metabolic processes so that inhabitants can fully engage in perceptual awareness and, ultimately, aesthetic enjoyment. "The central function of architecture is thus to lighten the very stress of life. Its purpose is to maximize our capacities by permitting us to focus our limited energies upon those tasks and activities that are the essence of the human experience."[5]

In his view, however, post-industrial architecture was failing to live up to this fundamental task. In "The Impact of Technology", Fitch expressed concern that modern architecture had fallen prey to formalism - a focus on building form to the neglect of optimal, and sometimes even basic, performance.[6] In pre-industrial society, comfort was of necessity achieved through architectural means, the careful manipulation of building form and fabric in relation to the surrounding environment. In post-industrial society, architecture's traditional role as environmental mediator had been replaced by mechanical building services. This had led many architects to use mechanical means, not to optimize building performance, but to correct for "basic errors of design". Fitch considered this an "abdication of (the architect's) historic responsibilities".[7] He argued that we should use architectural means to the extent possible before resorting to mechanical means and that this would not only result in an architecture of optimal performance, but also of beauty.

This is central to Fitch's argument - that physical well-being and aesthetic satisfaction were intertwined. "The esthetic enjoyment of an actual building (as opposed to a mere photograph of it) is not exclusively a matter of vision but of *total sensory perception*. Thus, to be truly satisfactory (that is, to be truly beautiful), a building must meet the demands of all the senses, not just those of vision alone. It is not the eye but the whole man who reacts to architecture."[8] This would require a deeper scientific, not just technical, understanding and approach to design.

Architects needed to move beyond simply trying to keep up with the onslaught of technological development and instead needed to develop architectural forms undergirded by "objectively verifiable" criteria. These criteria would grow out of a focus on building performance to meet biological and cultural needs. While Fitch never denied the importance of purely formal criteria in architecture, he stressed that culturally driven formal qualities should be disciplined by criteria derived from an understanding of human needs.

Fitch's conflation of building performance and human aesthetic experience in architectural form makes the case for continuing our environmental design approaches, as they are grounded in science. Architects need an empirical understanding of the natural environment, then, not just to avoid "basic errors of design", but also to maximize the potential of architectural form to optimally engage the human senses. This approach is not without its limits, though. It is primarily an analytical approach that alone is incapable of addressing broader cultural concerns. If taken to the extreme, it can become a technical determinism, marginalizing as opposed to simply disciplining purely formal aesthetic concerns. These are among the issues addressed by architect and academic Dean Hawkes.

Technique Conditioned by Cultural and Aesthetic Judgments

Hawkes was steeped in environmental design beginning with his time at Cambridge University and the Martin Centre for Architectural and Urban Studies from 1965-1995. The centre was unique in that the founder, Leslie Martin, believed that architectural research was not simply synonymous with building science, but that it could also be conducted on its own terms. "He set up no artificial opposition between the invention of architectural form and the rational analysis of what had been invented: in his view practical reason led on into speculative reason, without a break."[9] It is this mindset that opens the door for Hawkes to both accept the tenets of building science and address its limitations in architectural design.

Fitch and Hawkes agree on three things: first, architecture's primary responsibility is to mediate between an interior suitable for a variety of human activities and an exterior that is often hostile to those activities; second, this was historically accomplished through manipulation of building form and fabric in response to environmental forces; and third, this historical role has been lost. As did Fitch, Hawkes traces this loss to the adoption of mechanical building services, but he also traces it to increasingly quantitative environmental design methods. By the late 20th century, architects had further ceded environmental control to the engineer and the engineering mindset of objective analysis predominated. A technical determinism had taken hold which was severing connections between the interior and exterior environments, depriving architects of what had been, "in a profound sense, a primary generator of architectural form throughout history".[10]

Hawkes' solution to this problem is similar to Fitch's - use architectural means to temper the ambient environment before supplementing with mechanical means - but Hawkes' qualitative difference in environmental outcome holds the key to success. Fitch's stated goal was environmental *optimization* of the interior environment so that inhabitants could maximize their potential. His desired outcome was the same as the engineers', and has unfortunately been accomplished, not through architectural means, but through increased mechanization and at significant economic, environmental, and psychological expense. Ironically, so-called "active" mechanical systems led to static interior environments and passive inhabitants who no longer engaged with the natural environment, either directly or through the built environment

Hawkes' stated goal is "environmental *diversity* (italics mine), realized and experienced spatially and temporally. This envisages spaces in which environmental uniformity, in all its dimensions of heat, light and sound, is replaced by variations, within limits, which maintain, in the occupant, a sense of the dynamics of the natural climate, of the proper condition of humankind."[11] Hawkes' outcome is achieved by reinvesting inhabitants with environmental control. In this case, so-called "passive" architectural approaches lead to dynamic interior environments that encourage active participation on the part of the inhabitants to adapt the built environment to suit their needs and desires.

Mechanical systems are under the inhabitants' control as well to be used only as necessary. Hawkes' dubs the former engineering-driven approach the "'exclusive" mode and his latter hybrid approach the "selective" mode.[12] The "selective" environmental design approach, closely aligned with the adaptive comfort model developed by Michael Humphreys and others,[13] is essentially the more scientific approach to architecture called for by Fitch, but enabling architects and inhabitants, not just engineers.

It is through Hawkes' writings that we also understand the limits of a predominantly scientific approach to technical decision making in architecture. Hawkes asserts that at no point in time, even among the modernists, has aesthetic expression in architecture been simply the inevitable result of an objective, scientific approach to technology. In fact, inside of environmental extremes, Hawkes argues that technological concerns in architecture - broadly considered as environmental, material, and constructional - "are primarily *cultural* and *aesthetic* matters".[13] Through numerous analyses of 19th and 20th century architecture, Hawkes' illustrates the wide range of approaches that architects have taken to addressing technological considerations. He describes these approaches as falling along "an axis that has, at one pole, a position of extreme technical determinism - everything that is fundamental to a building derives from the statement and solution of technical needs - and at the other a view that declares...that architecture is fundamentally a matter of taste and that questions of technique are at best secondary concerns of architects...".[14] Two of Hawkes' most powerful examples are his analyses of Piano and Rogers' Centre Georges Pompidou (1977) and Louis Kahn's Yale Center for British Art (1974). Despite that they were contemporaneous and possess similar functional and technical demands, Hawkes makes evident that both their technical and aesthetic outcomes were largely the result of the architects' radically different viewpoints regarding the institutional nature of museums. Piano and Rogers were provocateurs looking to challenge museum traditions, which led to a generically flexible interior and a highly articulated and technologically expressive exterior. In contrast, Kahn was harkening back to the traditional daylit museum composed of discrete rooms. As a result, the interior exhibits careful attention to material and detail with concealed mechanical systems, and the exterior aesthetic is reserved.[15] These two works of architecture stake out the middle ground of Hawkes' axis where "questions of technique invest architecture with a necessary degree of objectivity and rigour, but...are in themselves deeply conditioned by cultural and aesthetic judgments".[16]

In his analysis of Venturi Scott-Brown's National Gallery Sainsbury Wing (1991), Hawkes indicates how far, in his mind, architects can stray from technical requirements as a basis for design decision-making before veering too far in the other direction. After describing seemingly architectural aspects of the museum that upon inspection are nothing more than postmodern artifice, Hawkes declares, "When scenography becomes this much more important than tectonics - when the appearances and the making of a building become so disassociated - I believe that the very nature and definition of architecture are at risk".[17] As with Fitch's concerns regarding formalism, Hawkes recognizes the danger of cultural and aesthetic considerations becoming untethered from technical considerations. However, for Fitch, the measure was the degree to which an architect's formal expression neglected building performance, but for Hawkes, it is the degree to which an architect's formal, spatial, and aesthetic expression are independent of material and constructional techniques. To further explore the relationship between architectural expression and techniques, and return to an explicit consideration of the dual role of technology in architecture, we turn to the work of Lance LaVine, Professor of Architecture at the University of Minnesota.

Literal Performance, Sensory Experience, and Symbolic Meaning Through Architectural Technology

Both Hawkes' and LaVine's thinking rests on the common foundation of Alan Colquhoun's architectural criticism. Although Colquhoun acknowledged that architects' cultural and aesthetic concerns were not entirely independent of an objective, scientific understanding of the world, he emphasized that functional and technical considerations alone were incomplete: "...a purely teleological doctrine of technico-aesthetic forms is not tenable. At whatever stage in the design process it may occur, it seems

that the designer is always faced with making voluntary decisions and the configuration which he arrives at must be the result of an *intention* and not merely the result of a deterministic process."[18] Revealing the multiplicity of architects' intentions and the varying influences of these intentions on both technique and expression became the impetus for so much of Hawkes' work. LaVine is interested in resuscitating a common theoretical basis for architects' intentions in order to place them on par with those of engineers, and he does so by establishing the importance of the unique role that technology plays in architecture.

Similar to Fitch's concept of architecture as the "third environment", LaVine describes architecture as a "technology of habitation", and as such, its primary responsibility is to provide inhabitants with a secure "place of residence in nature".[19] The fact that we inhabit these technologies is what distinguishes *architectural* technologies - the elements and assemblages that constitute the building form and fabric - from other types of technology and why they also must mediate between a quantitative, scientific world and a qualitative world of cultural significance. "Architectural technologies physically modify nature so that people might bodily inhabit this context, but in so doing, they create another realm of ideas that seek to locate people mentally, emotionally, and spiritually within nature. Buildings cannot fail to make such statements because their technologies are housed in physical forms that reside in nature and, in turn, house us. We are symbolic as well as physical creatures. We cannot help attempting to interpret the symbolic significance of a physical world that surrounds us even as we are subject to its measurable consequence."[20] Architectural technologies, then, are essential to architecture, not only because they are, or should be, the primary means by which we redirect the flow of environmental forces, but also because they are the means by which we make sense of our place in the world.

The problem, as LaVine sees it, is that engineering's compelling technological perspective has "confused and suppressed" architecture's "distinct technological voice".[21] Architects have tried to adopt engineering's methods to put toward their own, very different, objectives, but to little or no avail. In the meantime, engineers have had great success in achieving building performance objectives. As Hawkes notes, though, the subsequent loss of connection between inside and outside has deprived architects of a primary architectural form generator. Hawkes and LaVine both understand that architecture's environmental connectedness is also its primary source of meaning. For LaVine, the solution lies in reestablishing architects' historical approach to technology in design, one that uses architectural technology to convey a metaphorical understanding of our relationship with the natural environment.

Before this can occur, LaVine contends that architectural technology must meet two prerequisites. First, it must be used to literally moderate environmental forces. Thus, architecture fulfills its fundamental purpose, as Fitch put it, "to lighten the very stress of life". The engineer's scientific understanding of the natural environment and abstract, quantitative design methods have proven to be highly effective in this regard. Engineers and architects use structural frames to efficiently redirect the force of gravity; and weather envelopes, windows, and mechanical services to efficiently redirect the flows of heat, air, and moisture. LaVine considers it necessary for architectural technology to serve these practical purposes if it is "to take on symbolic meaning...Tool as origin ensures that technology as a form of architectural symbol making is not capricious. The ideas that grow from the use of architectural technology are not part of an unbounded speculation that is forced to establish its own constraints".[22] This is how the architect avoids formalism and its attendant problems. However, alone this condition is not capable of producing symbolic meaning. LaVine finds that attempts to reduce the meaning of architectural technologies to abstractions of "empirical facts, as in the functionalism of the twentieth century, have proved not to be so much wrong as not fecund. They fail to create the kind, level, and richness of formal ideas that allow people to reside in nature."[23]

Second, architectural technology must be used to convey a sensory understanding of environmental forces to inhabitants. This brings to mind Fitch's call for an architecture that meets "the demands of all the senses". However, Fitch's scientific and analytic methods were adopted from engineering and the numerical abstractions that these methods produce are not operative for architects in design. Instead,

LaVine calls for a return to the source of scientific and quantitative reasoning, which he terms "nature as felt force".[24] A "felt force" is an inhabitant's palpable awareness of an environmental force, that which existed before modern science and is still the basis for human experience. Returning to a sensory understanding of environmental forces allows architects to think about these forces in terms of characteristics or qualities that describe lived human experience, rather than exclusively in the measurable terms of modern science. This necessarily sacrifices the certainty of number to stimulate the architect's generative imagination. Architects are then able to use architectural technology - structural frames, weather envelopes, and windows - to express environmental qualities formally, spatially, and aesthetically for the benefit of the inhabitants. This is fundamental to achieving Hawkes' goal of environmental diversity and inhabitant participation in his "selective" environmental design approach. While LaVine's first prerequisite ensures that this diversity is reasonably constrained by performance considerations, his second ensures that inhabitants develop an awareness of the dynamics of the natural environment.

It is this palpable environmental awareness that opens up the possibility for architects to convey ideas about our relation to the natural environment that are beyond the measures of engineers. LaVine outlines how a set of general metaphors has arisen from our shared sensory experiences that connect particular architectural technologies to an understanding of our place in the world. The felt force of gravity is expressed through the structural frame and understood as "the rooted order of the earth", the felt force of sunlight is expressed through the window as "that which gathers all things into the human domain", and the felt force of climate is expressed through the weather envelope as "the boundary of touch".[25] To develop this argument, LaVine analyzes the floors, walls, roofs, frames, and openings of four houses via their formal characteristics and palpable environmental qualities to interpret the particular metaphoric connection between these architectural technologies and the inhabitants' understanding of their significance in the natural environment. For instance, after analyzing how the floor of each house literally performs as well as metaphorically expresses how inhabitants might "take possession of territory",

LaVine concludes, "In each of these cases, the floor separates people from the cold and damp ground, but in so doing, each places these inhabitants in a special relation to the earth. The being above of the Finnish log cabin, the being continuous with the terrain of Orinda, the being with the earth and floating above it of the Wall House, and the being placed between the earth and sky of Villa Savoye are all ways in which human beings reference their own existence to that which surrounds them."[26] Similar to Hawkes' analyses, LaVine's comparisons demonstrate that although architectural technologies perform the same physical tasks in each house, they are given different formal configurations in relation to their surroundings based, in part, on the differing cultural and aesthetic intentions of each designer. While LaVine's set of metaphors is admittedly incomplete and his interpretations are open to question, he leaves no doubt that architectural technologies can be used to convey metaphorical understandings of our relationship with the natural environment. Accordingly, he makes a strong case for returning this type of technological thinking to its former place of central importance in architectural design.

Toward an Architectural Technic

Fitch's, Hawkes', and LaVine's theories clearly demonstrate that architectural technology as empirical fact and interpreted value are both essential to architectural design. Without a technological approach grounded in a scientific understanding of the natural environment, architecture would not be capable of addressing the significant environmental concerns with which we are confronted. Yet, without a technological approach driven by a metaphoric understanding of our relation to the natural environment, architecture would be incapable of expressing any ideas outside of its own performance. When integrated, these technological approaches can be used to create high-performing, environmentally diverse, multi-sensory, and meaningful architecture.

The dual nature of technology in design makes clear that technology has as much to do with architectural expression as it does with building construction and interior environmental control. While this is essentially the argument put forth by Kenneth Frampton in *Studies in Tectonic Culture*;[28] Fitch, Hawkes, and LaVine expand Frampton's discussion of structural

and constructional concerns to include the entirety of environmental concerns in architecture. These theorists demonstrate that all building technology is essentially environmental in that the shared intent is to redirect the flow of environmental forces to create a built environment suitable for human habitation, and that any building technology is capable of participating in architectural expression. This broader definition of what is known as *tectonics* might best be labeled *architectural technics*, as a *technic* describes, along the lines of the late historian of technology Lewis Mumford,[29] the complex of interactions between a given set of technologies and a society.

Taken together, Fitch's, Hawkes', and LaVine's work reveals an architectural technic that has much to say about technology teaching in architectural design, particularly in regard to course content and the degree to which particular content should be emphasized. LaVine's concept of architecture as a "habitational technology" establishes an overarching framework that we can use to structure technology teaching in both technical and design coursework. That which sets *architectural* technologies apart from all others, the fact that we live within them, also engenders the need for design students to gain both an abstract, scientific and qualitative, experiential understanding of these technologies. The inseparability of this duality in architectural design challenges our essentially reductive architectural curricula, but this does not necessarily require radical curricular restructuring. In fact, it is possible to teach the dual role of technology in architecture while maintaining separate technical and design coursework as long as these two roles are addressed - albeit with varying degrees of emphasis - in each technical and design course.

Broadly considered, technical coursework should emphasize a scientific and empirical understanding of building technologies, but should frame these technologies in architectural, rather than exclusively engineering, terms. Scientific concepts and principles, and building technologies and their architectural applications must be situated within an architectural technic to engage design students and make it easier for them to transfer this knowledge to a design context. In addition, discussions of architectural applications must go beyond building performance concerns to address the experiential and qualitative aspects of architectural technology as well.

While LaVine acknowledges that architecture must perform physical tasks, it is Fitch and Hawkes that lend definition to what a scientific and empirical understanding should entail for design students. Fitch's concept of architecture as the mediating "third" environment between the natural and human environments clarifies the nature of this "habitational technology". Instead of viewing technology, particularly mechanical services, as something added to architecture in order to solve even basic environmental issues, architecture itself *is* an environmental technology. This is a biological rather than mechanical analogy in that it is about working in concert with the surrounding environment rather than physically overpowering it. This is the essence of the environmental design ethic, which requires architects to employ architectural means before supplementing with mechanical means. The building enclosure is once again an environmental filter used to foster connections between the interior and exterior environments. While once viewed as optional in our post-industrial society, this approach is now imperative due to climate change.

Hawkes' "selective" theory of environmental design incorporates this imperative, but further empowers inhabitants and architects with its emphasis on occupant control and spatial and temporal environmental diversity. As is Fitch's biotechnical approach, "selective" design and the related adaptive comfort model are scientifically grounded. However, the "selective" design goal of maintaining in inhabitants "a sense of the dynamics of the natural climate" redirects Fitch's approach in less deterministic, more architecturally productive ways.

This goal is akin to LaVine's second prerequisite - that architectural technology produce in inhabitants a palpable awareness of environmental forces - and is key to using architectural technology qualitatively to convey ideas about our relation to the natural environment. Toward these ends, design coursework should teach design students to think about environmental forces in qualitative terms that describe the desired experiential outcomes for it is these qualities that activate the generative architectural imagination. Then each architectural project becomes

an attempt to express these and other qualities to the inhabitants through architectural technologies, considered at ever greater levels of complexity and detail as design students move through the architectural curriculum. To be sure, each "habitational technology" must still perform physical tasks and remains subject to the world of empirical fact, but each is now capable of addressing broader cultural concerns and so is also subject to the world of interpreted value.

Notes:

[1] Dean Hawkes, "The Technical Imagination: Thoughts on the Relation of Technique and Design in Architecture," *The Journal of Architecture* 1, no. 4 (1996): 345.

[2] For a similar argument, see Edward Allen, "Closing Response," in *Proceedings from Cranbrook 2007: Integrated Practice and the Twenty-First Century Curriculum* (Cranbrook Academy of Art, Bloomfield Hills, MI: The American Institute of Architects and Association of Collegiate Schools of Architecture, 2007), 47–53.

[3] Alan Colquhoun, "Symbolic and Literal Aspects of Technology," in *Collected Essays in Architectural Criticism* (London, UK: Black Dog Publishing Limited, 2009), 26. First published in *Architectural Design* (November 1962).

[4] First mentioned in James Marston Fitch, "The Aesthetics of Function," *Annals of the New York Academy of Sciences* 128, no. 2 (September 1, 1965): 706–14.

[5] James Marston Fitch and William Bobenhausen, *American Building: The Environmental Forces That Shape It*, 3rd ed. (Oxford University Press, USA, 1999): 3.

[6] James Marston Fitch, "The Impact of Technology," *Journal of Architectural Education* 16, no. 2 (Summer 1961): 9.

[7] Ibid., 12.

[8] Ibid., 11.

[9] Robert Maxwell, foreword to *The Environmental Tradition: Studies in the Architecture of Environment* by Dean Hawkes, 1st ed. (Taylor & Francis, 1996): 7.

[10] Dean Hawkes, "Environment at the Threshold," in *The Environmental Tradition: Studies in the Architecture of Environment*, 1st ed. (London: Taylor & Francis, 1996): 102.

[11] Dean Hawkes, introduction to *The Environmental Tradition: Studies in the Architecture of Environment*, 1st ed. (London: Taylor & Francis, 1996): 18.

[12] See Dean Hawkes "The Theoretical Basis of Comfort in 'Selective' Environments" and "Building Shape and Energy Use" in *The Environmental Tradition: Studies in the*

Architecture of Environment, 1st ed. (London: Taylor & Francis, 1996): 28-35 and 36-45, respectively.

[13] See Fergus Nicol, Michael Humphreys, and Susan Roaf, *Adaptive Thermal Comfort: Principles and Practice*, 1st ed. (London; New York: Routledge, 2012).

[14] Hawkes, "The Technical Imagination," 345.

[15] Ibid., 340.

[16] Dean Hawkes, "Space for Services: The Architectural Dimension," in *The Environmental Tradition: Studies in the Architecture of Environment*, 1st ed. (London: Taylor & Francis, 1996): 72-87. See also Hawkes, "The Technical Imagination," 340-341.

[17] Hawkes, "The Technical Imagination," 340.

[18] Ibid., 341-343.

[19] Alan Colquhoun, "Typology and Design Method," in *Collected Essays in Architectural Criticism* (London, UK: Black Dog Publishing Limited, 2009), 47. First published in *Arena* 83 (June 1967).

[20] Lance LaVine, *Mechanics and Meaning in Architecture* (Minneapolis, MN: University of Minnesota Press, 2001): xviii.

[21] LaVine, *Mechanics and Meaning*, 6.

[22] Ibid., 17

[23] Ibid., 192.

[24] Ibid., 191.

[25] Ibid., 66-68.

[26] Ibid., 77-83.

[27] Ibid., 179-180.

[28] Kenneth Frampton, *Studies in Tectonic Culture: The Poetics of Construction in Nineteenth and Twentieth Century Architecture*, 1st ed. (Cambridge, MA: The MIT Press, 1995).

[29] See Lewis Mumford, *Technics and Civilization*, 1st ed. (New York: Harcourt, Brace and Company, 1934).

SESSION 08: HISTORY

Session Chair: Thomas Leslie
Iowa State University

Matthew Hall, Auburn University: "Intent vs. Interpretation: the Prosaic Poetics of Lewerentz and Nyberg."

Scott Murray, University of Illinois: "On the Role of History in Architectural Technology Education."

Clifton Fordham, Temple University: "Assessing the Aesthetic and Functional Contribution of Shading Devices to Richard Neutra's Library at Simpson College in Iowa."

Tyler Sprague, University of Washington: "Optimized Material, Expressive Forms: Precast Concrete Modern Architecture in the Pacific Northwest."

Intent vs. Interpretation:
The Prosaic Poetics of Lewerentz & Nyberg

Matthew Hall
Auburn University College of Architecture, Design and Construction

Abstract

Spanning three quarters of a century, Sigurd Lewerentz's architectural career left us with a body of uncompromising and mysterious work. Lewerentz rarely wrote and never lectured outside of informal discussions with colleagues on the job site. He has no lineage of direct followers, yet has indirectly inspired many through interpretations of his work. Operating outside of conventions and distanced from most of his contemporaries, Lewerentz's was neither rooted in dogma nor movement. In the wake of a rapidly changing cultural context and the increasingly pragmatic and production-oriented building industry of Sweden's welfare state in the 1960's, he consistently tested architecture's capacity for authenticity as a self-referential act, deploying archaic architectural moves in direct tension with modern materials and methods, interpreted as an internal conflict between the pragmatic and poetic. Familiar typologies and conventions were jettisoned because they simply were not useful given the architectural problems at hand. Each detail was purpose built, yet demonstrated refinement, self-editing and the progressive struggle to develop an appropriate architectural language.

A key source for understanding Lewerentz's intent is his relationship with Bernt Nyberg, an architect who had a short career of exceptional work on the fringe of post-war Swedish modernism. His close relationship with Lewerentz resulted in competition entries, conversations, and a mutual influence that changed the course of their architecture. Recordings of dialogs between the two architects and interviews with surviving collaborators have brought Lewerentz's voice to the surface for the first time, where through his own words we may potentially reconcile the inevitable rift between our interpretation and the architect's intent while gaining new insight on Bernt Nyberg as one of Sweden's most unique unknown architects. While the majority of the scholarship on Lewerentz's work is centered in an interpretive discourse on narrative, phenomenological theory and poetics, the dialogs and interviews suggest his intent was the exact opposite: an architect simply solving problems in a unique way resulting in open systems for interpretation. This paper proposes that Lewerentz and Nyberg are part of a rare lineage interested in orchestrating tension between technical refinement and innovation, rawness and precision, and honesty and contradiction. The aim is not to diminish the myriad of potential interpretations, but suggest that the resulting *poetry of the prosaic* incites an open dialog rather than didactic and precise meaning, The poetry one constructs through readings and experience, are in this case, the result of a precise yet challenging form of pragmatics left for us to decipher.

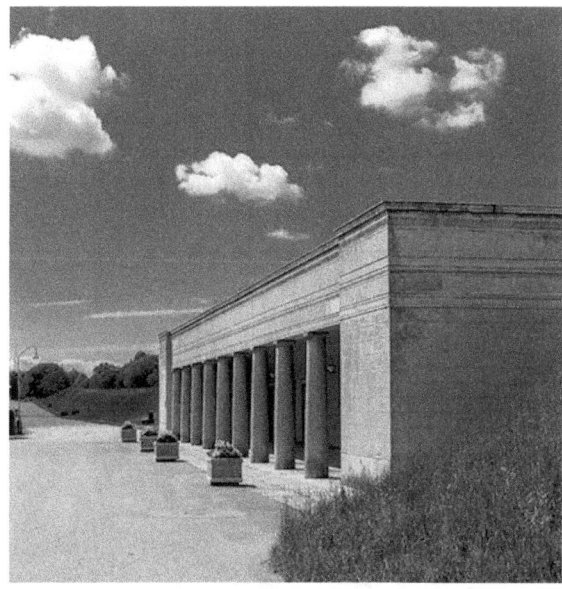

Fig. 1. The Chapel of St. Birgitta, 1918 at the Eastern Cemetery in Malmö

The struggle for language: the early work

Lewerentz practiced architecture from 1908 until his death in 1975. His subtle subversion of existing typologies and common materials became more extreme with age. One would expect the young architect to be radical by default, in search of new moves, forms and concepts in a struggle for autonomy and maturity. For Lewerentz, it is striking that his radical nature would most forcefully show itself in his late works through uncompromising formal and material unison. Concentrations of his work span decades at particular sites such as the Woodland Cemetery in Stockholm and the Eastern Cemetery in Malmö. Both served as laboratories for continuous experimentation where one can trace shifts in his design approach, realized often in confrontation with his previous solutions. Two examples in particular signal Lewerentz's abrupt departure for his masterful, yet subversive classical forms *Fig. 1*. At the Eastern Cemetery in Malmo, the twin chapels of St. Knut and St. Gertrude combined with a crematorium and the intimate Chapel of Hope form a disparate collage of aggregate pieces, breaking abruptly from previous referential classical forms. At this point his architecture engages the capacities and nature of materials with details that carefully orchestrate connections between differing assembles rather than rendering all surfaces, as was common in his early neo-classical architecture. At the twin chapels, an interior structural shell of golden Lomma brick is clad with scrap chips of marble, floored in bits of cork and wood, with an entry vestibule of filigree wood strips that wrap from wall to ceiling *Fig.2*. The wall's true make-up is only apparent at openings where the layers are revealed with mortar filling in the resultant gaps of contrasting masonry skins. *Fig. 3*.

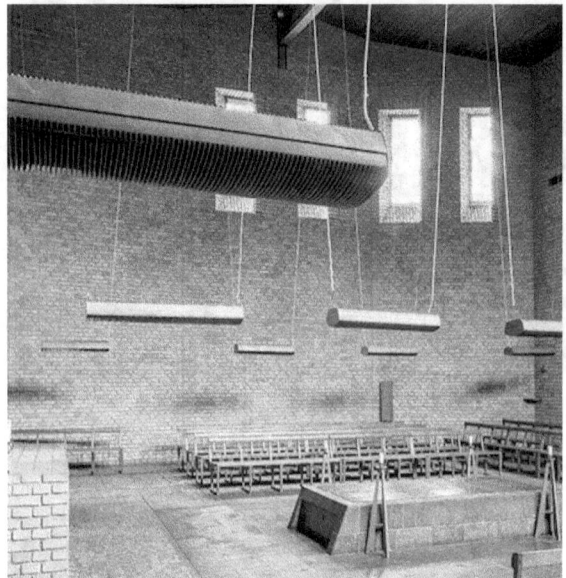

Fig. 2. Interior of the Chapel of St. Knut, Eastern Cemetery, Malmö, Sweden

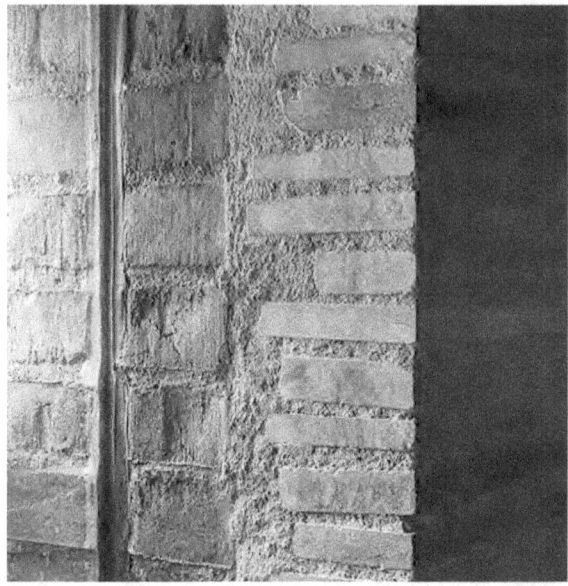

Fig. 3. Window detail at the Chapel of Hope, Malmö Sweden showing marble skin meeting brick structure

At his other life-long laboratory, the Woodland Cemetery in Stockholm, Lewerentz was tasked with creating a restroom addition to his 1925 masterpiece of "Swedish Grace," The Chapel of The Resurrection. Rather than connecting the new structure into a dialog with the existing complex of severe and stark classical volumes *Fig. 4* he stacked bricks with raw joints with the back, or "bad side" turned outwards, showing manufacturing marks and unfinished surfaces. *Fig.5*. These humble volumes are another example an aggregated architecture of unexpected material qualities that spark inquiry on the scale of the detail rather than reading a coherent and gestural form. These tendencies set the stage for what was to come in his later projects.

Strange Details: the late work

In 1966, Reyner Banham's *The New Brutalism* made the case for the budding Brutalist movement through a critical summary of international architecture. Banham described the movement as a new strain of modernism interested in directness and honesty where rawness and clarity were values that defined the overall aesthetic. In his chapter on the "Brick Brutalists" he refers to Lewerentz's Church of St. Mark in Björkhagen from 1960 as the "hardest case" of a building that would "greatly enrich the Brutalist canon if it could safely be included within it."[1] Lewerentz's work simply did not fit the clear ethical mold outlined in the New Brutalism, thus Banham considers the special case of Lewerentz to be a very "other" architecture, outside of conventions and distanced from his contemporaries. He was not the only Swedish architect to participate in the extensive church building of the 1960's, as many architects such as Johan Celsing used this venue to produce a high quality of work in the wake of an increasingly pragmatic and production-oriented building industry. Claes Caldenby refers to Sweden's extensive church building as a "haven of beauty" for architects who had ambitions beyond the practical, describing Lewerentz as an "emblematic artist-outsider."[2] He engaged critically with seemingly every *Zeitgeist* of the twentieth century by contributing to Sweden's transition from primarily Neo-classical architecture to most all of the early modernist identity crises. He tested their capacity for authenticity by constantly challenging himself through a balance of acquired expertise with fresh insight on each new design problem.

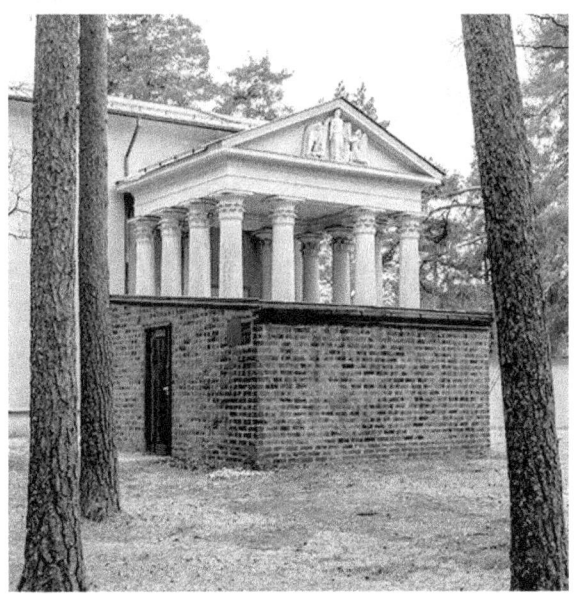

Fig. 4. Service addition (1952) designed in direct confrontation with the Chapel of The Resurrection, built over twenty-five years earlier (1925.) Woodland Cemetery, Stockholm, Sweden

With such a reputation coupled with a relatively small output of built works compared to his contemporaries, one is left with more questions than answers upon investigation. What is often considered an abrupt turn in his late work is suggestively foreshadowed in the moves of earlier experiments. Colon St. John Wilson

describes this turn as "extreme, unblinking, and absolute. His classicism was more refined, more deeply felt, more original than that of any of his contemporaries; his late work was more austere than any minimalist, more uncompromising than any Brutalist."[3]

Years of experience prepared Lewerentz to approach his late work with radical rigor. While he was not the only architect to work with Sweden's most readymade building material, the brick, Lewerentz gave it new meaning as a continuous fabric wrapping every surface of the sacred spaces, no longer relegated to traditional structural tasks. The two brick churches of St. Mark in Stockholm and St. Peter at Klippan are essays in how far one can push a single material in concert with contrasting pragmatic and compositional moves. Lewerentz was enamored with the massive archaic ruins of past civilizations where the lack of precision in hand-formed bricks necessitated wide mortar joints to adapt to the inconsistencies, which is evident in the walls of both churches where dimensions and openings follow no expected masonry dimensions resulting in wildly varying masonry joints as Lewerentz allowed no brick to be cut.

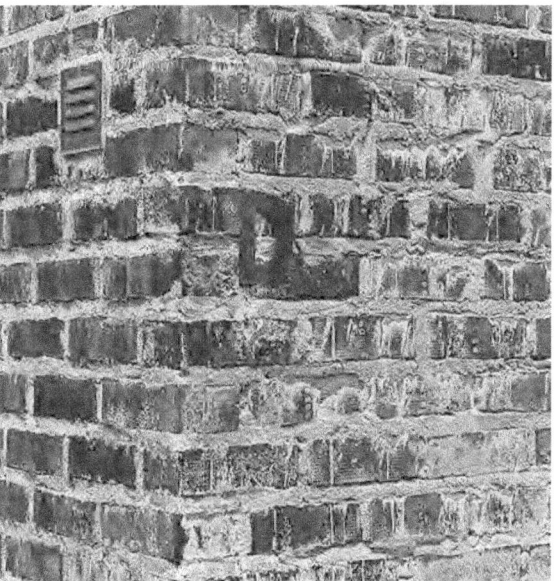

Fig. 5. Masonry at the restroom addition to The Chapel of The Resurrection, Woodland Cemetery, Stockholm, Sweden

Throughout his long career, Lewerentz dealt with fundamental themes: unit to whole, sterotomic vs. tectonic, and sacred vs. profane through the humble nature of his spatial and formal ideas enabled by the media used to imagine and construct them. It is impossible to divorce the form from it's materials, exacerbating the question of whether the material fills the form, or the form is a result of aggregated details that remarkably add up to a coherent spatial idea. While many details carry over from Lewerentz's earlier work here they are more refined with little reference to contemporary architectural themes. Brick and tile patterns vary wildly with drawings that suggest a precisely dimensioned starting point but no resolution for the patterns' end. *Fig.6.* In the sanctuary space, the floor undulates and breaks at the baptismal front as waves of brick articulate the vaults above. Caught between these vaults and the floor is a cross-like fabrication of weathered steel that sits upon two massive steel sections joined into one column. According to workers and others there during the construction, the steel assembly for the sanctuary was left outside for months to achieve a weathered state, which would have been impossible for an interior condition, thus adding the ruinous expression of the space.

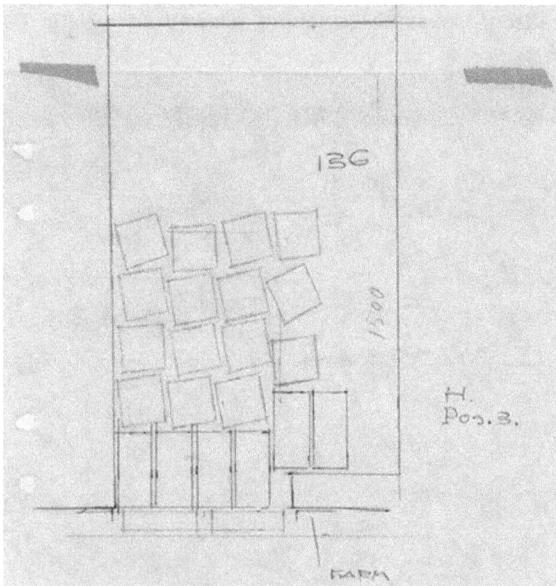

Fig. 6. Tile pattern drawing at St. Peter's Church. Image courtesy of the Swedish Center for Architecture and Design, Stockholm, Sweden

Some of the more discussed details of St. Peter's Church are the insulated glass panels simply clipped to the exterior of the wall with no clear compositional intent or frame other than a dripping bead of black

sealant. This enables the interior to read unenclosed, as the fragile panels of glass appear to float on the rough exterior brickwork. While the elimination of the window frame is an odd detail, it is even more astounding when one considers that Lewerentz spent decades designing and fabricating architectural components such window and door frames though his company IDESTA in Eskilstuna only to refuse to use any window frames at all in many late projects to include St. Peter's and the Flower Kiosk in Malmö. These, along with countless other details, suggest a struggle for more direct methods for joining contrasting materials without any mediating elements common to standard construction.

Lewerentz and Nyberg

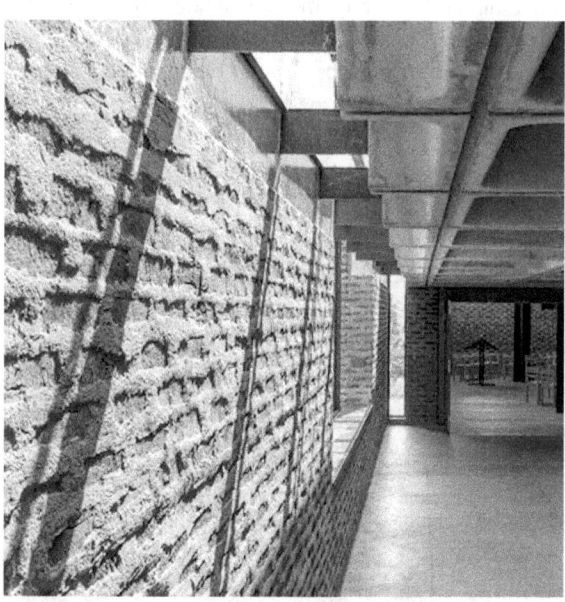

Fig. 7. Interior corridor of the Funeral Chapel in Höör, Sweden.

During the construction of the Church of St. Peter, a young architect named Bernt Nyberg began to show up at the site, slowly approaching the old master and gradually developing a relationship. Nyberg had his own architectural practice, but his eventual collaboration with Lewerentz would change his work dramatically. He did not follow in Lewerentz's footsteps, but instead asked similar questions about material, detailing and a building's place in culture. Like Lewerentz, Nyberg was enamored with archaic forms, ruins and the primal appeal of the brick in its most primal and raw form seeking innovative ways to solve simple architectural problems like the meeting of window and wall, or column and roof. This desire for a "new way" was not an attempt to be original, but rather the result of self-imposed challenges to create unique details for a precise context. While Lewerentz is best known for his religious structures and cemeteries, Nyberg's programs were primarily secular until he won a competition in 1970 for a funeral chapel in Höör, Sweden *Fig.7*. This building was realized at the height of both architect's collaborations, and Nyberg dealt with many of Lewerentz's themes by asking the same questions, but deploying a different solution.

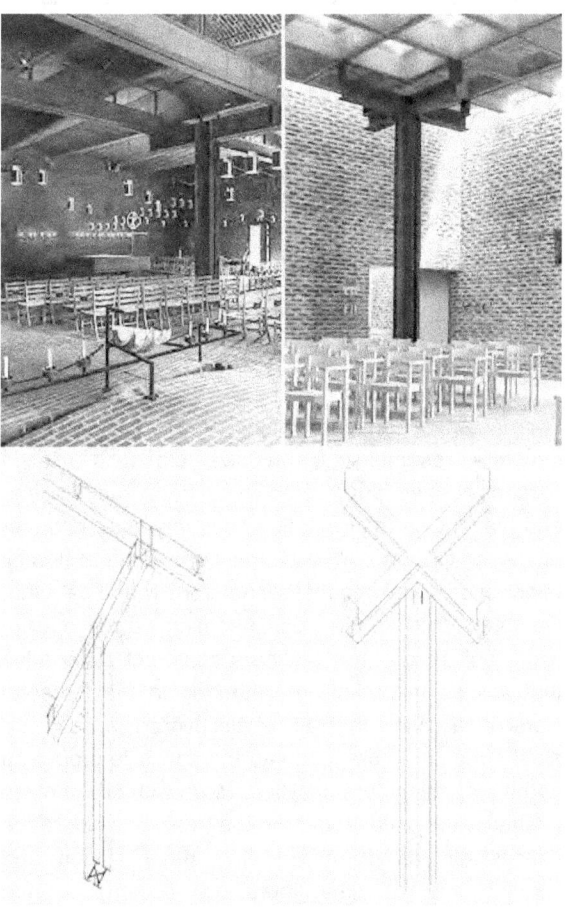

Fig. 8. Freestanding steel structure assembly comparison: Lewerentz's St. Peter's Church in Klippan and Nyberg's Funeral Chapel in Höör.

Lewerentz and Nyberg were interested in building an architecture that was neither abstraction nor symbol. Through self-imposed rules like never cutting a brick, or Lewerentz's obsessive requirement to leave all

weld joints visible, a clear respect for each material is demonstrated with equal appreciation for the hands that placed it. Nyberg for instance had a rule that hollow steel section should never be used, with a value for expressing edges and thicknesses which was a consistent feature of the steel detailing in all projects allowing for clear readings of structural forces and assemblies. Both architects had stringent yet contrasting ideas regarding masonry construction, and the nature of penetrations and systems integration. Lewerentz expressed each masonry unit, down to details that deployed single differentiated bricks for specific purposes. Did the wall facilitate the bricks or did the bricks allow for the wall? Conversely, Nyberg would often state, "why does the wall have to be about the individual bricks,"[5] as if dead set on a unified whole rather than an aggregation of parts. While this attitude is clearly evident in the smeared and projecting mortar joints that blur Nyberg's bricks into monoliths, upon careful investigation, there are more elusive dependencies between elements, such as the blossoming cruciform columns in the Höör chapel that support a coffered concrete slab held in precarious stasis on thin stilts of steel. This assembly is clearly derivative of the cruciform frame at St. Peter's but is dispersed into four freestanding elements rather than one total and centralized structural piece. *Fig. 8.* In both architects' work, subversions of the expectations we have about how walls meet ceilings and columns hold up buildings all serve to produce an equilibrium of the parts to the whole that is physically and conceptually indivisible, effortlessly obscuring origins and construction sequence for only acolytes to decode.

While simplistic interpretations of Nyberg's work suggest that he was imitating Lewerentz, the reality of the situation could not be more contrary from the truth. Long before his collaboration with Lewentz, Nyberg was dealing with similar issues constructing his own unique language. To this day, there are many myths about Lewerentz that are easily dispelled by understanding the relationship between these two masters. They had differing approaches to design, but shared a common interest in material as a communicative media un-divorced from it's historical connotations, and an approach to detailing based on the precise mediation between contrasting systems and formal elements, such as the immovable mass of a raw wall and the fragile ephemerality of the constantly changing reflective surface of insulated glazing units. *Fig. 9.*

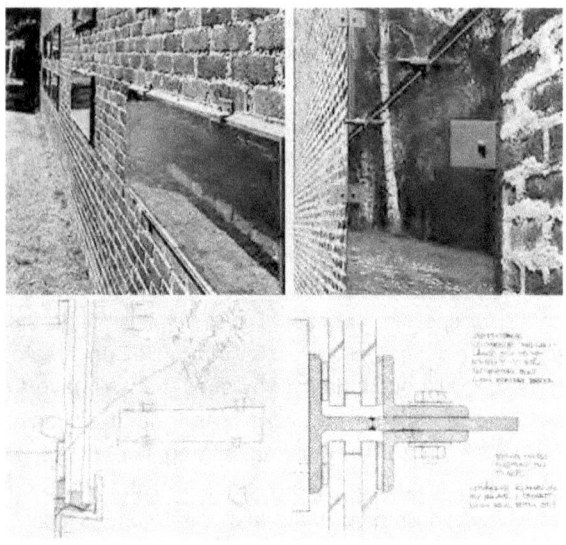

Fig. 9. Window detail comparison: Lewerentz's St. Peter's Church in Klippan, and Nyberg's Funeral Chapel in Höör. Drawings courtesy of the Swedish Center for Architecture and Design, Stockholm, Sweden.

Nyberg's relationship with Lewerentz offers us perhaps the earliest insight on Lewerentz as a man and a designer. Nyberg left us with documentary artifacts, objective film and candid recorded interviews. Nyberg had plans for a series of project monographs on Lewerentz beginning with the Church of St. Peter. The first book was to include academic texts by "Lewerentz connoisseurs" Per-Olof Olsson and Sven Ivar Lind (eventually published much later in other venues). The architects' viewpoints were then to be contrasted through "interviews with the collaborators and craftsmen from the building process. The occupants are also expected to contribute with their experiences."[4] In short, the plan was to contextualize the work beyond the iconoclastic struggles of a single canonical figure through the words and experiences of those who built and occupied the building.

Intent vs. Interpretation

Poetry is intense by default. Its concentrated, direct and precise use of language is often simultaneously vague, open and purposefully cerebral. A work of architecture can have these qualities through intent and purpose provoking a particular experience or

reading. A pragmatic approach is often at odds with the poetic, but in the case of Lewerentz and Nyberg, the pragmatics framed by a unique and uncommon set of architectural values yielded work that cuts past our normative perception of ordinary elements such as walls, columns and openings. These architects did not seek new forms, but rather, they focused on the prosaic in architecture. What we read from their efforts is of no consequence. What matters is that there is, in fact, something to read.

Architecture is often an unintentionally communicative medium. While it must convey the requisite functionary messages about use and way-finding, regardless of intent, architecture may also be read and interpreted, informing culture about those who conceptualized and made it. While it is natural to look for meaning, Lewerentz and Nyberg's work presents an overwhelming aura of strangeness begging for greater intent than a simple solution to a technical problem. Their architecture is one of dialog rather than discourse, as the forms seem so pregnant with symbolism prompting both occupants and architectural scholars to assign narrative, meaning and myth to the work.

For instance, at St. Peter's, the single column structure resembles a primitive cross. It sits in darkness, aged and rusted as if from another time and place. One interpretation sees this as a reminder of the crucifixion. "The solemn nature of the spatial experience speaks to the deeper sorrow and pain that was outworked on the cross, seemingly a reminder of what took place on it".[6] Others construct a narrative that follows the primitive: gathering in the forest to worship, a collapsing ruin is discovered; a decaying steel structure is dragged into the space to prop it up and the openings are hastily covered with bits of glass to shelter the occupants from the freezing winds.[7] The floor swells as if forces below have eroded and warped it over time, breaking violently at the baptismal with the module of the dark Helsingborg brick forming the line of the fracture. These details balance the perceived ad-hoc approach with a bloodless precision. Everything can be seen in two ways: as an obvious and clever solution, or a deep and symbolic operation. In a discussion with Bernt Nyberg, Lewerentz remarked disparagingly against a functionary who only conceived of one correct and absolute way of doing things stating with rare eloquence, "He had never understood that you can do it in a hundred different ways. That is what we must acquire. Knowledge."[8] In both Nyberg and Lewerentz's case, knowledge required practice, experimentation and dialog, and they chose to exercise all three silently through the act of building.

Per Olof Olson sums Lewerentz up well in the following theory: "He seems to be more interested in technical and constructive problems than esthetical, and is often shocking with "ugly" architectural solutions. He belongs to the few innovators to whom ugly or beautiful doesn't exist. It's all about finding an obvious solution to a problem.... Sigurd Lewerentz is a realistic technician and open-minded esthete."[9]

More pragmatic scholars perceive Lewerentz's details to be motivated by traditional notions of honesty and expression. The exposed conduit and steel suggest that the building has nothing to hide, yet the mechanical system is hidden and the openings follow no traditional or obvious notions of carrying masonry loads. The contradictions continue to add up and the interpretations have no end. For many the work is poetic, rich and meaningful with some from the congregation of St. Peter's inexplicably stating that the sanctuary space brings the "closer to god." For Lewerentz, it was simply a collection of reasonable solutions to obvious technical problems that he was both interested in and passionate about, with perhaps a keen awareness of their potential to satisfy more than mere functional requirements. Paradoxically, the problems are solved through unexpected and idiosyncratic methods, which seemed perfectly reasonable to the architect who neither pronounced nor assumed anything exceptional about his architecture.

The Dialogs

Other than interviews with surviving collaborators and the handed down tales of informal chats with masons, clergy, and others on the construction site, our only directly citable statements from Lewerentz exisit in the form of recently discovered recorded interviews conducted by Bernt Nyberg between 1964 and Lewerentz's death in 1975. These dialogs reveal a candid discussion devoid of any deep philosophical intent yet imply a tremendous care and interest regarding the consequences of construction. The

architect may have elaborate theories and intentions, but they should be left for others to read and discover which is evident in the discussion that focuses on results rather than intent. Nyberg followed suit, accompanying his work with dry descriptions of technical details, leaving the larger conceptual framework for the visitor to decipher. Lewerentz's unique way of dealing with questions he had no interest in answering can be summed up by his reply to an art historian's questions about why the lamps outside of St. Petri are leaning. *Fig. 10.* Often this is thought to be a symbolic bow to those who enter. Upon inquiry Lewerentz replied as if the answer was so clear that it did not need to be stated with a curt "Doesn't he see that?"[10] In addition to the interviews, Nyberg took extensive film of Lewerentz's late work under construction intending to create videos to educate young architects on construction methods; quite ironic given that such methods are perhaps impossible, if not inappropriate to duplicate.

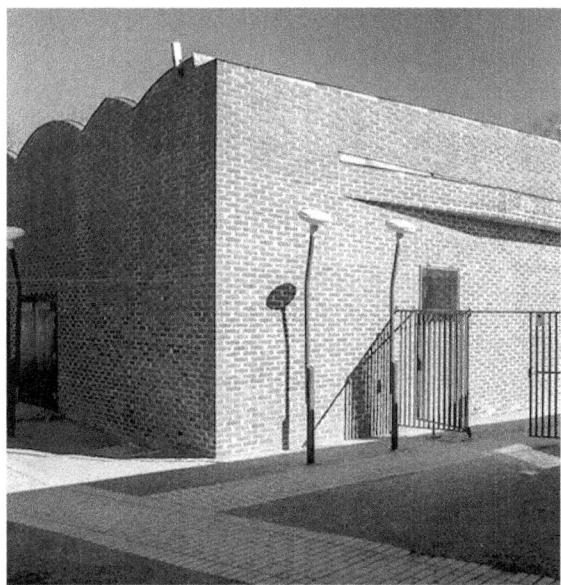

Fig. 10. Leaning lamps at entry gate to Lewerentz's St. Peter's Church

While many of the recorded interviews between Nyberg and Lewerentz have been and transcribed, sources have stated that many more must have existed. The majority of the dialogs consist of Nyberg struggling with Lewerentz to take the conversation deeper. Per Iwansson, a former colleague of both architects, described Lewerentz as gruff and not easily talkative about himself or his work with a refusal to discuss anything but technical solutions. It is fitting that in the context of hours there are only minutes of direct content about architectural intent. The mystery of the architecture truly does match the personality of the architect. Just as we must read into his work to find answers, we must read into his answers to understand the work. Both require the observer to take a position inevitably based in their own biases and experience.

One of the more discussed details in Lewerentz's late architecture is his approach to openings, previously described as devoid of frame, setting fragile glass in direct juxtaposition with massive walls. When asked, Lewerentz simply replied that it was much simpler to do it this way, continuing to state that it was not something that should normally be done, suggesting that this was a special case. Following is a short excerpt from the dialogs between Bernt Nyberg, (BN) Sigurd Lewerentz, (SL) and an unknown speaker on this detail and their relationship to the integrated heating system that was developed specifically for the building. It is translated verbatim.[10]

Unknown: I have been looking at the windows here. They are fine from the outside and from the inside. I think it is a good way of using new methods.

SL: Yes, but it is nothing to take after. It is one such exclusive thing. One can do it some time. Of course, it has to be hardened glass but it is expensive. But it is fun to be able to do some time. It is nothing you should do, you can place the whole frame on the outside, a common frame.

Unknown: How is it in the office-rooms? With ventilation and such things? They cannot open the windows. Has not anybody said anything about that?

SL: No I think it will work. Bacho will succeed in it (Bacho is the company which produced the heating and ventilation system). If anyone can do it, they can and they are working on it. At the time it has been very good. You don't have any maintenance. There are no radiators. There is nothing of the usual junk that show in the floors. Think about how it would look in a hundred years. You must then tear up all floors. So, it is practical with air.

BN: This double glazing on the outside. This silver lining. I heard that you wanted to paint over it. But there you have obviously changed your mind.

SL: Yes, I didn't think it hurt so much.

BN: No, I think it is quite elegant with the exactness.

SL: The drawback is of course that it has to be hardened glass. It is expensive. And easy to damage. It is nothing to take after.

BN: This? It is maybe nothing for normal housing. I think it is extremely stylish. The exact plate against the rough masonry.

SL: You could have another plate, a protection of the plate in some way. It is just fastened through... When the kids realize this... It is really more practical to put them inside.

BN. But this usually goes with jalousies that always gather dust, and you get four sides to polish. It is not right either.

SL: No, windows are troublesome in general. All should be single glass. It would be easier.

BN: This thick?

SL: But it doesn't help. There is not enough insulation value. They claim.

BN: With this small window area, it should...

SL: Downdraft.

BN: You can heat some more. Here the heating is in the floor, right?

SL: No it is in channels... There come out heating over there. I think it is a relief to get rid of all this with floor-heating, roof-heating, radiators and all that. It is hot air. It is comfortable I think. You avoid a lot of maintenance. You have to think about how such floor-heating looks in a hundred years. It is not fun to have such a thing.

The conversation continues to discuss the seemingly ad-hoc nature of the conduits for lighting at St. Peter's that are simply tacked onto the surface of the brick. Relatively banal power-strips and cords snake through spaces and up walls and across ceilings. One could read this as a mere afterthought if it were not for the precision of the installation. For the layperson it represents an aggressively banal way to solve the problem, while for the architect it is often interpreted as an attempt at integrity showing systems that would otherwise be hidden. The dialogs reveal Lewerentz's true intent further reinforcing his frank acceptance of the inevitable change that building systems will undergo.

BN: Lighting conduits are an eternally loved chapter in your churches (spoken no doubt with sarcasm.) Can I ask you? Is it on purpose in order to irritate people or what?

SL: Yes, you could say that.

BN: You don't want to show it off?

SL: No, it is because I think it is troublesome to put them in. Do you know when you make rooms like this, where the lamps shall be?

BN: Yes, you have to decide often these days. Then the lamps come.

SL. I never did that. The lamps have to come afterwards. And besides, these idiotic conduits which are drawn in the walls and which always come out in the wrong direction. I think that… It could probably be better done. It is a way to solve it, anyway.

Upon first reading of these and the many other discussions, one cannot help but feel that a myth is busted. It seems fitting that the architect himself would reduce our scholarly expressive and extensive rhetoric to a few brief statements. Perhaps another view of this realization is that the architect who thoughtfully considers the material and technical consequence of construction in unison with larger formal ideas can produce an architecture that gives us plenty to discuss, but does not rely on such rhetoric to be conceptually sound.

Both Nyberg and Lewerentz are clearly emblematic of a dying breed of architect that coupled a passion for an architecture that deals with prose before poetry. Mistakenly labeled as "Brutalists," they were, in fact, humanists interested in authenticity and a direct connection to human effort and struggle through the marks they made in architectural form. As a result, the work enjoys continued validity through both poetic interpretation and attempts at rational explanation.

"Lewerentz's late projects represent an unprecedented integration of making and thought. Like Matisse, who advised young painters to cut off their tongues and communicate with brush, paint and canvas, Lewerentz was famously laconic."[11] While Lewerentz and Nyberg understood that rhetoric is neither a meaningful substitution, nor an adequate explanation for a built language, these architects' life-long struggle for solutions is strangely analogous to our innate desire to question them. It is strangely satisfying that these dialogs and films have been hidden until recently as they may have otherwise stunted decades of rich scholarship. Ultimately, interpretation will always trump intent as visitors continue to occupy and interpret. Perhaps the most fitting dialog one can have with such an architecture is to experience it in respectful and fascinating silence.

Notes:

[1] Banham, Reyner. "Hard Cases, The Brick Brutalists." In *The New Brutalism: Ethic or Aesthetic?*, 125-127. New York: Reinhold Publishing Company, 1966.

[2] Caldenby, Claes. "Lewerentz and the Haven of Beauty." In *Lewerentz's S:t Petri at 50: Context, Fragments and Influence*, edited by Matthew Hall and Hansjörg Göritz, 47-53. Klippan: Municipality of Klippan, 2016.

[3] Wilson, Colin St John. "The Sacred Buildings and the Sacred Sites" In *Sigurd Lewerentz 1885-1975*, 11-34. Nicola Flora, Paolo Giardiello, and Gennaro Postiglione, Electa Architecture, 2001.

[4] Nyberg, Bernt, from description of the planned monograph of S:t Petri Kyrka. Book mock-up held at The Swedish Center for Architecture and Design, Stockholm, AKRM Nyberg, Bernt Box 01/AM 1985-16.

[5] Staffan Schultze (architect and close collaborator in the office of Bernt Nyberg), interview by Matthew Hall, December 2014.

[6] Baker, Reginald. "Precedent: Sigurd Lewerentz : St. Peter's Church," *reginaldbaker–architect* (blog), March 2, 2011 (04:23 a.m.), http://reginaldbaker-architecture.blogspot.com/2011/03/p-r-e-c-e-d-e-n-t-sigurd-lewerentz-st_02.html

[7] Mwenja, Waithera, precedent study drawings describing a narrative for the concept of St. Peter's Church.

[8] Lewerentz, Sigurd, in discussion with Bernt Nyberg and Karl-Erik Olsson (photographer), February 1967.

[9] Olof Olson, Per. "The Lewerentz Phenomenon" Originally intended to be published in the first monograph on Sigurd Lewerentz, edited by Bernt Nyberg.

[10] Iwansson, Per. Narrative and translation of interviews with Sigurd Lewerentz conducted between 1965-70 by Bernt Nyberg. In In *Lewerentz's S:t Petri at 50: Context, Fragments and Influence*, edited by Matthew Hall and Hansjörg Göritz, 111-115. Klippan: Municipality of Klippan, 2016.

[11] Caruso, Adam. "Sigurd Lewerentz and a Material Basis for Form." In *Sigurd Lewerentz, Två Kyrkor*, Claes Caldenby, Adam Caruso, Sven Ivar Lind, and Olof Hultin, 53-55. Stockholm: Arckitektur Förlag, 1997.

All photographs by author unless otherwise noted

On the Role of History in Architectural Technology Education

Scott Murray
University of Illinois at Urbana-Champaign

Abstract

As an inducement for discussion, this paper argues for the inclusion of history as a critical component in the teaching of architectural technologies. Traditionally, history courses are concerned primarily with the past, while technology courses are concerned primarily with the present (and sometimes the future), although it may be possible and beneficial to rethink these divisions. Whereas longstanding boundaries of architectural scholarship often place history and technology in wholly separate realms, indifferent if not oppositional to each other, a historical perspective can be used to effectively expand our understanding of contemporary technologies, linking current approaches to their antecedent developments and innovations. Technology thus becomes a more malleable and dynamic subject, rather than static, formulaic, or autonomous. In this way, students may understand current technologies as the result of a chain of experiments and breakthroughs, whether incremental or revolutionary, and thus view the contemporary practice of architecture and engineering as part of a continuum of technological and intellectual development.

The Nature and Function of Architectural History

In order to discuss the potential benefits of integrating historical studies within building technology education, I will begin by looking more generally at architectural history, its nature and function. Architectural history is concerned primarily with analysis of constructed buildings of the past (though, of course, unbuilt architectural projects and written works are also important subjects), commonly organized into subdivisions based on chronological time, geography, and/or common thematics.[1] But to interpret this concern as being focused solely or exclusively on the physical artifacts themselves (whether building, drawing, or text) is too limited. Many architectural historians view their work as a multivalent enterprise, understanding buildings as, on one hand, the end result of a complex process involving patronage,

design, and construction, and on the other hand, once built, as the setting for years, centuries, or perhaps millennia of daily human activity, with all of its cultural, political, biological, environmental, and technological manifestations.

The discourse of architectural history thus engages a full range of human endeavors. The historian Spiro Kostof, who taught for many years at UC Berkeley, has written that "the history of architecture partakes, in a basic way, of the study of social, economic, and technological systems of human history."[2] One may interpret from this statement that architectural history seeks to understand the interrelations of these three often overlapping systems: social, economic, and technological. Kostof believes that buildings, when viewed in this way, can serve as "palpable images of the values and aspirations of the societies that produced them."[3] In this interpretation, architectural history is not an autonomous, inwardly-focused discipline but one that – like architecture – operates and interacts within a broader context.

The historian Alberto Pérez-Gómez has noted that the disciplinary boundaries between architectural history and other types of history, including those of science, philosophy, and materials, are not solid but porous. For him, the essence of historical study is in hermeneutics, or knowledge through interpretation.[4] Likewise, in their book *Architecture: From Prehistory to Post-Modernism*, Marvin Trachtenberg and Isabelle Hyman define historical study as "a process of selection and interpretation" and "a dynamo of movement, influence, and climactic events."[5] Andrew Leach has described the enduring challenge faced by architectural historians of "writing into history a field that is marked by conceptual and technical fluidity," observing that "there is little in architecture that is consistent across all time and geography: appearance, building technology, materials, uses, status and so on."[6] The critical questions then become why do such changes occur, and what are the factors and influences that contribute to change?

These concepts of dynamism, fluidity, interpretation, and interdisciplinarity are key to the current discussion of history's potential role in technical studies. Another is the idea that history need not be perceived as separate from contemporary architectural concerns. Writing in a 1957 issue of the *Journal of Architectural Education*, Thomas Howarth lamented that too often "history is considered to be very much an academic subject, [merely] a cultural exercise unrelated to the world of today."[7] On the contrary, many historians today operate from a belief in the essential linkage or entanglement between history and contemporary practices—not through superficial formal mimicry or pastiche, but through a critical understanding of the forces that have shaped the present-day environment. Pérez-Gómez, a professor of architectural history at McGill University, has said that "in the end, for me, as an educator of architects, what matters is this interpretative framing of the historical material that connects in a dialogue with present questions."[8] Speaking to the Society of Architectural Historians of Great Britain in 1987, Mark Swenarton (a founding editor of the journal of the Construction History Society) argued for the development of an architectural history "marked by a critical interest in the present as well as the past," asserting to architects the educational and practical value of "historical understanding *per se*," and in fact looked ahead to the future, calling for "an architectural history adequate to the needs of the twenty-first century — and thereby one that will contribute to rather than obstruct the improvement of architecture and the environment."[9] This kind of call to engage current and future architectural questions or problems, aided by an understanding of history, is directly applicable to how students learn — or could learn — about architectural technologies.

The History of Technology

Within the broad field of historical studies, a new branch of inquiry emerged in the twentieth century, focusing on the history of technology as a sub-discipline. Although a comprehensive survey of this history is beyond the scope of this paper, it is useful to consider one of the earliest texts in the field: Oxford's *A History of Technology*, published in five volumes between 1954 and 1958, which has been credited with establishing the fundamental parameters of the subject.[10] An essential task for an emerging discipline is to clearly define its topic. The editors of *A History of Technology* offered a concise definition, though one with broad implications: "a history of how things have been done or made."[11] They argue, somewhat more poetically, for the value of "an understanding of the methods and skills by which man has attained a gradual easing of his earthly lot through mastery of his natural environment." (This phrase, though dated in its language and gender specificity, can also serve as a useful definition of building technologies.) The essays in the *History's* five volumes attempt a daunting task: to cover the development of human tools spanning more than half a million years.[12]

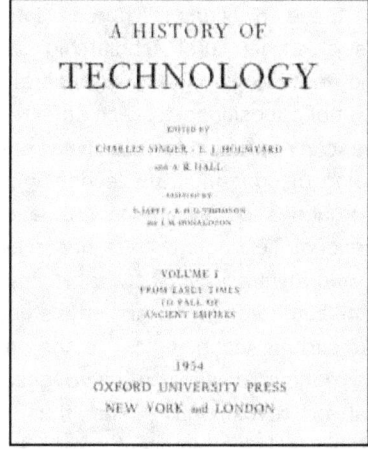

Fig. 1. One of the earliest comprehensive texts in the field of technology history: Oxford's *A History of Technology*, published in five volumes between 1954 and 1958.

Following this early encyclopedic approach, historians of technology have sought to both refine and expand the definition of their subject. In 1975, Angus Buchanan argued for emphasizing the active rather than passive nature of technological development, with "a revision of the definition in favor of a more general understanding of the technological relationship between things and their creators."[13] Translating Buchanan's definition through an architectural perspective, we may think of understanding the technological relationship between buildings and their designers, and further expand the relationship to the building's users. Conceptually, this establishes a network of technical and social relations between building technology, architects, and occupants, which can be a very useful framework through which to view technical education in architecture.

In 2005, Eda Kranakis noted a shift in historians' understanding of technology from passive artifact to active influencer, based on "a fundamental tension between our desire to understand technology as... hardware and our desire to analyze its role as a mediator and medium of historical change."[14] This means that technology should not be studied in isolation but rather through its interactions with its context, which the historian Barbara Hahn describes as "complex and multidirectional."[15] In Hahn's view, technology – the "systematic, purposeful, human manipulation of the physical world by means of some machine or tool" – is more accurately understood as a process, rather than an artifact. She cites as an example that "researching how a bridge came to be built in a particular place and way" would necessarily involve non-physical elements, such as how the engineers' design process may have been influenced by factors as diverse as zoning laws, funding sources, or community activists. Hahn further notes the value of studying not only technological successes but also failures, which can raise important questions of why certain technologies have endured while others fade away (and for whom do certain technologies work) as well as the value of experimentation. For Hahn, "the history of technology means to understand not only machines and tools but also the systems that make those devices work for and against human purposes." [16] Can this same approach to history aid in the study of building technologies?

History and Building Technologies

The call for an expansive history of technology that engages human experience and process has been embraced by many sub-disciplines, including some related specifically to building technologies, such as construction. The Construction History Society, based in the United Kingdom, has been publishing the journal *Construction History* since 1985. It promotes an understanding of construction as *technique*, resulting in physical artifacts that can be studied and analyzed, but also as a phenomenon influenced by social and economic factors, thus incorporating not only the physical building itself but also, for example, the development of guilds, contracts, working hours, rates of pay and conditions for workers, and their

training.[17] This organization and its publications provide clear examples of how the history of technology, and in particular those related to architecture, can explore the questions of how and why certain technologies come into existence and their influence on and by social conditions.

Although the mission statement of the Building Technology Educators' Society does not explicitly reference historical studies, it calls for the promotion of teaching and research that advance knowledge of the technologies of building design and construction and the promotion of critical discourse on pedagogic theory in architectural technology.[18] The breadth of its purview can be interpreted to include the various technological systems of architecture: structural, environmental, and enclosure systems, plus technologies of design and construction, such as digital design, building-information modeling, and fabrication techniques, and perhaps can also be expanded to include technologies of life-safety, accessibility, and communication systems, among others. Each of these technologies has a core set of principles and practices embodied through the physical reality of construction, developed through often complex procedures and methodologies, and codified over many years (centuries, in some cases). Each of these technologies therefore also has a history, which can be engaged to help illuminate how its core principles came to be.

Traditionally, architectural technology is most intensely interested in questions of what gets built today and how. The integration of historical studies into this framework can bring with it the implicit question of why things are the way they are and how they got that way (and likewise, how they might change in the future). A concept instructive for this discussion can be found in an article published in 1904 in *Architectural Review,* written by William R. Lethaby, an English architect and educator. Titled "Architectural Education: A Discussion," Lethaby's article proposed a curriculum for architectural education that prioritized the study of materials, craft, and detail. The examination of historical architecture was also an important subject, but, Lethaby wrote, "it should not be studied as history but as recorded experiment in building."[19]

This idea, "history as recorded experiment," provides a useful model for integrating history into technical subjects. Edward Allen has written of the importance of showing and discussing architectural projects in technical classes, noting that "students appreciate learning the thoughts and intentions that went into a project, how these were translated into materials, details, and structure, what went wrong, what went right, and how a given result was achieved."[20] Allen is essentially describing the experimental mode that Lethaby understood as inherent in the acts of design and construction, illustrated in works of the past. Through such an approach, the development of architectural technologies can be understood as an evolution, and students are encouraged to engage in critical thinking about why and how current technologies exist.

Edward Allen has also spoken of the danger of isolating technology subjects within architectural curricula, arguing that technologies such as structures are too often presented as purely mathematical in nature, located securely in the realm of science and separate from architectural design, when they should instead be presented and studied as a critical component of the design process.[21] In a similar way, understanding architectural technology through history is a way to re-connect technology with the larger concerns of architecture, to demonstrate its relevance to architectural design, and for it to transcend the limitations of its curricular compartmentalization. Allen's critique of technology education is that it has too often been inwardly focused and autonomous. History, as described above, seeks to make outward connections between architecture and the full range of human endeavors (including the social and technological), and can therefore assist in re-connecting and integrating technology courses with the larger discourse of architecture.

It is important here to make a distinction between *history* courses which address topics of technology within the context of studying architectural history of an era (such as construction techniques of the Renaissance, or the rise of iron framing in industrial buildings of the 19th century, for example) versus *building technology* courses which incorporate historical studies as a component of understanding a present-day technology. While both types can offer

great value, I wish to emphasize the latter, which is arguably less common and an area where great potential for enhanced understanding can be found. Architectural history courses can certainly benefit by including discussions of technology and construction, but if the history of technology is presented only in this context, it enforces disciplinary boundaries and discourages a fuller understanding of the relationship of current technologies to the experiments of the past.

The extent to which it is possible to incorporate historical study in technical courses depends, of course, upon many factors. The amount of technical content to be delivered within a limited time frame is often a major challenge in such courses and can lead to the perception that there simply is no space for the addition of a history component. I argue this is a shortsighted view; historical content can strengthen learning of technology and help students connect it to other aspects of their education in real time. But it should be noted that the history component need not be an exhaustive or comprehensive survey; on the contrary, targeted and specific historical examples can be integrated periodically to provide context for new concepts and topics. Also, in my view, "history" includes the very recent past, such as buildings completed in this century. The pace of technological change can be slow or rapid, and therefore useful historical examples may be found in previous centuries or last year, depending upon the technology under consideration.

The historian Alberto Pérez-Gómez has observed that "history is basically stories."[22] A building-technology educator has the freedom to choose which stories are most important or most instructive. The narratives of how architectural technologies have developed include protagonists (architects, engineers, manufacturers, code officials, and the public), plot (what happened and why), and setting (the site location and social context of the time). Using project-based historical analysis, telling the unique stories behind particular technologies, is often most effective: presentation and analysis of past buildings, how technologies were deployed, whether and how they succeeded or failed, and how these experiments led to how we currently utilize technology in buildings. Engaging such questions in a technology course introduces a critical-thinking component that enhances the overall learning experience and embeds technical thinking in a creative as well as analytical mode.

Examples and Application

The primary focus of building technology education is often placed appropriately on "best practices," meaning state-of-the-art systems, materials, and procedures that are in common use in practice today. Best practices are well-established with a proven record of performance. We also sometimes engage in speculation about expected or potential advancements in the future of a particular technology—these we might call "experimental practices." Because of continual research and development, we know that technologies evolve, new methods or materials are developed that outperform existing ones, and our definition of best practices transforms accordingly. Experimental practices imply forward progress in time to a future of new technological possibilities. But in addition to looking forward, we also have the possibility of looking to the past to understand what we can call "historical practices." The value in studying historical practices in technology is analogous to the value of architectural history in general described above: developing an understanding of how and why architecture changes, and learning to interpret and analyze current conditions in relationship to the past. While building technology education is obliged to focus on best practices (and for good reasons), I contend that its educational efficacy greatly benefits from finding connections among all three realms: best practices, experimental practices, and historical practices.

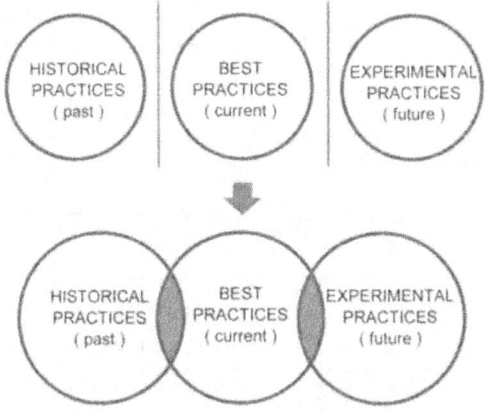

Fig. 2. Typical relationships among three types of practices (above) and proposed relationships (below).

To provide an example of this approach, I will discuss a course that I have taught in the School of Architecture at the University of Illinois in various forms beginning in 2006. The course, titled Curtain Wall Design & Construction, is offered in a weekly seminar format with approximately 15 graduate students in our M.Arch and M.S. degree programs. The seminar takes a materials-based approach to explore in-depth the processes of design and construction of building envelopes, with an emphasis on the theories and technologies behind leading-edge curtain wall systems in contemporary practice. Emphasis is placed on understanding curtain walls as a specialized type of building enclosure system with unique performance considerations (such as thermal, daylighting, wind-load resistance, moisture- and air-infiltration, and acoustic isolation) and unique fabrication and construction methods (such as stick-built, unitized, or point-supported systems, and their respective anchoring details). The objectives include ensuring broad understanding of the fundamental principles of curtain wall design and performance and the application of this knowledge through design exercises.

While the main focus of the course is on technological considerations in contemporary practice, the history of curtain walls is integrated throughout the course in several ways. The course follows a rationale that I describe in my book, *Contemporary Curtain Wall Architecture*, where I write that "developments in contemporary architectural design are best understood within their respective historical and technological contexts."[23] At the beginning of the semester, the topic of curtain walls is introduced by presenting and analyzing a number of recently built examples of innovative facades, which then leads us to go back in time and consider a comprehensive though quick survey of curtain wall history, augmented with readings and discussion. However, as suggested above, in addition to this initial survey, we do also periodically include micro-histories of particular aspects of building-envelope technology embedded directly within the context of technical discussions. For example, when we study the proliferation of glass fabrication techniques available today (from coatings of various types to insulating glass to lamination to bending, and so on), we also study the manufacturing process through which most architectural glass is produced today: the float process. This involves learning about the invention of the float process in the 1950s, its widespread adoption in the 1960s, the manufacturing techniques it superseded, and the reasons why this new process was such an improvement over previous methods of production.

Likewise, when discussing how low-e coatings can improve thermal and solar performance of glass through selective filtering of the solar spectrum, we also trace the history of reflective coatings on glass from their earliest adoption through buildings such as Saarinen's John Deere Headquarters (1964), Roche and Dinkeloo's College Life Insurance Building (1971), and Pei's John Hancock Tower (1976), considering each wall's aesthetic and technical performance and the details of its assembly. In the seminar, discussions of glass focus on technical issues of energy performance as well as strength and deflection parameters, but they also present an opportunity to consider the role glass and transparency have played in modern architectural theory by reading excerpts from texts such as Paul Scheerbart's *Glasarchitektur* (1914) and Arthur Korn's *Glass in Modern Architecture* (1929). Such historical treatises celebrating the potential liberation of modern architecture through the concept of transparency can encourage interesting discussion and critique among students when viewed in the context of energy consumption and contemporary aesthetic trends.

A fundamental categorization of contemporary curtain walls distinguishes between stick-built and unitized systems of assembly. The differences between these two major typologies are made apparent by viewing the installation process and by studying typical mullion details. The skill of "reading" architectural details requires practice but, once learned, can be deployed to comparatively analyze mullion details from historical buildings. Why are contemporary mullions fabricated and shaped the way we see them on manufacturers' websites today? How did the mullion, as a form of technology, evolve? In the seminar, we trace the development of curtain wall mullions from the beginning of the 20th century. In the earliest details, from buildings such as the Steiff Factory (1903), the Maison de Verre (1932), and MoMA (1939), we find mullions assembled in an

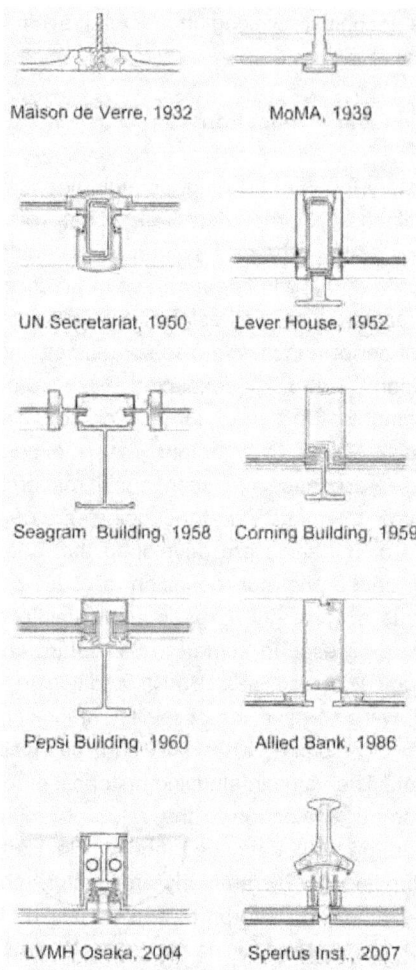

Fig. 3. Mullion plan details.

ad-hoc manner from stock steel profiles. Details of mid-20th-century curtain walls such as the UN Secretariat (1950) and Lever House (1952) illustrate how mullions adapted for glass-box skyscrapers, still structured by steel profiles but now clad in aluminum or stainless steel. In slightly later walls, like the Seagram Building (1958) and the Corning Glass Works (1959), we find the use of extruded metal and the concept of unitization gain prominence. By the 1970s, new technologies are deployed, such as the glass mullions and bolted-glass connections of the Willis Faber and Dumas Building (1975) and structural silicone glazing at the Allied Bank Tower (1986). In the 1990s and the early years of the 21st century we find an explosion of research and development leading to expanded possibilities for performance, both technical (in the form of more robust thermal breaks, for instance) and aesthetic (with the integration of media displays, for example). The steel and aluminum mullions at LVMH Osaka (2004) not only support unique cladding of translucent, thin veneer stone laminated to glass but also house integrated vertical light fixtures to illuminate the façade from within at night. Details of the Spertus Institute (2007) illustrate how mullions can be designed to accommodate the complex façade geometries made possible by today's digital design and fabrication tools. In each case, it is possible to make connections between and across this history in the ways this basic component of the mullion has been conceptualized.

These forays into history, embedded within a technical course, give students a fuller understanding of the materials used in curtain walls and instill a new way of looking at the building envelopes they design. An effective approach is to take a fundamental element or component of a building technology—in the example above, the curtain-wall mullion—and show how it has evolved over time, from the perspectives of construction (materiality, fabrication, installation, etc.) and performance. The study of recent history is formalized in the seminar through a Case Study project in which each student researches and analyzes the curtain wall of a project built since the start of the 21st century, preparing a set of drawings that describes the materials and assemblies of each system. Students are encouraged to find connections between these recent projects and earlier 20th-century examples studied in class.

Approaches similar to the examples from this curtain wall seminar can be applied in other technology-related subjects as well. Donald Friedman writes, "The history of technology as applied to structures includes... the development and industrialization of traditional materials such as wood and brick; the industrial development of iron and steel; [and] the development and industrialization of construction-site practices, such as excavation and hoisting."[24] For example, and more specifically, a technology course on steel structures could incorporate studying the post-fire Chicago building boom of the late 19th century, when architects experimented with various combinations of timber, masonry, iron, and eventually steel structural systems in taller and taller buildings. What characteristics of steel as a material made it a desirable choice for framing tall buildings? Additionally, studying changes in the steel-

manufacturing industry over the last 150 years, including the gradual rise and eventual decline of steel mills in the US, could help students comprehend the current global condition of steel construction.

Other applications may be found in a very different realm: accessible design. The requirements for accessibility in buildings, as defined by the Americans with Disabilities Act (ADA) and its design guidelines, are to a large extent based on technical issues: the slope of a ramp, the cross-sectional shape and placement of a handrail, the turning dimensions of a wheelchair, visible emergency signaling for the hearing-impaired, and so on. Accessibility should be a critical component of every design project, but it has the tendency among students and professionals to be seen as simply a list of dimensional requirements to be checked off. The value of accessibility and its potential impact on people can be illuminated, however, through an understanding of its history: an often dramatic and compelling story of people with disabilities and their advocates fighting for recognition of disability rights as civil rights, through protests, litigation, and legislation, leading to the 1990 enactment of the ADA. It represents a case where certain codified technical requirements for buildings, now understood as given, were once contentious and resulted from major shifts in social and political realities in the US. Such historical context can have a significantly positive impact on how students view both the technical requirements and ethical obligations of the architect in designing accessible buildings. Imagine the potential if similarly compelling histories could be drawn upon for the full range of architectural technologies.

Conclusion

Although there is a commonly accepted differentiation between *history* as the realm in which architectural ideas are identified and analyzed, and *technology* as the place where materiality and functional systems are studied, it can be productive and enlightening to rethink these distinctions and consider the overlaps. Mark Swenarton called upon historians to embrace an expanded view of history in which ideas and materials are interrelated, and "in which ideological and material elements alike can be handled as part of a common set of social relations."[25] Likewise, scholars and teachers of building technology could reconceptualize their field to embrace historical studies as a productive component of their methodology. As Swenarton wrote, "historical understanding is a necessary preliminary to informed action, in designing buildings… as much as in any other field of human endeavor."[26] This goal of "informed action" is precisely what building technology education should enable within design and construction processes, and therefore historical understanding of such technologies should be considered an important component of its study.

[1] For example, the authors of *A Global History of Architecture* describe as a goal of their work to help "develop an understanding of the manner in which architectural production is always triangulated by the exigencies of time and location." Franics D.K. Ching, Mark Jarzombek, and Vikramaditya Prakash, *A Global History of Architecture* (Hoboken: John Wiley & Sons, 2011), p. xi.

[2] Spiro Kostof, *A History of Architecture: Settings and Rituals* (New York: Oxford University Press, 1995), p. 7.

[3] Ibid., p. 19.

[4] See Saundra Weddle and Marc J. Neveu, "Interview with Alberto Pérez-Gómez," *Journal of Architectural Education* Vol. 64, No. 2, March 2011, p. 76-81.

[5] Marvin Trachtenberg and Isabelle Hyman, *Architecture: From Prehistory to Post-Modernism / The Western Tradition* (New York: Harry N. Abrams, 1986), p. 41.

[6] Andrew Leach, *What is Architectural History?* (Cambridge: Polity Press, 2010), p. 5.

[7] Thomas Howarth, "Some Thoughts on Teaching History," *Journal of Architectural Education*, Vol. 12, No. 2, Summer 1957, p. 12.

[8] Weddle and Neveu, "Interview with Alberto Pérez-Gómez," p. 78.

[9] Mark Swenarton, "The Role of History in Architectural Education," *Architectural History*, Vol. 30, 1987, p. 212-213.

[10] See Angus Buchanan, "Technology and History," *Social Studies of Science*, Vol. 5, No. 4, Nov. 1975, p. 489-499.

[11] Charles Singer, E.J. Holmyard, and A.R. Hall, eds., *A History of Technology, Volume 1* (New York and London: Oxford University Press, 1954), p. v.

[12] Ibid., v. Volume 1 opens with "the humblest beginnings of the making and use of tools, the most important of which is that most characteristically human tool called 'language'. Thus it starts more than half a million years ago, as man is becoming man."

[13] Buchanan, "Technology and History," p. 491.

[14] Eda Kranakis, "Surveying Technology and History: Essential Tensions and Postmodern Possibilities," *Technology and Culture*, Vol. 46, No. 4, Oct. 2005, p. 805.

[15] Barbara Hahn, "The Social in the Machine: How Historians of Technology Look Beyond the Object," American Historical Association, March 2014, https://www.historians.org/publications-and-directories/perspectives-on-history/march-2014/the-social-in-the-machine (accessed March 1, 2017).

[16] Ibid.

[17] From "What is Construction History?" The Construction History Society website: http://www.constructionhistory.co.uk/about-construction-history-society/construction-history/ (accessed March 1, 2017). An American branch of the society, called the Construction History Society of America, was started in 2007.

[18] From the Building Technology Educators' Society (BTES) website: http://www.btesonline.org/about.html (accessed March 1, 2017).

[19] W.R. Lethaby, "Architectural Education: A Discussion," *Architectural Review*, Vol. 16, 1904, p. 161.

[20] Edward Allen, "Some Comments Concerning Technical Teaching in Schools of Architecture," AIA/ACSA Topaz Medal Speech, March 4, 2005, http://www.sbse.org/announcements/documents/TopazMedalSpeech.pdf (accessed March 1, 2017). Allen writes, "the biggest mistake we've made in our schools is to divide architecture and the architectural curriculum into 'design' and 'building technology,' leaving a huge gulf between the two." Design courses often use the analysis of precedent projects as a form of historical research to influence a current design; technology courses can do the same. Using a similar form of historical research in both types of classes can help bridge the divide described by Allen.

[21] Ibid.

[22] Weddle and Neveu, "Interview with Alberto Pérez-Gómez," p. 80.

[23] Scott Murray, *Contemporary Curtain Wall Architecture* (New York: Princeton Architectural Press, 2009), p. 7.

[24] Donald Friedman, "A History of Building Technology and Preservation Engineering," *APT Bulletin*, Vol. 44, No. 1, 2013, p. 23.

[25] Swenarton, "The Role of History in Architectural Education," p. 210.

[26] Ibid., p. 210.

Assessing the Aesthetic and Functional Contribution of Shading Devices to Richard Neutra's Library at Simpson College in Iowa

Clifton Fordham
Temple University

Abstract

Richard Neutra is best known for beautiful houses inseparable from their location that incorporate details that speak to local conditions. Some of his houses, the majority constructed in the fifties and sixties in California, have benefited from widespread media exposure and have even been featured in Hollywood films. In contrast, his institutional buildings are less well known and are being demolished at a greater rate than the residences. Reflecting the austerity of post-war building construction, Neutra's institutional buildings melded sensible planning, exceptional detailing, and innovative solar control strategies. In retrospect, most of these seem modest, lacking the overall expressiveness expected in today's saturated high speed media environment. Like most reliable things that work well, buildings can be overlooked, or taken for granted.

This paper seeks to foster greater appreciation of Neutra's ability to synthesize performance and aesthetics through a study of his Simpson College Library building in Indianola, Iowa. In the era when Neutra designed the Simpson library solar design was largely an intuitive process, the efficacy of the devices assessed were crudely, if at all. With the development of digital analysis tools, verifying the effectiveness of devices is feasible during and after design, allowing greater potential for rationalizing building elements that can be viewed as decorative or superfluous. By meshing digital and traditional analysis, means for perceiving how poetics and pragmatics support each other are increased.

Introduction

Architect Robert Venturi coined the phrase "Less is a Bore" in his critique on the banality and visual austerity of mid-century modern architecture playing on Mies van der Rohe's caption "Less is More".[1]

Venturi's perspective centered on the communicative potential of architecture, and opportunities for play when building surfaces have been liberated from function and performance. Although he approached modernism from an academic perspective, popular opinion also had not completely internalized the image of modern architecture which had been widely adopted in post-war America, contributing to a return to traditional forms and symbolism.

Robert Venturi's writing ignored many forces that gave birth to modernism including technological innovation and social determinism. A dominant strain of the early modern movement embraced the possibility for new forms that technology permitted, advocated for expressive honesty, and saw new potentials for architecture to serve the masses. The potential for architecture to escape its past ties to elite power structures and decadence, opened possibilities for rational architecture striped of excess. The writings of Adolf Loos capture the move away from robust ornament, evident in his native Vienna, when he equated ornament with crime.

By the time Richard Neutra completed a library building for a small Iowa College in 1964, modernism had been adopted as a post-World War II answer to austerity and corporate rationality attributed to American success in the war effort.[2] The opportunity for Neutra to design in the mid-west came from fame he gained when his design for the Lovell Health House in Los Angeles was featured in the pivotal 1932 exhibition on the International Style curated by Philip Johnson at the Museum of Modern Art in New York. Despite Neutra's past and current status as a master architect, a significant number of his buildings have been demolished, or are threatened with demolition, a fate that many mid-century modern buildings face. Imminent loss of these works offer cause to examine their merit and liabilities better understanding what positive attributes can be retained or emulated.

Along with demonstrating deftness of composition, and exceptional ability to integrate buildings with surroundings, many of Neutra's designs incorporated shading strategies aimed at harnessing the impact of the sun. By applying technologically advanced details such as movable louvers, Neutra demonstrated a commitment to the performance of buildings and the integration of function and form. In an era where traditional ornament was considered superficial, contributing to pared-down facades, Neutra was able to offer responsible and integrated delight without resorting to formal expressiveness and literal figuration that Venturi and Denise Scott Brown later studied on in Las Vegas.[3] Nonetheless, Neutra's institutional designs appear modest by today's standards, challenging expectations of complexity often typified by busyness.

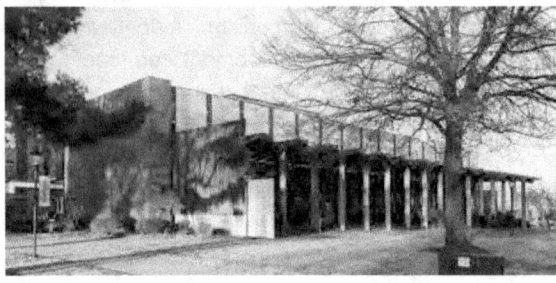

Fig. 1. Dunn Library.

In light of challenges appreciating modest buildings, this paper examines the relationship between ornament and performance through a study of Dunn Library at Simpson College. [Fig. 1] By utilizing digital tools to analyze the performance of building elements, their function beyond the decorative can be better understood. Without assessment that includes the material performance of buildings, the discussion of what constitutes good architecture occurs in separate spheres, where performance and the expressive components of buildings are discussed in isolation. Discourse architecture distanced from function also limits opportunities to justify ornament and understand how economical buildings can provide value for their owners and occupants as well as bring delight.

Toward Minimalism

With the exception of utilitarian structures, expressions of modern architecture prior to the emergence of European architecture encapsulated as the International Style, mid-century modernism, and corporate modernism, incorporated overt expressions of decoration albeit different from traditional notions of ornament. Louis Sullivan and later Frank Lloyd Wright represent early efforts to establish language appropriate to new building types such as the skyscraper, but also site conditions particular to the nascent cities of the new world.[4] The Auditorium Building (1887-9) designed by Louis Sullivan and Dankmar Adler is notable because of the rusticated Romanesque language at its base gives way to a sparse façade of the seven stories above punctuated by two levels of arched window openings and a simple classically inspired cornice. Sullivan later developed an ornamental vocabulary that displaced classical references exemplified in his design for the Guarantee Building (1895). Wright who apprenticed under Sullivan simultaneously developed an abstracted language for ornament which he carried into the latter half of the twentieth century.

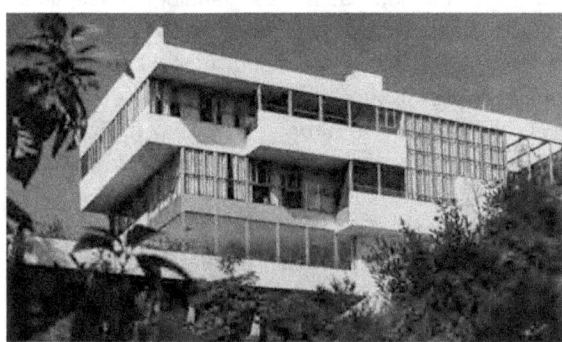

Fig. 2. Lovell Health House.

The 1932 International Style exhibition featured work reflecting a transition from architecture with minimal ornament and relief, to buildings absent of ornament entirely. Walter Gropius's Fagus Factory Building (1913) represents the former and Richard Neutra's Lovell House (1927) the latter. [Fig. 2] Along with Le Corbusier's Ville Savoye, Neutra's building had smooth white surfaces, windows set flush with the exterior surface, and absence of cornice and base details. The result was the appearance of pristine surfaces divorced from association with natural materials, and an appearance as if the building surfaces could have emerged from a factory assembly line.[5] Work of Mies van der Rohe who introduced an exceptional standard of industrial refinement, and would also play a pivotal role in the development of post-war aesthetic, was also exhibited.

Modernism and Machine Aesthetic

Hitchcock and Johnson's exhibition introduced minimalist architecture to a broader audience, but it had an alternative effect of divorcing visual outcomes from the forces that shaped them. The Bauhaus emerged out of the German culture of high quality mass production and messianic desire to create a classless community of industrial craftsmen. Inherent in the expression of industrial design and architecture was the notion of quality and refinement becoming available to a wider array of people.[6] Le Corbusier and Neutra were also interested in the potentials of industrial production to provide higher quality buildings for a greater range of people. Although their buildings were prototypes, the implied virtues of the architecture included efficiency and production, as well as harvesting natural light.[7]

Despite allusions to mass-production, and machine like functionality, Corbusier, Neutra and Mies were exceptionally talented architects, and established visual standards ordinary architects could not realistically attain. Prior to the work of early modern architecture, ordinary architects could rely on application of formal language and ornament appropriated from precedent. Ornament performed an expressive and communicative function by presenting a literal vocabulary, and also serving a practical role of mediating transitions between various building elements. Stripped of ornament, architecture could quickly become banal and oppressive although master architects realized that functional building details, such as sills and copings could become ornamental if aesthetically integrated within the larger composition.

Evaluating Modernism

In its evolution, the appropriateness of modern architecture was contextual, calling for building to better reflect the times and reconcile the visual with technical and cultural realities. Developments in the architecture profession however, reflected the schism between engineering and architecture resulting from highly technical expectations of buildings in which performance independent of expression occurred. Assessment and design of the building systems

related to performance became more scientific and difficult for architects to manage. In this context, Johnson and Hitchcock can be better understood as presenting modernism primarily as a visual reality where architects were relinquishing ownership of building technology, and fundamental functions such as serviceability were difficult to appreciate.

While a modern approach was appropriated by most architects in the US after the war, the expressive potential of details was often missed within a climate of delivering buildings cheaply, and quickly.[8] Without relief and delight, architecture was difficult to appreciate establishing ground for movement back toward expressiveness without a historical language through patterning and abstract figuration. However, failure of many architects to establish enough expressiveness in their buildings during the two decades after the war has contributed to an unfair rejection of positive characteristics of building of the period. In light of resource scarcities, and the aim of delivering architecture to the masses, modern architecture possessed positive characteristics that have been largely overlooked. Due to underwhelming visual impressions, assessing modest modern architecture is difficult if primarily pursued from a perspective privileging the visual and suppressing the functional. Renewed interest in building performance reflects challenges faced with moving beyond a primarily visual approach, while not factoring it out.

Reconciling Aesthetic and Performative

Tools for assessing building performance that do not rely primarily on observation, or tedious manual calculations are currently available permitting insight into the relationship of building function and form. This is particularly important when ornament and detail are linked to building performance as is the case with Neutra's Simpson Library. Evaluating buildings that integrate function and form is uniquely suited to architects because technology integration underpins the role of architecture despite attempts to diverge them.[9] Although there is not a single answer for every problem, architects and clients benefit from better understanding benefits provided by design decisions, and reasons to support investments in building components.

As a late modern building, Simpson Library was constructed at a period in which architects responded to problems introduced by loss of traditional ornament. The period also represented a transition from institutional buildings incorporating operable windows, and lacking air-conditioning, to buildings dependent on mechanical cooling and heating. The transition was primarily prompted by plentiful energy sources, and the benefits of mechanical cooling. Buildings after the 1950's also became more robust, reflecting greater optimism and more concern about outcomes beyond utility. Within these shifts, solar management strategies embraced during the immediate post war period were largely abandoned along with operable windows. In this light, Simpson Library is unusual in that it incorporates shading devices as building ornament, and different approaches at each exposure, while maintaining efficiencies of form consistent with the discipline of the prior decades.

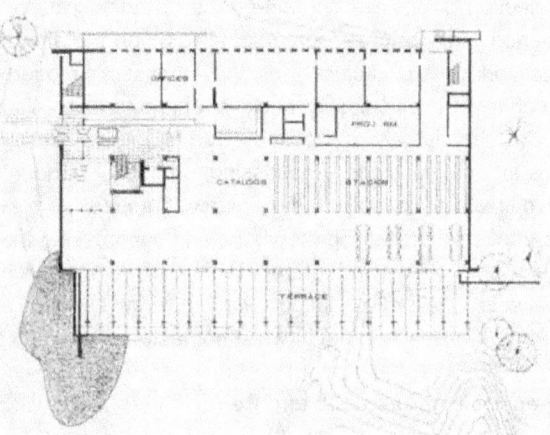

Fig. 3. Dunn Library ground floor plan.

Building Overview

The three-story building is rectangular in plan and oriented so that the long sides face the north and the east. [Fig. 3] It has a regular column grid arrayed on a twenty-two and half square module resulting in four zones that extend east to west in which the northern most bay is reserved for offices and conference spaces on all three levels flanked by exit stairs on the building ends. The main entry is on the west side of the building in the bay to the south of the northern bay and the monumental stair and elevator situated off the main entry. Book stacks and reading area on the first floor have been reconfigured since the building opened while the current second floor stack and reading desk layout reflect the original design. The

third floor that was designed to receive additional stacks leaving the area above the second-floor stacks open, contributing a sense of openness on the second level. A dormant catwalk for the future third floor book stack is isolated from the central core, along with the second floorplate, is set off the south side window wall.

Building Faces

All four facades are distinct in character with the east, north and west elevations primarily clad in vertically oriented brick running bond. The glazed building entry is on the west façade of the building and is clearly identifiable by a substantial cantilevered canopy. Windows above the canopy appear to extend to the parapet and are screened by vertical louvers that originally were programed to pivot. A slender vertical ribbon window separates the northern face of the building from the west face, and a concrete wall with a vertical wood trellis is set off the southern end of the west façade. [Fig. 4] The north face of the building is punctuated by staggered flush windows on the lower two levels and larger windows and precast panels on the third level. A one-story addition has been added to the east façade complementing what was designed as a plain façade with no openings, creating a design contingency for expansion.

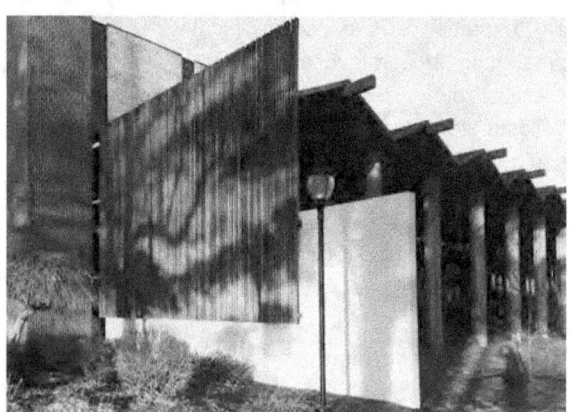

Fig. 4. Southwest corner.

Although it does not contain the main entry to the building, the south side of the building is the most unique elevation of the building and contributes to its dynamism. The signature characteristic is a continuous undulating trellis that fans across the elevation at the third level. It extends approximately twenty-five feet from the face of the building and is supported by concrete columns. The depth of the awning corresponds with the vertical trellis at the west end of the building. A continuous glazed window falls below the trellis and clad with precast panels above resulting in a v-shaped bottom to the precast panels.

Exterior Details

Neutra counters the tendency for boxy buildings in the post-war era to exclude both texture, depth, and difference on different facades. Instead of introducing materials that had more texture which was a common strategy in the sixties in the form of textured concrete, or pattern in material fields like Venturi, Neutra used other strategies. He creates texture through application of shading strategies, introduces pattern in expansive glass surfaces, variety in the exaggerated pre-cast cornice, and subtle playfulness by rotating the brick coursing vertically. Patterning in material systems that are otherwise mundane and predictable is a cost responsible way to counter predictability and foster uniqueness in a building. The oversized running bond pattern in the glazing is consistent with notions of austerity, and individual authorship.

The north elevation retains a reference to the internal column grid though repetitive precast panels and pilasters at the top of the building, relationships that reintroduces some of the expectations of a classical building *triparti*. In the brick field below the third level, staggered punched openings recall the running pattern in the south and west facades, as well as the vertical brick pattern. This obscures the location of the structure grid, since every third rectangular punched windows at second level is centered on a pilaster, while the rest are not. Concurrently, every third window on the second level is centered on an intermediate pilaster, while the rest on the same level are not. Apart from the protruding pilaster detail, the north façade is relatively flat reflecting the lack of need for shading in that façade pointing to a primarily decorative role.

The west face of Dunn Library faces an older campus structure and has only two fields of glazing, the vertical strip at the transition to the north façade, and the section above the entry storefront. Both window systems are set back slightly from the face of the buildings and along with the continuous nature of the glazing, distinguishing them from the flatness of the

north façade. At the northwest corner, the north wall appears to slip past the west face of the building resulting in an excess of wall that cannot be explained in terms other than compositional since there is no solar value created by extending the building there. The window setback introduces shade and shadow.

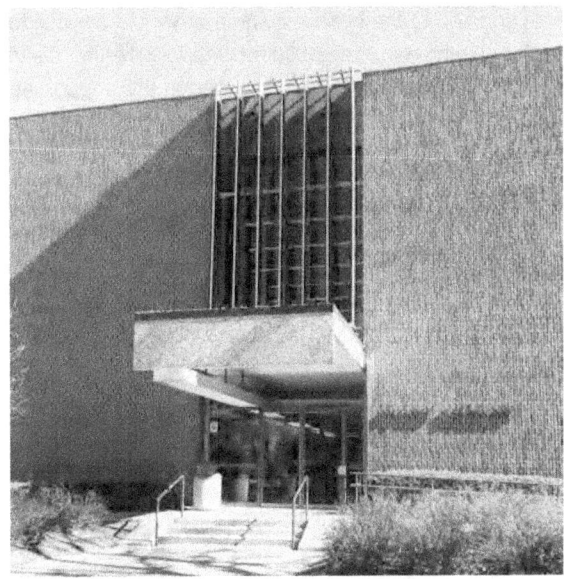

Fig. 5. West entry canopy and fins.

Although the entry canopy [Fig. 5] provides a visual signifier of the building entry and cover from the elements, both functions, the canopy also provides responsible relief from the otherwise flatness of the flanking brick fields. The use of glazing across the entry section also helps introduce visual continuity between the inside and outside of the building, a theme consistent in Neutra's residential buildings. Similarly, the glazing above the canopy introduces light into a reading area as well as views. By introducing vertical louvers in front of the curtainwall above the canopy [Fig. 5] Neutra interrupts the clarity of the views from the second and third levels. The vertical fins which are currently fixed so they are oriented in an east-west direction help mediate excessive late afternoon heat gain, demonstrating the architect's awareness of tensions between solar mediation, daylight, and views.

The glazing on the southern face of the building is comprised of a vertical running pattern set in front of columns that flows uninterrupted from a narrow brick section at the west of façade to an narrow section of precast at the east end of the building. It extends up to, and between precast panels that are pointed and correspond with the awning that are spaced off the bottom edge of the precast panels. The front portion of the awning appears as if it is draped over a steel beam that extends past concrete posts spaced eleven-foot three inches apart with every other column corresponding with the twenty-two and a half foot spacing of the interior column bays. At the inside of the awning, near the building wall, the awning shifts upward so that the high point is above the supporting beam. The posts are concrete and form a cross in section.

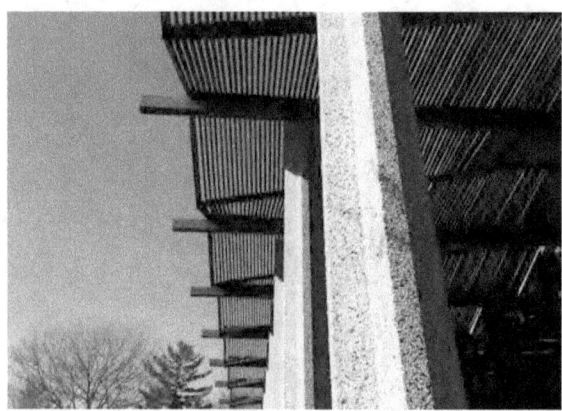

Fig. 6. Detail photo of south canopy.

The awning is the most unique part of the façade and provides the signature element of the project. It is comprised of 2x4 redwood slats that interlock at the beam extension creating space between and a sense of material lightness and connection to the sky from below. [Fig. 6] At the west end of the south awning, the wood slats intersect with vertical slats that are attached to a concrete wall below, both providing shading for the curtainwall from the western sun. As with most of the details in the building there is both a practical and decorative function. The concrete wall and vertical slats at the extension wall were originally set in a small pond which has since been filled.

Analyzing Performance

A key component of this study is the combination of traditional visual analysis with performance based analysis to determine how visual elements can be functional and not arbitrary. In this case energy analysis was utilized to determine the effectiveness of ornamental shading devices. To facilitate performance analysis a digital model of the building envelope was created in Revit. [Fig. 7] Revit was

chosen because it is compatible with Sefaira an analysis engine that allows for efficient comparison of design options and assessment of building assembly parameters.

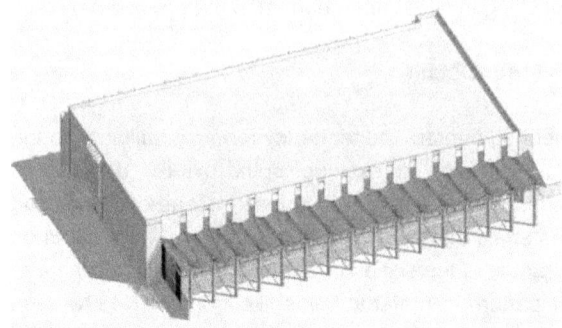

Fig. 7. Digital model.

Analysis was performed with three scenarios for comparison. A baseline model representing the original design with shading devices was compared to model without the horizontal southern shading elements, and a model without the vertical western shading elements. Results of the modeling indicated the southern shading elements contributed to positive energy savings with annual energy-use intensity (EUI) 0.28 percent lower than without the awning.

The western extension wall contributed to a 0.02 percent energy use increase which is slightly higher and correlates with greater electricity use to offset loss of daylighting. The western shading elements above the front door, currently in a fixed position contributed to a negligible performance difference which is expected to improve if operable.

A digital model permits efficiently correlating of the visual impact of design changes on both the literal experience of the building geometry and the effects of shade on the building surfaces. Sun studies of the south and west façade of the building were created with the Revit model for key points of the year (summer, fall, winter). Comparisons of the results of the studies demonstrate the impact of performance oriented elements on dynamic readings of the façade. The west elevation at the fall solstice at 3 pm is provided as a starting point. [Fig. 8A] For the purpose of understanding the visual impact of shadows on the building face, shading elements were gradually stripped away illustrating the importance of the devices to the visual complexity of the building by providing relief and interest.

An elevation with the vertical fins removed [Fig. 8B] results in almost no shadow at the west face of the building. The impression of verticality is also diminished above the canopy. Removing the vertical screen at the extension wall [Fig. 8C] also reduces vertical elements and suppresses the integration of wood into the west face. Deleting the concrete wall extension at the southwest corner of the building [Fig. 8D] further simplifies the reading of the west elevation harking to the banal boxes of the preceding two decades. Eliminating the horizontal trellis on the south façade [Fig. 8E] renders the west elevation banal, removes all play from the southern half of the west elevation and any indication of articulation at the southern elevation.

Relating Performative and Visual Analysis

Simpson library represents exceptional integration of ornament and performance in a way that dispels the notion that ornament is frivolous or tacked-on. It also counters the idea that ornament needs to give way to patterning, or ornament at figuration, which Venturi criticizes, in order to make buildings interesting. The ornamental shading devices in the liberty evade redundancy and boredom which is the case with many well detailed modern buildings. One of the ways in which this is achieved is the choice of materials, in the case of the south awning a warm Redwood two-by-four. The Redwood adds color variation to a the broader brick fields, glass window frames, and beige pre-cast panels, the latter of which too often play a role in contributing to the dreariness of late-modern buildings.

Neutra was particularly adept at mediating the transition between the horizontal slats and the west concrete wall extension by creating a screen made of slats that overlaps with the white painted concrete wall below. The wall extension also helps offset the potential mundaneness of the adjacent brick field, and serves as foil for the entryway section. [Fig. 10] The louvers, which could be dismissed as expressing technology, but not related to the specific building, overcome this dilemma by performing a vital solar function, as well as offering visual variety by introducing metal into the material pallet. The louver system also demonstrated the value of technology

transfer from the aeronautics industry to buildings, although the potential was lost largely due to the disappearance of shading devices from buildings in the 1960's.

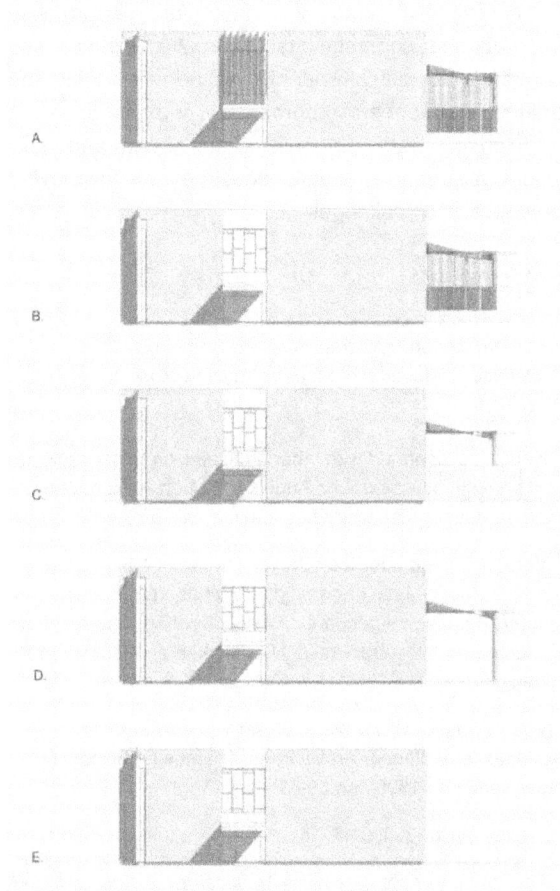

Fig. 8. West elevation study.

Debate about the benefits of building ornament has traditionally been within the purview of individuals assessing visual significance and merit. A dominant part of this critique since has included the notion that ornament is frivolous unless it helps individuals understand how a building is constructed. This critique which has shaped the development of modern architecture contributed to shifts toward fundamental structures after the war and appearances of utility. Efficient forms and non-frivolous façade articulation are virtuous if benefits to owners, occupants, and observers are greater over more articulated forms considering costs. If ornament contributes to a longer building life, better user experiences, and lower operating costs, it deserves a broader form of analysis than ornament purely evaluated for meaning.

Ornament can be integrated into a building, or appear applied and thus frivolous. In the case of the Simpson College Library, ornament in the form of shading devices are both visually and performativity integral to the building. The test for visual integration is comparative and the test for performative integration is computational. Visual integration can contribute to difficulty identifying benefits since the articulation appears appropriate and natural. A tradition of evaluating building for visual and non-visual performance simultaneously allows for moving beyond these challenges.

Notes:

[1] Venturi, Robert. *Contradiction and Complexity in Architecture.* Museum of Modern Art: New York, NY. 1977. p 16-17.

[2] Neutra collaborated with other architects on larger projects and projects outside of Los Angeles. Robert Alexander his most frequent collaborator had a role in this project.

[3] Venturi, Robert and Scott Brown, Denise. "A Significance for A&P Parking Lots or Learning from Las Vegas" in *Theorizing A New Agenda for Architectural Theory.* Princeton Architectural Press. New York, NY. 1996. pp 313–318.

[4] Wigley, Mark. *White Walls, Designer Dresses: The Fashioning of Modern Architecture.* Thames and Hudson: New York, NY. 1995. pp 60-63.

[5] Wigley. pp xiv-xxii, 3-4.

[6] Frampton, Kenneth. *Modern Architecture: A Critical History.* The MIT Press: Cambridge, MA. 1992. pp 109-110, 123.

[7] Frampton. pp 152-153.

[8] Wright, Gwendolyn. *USA: Modern Architectures in History.* Reakton Books: London, UK. 2008. p 151.

[9] The author elaborates on this point in a paper titled *Optimizing Early Design Process Decision Making through Effective Problem Framing* presented at the *2016 AIA/ACSA Intersections Symposium* and forthcoming proceedings published by ACSA.

Optimized Material, Expressive Forms:
Precast Concrete Architecture in the Pacific Northwest

Tyler S. Sprague
University of Washington

Abstract

This presentation will discuss the rise of precast, prestressed concrete in the Pacific Northwest in the late 1950s. Prestressing, new at the time, was a method of production that maximized the potential of high strength steel in tension and concrete in compression. Precasting concrete enabled new types of structures to emerge and fundamentally changed the understanding of concrete in the built environment.

The Northwest was well suited to the rise of precast concrete. With striations of compacted glacial till prevalent throughout the region and large deposits of clay and limestone in the North Cascades, reinforced concrete emerged as a modern material in the Northwest 1920s – giving rise to a new generation of concrete skyscrapers in downtown Seattle. In the 1950s, the Anderson Brothers (Arthur and Thomas) refined European prestressing techniques and built one of the first precasting plants in the country in Tacoma – Concrete Technology Corp. By pretensioning steel tendons before concrete is cast, prestressing compresses the entire section – eliminating concrete's persistent cracking, and drastically reducing the size of structural members. Prestressing could truly exploit the extremely high-strength concrete that was easily available in the Northwest.

While originally intended for bridges and transportation infrastructure, this new material began to rapidly re-shape modern architecture in the Pacific Northwest. With modern architects eager to explore new material and structural possibilities, precast concrete provided a new mix of thinness, malleability and durability that other materials could not offer. Precast concrete was quickly and experimentally used in, not only, industrial buildings and warehouses, but soon apartment buildings, churches, and most

dramatically, the US Science Pavilion for the 1962 Seattle World's Fair.

During this time, the building industry underwent a fundamental re-conception of concrete as a building material – a re-definition of proportion and scale possible. Concrete was no longer just a heavy, earthbound stereotomic material, but had the potential to become a lightweight, tectonic structural frame. Architects challenged structural engineers and concrete plant operators to push the limits of the technique, while finding new advantages in construction time and finish quality. Through these explorations, precast concrete became an essential medium of post-war modern architecture.

Origins

The history of precast concrete in the Pacific Northwest, beginning in the 1950s, draws on even earlier history of concrete innovation in the region. In the 1920s, it remained expensive to build in structural steel. Though some builders used high-rise steel to construct the first true skyscrapers of downtown (like the Smith Tower, 1914), the steel was often imported from the East. Some small steel mills opened in the Northwest, but the lack of significant iron ore deposits and the high cost of initiating the manufacturing of steel hindered its widespread use.

At the same time, entrepreneurs were discovering the mineral composition of the North Cascades – the mountain range to the northeast of the Puget Sound Basin. These mountains contained rich deposits of clay and limestone – the raw materials needed for the manufacturing of Portland Cement. When combined with the dense glacial aggregate base that underlies the lowland areas, the Northwest was soon producing some of the highest quality concrete in the nation. The towns of Baker and Cement City consolidated to form the city of Concrete in the late 1920s, giving the Northwest a reliable source for its own high-quality, and local, building material.

Post War in the Pacific Northwest

A flurry of building activity in reinforced concrete in the 1920s and 1930s was followed by a steep economic recession as a result of the Great Depression. With the onset of World War II, the economic prospects of the Northwest improved with the Boeing Company producing aircraft for the US military, but building activity still stalled. Following the end of the War in 1945, however, fortunes changed and flurry of building activity began. With an increasing population, the region had over 20 years of pent up demand for schools, libraries, houses, and office buildings.

This new interest in building aligned with a significant movement in architecture in the Northwest – Northwest Modernism. As in other places, young architects were trained in the tradition of the German Bauhaus and aligned themselves with the ideas of International Style. This interest in modern craft, industrial processes and abstract methods of composition created an openness to new technological possibilities within architecture – and created a market for innovative materials and structures.

Post War in the Pacific Northwest

Innovation came from many sources, and like earlier times, the most successful innovations were local. Arthur and Thomas Anderson were two brothers who grew up in Tacoma, Washington. Both attended the University of Washington as undergraduates in Civil Engineering and both went on to MIT for Masters degrees in structural engineering. After a year, Arthur continued for a doctorate in engineering while Thomas returned to Tacoma to begin business-related pursuits. Arthur studied with Roy W. Carlson, an expert in reinforced concrete, and continued at MIT as a researcher until 1941. Following these studies, he worked with the Belgian professor Gustave Magnel and saw some of the first prestressing activities taking place in Europe. Anderson began to understand the benefit of prestressing concrete – where steel cables are tensioned before the concrete is cast, and then embedded within a solid beam. This tensioning, when released, effectively placed the entire concrete piece in compression, reducing concrete's tendency to crack under tension stresses. This prestressing

also meant that concrete could be thinner than ever before. The bulky, heavy associations with concrete structures could now dissolve in to thinner, prestressed elements with the potential to be both more efficient and more slender. Anderson, alongside Magnel, also helped oversee the instrumentation for the Walnut Lane Bridge in Pennsylvania in 1948 – a structure widely considered to be the first prestressed concrete bridge in the United States.[1]

Following this extensive experience, Anderson returned to Tacoma and reunited with his brother to form their own prestressed concrete plant – named Concrete Technology Corporation. They also founded a complimentary engineering firm Anderson Birkeland Anderson to design with the new material. This new precast, prestressed concrete had complications but also potential: the Anderson Brothers had to not only discover a way to economically produce these new concrete elements, but effectively market them for architectural and engineering purposes. In 1950, the Anderson brothers toured Europe, visiting several precasting prestressing plants in Italy, France, Belgium and England - gaining insight into successful engineering and production companies. With flexible building codes in the Northwest, characteristically open to new ideas, the Anderson Brothers were able to apply their emerging expertise to office buildings, bridges, waterfront structures, grandstands and warehouses. The Anderson Brothers had to constantly innovate to execute new ideas, trying things in prestressed concrete that had never been done before. Their success as a company was based soley on their ability to communicate why prestressed concrete was a good idea and how it could change the way the Northwest used concrete.

The Norton Building, Seattle, 1958

In 1958, the economic fortunes of Seattle had rebounded from the Great Depression and wartime austerity measures, and construction activity had restarted in downtown. The Norton Building was one of the first tall buildings built in over 20 years, designed by the San Francisco office of the Chicago design firm Skidmore Owings and Merrill (Myron Goldsmith, design principle). The 21-story steel and glass curtain wall building resembled similar designs the firm had completed in San Francisco (Crown Zellerbach), but the interior of the building is quite different - using prestressed concrete beams instead of long span steel. Goldsmith's interest in concrete (begun in Italy with Pier Luigi Nervi) combined with the casting capability the Anderson Brothers had established in Tacoma to create a truly unique building. These beams span 70' in three bays to create an entirely column-free interior floor. Several large openings were cast within the depth of the beam to allow mechanical and electrical systems to pass through, and minimize the floor-to-floor height.[2] All the beams were cast in Tacoma, and was the first time that prestressed concrete was used in a building over six stories tall in the United States.

The Norton Building showed that precast, prestessed concrete clearly had a functional, utilitarian role within modern architecture.

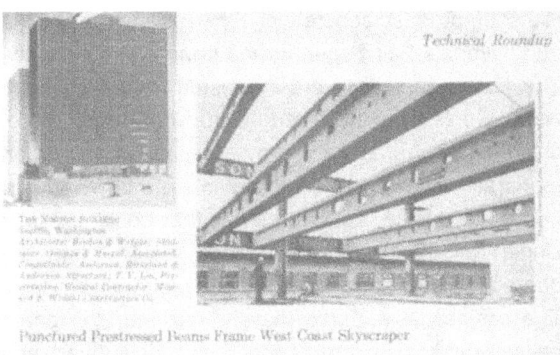

Fig. 1. Norton Building Beams & Exterior[3]

Cheney Grandstand, Tacoma, 1959

The Anderson Brothers were convinced however, that precast concrete could become more of the structure than just long-span beams. In 1959, the city of Tacoma was interested in bringing Triple-A baseball to the city, but needed a cost-effective grandstand structure to serve as a stadium. Under a tight deadline, the Anderson Brothers quickly developed a column-free concept that could be executed quickly in precast concrete. The Anderson brothers turned their experience casting concrete into a design approach, beating out several other design proposals on cost, schedule and performance. The design could be produced and built in only 99 days.

The design was a simple assembly of individually cast elements: an angled back column, an inclined seating riser, and an overhead cantilevered canopy. Each one of these pieces was prestressed concrete, pieced together with post-tensioned cables. All together, 1650 pieces came together to create a grandstand with clear, unobstructed views from every seat.

The result was a slender, utilitarian structure, yet in it's exposed state, reveals the language of precast as a free-standing structure. With no associated architect, the building is devoid of ornamentation or detailing, but hints at an emerging expressive potential. Through this stadium, architects began to see the benefits of precast concrete as more than just individual elements but fully a part of a work of architecture.

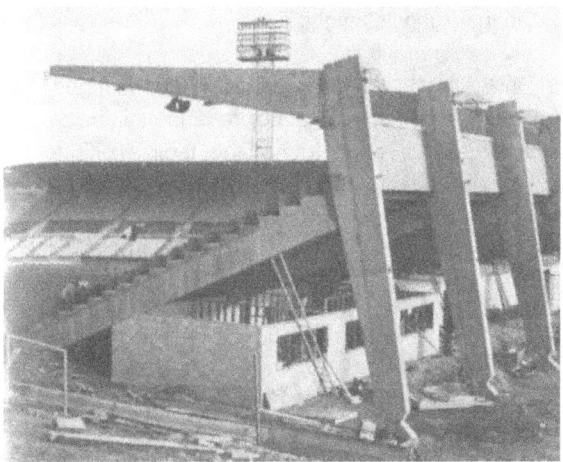

Fig. 2. Cheney Grandstand[4]

Our Lady of the Lake, Seattle, 1960

By 1960, precast concrete was flourishing. The architects Roger Gotteland and Roy Koczarski, French and Polish immigrants to the region, were commissioned to design a new gathering space for the Catholic church, Our Lady of the Lake. The architects faced the issue of increasing the capacity of a church parish hall on a severely limited site, with a tight budget, while wanting to explore a modern spiritual expression. In this vein, the architects defined concept of the church to match their interest in using innovative materials. They stated: "The principle aim of contemporary architecture is to be functional. By functional is meant that there is no superfluous use of materials or ornamentation. There is a structural or functional purpose for everything that is done."[5] To execute this concept, they turned to precast concrete.

The church is a single volume space, 40 feet tall, 80 feet wide and 135 feet long, defined by of a series of precast concrete arched frames, spaced 20 feet apart. Each individual frame was cast in two pieces in Tacoma, trucked to the site, and joined together at the center point of the span - effectively creating a three-hinged arch. These frames, painted white, are infilled with a dark brick and windows.[6]

An eighty-foot tall bell tower marks the corner of the site. The tower is composed of three prestressed concrete elements (also cast at Concrete Technology, in Tacoma), brought together and jointed at four locations along its height.

In this church, prestressed concrete changed the relative proportions of structure and volume. The slenderness of each frame and their ability to be assembled on site changed the nature of the interior space, making a truly modern worship hall.

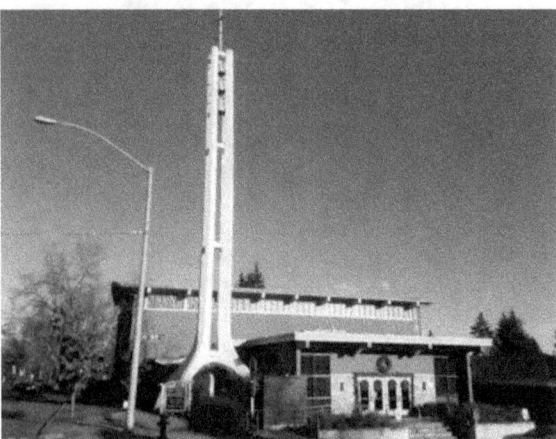

Fig. 3. Our Lady of the Lake Exterior

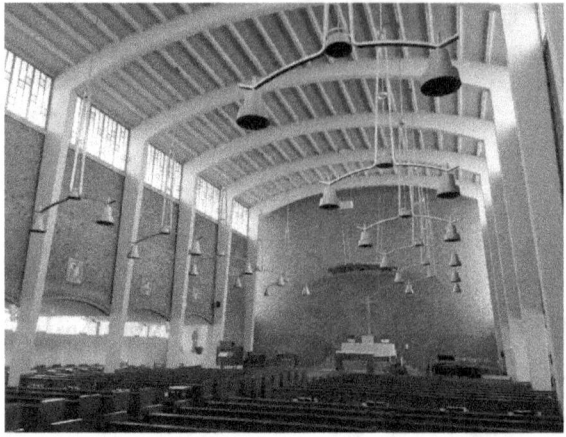

Fig. 4. Our Lady of the Lake Interior

Seattle Monorail, Seattle, 1962

But the Anderson Brothers did not forget the utilitarian roots of precast concrete. When planning for the 1962 World's Fair began, urban transit was a priority. The Fair organizers were interested in changing the way people moved through the downtown core, choked by traffic, so they proposed an urban monorail. The Alweg company in Germany had just begun producing a monorail car that could follow a single rail track along a curving route – and the offered to build and operate the monorail for free. The car design required that the car 'hug' the beam below – rolling on top of the beam for support and guided by wheels rolling on either side of the beam. While the cars would be made in Germany, the monorail track would have to be built locally. Given the nature of the design, the precision of the beam would have to exactly match the precision of car – the design of the two was inseparable.[7]

In laying out the route between the Fairground and downtown Seattle, the Monorail would have to twist and turn through the downtown buildings on elevated pedestals, meaning each segment of track would have to be different – with different degrees of curvature and torsion. At the time, many people thought it was impossible to prestress a curved beam. But it turns out, given the mechanics of the beam, it is possible and the Anderson Brothers figured out how to cast them. To reduce the self-weight of the beams, each beam was cast with a large void in the middle making them hollow.

The adventurous designs in architecture – challenged to cast and transport different shapes and forms – helped the Anderson Brothers form the monorail beams. Their ability to innovate in precast concrete was opening the eyes of the public to the material possibilities.

US Science Pavilion, Seattle, 1962

It is ironic that the most well-known precast concrete work of modern architecture was not completed by the Anderson Brothers by by a competing firm. Concrete Technology and the associated engineers had proven the market and opened the door for other engineers and producers to try their hand at designing and creating precast concrete.

This fact is evident at the federally funded US Science Pavilion - one of the largest complexes on the Fairgrounds for the 1962 World's Fair. The Fair promotional material stated that the US Science Pavilion "will be a large, ultra-modern building designed to reflect the concept of its contents – the world's scientific vistas," and express "the role of science in the Space Age."[8] Sited on the south end of the fairgrounds, on the corner of Second Avenue North and Denny Way, the building was intended to express and display the promising technological future of the United States enabled by science – a government showpiece at the core of the Fair's cultural mission.

In 1959, the federal government awarded the design of the US Science Pavilion to Minoru Yamasaki. To execute the project in Seattle, Yamasaki partnered with the architects at Naramore, Bain, Brady, and Johanson. Yamasaki was classmate of Perry Johanson at the University of Washington and the two remained close. In need of a good engineer to execute a technologically advanced building, Johanson introduced Yamasaki to John Skilling, and the engineers at Worthington Skilling Helle and Jackson – most specifically, Jack Christiansen.

Yamasaki was more interested in using his design to create a peaceful setting. He wanted to harness the advancing technology and use it to create a human-centered experience. In his evolving perspective on modern architecture, Yamasaki stated that he aimed to create buildings to "love and touch."[9] He wanted his buildings to have a sensitive, tactile quality. He was interested in combining the high-quality texture and finish of precast concrete, with the thinness of shell construction, in the creation of a serene environment.

Yamasaki was also influenced by his experience as a visitor at previous World's Fairs in other cities – where each architect was "vying to be more spectacular than the next, with chaotic results."[10] As a result, Yamasaki chose to design not a singular building, but a central courtyard space surrounded by five separate buildings. The visitor would enter a somewhat enclosed space on a series of elevated platforms, with soaring arched towers overhead, and fountains and pools below. Yamasaki stated: "We wanted visitors to be intrigued as they first see the five towers of the pavilion- and then the visual surprise of pools and fountains."[11] The courtyard was intended to be an "oasis in a rapidly growing Seattle."

Thinness was held paramount to Yamasaki, who designed the curving ribs and columns as a delicate pattern. Yet these ribs would have to be structural as well – strong enough to carry the loads from the roof and floors of the buildings to the foundation. To achieve the desired thinness, Christiansen would have to use the pattern as the beginning of his structure design – placing the reinforcing steel and prestressing tendons within the pattern of Yamasaki's design, with little flexibility to alter the overall form.

The building facades that faced the interior of the complex would shape the pristine environment of this courtyard. Yamasaki wanted these building surfaces to be precast concrete, yet as thin and delicate as possible. To minimize the number of elements and attain this refined aesthetic, the structure would have to become the façade – an opposing strategy to the non-structural glass curtain wall Yamasaki had used on the American Concrete Institute headquarters. The buildings each became a strikingly simple assembly of thin, precast concrete bearing walls supporting long-span, prestressed concrete girders overhead. The buildings have no interior columns, leaving wide-open floor plans for exhibits of different sizes.

The walls are articulated by a pattern of tightly spaced columns or studs, only 3 feet apart, giving the walls a 'pin-striped' appearance. Curving ribs trace out pointed arches in between the columns. The flat wall surface in between the columns is solid in some places, open in others – allowing for colonnade-like walkways and windows in different locations.

The wall panels – each five feet wide - were cast in fiberglass forms with a structural steel support. A relatively new firm in the Seattle area - Associated Sand and Gravel - designed custom prestressing equipment to match the tight tolerance and exact rib geometry. They experimented with different mixes of concrete to get the correct balance of strength, and brilliant exterior finish – selected to be a crushed white quartzite. The panels were cast in a plant in Everett and trucked to the Fairgrounds for simple assembly.

The result is a courtyard that is surrounded by the thin tracery of columns and ribs. The buildings are delicate, yet substantial – enclosing exhibits while shaping the experience of the visitor.

In the center of the building complex, Yamasaki designed a series of five, delicate towers that marked the entrance to the central courtyard. Continuing his interest in lightness and thinness, Yamasaki designed pointed arches filled with a thin lattice.

Each tower was composed of four, supporting corner columns topped with connecting arches that rise higher than the surrounding buildings – over 70 feet tall. The arches come together to create an open, dome-like shape, filled in with a thin tracery similar to the pattern of the building walls below. Despite their delicate appearance, the towers are made entirely of precast, prestressed concrete. Each individual piece was brought to the site and assembled together in place. A light fixture part of the way up links the lower legs of the towers and resolves any outward thrust developed from the top.

The buildings, towers and entrance platforms created a powerful composition, all executed in prestressed concrete. The architectural critique of the US Science Pavilion recognized the modern technological methods used to create the pavilion.[12]

Conclusion

This progression of buildings and projects demonstrates the evolution of precast concrete as a medium of modern architecture. Through the

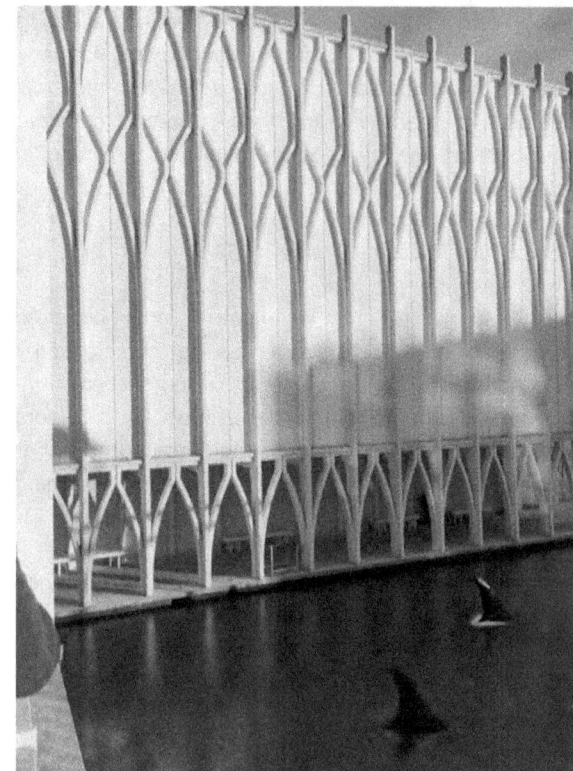

Fig. 5. US Science Pavilion Walls

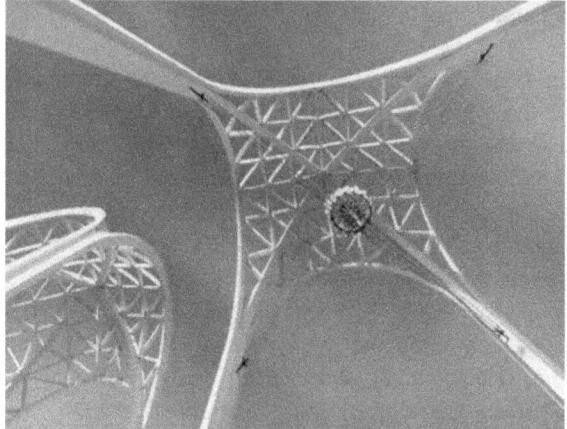

Fig. 6. US Science Pavilion Arches

ingenuity of the Anderson Brothers, and the unique strand of Modern architecture that emerged in the Pacific Northwest, the late 1950s and early 1960s became a 'golden age' for precast concrete. During this time, there was an alignment between design intent and production capability, with both architecture and engineering professionals working towards a shared goal – one that maximized the potential of a new building material. Treated as an honest expression of structural form and finish, precast prestressed concrete fundamentally changed the modern architecture of the Northwest. As new materials continue to emerge in the current context, it becomes evident that a similar shared vision between professionals is essential to realizing exciting and efficient buildings.

Notes:

[1] Lightbourne, Alesa. *Ideas into reality: the BERGER/ABAM story*. Kent, Wash: Amica Inc. 1990. 5.

[2] Anderson, Arthur, "Part 7 – An Adventure in Prestressed Concrete", in "Reflections on the Beginning of Prestressed Concrete in America", *PCI Journal,* January-February 1979. 189-255.

[3] "Punctured Prestressed Beams Frame West Coast Skyscraper", *Architectural Record,* March 1960, 225.

[4] Anderson. 243.

[5] "Unity is Key to Design of Our Lady of Lake Church", *Seattle Times,* March 19, 1961. 35.

[6] "Architecture", *Our Lady of the Lake Parish History,* Seattle, WA. 1962.

[7] Anderson, Arthur, "Casting Curved Prestressed Monorail Beams", in "Concrete Construction for the Century 21 Exposition", *Proceedings from 15th Fall Meeting, American Concrete Institute,* September 27-29, 1962. 11.

[8] *Century 21 Exposition,* Century 21 Exposition, Inc., California Institute of Technology, 1959. 10.

[9] "UW Alumnus of the Year Was 'Regular Fellow', *Seattle Times,* June 6, 1960. 12.

[10] Yamasaki, Minoru. *A Life in Architecture.* 1st ed. New York: Weatherhill, 1979. 70.

[11] "Architects 'Tickled to Death' With Their Science Pavilion", *Seattle Times,* April 5, 1962. 12.

[12] " 10. Architectural Critique of the Pavilion", *U.S. Science Exhibit – Seattle World's Fair Final Report,* US Department of Commerce, Library of Congress Catalogue Card No. 63-60022, Washington D.C., 1963. 51-56.

SESSION 09: ATMOSPHERES

Session Chair: Naomi Darling
Five Colleges—Hampshire, Mt. Holyoke, UMass Amherst

Chad Schwartz, Southern Illinois University: "Intersections."

Andrew Cruse, Ohio State University: "Comfort Zones and Weather Patterns."

Peter Raab, Texas Tech University: "The Beginning Is Place."

Intersections

Chad Schwartz
Southern Illinois University - Carbondale

Abstract

In *Thinking Architecture*, Peter Zumthor states that "buildings are artificial constructions. They consist of single parts which must be joined together."[1] Within this discussion, Zumthor poses that the quality of a finished project is a direct resultant of the quality of the joints holding together the assembly. As such, the architectural joint sits at the confluence of the poetics and pragmatics of our built world. It concurrently provides – as Marco Frascari, Edward Ford, and others have also so eloquently professed – the structural connectivity for our buildings as well as the seat of identity for our understanding of the spaces we inhabit.

In an entry-level building technology course, a seemingly simple question has been posed to a group of second year architecture and interior design students: How do you join together two lengths of 2x4? The responses to this challenge, which were inspired by typical connections the students see and utilize every day (drawer hinges, skateboard trucks, bra straps, sketchbook bindings, carabineers, shotguns), provided the students not only with ideas about the poetic assembly of architecture and the careful fabrication of joints, but also about the seemingly infinite number of opportunities available for crafting the constructed environment. This paper examines the relevance of the assignment and the student's responses in the context of a course centered on experiential learning. By learning through the physical crafting of these joints – paired with sketching and targeted readings – this assignment has the potential to embed threads of poetic understanding in what can be a very pragmatic curriculum of building technology while also forcing the students to think about the materials of construction with much broader seeing, yet deeper penetrating eyes.

Introduction

What is an architectural detail? In his seminal work, *The Architectural Detail*, Edward Ford outlines five definitions or types of details: the detail as abstraction, the detail as motif, the detail as an order, the detail as a joint, and the detail as a subversive activity.[3] While Ford argues that all of the typologies of the architectural detail are useful and important in our built environment, he finds that the detail is at its most meaningful when considered as either a joint or an autonomous condition.[4] This sentiment is paralleled by Peter Zumthor who praises the art of joining and the nature of architecture as an assembly of parts that must be affixed to one another.

> Construction is the art of making a meaningful whole out of many parts. Buildings are witnesses to the human ability to construct concrete things. I believe that the real core of all architectural work lies in the act of construction. At the point in time when concrete materials are assembled and erected, the architecture we have been looking for becomes part of the real world.
>
> I feel respect for the art of joining, the ability of craftsmen and engineers. I am impressed by the knowledge of how to make things, which lies at the bottom of human skill. I try to design buildings that are worthy of this knowledge and merit the challenge to this skill.[2]

Marco Frascari states in "The Tell-the-Tale Detail" that it is possible to observe that any architectural element defined as a detail is always a joint.[5] The adoration of the joint is also significant in Gottfried Semper's philosophy of dressing, a primary catalyst for the development of architectural tectonics. Semper believed that one of the oldest technical symbols of human culture, and an inspiration for the development of the built environment, could be found in the original joint or architectural detail: the knot.[6]

This paper outlines a building technology project that asks students to explore the notion of the detail as joint, a condition examined for its ability to join together discrete parts of our built environment. Frascari separated this classification into two distinct arenas: material joints such as the bolt connecting a wood slat to its support or the connection of the capital of a column to a beam and formal joints such as the entry porch that connects the exterior and interior environments of a home or the bridge that connects the farmland on the east side of the river to the city on the west.[7] This exercise is focused distinctly on the material classification of the architectural joint, with an effort on helping students reconnect the pragmatics of assembly with the poetic and aesthetic potential of the intersection of the individual components that make up our built environment.

It can be argued that the contemporary construction and manufacturing industries have had a distinct impact on the presence and impact of the architectural detail. Our buildings are often filled with stock / typical / off-the-shelf / standardized / manufactured details, details selected out of a catalog or library rather than originating through the process of design in a way that is project specific. How do we teach our students to balance the use of standardized components (and their installation specifications) with the design or connections that are expressive and add to the qualities of a space? We need to encourage them to take what is given and rework it to fit the needs of a specific place, a specific project, a specific client. Students must be taught to think beyond their preconceived notions of "typical" assembly practices and explore the virtually infinite number of ways we can construct.

Architecture is a series of connections; at a base level, it is the joining of elements to create a whole. The means and methods of making the connections, however, are far from simple. The way we connect two elements together has major ramifications on how we experience space, how we construct architecture, and on the relationship of the parts to the overall project. In a second year building technology course, architecture and interior design students are asked to explore the dialogue between two modest elements as they attach one to the other. This assignment takes a different approach to detailing than would be

traditionally implemented in a building technology course (Figure 1). This assignment is about the poetics of construction.

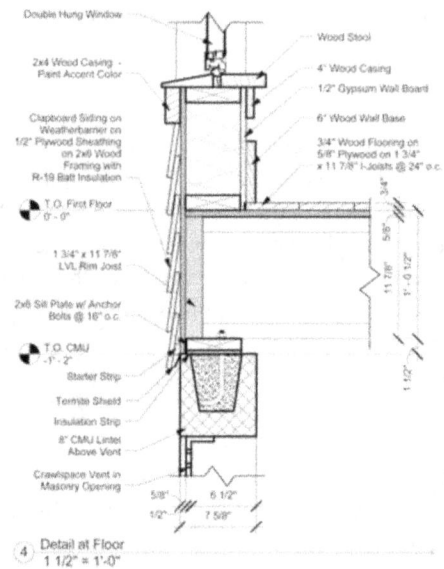

Fig. 1. Traditional technical architectural detail. Drawing by E. Hall-Skank.

The Course and the Assignment

Students enroll in their first building technology course in the fall semester of their second year in the architecture and interior design programs at Southern Illinois University. The course centers on the study of wood construction technology and is delivered through a lecture and a lab, each attended twice a week. The lectures provide the students with the technical fundamentals of wood light frame construction as well as a forum for quizzes and tests. The lab sessions are utilized for the development of project content and for introducing the students to the use of BIM software in the development of the technical drawings for a small design project.

At the time the students take this course, most have never built anything using real materials and some have never before used power tools (or even hand tools for that matter). As such, during the first week of class, the students go through a shop tutorial and are introduced to safety procedures, best practices, and how to use the shop's complement of tools.

Each of the three projects the students work on in the course contribute to their overall understanding of the potential impact of construction and documentation in architecture and interior design (Figure 2). The primary individual project undertaken during the semester asks the students to translate a design project created in their studio into a set of working documents, while the course's group project involves the designing and building of a small-scale structure, which has taken a variety of forms over the years.

These two larger endeavors are preceded by an introductory project intended to spark the imaginations and intellects of the students at the beginning of the semester. In this project, the students are asked to design and construct a joint connecting two, 2'-0" lengths of 2x4. Each student begins the assignment by finding examples of joints in their everyday lives that can inspire their own work, i.e. a carabineer clip, a door lock, a guitar tuning knob, a zipper, or a shoelace. These elements must be able to be experienced and manipulated first-hand (no Google-searching allowed). The students present several examples for critique by the class and faculty. After this initial investigation, each student must select a single inspiration to use as a catalyst for the project, photograph the joint, and study it to thoroughly understand how it works. The students then start the construction process. They use their sketchbooks and raw materials to craft two versions of a joint that is inspired by – not a copy of – their inspirational example. The first version of the joint must be made entirely out of wood, although they are permitted to use other wood in addition to the 2x4s. The second version of the joint must use a material other than wood to make the connection. The two constructions are then presented in class for critique. After the discussion, the students refine their work and create a final version of the 2x4 joint constructions (Figure 3).

Fig. 2. Breakdown of course learning objectives for Building Technology I.

This project has been utilized four times in the past six years of teaching this course and each time the delivery of the project has been refined. In the first iteration, the students created the first versions of their pair of connections at the beginning of the semester. Their final versions of the two joints were then created at the end of the semester after most of the substantial course learning objectives had been

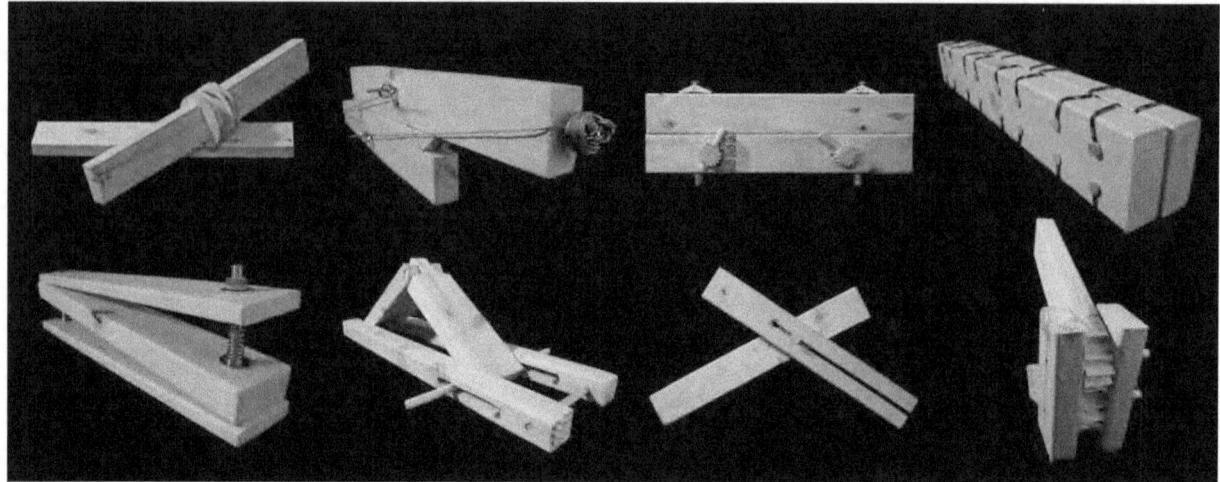

Fig. 3. Final 2x4 constructions. Photographs by Author. Constructions by (clockwise from upper left) A. Weitnauer, L. Henson, R. Mason, H. Pence, R. Pruitt , L. Ovca, E. Hamilton, and W. McGuire.

conveyed to the class. Although the intent was to allow the students to gain experience before creating their final constructions, the time gap in between the initial and final submissions ended up being too great and the minimal gains did not end up warranting the project spanning the entire semester.

In the second iteration, the project timeframe was truncated and both the first and second versions of the project were delivered back-to-back in the first few weeks of the semester. Although the timeframe worked better, building four complete joints in a short timespan proved to be a bit too much work for many of the students. As such, in the third iteration, after the presentation of the initial constructions, each student had to choose one of their two detail designs to produce as a final version. This modification reduced the demand on the students and allowed them to focus their efforts in refining the final product of the project.

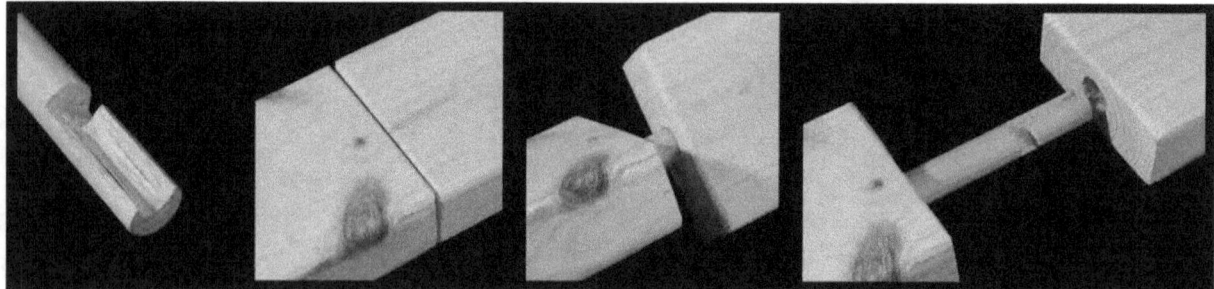

Fig. 4. Final construction assembly sequence. Photographs by Author. Construction by R. Bdair.

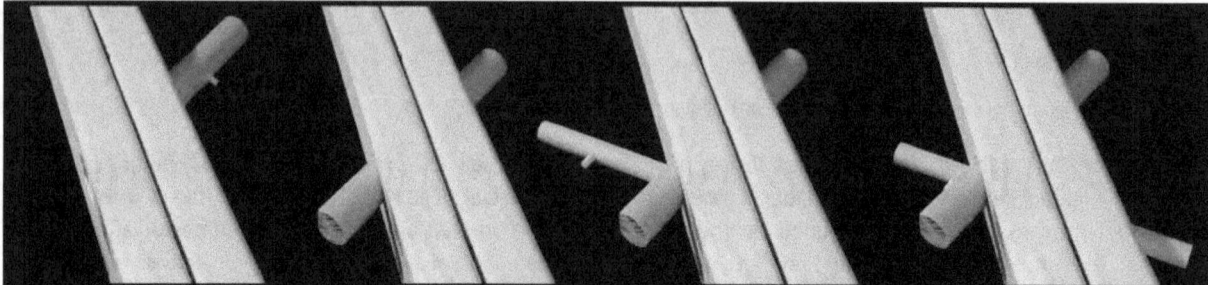

Fig. 5. Final construction assembly sequence. Photographs by Author. Construction by J. Gossman

In the latest iteration of the project, the students followed the same process undertaken in the third iteration with one additional responsibility. In addition to the single final construction, each student was responsible for generating a single 11x17 sheet of drawings of the joint – which included an elevation, a section, and two details – based on a given CAD template file. The addition of the very small set of drawings helped tie the exercise to the other projects in the course and served as an instigator for the initial discussions of technical documentation occurring both in lecture and lab over the first half of the semester.

Lessons Learned

There are a handful of critical lessons that students have had the opportunity to learn by engaging with examination of the architectural detail. The first realization that many of the students have come to is the diversity of connections utilized in our environment. They find joints that are static and others that are dynamic. Some static joints are meant to be permanent, others offer the ability to be released or repositioned. Dynamic joints operate in a multitude of ways, through rotation, sliding, compression, and so on (Figures 4 and 5). As certain as there is variety, there are also themes that carry through connection details, with many very diverse constructions utilizing similar means of attachment, but perhaps in different ways or for different reasons. These realizations are essential to the assignment, which seeks to break down preconceptions of how we build and to illuminate to these novice students the possibilities existing around them in plain sight (Figures 6, 7, 8, and 9).

A second core lesson learned is the complexity involved in and the skill required to connect two things together. Most expressed joints, assuming that they are to be built at finish quality, require precision and careful planning. Each of the students goes into the construction phase of this assignment with an intended plan. When they start using the tools, however, very often they find their plan for the construction does not match either the operational limits of the tools available or the skill of the operator (or both). The process of learning how to fabricate an idea is eye opening. What is so easily drawn in a sketchbook can become incredibly cumbersome when sitting in the woodshop if fabrication is not taken into account during the design process. And, as many of these students have never built anything using traditional construction materials before, this opportunity marks their first chance to understand this point.

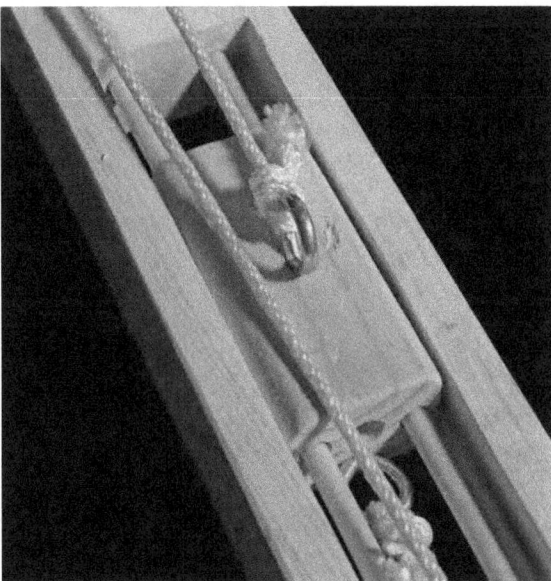

Fig. 6. Detail of construction. Photograph by Author. Construction by D. Christensen.

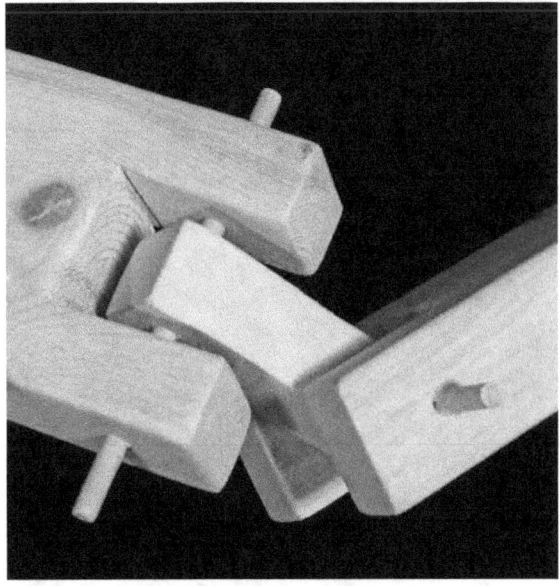

Fig. 7. Detail of construction. Photograph by Author.

In addition to the process of fabrication, each student becomes aware of the opportunities and limitations of wood and manufactured lumber through this exercise. The first constructions are typically littered with examples of wood that has been pushed past its structural limitations, wood that has been left too thin to stand up to the impact of movement or even just transportation to class. Wood is a natural material that is unequal at all parts. How do you avoid knots and other inclusions in the wood or, perhaps, include them in the design? The students also learn quickly that wood is not equally strong in all directions. Cutting along the grain or against it becomes critical to the ultimate stability and success of a given design.

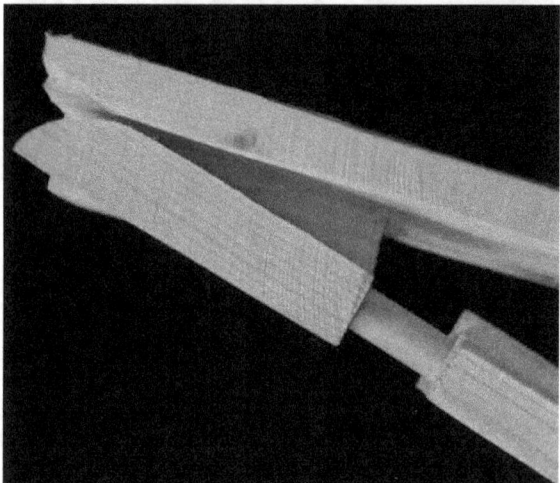

Fig. 8. Detail of construction. Photograph by Author. Construction by A. Michael.

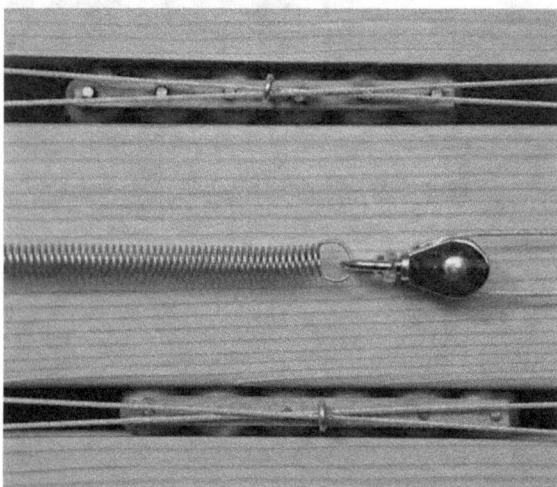

Fig. 9. Detail of construction. Photograph by Author. Construction by M. Ollmann.

As important as it is for the students to learn the qualities of wood and its potential as a construction medium, by having them create two separate constructions in the first build phase, they also start to make comparisons between wood and other materials. The most prominent examples of this comparison often come when a student builds a construction utilizing a material that is thin, but strong in tension like aluminum or cable of some sort and finds a successful solution. Pleased with the results, he or she tries to do something similar with the all wood connection only to find that the only way it will work is if the wood used to create the attachment is significantly more bulky to avoid it splitting. Although the project is centered on beginning to understand the properties of wood, some of these realizations are better learned when set in comparison with other materials performing in similar conditions.

More abstractly, the project provides a forum for the students to learn how to properly convey a series of instructions to those who will be constructing or fabricating a project in the field. What responsibility do architects and designers have for ensuring the overall quality of the final product? If students begin to consider what will happen in the process of fabrication during the early stages of their education, the opportunity arises for more thoughtful consideration of the process of construction later in their professional careers. In this simple assignment, with little to no future ramification, the students are asked to build their conceived detail with their own hands. This haptic, first-hand experience, where mistakes cannot be hidden away, illuminates the complexity of fabricating and assembling our built environment.

In addition, as is stated in the opening section of this paper, the students must create joints that are both structurally sound (pragmatic in their assembly) and that convey the idea of their inspiration without creating a copy of it (the poetics of construction). This pairing epitomizes the nature of architecture as a practice and the hope is that it will serve as a springboard for these students to continue to consider these dual roles as they move forward in their architectural explorations.

Final Thoughts

In the closing lines of *The Architectural Detail*, Ford states:

> Detailing that is stylized, perfect, invisible, or accomplished with motifs will succeed only where it is inconsistent, imperfect, exaggerated, and contains non-conforming parts. The good detail is not consistent, but non-conforming; not typical, but exceptional; not doctrinaire, but heretical, not the continuation of an idea, but its termination, and the beginning of another.[8]

A significant portion of the building technology that most of us teach deals with the practicality of building in the contemporary world. We teach how architecture is assembled and how to create representations that will serve as a set of instructions to those who do construct the ideas that we conceive. Understanding the standards of assembly is essential for any young architect. Equally important, however, is understanding that the articulation of a detail or the development of a connection between elements has the potential to move beyond mere assembly, beyond the typical to the exceptional. Through this elevation, the detail also then has the potential to have an impact on how the users experience and remember the space.

This assignment is deceptively simple. Take the most mundane of building materials and elevate it to something unique, something special, something inspired. This fundamental strategy has been utilized by some of our greatest architects and can be found within a number of spectacular pieces of architecture such as E. Fay Jones' Thorncrown Chapel. Outside Eureka Springs, Arkansas, Jones took a pile of dimensional lumber, had it carried into the forest, and fabricated into a classic piece of American architecture. This exquisite artifact is not cherished for its luxurious materials, but for the creative and intricate way in which thoughtful details have transformed a pile of 2x's into an awe-inspiring space. At the end of the semester, no one in the class is going to claim to be the next Fay Jones, but each will have had the opportunity to get a first impression of the potential embedded in the joining of two elements to each other.

Notes:

[1] Peter Zumthor, *Thinking Architecture*, 2nd ed. (Boston, Massachusetts: Birkhauser, 2006), 13.

[2] ibid, 11.

[3] Edward Ford, *The Architectural Detail* (New York: Princeton Architectural Press, 2011).

[4] ibid. p 45.

[5] Marco Frascari, "The Tell-the-Tale Detail," in *Theorizing a New Agenda for Architecture: An Anthology of Architectural Theory 1965-1995*, ed. Kate Nesbitt (New York: Princeton Architectural Press, 1996), 500. Originally published in *VIA 7: The Building of Architecture* (1984): 23-37.

[6] Gottfried Semper, *Style in the Technical and Tectonic Arts: Or Practical Aesthetics*, trans. Harry Francis Mallgrave and Michael Robinson (Los Angeles: Getty Research Institute, 2004), 219. (Originally published as Semper, Gotfried. *Der Stil in den technischen und tektonischen Kunsten; oder, Praktische Aesthetik: Ein Handbuch fur Techniker, Kunstler und Kunstfreunde*, 2 vols. Frankfurt am Main: Verlag fur Kunst & Wissenschaft, 1860.)

[7] Frascari, "The Tell-the-Tale Detail," 500, and Chad Schwartz, *Introducing Architectural Tectonics: Exploring the Intersection of Design and Construction* (New York: Routledge, 2016), lvii.

[8] Ford, *The Architectural Detail*, 312.

Coenesthetic Comfort: Between Climate and the Body

Andrew Cruse
Ohio State University

Abstract

This paper proposes coenesthetic comfort as a nexus between climate and the body. A coenesthetic experience is one arising from the sum of our bodily impressions and experiences, rather than from a single input. Coenesthetic comfort differs from the dominant model of thermal comfort found in most buildings. While thermal comfort specifies a homeostatic relationship between a building's interior climate and the body's involuntary physiological processes, coenesthetic describes for a heightened awareness of both the environment and our experiences of it. As such, it links climate patterns—from seasonal change to climate change—with corporeal experiences—from concerns for health to the possibilities for pleasure. The paper contrasts two approaches to comfort, human biometeorology and thermal comfort, through a discussion of the 18th century bathing machine and the 20th century psychrometric chamber. It continues to examine how these two approaches are combined in the Adaptive Thermal Comfort model, and as part of several innovative architectural practices. The paper concludes by discussing how discomfort is an important aspect of coenesthetic comfort.

Introduction

It is said that architecture improves the weather. That is, the sealed and insulated envelopes of modern buildings contain vast quantities of conditioned air that provides optimal atmospheric conditions for the human body. Since, as a global average, working people spend approximate 90% of their lives indoors,[1] we can more accurately say that architecture replaces the weather. Yet today the effects of weather cannot be so easily eliminated from our lives. Indeed, weather is at the center of the great drama of our time, climate change. And changes in the weather are affecting how we as architects design and construct buildings. This is most commonly seen in approaches to architectural sustainability and resilience. Here I want to propose coenesthetic comfort as a rich and largely untapped way to relate architecture to larger climate patterns, and to our own corporeal experiences. Coenesthetic comfort is the nexus between climate and the body. A coenesthetic experience is one arising from the sum of our bodily impressions and experiences, rather than from a single input. Current thermal comfort standards in architecture call for our body's physiological processes to reach homeostasis with a static interior climate without our conscious attention. (Homeostasis describes the ability to maintain an internal state of stable equilibrium when faced with external change.) An engaged idea of coenesthetic comfort can have the practical effect of reducing energy needs, and the poetic one of heightening our architectural experiences in ways that pique public consciousness and provide personal pleasures.

To unpack the relationship between our bodies and climate in an architectural context, I want to weave together two historical narratives, that of human biometeorology and thermal comfort standards. While the first studies the interaction of the body with the natural atmospheric systems, the second studies the interaction of the body with a building's artificial mechanical ones. Historically, these two narratives have been separate. The study of human biometeorology began in the west with the Greek physician Hippocrates in *On Airs Waters and Places* (second half of 5th century BCE). It greatly expanded in the 18th century when natural scientists (most famously Alexander von Humboldt) linked the distribution of species with different ecosystems. It also relied on the invention of measuring devices, such as the thermometer and the barometer, that allowed health and weather to be objectively recorded and analyzed. At the start of the 20th century, the shift from a natural to mechanical basis for comfort was spurred in part by the development of air conditioning (that is the ability to control the temperature and humidity of air). However, the technology itself was not solely responsible for this change. Instead, it resulted from a complex interplay of political, cultural and energetic narratives, in which architecture was intimately involved. Collectively, these led to architecture replacing the weather through interior environments designed to meet thermal comfort standards. Two simple spaces can help to explain these different approaches to comfort, the bathing machine and the psychrometric chamber.

Spaces for Comfort

The bathing machine was invented in the 1720's along the southern coast of England as a means of taking people from the shore to the sea inside a private and secure environment. [Figure 1] It was part of the larger rush to the sea that was spurred by contemporary medical theories which described the benefits of sea water bathing as a cure for various ailments. Technologically, the bathing machine was quite simple. It consisted of a small closed wooden carriage, often moved by a horse between the shore and the water. Its designation as a machine referred to a moveable awning that could be lowered over the door, allowing the bather to enter the water without being seen. However, as the architectural platform for a coenesthetic experience, the bathing machine was anything but simple. It provided a transition from a fixed, terrestrial world to a mobile, aqueous one, thus facilitating both therapeutic and aesthetic experiences. The therapeutic benefits were first discussed by the physician Richard Russell in his book, *A Dissertation on the Uses of Sea-Water in the Diseases of the Glands* (1755). The thermal and physical shock of the water and waves were thought to bring vigor to the body, helping to cure the bather of gout, jaundice and other glandular problems, as well as treating more existential aliments related to urban living such as melancholy and excess spleen.

Aesthetically, the sea held very different connotations in the 18th century than it does today. Unlike the garden, the sea could not be tamed. It was a remnant of the Biblical Flood, the primitive state of the world that existed before history began. To experience of the sea was to experience the sublime, that is the combination of awe and terror that emotionally and intellectually moved the subject, forcing them to make sense of their experience. As an architectural platform for the sublime, the bathing machine created a relationship between one's body and the outside world that had both medical and philosophical dimensions. This was not a comfort of ease,

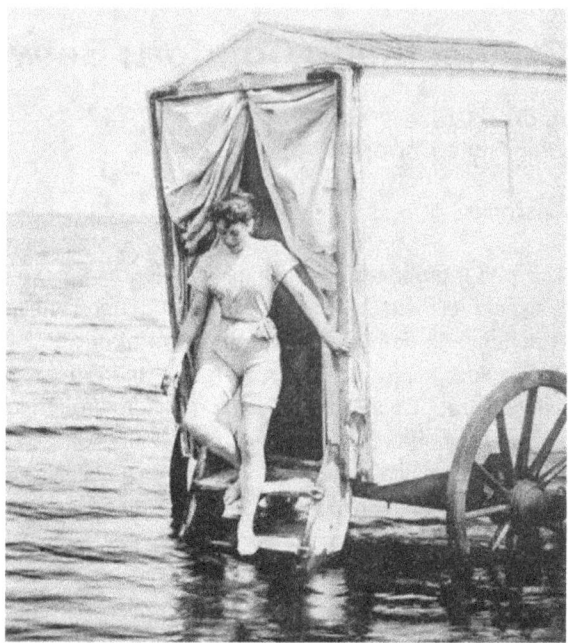

Fig. 1. Bathing Machine

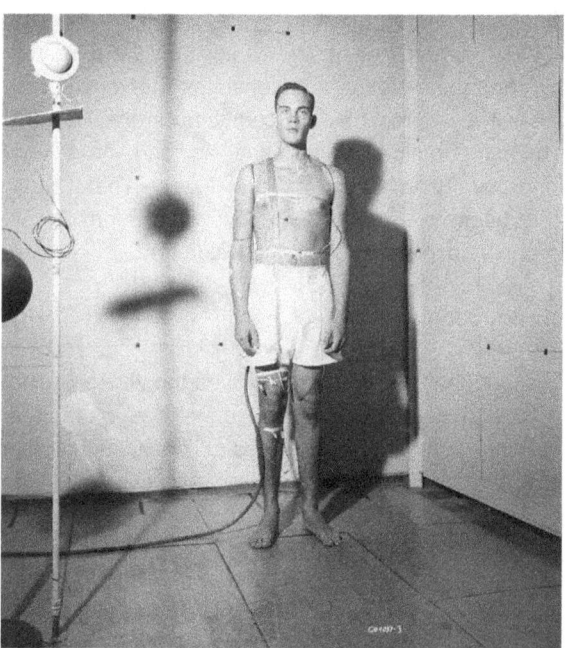

Fig. 2. Psychrometric Test Chamber

relaxation and luxury. Instead, as the historian Alain Corbin has discussed, "a new world of sensations was growing out of the mixed pain and pleasure of sudden immersion [in the sea]. Here, for the benefit of the leisured classes, a new way of experiencing one's body was developing, based on rooting out the desires to disturb it."[2]

While the bathing machine provided experiences to disturb the body, the psychrometric chamber was designed to silence it. Invented in the early 20th century, the psychrometric chamber was used, in part, to settle a professional dispute that had arisen between the medical community and the emerging profession of ventilation engineers about how best to ventilate public school classrooms. While physicians favored natural ventilation through open windows, the engineers favored artificial ventilation using mechanical equipment. Engineers saw the development of rational comfort standards as the best way to establish the superiority of mechanical systems, and to gain public confidence in their professional authority.[3] Built by the American Society of Heating and Ventilating Engineers (ASHVE), the first psychrometric chamber was a laboratory device to determine quantitatively a thermal comfort standard. It consisted of a sealed, insulated, windowless room in which temperature and humidity could be precisely set and independently controlled using the new technology of air conditioning. [Figure 2] Test subjects would spend a set period of time in the room at specific temperature and humidity levels. On leaving, they were asked if they found those conditions comfortable, and, if not, if it was too warm or too cold. ASHVE researchers recorded this data and, by 1924, published the first comfort chart. They continued to refine this chart into the 1960s.

Like the bathing machine, the psychrometric chamber was related to a new medical theory of the day. By the late 19th century, germ theory, which explained the spread of disease by microorganisms, had replaced miasmatic theory, which attributed disease to bad air. With this shift, the medical profession began to focus on the physiological effects of air caused by temperature and humidity. Looking to establish their professional expertise, ventilation engineers seized on this, proposing a model of thermal comfort based on heat balance between the body and the surrounding environment. That is when the heat produced by metabolism was balanced with a room's air temperature and humidity, people felt comfortable. Mechanical air conditioning in a building's closed environment was an ideal way to

provide such comfort since it could maintain ideal steady-state air conditions, regardless of location or season.

In advocating for the superiority of mechanical ventilation, engineers and mechanical equipment manufacturers vilified the weather as unpredictable and often uncomfortable. For the mechanical system to function optimally, the effects of weather needed to be eliminated from buildings by separating interior and exterior climates, that is by sealing the building envelope. This lead, in the opinion of building owners and operators, to satisfied tenants and productive employees. As one commentator succinctly put it, when a building has operable windows and no air conditioning, employees tend to blame nature for their discomforts. But when a building has air conditioning, they blame the building's management.[4] Eliminating the weather from a building's interior climate allowed for its mechanical systems to provide an optimal amount of thermal comfort.

The type of thermal comfort measured in the psychrometric chamber had no aesthetic aspect equivalent to the sublime experience of the bathing machine. In fact, quite the opposite. Psychrometric chambers were used by building science researchers to determine which interior climates eliminated such conscious consideration of comfort. They did this by working with the body's involuntary physiological response systems to achieve thermodynamic equilibrium between the body and the interior climate with as little personal energetic cost as possible. Researchers proposed that test subjects exiting the chamber report not the presence of comfort (which would require them consciously thinking about what was or was not comfortable) but report only if they felt uncomfortable. That is, when their involuntary physiological responses were not able to achieve heat balance, and produced a sensation of thermal discomfort that entered their conscious mind. Under this model, building occupants were the unconscious, passive recipients of comfort conditions. Such an approach to homeostatic thermal comfort underlies the two most widely used engineering comfort standards today, the ASHRAE 55 – Thermal Environmental Conditions for Human Occupancy and ISO 7730 Moderate Thermal Environments.[5] The 20th century development of architectural comfort that is embodied in building standards has reduced the prevailing contemporary understanding of comfort to focus on laboratory experimentation in psychrometric chambers, mechanical equipment and sealed building facades, while excluding conscious aesthetic experience and exterior climate.

Mixing the Mechanical and the Meteorological

Beginning in the 1960's, building professionals sought novel ways to expand the dominant notion of artificial thermal comfort by integrating elements of outdoor climates with indoor ones. The desire for this expansion grew both from the heightened environmental awareness of the 1960's, and the increasing energy costs due to the oil embargo of the early 1970's. This expansion happened in two ways. First, building science researchers developed the Adaptive Thermal Comfort model based on expanded research methods. And second, architects used ideas of comfort as generative in their design work.

While the dominant thermal comfort model for buildings grew from laboratory experiments, the idea of Adaptive Thermal Comfort built on this knowledge while also incorporating field studies of building occupants. Starting in the 1930's, ASHVE researchers had noted differences between expected thermal comfort conditions based on laboratory research, and what they observed occupants in air conditioned buildings wanted. However, it was not until the 1980's that such differences began to be systematically formulated into the Adaptive model. Building scientists found that occupants of naturally ventilated buildings (buildings with direct connections between the inside and outside such as operable windows) were comfortable over a wider range of conditions than anticipated by existing thermal comfort models. In highlighting this difference, they proposed that comfort results from feedback loops, in addition to physiological heat balance. Input for this feedback includes expectations conditioned by climatic and geographic differences, and personal preferences based on age, gender, metabolism and other individual characteristics. By proposing building occupants as active agents in creating their own comfort, the Adaptive model elevated comfort to an environmental quality building occupants consciously consider, and over which they could and indeed should, have a degree of direct control.[6]

Adaptive Thermal Comfort proponents looked to building standards and codes as the best way of turning research into practice. This was the path followed by earlier thermal comfort researchers. In this, they have succeeded despite not having the degree of professional and industry support enjoyed by earlier comfort researchers. The Adaptive Thermal Comfort model was included in the 2004 revision to the ASHRAE 55 Thermal Comfort standard as an alternative compliance method. However, the standard stipulates the Adaptive option is only applicable to buildings that do not have mechanical cooling systems. In addition, it can only be used when the heating system is not in operation, and when the prevailing mean outdoor temperature falls between 50° and 92°F. Such restrictions limit when and where the Adaptive Thermal Comfort method can be used.

In part as a reaction to its limited applicability, some progressive engineering design firms are proposing other comfort standards that integrate indoor and exterior climates. Often these are meteorological comfort models. For example, Transsolar Climate Engineering uses SET (Standard Effective Temperature) and UTCI (Universal Thermal Climate Index) standards to help establish and design comfort conditions for both interior and exterior spaces.[7]

Recovering Comfort from the Laboratory

The exterior climate is finding its way into the interior as designers recover coenesthetic comfort from the laboratory, and integrate it into their practices. In some cases, high profile design practices are including operable windows in commercial and civic building. Such connections can be seen in Herzog & de Meuron's Elbphilharmonie (2016) and OMA's De Rotterdam office building (2013) to name but two.[8]

For others, novel connections between inside and out, and between climate and body, are central to the design proposals. The French firm Lacaton & Vassal have made a career using simple, industrial materials for a wide range of project types, from single-family houses to public housing, educational and civic buildings. As architects, they see themselves as "climate optimists," more like the greenhouse designers, who attentively shape the interior environment in a relationship to the exterior, than mechanical engineers, who design to protect from worst case weather conditions. Their projects often include a layering of thermal spaces that is integral to the architectural approach. [9] In one example, the FRAC museum in Dunkirk France, they maintain an existing industrial hall while mirroring it with a new light and translucent "ghost" building with a range of interior comfort conditions. [Figure 3] This strategy allows them to preserve the civically important interior volume of the existing structure for a single monumental space, while providing smaller gallery, work and event spaces in the new volume. Through nesting and layering, these new spaces create a variety of interior climates within the building that are calibrated to program and schedule, as well diurnal and yearly exterior climate conditions.

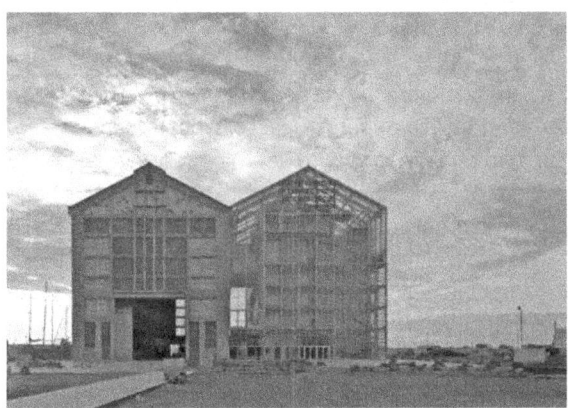

Fig. 3. Lacaton & Vassal, FRAC, Dunkirk France (2013).

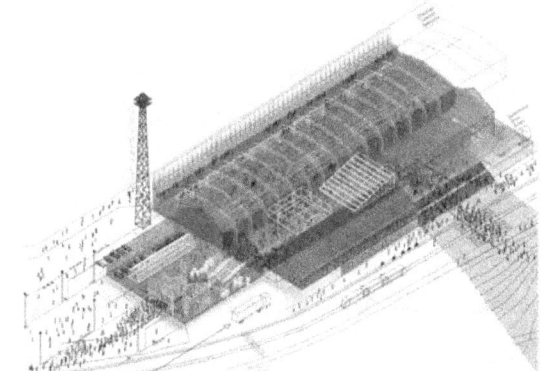

Fig. 4. Fake Industries, 47 Rooms, Guggenheim Helsinki competition (2014).

The firm Fake Industries' entry for the Guggenheim Helsinki 2014 competition (which was one of six finalists) takes a similar design-based approach to comfort. While recognizing the tight environmental controls necessary for many gallery spaces, their proposal, called "47 Rooms," designed different thermal experiences as part of the civic space of the museum. [Figure 4] Using the model of the Finnish sauna as a public space, the designers created a series of thermal onions where areas of tighter atmospheric control are nested within areas that have less control. These conditions were realized using a mash-up of environmental control devices including mechanical equipment, greenhouse and sports hall technologies, as well as landscape and furniture elements.[10] Their drawings of the project, at both a building and urban scale, demonstrate this intent.

In both examples, the architects use greenhouse-like structures to create a variety of coenesthetic experiences, while also tapping into their cultural and symbolic meanings. We are reminded that the "greenhouse effect," which describes the literal phenomena of trapping radiant energy in a glass building, is also an architectural metaphor describing the process behind global warming. Here two civic institutions are shaped by the positive thermal experience of the "greenhouse effect" in ways that project new relationships between the public realm and environmental phenomena through the experience of coenesthetic comfort.

A similar framing of experiences that blurs the boundaries between constructed and natural comfort conditions can be found at the Taichung Gateway Park in Taiwan. Designed by the French landscape architect Catherine Mosbach and Swiss architect Philippe Rahm, the park modulates the sub-tropical climate with overlays of cooler, dryer and cleaner zones. Beginning with the park's existing microclimates, the designers create varied atmospheric conditions related to new programmatic activities. They do this both with trees, as well as a collection of "meteorological devices" including atomizers, dehumidifiers, radiant panels and ultrasonic bug zappers. Such an approach to comfort based on landscape design recalls the landscape ideal of the Picturesque. First formulated by in 1768 by the artist and priest William Gilpin, the Picturesque gave designers creative freedom from the formal imperatives of symmetry, hierarchy and canonical style to explore the subjectivity of comfort and to satisfy a new-found interest in the exotic.[11] In a video produced about the Taichung Gateway Park,

Mosbach and Rahm say: "to go to the park is like traveling instantly to other latitudes, altitudes, seasons where the climate is more comfortable."[12] The park's naturally and technologically mediated climate connects visitors with other geographical spaces as well as historical and seasonal times through coenesthetic comfort.

The Comfort of Discomfort

While creating a weatherless society was once the dream of science fiction writers like H.G. Wells, in many respects, thermal comfort standards have helped to realize this dream by replacing the weather with architecture. In creating a thermal comfort standard, researches focused on a limited notion of homeostatic comfort resulting from involuntary physiological responses, rather than a fuller sense of what I've called coenesthetic comfort. While most of the discussion so far has been how this idea of comfort can address a wider range of exterior climates and bring greater consciousness to the experience of comfort, I want to conclude with some speculation about how coenesthetic comfort understands the body differently from thermal comfort. More than raising individual attention to comfort above an unconscious level to pique individual and collective consciousness, coenesthetic comfort proposes, paradoxically, that discomfort is a vital element of true comfort. However, such attitudes towards discomfort have yet to be clearly expressed in contemporary architectural design.

Medical theories have long formed a significant impetus for comfort theories. The bathing machine provided a literal platform for therapeutic water treatments advocated by doctors in the early 18th century, while the psychrometric chamber used conditioned air to produce optimal skin effects studied by doctors of the early 20th century. Following the medical advances of the past fifty years, lower human mortality from deadly diseases is being replaced by higher morbidity from diseases of excess such as Type 2 diabetes and obesity. The current notion of thermal comfort contributes to this morbidity by appeasing our desire for homeostasis. This desire is a product of our biological evolution. In a situation with limited resources, the human body has evolved to favor those environments that require the least energy to be used for thermoregulatory processes. Recent

thinking has argued that the most potent form of evolution today is not biological, but cultural evolution, where we develop novel behaviors and environments that we then pass on to subsequent generations.[13] Thermal comfort standards are a product of this cultural evolution. While on a biological scale, homeostasis was valued as an exceptional experience, requiring that one face challenges and overcome hardships to achieve it, today the cultural evolution of thermal comfort has made homeostasis a common experience that is easily had without any effort. Achieving environmental homeostasis without stress has led to mismatches between our comfort and our well-being in that remaining indoors and largely inactive, although associated with thermal comfort, is a leading cause of disease and disability according to the World Health Organization.[14]

The thermal comfort that exacts such a high price in terms of building energy use, also has a dark side for our personal health. Medical research has begun to explore how the "thermal neutral zone" (the ideal zone for comfort described in the thermal comfort standard) is negatively affecting human health. Some researchers have suggested lowering recommended thermal comfort temperature recommendations can be used to raise resting metabolic rates and reduce obesity.[15] However, such an approach simply tweaks the existing homeostatic ideas of thermal comfort, and does not address beneficial connections between indoor and outdoor climates.

Elsewhere, public health officials and physicians are recognizing the benefits of discomfort, or environmental stressors, for health and well-being. From common recommendations for increased physical activity and challenging mental tasks to maintain neural plasticity, to extreme feats of endurance and exposure to temperature extremes, today's culture of wellness is fostering a growing awareness that some degree of discomfort is an important part of wellbeing.

Coenesthetic comfort requires recognizing the positive aspects of discomfort when it comes to the healthy functioning of the body. Apart from specialized building typologies such as saunas and thermal baths, such thinking has yet to enter larger architectural discussions where homeostatic thermal comfort remains the dominant model. Recalling the bathing machine, which linked body and climate, medical and aesthetic, discomfort and well-being, architects can look to an enlarged approach to coenesthetic comfort as a means of addressing the practice of and finding poetry in building that work with the weather and with ourselves.

Notes:

[1] Neil E. Klepeis et al. "The National Human Activity Pattern Survey (NHAPS): a resource for assessing exposure to environmental pollutants," *Journal of Exposure Analysis and Environmental Epidemiology* no. 11 (2001): 231–252.

[2] Alain Corbin, *The Lure of the Sea: The Discovery of the Seaside 1750-1840*, trans. Jocylyn Phelps (New York: Penguin Books, 1994), 95. See also Corbin "L'Emergence du désir du rivage ou la spécificité d'une form de fascination de la mer," in *Le Ciel et la mer*, (Paris: Flammarion, 2014), 39-63.

[3] For a description of this debate, see Gail Cooper, *Air-Conditioning America: Engineers and the Controlled Environment, 1900-1960.* (Baltimore: Johns Hopkins UP 1998), 51-79.

[4] Charles S. Leopold, "Conditions for Comfort" *ASHVE Transactions*, no. 53 (1947): 304.

[5] Both standards rely, in large part, on the Predicted Mean Value method for determining thermal comfort. Based on empirical research using psychrometric chambers, this model was developed by the Danish researcher P.O. Fanger. See his *Thermal Comfort: Analysis and Applications in Environmental Engineering*, (New York: McGraw-Hill Book Company, 1972).

[6] Richard de Dear and Gail Brager, "Towards an adaptive model of thermal comfort and preference" *ASHRAE Transactions,* vol. 104 no. 1 (1998): 145-167.

[7] Erik Olsen (principal, Transsolar Climate Engineering) in discussion with author, October 2016.

[8] "Opening the un-openable window: Matthias Schuler" by Tiffany Obser in Rem Koolhaas et al eds. *Elements of Architecture*, (Venice: Marsilio, 2014), 720-729.

[9] Anne Lacaton and Jean-Phillippe Vassal were educated in the energy-conscious 1970's, and attribute their interest in the design of the thermal environment to this training. See "Two Conversations with Patrice Goulet" in "Lacaton &

Vassal" *2G Libros*, (Barcelona: Editorial Gustavo Gili, 2010), 130-155.

[10] "47 Rooms" http://designguggenheimhelsinki.org/images/static/stage-two-submission/3-pdfs/GH-5059206475.pdf accessed February 18, 2017.

[11] John E. Crowley, *The Invention of Comfort: Sensibilities & Design in Early Modern Britain & Early America* (Baltimore: Johns Hopkins UP, 2001), 203-230.

[12] "Phase Shifts Park: An Atmospheric Fable" https://www.youtube.com/watch?v=UDr-6UtlUu8 accessed February 18, 2017.

[13] While this discussion falls generally into the different evolutionary ideas of Jean Baptiste Lamarck and Charles Darwin, for its relevance to the human body see Daniel Lieberman. *The Story of the Human Body* (New York: Penguin) 2013.

[14] "Physical inactivity a leading cause of disease and disability, warns WHO" http://www.who.int/mediacentre/news/releases/release23/en/ accessed February 19, 2017.

[15] Francesco S. Ceil et al. "Minimal changes in environmental temperature result in a significant increase in energy expenditure and changes in the hormonal homeostasis in healthy adults" *European Journal of Endocrinology* no. 163 (2010): 863-872.

Beginning is Place

Peter Raab
Texas Tech University

Ill fares the land, to hastening ills a prey,
Where wealth accumulates, and men decay:
Princes and lords may flourish, or may fade;
A breath can make them, as a breath has made;
But a bold peasantry, their country's pride,
When once destroyed, can never be supplied. [1]

"Sweet Auburn", Oliver Goldsmith (1730-74)

Abstract

Increasingly architecture has looked at the past with newfound promise. Not as a way to simply copy, or borrow ideas from past architectural successes, but looking deeply at ways in which both formally-trained and architects and locally skilled builders have established local material cultures throughout the history of place.

This paper will examine the tectonic culture of an historic regionalist architecture of southwest Ontario, specifically looking at two original bank barns located in Seaforth, Ontario that are slated for deconstruction in the spring of 2017. With thousands of linear feet of old growth timber, the deconstruction, cataloguing and investigation of potential future uses of this material that continues to evoke local cultures, histories and narratives of local sustainability will be expressed.

Pre-History

As the European settlers descended upon North America, bountiful amounts of land, old-growth trees, freshwater lakes and rivers from the Eastern Seaboard to the Great Lakes region provided an abundance of natural materials to be utilized in the construction of the "New World". While the Native Americans were living in a symbiotic relationship with the natural world, the settlers, arriving with more advanced technical means, and disease, overtook these natives, cleared fields for agriculture and built villages with houses both for people and livestock, thus altering the relationship of man and nature. Over several hundreds of years, this agrarian way of life dominated the wide-open spaces of North America as millions came seeking newfound freedoms and bountiful lands of promise.

During the last one hundred years, people worldwide have become more urban. With industrialization, wealth, safety, culture and comfort afforded by cities, now - for the first time ever - over half of the world's population live in urban areas.[2] In the United States, this figure is even higher, as of the 2010 census, 80.7% of Americans live in urban areas, while in Canada, 81.7%.[3] This once agrarian society, consisting of family farms, homesteads and barns is now vanishing. These historic structures, their old materials, are being decimated to make room for industrial-sized farming operation. Each structure, upon close inspection offers a mapping of place and culture. Knowing that each piece of wood was sourced locally, each log cut manually, carved and assembled, offers a special material resonance containing the tectonic DNA both of time and place. We can clearly see the collective aspirations of a culture within these old, disused relics.

As was true with the majority of North America, pre-Columbian landscape in southwestern Ontario was heavily forested. As early as 10,000 BC, people lived in the eastern woodlands of spruce and have been classified by archeologists as Early Palaeoindian; utilizing stone tools for construction.[4] Thusly, the technological means and material limits led to the crudely composed wooden structures. The region of Huron County was controlled by the *Attawandaron* by the Huron, however European explorers named them Neutral Nation, "...on account of enjoying peace with the Hurons and with the Iroquois...".[5] These natives were related to the Iroquois Confederation and were known to create permanent settlements and farm the land. This architectural permanence due to the agricultural aspirations of the peoples allowed for the development of such architectonic constructions as the palisade fence and the longhouse. The first Europeans known to have explored southern Ontario in 1610 AD was Étienne Brûlé, a French explorer, interpreter and guide that ventured to the Georgian Bay and Lake Huron and lived among the Algonquins until 1629 AD. The majority of the 40,000 Neutral Nation lived within a 32 km radius of present day Hamilton, Ontario, 100 km and 200 years before the settlement of Seaforth, and another 100 years before the raising of the bank barn in Seaforth.

Ecology of Place

Some may suggest that we should transport this landscape back to its original, forested state, that the true ecology of the place is one of woodlands, streams, native creatures and fauna. However, this naïve supposition negates the centuries of

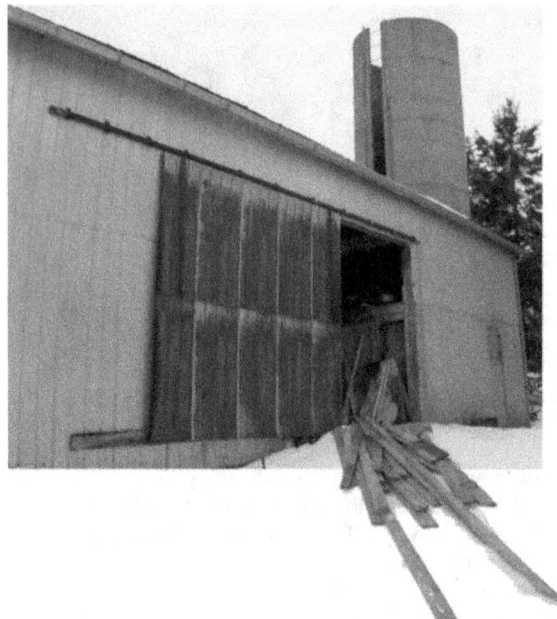

Fig. 1. Beginning to non-structural wood removal.

European and pre-Columbian history and involvement of man within the place. from a standpoint of opposition to his environs, to working with nature, before eventually taming his surroundings and allowing it to work for him. In this hypothesis, the absence of human beings from the existing ecological construct is essential to the current comprehension. It is essential to both consider human existence as contextual, nested within larger systems, no matter how small the interposition.

It is only through thorough investigation of the ecology of a precise place that it can provide a contextual understanding of the cultural and biological diversity to ensure designs respect the larger social and cultural patterns and preserve the essence of the local. As David Orr points out; "an ecological design is the careful meshing of human purposes with the larger patterns and flows of the natural world and the study of those patterns and flows to inform human actions."[6] Therefore we must both understand the history of place, and the technological culture of the people who construct its realities.

Tools and Constructs

With the arrival of Europeans in North America, so came the Iron Age, and with it the ability to shape wood using metal tools. Also brought to the "New World" was the ability to farm with metal-tools and livestock, and a most elegant architectural solution to combine grain and animal under one roof - the two-story bank barn. The first incidences of this new configuration can be traced to the upland areas of Britain, in Cumbria by the 1660's.[7] These structures

were also called basement barns due to their exposed bottom floor and included a threshing chamber within the central bay of the second story, flanked by one or two mows (or loft spaces) for grain storage and doors at either end, and a bottom floor left solely for livestock.[8] This multistory bank barn was indelibly connected to the landscape, firmly planted into the hillside so that both grain and herd had ground-level access. The benefits of stacking these programs was twofold: 1) Heat generated by the livestock below warmed the threshing level above, and 2) opening the threshing floor allowed for feed to be tossed down to the livestock.[9]

The temperate climates of northeast Canada and United States, where these barns originated, demanded specific orientation of the structures in combatting cold, wet winters. Preferably these barns are banked to the north to minimize exposure from these icy winds, while leaving the south and east sides as two stories filled with operable doors and windows to light the various daily activities and passively heat the loft space during the colder months.[10] This two-and-a-half story structure divides the upper level into three bays with entry happening in the central threshing unit. A double wagon door was added opposite the entry doors for increased airflow and light to assist in the threshing process.[11] Widespread adaptation during the late 18th century and early 19th century saw this typology employed from Pennsylvania to Iowa, and from Virginia up to Ontario, Canada. The barn in Seaforth follows this typology in both pragmatics and poetics.[12]

Changing Demands

The invention of hay-baling machines from the 1870's to the 1930's made large loft barns unnecessary and undesirable due to the reduced bulk yet increased weight of hay to be stored.[13] Soon barns were only needed to provide shelter for livestock during inclement weather, and this decoupling of programmed space meant lower, simpler structures could be utilized. Lower single-story pole barns, and the transverse crib barn began to replace the earlier, bigger barns, especially in regions lacking large timber resources, while developments in hay-baling techniques reduced the need of the hay-loft as much of the cut hay was dried and rolled in the fields until the livestock were brought to pasture, saving fuel, labor and the need for large storage facilities. The growth of industrialized farming practices, and migration of people from rural areas to urban centers have further allowed these historic artifacts to be left to ruin. Why is it important to study these relics, or even consider saving / preserving them?

Material Culture [of stone, wood, soil + water]

Materials are the physical manifestation of spatial

constructs, each holding the specific ecological signature telling a story of locale, history and the embodied energy. Each structure, each wooden member, stone mass, and piece of forged iron was sourced and fabricated locally. Each piece manually cut, carved and assembled, containing the human handprint of a time lost. Barns imbue particular material constraints and functionalist needs of the region, indelibly connected to the climate and culture and rooted to the very land it occupies. Paul Oliver points out that it is absolutely fundamental that architecture express local culture, which can be read as the vernacular – tuned to place, climatically and ecologically imbedded – and that failure of much of architecture is that many architects are only interested in "architecture as some abstraction, separate in a sense from the values or the qualities that the peoples of the various cultures require in their building."[14]

Materials have an intrinsic and direct connection to architectural positioning within local environs. In his seminal book, "Dwellings", Oliver investigates the architecture of the common man, documenting vernacular architectural solutions across the world drawing connections from materials, climate and culture to inspect how "90 percent of the world's buildings" are built and lived. [15] These dwellings tend to blur geo-political borders and align more so with ecological zones or regions. In this sense, the architectural solutions are less stylistically derived, and more a function of locale, technology and designing with natural systems already present. There is an evident and pronounced interrelation of site and culture, as well as social equity and community exemplified within the projects presented in the book. Out of necessity, these solutions are very much tuned to the site, temporality and ecology.

Through the process of documentation and cataloguing, the hope is to rediscover the collective aspirations of a culture rooted within these ancient, abandoned relics. By taking cues from this material and cultural resonance through the thorough understanding of the underlying ecology of place we can demonstrate integral relationships of site and material. This understanding is paramount to balancing local needs, materials and techniques. When this knowledge is combined with a broadened perspective and modern knowledge, these ecologically-based solutions can resonate with site-specific solutions for an impact on a global scale.

The Poetry of the Pragmatic

The threshing floor level and loft space *[or mow]* has a proportionally high height in relation to its width - typical for barns of this era. The reason being extremely practical and twofold; a larger area plan would have meant much wasted space after the

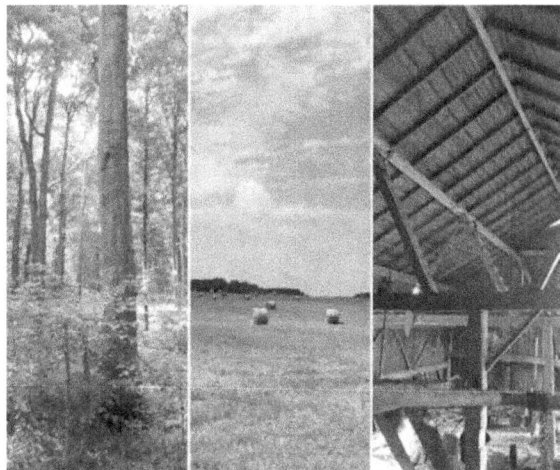

Fig. 2. From woodlands to agricultural land and implements.

considerable settling of the freshly-cut hay, and consequently the smaller plan area meant a smaller roof, and therefore a less complex roof structure.[16] "Framing typically followed a preordained arrangement with two major considerations governing factors. One was the heavy static load to be carried by the structure when filled; the other was the great wall and roof areas that were exposed to wind. Complete and thorough bracing, both lateral and transverse, was essential. It is to the credit of the early builders that so many old structures are still perfectly plumb and true after many years of service. It will be noted that in frame barns the ridge board was generally omitted, the roof being framed in pairs of rafters." [17]

It is with this understanding the pragmatism of the design of the barn that we can explore the poetry of the joinery methods used within the structure, from the bottom up.

Foundation

The foundations of early barns were often no more than large boulders, usually found during excavation or in clearing the fields for planting, and laid in shallow trenches. These foundations would often move greatly as they were above the frost line, and the seasonal freeze/thaw cycles would move the large structures. This would have been less apparent with the natural warmth of the livestock below, acting as 400-pound heaters and modulating some of the diurnal temperature swings and preventing water/ice penetrations. Timber sills are placed over these stones and served to tie together the barn's posts to keep the entire structure intact despite seasonal fluctuation.

Mortise and Tenon Joinery

The most typical demonstrated joint in timber framing are the mortise and tenon joints. These often are with

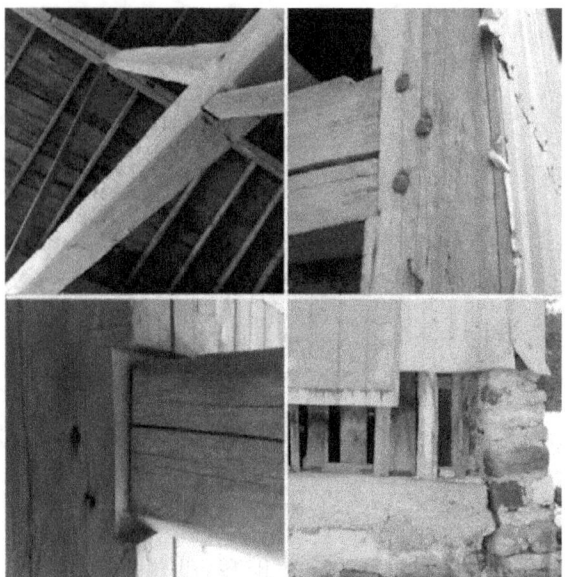

Fig. 3. Details: knee braced roof, mortise and tenon joint with full shoulders, and stone foundation, amended with concrete.

full shoulders into the post to allow the shear force to be moved across the entire width of the beam and not solely depend on the tenon for shear support, while avoiding the critical corner stress within a notched anisotropic beam.[18] This type of joint could work in tension or compression, and offered the ability to connect wood-to-wood without other materials. These joints have several variants.

Spline Mortise and Tenon

When two girts *(beams)* are joined to a post at the same height, often there is insufficient cross sectional width in the post to allow for each girt to have a tenon of sufficient length. The solution demonstrated here offers a spline joint to create a solid connection, which is capable of resisting tensile force within the beams.

Lateral and Transverse Forces

Knee brace is a crucial element of the timber frame; providing rigidity to the frame through triangulation, these diagonal members are used wherever major beams meet posts. The mortised knee brace joint shown here is much stronger than a half-lapped variant.

Scarfed Joints

The whole purpose of this joint is to join two pieces of wood when one, longer piece is either unavailable or too difficult to handle during the erection process.

No Ridge Beam

As typical with English and German barns of the era, no ridge beam is present, while the rafters maintain half-lapped rafter connections at the peak.

Ventilation of these barns were of the utmost importance for the drying process of the hay and straw, and therefore most barns had vertical boards on the exterior with small gaps, along with the double doors on the long axis of the threshing floor as previously mentioned.

Education through Un-Construction

"Therefore, when we build, let us think that we build forever. Let it not be for present delight, nor for present use alone; let it be such work as our descendants will thank us for, and let us think, as we lay stone on stone, that a time is to come when those stones will be held sacred because our hands have touched them, and that men will say as they look upon the labor and wrought substance of them..." [19]

When Ruskin penned these words, he likely spoke of less utilitarian structures than the common barn, however with the process of building so clearly evidenced through the handprint of the worker, an uncommon practice today, it is this mark of history that needs to be restored or reclaimed for our culture.

Recycling vs. Down-Cycling

Glenn Murcutt designs his rural architectural interventions using steel members, typically composed of a high percentage of recycled content, which are trucked-in and bolted together under the auspicious of being fully recycled again after the life of the building. In a perfect world, we could reuse every 2x4 as a 2x4, but the unfortunate reality is that with the cost of labor in North America, it is faster and cheaper to raze rather than to reclaim.

While wood is a renewable resource, and most wood products represent a carbon sink, there are still the life-cycle costs of turning a tree into a building product. Is it not equally important to recycle our already harvested old-growth forests with its embedded history? The structure has several beams and girts that measure a full foot square and span thirty feet, which are extremely difficult and costly to source as singular members. Naturally weathered, hand-hewn members are only found within these older structures and we cannot replicate the history once destroyed.

Speaking of raw costs - the added labor cost of deconstruction typically offsets any material savings, however it is my opinion that the imbedded history of the materials is truly priceless. The memory a place, or time past can sometimes be enough impetus for some of these structures to be catalogued, deconstructed and shipped to a new region, or country, reincarnated as a residence, cabin or office –

which aside from reuse as a barn is likely the highest re-use of material – beam for beam, post for post, etc.

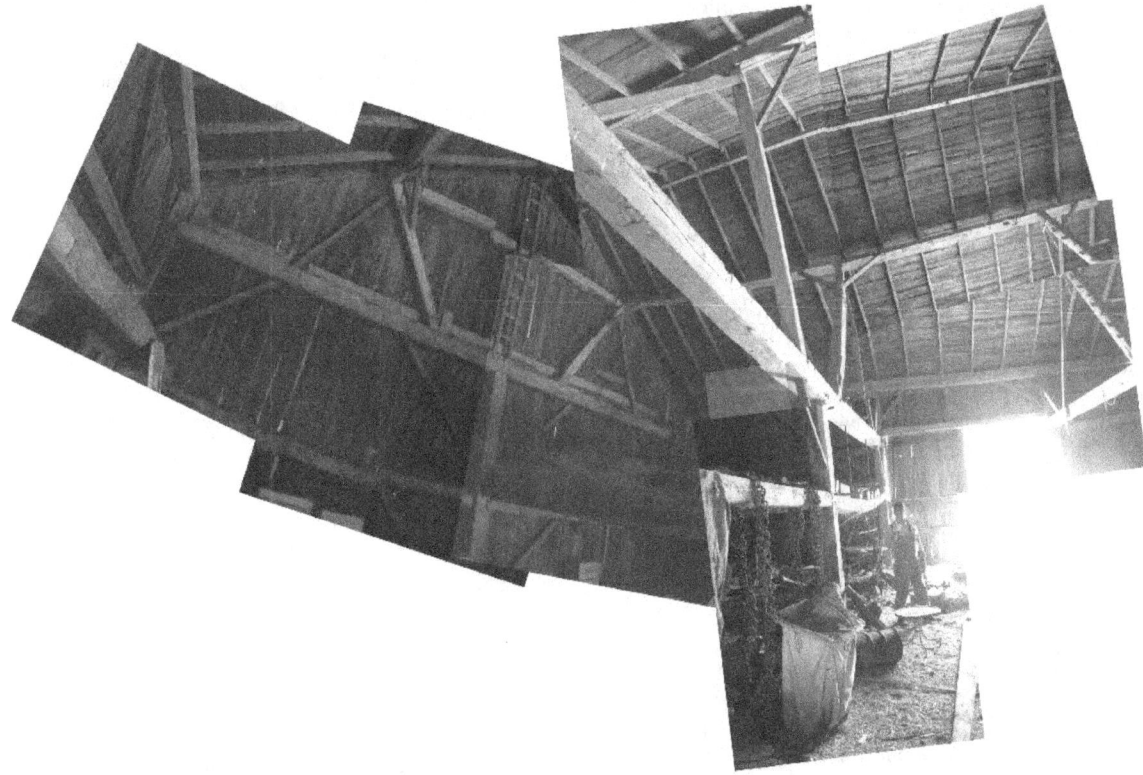

Fig. 2. Large Barn Montage – showing one half of one barn, the loft space and threshing floor.

However, all too often these beams are cut to remove the outermost, hand-hewn layer, as a finish, encasing a beam, a feature wall, or simply reduced to furniture or a mantle – for those looking for instant rusticity.

Future Plans

It is the hope that this barn, which has been intact for over 100 years, will find a new life through this deconstruction, documentation and history in educating of future architects about a nearly lost time in North American agricultural architecture, and a further life in the reconstruction within southwestern Ontario as a construction for the next 100 years. After the safe deconstruction of the barn and cataloguing, it is the intention to use this artifact to teach through construction of a future project as a design-build studio linked to culture, maintaining its connection to place and history with a view towards the future.

Architecture is a field based on a cumulative history. In order to be well-versed in present practices we must understand the long lineage of architectural thought and historic precedent. This is especially important for teaching building technologies. The process of constructing heavy timber barns in the 19th century is a unique one that speaks to craft, tectonics

and a complex coupling of program within its architectural design. In the same manner, there is much to be learned from the deconstruction of a building, almost as much as through the construction process.

It is becoming more and more rare for architecture students to participate in actual, full-scale constructions during their education. This construction experience could come from precedent study, or even through full-scale deconstructions of built work. The ability to see, touch, and experience the weight of the built world provides an empirical understanding about architecture construction, which I have written about previously. The true benefit of this experience is the student's ability to translate this knowledge within their designs and adds a certain gravity to their lines, and models.

Conclusion

While it is difficult to imagine a time when architectural thought and design was so indelibly tied to place, as our never in the history of mankind have we ever been so divorced from nature. Our current generation can within seconds view materials and products on a video screen, and have them delivered to a doorstep across the planet within a few days – sometimes without even touching a human hand. This does not mean that local ecologies, resources and climates should be ignored. Much can be learned from the sensitive pragmatic design solutions related to siting, programming and the wise utilization of materials for their distinct properties and possible re-deployment at the end of their useful life. There is something poetic about working within an existing context, using wood to join wood, stacking local stones for foundation walls, and fabricating grand structures using manpower.

Architecture's power and promise is in its resonance with local culture and ecology – of place. If we, disavow our historical context, discarding the old for the new without care we limit our future potential. Current population projections envision the world needs outstripping the current material supplies, and we must educate the future generation of architects to respect the past and build intelligently for the future.[20]

With the imminent collision of a growing population - projected to reach 10 billion in the year 2056 – and escalating material expectations with a limited ecological capacity, development must create more reciprocity with the existent world around us. Design must become more ecologically sensitive - taking account of the existing patterns and interrelating both site and culture, "not just about how we make things, but how we can make things fit harmoniously within an ecological, cultural and moral context."[21] Understanding how architecture may have second [and third] lives beyond the immediate needs of today are valuable tools and likely begin with study of successful feats of the past. In each of these architectures, the beginning is place.

Notes:

[1] Bartleby.com. *English Poetry II: From Collins to Fitzgerald. Vol. XLI, 1909–14.* The Harvard Classics. P.F. Collier & Son: New York, 2001. www.bartleby.com/41/. [September 16, 2016].

[2] United Nations. Today, 54 per cent of the world's population lives in urban areas, a proportion that is expected to increase to 66 per cent by 2050. *2014 Revision* of *World Urbanization Prospects* (United Nations, 2015). https://esa.un.org/unpd/wup/, [July 22, 2016].

[3] Ibid.

[4] Thwaites, ed. (1898). Travels and Explorations of the Jesuit Missionaries in New France 1610–1791. Cleveland: The Burrows Brothers, Museum of Ontario Archaeology, [March 12, 2011].

[6] Orr, David. *"Architecture, Ecological Design and Human Ecology."* Part 1 In The Green Braid. New York: Taylor and Francis, 2007, 21.

[7] Lake, Jeremy. Historic Farm Buildings: An Introduction and Guide in association with the National Trust. Blandford Press, Cassell, London. (1989): 99-101. Print.

[8] Sloane, Eric. An Age of Barns. New York: Ballantine, 1975, 50.

[9] Ibid, 50.

[10] Raab, Peter. "Barns as an Adaptive Archetype" in *Discovering Architecture: Built Form as Cultural Reflection.* Edited by Frank Jacobus. Kendall Hunt Publishing, Co., 01/2014. VitalBook file.

[11] Noble, Allen G. Wood, Brick and Stone: The North American Settlement Landscape, Volume 2: Barns and Farm Structures. New Brunswick, NJ: Rutgers UP, 1995, 24-25.

[12] Ibid, 25.

[13] Ibid, 37.

[14] Oliver, Paul. "International Dialogues," lecture at Oxford Brookes 2010.

[15] Oliver, Paul. *"Dwellings: The Vernacular House Worldwide."* Phaidon Press, 2003, 14.

[16] Rempel, John I., Building with Wood, and Other Aspects of Nineteenth-Century Building in Central Canada, Revised Edition. University of Toronto Press, Toronto. 1980, 201.

[17] Ibid, 205.

[18] Foliente, Greg C. and Thomas E. McLain. Design of Notched Wood Beams, Journal of Structural Engineering, 1992.118, 2407

[19] Ruskin, John. "Chapter VI. The Lamp of Memory" in *Seven Lamps of Architecture* Dover Publications: New York. 1989, 81.

[20] The United Nations Population Division of the Department of Economic and Social Affairs every two years calculates, updates, and publishes estimates of total population in its *World Population Prospects* series. These population estimates and projections provide the standard and consistent set of population figures that are used throughout the United Nations system.

[21] Orr, David. *"Architecture, Ecological Design and Human Ecology."* Part 1 In The Green Braid. New York: Taylor and Francis, 2007, 31

SESSION 10: TECH PEDAGOGY

Session Chair: Patrick Tripeny
University of Utah

Ryan Smith and Keith Diaz Moore, University of Utah: "Building Science Education Entrepreneurism."

Diane Armpriest and Carolina Manrique, University of Idaho: "Towards a Multi-Faceted Integration Model for Teaching Architectural Design and Technology."

Patrick Tripeny, Robert Young, Ryan Smith and Erin Carraher, University of Utah: "Building Technology within a New Architecture Curriculum."

Designing Curriculum for Building Science

Ryan E. Smith, Keith Diaz Moore & Joshua F. Workman
University of Utah

Abstract

This research represents background data that was gathered and analyzed for the development of a unique degree offering, the Bachelor of Science in Building Science at the University of Utah. The purpose of the degree is to meet the growing demand of knowledge of building science in building professionals and respond to the university's budget models to support productivity. This research found that the most robust peer reviewed effort to date to outline knowledge areas and learning objectives that a building science program might fulfill is the DOE effort in "Building Science 101". The DOE learning modules were used as a comparison to 14 other building science related programs nationally. The University of Utah was the 2nd most effective program among the 14 programs reviewed at achieving the DOE goals with existing course work. It is therefore, positioned well to leverage existing course work augmented by few additional classes to deliver an excellent building science curriculum.

Introduction

Importance of Building Science Education

Buildings account for 38% of carbon dioxide emissions in the United States and consume 40% of the energy used.[1] Since the vast majority of energy consumed by North American buildings is fossil-based, there is a clear and almost direct connection between decreased energy use and reduced carbon emissions.[2] In 2013 ambient CO2 levels in the atmosphere reached 400 ppm for the first time in recorded history.[3] As climate change becomes continually more apparent, the importance of smart and sustainable design strategies to respond to this challenges becomes more important. Progress toward improving the efficiency of buildings needs to advance more rapidly to combat climate change and other natural hazards that are exacerbated by human actions.[4]

Architects and engineering designers are ultimately the ones who specify which systems will be used in a building. Architects, in particular, have responsibility for decisions of building orientation, and building envelope detailing, two of the primary drivers that determine building performance. Despite this responsibility, 86% of A/E firms report difficulty finding employees equipped with the knowledge and skills needed to achieve the American Institute of Architect's adopted 2030 Challenge.[5] Professional education needs to adapt to include increasingly the principles, strategies and practices of building science. However, professional education is already oversubscribed with important content [6] and the accreditation bodies (NAAB and ABET) have difficulty adapting quickly to this immediate need for action in building performance.

This paper outlines a process for developing a unique undergraduate degree, the Bachelor of Science in Building Science, that if designed properly, will equip students with the knowledge necessary to create smart and sustainable buildings that will perform well and reduce the negative impact on the environment. Other academic degrees in the built environment, such as architecture, architectural engineering or construction management, seek to teach students about buildings through the context of a professional education, but can fall short of the scientific knowledge that makes a cost-effective high-performance building.

University Context

University departments, especially at state institutions, are under increasing pressure from central administration to increase productivity.[7] Architectural education, rooted in a studio based model, relies on a high student to instructor ratio that consumes large amounts of floor area and requires additional resources such as a fabrication shop, large format plotter space, and gallery space for jury reviews. Often budget models are tied to student credit hour production which favors large lecture courses with minimal student and instructor interaction.[8]

Further, undergraduate education trends on university campuses are encouraging early declaration of major and admission to departments. Research evidence demonstrates that early admission aids undergraduate students in success to completion of their respective degree programs.[9] Historically, architecture departments have admitted students to their programs after the first or second year with a stage gate portfolio submission process. This requirement ensures that students who have acquired the skills for upper division study in architecture are accepted, but it also limits some students with an interest in the built environment from continuing with an architectural education.

The Bachelor of Science in Building Science is envisioned as a program that builds upon the technical course work in a traditional 5-year accredited Bachelor of Architecture or 4-year Bachelor of Arts/Sciences in Architectural Studies. It removes the requirement for studio. The BSBS relies on larger lecture courses, or could be taken online completely. The degree allows students to be admitted to the Department of Architecture as Freshman and finish their degree in 4 years. There is no portfolio requirement. Students are able to learn building technology from an architectural perspective, with a focus on preparing for graduate school in architecture or a related discipline, or prepare for work as a building science professional.

Method

The research in preparation for curriculum development of the BSBS degree included two phases: Phase 1 - literature review of building science education learning objectives; and Phase 2 - comparative analysis of current building science degree offerings nationally. In Phase 3 the learning objectives and comparative analysis will be used to develop a Building Science undergraduate curriculum in the School of Architecture at the University of Utah.

Phase 1 - Literature Review

A review of literature regarding building science education was undertaken in order to identify the building science knowledge areas. There are a number of initiatives that identify the topics under the umbrella of the term building science. The literature review was separated into peer review journal publications and online resources. The journal publications identify early definitions of building science and the evolution of the thinking behind building science topics. The most current thinking on building science knowledge areas is found in online resources including the Joint Committee on Building Science Education with its related DOE Building Science Education Initiative and outcome of learning objectives. This committee and the resultant resources were developed from a multi-organizational effort over a number of years to determine learning objectives for building science education published by the DOE. Therefore, this effort and its publications and resources provided the primary reference for Phase 2 comparative analysis.

Phase 2 - Comparative Analysis

This portion of the research was focused on comparing current four-year institutions that offer education in the building and construction industry. The objective was to see how the different programs compared to one another in terms of what courses are taught; how they perform in fulfilling the learning objectives defined by Phase 1 of the research; and how the University of Utah School of Architecture current course offerings compared to these peer institutions.

Phase 2.1 – Peer Institutions Learning Objectives

Using the Google search engine, 14 university degree programs were identified that offer bachelor's degrees in building science related subjects including: Building Science, Construction Science, Construction Science and Management, Building and Construction Technology, Construction Management Technology, and Architectural Engineering. Curriculum paths outlining the courses in the degree program were gathered from each of the respective university websites. Course descriptions for classes were also collected.

Each course was analyzed and classified based on the course title and description. The intent was to gain an understanding of the general content of each course across all institutions being examined and compare them to one another. Classes described as covering similar content were grouped together. Upon completing the classification over 350 courses across the 14 universities, a frequency analysis determined how often each learning objective was taught. Sorting the data numerically made it possible to see which classes were most commonly taught across the spectrum of degrees being researched.

Further, the research analyzed the academic degrees at each of the 14 peer institutions to determine how their curriculum compares to the curricular objectives identified in Phase 1. The intent was to develop a basic understanding of how well each of the 14 programs fulfill the learning objectives of the Joint Committee on Building Science and the DOE.

Phase 2.2 – Utah Learning Objectives

In the next step, it was determined which current courses could be cross-listed or need to be slightly adjusted within the School of Architecture, and other departments on campus. This analysis revealed the new courses that need to be created at the University of Utah in order to fulfill the learning objectives identified in Phase 1. In addition to the School of Architecture, the University of Utah College of Engineering has Departments of Electrical, Mechanical and Civil (structural) Engineering. An idealized Building Science curriculum would include as many of the learning objectives outlined by the Joint Committee on Building Science as possible to ensure that graduates of the program are meeting the highest standard. Phase 3 is future work to develop a BSBS curriculum for delivery in Fall of 2019.

Limitations

It was quickly discovered that assigning a peer institution course to specific learning objectives presented a challenge. The learning objectives are quite specific, while course descriptions are, by nature, very general. Without having access to a detailed syllabus for each course, it was necessary that an inference be made as to which learning objectives are *most likely* to be met by a given course. Since this is often difficult to infer, each class was assigned to one or more of the DOE learning modules which it likely covered, rather than specific learning objectives within that module. This, unfortunately, gives an under-developed view of each program, since it only shows which modules are likely to be included in each program, but doesn't demonstrate whether only one of the learning objectives within the module is met or whether all of them are met.

Results

Literature Review

As a discipline, building science started during the 1920s and 1930s when the new practice of insulating wall cavities caused paint to peel due to vapor transmission.[10] Subsequently, in addition to moisture, other issues became important to building occupants' health including indoor air quality, heat flows, air flow, and exterior water management.[11] The term building science has not consistently been used throughout its short history.[12] The simplest definition of building science, "science applied to buildings" is so broad as to not be much help at all in defining a knowledge scope for the discipline. Rose notes that the term corresponds to what is called "building physics" in Europe.[13] Best Training School defines building science by its purpose: to provide a predictive capability to optimize building performance and understand or prevent building failures in structure, and envelope. The scope of knowledge of the discipline of building science is still relatively immature and continues to be redefined even today.[14]

The most contemporary comprehensive effort to define and scope the knowledge areas that make up building science is by the US Department of Energy (DOE). The DOE interest in building science education stems from their history with Building America, a 20+ year effort to create innovative energy efficient and cost effective solutions for production housing in the US. The program found that one of the primary barriers to market transformation toward high performance homes can be attributed to the limited building science knowledge among stakeholders that design and produce homes. A notable effort by the DOE to affect building science education was in 2005 in collaboration with the Association of Public and land-Grant Universities (APLU) producing an outline for a university semester-long course in building science called "Building Science 101".[15] This outline defines the expectations for a quality building science program by establishing criteria for learning excellence. The outline includes 19 learning modules broken down into some 162 specific learning objectives that would be met throughout an idealized building science educational program.

The learning modules defined by the DOE are as follows:

1. Energy Issues and Building Solutions
2. Introduction to Sustainable Design & Building
3. Flows: Air, Heat, Water, Vapor
4. Building Materials and Their Properties
5. Climate and Designing with Nature
6. Building Design & Systems Engineering
7. Commissioning; Site: Drainage, Pest Control, Landscaping
8. Foundation: Moisture Control and Energy Performance
9. Building Envelope: Moisture Control and Energy Performance
10. Windows, Doors and Other Penetrations
11. Mechanicals, Electrical, & Plumbing Systems
12. Electricity Payload
13. On-site Power Generation
14. Field Issues
15. Construction Management, Codes, and Other Regulatory Matters
16. Benchmarking performance: meeting and exceeding the norm
17. Community Scale; Putting it all Together: Experiential Learning in the Field / Office
18. Homeowner Education (Communicating with the Consumer)
19. Conclusions, Implications, sources of further learning and continuing education

Peer Institutions

Steps 1 and 2 in the research resulted in a matrix of building science-related programs and the course content that each of the 14 programs have in common. Once all of the courses were classified and grouped based on their content, a frequency percentage could be calculated to describe what portion of the programs being studied are teaching similar content to each other. Figure 1 represents the top 10 most commonly taught classes, showing the frequency at which they are taught across the spectrum. As may be noted in Figure 1, there is not a single class which is taught by all 14 programs.

Interestingly, although there is a trend of what the various programs value as demonstrated by their

curriculum content, the trend doesn't align well with the learning modules that the DOE has defined in their ideal curriculum. For example, the DOE learning modules do not address structures, computer

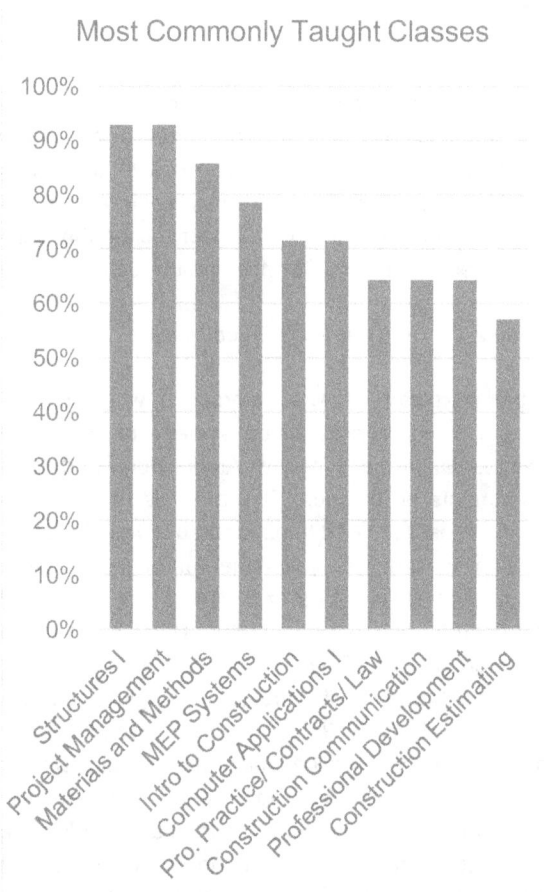

Fig. 1. Most commonly taught classes across all programs.

applications, law and professional practice,

construction communication, professional development, or construction cost estimating. In other words, 6 of the 10 most commonly taught classes do not fulfill any of the learning module topics suggested by the DOE. Although these subjects may not at first glance appear to be building science related, they might be considered contextual courses without which the question of "why" building science is relatively unimportant.

Step 3 was to use each course title and description as a reference to compare to the DOE learning module(s) that it addresses. Figure 2 demonstrates that no program meets all of the DOE learning modules. This means that they are not only falling short of a few of the specific learning objectives in a given module, but they are ignoring entire modules that peer review has determined is important for excellence in building science.

Of all the programs studied, Algonquin College's Bachelor of Building Science degree meets the most learning modules at 80%. Weber State University's Bachelor of Construction Management Technology degree meets the fewest DOE knowledge areas at

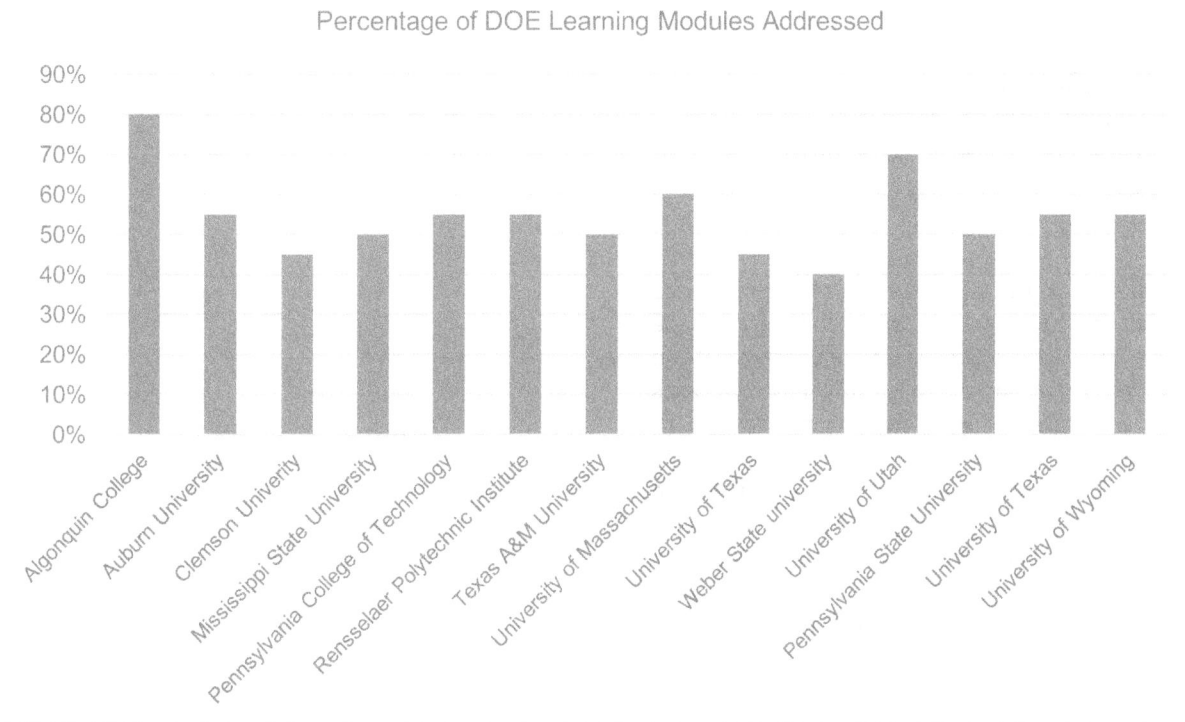

Fig. 2. This chart describes how many of the DOE's learning module topics are addressed, at least in part, by each program.

40%. The average across the spectrum is 54%.

Figure 3 illustrates the number of classes in each program that address content defined by at least one DOE learning module, versus the number of classes that address zero learning modules.

The fact that peer institutions are neglecting to fulfill the basic learning objectives defined by the DOE, while teaching multiple courses that fulfill no recommended learning objectives underscores the DOE's assertion that the current building science education lacks consensus, focus and direction.[16]

Current Offering

Step 4 in the study was to look closely at building science content courses currently being offered on campus in both the University of Utah's Bachelor of Science in Architectural Studies program and programs in the College of Engineering including B.S. in Civil Engineering, Mechanical Engineering and Electrical Engineering. These program courses were evaluated to determine how they addressed the DOE learning objectives. Overall, Utah performs quite well compared to their peer institutions, addressing 65% of the DOE modules. Table 1 outlines the DOE learning objectives and which current offerings at the University of Utah by number and name fulfill these learning areas.

One area in which the University of Utah's course offerings are lacking deals with "building envelope design" and "window and door penetrations". While these topics are addressed to an extent in classes such as Materials & Construction, Sustainable Design, and Building Performance Analysis, the subjects are not addressed as in depth as described by the DOE learning objectives defined in these two modules. The program could benefit from an increased focus on this significant area of building performance including field assessment and energy modeling activities.

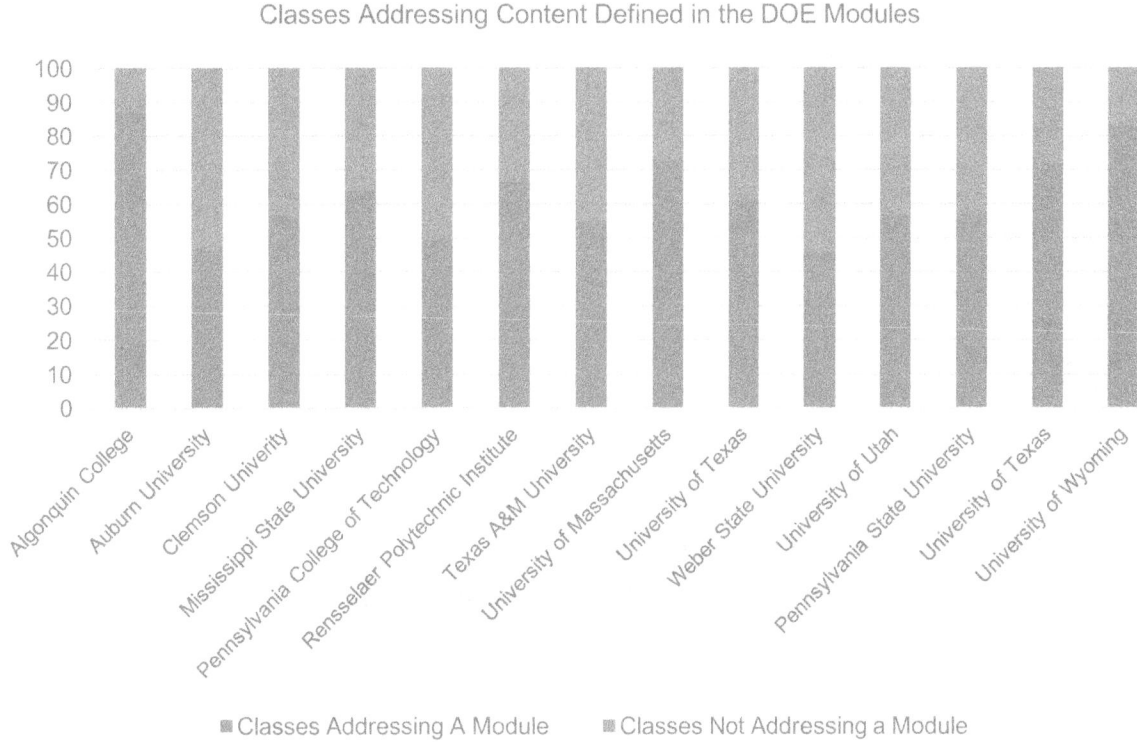

Fig. 3. This chart compares the number of classes that address DOE learning module topics with the number of classes that address zero learning module topics.

Another module which Utah is lacking is "Community Scale," which addresses how a building's energy use and performance is related to the community and existing infrastructure, amongst other large-scale issues in energy and other resource use.

"Homeowner Education" is also noticeably missing from current course offerings at the University of Utah. This module is intended to help students gain an understanding of the housing market and how to explain housing-related principles to consumers that they may interact with in the future.

Utah is also lacking in classes that allow ample opportunity to apply knowledge gained throughout the program in a real-world scenario or capstone project. The "Putting it all together" and "Conclusions" modules described by the DOE allow for students to shadow business professionals and learn more about specific jobs and responsibilities in the field. They help students be able to synthesize and reinforce some of the most important lessons learned throughout the program.

Curriculum Design

The next phase in this research is to develop a new curriculum that leverages the current offerings on the Utah campus, and provides new courses that meet the knowledge areas by DOE that are not available in offerings on campus. The BSBS program will then be submitted for university approval during the 2017-2018 academic year for its first-year degree offering in 2018-2019 academic year.

Conclusion

This research represents background data that was gathered and analyzed for the development of a unique degree offering, Bachelor of Science in Building Science. The purpose of the degree is to meet the growing demand of knowledge of building science in building professionals and respond to the university's budget models to support productivity. A BSBS degree is envisioned as a non-studio based program that leverages existing course work on campus in architecture and engineering for a high return on investment.

Building science is an evolving and maturing discipline. Although building science was born from issues of moisture migration, indoor air quality, thermal comfort and durability, the domain requires much background knowledge in understanding the content of building development and stakeholder engagement. This research found that the most robust peer reviewed effort to date to outline knowledge areas and learning objectives that a building science program might fulfill is the DOE effort in Building Science 101. The University of Utah was the 2nd most effective program among the 14 programs reviewed at achieving the DOE goals with

existing course work. It is therefore, positioned well to leverage existing course work augmented by few additional classes to deliver an excellent building science curriculum.

Table 1. DOE Learning Module Areas fulfilled by University of Utah current offering.

DOE LEARNING MODULE	UNIVERSITY OF UTAH COURSE NO.
Energy Issues and Building Solutions	ARCH 6352 – Advanced Tech: Sustainable Design
Introduction to Sustainable Design & Building	ARCH 6352 – Advanced Tech: Sustainable Design
Flows: Air, Heat, Water, Vapor (Site related)	ARCH 3371 – Materials and Construction PHYS 2210 – Physics for Scientists and Engineers I PHYS 2220 – Physics for Scientists and Engineers II
Building Materials and Their Properties	ARCH 6360 – Advanced Technology: Construction ARCH 3371 – Materials and Construction CVEEN 3510 – Civil Engineering Materials CVEEN 2140 – Strength of Materials ME EN 3300 – Strength of Materials
Climate and Designing with Nature	ARCH 4350 – Environmental Controls
Building Design, Systems Engineering	ARCH 6353 – Advanced Tech: Building Performance ARCH 2611 – Design of the Built Environment ARCH 6720 – Project Finance
Commissioning	ARCH 6353 – Advanced Tech: Building Performance
Site: Drainage, Pest Control, Landscaping	ARCH 4112 – Site Planning and Urban Design CVEEN 3310 – Geotechnical Engineering
Foundation: Moisture Control and Energy Performance	CVEEN 3310 – Geotechnical Engineering
Building Envelope: Moisture Control and Energy Performance	
Windows, Doors and Other Penetrations	
Mechanicals/Electrical/Plumbing Systems	ARCH 4372 – Building Technology in Architecture ECE 2210 – Electrical & Computer Engineering
Electricity Payload	ARCH 6353 - Advanced Tech: Building Performance
On-site Power Generation	ECE 5074 – Photovoltaic Materials & Solar Cells
Field Issues: Construction Management, Codes, and Other Regulatory Matters	ARCH 6710 – Project Management ARCH 6809 – Leadership, Risk & Delivery
Benchmarking performance: meeting and exceeding the norm	ARCH 6570 – Building Condition and Assessment ARCH 6353 – Advanced Tech: Building Performance
Community Scale	
Putting it all Together: Experiential Learning in the Field / Office	
Homeowner Education (Communicating with the Consumer)	
Conclusions, Implications, sources of further learning and continuing education	
Classes not used to cover learning module content	ARCH 1615 – Intro to Architecture

areas	ARCH 1630 – Architectural Graphics
	ARCH 3050 – Architectural Communications I
	ARCH 3052 – Architectural Communications II
	ARCH 3210 – Survey of World Architecture I
	ARCH 3211 – Survey of World Architecture II
	ARCH 3310 – Architectural Structures I
	ARCH 4311 – Architectural Structures II
	ARCH 6050 – Visual Communications
	ARCH 6054 – Contract Documents
	ARCH 6055 – Intensive Architectural Communications
	ARCH 6059 – BIM and GIS
	ARCH 6301 – Advanced Structures Materials
	ARCH 6302 – Advanced Structures Technology
	ARCH 6700 – Professional Practice for Architects
	CVEEN 2010 – Statistics
	CVEEN 2300 – Engineering Economics
	CVEEN 4221 – Concrete Design I
	CVEEN 4222 – Steel Design I

Notes:

[1] Department of Energy. "Buildings of the Future." Energy.gov. Accessed February 22, 2017. https://energy.gov/articles/buildings-future.

[2] Kwok, A., Tepfer, S., Grondzik, W. Zero net energy education: mind the gap. ARCC/EAAE 2014 | Beyond Architecture: New Intersections & Connections Methods: Agents of Change in Changing Paradigms. Scientific, Technological, Strategic, Intuitive, and Pragmatic. 2014: Pp. 354 – 362.

[3] NASA News: Scientists react to 400 ppm carbon milestone. National Aeronautics and Space Administration. http://climate.nasa.gov/400ppmquotes/ 2013.

[4] Anderson, M., T. Collins, and A. Kwok. "Zero Net Energy Education: a survey of building science curricula," Proceedings of National Solar Conference—Solar 2013, American Solar Energy Society, Baltimore, Maryland, April 16–20, 2013.

[5] Kwok, A. et al, 2014. & Architecture 2030. http://www.architecture2030.org/ 2013.

[6] Nicol, D. and Pilling, S. Changing Architectural Education: towards a new professionalism. London & New York: E&FN Spon Taylor & Francis Group. 2000.

[7] Levin, H. Raising Productivity in Higher Education. The Journal of Higher Education Vol 62:3, 1991: 241-262.

[8] Toth, L. & Montagna, L. Class size and achievement in higher education: a summary of current research. College Student Journal Vol 36:2 June 2002: p.253-260.

[9] Jacoby, M. Mentoring and Undergraduate Academic Success: A Literature Review. Review of Educational Research, January 1991. Sage Publishing.

[10] Ireton, K. "The Trouble with Building Science." Fine Homebuilding 227, 2012: 70-5.

[11] Institute of Medicine (US) Committee on Damp Indoor Spaces and Health. Damp Indoor Spaces and Health. Washington: The National Academies Press. And Florida Solar Energy Center. n.d.. "Building Science Basics." Florida Solar Energy Center. 2004. Accessed 04.15.17. http://www.fsec.ucf.edu/en/consumer/buildings/basics/index.htm.

[12] Laquarta, J. The Need for Building Science Education. Journal of Civil Engineering and Architecture 9, 2015: 775-779.

[13] Rose, W. "Research, Building Science and Architecture. Housing Knowledge Community Webinar Series." American Institute of Architects. 2012.. Accessed November 11, 2012. http://network.aia.org/AIA/Resources/ViewDocument/?DocumentKey=89904d0f-70dc-4c4f-906a-c44e1556ec19.

[14] Lstiburek, J. "Forward." In Building Science for Building Enclosures, edited by Straube, J., and Burnett, E. Westford: Building Science Press. 2005.

[15] Department of Energy. "Building America: building science education roadmap". April 2013.

[16] Ibid, 2013.

Towards a Multi-faceted Integration Model for Teaching Architectural Design and Technology

Diane Armpriest, Carolina Manrique
University of Idaho

Abstract

Our architecture program recently engaged in the redesign of the curriculum, with a particular focus on rethinking the integration of design studio and technology at the undergraduate level of the professional M. Arch. Degree. The goal was to transition from having technology courses that were somewhat disengaged from the design sequence, to a curriculum where construction and structures would become more fully embedded and engaged in other areas of study. More specifically, we wanted to accomplish these changes while maintaining the strong design focus of our program. This process was facilitated by the opportunity to hire two new faculty members. Our position announcement – which echoes the program's mission statement - set the tone by stating that we "value design excellence centered in the poetic merging of the arts and technology" and are seeking "educators who are enthusiastic about architecture, excited to teach design, love working with students, have a strong desire to work collaboratively, and are determined to make a difference in the world". During the search process, members of the faculty were actively engaged in setting the stage for change: researching and experimenting with alternative approaches to design focused structures and construction education, meeting with innovative educators, visualizing curricular opportunities and implementing changes. It required about a year to hire two enthusiastic and well-prepared faculty members who would be instrumental in implementing this new vision upon their arrival. The initial changes were to move from four structures courses to two, expand from one construction course to two, and revise the second and third years of the design curriculum.

The curriculum as implemented included developing a building technology sequence that is tied horizontally and vertically with design studios. Integration in second year aims toward exploring the constraints and opportunities of building materials at full-scale through the direct experience of making (small scale design-build); integration in the third year design studio encourages explorations on the poetic implications of structure and construction systems in architectural design through the use of project-based methods and case-examples in architectural history introducing concepts linking "form and forces" (e.g. Allen, Sandaker, etc.). During fourth year, after students have completed structures and are studying environmental control systems and taking vertical design studios, they focus on building assemblies – taught in relationship to design and detailing of enclosure systems. Other initiatives include an Integrative Design Studio and Technical integration courses that are part of the graduate program, and a design-build elective in progress.

This paper presents the experience of making program changes and includes a summary of the original and new curricula, and discusses strategies implemented to improve student learning at the intersection of art and technology. Included in the discussion are the content and delivery of the courses and results of the changes that included embedding design in technology courses, technology in the design studio, reconfiguration of two industry sponsored design competitions, and increased industry support for these changes. It also introduces preliminary findings based on course and program assessments, and input from visiting educators, practitioners and critics.

Introduction

Part of the mission statement of the Architecture Program at the University of Idaho reads that we *"value design excellence centered in the poetic merging of the arts and technology"*. We took this as a mandate as we transitioned from a construction and structures technology course sequence that was disengaged from the design sequence, to a curriculum where construction and structures would become more fully embedded and engaged in studio and other areas of study. This opportunity came about as the result of the retirement of two adjunct instructors who had previously taught 3 of 4 of our structures courses, and the loss of a tenure track faculty member to another university. With the potential for two new hires we were well positioned to implement curricular changes.

In order to accomplish these changes and make more advances in student achievement of design excellence, we needed to plan for the future and simultaneously, to initiate a search for two new tenure-track faculty members. To facilitate the transition, we began by assessing our existing curriculum in terms of the sequencing of design studio and technology courses, identifying ideas for integrating design and technologies experimented within the past, and exploring opportunities that exist with current and potential industry collaborations. We also reached out to learn from the experiences of others in teaching structures in the context of design.

This allowed us to develop new position descriptions we hoped would attract the types of faculty who could take the lead in moving the curriculum forward.

In retrospect, we laid the groundwork for articulating the *multi-faceted integration model* described in this paper, and which is also now being used as a tool for assessing progress toward the goal of achieving design excellence through the poetic merging of arts and technology.

Background

The curriculum that was in place before changes were implemented (illustrated as the 2014 Curriculum in Figure 1) was not unlike many that exist in accredited 4 + 2 professional programs. In assessing the existing curriculum, we identified several ways in which we could better implement the design and technology courses: changing the structures courses from materials focus to systems focus, integrating classes horizontally, appropriate sequencing of courses, and developing closer ties to industry.

2014 Curriculum

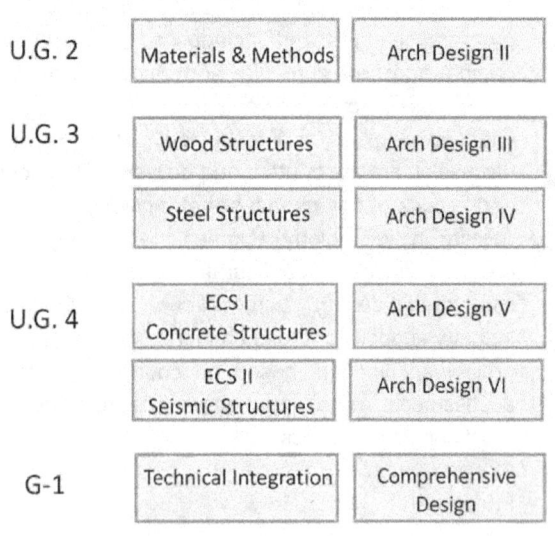

2016 Curriculum

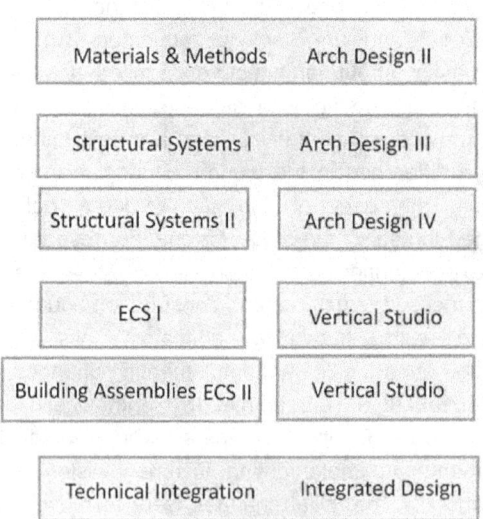

Fig. 1. Design and technology curricular diagram illustrating transition from 2014 to 2016. Note four areas of the 2016 curriculum where intentional links could be made between technology and design in new or revised courses.

Implementation

The original plan in rolling-out the new curriculum was to implement changes first in the collaborative Architectural Design III and Structural Systems I, which is the focus of this paper. However, we quickly realized that between the addition of new faculty members and the curricular change process there were more opportunities for integration than originally envisioned. For instance, we discovered the potential to integrate Materials and Methods of Construction with Architectural Design along the way, the availability of a new student centered classroom made it possible to take a more hand's-on and design-focused approach to Building Assemblies that built on content from ECS I and ECS 2, and that Technical Integration would once again be linked directly to the Integrated Design Studio. The result was that the number of the course offerings during this school year became experimental as we worked toward the integrated model approved by the University for delivery beginning in 2016. See the graphic comparison of the two approaches as illustrated in Figure 1.

As we began our assessment of Architectural Design III and Structural Systems, our goal was to build a framework that would enable the students to improve their ability to explore the poetic opportunities at the intersection of technology and design. There were a

number of obvious changes that were required: refining the design studio and structures classes and building stronger connections between the two courses. During the assessment process we came to better understand the complexities of the task, and began to define the multiple factors at play. As a result, we began to envision the interactions of these factors in terms of a multi-faceted model that we could use to continue to develop and assess progress in these two classes, apply to the curriculum, and guide our aspirations to develop a center for excellence within our program.

The multi-faceted integration model

The primary influences (factors) we identified are those which come from within (internal) and outside (external) of our curriculum and program, the relationships which exist between courses and content that precede or follow each other (vertical relationships) and the relationships that exist between courses and content offered at the same time in the curriculum (horizontal relationships). Table 1 represents a conceptual model for clarifying the relationship among these factors and their interactions with the 2016 curricular diagram in Figure 1. The strategies that comprise the model are summarized below. Some have been implemented and some are aspirational.

Table 1 Summary of Integration Strategies

Integration Types	Strategy	Level(s)	Course(s)
Internal – Horizontal	Design thinking to structures	U.G. 3	Structures I - II
	Structures to design studio	U.G. 3	Arch Design III
Internal – Vertical	Design thinking to materials and methods	U.G. 2	Materials and Methods
	Building assemblies to upper level design studios	U.G. 3	Building Assemblies
External – Horizontal	Industry partnerships in design studio	U.G. 3	Arch Design III
	Industry partnerships in building technology courses	U.G. 3	Structural System I
External – Vertical	Industry partnerships with architecture program	U.G. 3-4; Graduate (M.Arch & MSIAD)	Arch Design; Building Technology; Research
	Industry partnerships with College of Art and Architecture	U.G.; Graduate; outreach	Arch Design; Building Technology; Research

1. Internal-horizontal integration

a) Introducing design thinking into the new structures sequence:

The structures sequence was changed from four courses that were organized around materials and the related methods of structural design that were primarily based on calculations, to a two-course (one-year) structural systems sequence that is project based and more closely aligned with architectural design. This approach aims to bridge the gap between technology and design through a problem-solving methodology that introduces the fundamental principles of structures (loads, stress, etc.) as needed in the investigation of case study examples, and is inspired by the work of M. Salvadori, F. Moore, E. Allen, B. Sandaker and others. Their works recognize the structure as an intrinsic component of a building that is developed from the initial stages of the design process rather than solved by others as an afterthought.[1]

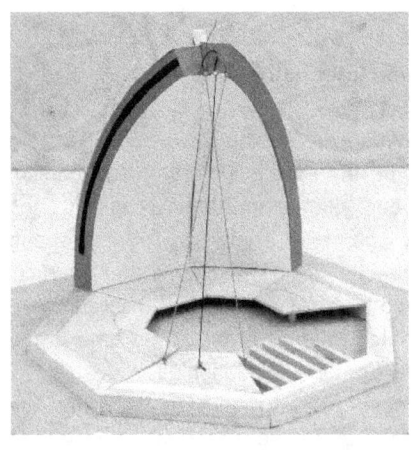
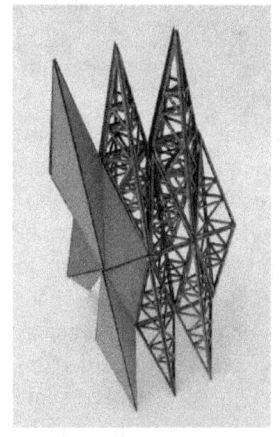
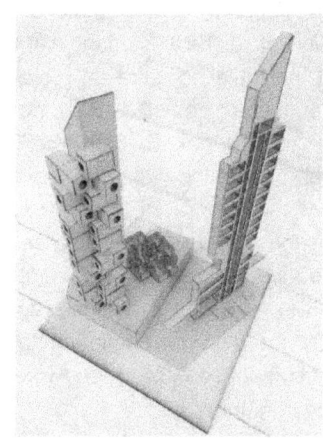
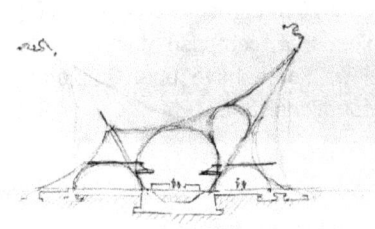
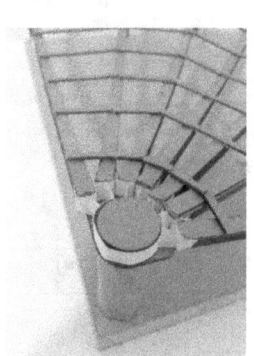
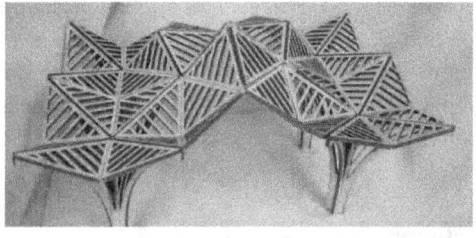

Fig. 2. Student work in Structural Systems–I. Study of precedents (fall 2015, 2016): a) Brunelleschi Dome construction (Alenazi and Beesley); b) Air Force Academy Chapel (Newcomb and Reed); c) Nakagin Capsule Tower (Xu and Hu). Structural Systems-I (fall 2016). Project #2 requires proposing an exciting, interesting and expressive structural solution to cover an area of approximately 8,000 sq-ft (varies). Students were assigned dimensions and material (wood or steel); d) 70 ft x 110 ft wood (Rott and Collie); e) 90 ft x 90 ft wood (Behrens and Corr); f) 30 ft x 260 ft wood (Sawadogo and Duclos).

The learning outcomes specify that students will demonstrate: an understanding and application of the fundamental principles of structural design using graphic statics and introducing numerical methods where needed; an understanding of the key concepts and related equations necessary to communicate with engineering professionals; and a synthesis in the application of structural design principles in architectural design.[2]

These were accomplished by: using two complementary textbooks that introduce the fundamental principles of structural design through project-based design challenges (Allen, 2009[3]), and classic and contemporary examples in architectural design (Sandaker, 2011[4]); using physical models for analysis of architectural precedents (e.g. Brunelleschi Dome) and structural design proposals that have a structural and construction focus as illustrated in Figure 2; using references that situate architectural precedents in history based on the contribution of structural explorations in form-finding (e.g. Gaudi, Nervi and others), or other architecture and structure relationships (e.g. Ching, 2014[5]; Macdonald, 2001[6]); exams and projects that require the use of both graphic and written explanations to evaluate understanding and application of structural concepts. Class lectures promote understanding structural design as an iterative process requiring refining each stage to avoid focusing on single values (e.g. efficiency), awareness of the simplification in gravity-free architectural design software, and reassessing the history of architecture from the values of a material and technological thinking.

In the future, digital tools will be introduced that use graphic statics and software applications to evaluate structural performance *during* the form-finding process.

b) Integrating structures in design studio:

Architectural design III (fall) has two 8-week material-based projects that are each supported by industry sponsors and which include design competitions. The Idaho Concrete Masonry Association (ICMA) explores the creative design possibilities related to the use of concrete masonry units, and the Idaho Forest Products Commission (IFPC[7]) promotes the inventive use of Idaho wood products in architecture. These two materials suggest the building types to be assigned as the design challenge (e.g. fire station; city market), and set the boundaries and possibilities of explorations in the relationship between structural systems and form-finding. Early investigations for each project involve a careful analysis of the expressive use of the particular structural system and material conducted simultaneously with an exploration of the potential for spatial definition based on structure type.

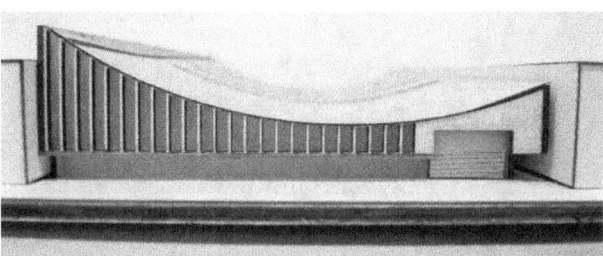
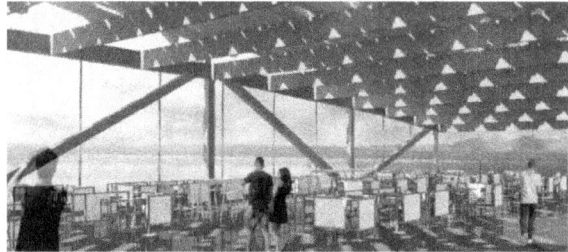
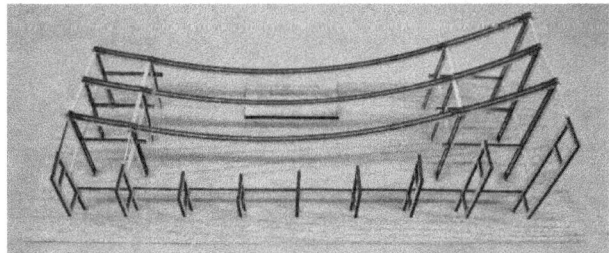
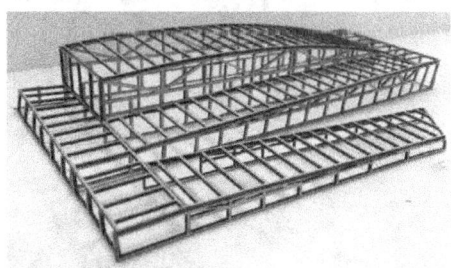

Fig. 3. First place IFPC design competitions: a & c) Ehly, fall 2015; b & d) Du, fall 2016.

The learning outcomes specify that students demonstrate: the ability to apply basic organizational, spatial, structural, and constructional principles to the conception and development of interior and exterior spaces, building elements, and components; the ability to respond to natural and built site characteristics in the development of design solutions; an understanding of the basic principles of structural behavior as applied to the specific design projects; the ability to assess, select, configure, and detail –

integral to the design solution – appropriate combinations of building materials, components, and assemblies; and an understanding of the design of sites, buildings, and systems that are responsive to relevant codes and regulations.[8]

One of the challenges with integrating structures and design studio at this level is the fast-paced and complex explorations required for each building type (e.g. a fire station in concrete masonry), and the topic and order in which fundamentals of structural design topics are delivered in Structural Systems I. These issues are addressed through kick-off and keynote awards lectures that focus on the expressive possibilities, and current challenges and opportunities for each material; visits to manufacturing plants for key materials (e.g. wood and concrete masonry) that provide for hands-on experience with material properties; and the application of fundamental concepts in structural design through the use of "preliminary design charts" (e.g. Architect's Studio Companion in Allen, 2012[9]). These tactics provide students with an expanded repertoire of structural systems in design studio early in the semester when the fundamental concepts are introduced in Structural Systems I.

In the future, a regular series of design studio lectures that complement the topics addressed in Structural Systems I will be introduced. (e.g. spatial implications of structural systems).

2. Internal-vertical integration

a) Introducing design thinking into materials and methods:

One of the objectives in Materials and Methods offered in the second year is to explore the "constraints of real materials at full-scale"[10], and those materials included concrete masonry and wood. In this class, students designed and built concrete masonry blocks using standard dimensions, while exploring intentional design solutions. They also explored the use of wood in a small-scale design-build project. Both of these projects supported work that would be done in Architectural Design III the next semester, so they had theoretical and practical preparation for the next design project (figure 4).

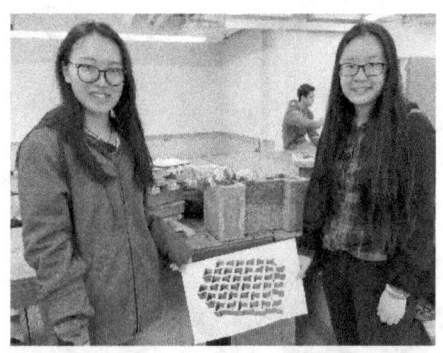
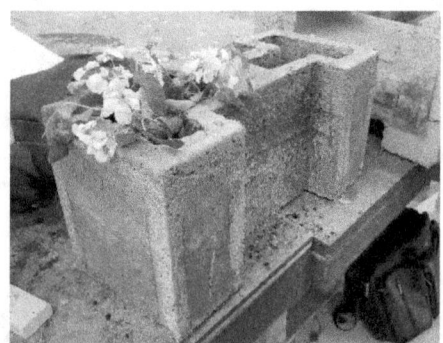
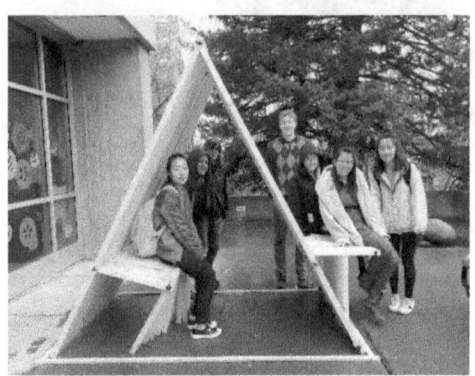
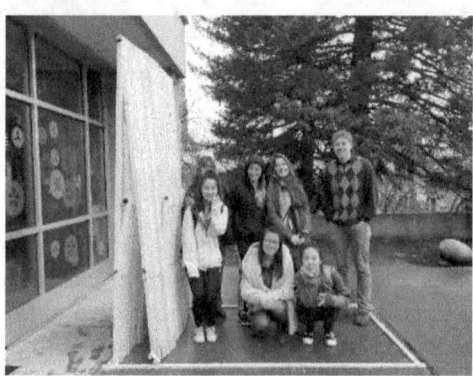

Fig. 4. Materials and Methods of Construction; a & b) CMUnit project (Miller, spring 2016); c & d) Wood: "To-fold" (Miller, spring 2016).

b) Creating a Building Assemblies course to support advanced construction skills in upper level studios:

The sequencing of building technology was adjusted to relate to goals of design studios at various levels of curriculum. A new Building Assemblies course (3 credit) was added to the curriculum in 4th year to replace the structures courses (4-credits) dropped from the curriculum. The focus is on students developing the ability to make design decisions and develop technical documentation skills for building enclosure systems and assemblies that are responsive to site and climate, consider environmental stewardship, and integrate environmental control and structural systems. The classroom is semi-flipped so students focus in developing knowledge through reading and online study tools outside class and develop design and detailing skills through in-class exercises and group discussion. Three design problems and a semester long construction observation project are also assessed with feedback provided throughout the semester.

3. External-horizontal integration

a) Industry partnerships in design studio:

The Third Year Design Studio now has two industry sponsors, each of which sponsor design competitions.

The Idaho Concrete Masonry Association has sponsored a design competition for 48 years, introducing students to CMU materials and assemblies, and providing technical support, hosting a visit to the Basalite CMU plant in Boise, Idaho (see hand's-on exercise and awards in Figure 5, and providing $1,000 in scholarships for student design projects awarded at a closing banquet. Entries are judged by industry members and the architecture faculty.

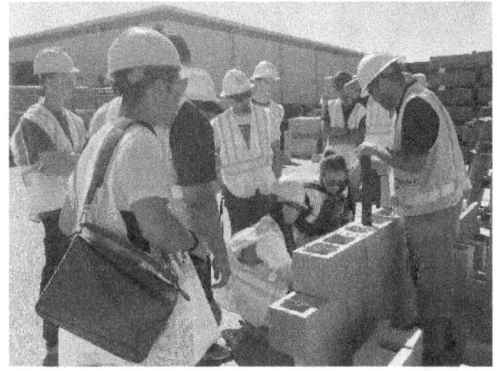
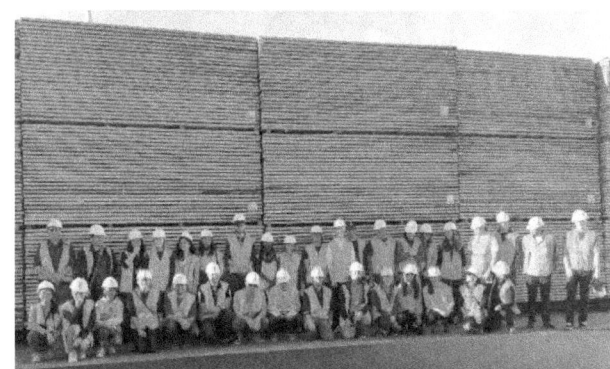
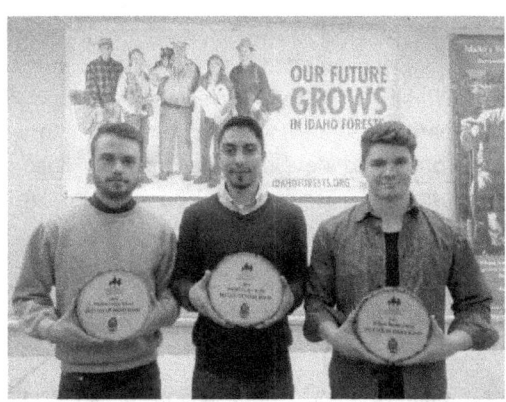
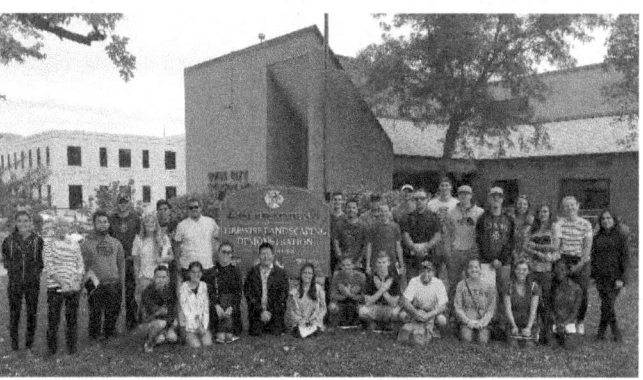

Fig. 5. - ICMA and IFPC competitions in Architectural Design III, fall 2016: a) ICMA Basalite CMU plant visit, Boise, ID b) IFPC Lumber Mill visit Lewiston, ID c) ICMA competition fire station site visit Boise, ID. d) IFPC Design Competition winners fall 2015.

The Idaho Forest Products Commission initiated a similar program in 2013 and it was moved to the Third Year studio when we made curricular changes. The focus of this project is to inform students about the design possibilities related to Idaho Forest Products is part of a larger program to promote architectural uses of forest products statewide. The student design competition includes both a lumber mill and forest tour as shown in Figure 5 as well as technical support and an awards luncheon. Student work is judged by a panel of that includes an industry representative, architecture faculty member, AIA representative and a keynote speaker who is a regional leader in the use of wood in architecture.

These sponsored studios bring resources and incentives that challenge the students to excel and at the same time focus on high aspirations for design that emphasizes structure and materials (figure 5).

b) Industry partnerships in building technology courses:

In addition to industry partnerships with design studio, the third-year field trip provides students with opportunities to learn more about materials for those who had no access to manufacturer locations during second year when Materials and Methods is taught. Students visited a precast concrete manufacturing facility and steel fabrication plant (figure 6).
The structures course partners with Simpson Strong-Tie for a guest lecture and offers scholarships to individual applicants.

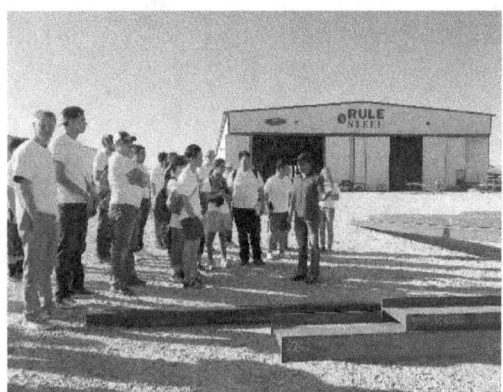

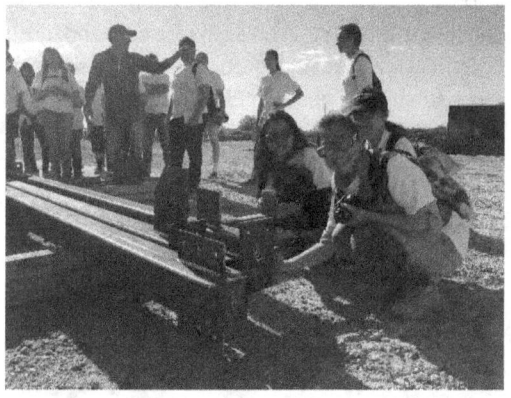

Fig. 6. *Architectural Design III: Rule Steel visit, Boise, ID (fall 2016).*

4. External-vertical integration

a) Industry partnerships with architecture program:

Industries partner with architecture program to support teaching (e.g. ICMA TA - 2017)

As part of a program-based strategy to expand industry and professional support for teaching and research, we proposed an enhanced sponsorship to ICMA, our longest standing industry sponsor. The goal was to fund at a higher than typical TA/RA rate that can be used to recruit highly skilled M.Arch students to our program, and at the same time support teaching and research initiatives. After more than a year of discussions and negotiation, an agreement was finalized, and it will be implemented next year starting in fall 2017.

b) Industry partnerships with College of Art and Architecture:

At a higher level, the Architecture Program and College of Art and Architecture, in alliance with three other University Colleges, have been working for several years with the timber and energy sectors to craft a proposal to develop and fund new lines of research through collaborative partnerships (e.g. IGEM[11] proposal – Idaho wood Industry).

Conclusion

The development of this *multi-faceted integration model* resulted in the identification of integration strategies that were used *informally* to develop the concept for integrating technology and design, assess the first year teaching experience and redesign the course for 2016. It has now been formalized and is being used as a framework for further development of the collaborative offering and with program level support might be used throughout the curriculum. The additional use of SWOT analysis (strengths, weaknesses, opportunities and threats) as a strategic planning technique, contributed to the assessment of external and internal interactions. An example of this was identifying the necessity of extending current industry partnerships beyond the usual expectation of just sponsoring design competitions. It was recognized that the value contributions from ICMA had not increased for 47 years, and this realization was used as leverage to increase their contribution by funding the ICMA Graduate Research Assistantship with annual contributions beginning in fall 2017. The development of the model initially focused on the undergraduate program in architecture, but has led to the identification of new opportunities for increased participation in both the professional and post professional graduate programs and allow us to envision a future that might include developing strong research focus that includes a PhD program.

During the process of development of this model, it has become evident that existing efforts to achieve design excellence as stated in the architecture program mission could be *formalized* using the model to help insure continuity (e.g. faculty turnover), establish clear indicators for evaluating the effectiveness of ongoing implementation of strategies for improvement, and provide a framework for managing increased resources (e.g. funding; partnerships). In addition, it could be *inserted in a broader plan* where the proposed model acts as a baseline (stage-1) to build-on the experience and network developed so far by the architecture program and move us forward to higher impacts contributing to University of Idaho's goal of becoming a Carnegie R1 (Highest Research Activity) institution. [12]

In addition to using the multi-faceted model to guide strategic program development, it provides a useful framework for assessing learning outcomes focusing on continuous improvement. The University of Idaho has recently restructured its assessment program and the focus is on "assessment for [program] improvement" based on the University student learning outcomes. Our new model, which is motivated by the goal of achieving design excellence in the poetic merging of art and technology, can also

be applied to program level as well as individual courses to support University goals. [13]

Notes

[1] From Arch 361 Structural Systems I (Manrique, 2016), syllabus and catalog description.

[2] From Arch 361 Structural Systems I (Manrique, 2016), syllabus.

[3] Allen, Edward, and Waclaw Zalewski. *Form and Forces: Designing Efficient, Expressive Structures.* Hoboken: Wiley, 2009.

[4] Sandaker, Bjorn N., Arne P. Eggen and Mark R. Cruvellier. *The Structural Basis of Architecture.* New York: Routledge, 2011.

[5] Ching, Francis D.K., Barry S. Onouye, and Douglas Zuberbuhler. *Building Structures Illustrated: Patterns, Systems and Design.* Hoboken: Wiley, 2014.

[6] Macdonald, Angus J. *Structure and Architecture.* Woburn: Architectural Press, 2001.

[7] Idaho Forest Products Commission (IFPC). Accessed February 13, 2017. http://www.idahoforests.org/

[8] Armpriest, Diane and Carolina Manrique. Architectural Design III Syllabus for fall 2015 and 2016. Learning objectives are complex and holistic in the design studio, but all accredited professional programs in architecture are accountable to the educational performance criteria as outlined by the National Architectural Accrediting Board (NAAB).

[9] Allen, Edward, and Joseph Iano. *The Architect's Studio Companion Rules of Thumb for Preliminary Design.* Hoboken: Wiley, 2012.

[10] Miller, Matthew (2016). CMUnit Project. Materials and Methods of Construction.

[11] IGEM (Idaho Global Entrepreneurial Mission) request for proposals from the State Board of Education to be awarded by the Higher Education Research Council (HERC).

[12] Carnegie Classification of Institutions of Higher Education. Accessed February 13, 2017. http://carnegieclassifications.iu.edu/

[13] University of Idaho, Office of the Provost & Executive Vice President. "Strategic Plan 2016-2025." Accessed February 13, 2017. http://www.uidaho.edu/provost/strategic-plan

Building Technology within a New Architecture Curriculum

Erin Carraher, Ryan E. Smith, Patrick Tripeny, Robert A. Young
University of Utah School of Architecture

Abstract

Faculty in the School of Architecture (SoA) at the University of Utah are in the process of conducting a major curriculum revision of both the 4-year undergraduate Bachelors of Science in Architectural Studies as well as the 2-year accredited Masters of Architecture programs. This marks the first holistic review of the entire curriculum in almost twenty years. With guidance from the university's teaching center, the faculty established a collective goal to develop a contemporary curriculum geared toward educating students to not only survive but thrive in the constantly evolving nature of architectural practice today.

The process being undertaken to develop the new curriculum is known as a 'backward design.' This begins at the macro scale, examining the program's overall goals and objectives. From these, faculty develop a series of learning objectives students are expected to achieve during the course of their studies. Once the objectives are set, they are grouped, first in chronological sequence and then in clusters that form the basis for a new sequence of classes. This initial process will take place over the course of the fall semester while the spring semester will focus on developing the new courses themselves.

The building technology faculty are actively involved in the curriculum redesign process and are also working together to rethink the overall technology sequence and delivery. Much has changed in architecture in the last twenty years; these changes include the incorporation of digital technologies a part of the building technology sequence with the development of BIM and digital fabrication tools. Exterior skins and methods of construction have also changed greatly, necessitating a constant recalibration of content and delivery methods that draw the connections across the domains of contemporary building technology education.

Instead of keeping our various technologies siloed, we are developing strategies that may change the way we deliver content as a more collaborative process and break down traditional courses with discrete subject areas. As part of the curriculum redesign process, the authors conducted a national survey of how building technology is taught within programs across the country to identify leading schools and innovative coursework for further examination. The building technology faculty will also conduct a series of case studies and interviews of faculty at other institutions to find out what is working well and where there is still room for improvement – always with an eye on advancing academic and professional practices, not just meeting the needs of today's practice. The end goal is to develop a strategy for linking learning objectives in order to find a new curriculum. This paper will present the framework that has been developed for the new curriculum as well as the findings of the survey.

Curriculum History

The College of Architecture + Planning at the University of Utah (and its predecessor, the Graduate School of Architecture) has a long tradition of periodically revising its curriculum. While most revisions have been in response to or preparation for a NAAB accreditation visit, the most recent major curriculum revision occurred in 1999-2000 as the University of Utah converted from a quarter-based system to a semester-based schedule. During this conversion, all areas of the curriculum were reviewed to determine how to best transition from 12-week quarters to the corresponding curriculum based on semester-based units of 15 weeks of instruction.

Before this change took place, the technology-based portions of curriculum (e.g., materials and construction, environmental controls, and structures) each had been taught by a single tenure-line faculty member or affiliated adjuncts in a year-long sequence of three courses. These courses were directly converted into two 15-week semester-length courses.

Design studios were similarly transitioned from quarters to semesters with project sequences defined by topic areas that collectively worked toward meeting the overall expected learning outcomes for that particular year of the program. Lastly, other courses, such as those in history, theory, and criticism (HTC), communications, professional practice, and special topic seminars were either expanded to a full semester length, merged with other thematically compatible topic-based courses, or reduced to what became known as "session" or half-semester long courses. The session structure was applied across the curriculum when appropriate in design studio, professional practice, and some HTC and communications courses. These 7.5 week intensive courses enabled specific short term instruction on emerging and relevant concepts from design research and practice.

In 2007-08 academic year, as a result of several faculty retirements and new hires, the program was revisited to reflect the then current research and practice direction of the faculty. As the strengths and weaknesses of the prior curriculum structure for the session courses and the overall sequencing became evident, the curriculum was again reviewed and reorganized to accommodate learning foci. For example, as part of an integrated studio process for the final semester, a final "Technology in Architecture" course was devised to accommodate the opportunity to provide concurrent and complementary instruction to the design studio together fostered a capstone experience for undergraduate students. In the previous version, many of the fundamental aspects of architectural design education were covered in a rigid curriculum directed at undergraduates. The new approach enabled great latitude with course offerings and experimentation in the graduate program.

Once again the effectiveness of this curricular structure was reviewed and as part of the outcome of accreditation visits in 2013 and 2016 at which point the faculty determined that there was both need and opportunity to undergo a holistic review of the overall program, leading to the curriculum redesign process currently underway.

Current Curriculum Structure

The curriculum structure prior to the re-imagining process was a "2+2+2" model with two years of pre-major undergraduate general education classes and prerequisites required before students applied to the architecture major at the end of their sophomore year. This was then followed by two years of highly-structured and coordinated coursework in the junior and senior year. This structure also allowed for students transferring into the program from local and regional schools with articulation agreements to do so seamlessly. Historically, a large percentage of graduate students in the program, which is the only accredited architecture program in the state, matriculated through the undergraduate program. As such, the graduate sequence was structured more loosely to allow students to take a more self-directed path through the program, with a few signature programs such as DesignBuildBLUFF as key milestones.

Early in the curriculum redevelopment process, faculty confirmed their collective desire to both serve the in-state population as well as increasing the diversity of out of state and international students. In relation to this, the faculty determined that there needed to be better distribution of the technical coursework relative to the B.S. versus M.Arch degrees.

Learning Context

There were several contributing factors that were required to support this process including full faculty buy-in, administrative support, an 8-year accreditation term, and a transition at the university level that shifted the previous junior-year application to freshman admission into the college.

Designing environments for optimal learning requires a learner-centered approach; clarity in what is taught, why it is taught, and what competency entails; understanding where students are coming from in their personal experience and educational background; and fostering a supportive and collaborative context[1]. At the University of Utah, a learner-centered approach is supported at each scale – university, college, and department. Under the current president, there is a university-wide mandate to "offer every entering high school student the opportunity to participate in at least one signature experience — a genuine and deep engagement outside the classroom[2]." These project-based and experiential learning opportunities are not meant as extra-curricular or optional but as ways of augmenting or restructuring the traditional lecture course (or studio) framework to provide students with a transformative learning experience.

The College of Architecture + Planning has a value- and place-based approach to structuring the educational experience: "We believe that innovative processes predicated on human-centered, evidence- inspired, integrated, collaborative inquiry and harnessing emergent technologies to enhance these processes are essential to preparing the design mind of the future. These processes must be tested in real- world applications—such as problem-based community engaged learning, applied research and reflective practice—so as to both respond to the needs of our local, regional and global communities and to provide immersive educational experiences that create a strong foundation for life-long learning."[3]

Grounded in this context, the School of Architecture faculty support students through highly-impactful teaching approaches intended to help students connect "their values with making and the production of space." The SoA faculty believes an architect should be "a dedicated team player that seeks to elevate everyone in the community through collaboration. [Future architects] should be constantly curious, learning and expanding their understanding of culture and the impact of architecture on communities."[4] It is worth noting that all academic units in the college—School of Architecture, Department of City and Metropolitan Planning, and Multi-Disciplinary Design Program—are undergoing concurrent curriculum restructuring, which allows for integration not only within programs but also across disciplines.

Curriculum Development Process

The groundwork necessary for such a massive project began years in advance of the formal kickoff of the process. This is typical for curriculum revision to any degree regardless the discipline. Beginning in summer 2011, a series of college- and school-wide retreats specifically dedicated to discussions of overall objectives and visionary curriculum approaches have been conducted internally as well as with facilitation from university offices.

Though the undergraduate and graduate architecture curricula had been regularly reviewed, changes that taking place in the five years prior to this effort had been isolated adjustments meant to address specific issues. Over time, it became clear that a more substantial change was needed. The department chair, Mira Locher, thus invited the university's Center of Teaching and Learning Excellence (CTLE) at the University of Utah to play the role of curriculum development leadership and moderators. CTLE's Associate Director, Pamela Hardin PhD, is leading the school through the process.

CTLE's process is based on what is known as the backward design model of curriculum development. The term backward design may be confusing to an architect. From an instructional designer's perspective, it is "backward" in that it begins with intended outcomes, moves toward methods of assessment of those outcomes, and finally develops instructional methods for teaching this to students. This approach is reversed from the traditional methods of instructional development. Backward design was first coined by Jay McTighe and Grant Wiggins in their book *Understanding by Design* and was furthered by L. Dee Fink in his book *Creating Significant Learning Experiences: An Integrated Approach to Designing Colleges Courses*. Both of these precedents used a similar process to that described in this section but at the scale of a course. CTLE has adapted the approach to apply to curricula.

Backward curriculum design begins with the program objectives, which include items universal to all programs in the discipline (i.e. accredited architecture degree programs would have as a program objective to be NAAB accredited) and also include outcomes particular to each school such as addressing the high desert landscape of the Intermountain West where the SoA is located. Once program outcomes are set, faculty begin discussing how they can be measured and defining the learning objectives that will allow students to meet the program objectives. These learning objectives are developed for each general area of the curriculum such as design, technology, communication, HTC, professional practice, etc. Once learning objectives are defined within curriculum areas, they can be ordered within the 4-year undergraduate and 2-year master's degree structure. The final step involves sequencing the learning objectives and determining how to group them in clusters, which will form the basis for the program's courses. Currently, the SoA has completed the program objective definition and is finalizing learning objectives across the undergraduate and graduate programs. Course and project development will take place over the 2017-18 academic year with the new curriculum to begin in fall 2018. No curriculum development process is as easy as the milestones described above. Curriculum development is a personal process to the faculty within any program and rarely proceeds in a perfectly linear way.

Curriculum Survey

In spring 2017, a survey was distributed to building technology educators nation-wide. Over sixty faculty members responded to the questions, the results of which are outlined below.

The majority of the accredited degrees offered by the survey respondents are Master's of Architecture with nearly half also offering Bachelor's of Architecture. Very few programs offer an accredited Doctor of Architecture program. (Fig.1)

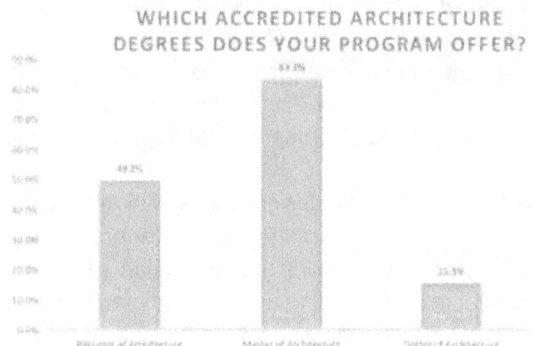

Figure 1. Accredited degree programs taught among respondents

Many accredited programs in architecture also offer non-accredited tracks and degrees. The non-accredited degree programs include the greatest number to least: Bachelor's of Science

in Architectural Studies, Bachelor's of Arts in Architectural Studies, Bachelor's of Environmental Design, and Bachelor's of Building Science. Respondents also wrote in other options that includes from greatest number of responses to least: MS or post professional degree in architecture, PhD, and various dual degree options. (Fig.2)

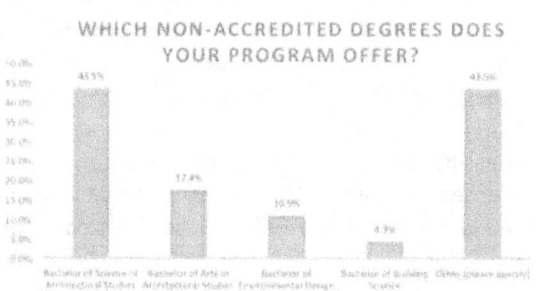

Figure 2. Non-accredited degree programs offered by the respondents' departments.

Building technology is taught by wide majority as a stand-alone subject matter. Structures, materials and construction and environmental controls tend to be discrete courses not integrated with one another or with the design studio. Less than 50% of respondents indicated that technology courses are integrated or aligned with design studios. (Fig. 3)

Open ended responses from those surveyed indicate that there are a number of ways in which to integrate technology courses with design studio. These include strategic semesters at which course content from technology supports the design studio project that ranges anywhere from two semesters to each semester in an accredited degree. Further, some building technology courses are integrated and others are not depending on the expertise of the studio and technology instructor.

Another model leverages lab assignments to investigate technology aspects of the students' studio projects. Best practices indicate overlapping and in some cases shared grading rubrics for integrated assignments so that students are working in a cohesive manner on both the design and technology integration.

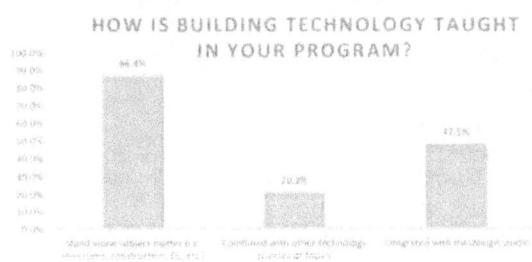

Figure 3. How building technology is taught in architectural degree programs.

Respondents indicated that building technology themed studios are popular with over 65% of reporting programs offering such optional or required studios to students. (Fig. 4)

Comments provided by respondents indicate that many programs are having trouble realizing an integration between technology and design studio in a consistent way. Respondents attributed this to a lack of consistency in the teaching approaches and shared objectives of faculty teaching across the studio and technology courses. This also points to the lack of learning objectives and rubrics that tie design and technology courses together in a standardized curriculum.

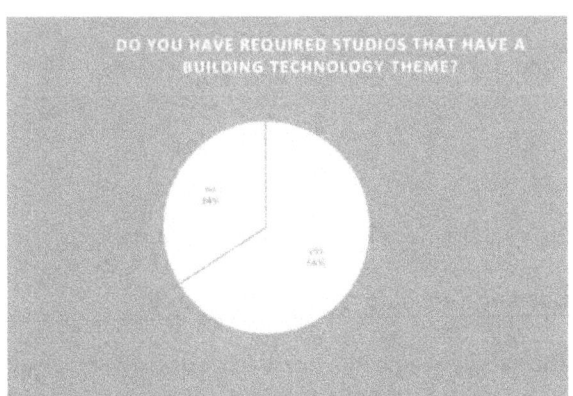

Figure 4. Building technology themed studios.

One of the questions asked was how the accredited degree program fulfills the Integrated Design Student Performance

Criteria introduced in the NAAB 2014 Conditions for Accreditation. Most programs report targeting a specific semester focused on this outcome, though the location of this within the curriculum is inconsistent. No clear pattern can be determined through B.Arch programs generally offer this later in the sequence and M.Arch programs offer it earlier. An emerging best practice model is to utilize outside consultants from the professional community, which models relationships students will have with consultants once they enter practice and builds these practitioners' investment into the program.

Almost half of the respondents reported reviewing learning objectives every five years. Twenty percent indicated they review learning objectives each semester, while 16% indicate they review objectives every other year. A small minority indicated that they review learning objectives every 10 years or more. (Fig. 5)

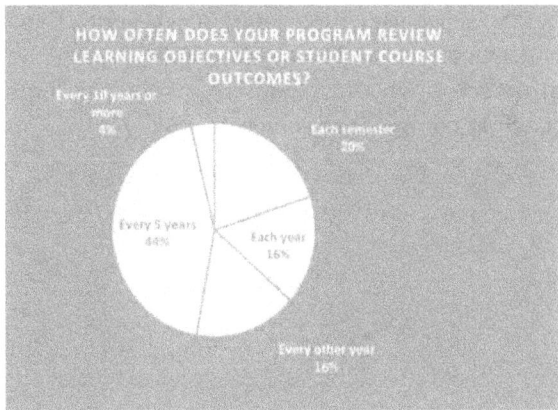

Figure 5. Frequency with which program review of learning objectives is occurring.

Curriculum revision is time consuming and therefore not performed as frequently as learning objective review. The survey results indicate that 35% of respondent institutions undertake a holistic curriculum revision every 6-10 years. A slightly lower percentage of programs review every 3-5 years, while the minority review very 10 years or more. A few outlying programs holistically review their curriculum every year or every other year.

Surprisingly, 14% indicated that their faculty never review the curriculum holistically. (Fig. 6)

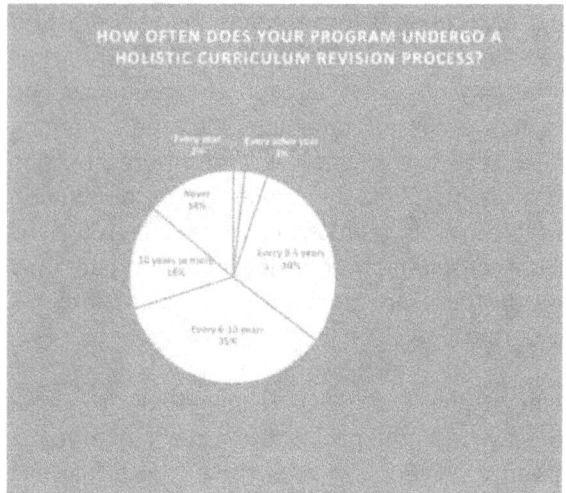

Figure 6. Frequency of holistic curriculum revision.

The respondents represent instructors across a variety of building technology topics: over half of the respondents teach in the area of environmental controls or environmental systems, nearly 40% teach in materials and construction, while nearly 30% teach in structures, while a minority of respondents teach in computational design. (Fig. 7)

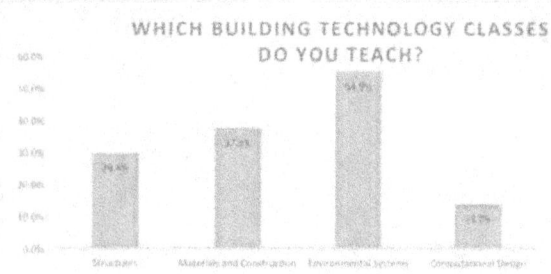

Figure 7. Respondents' teaching areas.

The experience level among building technology instructors who responded to the survey is wide ranging. The largest percentage are instructors who have been teaching 5-10 years, followed by instructors who have taught 10-20 years. Instructors who have been teaching for 20 years or more constitute nearly 30% of the pool. The smallest portion of respondents have taught 2-5 years. (Fig. 8)

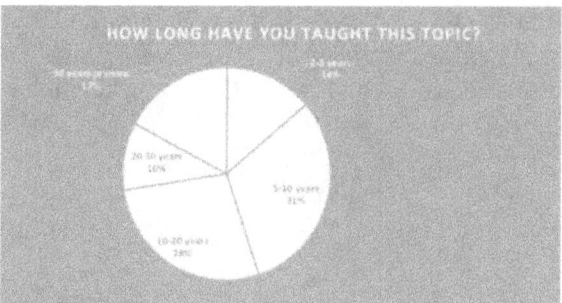

Figure 8. Experience teaching in building technology.

Respondents indicated the methods they are using in delivering building technology content. Lecture format is the most widely used. Less than 50% of respondents use methods including workshops, field trips, seminars, design-build, hybrids and modules. A small percentage of respondents use externships and online education as well as other newer modes of education.

Open-ended responses indicate that other methods are being used for building technology learning. These include: labs in addition to the core course content delivery, simulation projects for building performance analysis, flipped classrooms whereby class time is dedicated to hands-on activities, and community engagement projects.

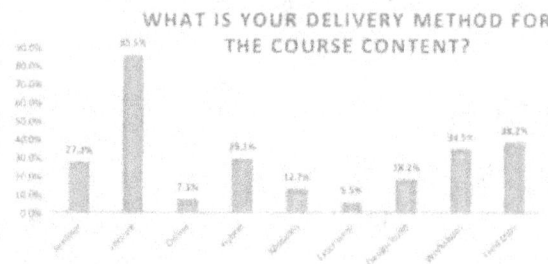

Figure 9. Delivery method for course content.

Building Technology Curriculum Area

The faculty members who teach building technology have been working to redesign the delivery of content in this area. As of now, the proposal is for two courses early in the undergraduate sequence classes that are more "intuitive" in their approach to technology. The first will likely be an introductory general education course that explores how buildings work. The second will be a transitional course for the first-year in-major students presenting general parameters of building technology. The purpose of the second class will be to give students the needed support to integrated building technology at a fundamental level in their studio projects. Both of these classes will teach all aspects of building technology in an integrated rather than siloed way. Toward the end of the undergraduate curriculum and in the beginning of the graduate curriculum, more discrete subject matter will be presented through courses on Materials and Assemblies, Applied Mechanics and Strengths of Materials, Passive and Active Environmental Systems and Building Codes. These will be streamlined versions of current technology courses that have a more rigorous approach to quantative information.

The final type of course being proposed will take place in the middle of the graduate curriculum and will synthesize technology with design and theory. The first of these will be a Typology and Technology course, which will synthesize technology and design. In this course, a certain building typology will be investigated through a deep dive into each area of the technology curriculum. Suggested typologies include highrise, longspan, high performance buildings, medical or research buildings, clean room buildings, etc. The final course being discussed would be a HTC seminar on Culture and Technology.

Conclusions and Next Steps

The SoA faculty are roughly half-way through the development phase of the curriculum re-envisioning process, as outlined in this paper. This will be followed by the rollout of the new curriculum in the 2018-19 academic year. The outcomes of each course as well as the overall program objectives will be evaluated and adjusted as needed on a regular basis.

Notes:

1 Bransford, J., Brown, A., and Cocking, R., eds. *How People Learn: Brain, Mind, Experience, and School.* National Academy Press: Washington, DC, 2000, p. 25.

2 "Pershing's Proposals," *Daily Utah Chronicle*, October 26, 2012. http://dailyutahchronicle.com/pershings-proposals/, accessed October 5th, 2016.

3 Diaz Moore, Keith. "College of Architecture + Planning Vision: Designing to Make a Difference" http://www.cap.utah.edu/visiongoals/

4 "Vision and Mission of the School of Architecture." http://soa.cap.utah.edu/vision-and-mission/

SESSION 11: STRUCTURES

Session Chair: Rob Whitehead
Iowa State University

Ming Hu, University of Maryland: Performance-driven Structural Design – Biomimicry in Super High-rise Structure Design

Caryn Brause, University of Massachusetts: "Constructing Relationships: Examining Project Structures to Align Design Conception and Realization."

Marci Uihlein and Patrick Tripeny, University of Illinois at Urbana-Champaign, University of Utah: "Building Structural Education: An Examination of the Books Used to Teach Structures to Architectural Students."

Deborah Oakley, University of Nevada - Las Vegas: "Chasing Time: The Forgotten History of NAAB and the Evolution of the Structures Student Performance Criteria."

The Art of Performance-driven Design – Biomimicry and Structure

Ming Hu
University of Maryland

Abstract

Since last century, one of the iconic dichotomies that divides architectural designers into two groups is performance and appearance. It is to our benefit to reconcile the performance-appearance debate and to provide an unambiguous definition of the related notions. A natural organism and system is a great model to follow. Biomimicry is the study of emulating and mimicking nature, which has been used by designers to help in solving human problems [i]. Biomimicry as an emerging field since the late 1980s has been looking at advanced technologies derived from bio-inspired engineering at different levels. However, the research on biomimicry applications in the structure design field is lagging behind other design-related fields such as product design and material design. This paper provides a review of recent studies of biomimicry applications in structure design and proposes a framework to answer these questions: How do we make biomimicry concepts practical in the context of structural design and from what key perspectives, especially in super high-rise building design? It will also address how performance and appearance could be blended into one and measured and verified as a whole.

Numerous case studies will be used to demonstrate a variety of strategies corresponding to different levels of performance-driven structure design based on bioengineering. This paper aims to integrate material science and biology studies into the research of architectural structure design.

Introduction

As pointed out by one of the greatest physicists of this century, Freeman Dyson, "It has become part of the accepted wisdom to say that the twentieth century was the century of physics and the twenty-first century will be the century of biology…. Biology is also more important than physics, as measured by its economic consequences, by its ethical implications, or by its effects on human welfare" [ii]. In the natural ecology system, performance is the overarching goal of all independent parts and of the system, all organisms and structures. It is also the underlying measurement to determine the opportunity for survival and evolvement. Biomimicry argues that nature is the best, most influential guaranteed source of innovation for designers. As a result of nature's 3.85 billion years of evolution, it holds vast experience in solving problems of the environment and its inhabitants [iii]. Architects have been looking to nature for solutions to their complicated condition of needing more innovative structures, and they have started to benefit from mimicking forms and shapes from nature to create more efficient and resilient structures to fit different programmatic needs.

1.0. Previous research on biomimicry in design

Nature can provide us with infinite inspirations and lessons from its 3.8-billion-year evolution. "Biological organisms can be seen as embodying technologies that are equivalent to those invented by humans" [iv]. In nature, embodying technologies can be found everywhere in the optimization of the geometrical form and efficacy of energy and material distribution. For instance, in nature, building tall and slender structures presents a special challenge. In order to ensure those structures remain economically viable and sustainable, nature has found a pathway through evolution, one designers could draw their inspirations from. Several research teams have focused on studying a variety of cactus species. They found some types of cactus such as the Saguaro Cactus could grow to 15 meters or taller with aspect ratios (height/diameter) over 20 [v vi vii viii]. Cactus-inspired shapes with 24 circumferential grooves have been seen to have a large reduction, around 20% for mean and fluctuating, in wind-based shear and overturning momentum. The inspiration from the cactus certainly taught the use of the least material to build the highest possible structure [ix]. Regardless

Title	Authors	Year	Main objectives	Focus
Beehive, New innovated structural system for tall buildings	Peyman Askari Nejad	2016	Proposes a novel structure system for tall buildings.	Structure
A biophysical framework of heat-regulation strategies for the design of biomimetic building envelopes	Lidia Badarnah	2015	Presents a structured framework of thermal solutions for buildings taking a biomimetic approach.	Thermal
Bio-mimicry inspired tall buildings: The response of cactus-like buildings to wind action at Reynolds Number of 10	C.W. Letchford; D.C. Lander; P. Case; A. Dysonc; M. Amitay	2016	Studies cactus-like buildings for aerodynamic, wind design.	Aerodynamic
Biomimetic Potentials for Building Envelope Adaptation in Egypt	Nour ElDin. N., Abdou. A., Abd ElGawad.	2016	Studies how biomimicry design could help building envelope design in Egypt.	Thermal
Biomimicry, an Approach, for Energy-Efficient Building Skin Design	Gehan.A.N.Radwana, Nouran Osama	2016	1. Deep research on biomimicry applications in building skins 2. International studies 3. Concludes the guideline for building-skin biomimicry design.	Thermal, energy efficiency
Biomimicry as a Problem-Solving Methodology in Interior Architecture	Rasha Mahmoud Ali El-Zeiny	2012	Reviews key points and case studies of applications of biomimicry in interior architecture.	Interior
Biomimicry as an approach for bio-inspired structure with the aid of computation	Moheb Sabry Aziz, Amr Y. El sherif	2015		Structure
Biomimicry in Architectural Design Education	Cengiz Tavsana, Filiz Tavsanb, Elif Sonmezb	2015		Architecture education
Biomimicry in Furniture Design	Filiz Tavsana, Elif Sonmez	2015		Furniture design
The Load-Bearing Duct: Biomimicry in Structural Design	Gary R. Hunt, M. Ahmer Wadee, Stylianos Yiatros	2007	Proposes the possibility of biomimicry design use in buildings: material, shape, and process.	Structure
Hydromorphic materials for sustainable responsive architecture	Artem Holstov, Ben Bridgens, Graham Farmer	2015	Explores the possibility of adaptive building systems based on incorporation of hydromorphic materials and argues that they present opportunities for architecture design.	Structure
Tree-inspired dendriforms and fractal-like branching structures in architecture: A brief historical overview	Iasef Md Rian, Mario Sassone	2014	Discusses the biological functions and mechanical properties of trees with regard to their shapes.	Structure

of the long-standing history of the division between appearance and performance, form and function, there have been many examples showing how both architects and engineers have been trying to bridge the gap for many years. The research on biomimicry principle applications in the design field are diverse. Lurie-Luke provides an eco-system-based analysis of biomimicry-inspired technology and production innovation [x]. He identifies the three most successful areas of biomimicry applications: material development and locomotion and the emerging fields of smart materials and sensors. Yiatros and team use a multi-story office building as a case studying the integration of structural design and building services (ventilation, thermal cooling) They look at trees as a model. Trees are the most abundant cantilevers in nature and distribute internal stresses due to gravity and live loads with great efficiency as the size of the branches and trunk increases because the stresses are transferred down toward the base [xi]. Holstov and team explore the possibility of adaptive building systems based on incorporation of hydromorphic materials and argue that these present opportunities for architecture that is passively attuned to the variable natural rhythms of the internal and external environments [xii]. Rian and Sassone discuss the biological functions and mechanical properties of trees with regard to their shapes and point out the most inspiring feature of a natural tree undoubtedly is its capacity to carry a large surface supported by a narrow element (trunk) through a fractal-like branching configuration instead of the shape and appearance most architectural and engineering communities focus on right now [xiii]. Nejad proposes a novel structure system for tall buildings that takes inspiration from the ability of a hexagrid to resist lateral forces that can bind in bee hives [xiv]. Aziz and Sherif look at current work that focuses on the mimicry of structural forms from nature and use digital tools as a source of defining and applying simulations to these complex structures [xv].

In other building-design-related research, Badarnah proposes a structural framework for thermal solutions for buildings taking a biomimetic approach [xvi], Abdou and team study how biomimicry design could help building envelope design in Egypt [xvii], Osama and Radwanan propose a design guideline for building-skin design using biomimicry principles [xviii], Rasha Mahmoud reviews key points and case studies of applications of biomimicry in interior architecture [xix]

and Tavsana and Sonmez study biomimicry in future design [xx]. Table 1 list some research findings in recent years.

1.1 Definition of Performance

Performance-driven design is based on understanding that architectures or structures unfold their performative capacity by being integrated in a system, which could be a single building or a nested group of buildings [xxi]. The relationship between a building's primary framework-structures and the external environment factors is set on a spatial organizational level. Materials and patterns of individual elements are secondary. When we define the performance of a building's primary organization we should take into consideration the material-specific exterior-to-interior relations, as well as the order and hierarchy of the form-to-function extension. All of the above live within a dynamic environment.

In reality, the majority of today's designs are perceived and achieved as discrete objects, and the performances of the buildings have been divided into separate categories and measured by separate metrics: energy performance, material performance, structural performance, aesthetic performance and occupancy satisfaction are designed and measured individually. One of the most fundamental consequences of the dominance of isolation and individual measurement is that the building performance becomes locked in the stringent definition between the natural versus man-made, quantitative versus qualitative, unlike in nature where the efficient, safe and aesthetically pleasing structure can be found everywhere and the attributes are always regarded as a whole. The challenge of learning from nature, however, is to quantify these understandings of the natural form and derive the structural behavior from it and then modify and adapt it to buildings. "These organically-inspired structural systems typically exhibit intersecting aesthetic qualities which are not necessarily intuitive" [xxii]. In some projects, individual performance metrics have been blended better than in others. Two approaches within structural design have particularly shown a promising model for how performance could serve as a linkage among all concerns, including energy, functionality, stability and constructability. The two approaches are form-finding and material-centric. In the next section, the author will focus on form-finding.

1.2 Form-finding: biomimicry structure design

Form-finding is a basic skillset that a building designer would inquiry during the training. It falls somewhere in between the theory and practice of architecture. It can be described as the study of the emergent properties of complex systems to establish a more intelligent, correct and robust form [xxiii]. Form-finding requires not only years of training, but also drastic changes in the way designers think about structures and their stability and their resistance to external forces. It is not metaphor of the arts; it is not a piece of poetry of surrounding. Instead, it is rooted in necessity and survival. As pointed out by Julian Vincent, one of the leading thinkers in biomimicry, "materials are expensive and shape is cheap" in nature [xxiv]. Professionals in the building industry often ask "what the most economical and efficient way to build is" [xxv]. Form-finding is part of the answer to the question. Leaves, waves, shells might not appear to us as architectures. However, nature produces extremely efficient, organic and beautiful forms. At the same time, nature makes the most economical use of the limited local materials available and the economy is achieved by weaving material properties into the forms. As the global population increases, especially at urban levels, it has become increasingly imperative that we find a more efficient way to use finite materials within a limited physical environment.

"The straight line belongs to man, the curved line belongs to God," –Antonio Gaudi. Antonio Gaudi is one of the great architects and structural engineers who started learning from nature from a performance perspective instead of a merely aesthetic perspective. Gaudi has a famous approach to taking inspiration from natural objects such as trees and flowers. In his structures, one can find a clear indication of natural inspiration. Before form-finding—which was later practiced by Frei Otto—Gaudi tried to invent his bio-spired structures by conducting experiments. For instance, he suspended inverted structures using cables and left gravity to do its job in determining the resultant organic form. He often applied a form called "inverted catenary arches," which is the mirror image of catenary arches, because of the form's ability to be made of minimal materials and support tremendous weights. The key is the system's active form and pattern that resist external forces. One can find inverted catenary arches everywhere in the nature, such as a spider web.

In early twentieth century, long before the concept of biomimicry was introduced in architectural design field, numerous architects started to explore innovative approaches using nature as a guiding principle to come up with form and structural systems. Frei Otto calls for an architecture of necessity, saying, "Good architecture is more important than beautiful architecture…. The ideal is ethical architecture that is also aesthetic" [xxvi]. As a pioneer of lightweight construction, Otto focused on finding the most force-resistant efficient building. Without his invention of several tensile structures, lots of modern buildings would not be possible. His building are all form-active buildings that use the entire form to resist external forces. Other architects, such as Eero Sarrinene's Dulles Airport and Frank Lloyd Wright's Johnson Wax Building, took the first step toward emulating the natural forms—the former's was birds and latter's was trees.

2.0. Levels of Biomimicry

The term "biomimcry" first appeared in scientific literature in 1962 [xxvii] and later was adopted by material scientists in the 1980s. In 1997, Janine Benyus published a book, *Biomimicry Innovation Inspired by Nature*, that reintroduced the term and broadened the usage of its application. In her book, biomimicry was introduced as a new discipline that analyzes nature's best ideas and adapts them for human use—such as weaving fibers like a spider or gathering energy like a leaf [xxviii].

According to Benyus, the inspiration from nature could be drawn from three levels. The first level is the organization level, which can also be seen from the biomimetic technologies and techniques. At this level, we could mimic the whole organization or certain parts of the whole. The second level is the behavior level. At this level, we could learn from how pine cones open up due to the shrinkage rate difference and apply this to responsive façade design. The third is the system level. This level is considered the most difficult level, as it focuses on a functionally difficult issue to mimic. Five

Table 2 Biomimicry Structural Projects

Project Names	Location	Natural Inspiration	Level of Biomimicry
HSB Turing Torso	Malmo, Sweden	Human Spine	Organizational Level
Hungerburg **Funical [Funicular?]** Station	Innsbruck, Austria	Natural ice formations	System level
ICD-ITKE Research Pavilion	Stuttgart, Germany	Lobster exoskeleton	Organizational Level
Munich Olympic Stadium	Munich, Germany	Soap bubble	Behavior level
L'Oceanografic	Valencia, Spain	Hyperboloid shell structure	Behavior level
Metropol Parasol	Seville, Spain	Mushroom morphology	Organizational Level
Palazzetto Dello Sport	Rome, Italy	Lily pad	Behavior level
Swiss Re Building	London, UK	Sea sponge	Organizational Level
Times Eureka Pavilion	London, UK	Leaf	Organizational Level
Esplanade Theater	Singapore	Durian fruit inspired responsive roof and envelope	Organizational Level
2008 Beijing Olympic Stadium	Beijing, China	Bird's nest	Organizational Level

dimensions could be applied to each of these three levels to determine to what extent mimicry exists. The design is listed as biomimicry in the way it looks (form), what it is made of (material), how it is made (construction), how it works (process) and what its capability is (function) [xxix]. These levels are very important, and they complete the biomimicry approach. They all exist in the structure-design context as well. In table 2, the difference between each level of biomimicry in the structure-design context is described and exemplary projects and their related natural inspirations are listed.

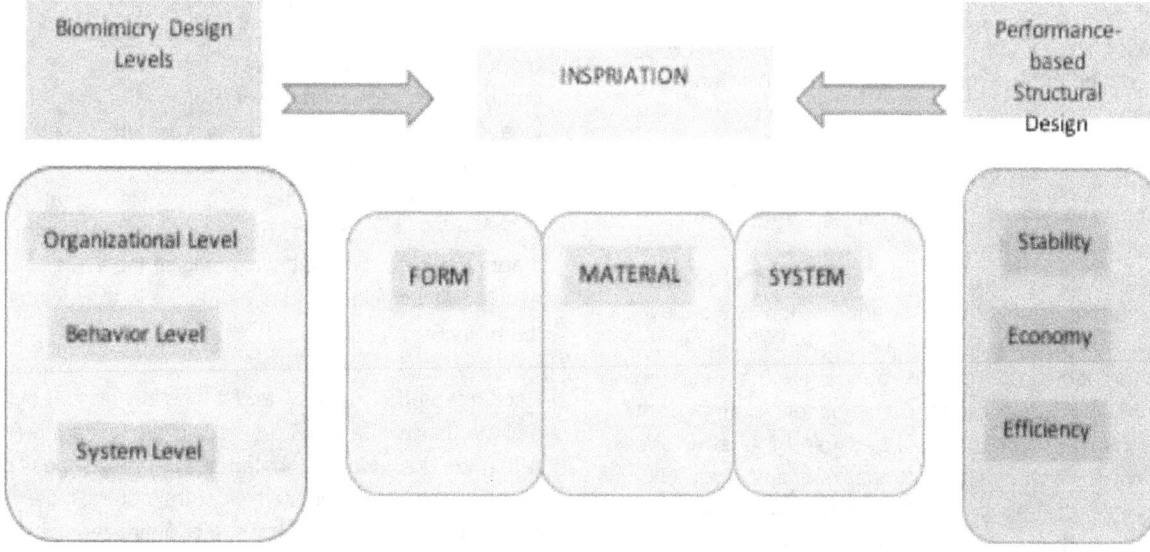

3.0. Proposed framework for understanding biomimicry application in architectural structure design

A framework for understanding the different forms of biomimicry has been developed and is used to discuss the application of biomimicry in architectural structural design with a focus on form-finding and material-centric. (Figure 1 Framework of understanding biomimicry approach in structural design)

3.1 Form-finding - structure lesson

In structure design, there are several structural systems that use its form to resist external load, both flexural and transversal load. The funicular structure and reciprocating structure are two of most obvious examples. A reciprocating structure is a system that's overall span is longer than that of its individual pieces. In nature, a bird nest is a reciprocating structure. In construction, a truss system is a reciprocating structure.

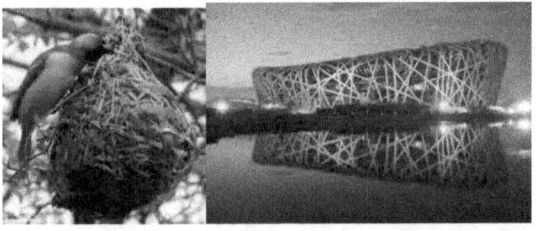

Fig. 2. Bird's nest and building truss

Imitating shape and form from nature is the most well-known type of biomimicry in architecture and structure design. The natural environment in fact inspires a number of structural systems that are considered great man-made achievements, such as Sydney Opera House. Suspension structures, such as long-span suspension bridges, share the same structural principles as spider webs. Membrane structures, such as modern stadium roofs and canopies, behave similarly to cell walls, gaining strength by maintaining constant tension. Someone could argue that even the Pantheon of Rome is indeed a biomimetic example, not in terms of its materials but because of its structural behavior, which is similar to that of a sea shell. Like seashells, the roof of the Pantheon gains its strength from its multi-dimensional curvature, which results in a structure that does not require extra reinforcement. Hence, it is much lighter than conventional reinforced concrete spanning structures [xxx]. Most recently, in SOM's competition scheme for the China World Trade Center, the design team took inspiration from bamboo as a form and for structural organization and created a high-rise that could scale up the bamboo's resilience through a deliberate form. Through study, the team discovered the natural formation of bamboo reveals unique structural characteristics. Long, narrow stems provide support for large foliage during its growing life and also provide strong and predictable support for man-made structures after harvesting [5].

When encountering tremendous lateral loads such as tsunamis, bamboo structures respond in a very resilient way with minimal materials required. The resilience is rooted in the genius of its natural structural organization. When one examines the cross-section of bamboo, one can recognize the mathematically laid out position of nodes and diaphragms. These elements are not evenly space over the entire height of bamboo. They are closer at the base and top and in the middle they are further apart. If we construct a buckling diagram of bamboo, one can find the diaphragms are located to prevent excess buckling when subjected to transversal and lateral loads. Bamboo consists of several stems that are divided by diaphragm into internodes. From outside, nodes mark the location of diaphragms and provide the location for new growth. The small diameter change happens at the node location, typically from large to small from the bottom to the top. This growth pattern is common to all bamboo regardless of the different subspecies. The wall thicknesses and diameter of the culm are also in the proportion needed to "meet" the slender ratio for bamboo. All equations that define the diaphragm locations, diameter and wall thickness are based on a quadratic formulation [xxxi]. A study conducted by David Taylor and team suggests "that the morphological features of the node—the internal diaphragm and external thickening of the culm—have evolved as an attempt to avoid failure in the vicinity of the branch...." [xxxii]

Each internode is hollow, and the hollow portion forms an inner cavity surrounded by a culm wall. The material within the culm wall is located at the farthest position, which is away from the stem's central neutral axis. The distribution and form follows the optimized bending resistance moment and allows the transversal load to be transferred through the exterior skin of the stem.

The fast transference of load, meanwhile, also impedes the uplift wind force. The combination of hollow structure and material distribution provides the strongest bending resistance with minimal weight. The cellular structure of the bamboo wall reveals tighter cellular density near the outer surface of the wall and less density near the inner wall—once again reinforcing the idea of maximum material efficiency when subjected to bending loads [18]. If we plot the bamboo stem and diaphragm section onto a bending moment diagram, with similar height, diameter and material thickness, one can clearly see the shape of the bamboo step is the representation of bending and shear force diagram of a cantilever object. The cantilever object could be a beam; it also could be a high-rise building. The structural principle is the same for bamboo and other cantilevered objects.

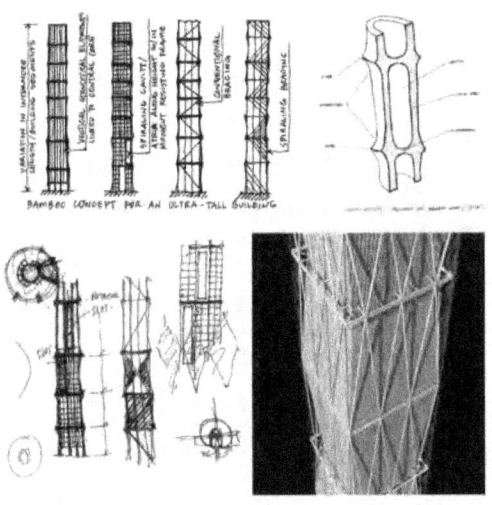

Fig. 3. China World Trade Center [18]

The group of architects and engineers from SOM applied the geometric principles of bamboo in a high-rise design competition: the China World Trade Center Tower. "The tower is divided into eight segments along its height. The structural demand from the lateral load is highest at the base of the culm (or tower), therefore internode heights are smaller compared to the mid-height. Smaller spacing increases moment capacity and buckling resistance. Beyond the mid-height of the culm (or tower), the heights of the internodes decrease proportionally with the diaphragm diameter. Thus, the form of the culm (tower) responds to structural demands due to lateral loads…" [5]. The competition

scheme is a large assembly of bamboo with an inner core connected to perimeter structure-tubes and the connections are mathematically defined to brace the structure against the lateral load and reduce the buckling, just as bamboo grows and resists wind load in an extremely efficient way.

4.0. Conclusion and Discussion

Various natural organisms and structures succeed in maintaining an adequate balance between rigidity and flexibility to resist external forces while adapting to the changing environment. Various biomimicry design strategies can be found in nature for stability, strength, growth, stiffness and prevention, which are accomplished by physical and morphological means. This paper provides an overview investigation of the biomimicry approach in structure design. The in-depth look into the natural way of dealing with structural stability and adaptiveness provides a broad understanding of how structural elements interact with each other and function together rather than being limited to a specific natural organism. Biomimicry does not always offer universal solutions. Understanding the local conditions and adapting to surroundings are the keys for success in using biomimicry principles in structural design. The proposed framework could serve as a roadmap to be used by architects and engineers. Performance-based design cannot be achieved by means of stand-alone technologies that only aim at saving energy. Instead, it requires application of design strategies, methods and materials that allow simultaneous consideration of a wider range of multi-dimensional issues [5], and it requires the design team to take a life-cycle approach that considers both formal/code requirements as well as contextual requirements such as financial feasibility, constructability, aesthetic value and adaptability to future change.

The biomimicry principle's application in structural design has a long way to go—perhaps a difficult way—that includes model testing, structural analysis, mathematical and computational modeling, fluid-dynamics testing, and whole-life cycle analysis. A good ecological solution that takes a million years of evolution and a truly integrated and efficient design approach also needs generations of practice, especially when the current form-function design approach has dominated the design and engineer

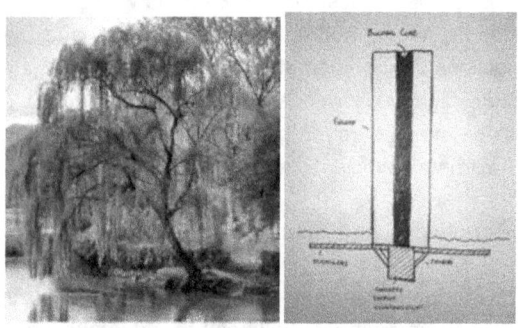

Fig 4. High-rise building foundation design inspired by tree taproots(student work)

Fig. 3. New floor structure inspired by horse hoof (student work)

industry for more than hundred years. To expand biomimicry's influence in architectural structural design, education can play a significant role. In this last section of this paper, the author has demonstrated some examples from the in-classroom design charrette in the structure course to illustrate the potential benefit of integrating biomimicry design as a component of structure teaching.

Notes:

[i] Aziz, Moheb Sabry, and Amr Y. El Sherif. "Biomimicry as an Approach for Bio-inspired Structure with the Aid of Computation." Alexandria Engineering Journal 55.1 (2016): 707-14.

[ii] Dyson, Freeman. "Our Biotech Future." The New York Review of Books. July 19, 2007. Accessed September 19, 2016. http://www.nybooks.com/articles/2007/07/19/our-biotech-future/.

[iii] Benyus, Janine M. Biomimicry: Innovation Inspired by Nature. New York: Morrow, 1997.

[iv] Pawlyn, Michael. "Biomimicry in Architecture". RIBA Publishing. 2011

[v] Abboud JE, Karaki WS, Oweis GF. Particle Image Velocimetry Measurements in the Wake of a Cactus-Shaped Cylinder. ASME. J. Fluids Eng.2011.

[vi] Levy, Benjamin, and Yingzheng Liu. "The effects of cactus inspired spines on the aerodynamics of a cylinder." Journal of Fluids and Structures39 (2013): 335-46.

[vii] El-Makdah, Adnan M., and Ghanem F. Oweis. "The flow past a cactus-inspired grooved cylinder." Experiments in Fluids 54, no. 2 (2013).

[viii] Hodge, C., 1991. All About Saguaros. Arizona Highways Publisher, Phoenix.

[ix] Letchford, C.W., D.C. Lander, P. Case, A. Dyson, and M. Amitay. "Bio-mimicry inspired tall buildings: The response of cactus-like buildings to wind action at Reynolds Number of 104." Journal of Wind Engineering and Industrial Aerodynamics 150 (2016): 22-30.

[x] Lurie-Luke, Elena. "Product and technology innovation: What can biomimicry inspire?" Biotechnology Advances 32, no. 8 (2014): 1494-505.

[xi] Yiatros, S., M. A. Wadee, and G. R. Hunt. "The load-bearing duct: biomimicry in structural design." Proceedings of the Institution of Civil Engineers - Engineering Sustainability 160, no. 4 (2007): 179-88.

[xii] Holstov, Artem, Ben Bridgens, and Graham Farmer. "Hygromorphic materials for sustainable responsive architecture." Construction and Building Materials 98 (2015): 570-82.

[xiii] Rian, Iasef Md, and Mario Sassone. "Tree-inspired dendriforms and fractal-like branching structures in architecture: A brief historical overview." Frontiers of Architectural Research 3, no. 3 (2014): 298-323.

[xiv] Mashhadiali, Niloufar, and Ali Kheyroddin. "Proposing the hexagrid system as a new structural system for tall buildings." The Structural Design of Tall and Special Buildings 22, no. 17 (2012): 1310-329.

[xv] Aziz, Moheb Sabry, and Amr Y. El Sherif. "Biomimicry as an approach for bio-inspired structure with the aid of computation." Alexandria Engineering Journal55, no. 1 (2016): 707-14.

[xvi] Badarnah, Lidia. "A Biophysical Framework of Heat Regulation Strategies for the Design of Biomimetic Building Envelopes." Procedia Engineering 118 (2015): 1225-235.

[xvii] Eldin, N. Nour, A. Abdou, and I. Abd Elgawad. "Biomimetic Potentials for Building Envelope Adaptation in Egypt." Procedia Environmental Sciences 34 (2016): 375-86.

[xviii] Radwan, Gehan.a.n., and Nouran Osama. "Biomimicry, an Approach, for Energy Effecient Building Skin Design." Procedia Environmental Sciences 34 (2016): 178-89.

[xix] El-Zeiny, Rasha Mahmoud Ali. "Biomimicry as a Problem Solving Methodology in Interior Architecture." Procedia - Social and Behavioral Sciences 50 (2012): 502-12.

[xx] Tavsan, Filiz, and Elif Sonmez. "Biomimicry in Furniture Design." Procedia - Social and Behavioral Sciences 197 (2015): 2285-292.

[xxi] Hensel, Michael. "Performance-Oriented Architecture." Willey and Son, 2013.

[xxii] Sarkisian, M., P. Lee, E. Long, and D. Shook. "Organic and Natural Forms in Building Design." Structures Congress 2010 (2010)

[xxiii] Isaacs, Allison Jean. "Self-organizational Architecture: Design Through Form-Finding Methods". Master Thesis, Georgia Institute of Technology, 2008

[xxiv] Vincent, Julian F. Structural Biomaterials. New York. Wiley, 1982.

[xxv] Peters, Brady; Peters, Terri. "Inside Smartgeometry: Expanding the Architectural Possibilities of Computational Design." Willey and Son, 2013.

[xxvi] Drew, Philip. "Frei Otto: Form and Structure" Boulder, CO: Westview Press, 1976.

[xxvii] McCulloch, W. S., in Biological prototypes and synthetic systems, E.E. Bernard, Morley and R. Ka eds., vol. 1, Plenum Press, New York, 1962, pp. 393-97; quot. p. 393.

[xxviii] Benyus, Jane. "Biomimicry Innovation Inspired by Nature" HarperCollins. 1997

[xxix] Moheb Sabry Aziz, Amr Y. El Sherif. "Biomimicry as an approach for bio-inspried structure with the aid of computation". Alexandria Engineering Journal. Vol 55 (2016): 707-714

[xxx] Yiatros, Stylianos, M. Ahmer Wadee, and Gary R. Hunt. "The load-bearing duct: biomimicry in structural design." Proceedings- Institution of civil engineers engineering sustainability. Vol. 160, 2007

[xxxi] Sarkisian, Mark. "Designing Tall Buildings: Structure as Architecture". Routledge. 2012

[xxxii] Taylor, D., Kinane, B., Sweeney, C. et al. Wood Sci Technol (2015) 49: 345. doi:10.1007/s00226-014-0694-4

Constructing Relationships: Exploring the Correlation between Project Structures and Design Outcomes

Caryn Brause
University of Massachusetts Amherst

Abstract

As the profession develops ever more collaborative project structures and delivery models, it is necessary to consider how the ultimate value of these models will be transmitted to current and emerging practitioners. This paper documents pedagogical research that employs an experiential model for integrating these professional practice issues into design curricula. Original objectives of the *Voices from the Field* course focused on introducing students to the relationship between concept design and technical execution. Testing the format across varied project types, delivery methods, scales of operation, and practice models with a range of practitioners, however, addressed a much larger realm of concerns than initially hypothesized. The focus of the course has thus expanded, with an increasing emphasis on examining the connection between the quality of collaborative working relationships and the successful manifestation of design intent. The paper posits that, among professional practice topics, contracts and delivery methods may seem abstract and difficult to grasp for students who have little practice experience. It explores whether experiencing the realization of spaces, details, and materials that are a direct result of the project structures would make these relationships more understandable to students. By sensitizing students to the value of collaborative behaviors as an essential ingredient to creating advanced architecture, the course supports the shift in the culture of the building industry toward greater and more productive collaborative practices.

Introduction

For the multiple agents involved in contemporary design and construction projects, the task of transforming a design concept into a constructed reality remains an ongoing challenge. Design activities rarely end at 100% completion of the contracted design phase of a project; often they continue throughout its construction and even occupation. In this context, the building process may be reconceived as a series of information operations in which "the initial building representation is progressively enriched and completed through a process of accretion by bits and pieces that takes place during and by means of the interaction of project participants."[1]

Traditional tactics for bridging poetic conception and pragmatic realization emphasize clarity and rigor in the production of documentation that communicates design intent to fabricators and constructors. This is followed up with an uncompromising attitude toward construction administration, which is frequently learned on the jobsite through modeling and mentoring. At a more detailed level, the design team may employ mechanisms such as construction mockups early in the design process, as well as punchlists at its conclusion, to further align concept and realization. A tactic less visible and yet highly effective in ultimately assuring the successful execution of design decisions is the careful structuring of relationships among the project's various agents.

This paper documents pedagogical research that makes a clear connection between successful collaborative working relationships and the manifestation of design intent. The research examines the *Voices from the Field* course, an experiential model for integrating professional practice issues into the design curriculum. Original course objectives focused on introducing students to the relationship between conceptual and technical execution by reviewing project documentation and then visiting construction sites to discuss issues of design, materials, methods and constructability. However, while testing the course format through several semesters and across varied project types and delivery methods, and by interacting with a range of project agents, the focus of the course notably shifted, with an increasing emphasis on project structure and relationships.

This paper will focus on two of the projects examined in the course, which feature different project types and contract structures. The first project involves a higher educational residential building executed by a nationally recognized design firm working collaboratively with a local associate architect. The second project examines a complex hospital project executed through an IPD contract. By analyzing student assignments, both quantitatively and qualitatively, for evidence correlating relationships among project agents to successful design realization, the paper establishes a pedagogical method for connecting these professional practice issues to design concerns.

Practice Context

On the search for technological workflows and delivery modes that facilitate a move toward greater integration of design and building, Marty Doscher, Vice President at Dassault Systemes, writes,

> "The act of design is a complex network of interactions across teams. The architect is becoming an integrator of increasingly complex design information generated by ever larger and more diverse teams. This role seems to have arisen not by choice but as a pragmatic response to the growing complexity of executing built work, and the desire to get through the construction process with the design as intact as possible."[2]

Whereas architects aim to preserve their design agendas, owners seek more predictable results from construction projects, such as higher performance and lower project risk. To achieve their goals, owners look to project structures that ensure greater integration between team members. Methods that provide for the early integration of all disciplines, combined with better communication and collaboration among all parties, provide some of the most effective mitigation of overall project risks.[3]

Many architects, owners, and contractors achieve high levels of collaboration regardless of contract or delivery method. However, research shows that collaborative team behaviors can be fostered by IPD contracts when these are aligned with practices that support a team culture wherein members are willing and able to engage in collaborative problem solving to address project challenges.[4] Projects delivered by IPD currently account for only a small share of the construction market: in 2015 only three percent of projects by dollar volume used this method.[5] This approach is expected to increase in the coming years, however, particularly as its concurrent use with BIM becomes more widespread.[6] Moreover, the collaborative strategies of IPD are impacting the industry: many project teams are adopting similar structures and employing similar strategies in order to build mutual trust and respect, foster communication, and increase knowledge sharing.[7]

Voices from the Field

The *Voices from the Field* course was originally developed as a response to the *2012 NCARB Practice Analysis Education Report*. The *Practice Analysis* findings identified eight areas requiring additional focus and reinforcement in academic curricula: collaboration, as well as communication, professional conduct, practice and project management, site design, constructability, sustainability, and technology.

The initial objective of the course, which was piloted in the Spring semester of 2014, was to bridge education and practice by increasing students' understanding of the relationship between concept design and technical execution. Whereas constructability was certainly a primary focus, the intention was to expose students to the complex web of factors that go into taking design decisions to realization. The structure of the course combines classroom time with fieldwork. First, students review project documentation to understand its role in communicating design detailing for construction. Then, they attend site visits with project agents such as architects, construction managers, owner's project managers, and engineers. This enables students to gain direct experience of the construction process and to become familiar with roles of various agents during construction.

Students are evaluated on several individual and group efforts: general participation and contribution to the discourse; team facilitation of a pre-site visit seminar to present context for the project; submission of individual field reports following each site visit; and a final project comprising a short, reflective paper or an instructor-administered survey, designed to synthesize their experiences. The final two deliverables provide an opportunity to measure student learning outcomes with respect to established and emerging course objectives.

Research Questions

After its initial offering in Spring 2014, *Voices from the Field* was tested again in Fall 2014 and further developed in Fall 2015. Early stages of the research inquired as to whether sampling available projects from a mostly rural region would enable the course to cover a sufficiently broad spectrum of project types, issues, and professional roles to address the *Practice Analysis* Recurring Themes.[8] Ongoing research investigates whether the situated learning that occurs through personal observation and interaction with practitioners on the construction site yields a deeper integration of concepts typically covered in a comprehensive but compartmentalized manner.[9] In this paper, the author looks more closely at two course deliverables in order to evaluate how this method of teaching can contribute to student understanding of the relationship between project structures and design outcomes.

Exploring the Correlation between Project Relationships and Design Outcomes

As suggested above, the student-created Field Reports provide one important method for assessing students' increasing understanding of the correlation between project structures and relationships to design outcomes. In their reports, students juxtaposed photographs with annotated excerpts from construction documents and added written descriptions of the transformations that occur from drawing to construction. In their reports, they also illuminated aspects of the design and construction process that were not readily apparent from the documentation alone: in particular, issues of project management and delivery, construction scheduling,

collaboration, the role of technology, and professional conduct.

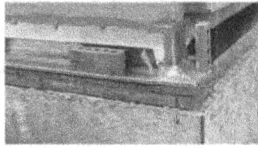
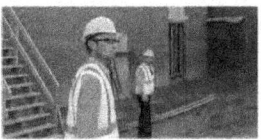
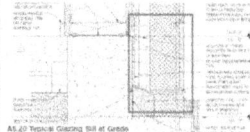

Fig. 1. Field Report: "Observation" documenting the role of the Associate Architects (Dylan Brown, 2015).

Each Field Report comprised eight to ten distinct "Observations," and students were required to submit five reports per semester; some students made multiple points per "Observation." (Fig. 1) In 2014, there were fourteen students in the spring course and twelve students in the fall course; each project's Field Reports yielded 120-40 observations, a total of 1492 data points. With eight students in the Fall 2015 course, each project's Field Report yielded 50-60 observations, yielding a total of 350 data points. At the end of each semester, these data points continue to be analyzed with respect to how often the eight areas identified by the 2012 Practice Analysis requiring additional focus and reinforcement in academic curricula are discussed. Additional recurring thematic issues emerge each semester and these are added to the coding process.

The emergent themes that are brought forth through the data in Field Reports has led to new final deliverables that can best address the course cohort and respond to refinements in the instructor's research paradigm. During the initial offering, students were required to submit an essay reflecting on their overall experience. Many students wrote about how their perspective on practice had changed and how the course affected their thinking about their future plans. In an effort to analyze more precisely the relationship between student learning and the topics identified in the *Practice Analysis*, the culminating assignment of the Fall 2014 course offering was changed from an essay to a survey. Questions employed specific language adopted from the *2012 Practice Analysis*.

In the course's third iteration, Fall 2015, the final deliverable comprised a short paper and accompanying diagram that considered one or more of the studied projects in the larger context of architectural design and realization. Students were asked to analyze their collected evidence regarding the project team, their roles, how the projects were structured, and their collaborative processes. They were also instructed to reflect on the specific ways that they understood these relationships to have impacted the project outcomes. In these papers, students were able to draw connections across multiple projects and had considerably more freedom than in the prescriptive Field Reports to choose practice topics that broadly interested them.

Students visit five projects per semester; the course has revisited projects in a subsequent semester to observe a different phase of construction such that twelve projects have been analyzed over three semesters. As a result of valuable data from the Fall 2014 semester studying an IPD project, this project was revisited and a new deliverable was introduced in Fall 2015. Two of the projects from this most recent semester are particularly worthy of closer analysis. These feature different project types and contracts, which help in considering whether this method of experiential learning—through interaction with practitioners and personal observation on construction sites—yields insights into the essential role played by relationships among project agents to successful design realization. By first analyzing deliverables from each project and then discussing them in aggregate, certain learning outcomes become apparent.

Residential Housing Complex

In Fall 2015 students visited a residential building complex at a higher educational institution comprising twenty apartment units in five buildings. Prior to visiting this $11.3 million, 34,000-square-foot project, most students had only limited experience on construction sites and no knowledge of the architect's role during construction. This proved an auspicious start to the course, as students were able to witness every phase of construction, from wood framing, MEP work and brick cladding to window installation, insulation and interior finishing. In one largely completed building, students experienced the near-final realization of the design.

Filled with details of materials and methods they encountered on site, the students' Field Reports bear evidence of their learning. Out of the sixty reports submitted, more than half concerned constructability, with brickwork, insulation, window details, flashing, and roof details claiming the most interest. Interestingly, most students also wrote in detail about the nuances of the relationships they observed between the project agents. These agents included a nationally-recognized architecture firm working collaboratively with a local associate architect. The project departs from standard practice, in which a client hires a Design Architect to create a design which is then handed off to a local Architect-of-Record for construction documentation and supervision. Instead, on this project the Design Architect produced the construction documentation and the local Associate Architect worked with the Design Architect continuously from the Schematic Design phase through Construction Administration.

After touring the project with members of the Associate Architect's firm, students commented in their Field Notes on the productive and valuable nature of the team structure they witnessed: the Design Architects contributed their exacting design sensibility, their attention to details, and their broad vision, while the Associate Architects contributed their commitment to advanced building performance standards, knowledge of local building culture, and a longstanding and trusting relationship with the client.

Several students, for example, pointed in their Field Report to the Associate Architect's success in brokering a new detail for flashing included at the bottom of a brick wall. The original plan was to paint the flashing, but anticipating the client's objection to ongoing maintenance costs associated with paint, the Associate Architect advocated substituting a lower-maintenance material. The Associate Architect was then able to redirect the money saved by this change to reintroduce canopies important to the

Design Architect but value-engineered out of the project at an earlier stage.

Several students pointed out other examples of the Associate Architect acting as an "advocate" for the Design Architect during the decision-making process. For example, each of the buildings features small bedrooms and a large living room. To emphasize the importance of the communal space, the Design Architect provided a double-height space with a large bank of windows. Achieving this composition required some additional drywall framing, leading the contractors to question the time, money, and effort required to achieve it. The Associate Architects argued successfully for this work in order to meet the designers' spatial and daylighting objectives. Walking through the finished space, students appreciated how this extra effort contributed to the quality of the space; many described the Associate Architect's intervention in their Field Reports.

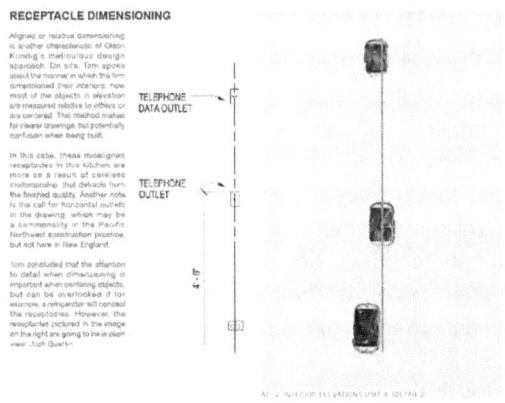

Fig. 2. Design tolerances (Josh Guertin, 2015)

Students also perceived instances where the Associate Architect acted as a "translator" for the Design Architect, communicating their particular approach to other agents. For example, the Design Architect employs tight tolerances and alignments to achieve their clean minimalist detailing. The contractors were less familiar with this meticulous method of detailing. This required the Associate Architect to act as a translator to insure that the contractors successfully complied. Students recorded observations of these interventions in areas ranging from brick coursing and window buck

detailing to the alignment of receptacles, light fixtures, and other interior features. (Fig. 2)

Students also recorded in their Field Notes other occasions in which the Associate Architect advocated on behalf of the contractor. This ability of one party to operate on behalf of another selectively (students frequently made reference to "both sides," meaning both client and Design Architect, or both contractor and Design Architect) demonstrated the complexity of relationships on the jobsite and the critical value of navigating them skillfully. These real world examples made clear to students that the successful navigation of project relationships leads to better overall design outcomes

Healthcare Fit-Out

In Fall 2014 and Fall 2015, students visited a 90,000-square-foot addition to a healthcare facility, which included a new inpatient pharmacy. This $40 million project is unique in that approximately forty-five percent of the building area was designed as shell space for future growth. During the 2014 visit, students saw many different stages of construction including framing, drywall, insulation, flooring, and utility rough-ins. They also observed a mock-up patient room, which was used for collaborative problem solving as well as to gain consensus among project stakeholders regarding design options and material choices. During the Fall 2015 visit, students were able to observe more of the design realization and compare it with the shell space. While this was the most complex project visited throughout the course, it was also the last: armed with additional site experience, students were able to identify many of the typical construction details they had observed elsewhere and focus on those that were particular to the project at hand or healthcare facilities generally.

The project was delivered through a tri-party Integrated Project Delivery (IPD) contract. IPD partners included the Owner, the Architect, the Construction Manager, the Mechanical Contractor, the Electrical Contractor, and the MEP Engineers. Both semesters, students met with the Project Manager and several of the architects to learn about the principles of IPD and its implementation on this project. Greater design quality, client satisfaction, and cost savings, as well as an accelerated schedule emerged in these discussions as benefits of the project's use of IPD.

Student Field Reports from both semesters as well as final papers from the Fall 2015 semester provide evidence of student learning. Reports remarked on the intensive MEP coordination necessary for a project of this complexity. Students were also impressed with the care given to design for occupant comfort. (Fig. 3) They paid particular attention to the hospitality-like indirect lighting strategies that they experienced. They were also impressed by the unique hospital features such as the narcotics vault, the network of pneumatic tubes for prescription delivery, the detailing of bariatric rooms, and the pre-fabricated headwall panels.

Because the project progressed from one phase of construction to the next, student observations differed. Fall 2014 reports focused heavily on construction, with a great many students noting the difficulties associated with managing an active construction project in the midst of an operational hospital. Over sixty percent of data points concerned constructability while twenty-seven percent focused on project management, collaboration, and project delivery; only eight percent focused on design. By Fall 2015 many areas of the project were complete; more students focused on design realization, with a greater interest in finishes. These reports also demonstrated an understanding of unique concerns for healthcare projects, such as maintenance, security, and sanitary requirements. Thirty-seven percent of data points focused on design, while twenty-three percent concerned constructability and seventeen percent focused on project management, collaboration, and project delivery.

The Fall 2014 Observations clearly document student understanding of the collaboration required to reach the client's goals and realize the designers' intent. Almost all students wrote about the full-scale patient room mockup: the mockup sequence started out rough, in cardboard, and was gradually refined as materials were applied and tested. Students recognized that this iterative process was used to both solicit end-user feedback as well as refine details in order to achieve a forty-six percent cost savings compared to earlier project phases. Nearly all students recognized that the high level of early

trade engagement provided input to achieve very integrated solutions. For example, most Field Reports documented the prefabricated headwall panel that supplies utilities at each bed; students noted that this solution integrated early MEP and millwork trade expertise to save time on future field coordination issues while maintaining finish quality.

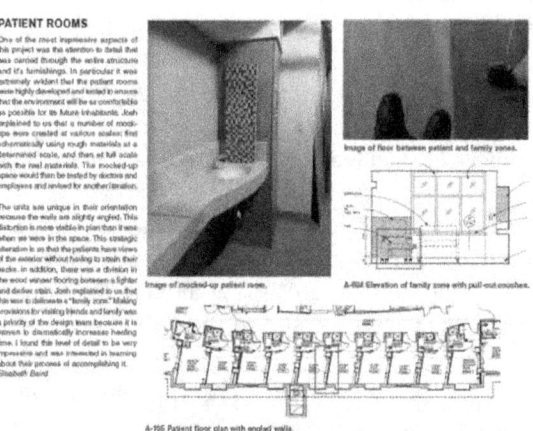

Fig. 3. Patient Room development (Elisabeth Baird, 2014).

Field Reports from the Fall 2015 semester which documented the impact of the IPD method focused on project efficiencies, including increased communication, easier coordination of trades, and reductions in cost and schedule. Student observations indicate they understood the value to design afforded by cost estimating in real time rather than after design is complete, which the team had identified as central to the project's success.

Along with the Field Reports, in the Fall 2015 final paper and accompanying diagram, students reflected on specific ways they understood the structuring of project relationships to have impacted the project outcomes. Half of the students focused on the healthcare project and its delivery method, whereas a few compared the outcomes of IPD with the delivery methods used on other projects they had studied during the semester.

While the Field Reports examined specific design and construction elements, the paper and diagram permitted students to reflect on the larger project context. First and foremost, students noted how in the IPD project the shared risk and reward structure seemed to them to mean that everyone was working toward a single goal. They also focused on the significant difference in project timelines, pointing out that the IPD structure "leveraged early contributions of knowledge and expertise." (Fig. 4) One student noted, "Designers fully understand the ramifications of their decisions at the time the decisions are made and the contractors know how to organize construction based on the architectural design." Students perceived a clear benefit to the architect: "IPD allows for more extensive pre-construction efforts related to resolving potential design conflicts that traditionally may not be discovered until construction." This eliminates the need for "hacking off design elements deemed too expensive" or "sacrificing design intentions" during value engineering. Students found evidence that IPD reduced conflicts, especially over design goals.

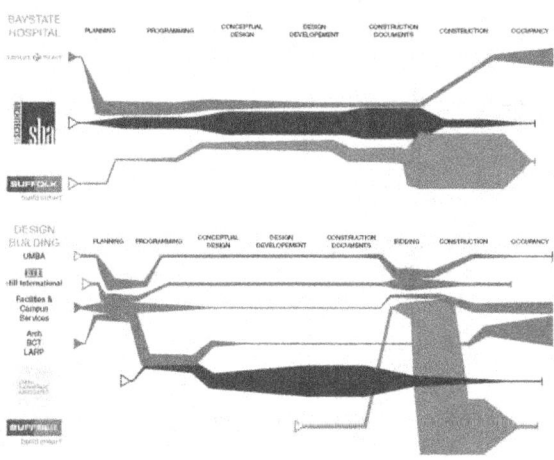

Fig. 4. Comparative timeline for the integration of team members. (Dylan Brown, 2015)

Comparing this project to the *Residential Housing Complex*, another student wrote, "[At the Hospital Fit-Out] I picked up on the support and flexibility of problem solving. The constant conversation that occurs before and during construction amongst all parties enables a more fluid operation. In comparing the tone, coordination and problem solving experienced on both sites, IPD proves...superior... This flexibility sets the tone of the project. There was a willingness to adapt the design to the wants and need of the occupants of [the hospital project]. There was a more rigid tone within the Housing Project...I sensed a more practical tone in the suggested changes of the design." Students found evidence that project structures directly influenced collaborative behavior, which they increasingly valued.

Discussion

Architectural educators employ experiential projects to increase student understanding of a variety of subjects, from site, culture and sustainability to structures, materials, and detailing.[10] By comparison, professional practice topics have been less typically explored through these means. Abstract and intangible in nature, subjects such as contracting, scheduling, project structuring and delivery may be among the most difficult for students with limited exposure to practice to "experience." However, as the profession looks for ways to shorten the licensure process, eliminating months or even years of internship in a practice setting, it is necessary to examine how these issues may be addressed in a situated learning environment within the academy. By locating professional practice learning within active construction projects, and by allowing students to experience the spaces, details, and materials that result directly from varied project structures, students are better able to visualize the impact of project relationships on design outcomes.

Analysis of the data extracted from the course deliverables demonstrates an increased understanding of this relationship among *Voices from the Field* participants. Although the course will continue to explore materials and methods as its baseline, in order to more fully investigate issues such as interaction among project agents, some experimentation is still needed. The Fall 2015 deliverables enabled students to engage the topic more deeply when students grappled with constructing the web of project relationships graphically to produce the assigned diagram. The most successful papers and diagrams were those created by students who chose to compare multiple projects, as they needed to identify project and team variables, and connect those variables to project outcomes. These successes suggest that future assignments might, at minimum, require comparisons between projects to enable students to assess evidence of each teams' achievement of project goals across several dimensions—for example, time, budget, building performance metrics, user satisfaction, and quality of design.

Future course experimentation might also include helping students develop a more rigorous interview methodology in order to extract richer material from their interactions with practitioners. Prior to site visits, students currently generate a collective list of questions for the practitioners with whom they will meet. In the future, students might be encouraged to standardize the list of questions; more in-depth, project-specific questions might be added subsequently. The setting for the interview may also be reconsidered. Interaction with practitioners typically occurs on the construction site, when students are excited and overwhelmed by construction activity. Practitioners have occasionally met with the class in advance in a seminar setting. One variable that has not yet been tested involves interviewing practitioners after the site visit, when students have had time to reflect on the experience; this might produce a different set of understandings. A final modification might relate to documentation. Some site visits were videotaped with recordings available afterwards to students. Field reports from recorded and non-recorded site visits might be compared to see if recording yielded greater integration of knowledge.

Conclusion

The experiential format of the *Voices from the Field* course provides an opportunity for students to gain an understanding of the dynamics of design decision-making as projects progress from inception to realization. The course has continued to shift and refine its focus on project relationships by altering the final deliverables, recalibrating and deepening student learning in an area that often remains opaque to students. By applying what we know to be an effective pedagogical method of experiential learning to professional practice topics, and especially to issues surrounding project agent interaction and relationships, we can heighten student awareness of the collaborative aspects of contemporary practice. One emerging goal of the *Voices* course is to advance this shift in the culture of the industry by imbuing students about to enter the workforce with not only an understanding of collaborative processes that will increasingly typify twenty-first century building but also an appreciation for the value of collaborative behaviors as essential ingredients from which to create better designed, more advanced, and highly innovative architecture.

Notes:

[1] Pietroforte, Roberto, Paulo Tombesi, and Daniel D. Lebiedz. "Are Physical Mock-Ups Still Necessary to Complement Visual Models for the Realization of Design Intents?" Journal of Architectural Engineering 18, no. 1 (March 2012): 34–41.

[2] Doscher was previously Technology Director of Morphosis Architects for eight years. Marty Doscher, "Disposable Code; Persistent Design," in Digital Workflows in Architecture: Designing Design -- Designing Assembly -- Designing Industry, ed. Scott Marble (Basel: Birkhäuser, 2012), 211.

[3] A 2017 study of construction industry risk found that 91% of respondents agreed that the most effective risk mitigation strategies are those that enhance collaboration. "Managing Risk in the Construction Industry," SmartMarket Report (Bedford, MA: Dodge Data & Analytics, 2017), p.1-5, 37. http://www.bim.construction.com/research/.

[4] See Renee Cheng, "Motivation and Means: How and Why IPD and Lean Lead to Success" (University of Minnesota, 2016), http://arch.design.umn.edu/directory/chengr/documents/motivation_means2016.pdf.

[5] American Institute of Architects, "The Business of Architecture 2016: AIA Firm Report" (Washington, DC, 2016), 74.

[6] "Project Delivery Systems: How They Impact Efficiency and Profitability in the Building Sector," SmartMarket Report (Bedford, MA: McGraw Hill Construction, 2014), http://construction.com/about-us/press/construction-project-delivery-systems-vary-widely-in-benefits.asp.

[7] See Renee Cheng and Katy Dale, "IPD Case Studies" (AIA Center for Integrated Practice, AIA Minnesota, and University of Minnesota School of Architecture, 2012), http://www.aia.org/about/initiatives/AIAB087494.

[8] Brause, C., "Intern Architects in the Academy: Preparing for Future Practice," Future of Architectural Research: Proceedings of the 2015 ARCC Conference, Chicago, IL 2015, 627-634.

[9] Brause, C., "Foraging for the Curriculum: Sourcing Local Projects for an Integrated Understanding of Issues Central to Practice," Intersections and Adjacencies: Proceedings of the 2015 Building Technology Educators' Society Conference, Salt Lake City, UT, 2015, 167-174.

[10] On architectural education's emphasis on learning by doing, see Simon, Madlen, "Design Pedagogy," in Architecture School: Three Centuries of Educating Architects in North America, ed. Ockman, Joan and Williamson, Rebecca (Cambridge, MA: MIT Press, 2012), 276–85.

Building Structural Education: An Examination of Textbooks Used to Teach Structures to Architectural Students

Marci S. Uihlein
University of Illinois at Urbana-Champaign

Patrick Tripeny
University of Utah

Abstract

For almost as long as there has been university architectural education within the United States, there have been textbooks on structures. These textbooks cover basic, centuries old subjects such as statics and stress, but also give an indication of the time in which they are written. This paper examines architectural structures textbooks to gain insight and knowledge on the development of the teaching of structures. There is a lineage of textbooks begun in a search not only for the earliest structural textbooks, but for what inspired them. N. Clifford Ricker's *Elementary Graphic Statics and the Construction of Trussed Roofs* (1885) was influenced by Culmann's *Die graphische Statik* (1865), and *Simplified Engineering for Architects and Builders* began in 1938 by Harry Parker with the twelfth edition by Ambrose and Tripeny issued in 2016. A case study of the architectural program at the University of Illinois gives examples of what textbooks were used at the turn of the twentieth century. Besides historic examples, contemporary textbooks are many and vary from the image oriented, such as Francis D.K. Ching's *Building Structures Illustrated*, to the more engineering based like Beer, Johnson, and DeWolf's *Mechanics for Engineers – Statics*. This textbook study will give an idea of what and how structures have been taught, and an indication of who is shaping the educational knowledge.

Introduction

This paper began with a curiosity about the evolution of structural textbooks, primarily those used to teach architects about structures. Who wrote them; what is the taken perspective; and how have these books and instruction methods changed over time? An analysis and investigation of these pedagogic tools could be expected to reveal the teaching emphasis of the author, reflect something about the state of practice at the time it was written, and identify the ubiquitous construction materials. Thus, a textbook is interesting not only for the subject it covers, but for the information embedded within its text and/or omissions. The research into structural textbooks is equally engaging as it is an investigation into historic educational and curricular models as well as a genealogy of thought, passed from one author to another. Also, some knowledge of publication history is needed. The work presented here represents the initial investigation into the subject. While not comprehensive at this stage, the findings thus far are presented through an examination of a lineage of structural textbooks and a case study on structural texts from 1891-1911 at the University of Illinois at Urbana-Champaign. Structural textbooks have a rich history that demonstrates the attempt to balance engineering and architecture.

Historic Roots

The roots of structural knowledge are apparent in the subjects that are taught today. Galileo's (1564 - 1642) book *Discorsi e Dimostrazioni Matematiche, intorno a due nuove scienze*, or *Discourses and Mathematical Demonstrations Relating to Two New Sciences* (1638), highlighted the strength of materials as one of the new sciences. In this work, tensile and bending tests of structural members are illustrated in such a way that they would be recognized in any structures class today. In 1687, Isaac Newton (1642 - 1726) published his work *Mathematical Principle of Natural Philosophy*, which includes his three laws or axioms. Robert Hooke's (1635 - 1703) work on elasticity, and Hooke's law ($\sigma = \varepsilon * E$) is seen as the "foundation" of elastic materials.[1] The *Ecole Polytechnique* became an influential force in education at the end of the eighteenth century, with French and English engineering experimentation advancing the field into the nineteenth century. It is the development of German engineering schools after the Napoleonic Wars that yield the seeds of structural textbooks. As engineer, author, and engineering scholar Stephen P. Timoshenko states, these German engineers wrote "more practical books in engineering mechanics."[2]

These researchers, educators, and engineers did work in discrete areas of applied mechanics such as suspension bridges, but no text brings it together in a single document or book until Julius Weisbach (1806-1871).[3] In 1845, he published an encyclopedia of applied mechanics that carries an English title of *Principles of the Mechanics of Machinery and Engineering* with an English edition following in 1847.[4] Weisbach follows this up with an engineering manual that was meant to be a compendium to the encyclopedia in 1848 with the work titled *Der Ingenier* (the Engineer). This was a compact and orderly compilation of carefully selected rules, formula and tables. Intended to be used by a working engineer, there were three parts to volume (arithmetic, geometry and mechanics). Of note, Weisbach was the first person to represent bending moments in beams graphically. Other manuals were produced similar to Weisbach. In the United States, this included *The Civil Engineer's Pocket Book* by John Trautwine in 1887.[5] This book was replaced in 1912 by Mansfield Merriman's *American Civil Engineer's' Pocket Book*.[6] The German authors refer to their books as "brochures" while the American authors refer to them as "pocket books." Both of these terms are a bit deceiving from the contemporary perspective as they typically more than a 1200 pages. A contemporary book familiar to many that would be equivalent in length and content would be the "Steel Manual" by AISC.

These manuals might be considered the beginning of the genre of textbooks for civil engineering in the United States. These texts could be considered the single text for civil engineering as they contain topics related to structures but also other civil engineering topics including steam locomotion, surveying, dredging, drilling, etc. They are much greater in content than one would find in a contemporary structures textbook either for civil engineers or architects. But is in these books that there are chapters that could be used to teach structures to architecture students today. Notation has changed and graphics within the books is limited but the concepts and equations are already set. In Trautwine's 1875 book, there are chapters on Statics, Dynamics and Strength of Materials. He includes a table of moment and stress that could be taken directly from any contemporary textbook (Figure 1). Trautwine's book is filled with the graphical methods of analysis including truss analysis and determining reactive forces. There is plenty of algebra and trigonometry but is solutions common to forces and force systems are graphical. There is no reference to the Methods of Joints or Sections in the truss analysis. The Euler equation of buckling is recognizable but is not in a fashion commonly adopted now. Bending moment and shear diagrams are taking as a series of free body diagrams and then plotting the results. Typically, the bending moment diagram appears above the shear diagram. By the time Merriman's book is published in 1911, many of these differences have evolved into concepts and equations that are easily recognizable to a contemporary structures student. Trusses are solved first by the graphical method but then are also solved using algebraic methods. The solving of reactive forces is done by summing moments and forces vertical. The construction of shear diagrams is directly related to the loading diagram while the bending moment diagram is still constructed by plotting free body diagrams. Merriman's includes an early inclusion of live loading codes and values. These live loads are for the cities of New York City, Chicago, Philadelphia and Boston as there was no uniform code.

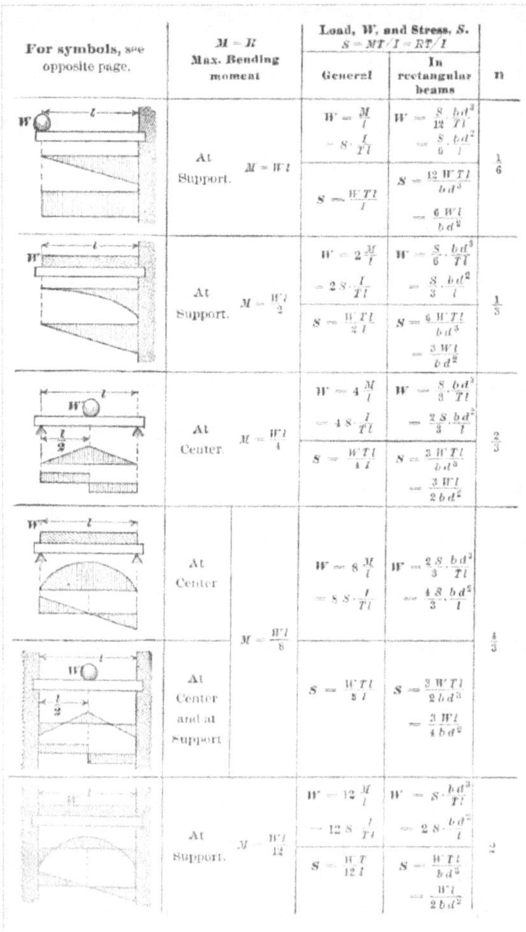

Fig. 1 - Trautwine's Table about Bending Moments and Shear Diagrams.

The first book discovered during this project that limited its content to that of structural engineering for architecture was Harry Parker's 1938 book *Simplified Engineering for Architects and Builders*.[7] In this book Parker removes all aspects of civil engineering not directly related to architectural structures, and it is structural knowledge as opposed to it being combined with construction subjects. By doing so, he produced a book that was under 250 pages. He boils it down to four sections: Principles of Mechanics, Wood, Steel, Reinforced Concrete and Roof Trusses. Parker was a Professor at the University of Pennsylvania and refers to the readers of his book as students as opposed to practitioners or engineers. While this might not have been the first text in America textbook on architectural structures, it was the first widely distributed without containing materials for a larger ivil engineering audience. Parker quickly followed this

book with more in depth separate texts of similar size on timber, steel, reinforced concrete and roof trusses.

An Example, the University of Illinois

As part of this research, it is necessary to collect the titles of textbooks that various architectural institutions have used. The University of Illinois at Urbana-Champaign will be used here to illustrate an example of the selection of structural course books. This institution was chosen in part for the ease of access to historic sources, and because this university (1868) was one of the first five architectural educational programs alongside MIT (1865), Cornell (1871), Syracuse (1873), and Columbia (1881).[8] The age of University of Illinois means that if the records could be found, it is possible to trace the selection and the changes of focus happened over a period of one-hundred years. However, for the earliest years, information is scarce for architecture program and the University. After 1873, the curriculum becomes more detailed as are the educational aims. In terms of being able to find textbook usage, information can be found starting in the 1890s. The sources that was the most fruitful has been the *Course Catalog*, also known as the *Annual Register*, or *Catalogue and Circular*.[9] These documents originate with the start of the university, and in the early days contain information about the intention of the university, curricula of various programs, and lists of students. By 1891, the courses are starting to be described more fully with learning objectives, instructors, and textbooks. The architecture curriculum had undergone a revision in 1890 with the addition of an architectural engineering program the same year. With the educational specialization in a more technical education, the architectural program was able to relax some of these requirements for architects. The listing of textbooks continues in the course descriptions until 1914.

From 1891/92 to 1910/11, there were five courses that would be recognized as part of the structural education for architects, and during this time the structures curriculum, mostly, appears to be constant. In fact, there seemed to be little change to the entire architectural curriculum, and while the department grew, the actual and intellectual leadership was held by one person. N. Clifford Ricker (1843 - 1924) was head of the department for nineteen of twenty of those years, and strictly governed the pedagogic philosophy. The faculty did grow from two to six with Ricker and James McLaren White as key faculty members for the period. As part of the structures education students took two courses taught in Civil Engineering: "Applied Mechanics" and "Strength of Materials." Both were described as softer or less technical versions of the engineering ones by similar names. The three course were taught within the Architecture Department: "Wood Construction," "Masonry and Metal Construction," and "Roofs." The courses addressing materials included a range of topics from uses, construction methods, joinery, and structural design tables.[10]   The course on Roofs include structural standards such as reactions, bending moments, and moments of inertia. Graphic statics was the basis for instruction and used to design roof trusses of metal and wood. The School of Architecture at the University of Illinois was one of the architectural programs started in a College of Engineering, and the influence of engineering can be seen in the number of scientific and mathematical classes required.

Like the courses themselves, the textbooks that were used did not vary greatly during this time (see Table 1).   The Strength of Materials course used one textbook consistently over twenty years, the material courses used two, and it was the Roofs course that varied the most.   The textbook for Strength of Materials was listed as "Merriam's Mechanics", and by 1892, this book was on its fourth edition. The full title was *A Text-book on the Mechanics of Materials and of Beams, Columns, and Shafts*.[11] Mansfield Merriman, a professor of civil engineering at Lehigh University, had not only written this standard and "pocket book" described above, but books on hydraulics, roofs and bridges, and retaining walls and dams. Merriam's Mechanics is a basic introduction to elastic behavior, and addresses structural member performance with bending, shear, deformation, tension, and compression. While variables are not entirely those used today, the arrangement of the subjects, the formulae, and visual examples could be easily recognized and used in the contemporary classroom (Figure 2). Subjects also include those that are specific to that era of construction such as rivet design and the use of wrought-iron sections.

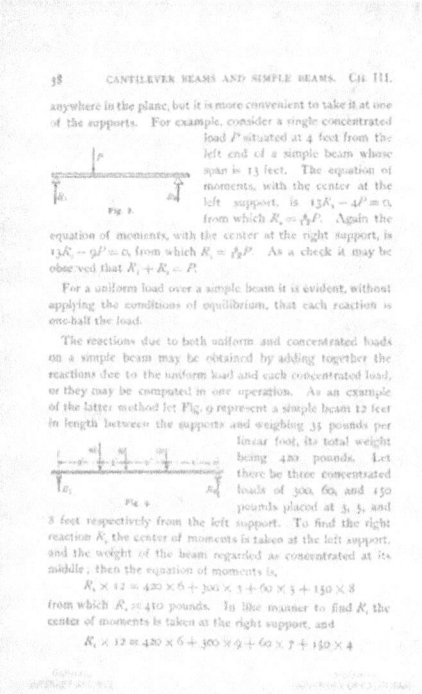

Fig. 2 – Merriman's calculation of reactions.

Ricker's Wood, Stone, Brick, and Metal Construction. was unlike other books referenced in this paper.[12] This work was written by Ricker, but reproduced through something called the "blue" process. Invented around 1878, this method was the predecessor to the blueprinting method with the majority of the page in blue with the text and drawings conveyed in white through a chemical extraction of the image. By 1880, Ricker had adapted the original method and was using it to make lecture notes for architectural and other students in the College of Engineering. The use of this method, rather than a textbook, gave the ability of the professor to transfer his knowledge completely and to provide updates quickly, rather than wait for a textbook. This speed was important during a time when changes in construction were significant and happening quickly. This "book" on materials was a holistic approach that encompassed how materials were manufactured and detailed, properties of materials, and structural design tables or formulae.   Ricker, known for his emphasis the technical aspects of architecture, saw all of information as integral to architectural education.

Architectural Structures Courses				
Applied Mechanics	**Strength of Materials**	**Wood Construction**	**Stone, Brick, and Metal Construction**	**Roofs**
Bowser's Analytical Mechanics (1891 – 1894) Peck's Elementary Mechanics (1894 – 1897) Wright's Mechanics (1897 – 1906) Morley's Mechanics for Engineers (1906 – 1911)	Merriam's Mechanics of Materials (1891 – 1911)	Ricker's Wood, Stone, Brick and Metal Construction (1893 – 1898) Kidder's Building Construction and Superintendence, Part II (1898 – 1911)	Ricker's Wood, Stone, Brick and Metal Construction (1891 – 1898) Kidder's Building Construction and Superintendence, Part I and II (1898 – 1911)	Ricker's Trussed Roofs (1891 – 1902) Ricker's Notes on Graphic Statics (1894 – 1898) Ricker's Elementary Graphic Statics (1898 – 1903) Howe's Simple Roof Trusses (1902 – 1903) Sondericker's Graphic Statics (1903 – 1910) Ricker's Notes on Graphic Statics (1909 – 1911)

Table 1. Textbooks used in Structural Courses at the University of Illinois from 1891-1911.

Ricker's *Elementary Graphic Statics and the Construction of Trussed Roofs* is aptly named.[xiii] The first section is a detailed lesson in learning graphic statics with examples to determine moments, centers of gravity, and moments of inertia (Figure 3).

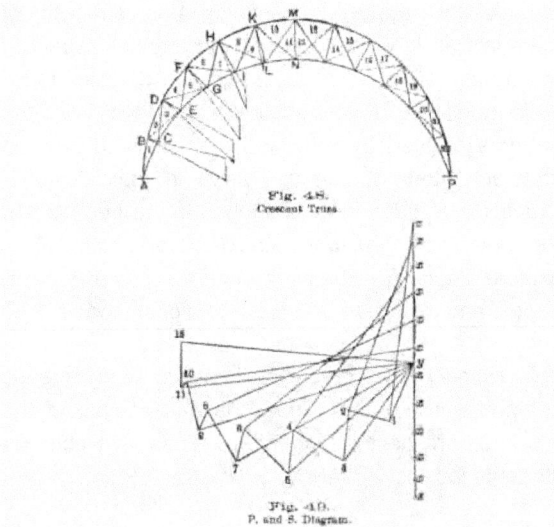

Fig. 3. Crescent truss design using graphic statics.

In continuing to reinforce his approach to a larger framing structural knowledge, there are also explanatory sections on the construction of roofs and the trusses themselves. The book concludes with graphic examples of truss details and the calculation of their strength. (Figure 4). This book was a "how-to" for designing and building roof trusses.

Ricker's notes for materials and even graphic statics books were influenced by his experience of traveling in Europe, seeing the architecture, and visiting the *Bauakademie* in Berlin in 1873 where he was inspired by its library. In addition to being a fixture in early architectural education, Ricker saw the importance of collecting and translating important architectural tomes.[xiv] In his career, he had translated thirty works including books on graphic statics by H. Muller-Breslav, H. *Graphische Statik*, vol. 1, and Wittman's *Statics*. In addition, Carl Culmann's *Die graphische Statik* is also present in Ricker's books. The early architectural education at the University of Illinois saw the influence German engineers and their publications translated through the American perspective of Ricker and the materials being used to construct buildings in the United States during the late nineteenth century.

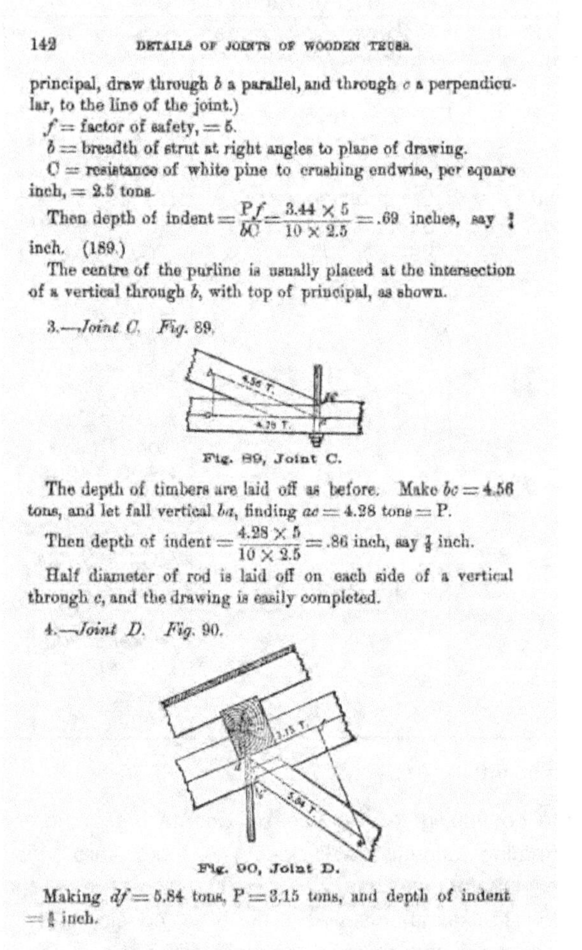

142   DETAILS OF JOINTS OF WOODEN TRUSS.

principal, draw through b a parallel, and through c a perpendicular, to the line of the joint.)

f = factor of safety, = 5.

b = breadth of strut at right angles to plane of drawing.

C = resistance of white pine to crushing endwise, per square inch, = 2.5 tons.

Then depth of indent $= \dfrac{Pf}{bC} = \dfrac{3.44 \times 5}{10 \times 2.5} = .69$ inches, say $\frac{3}{4}$ inch. (189.)

The centre of the purline is usually placed at the intersection of a vertical through b, with top of principal, as shown.

3.—*Joint C. Fig. 89.*

Fig. 89, Joint C.

The depth of timbers are laid off as before. Make $bc = 4.56$ tons, and let fall vertical ba, finding $ac = 4.28$ tons = P.

Then depth of indent $= \dfrac{4.28 \times 5}{10 \times 2.5} = .86$ inch, say $\frac{7}{8}$ inch.

Half diameter of rod is laid off on each side of a vertical through c, and the drawing is easily completed.

4.—*Joint D. Fig. 90.*

Fig. 90, Joint D.

Making $df = 5.84$ tons, P $= 3.15$ tons, and depth of indent $= \frac{5}{8}$ inch.

Fig. 4. Truss connection detailing and calculations.

Contemporary Textbooks

As discussed earlier in this paper, not much has changed with regards to the content of applied mechanics and strength of materials since the early parts of the twentieth century. Through the years, various aspects of what is taught has changed but the actual content has largely remained the same. An example of a subject that lost favor and then regained it is the use of graphic statics in particular with regards to the analysis of trusses. Many textbooks removed it during the second half of the twentieth century only to have it return to favor after Zalewski and Allen's book *Shaping Structures: Statics.*[xv] Contemporary textbooks are at least twice the size of

Parker's 1938 book while some are approaching the 1200 pages of the civil engineering texts of late nineteenth and early twentieth century. The question is what is it that they are adding to their texts to fill this space?

Many texts are following Parker's outline and including sections of their books devoted to Wood, Steel and Concrete. Not surprising that one of these is Ambrose and Tripeny's twelfth edition to *Parker's Simplified Engineering for Architect and Builders.*[xvi] Added since Parker's original text is a section on designing within a context of architecture. Another text that continues in this area is Underwood and Chiuini's text *Structural Design.*[xvii]

Another common addition to supplement the applied mechanics and strength of materials is with a greater context within architecture. Texts in this area include Onouye and Kane's *Statics and Strength of Materials for Architecture and Building Construction*, Shaeffer's *Elementary Structures for Architects and Builders*, and Sandaker and Eggen's *The Structural Basis of Architecture.*[xviii]

A structural typology approach is taken by a few architectural textbooks. In these textbooks past the mechanics, the authors explore typologies such as highrise, longspan and membrane. Schodek and Bechthold *Structures* and Schueller's *The Design of Building Structures* are both notable in this area.[xix]

A final category are textbooks that either downplay or remove the applied mechanics and strength of materials all together, focusing on another aspect of structures. Ching, Onouye and Zuberbuhler focus their book *Building Structures Illustrated* on the patterns created by structural systems and how an architect (student) can use them in their design.[xx] Cruvellier, Sandaker and Dimcheff in the book *Model Perspectives: Structure, Architecture and Culture* explore structural systems through a series of essays, photos and elaborate physical and digital models.[xxi]

This listing of contemporary texts is by no means comprehensive but are used as an example of the types of architectural structures texts available for students today.

Conclusion

This study has been filled with fascinating research into early reference texts and textbooks from the nineteenth and twentieth centuries as well as diving into the archives at the University of Illinois. It was easy to find a text and just get lost exploring various facets of it. This work was made possible partially by the ready access to many of the early works via HathiTrust's digital library (www.hathitrust.org). Through this venue, it was possible to trace the beginnings of the structures textbooks for architects from the encyclopedic reference material in Germany to the pocketbook reference material for civil engineers in America and finally to Parker's textbook meant to teach structures to architecture, architectural engineering and construction students in pre-World War II America. The search of the archives at the University of Illinois turned up many interesting observations on how faculty taught the subject of structures and how they developed their own texts before one was readily available via a publisher.

The study fell short of some of its original goals of tracing how structures was taught over time. The next phase of this study is to examine how various concepts change in the corresponding historic era. An example will be the representation of the end condition in Euler's equation for buckling. In the 1912 edition of Merriman's text, it is represented in the numerator instead of the denominator (n=1/k). How, when, and why did this change happened? Another topic would be the development of the relationships between loading, shear and bending moment diagrams. In 1938, Parker suggests to construct the shear diagram until one finds the zero shear point so one knows where to take a free body diagram to find the maximum bending moment. Other topics might include notation used in the graphic methods, representation of bending stress, teaching of non-determinate structures, etc. Finally, it will be important to examine textbook selection at other Schools of Architecture. Together, this areas of research will give a historic context to architectural educators and building structures as well as how the subject is represented in the texts used in the classroom.

Notes:

[1] Timoshenko, Stephen P. *History of Strength of Materials.* Dover Publications: New York, NY, 1983 reprint.

[2] Ibid.

[3] Weisbach, Julius. *Mechanics of Engineering and Machinery – Volume 1 and 2*, D. Van Nostrand, New York, NY, 1878.

[4] Kurrer,Karl-Eugen. *The History of the Theory of Structures: From Arch Analysis to Computational Mechanics*. Ernst & Sohn Verlag Für Architektur und technische Wissenschaften: Berlin, 2008.

[5] Trautwine, John C. *The Civil Engineer's Pocket-book*, Trautwine Company: Philadelphia, PA, 1887.

[6] Merriman, Mansfield, *American Civil Engineers' Pocket Book*, John Wiley and Sons: New York, NY, 1912.

[7] Parker, Harry, *Simplified Engineering for Architects and Builders*, John Wiley and Sons, New York, NY, 1938.

[8] Ockman, Joan. Architecture school: three centuries of educating architects in North America. MIT Press: Cambridge, MA, 2012.

[9] For example: University of Illinois. *Catalogue of the University of Illinois 1892-93*, The University: Urbana, IL, 1893.

[10] University of Illinois. *Catalogue of the University of Illinois 1897-98*, The University: Urbana, IL, 1898

[11] Merriman, Mansfield, *A Text-book on the Mechanics of Materials, and of Beams, Columns, and Shafts*, John Wiley and Sons, New York, NY,1892.

[12] Ricker's work can be found in Record Series 12/2/21, Box 1-4. University of Illinois Archives.

[xiii] Ricker, N. Clifford. *Elementary Graphic Statics and the Construction of Trussed Roofs*, William T. Comstock: New York, NY, 1892.

[xiv] Quinn, C. J. "Nathan Clifford Ricker: Translator and educator." *Arris: Journal of the Southeast Chapter of the Society of Architectural Historians*, 11 (2000): 40-54.

[xv] Zalewski, Waclaw and Edward Allen. *Shaping Structures: Statics*, John Wiley and Sons. New York, NY, 1998.

[xvi] Ambrose, James and Patrick Tripeny. *Simplified Engineering for Architects and Builders*, John Wiley and Sons: New York, NY, 2016.

[xvii] Underwood, James R. and Michele Chiuini. *Structural Design: A Practical Guide for Architects*, John Wiley and Sons: New York, NY, 1998.

[xviii] Onouye, Barry and Kevin Kane. *Statics and Strength of Materials for Architecture and Building Construction*. Prentice Hall: Boston, MA, 2012.

Shaeffer, R.E. *Elementary Structures for Architects and Builders*, Pearson: New Jersey, 2007.

Sandaker, Bjorn and Arne Eggen. *The Structural Basis of Architecture*, Watson-Guptill Publications: New York, NY, 1992.

[xix] Schodek, Daniel and Martin Bechthold. *Structures*, Pearson/ Prentice Hall: Upper Saddle River, 2008.

Schueller, Wolfgang. *The Design of Building Structures*, Prentice Hall: Upper Saddle River, 1996.

[xx] Ching, Francis, Barry Onouye and Douglas Zuberbuhler. *Building Structures Illustrated*, John Wiley and Sons: New York, NY, 2009

[xxi] Cruvellier, Mark, Bjorn Sandaker and Luben Dimcheff. *Model Perspectives: Structure, Architecture and Culture*, Routledge: New York, NY, 2017.

Chasing Time: The Forgotten History and Evolution of the NAAB Structures Student Performance Criteria

Deborah Oakley
University of Nevada, Las Vegas

Abstract

Over the decades since its inception, the history surrounding the developments of what we know today as the Student Performance Criteria (SPC) as outlined by the National Architectural Accrediting Board (NAAB) has become somewhat lost to time. Though the NAAB was formed in 1940, it was not until the very late postwar period that the forerunner of the current SPC was first implemented in the form of "Achievement-Oriented Performance Criteria," beginning in 1982. The precise details of this evolution have unfortunately been for the most part lost and forgotten, with most of the pre-1982 archival records destroyed. The specifics surrounding much of the evolution of the Structures SPC are similarly little known.

Furthermore, with the retirement and passing of individuals involved in crafting the earlier versions, much of thinking behind this prior evolution is opaque to younger generations of structures teachers. It is little known, for instance, that in 1983 there were nine criteria related to structures out of the 88 overall, or more than 10% of the total. Through subsequent iterations over the next fifteen years, this number was reduced first to six in 1984, 1986 and 1988, then to four in 1991 and 1995, and then to a single criterion in 1998. With the 2014 *Conditions*, the sole structures criterion is now less than 4% of the 26 overall. With minimal alteration in scope and language since the publication of the 1988 Conditions, for nearly 20 years this criterion for structures has been largely unchanged.

Through a review of the existing NAAB archives and discussion with the current executive director and a past NAAB president, this paper summarizes this evolution and consolidates the changes in the structures SPC over the past several decades. It speculates on the impact that the structures SPC has had on the place and role of the principles of structural engineering in architectural curricula, thereby providing a context for future discussion.

Introduction

How much does an architectural student really need to know about structure in architecture? This has been a topic of debate for as least as long as there has been accreditation of architectural schools. The range of approaches is as varied as the many accredited architectural programs themselves, with some providing highly technical civil engineering-level coursework, while others far more conceptual. Furthermore the expectations of the NAAB SPC have evolved considerably over the past decades leading one to continued reflection on the question.

While there is no definitive agreement, one observation is that there have been arguments by distinguished individuals that an engineering calculation-based approach by itself does not serve the majority of architectural students, and in fact may cause harm in the form of students who become disengaged or even turned off to the subject. For instance, the acclaimed engineer, mathematician and Columbia University educator Mario Salvadori wrote in 1991 that "After years of trying to teach structures to architects on the basis of a mathematical approach (which was natural to me because I am a mathematician), I became convinced that the only way to introduce structures (or any other technical subject) to architects is by appealing to their sense of physical reality and presenting all of the basic principles, both elementary and sophisticated, without using mathematics. I was comforted by the results I achieved after shifting from the mathematical to the physical (some call it intuitional) approach: the students learned without trouble a subject they considered obnoxious before, became interested in the problems they at long last understood and could deal with intelligently, and, miracle of miracles, could talk with and understand me when I spoke as an engineer."[1]

Similarly, the renowned author, educator and architect Edward Allen, FAIA, has long argued that technical education must be taught as an act of design, not simply based (in the case of structures) on the mathematics of member sizing, and that by promoting such conventional education we inadvertently "destroy most students desire to learn the technology of architecture."[2]

Prior studies[3] have indicated that the majority of structures educators are themselves engineers, and thus by training lean toward a form of engineering education, even if tailored to architecture students. Many early career academics enter into a mature architectural program with an established curricular organization. This often has its basis in a traditional civil engineering format, thereby further reinforcing this approach.

Program evaluation is of course measured against requirements stipulated by NAAB. In the earliest implementations, these requirements were quite prescriptive and highly specific in the content of structures education, but over the decades have became more sweeping and general to the point where seemingly any approach is acceptable. But do many continue the calculation-based approach simply out of inertia or habit? This is not to in any way impugn those who teach a traditional engineering format, for there are many excellent and dedicated teachers who want only the best for their students. But does this approach ultimately serve the profession of today as well as it can?

The current solitary criterion for structures has existed virtually unchanged for nearly two decades, perhaps giving the impression to younger professors that it has always been this way. As will be shown, however, nothing could be further from the truth. In fact, the evolution was continual for the first 16 years and six distinct publications of the variously named *Criteria and Procedures* (years 1982, '83, '84, '86, and '88) or *Conditions and Procedures* (years 1992 & '95). It was only with the publication of the 1998 *Conditions and Procedures* that the current sole criterion emerged.

The question of what architecture students really need to know about structures is beyond the scope of this study, however the document sets the stage for such continued important discussion. "How we got to now" (to exploit the title of the popular historical science book of Steven Johnson) is a relevant background to "Where do we go from here?"

History

The early history of NAAB is documented in the 1975 "Restructuring NAAB" report[4], where it is recorded that "The National Architectural Accrediting Board was founded in 1940 by an agreement between the American Institute of Architects, the Association of Collegiate Schools of Architecture, and the National Council of Architectural Registration Boards. Its duties delineated at that time were to publish a list of accredited schools of architecture, with the general objective *'that a well integrated and co-ordinated program of architectural education be developed which will be national in scope and afford opportunity for architectural schools with widely varying resources and operating conditions to find places appropriate to their special objectives...'*"

During the years of WWII however, for obvious reasons there were no formal visits or any sort of implementation of accreditation until 1945. Specifics of any activities and developments during the postwar period for the next 22 years, however, have been completely lost with all archival documents destroyed.[5] What is known, though, is that in 1967 the NAAB was an office inside the AIA with all appointments made by the AIA director. In 1967, the NAAB was formally organized as a separate body with its own governance structure and Executive Director.

A comprehensive and significant review of the NAAB mission, policies and procedures was undertaken starting with the work of a Special Task Force on Education in the early 1970s. With input from a number of prominent academics and professionals from NAAB, ACSA, NCARB, AIA and Student Chapters of the AIA (known today as AIAS), the outcome of this review was the 1975 "Restructuring NAAB" report, which laid the foundations for the evolution of the SPC as we know them today. The stated objectives in this report were to address "the growing complexity of architectural education, along with an ever increasing role in the accreditation process [which] has pressured the boundaries of these duties and extended the responsibilities of NAAB." It further sought to more clearly identify the relationship between the NAAB and the AIA, ACSA, NCARB, AIAS (as later named), and the Public and Community.

Thus the first modern Conditions for Accreditation are actually relatively recent, dating back only 35 years beginning in 1982. In this initial publication of the Conditions[6], there were no bullet point or enumerated criteria as we now know them, and the format is barely recognizable by today's standards. The first reference to structures is found under article 2.1 "Accreditation Perspectives" in a statement that students "…*should also have a working knowledge of the principles and theories of structural technology, materials and methods of construction and of environmental control systems.*"

Article 2.2 identifies the "Criteria for Program Evaluation" and is categorized into seven topical areas (identified by letters A through G), and the SPC are very broadly defined. For instance, structural technology is found within Category C, which states, "*The program should develop student awareness of, and responsibility for, the public welfare — social, health, safety, and quality of the environment — in the practice of architecture.*" The specifics relating to structures in this category are extremely vague in nature reading "*NAAB also expects to find a knowledge of the engineering disciplines that is appropriate to building design and construction.*"

A review of all of the *Conditions* documents in the NAAB archives indicates that significant evolution has occurred in the SPC overall since the first 1982 issue, the first subsequent editions being highly detailed and prescriptive with respect to structures. Between the years 1983 and 1998, the total number of SPC overall was high and written in very precise language, starting with 88 SPC in total and gradually consolidating to 54 in 1995. The 1998 Conditions brought the most significant change to the organization of the SPC since the initial 1982 edition, among other things formalizing the essential language of the single structures criterion as it remains today.

For the purposes of the present study, it is noted that this evolution can be viewed in two distinct periods, corresponding to both the development of language in the SPC requirements as well as total number of criteria and overall configuration. This organization is used solely within the present paper and does not reflect any actual formal categorization by NAAB. The two periods are being referred to here as, first, a "Formative Period" of fifteen years, lasting from 1983 to 1998, followed by a "Contemporary Period," beginning in 1998 and continuing through the present. The 1982 Conditions are not further addressed, since the format is so significantly different and wording more sweeping than anything that followed.

Formative Period: 1983–1998

During the Formative Period of the Conditions, the specific criteria were organized within distinct categories. Between the years 1983 and 1988, there were four such categories employed in four iterations in 1983, 1984, 1986 and 1988. In the 1983 and 1984 editions the categories were:

- History, Human Behavior & Environment
- Design
- Technical Systems
- Practice

In 1986 and 1988 the categories were essentially the same, however the wording was simplified to:

- Context
- Design
- Technology
- Practice

The 1991 and 1995 Conditions similarly used distinct categories, but the number increased from four to seven and the names were again changed:

- Social
- Environmental
- Aesthetic
- Technical
- Design
- Communication
- Practice

The structures criteria in all cases fell within the "Technical Systems," "Technology," or "Technical" categories.

In the 1983 Conditions[7], the prelude paragraph in Structural Systems reads "*Structural systems include the basic structural elements of buildings, their interaction as a support system, the forces that act on and in buildings and the principles and theory upon which an understanding of these systems is based.*"

There were nine specific SPC for structures:

- *be aware* of behavioral and computational analysis and design;
- *be aware* of current and developing structural systems;
- *understand* structural behavior of typical systems;
- *understand* theory and principles in the areas of statics, dynamics and strength of materials;
- *understand* theory of simple structures;
- *be able* to design simple building elements utilizing a variety of materials to include the full range from footings and foundations to building frames, bearing walls and structural floor systems to roofs and ceiling systems;
- *be able* to analyze structural systems in frequent use, such as post and beam, rigid frame and others;
- *be able* to organize building systems to withstand lateral forces in connection with wind and earthquake conditions;
- *be able* to select, integrate and coordinate structural systems with other building systems.

It is evident that in this earlier period, those involved in crafting the SPC strongly believed that architects should be able to actually design basic structural systems, and should understand not only statics and strength of materials but also dynamics...in other words, the basics of engineering that a civil engineering structures graduate would find familiar, even if in a simplified format.

The 1984 Conditions[8] reduced this total number down to six, and also was the first edition to employ enumerated SPC. The prelude paragraph is the same as in 1984, and was maintained in both the 1986 and 1988 Conditions, where the total number of structures SPC was also six, although specific wording changed.

The six structures SPC in 1984 were:

37. *understand* theory of simple structures and the structural behavior of typical systems.
38. *be able* to design simple building elements utilizing a variety of materials to include a full range — from footings and foundations to building frames, from bearing walls and structural floor systems to roofs and ceiling systems.

39. *be able* to analyze structural systems in frequent use, such as post and beam, rigid frame, and others.
40. *be able* to organize building systems to withstand lateral forces in connection with wind and earthquake conditions.
41. *be able* to select, integrate and coordinate structural systems with other building systems.
42. *be aware* of current and developing structural systems and the associated methods of behavioral and computational analysis and design.

The six structures SPC in 1986[9] read:

32. *be aware* of the significance of appropriate structural systems in guaranteeing human comfort and safety, and of the traditional role of those systems in relation to architectural form;
33. *understand* the theories of simple structures and the structural behavior of typical systems;
34. *be able* to select, integrate and coordinate structural systems which may be designed by others, with other building systems;
35. *be able* to analyze structural systems in frequent use such as post and beam, rigid frame, and others;
36. *be able* to design simple building elements, utilizing a variety of materials, including footings and foundations, building frames, bearing walls, structural floor systems, and roof and ceiling systems; and
37. *be able* to organize building systems to withstand lateral forces resulting from wind and earthquake conditions.

The 1988 structures SPC[10] is identical in wording, however the numbers run from 39 through 44 due to insertions and deletions of preceding SPC in other categories.

Although wording and specifics changed during this initial period, the essential concept that architectural students should possess the capability to perform basic engineering design remained in the language. This in itself in part may represent a legacy of why the "structures as basic engineering" approach continues to be taught with frequency.

Beginning in the early 1990s, the number of structures SPC was again reduced, this time from six to four, and the language became broader. In conversation with Linda Sanders, FAIA, who was NAAB president in 1991-1992, it was conveyed that one of the problems faced by NAAB at this time was that many students were simply unable to rise to this level of basic engineering competence as outlined in the structures SPC. A strong desire to find language that would meet the objective of understanding and integrating structure into architecture by the majority of students *without* a reliance on calculations was the objective. Furthermore, a desire to become more closely integrated with the Canadian Architectural Certification Board to better permit reciprocity for Canadian graduates to work across national boarders in the US led to a "softening" of the criteria to be less prescriptive in engineering specifics[11].

The 1991[12] and 1995[13] editions of the Conditions are identical in numbering and text, with only a slight variation in the prelude wording. This may be seen as a response to the challenges of students meeting the earlier, more prescriptive, criteria noted above.

We now find that "Structural Systems" has been replaced by the more global term "Technical," which includes not only structures, but also materials and methods of construction and environmental control systems. The 1991 edition "Technical" prelude reads: *"The technical context is defined by the NAAB as the physical systems necessary to create a beneficial environment that responds to both human behavior and the laws of nature. For the purposes of NAAB accreditation, graduating students must:*

19. *Understand the principles embodied in the natural laws affecting the science of building.*
20. *Understand the basic theories of structures and the structural behavior of typical systems.*
21. *Be able to organize and design simple structural systems to withstand gravity and lateral forces.*
22. *Be aware of relevant codes and regulatory standards and their application to physical and environmental systems.*

The criterion of structural-architectural integration was also moved from the Structural Systems category to the Design category as SPC 35: *Be able to assess, select and integrate structural and environmental systems into building design.*

Contemporary Period: 1998–Present

The most radical change in the criteria occurred in the 1998 revision[14] where any reference specifically to the design of structural elements was removed in entirety. With only slight changes in wording, this sole criterion has remained essentially unmodified since this time. The specific reasoning and discussions behind this change have yet to be fully uncovered as of this writing; however, much of the reasoning is likely to be seen as a continuation of the process begun with the 1991 conditions, in response to the previously noted challenges of meeting the stringent earlier requirements.

The 1998 edition also saw the removal of the distinct categories, which had been in use in the Formative Period of the preceding fifteen years. The prelude paragraphs for all criteria were also removed with this edition, replaced instead by sequential numbering throughout the document.

The wording of the structures SPC in the 1998 and 2004 Conditions[15] is identical except for a change in numbering (2004 was SPC number 18). The structures SPC for 1998 reads:

12.17 Structural Systems

Understanding of *the principles of structural behavior in withstanding gravity and lateral forces, and the evolution, range, and appropriate applications of contemporary structural systems*

According to NAAB Executive Director Andrea Rutledge, the 2003 Validation Conference was a formal affair that involved presentations and discussions, and there was a good deal of bargaining and aggressive lobbying by observers to delegates to influence decisions one way or another, not always for the best. One of the first efforts by Ms. Rutledge (hired in 2007) was to avoid this situation by reorganizing the Validation Conference. Substituting interactive small group discussions for presentations, significant levels of agreement were reached for another major reconfiguring of the entire document.[16]

The 2009 Conditions[17] thus saw the first major reorganization into the "realms" A, B, and C, with Realm B addressing "Integrated Building Practices, Technical Skills and Knowledge." In a way, this was a return to the earliest categorizations of the early 1980s, although defined differently. The criterion for structures remains essentially unchanged from 2004, however it is now even slightly less specific in that "principles of structural behavior" are now "*basic* principles of structural behavior":

> B.9 Structural Systems: Understanding *of the basic principles of structural behavior in withstanding gravity and lateral forces and the evolution, range, and appropriate application of contemporary structural systems.*

The most recent 2014 NAAB Conditions[18] have maintained the realms of 2009, but a slight change of wording to the structures criterion has been made as follows:

> B.5 Structural Systems: Ability *to demonstrate the basic principles of structural systems and their ability to withstand gravitational, seismic, and lateral forces, as well as the selection and application of the appropriate structural system.*

We now see the substitution of "basic principles of structural behavior" with the "basic principles of *structural systems*," and a clear indication of withstanding not simply lateral forces but specifically seismic forces. The phrase "...and the evolution, range and appropriate application of contemporary structural systems has been replaced with the "...selection and application of the appropriate structural systems," all of which harken back to much earlier versions of the structural SPC, but without specific mention of member or element sizing.

What is perhaps most notable is that for the first time since the earlier SPC editions of the 1980s, the criterion has been elevated to "ability," yet the ability is to "demonstrate the basic principles of structural systems," which to this author and a few others seems a rather strange wording. How exactly does one demonstrate the principles of structural systems? Perhaps what is really meant is to "demonstrate an *understanding* of the basic principles of structural systems." While becoming slightly more specific than the

previous three editions dating back to 1998, the structures criterion remains (no doubt intentionally) very open-ended with regard to what work specifically is expected to meet it.

Summary and Implications

The future of the accrediting criterion or criteria for structures has of course yet to be written and will continue to evolve as has occurred for the previous 35 years. This author wonders, though, if perhaps the needle has swung too far from the initially highly prescriptive requirements to one that is nearly as vague as the first 1982 SPC. The pass rates of reviewed architecture programs with regard to the structures criteria are an interesting metric in this regard.

Though the specifics of any one program's accreditation visit are private, the global pass rates have been made available. In the period from 1999 to 2003, of 92 schools evaluated (or 80% of all accredited schools in the U.S.), there were zero (0) schools that failed to meet the structures criteria.[19] Similarly, in more recent years, between the years 2001 and 2016, of 152 visits representing the majority of all accredited programs, only two failed to meet the structures criteria.[20]

If in essence then virtually *all* schools meet the SPC for structures, does this imply that the criterion is so all encompassing that virtually *any* presentation of structures is acceptable? It is notable that in anecdotal conversations with colleagues teaching structures, no one is aware in recent memory of a structures-focused faculty being involved in the crafting of the structures SPC.

So a question is left on the table from this historical review: Does the structures SPC merit revisiting by those directly responsible for teaching the subject area, or do the majority of today's professors consider the opportunity to address structures in the broadest possible interpretation (i.e., maintain the open-ended wording of the criterion) the way to go?

An open discussion at the BTES 2017 Conference is planned to in part address this very topic. As the experts in this subject area, it is incumbent upon us to set the agenda for NAAB regarding the structures criterion and not the other way around. It is hoped that this summary document of "how we got to now" may help inform this and future discussions around this important, yet often neglected, aspect of architectural education.

Notes:

[1] Salvadori, Mario. Introduction in *Bridging the Gap*: Rethinking the Relationship of Architect and Engineer. The proceedings of the Building Arts Forum/New York symposium held in April of 1989 at the Guggenheim Museum. New York: Van Nostrand-Reinhold. (1991)

[2] Allen, FAIA, Edward. *Some Comments Concerning Technical Teaching in Schools of Architecture.* Topaz Medallion Award Acceptance Speech. Washington, D.C.: ACSA News. (May 2005).

[3] Theodoropoulos, Christine. *Seismic Design Education in U.S. Schools of Architecture.* Proceedings of the 2006 Building Technology Educators' Symposium. (2006)

[4] National Architectural Accrediting Board, *Restructuring NAAB.* Washington, D.C.(1975)

[5] Rutledge, Andrea. Interview by Deborah Oakley. In person Interview. NAAB Headquarters, Washington, D.C. January 5, 2017.

[6] 1982 *NAAB Criteria and Procedures.* Washington, D.C.:National Architectural Accrediting Board (1982)

[7] 1983 *NAAB Criteria and Procedures.* Washington, D.C.:National Architectural Accrediting Board (1983)

[8] 1984 *NAAB Criteria and Procedures.* Washington, D.C.:National Architectural Accrediting Board (1984)

[9] 1986 National Architectural Accrediting Board, *Criteria and Procedures* (1986)

[10] 1988 *NAAB Criteria and Procedures.* Washington, D.C.:National Architectural Accrediting Board (1988)

[11] Sanders, FAIA, Linda. Interview by Deborah Oakley. Telephone Interview. February 22, 2017.

[12] 1991 *NAAB Conditions and Procedures.* Washington, D.C.:National Architectural Accrediting Board (1991)

[13] 1995 *NAAB Conditions and Procedures.* Washington, D.C.:National Architectural Accrediting Board (1995)

[14] 1998 *NAAB Conditions and Procedures.* Washington, D.C.:National Architectural Accrediting Board (1998)

[15] 2004 *NAAB Conditions for Accreditation.* Washington, D.C.:National Architectural Accrediting Board (2004)

[16] Rutledge, Andrea. Interview by Deborah Oakley. In person Interview. NAAB Headquarters, Washington, D.C. January 5, 2017.

[17] 2009 *NAAB Conditions for Accreditation.* Washington, D.C.:National Architectural Accrediting Board (2009)

[18] 2014 *NAAB Conditions for Accreditation.* Washington, D.C.:National Architectural Accrediting Board (2014)

[19] Theodoropoulos, Christine. *Seismic Design Education in U.S. Schools of Architecture.* Proceedings of the 2006 Building Technology Educators' Symposium. (2006)

[20] Rutledge, Andrea. e-mail message to author, January 5, 2017.

SESSION 12: DIGITAL TOOLS II

Session Chair: Kris Nelson
University of Florida

Robert Holton, Louisiana State University: "An Architecture of Performance."

Andrzej Zarzycki, New Jersey Institute of Technology: "Hackers and Makers: Prototyping with Emerging Technologies."

1:1 Drawing   An Architecture of Performance

Robert Holton
Louisiana State University, College of Art & Design, School of Architecture

Abstract

"How can an understanding of material attributes, assembly techniques, and environmental conditions inherent in the 'act' of 1:1 building be evidenced in the 'act' of 1:1 drawing?"

Material attributes profoundly define the experiential process of building. The human scale of a brick allows it to be placed and set by hand. The heavy weight of a beam requires mechanization for alignment and placement. The soft density of a stone necessitates a delicacy of handling. The hot temperature of asphalt defines the temporal extent of application. The sharp edge texture of glass mandates cautionary and protective measures. Can the ability to develop a *sensibility* for the application of materials, linked to their distinct properties, be revealed in 1:1 drawing?

Assembly techniques delineate the construction sequences in the performance of building. Connections are an outcome of the actions utilized in placing materials and the detail is the confluence of these histories. Joinery describes a relation between specific surface conditions and an understanding of tolerances. Fasteners elucidate material properties through the movement and resistance of securing. Can 1:1 drawing promote the ability to comprehend necessary assembly *sequences* relative to specific construction techniques?

Environmental conditions impact the routine and course of actions in the feat of building. Temperature can make unavoidable the restrictive use of additional layers that slow movement.   Moisture and temperature impact soil consistency and the ease of workability.   Wind can impinge precision causing hazardous conditions and increased production time. Can 1:1 drawing demonstrate an understanding of the physical *context* that guides building construction?

The objective of the building technology exercise seeks to investigate material attributes, assembly techniques, and environmental conditions intrinsic in the *'act'* of building: realized in the *'act'* of drawing. Drawing techniques are explored with an emphasis on the ability to communicate the processes inherent in the practice of making architecture: *pragmatics & poetics*. The *'act'* of 1:1 drawing is our format.

Approach

"How can an understanding of material attributes, assembly techniques, and environmental conditions inherent in the 'act' of 1:1 building be evidenced in the 'act' of 1:1 drawing?"

'Architectural Systems', an introductory course in materials and constructions, emerged around this question and is based on an understanding of specific conditions, an iterative process of application, and the resulting outcome.   The pedagogical approach is grounded in the conviction that the processes by which something comes to be is critical to what it is. The method towards developing this technique of critical thought is the presentation of knowledge, *'what is something'*, and the practice of application, *'why is something'*. The approach strives to understand the potential of architectural drawing as a means to communicate physical conditions, the processes by which they are achieved, and the physical and cultural parameters in which they exist.   The corresponding relevance of setting, performance, and result are expressed in a quote by Peter Gluck published in the monograph, The Modern Impulse.

"Architecture has often been likened to frozen music. If so, the construction of a building is the equivalent of a musical performance, which is in fact the only thing that makes it real. To realize a design, the architect ought to be not only the composer but also the conductor, the more so because with a building there is only one performance. The best way to maintain whatever balance the architect has managed to achieve during the design phase is to direct the architectural process from initial conception to final construction. This makes it possible for the constant

interaction among the various attributes to continue until the building is completed, so that issues of cost, technique, and construction help to inform the design and insure its integrity rather than impede its realization. The responsibility for the alignment of attributes in the completed building lies with the architect. And the goal of this complex process is the building it produces – a building that resolves the overlapping attributes in so strong and elegant a manner that experience of it is all the explanation it needs."

In the example of audible constructs, lines, signs, and characters set out the pitch, rhythm, and tempo of a composition. This notation describes a specific sequence of actions as a way to perform the resulting composition. The simultaneous existence of both the process and the result is an inherent quality of a musical score. In the example of physical constructs, lines, symbols, and annotations are conventions used to set out the shape, size, and arrangement of a composition. This notation describes a specific completed work, however the sequence of actions, as a way to perform the resulting composition, is often traditionally undefined. Through the inclusion of processes of generation and contextual parameters in conjunction with material characteristics, the act of architectural drawing has the potential to question why specific conditions are relevant in the complex union of multiple variables. This dynamic set of relations is fundamental to the practice of making and constructing architecture.

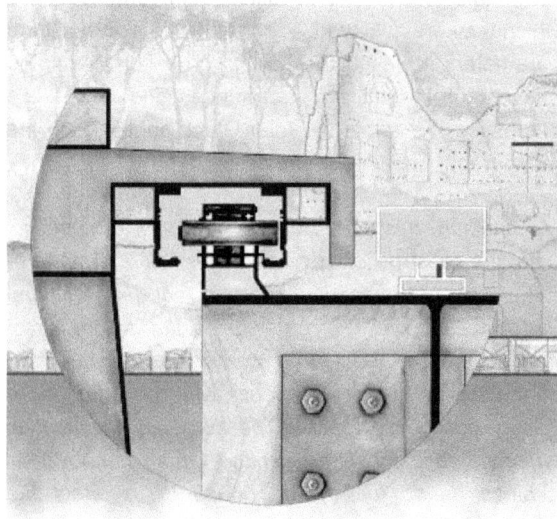

Fig. 1 Enlarged connection detail

Objectives

The course objectives of 'Architectural Systems' seek to investigate material attributes, assembly techniques, and environmental conditions intrinsic in the construction of architecture and apply the findings through the varied processes of architectural drawing. Drawing techniques and objectives are explored with an emphasis on questioning the procedures inherent in the practice of making architecture: *pragmatics & poetics*. The following primary objectives are focused around both tangible and abstract concepts fundamental to design thinking.

• *Ability to develop a sensibility for the application of materials linked to their distinct properties.*
• *Understand and evaluate factors that influence material selection and assembly methods.*
• *Ability to comprehend necessary assembly sequences relative to specific construction techniques.*
• *Develop an understanding of fabrication processes, tools, and established communication procedures.*
• *Understand the means by which building systems and assemblies influence one another.*
• *Understand the implied possibilities implicit in transferring a material from one application to another.*
• *Demonstrate an understanding of the physical and social context that guides building construction.*
• *Understand the environmental, historical, and cultural impact on an applied tectonic language.*
• *Develop an ability to investigate the built environment through a series of detailed drawings.*

Context

Organized around the goal of developing an awareness of the built environment, 'Architectural Systems' examines the means by which materials, assemblies, and context influence design thinking. The course initially presents topics that explore the elemental qualities of physical building components and the varying processes by which they are both manufactured and standardized. This beginning inquiry is built upon through additional topics that investigate the parameters and possibilities by which components may be combined. Contextual questions related to environment, cultural methodology, and proximity are introduced through historical case studies. Drawing on this knowledge, assignments provide an opportunity for creative synthesis based on unique design queries. The assignments intend to engage a tectonic language and seek to establish a vocabulary capable of communicating complex issues of selection, technique, fabrication, and assembly. The course utilizes the decision processes inherent in the act of drawing and aspires to address the many associations essential to developing architecture.

The material presentations offer a foundation of knowledge intrinsic to an architectural process of formulating questions and making decisions. Each presentation is structured around three categories titled *'Properties, Manufacturing, and Standards'*. The objective is to develop an understanding of natural materials, the methods by which they are transformed, and then subsequently regulated.

'Properties' focuses on basic material attributes. Classifications are presented to relate material types of similar qualities as in the cases of hardwood and softwood or ferrous and non-ferrous metals. Compositions are introduced to reveal a commonality of elements across materials as evidenced in the silica, soda, and lime makeup of glass in comparison to the lime, alumina, and silica makeup of a brick. Attributes are specified to define unique material characteristics of strength, stability, and performance. Awareness of distinct aspects of strength, such as compression and tension, are vital to the selection of concrete, steel, or wood structural components. The stability of materials is important to ensure dependable enclosures and requires the separation of certain metals, especially aluminum and steel, to prevent galvanic action. Understanding the performance characteristics of a material, including expansion and contraction, is critical to proposing appropriate components in response to specific environmental conditions. Each of these aspects plays a pivotal role in the inquiry towards why a specific material is appropriate for a particular application.

'Manufacturing' highlights techniques that have been used to transform primary material elements into composite building materials. A historical evolution of fabrication technologies, from manual to mechanized processes, is presented to address advancements in quality, time, and expense. One example is the advancement of masonry production processes from soft-mud to stiff-mud to dry-press to the highly automated contemporary brick fabrication assembly line. These modern assembly production sequences are shown to articulately describe the current practices of converting raw materials into finished building components as illustrated in the process of producing float glass or rolled steel sections. The location where materials originate and how they are extracted from specific sites is emphasized. Of significant importance to understanding the management of natural resource sites such as forests or mines are issues of sustainability. Sustainable matters in question include harvesting expenditures, renewability of resources, site resiliency, and relative locale. Understanding the processes, including energy expenditure and renewability, by which materials are brought into existence is vital to asking why a material is suitable to a certain demand.

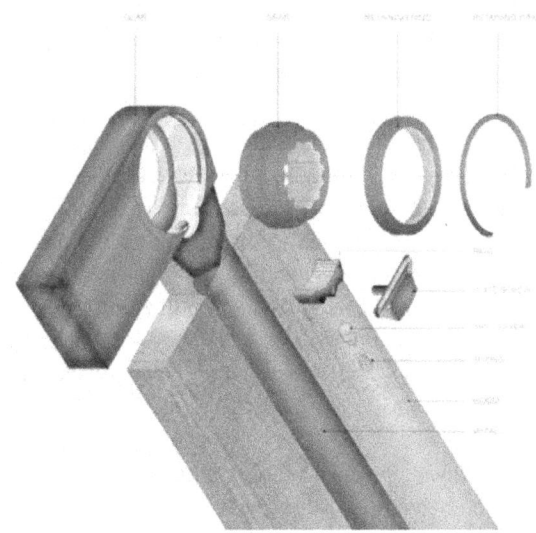

Fig. 2 Exploded connection detail

'Standards' concentrates on the norms, customs, and regulations to which building components are manufactured. Benchmark dimensions of wood, steel, concrete, masonry, and glass are considered as a set of parameters to work with in the development of architectural concepts. An awareness of nominal and dressed wood dimensions provides a relevant link between the manufacturing processes and the regulated sizing nomenclature. The intrinsic necessity of buildings to transfer loads from the structure to the ground is similarly based on an

understanding of sizes. In steel construction, simple rules of thumb can be used as a way to preliminary size components and realize the dimensional impact of design goals. Steel shapes ranging from a W-section to a tube are similarly significant in the determination of structural performance. Material types are presented to realize that material properties are commonly modified and specialized to meet the demands of particular applications. The modification of annealed glass to heat strengthened or tempered exemplifies the refashioning of a material to meet specific security needs. Quality specification and determination is a critical part of the construction process as represented by the process of cylinder testing concrete samples over a series of daily intervals. Correspondingly, material grading is a method used to specify the strength or appearance of a building component and is often linked to the means by which it is distributed and sold as is in the case of timber. A cognitive understanding of the standards that articulate material properties is fundamental to inquiring why certain physical attributes are necessary to achieve unique design decisions.

The assembly presentations are of equal importance in the learning of knowledge that is essential to the processes of formulating questions and proposing techniques. The presentations are structured around categories of architectural components titled *'Foundations, Floors, Walls, and Roofs'*. The aspiration is to achieve a level of knowledge that can be applied in the development of constructible building systems.

'Foundations' focuses on the means by which an interface between buildings and the ground they are placed within is established. An understanding of both land composition and building characteristics is critical to how they come together. An analysis of soil classes and types is discussed to reveal that a particular site may be made up of various materials with differing characteristics. The different behavior of fine or course material is critical to the load bearing capacity of a soil. Likewise, the contrasting performances of sand and gravel to silt and clay play a vital role in soil stability. The composition of the material that supports a structure plays a key role in the transmission of live and dead loads from the building to the earth. The importance of geographic location is introduced as a factor in the determination

of a particular foundation type. The knowledge of Northern freeze and thaw cycles bares a relevant factor in the degree to which a foundation extends into the earth, necessitating foundation designs of greater depth compared to Southern regions with warmer climates. All of these attributes contribute to the formulation of questions into why a particular set of foundation specifications is needed for a specific building site.

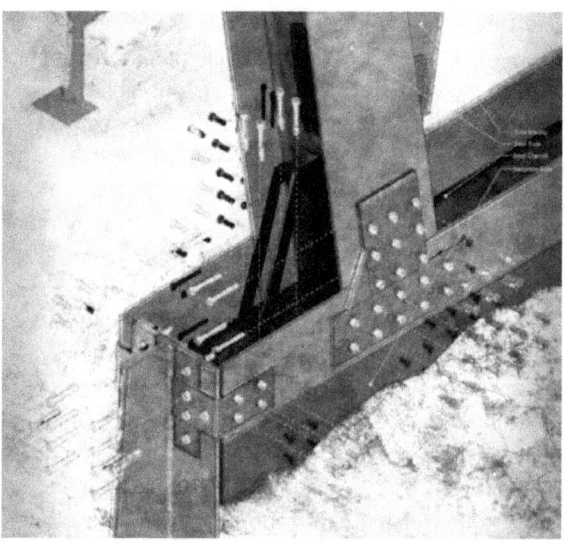

Fig. 3 Exploded foundation assembly

'Floors' is centered on structural concepts and explores the spanning capacity of beams, joists, and slab compositions. Wood, metal, and concrete components are presented along with the relative merits of each material. Wood framing standards are oriented relative to individual applications to call attention to questions of performance relative to corresponding joist span and depth. An investigation of different framing types leads to questions and tradeoffs associated with considerations of schedule, economics, and aesthetics. Metal systems are similarly presented through questions of performance linked to different types of structural members as seen in the application of W-section beams to transfer heavier loads and open web joists to transfer lighter loads. The use of a moment or shear steel connection is investigated as a response to resolving structural forces of varying floor configurations as in the case of cantilevered areas. Properties of concrete elements are described to apprehend the strength and means by which forces are transferred through

different slab configurations. Recognition of precise attributes of structural capacity is vital to the selection of a slab type, such as flat plate or waffle, relative to specific programmatic requirements.

'Walls' discusses assembly types oriented around the many plies that define the multiple layers of an enclosure system. Both the structural and insulating properties of wood, metal, masonry, concrete, and glass components are considered. For example, wood is a material with limited load bearing capacity compared to steel, masonry, or concrete, but it's ease of on site workability make it a common selection for small structures. Also, relative to the other materials, the cellular composition of wood acts as a thermal barrier reducing a temperature exchange from one side of a wall to the other. Metal framing has the capacity to carry great loads while having the advantages of being lightweight, noncombustible, and damp proof. The capacity of structural steel shapes to carry greater loads makes them a frequent selection for large structures, however the performance of the components under high heat requires added layers of fire protection. Load bearing masonry walls perform well in compression, but a reduced capacity to transfer tensile forces requires the inclusion of lintels to form openings. With the pairing of steel and concrete walls perform well in both compression and tension, however the process of forming and curing is often not cost effective and beyond scheduling constraints. An understanding of the structural role a component can play and how it responds to environmental conditions is key to questioning why it is applicable to a particular use.

Comparable to 'Walls', 'Roofs' are assembly types that can also be described as a series of layers in the composition of an enclosure. The oblique surface, with a minimal required slope to manage runoff, must transfer dead and live loads and protect against environmental conditions. Questions of where a wall ends and a roof begins are critical to adequately shedding water off a building and preventing inundation. The parapet is the resolution of this meeting and can result in a range of connection details from the unnoticeable to the profound. Roofs are constructed by way of both tectonic and stereotomic systems. The selection of a technique has as much to do with local culture and traditions as an economy of means. A roof can be viewed as the culmination of a building proposal, take on many forms, be both structurally and environmentally responsive, and conceptually guide a design inquiry from formulation to constructed outcome.

Assignments

The assignments intend to link the course learning objectives and activities through the application of knowledge in a series of drawings that respond to specific architectural questions. The questions are presented as sequential investigations toward the development of drawings that begin by exploring material attributes, then incorporate assembly techniques, and culminate with the inclusion of environmental conditions. The goal is to put into practice presented knowledge, approaches, and circumstances in the formulation of unique architectural proposals.

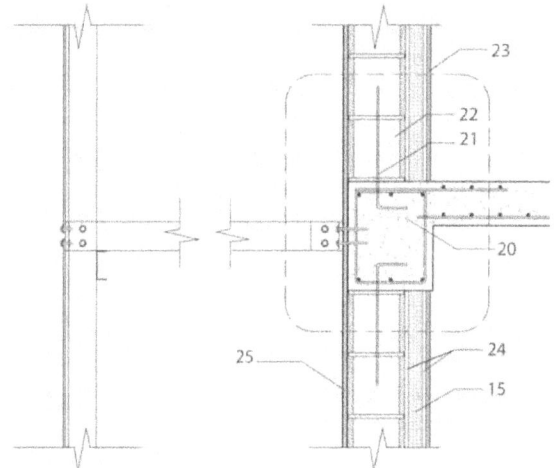

Fig. 4 Wall section

The initial inquiry is based on the development of a wall section drawing that communicates the integration of systems required to meet the specific needs of a design generated by each student in studio coursework. The wall section is intended to be holistic and include all necessary components in the composition of foundation, wall, floor, and roof assemblies. Special consideration is given to questions of materials, structure, enclosure, and construction. Drawing explorations focus on materials with unique qualities and how they are assembled to communicate a clear architectural proposal. Ideas of structure and enclosure are advanced relative to one another and take into consideration specific site conditions by way of drawn layers in each assembly composition. The processes of sequencing construction and assembling material components are researched and expressed through conventions of line styles and weights. This initial set of drawings strives to investigate the integration of and relationships between site conditions, material qualities, structural forces, and construction processes.

Continuing the focus on a unique design generated by each student, the subsequent inquiry is established on the development of a series of detail drawings that present the interface between primary building components. These details include the connections of foundation to wall, wall to floor, and roof to wall. The details aspire to show the connections between components as part of the multiple systems necessary in the articulation of a design proposal. Attention is now given to questions of materials, structure, enclosure, and construction at a finer scale. Drawings seek to emphasize the connections between materials and why certain affiliations are appropriate. A series of joints between the structure and enclosure are included in the drawings as an expression of exterior and interior environmental conditions. The process of installing connection fasteners is understood through the drawing of spaces and gaps to illustrate construction tolerances. This iteration of drawings develops enlarged detail connections in the demonstration of a tectonic language equally responsive to material logics and environmental conditions.

The culminating inquiry is positioned on the generation of a comprehensive exploded perspective drawing that includes the specific components of foundation, wall, floor, and roof along with the necessary connections to define and communicate the process of assembly. The exploded perspective continues the design exploration into the unique proposals of each student based on materials and techniques and orients the process of assembly within an exact contextual framework. The final series of drawing iterations works with the following questions that strive toward a synthesis of previous investigations and incorporates the complex set of contextual parameters deep-rooted in the practice of constructing architecture.

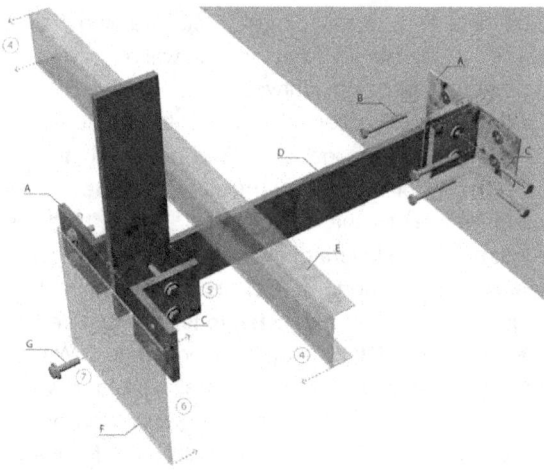

Fig. 6 Exploded wall assembly

Material attributes profoundly define the experiential process of building. The human scale of a brick allows it to be placed and set by hand. The heavy weight of a beam requires mechanization for alignment and placement. The soft density of a stone necessitates a delicacy of handling. The hot temperature of asphalt defines the temporal extent of application. The sharp edge of glass mandates cautionary and protective measures. Can the ability to develop a sensibility for the application of materials, linked to their distinct properties, be revealed in 1:1 drawing?

Assembly techniques delineate the construction sequences in the performance of building. Connections are an outcome of the actions utilized in placing materials and the detail is the confluence of

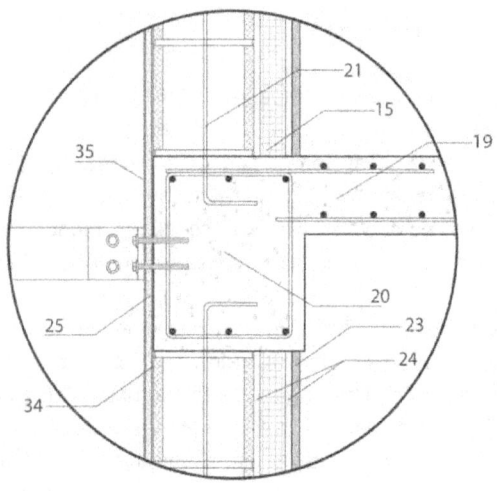

Fig. 5 Detail

these histories. Joinery describes a relation between specific surface conditions and an understanding of tolerances. Fasteners elucidate material properties through the movement and resistance of securing. Can 1:1 drawing promote the ability to comprehend necessary assembly sequences relative to specific construction techniques?

Environmental conditions impact the routine and course of actions in the feat of building. Temperature can make unavoidable the restrictive use of additional layers that slow movement. Moisture and temperature impact soil consistency and the ease of workability. Wind can impinge precision causing hazardous conditions and increased production time. Can 1:1 drawing demonstrate an understanding of the physical context that guides building construction?

Results

The opening question proposed by the course, *"How can an understanding of material attributes, assembly techniques, and environmental conditions inherent in the 'act' of 1:1 building be evidenced in the 'act' of 1:1 drawing?"*, inspired drawing investigations founded in an understanding of natural order, a system of repetitive takes, and an aspiration for conclusive results. The assignment outcomes are a materialization of the goal to simultaneously investigate materials, assemblies, and context intrinsic in the act of building through the act of drawing. Knowledge of material properties, fabrication practices, and component standards gave way to design proposals grounded in actual real world parameters. Along with illustrating the relationship between dimensioned architectural components, the drawings also represent projected interactions between adjacent materials and environmental conditions. The drawings are enriched with a myriad of surface textures, hues, and values that bring to light a series of both temporal and performance questions.

An understanding of assembly methods and precise construction sequences resulted in the development of buildable connection details with an allowable amount of room for fabricators to maneuver. The effect of drawing connection fasteners installed and then pulled apart along sequential lines of assembly brings in an understanding of the necessary

tolerances to the picture. The drawings visually illustrate the means by which an assembly goes together. Realization of contextual factors allowed for appropriate design strategies relative to specific environmental and cultural conditions. Geographic location is annotated as *'degrees North'* with probable atmospheric conditions both rendered and reflected in the materials. This approach sheds light on the individual experience of putting together components within a variety of contextual factors. The methodology of staging assignments with complimentary objectives innately reinforces a cyclical process of applying knowledge, reflecting critically, and then reapplying design strategies with a revised awareness. The series of drawings that commence with wall sections that address architectural components, then move to details that speak to connections between components, and then advance to exploded axonometric diagrams that articulate sequencing allow for a continued focus on a subject through the perspective of multiple frames. The resulting architectural drawings reveal a gradual refinement of initially proposed design and construction strategies.

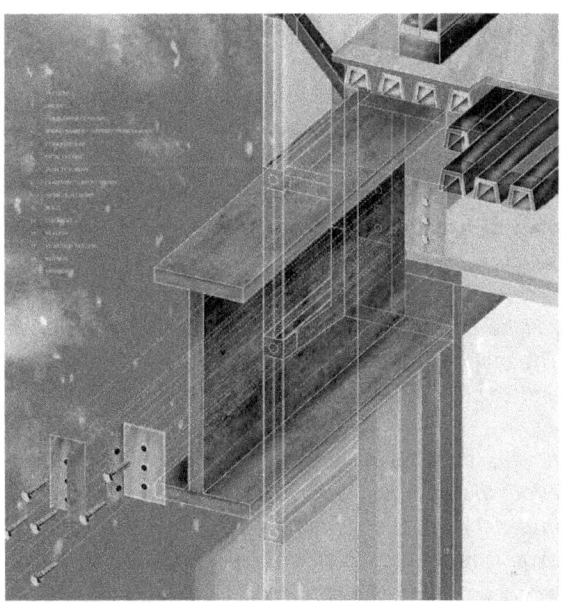

Fig. 7 Exploded floor to wall connection

Conclusion

To conclude, a personal learning assessment was developed by each student through reflecting on three considerations expressed in the following question. *In* the exploded perspective drawing, qualitative characteristics of material attributes, assembly techniques, and environmental conditions were investigated as a means to further explore the quantitative attributes of size, dimension, and connections from the wall section and detail drawings. In what ways did the three considerations of sensibility, sequence, & context transform how you think about building assemblies? The written contemplations offer an insight into the learning of each distinct individual.

Sensibility, for the application of materials:

"My great revelation was how materials do not exist in a vacuum. Steel conducts heat from the sun. Wood expands when rained on. You can choose certain materials to work along side the environment, you don't have to fight it."

"I began to understand in real life how something would be built which added to my understanding of what the limits of a building supposedly are and how I can engage and challenge that."

Sequence, relative to construction techniques:

"In creating the detailed axon and wall sections, there was a lot of change in scale. The whole structure has to make sense as well as the placement of a bolt. I found it easiest to start from the bottom and work upward because it makes you think about the actual construction of your building."

"Cliché as it is buildings don't appear out of thin air. Thought has to be put into what is first what is second and so on."

"It was impossible while I was drawing to not think about the assembly and construction sequence of the material components. In this way I feel the exploded axon is really great in trying to understand how things would actually be constructed."

"There was order in a process that didn't exist beforehand. I would begin to understand the logic of structure and visualize it somewhat like Tetris."

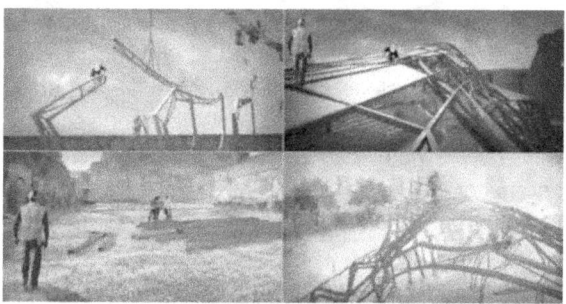

Fig. 8 Construction sequencing

Context, that guides building construction:

"Considering the environment of Chicago helps to determine the materials used to compose the buildings, but also how they would actually be constructed. Different locations have different requirements for their buildings. Structure in many ways expresses the people within a region."

"While people are out in the world constructing our beautiful creations the weather doesn't always cooperate. We need to understand the sequencing so fully that we can begin to alleviate outside variables for the people trying to assemble these buildings."

Through the learning outcomes and learning assessments it is evident that the systemic application of knowledge, exemplified by the process of drawing, acted as a linkage between the learning objectives and the learning outcomes. Inspired by the individual inquisitiveness of the students the investigations uncovered unique conditions relative to a specific context. The iterative process of questioning the subject and developing the drawings shifted the course focus from teaching to the eccentric learning of each individual design student.

Notes:
Fig. 1 Tina Naraghi-Pour, LSU School of Architecture.
Fig. 2 Xueru Lan, LSU School of Architecture.
Fig. 3 James Babin, LSU School of Architecture.
Fig. 4 Fernando Chavez, LSU School of Architecture.
Fig. 5 Fernando Chavez, LSU School of Architecture.
Fig. 6 Fernando Chavez, LSU School of Architecture.
Fig. 7 Madeline Luke, LSU School of Architecture.
Fig. 8 James Babin, LSU School of Architecture.

Prototyping Construction Assemblies with Emerging Technologies: An Educational Perspective

Andrzej Zarzycki
New Jersey Institute of Technology

Abstract

This paper presents a number of research case studies that integrate building assemblies with distributed sensing and actuation systems in the context of smart buildings. It looks into prototyping a vehicle to creatively engage architectural design and traditional design process. This is achieved through an emphasis on increased design resolution where designers are responsible for the definition of an actual performance and for the behavior of the designed systems. This approach extends the field of architectural design beyond form- and pattern-making, or designs based on hypothetical users, and focuses on data-driven building behavior. Design responds to outside and changing needs, with the ability to supersede initial designer thinking.

Introduction

The role of prototyping as a design methodology has been on the rise since early digital fabrication processes in architecture. Conceptualizing, making, testing, and rethinking based on these processes have become necessary milestones of an effective design process. While for some this may seem to significantly differ from past modes of creativity, the meaning of "making" and "testing" has evolved to include technological methods with scientific rigor. In more recent years, fabrication processes not only have provided designers with direct access to means of production and the ability to control design outcomes, but more importantly have allowed a feedback loop characteristic of past craftspeople involved in creating-making processes. This feedback loop allows for developing a close connection between the intent, the method, and the outcome.

This paper discusses a number of research case studies that focus on prototype developments and the integration of interdisciplinary knowledge into architecture. What distinguishes discussed projects is not the use of fabrication techniques or a learning-by-doing approach, which both are important, but the emphasis on bringing the design resolution to the higher level of reality where designers are responsible for defining an actual performance and the behavior of the designed system. In these scenarios, design as conceptual proposition is followed by an increased design resolution through prototyping of building assemblies. This approach extends the field of architectural design beyond form- and pattern-making, or designs based on hypothetical users, and focuses on data-driven building behavior. Design responds to outside and changing needs with the ability to supersede initial designer thinking.

Making as Reflective Learning

In disciplines outside architecture, learning cycles or reflective models are commonly applied to reinforce experiential learning. Terry Borton (1970), in his book *Reach, Touch, and Teach: Student Concerns and Process Education*, framed experience-based knowledge formation through the following three questions: "What?" "So what?" and "Now what?" (fig. 1), an approach inspired by Gestalt therapy practices. This model was later adopted in other disciplines, including nursing, by Gary Rolfe (2001). In parallel developments, reflective models were connected with the experiential learning model (ELM) developed by David A. Kolb and Ronald Fry (1975), who drew heavily on the works of John Dewey, Kurt Lewin, and Jean Piaget (Dixon et al. 1997). ELM was composed of four actions as a learning loop: (1) concrete experience, (2) observation of and reflection on that experience, (3) formation of abstract concepts based upon the reflection, and (4) testing the new concepts. This model can be expressed in simplified terms such as doing, reflecting, concluding, and planning. Later and along the same lines, the 5E model [1] was developed by the Biological Science Curriculum Study (BSCS) team led by Roger Bybee. The 5E stands for five stages of building understanding through experience:

Engage: capturing interest and engagement with investigated topic,

Explore: building understanding and knowledge through questioning and observation,

Explain: forming and communicating explanations about discoveries and lessons learned,

Extend: applying lessons learned to similar situations outside current knowledge or study,

Evaluate: assessing what has been understood and learned at previous stages.

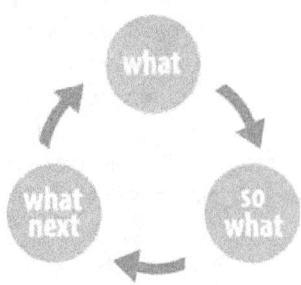

Fig 1, Terry Borton's reflective model.

While the 5E model was developed primarily for science teaching, it could, and should, be extended to other fields, including creative disciplines such as architecture and design. This is particularly important in the moment when technology becomes a prevailing mode of creative thinking in design disciplines, as evident in developments in fabrication technologies, material sciences, data-driven design, buildings as autonomous robotic agents, and an increased interest in user-based design. While maintaining its social and creative dimensions, architecture also needs to examine its impact on the environment and society. When measuring and evaluating this impact, architects need to consider scientific methodologies, data-driven design drives, and user feedback.

Architectural Process

Creating-making becomes a form of the research-design triage that allows for almost instant idea testing with rapid prototyping providing bases for a significant acceleration of innovations. There is a hidden value, often overlooked but revealed by the current fabrication technologies, of closing the feedback loop while still in the design or early implementation phases. The traditional feedback loop informed by building construction and on-site experience comes usually at a very late stage of design production, often years after its completion. It provides limited value for the quality improvement of design and construction processes, as well as advancement of new ideas and technologies in architecture. This delayed feedback often resulted in lost knowledge and. In that paradigm, designers are often faced with the dilemma of either following a conservative practice approach or experimenting and being exposed to the liabilities of malpractice. However, an even greater point of concern is the inadequacies of the design production. While architecture as a discipline has accumulated a significant body of knowledge and established practices for design processes (ref), there is relatively limited architectural literature on how to make this process reiterative and self-reflective as well as innovative. A process that functions as autonomous self-guiding and self-improving systems analogous to scientific research paradigm. Definitions of what constitutes the architectural design process vary significantly, yet they often converge on what the American Institute of Architects (AIA) defines through the sequence of five consecutive phases: Schematic Design, Design Development (DD), Construction Documents, Bid and Negotiations, and Construction Administration (2007). It is understood that the design process ends with the completion of construction and revolves around the client-architect relationship and contractual obligations. It is linear and algorithmic rather than reiterative, informed by quantifiable data and justifiable through a long lineage of design reasoning. The traditional design process does involve testing ideas, usually through visual means, and occasionally developing mock-ups to evaluate various design alternatives. However, the process heavily relies on past experience as tacit knowledge that is seldom evaluated and quantified beyond basic values representing budgets or per-square-foot costs. Similarly, user group studies performed during the DD phase generally rely on individual interviews rather than more scientific data collecting systems. The introduction of post-occupancy evaluations, either through the use of building information modeling (BIM) data sets as part of the facility management or through Leadership in Energy and Environmental Design (LEED) green building certification validation, creates opportunities for closing a design feedback loop in more informed ways. However, these opportunities are not explicitly and widely integrated into the design process nor seen as necessary credentials when evaluating the projects themselves.

The relative lack of quantitative methods and evidence-based design processes contributes to a slow development and implementation of new technologies in architecture and construction, partially due to the inability to reduce the risk associated with introduction of new materials and technologies. The use of the construction mock-ups to alleviate this risk provides only partial benefits. Extending this approach by developing fully functional prototypes with embedded systems, sensors, and actuators would allow for end-to-end technology development and testing. It would provide immediate feedback that could be used to validate design alternatives as well as long-term value by tracking the fidelity of the initial prototype testing in the relationship to finalized designs and their performance. More significantly, the inclusion of technology innovation—an architectural research and development component—into the design process would drastically change the outcomes as well as dynamics and outlooks of design teams.

While end-to-end prototyping as part of the design process is not a new approach, the extent and degree to which it is practiced as well as the professional readiness of architects to engage it remain low as compared to scientific, engineering, and even product design disciplines. Perhaps it is not a coincidence that a significant portion of innovations in architecture are powered by engineering firms such as ARUP or Buro Happold. The case studies discussed here represent an attempt to realign architectural design curriculum with the demands of contemporary technology-driven and science-informed practices, partially in response to new expectations toward sustainable and resilient developments and user-centered design. They also aim to discuss the methods and goals of research-driven design education today.

The Shift: Designers as Makers

The recent renaissance of maker and do-it-yourself (DIY) culture also permeates into design disciplines, including architecture. An increased interest in project-based curricula recognizes reflective learning as well as the artistic philosophy of working with a

medium, as evident in the adage attributed to Michelangelo: "I saw the angel in the marble and carved until I set him free." This revelation points to a set of experiences and creative or intellectual processes that can only be enabled by working directly with a particular medium or context. This could be expressed through the creating-making continuum that questions the need for detachment from direct engagement with materiality. Yet materiality in the new paradigm could be interpreted not only as physical and tangible but also as virtual contextualization. Consequently, the creating-making continuum becomes the subject to Friedrich Nietzsche's tools-and-thoughts predicament, "our writing tools are also working on our thoughts" (Kitter 1999), which recognizes a close and direct relationship between "how" and "what" in human creative processes.

It reconnects the process of conceptualization with making, constructing, and developing: tasks that were traditionally separated from labor to bring "professional" status and standing to architects and designers. While there are definite benefits of this separation—the abilities to participate and guide without taxing labor—there are also impediments caused by the separation of creative thinking from the direct execution and, more importantly, from the uninterrupted feedback loop that inspires and informs design. This creative reinforcement enabled by the feedback loop draws from making processes, material handling, and the discovery moments that occur when unexpected or unintended substitutions and occurrences happen. This dilemma and dichotomy of being both involved (as a maker) and detached (as conceptualizer and idea generator) can be effectively bridged with recent developments in (fabrication) technologies and electronic networks: collaborative culture where the connection from the ideation to implementation is significantly shortened, streamlined, and able to be handled by a single designer or a small team of designers.

Making Technologies

3D printing, computer numeric control (CNC) machining, laser cutting, and customized fabrication with short-run orders redefine what designers can do and to what extent they need to rely on a middleman to facilitate manufacturing. While this is already an established practice, particularly for small experimental firms, there is still a lot to be formulated about effective ways to harness these technologies. Showcased projects illustrate how emerging fabrication technologies can be used not only to develop individual products but also to integrate various separate components or systems. While students rely heavily on already existing components/parts, there is usually a need to adopt them into a particular implementation or arrangement. This means designing assembly systems or individual elements that "glue" various technologies together (fig.2). Using ready-made technologies and solutions significantly speeds up the process of prototyping and makes it possible to develop solutions that focus on filling the gap in between systems and provide an interface to effectively interconnect them. An important benefit of this approach to design is that it transcends materiality and disciplinary boundaries. It applies to both physical and virtual prototyping. Virtual making and creativity follow similar innovative frameworks, informed significantly by scientific and engineering disciplines, where innovation is seen as a unique, yet incremental development of past precedents. It is an extrapolation of the known and an interpolation of diverse and distinct disciplinary threads. While it is new and original, it is also contextualized and tied into an existing body of knowledge. In this scenario, an innovator—a designer, engineer, or scientist—functions as knowledge manager ensuring the ways various technologies interface and seamlessly bridge.

This creative use of existing knowledge and technologies is evident in the Invisalign-like project by Amos Dudley. The project gained almost instant media attention, including publicity from CNN [2] and the Washington Post as well as engaged discussions on various public forums and blogs. This example represents a creative and entrepreneurial mindset that capitalizes on technological opportunities available to everyone and easily obtainable. However, 3D printing of Invisalign-like orthodontic treatment by Dudley would not be possible without easy access to know-how and technological means of production. It would not be as impactful without an almost instant and often viral information sharing. While it is innovative and empowering, it is fully based in already established technologies (3D printing) and digital 3D modeling as well as materials used for orthodontics.

The innovation or creativity is achieved through the realization that professional and specialized knowledge is available to everyone and that anyone can replicate results given enough effort and research commitment. However, this democratized knowledge is a result of technological forces that enable sharing and collaborative authoring.

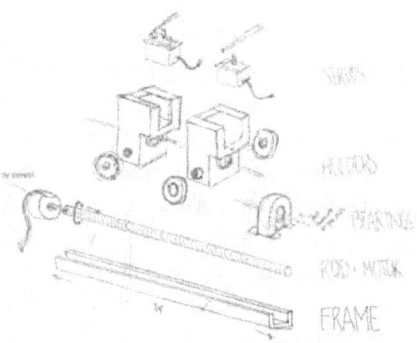

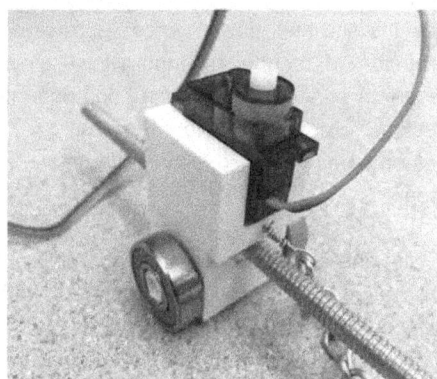

Fig.2, Students designed and fabricated a number of custom elements to provide an efficient integration of various mechanical and electronic components.

Sharing Culture

The digital creating-making relies on the genetically diverse primordial soup of technologies that can be adopted into various configurations. The creative effort is often focused on reusing open-source contributions and adopting them into new designs. It resembles a system management approach where new knowledge is created by operations on complex assemblies, not on individual elements, atoms, or particles. It is about building relationships between objects or transforming them rather than creating them from scratch. This approach requires access to diverse expertise and object histories in order to effectively adapt or combine them. It also needs almost real-time sharing of this knowledge extended by crowd-sourcing and collective authoring that puts a designer into the position of managing technologies and expertise that exceed single-person capabilities. Interestingly, this is very similar to the role architects currently find themselves in, coordinating various trades and professions. However, there is also a difference between project management or delivery and fostering innovation or development of new knowledges. To achieve the latter, architects and designers need to reconnect with their scientific and engineering selves and develop research-based design processes that consider both qualitative and quantitative factors. They also need to be able to establish innovative and ambitious design goals as well as methodologies to achieve them. In a similar way that a software product brings new features and improvements with each consecutive release, buildings and individual design practices should be able to advance their offerings, superseding their past projects. This attitude is evident in a number of "zero energy" or "zero carbon" initiatives that propose goals and timelines for buildings and architectural practices. These goals are framed around continuously increasing benchmarks and standards. However, this approach needs to go further in redefining current architectural modes of production and conceptualization to avoid marginalization or the perception of being yet another practice subcategory. The discussed technology- and research-driven design curricula reignite these science and engineering sensitives and project a path forward for expanded roles architects can play.

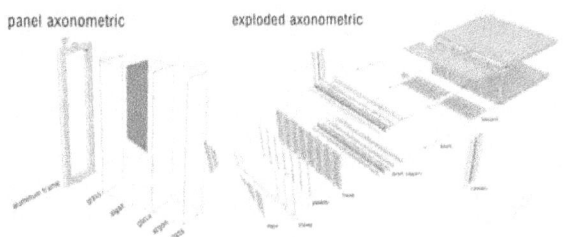

Fig. 3: Algae panel geometries and design.

Case Studies

The Algae Façade project (fig. 3) integrates façade and building technology research (performance, materiality, and feasibility) with embedded systems (sensors, actuators, and microcontrollers) (fig. 4). It deploys a double-skin building façade as a harvesting surface for algae growth for subsequent conversion into biofuel (BIQ House in Hamburg, Germany) or as a simple carbon-footprint offset by absorbing carbon dioxide from the atmosphere. The algae façade functions as an adaptive building skin that optimizes sun exposure for algae panels and reduces solar gains in the inner skin of the double façade.

There are a number of objectives that this design needed to achieve. In addition to tracking sun location and providing shading, it also had to monitor the growth of biological agents (algae). This meant aerating water inside the algae panels and collecting temperature data throughout the façade assembly, while allowing for various functionality overrides to maintain optimal building skin performance (fig.5). These overrides included both user inputs and negotiations between various building performance needs and criteria. For example, if the water temperature inside dropped to 29°F, the panel would drain to prevent the algae solution from freezing.

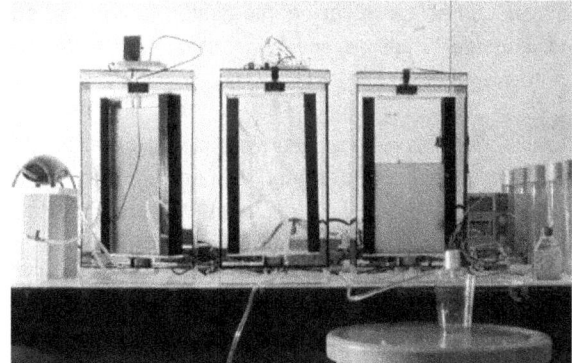

Fig. 4, Algae panel prototypes; each tests a different panel functionality.

This sophisticated and complex behavior required comprehensive design and problem-solving thinking with research into several disciplines. It involved understanding of (1) biological processes behind algae growth, including species selection; (2) embedded electronic systems using microcontrollers with actuators and distributed sensors continuously monitoring building performance; and (3) construction assemblies with research into high-performance buildings.

This experience gave students an insight into comprehensive design thinking that sees architectural design outcomes as products of diverse expertise drawn to a significant degree from other disciplines. Through the process of prototyping—building and testing—they were exposed to the notion that design can emerge out of algorithmic and adaptive processes driven in response to gathered data rather than by a priori assumptions. This process also required students to engage with the project not only physically, by understanding building performance and construction assemblies, but also biologically, by working with actual algae specimens obtained from a biology lab (growing them over a period of several months) and algorithmically, by defining operational procedures and feedback loops.

This emphasis on algorithmic thinking and understanding a broader topology of possible scenarios (fig. 6) in defining the adaptability of the façade triggered a perception shift among students about building design as a highly interconnected and interdependent system with a strong inner logic. Defining adaptive panel behaviors as a resultant of diverse and competing factors, such as sun exposure versus shading or double-skin ventilation needs, introduced system thinking into design. Students had to consider multiple scenarios that impact design outcomes.

While the Algae Façade project is reflective of the bioreactive façade designed by Arup for the BIQ House in Hamburg, the focus of student work was on extending existing precedent into more adaptive and autonomous building skin.

Fig. 5, Testing early prototypes (left), algae cultivation, showing 14-day cycle of growth (right).

This work represents an educational philosophy that starts with an in-depth precedent study as a holistic design solution (fully functional mechanism), not only as an inspiration (visual and metaphoric). Then it uses the precedent as a vehicle for innovation by extending its concept through new functionalities and/or capabilities, with the ultimate goal of producing precedent 2.0. Not unlike in evolution and natural processes, new designs build upon previous successful designs—not only phenotypically but also genetically, by understanding and improving the inner workings of buildings. Furthermore, using the BIQ House as a design springboard allowed students to dive directly into more sophisticated design issues and research work. To some extent, this approach put aside the discussions of "what" and "why" to concentrate on research and prototyping to answer the "how" question. While the design process certainly involves all these and other questions, the nature of architectural education and even practice usually privileges the "what" and "why."

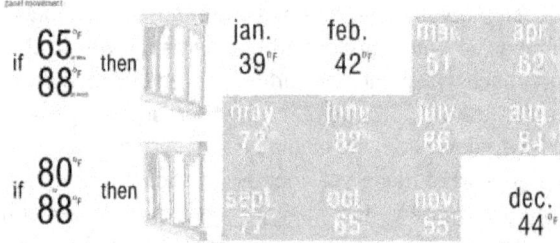

Fig. 6: Defining algorithmic operabilities of adaptive panels (left) and addressing the seasonal nature of the design assembly (right).

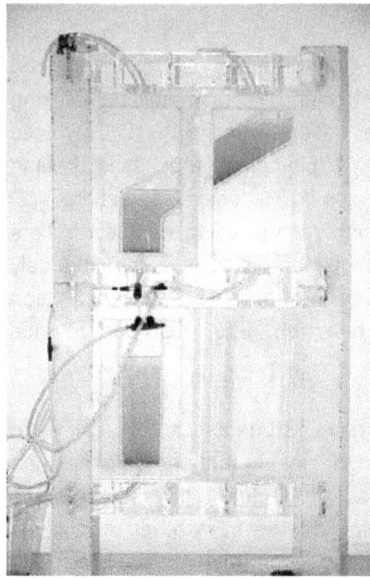
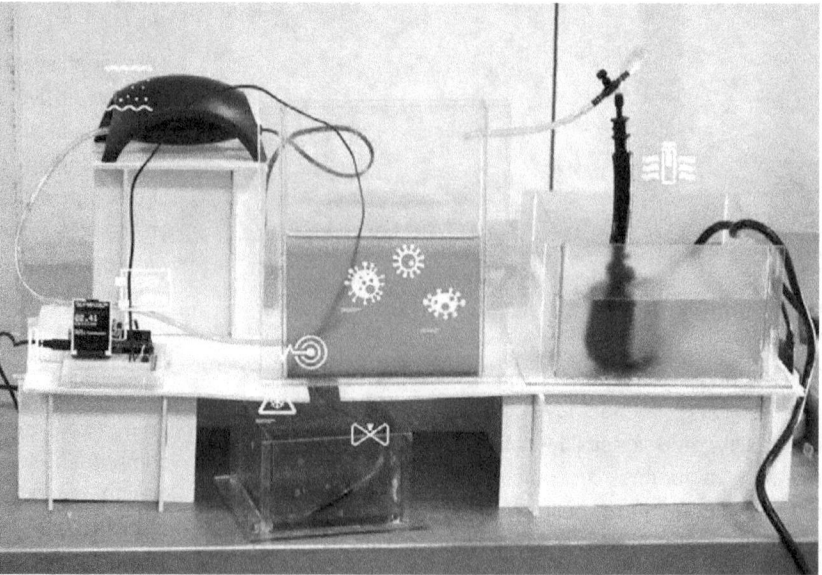

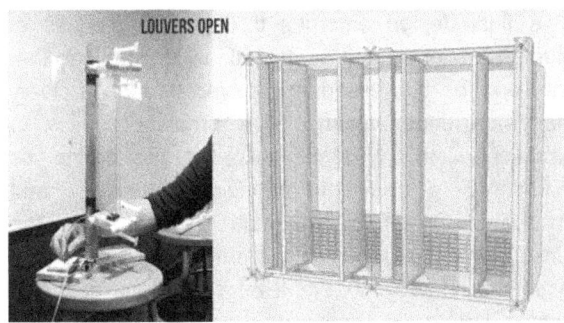

Fig. 7, An adaptive shading component. This photograph shows a researcher testing individual façade functionality—a subcomponent of a larger assembly as a form of scalable and progressive prototyping (left). Multiple components forming a façade element (right).

In the Adaptive Façade projects (fig. 7), designers investigated an integration of kinetic shading adaptability with embedded media components to provide visual displays that could also address glazing privacy and energy needs through photovoltaic frits. Similarly, these projects extended existing precedents by identifying additional functionalities and characteristics that could enhance the original façade. One of these characteristics is the ability of the façade to alternate between single- and double-skin states based on the season, on the time of day, and on what may be a more beneficial arrangement from the perspective of a user or building performance. In the single-skin phase, adaptive panels function as shades doubled with solar energy harvesting or as privacy and media screens during evening hours.

The expanded functionalities and adaptive states of the façade bring a number of competing criteria into consideration, particularly when balancing between individual and group (overall) interests. The educational value of this exercise lies not only in identifying all performance- and user-driven considerations but also in developing a conceptual framework of how to negotiate and reconcile various needs. This not only shifts significantly a set of criteria used by students to evaluate buildings and engage in the design process but also frames a new mindset that sees design outcomes as a set of objectives that are being addressed.

Since the project approach is outcome driven, it focuses on technology adoption and integration. Students are asked not to reinvent already known

solutions but rather to research their benefits and limitations, find the ways to adopt them from other disciplines, and reappropriate them into architectural and building technology applications. This leads to a modularity approach in design thinking and processes, where the final product is made of a number of integrated technologies. It is similar to the process of designing products that often require inputs from various engineering and scientific disciplines with constant prototyping. Another aspect of this approach is scalability—establishing various scales and degrees of deployment. It often translates to positioning a design product in a timeline of what technologies and solutions are achievable now and what would need significantly more time and resources to be implemented. This is an important feature that transforms the traditional design process into a cumulative, reiterative research and development methodology with each project, course, or student thesis, addressing a particular section of the research/innovation continuum. However, any in-between prototype is, and should be, considered as a fully functional deployment that at the same time supports future enhanced versions or implementations—a form of the forward and backward conceptual compatibility.

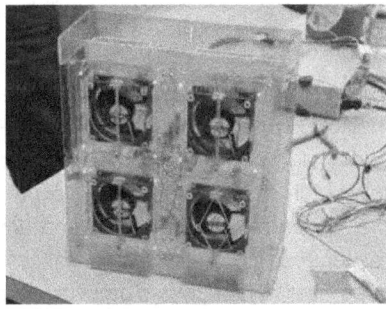

Fig. 8, A prototype integrating mechanical and electronic components with full kinetic operability.

Since prototypes involved an integration of various mechanical, electronic, and material technologies (fig. 8), they provided an opportunity for a more expressive design language, with many reappropriated components, such as fans and motors, playing a central role as functional (performative) and aesthetic features. This also forced students away from an overly stylized approach to design and design representation, since the majority of the design process relied on sketched and simplified conceptual prototypes, often testing a single action or mechanism, before an immediate shift toward developing more involved assemblies. Technical drawings and computer renderings were usually produced post-factum to represent and register technical knowledge developed through prototyping. However, fabrication did rely on the development of CAD drawings and 3D models of individual components. Additionally, 3D assembly models were used as dimensional sources for calculations of kinetic movements and component geometric information (fig. 9).

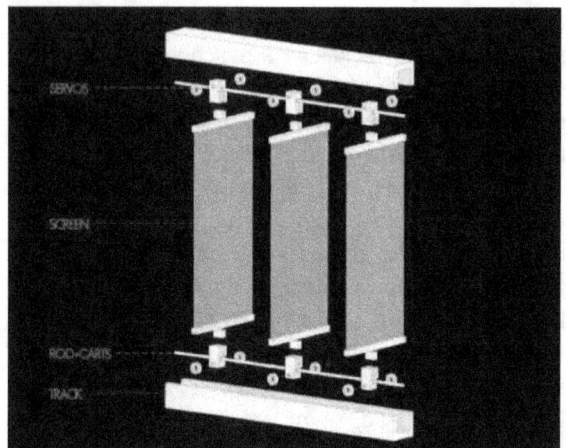

Fig.9, 3D assembly models were also used as dimensional sources for calculations of kinetic movements and component geometric information.

The prototyping process involved constructing multiple working mock-ups and testing their kinetic and electronic assemblies. Each subsequent reiteration focused on refining a particular aspect of the assembly performance and improving façade responses by fine-tuning sensor and actuator integration. Through this process, students developed an understanding about designing for tolerances, material fatigue, and the precision required to make kinetic connections, which need to be considered and continuously addressed when prototypes undergo prolonged-time testing. Students quickly learned that prototypes that are exposed to extended real-life operations (actuations) fail relatively quickly if they are not designed and fabricated with material performance in mind.

Prototyping and learning from implementation failures provide design feedback both performative and aesthetic. The iteration is what allows for design variation, and the iteration is what makes it perfect.

The final design emerges through the process of human, material, and computational interactions that can only be addressed and solved through a close, hands-on understanding of a problem. This also underlines an important value of prototyping as compared to traditional methods of drawing and modeling. Sketches and models may refine the design intent—the look and the feel—but do not significantly advance the level of design resolution (actuation) as compared to prototypes. The conceptualization without an engagement of materiality and performance feedback isolates design from effective actualization. An increased reliance on drawings to define building design also runs the risk of reducing technological innovations in materiality and physical construction, as suggested by David Pye (1968) in his book *The Nature and Art of Workmanship*.

While the drawings in figure 10 may look like typical conceptual design sketches, they show students' concern about dimensions and distances between various components. Since these components were to be fabricated (3D printed) and integrated into a kinetic assembly, tolerances became an important part of design discussion. Another important consideration involved understanding fabrication process, since various spatial configurations within the 3D printer module impacted assembly precisions, the need for post-processing, and the overall aesthetics.

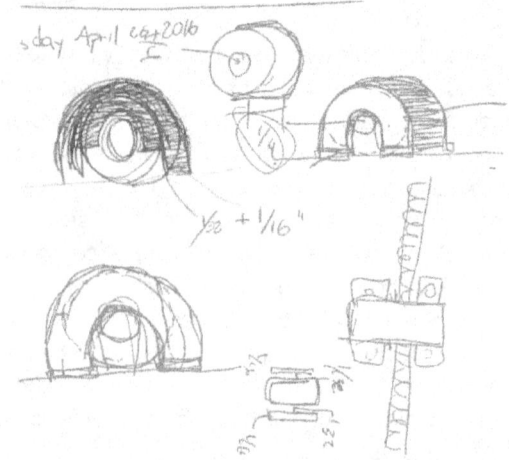

Fig. 10, Conceptual sketches of the ball bearing mounting and the leadscrew connection.

Most of the elements proposed in learning cycles, reflective models, or experiential learning are also present in current methodologies of designing through prototyping. The focus on (1) questioning and reflection, (2) synthesizing observations into new concepts, and (3) assessing what has been achieved is consistent with creative, yet scientifically rigorous, inquiry into architectural production.

These emerging prototyping technologies, coupled with crowdsourced and open-source electronic culture, provide a new take on the architectural design process. This process that brings architecture closer to product design by focusing on the development of end-to-end solutions and recognizing the front-end (human interface) design aspects as well as the back-end technological framework as necessary components. The standard architectural design model, an architect defines design intent (the "what") and a contractor provides the implementation (the "how"), no longer supports the innovative needs of profession and society.

As is evident with the approach to the Algae Façade project—using a precedent as a starting point for design—maker and hacker culture ultimately will penetrate the traditional inert notion of architecture. The environment will not be built from scratch, but rather will be tweaked and reappropriated from existing or mass-produced elements with strong adaptive features. This will become even more pronounced at the point when the built environment is defined not only by its built form—hardware—but also its software: embedded electronic and media functionalities.

Conclusions

The works discussed above focused on several educational objectives: (1) grounding design in a higher level of technical and physical resolution by promoting the creating-making processes, (2) emphasizing research that goes beyond inspirational visuals and addresses the *whys* and *hows* of architecture, (3) using design as a springboard to ask inquisitive questions—the adoption of the reflective model: "What", "So what", and "Now what?" and (4) finally, using design to motivate and advance architectural research. In this context, a prototype becomes a form of design proposition that can, and should, be tested to derive knowledge informing design performance, its innovative framework, and the ultimate actualization. Furthermore, to maintain its

integrity and solvency within the profession, the architectural design process needs to involve the creation of new knowledge that is verifiable and relevant to society.

Acknowledgments

The following projects were developed as part of the College of Architecture and Design at NJIT curriculum: the Algae Façade project by Samantha Bard, Mary Lopreiato, and Libertad McLellan (figures 3-6), the Adaptive Media Façade projects by Anthony Morrello and Anthony Samaha (figure 7) and Kevin Suqui and Alfredo Silva of NJIT (figures 2, 9, and 10). The Kinetic Assembly was developed by Leland Greenfield and Edward Perez (figure 8)

References

American Institute of Architect (AIA), Defining the Architect's Basic Services, July 2007 www.aia.org/aiaucmp/groups/secure/documents/pdf/aiap026 834.pdf

Borton, Terry (1970). Reach, touch, and teach: student concerns and process education. New York: McGraw-Hill.

Dixon, Nancy M.; Adams, Doris E.; Cullins, Richard (1997). "Learning Style". Assessment, Development, and Measurement.

Kittler, F. A. Gramophone, Film, Typewriter, trans. Geoffrey Winthrop-Young and Michael Wutz (Stanford, CA: Stanford University Press, 1999), 200–208. Quoted in Patricia Falguières, "A Failed Love Affair with the Typewriter," Rosa B, Friedrich Nietzsche, letter toward the end of February, in F. Nietzsche, Briefwechsel: Kritische Gesamtausgabe, ed. G. Colli and M. Montinari (Berlin, 1975–84), pt. 3, 1:172.

Kolb, David A.; Fry, Ronald E. (1975). "Towards an applied theory of experiential learning". In Cooper, Cary L. Theories of group processes. London; New York: Wiley.

Rolfe, Gary; Freshwater, Dawn; Jasper, Melanie (2001). Critical reflection for nursing and the helping professions: a user's guide. Houndmills, Basingstoke, Hampshire; New York: Palgrave.

Pye, David. (1968). The Nature and Art of Workmanship. Cambridge: Cambridge University Press.

Schön, Donald Schön (1983). The reflective practitioner: How professionals think in action. New York: Basic Books.

Notes

[1] nasaeclips.arc.nasa.gov/teachertoolbox/the5e.

[2] money.cnn.com/2016/03/16/technology/homemade -invisalign/

SESSION 13: SKINS

Session Chair: Scott Murray
University of Illinois at Urbana-Champaign

Martina Decker, New Jersey Institute of Technology: "Bio-Enabled Façade System integrated into the Internet of Things (IoT)."

The Role of Testing and Validation in the Development of Bio-Enabled Façade Systems

Martina Decker
New Jersey Institute of Technology, College of Architecture and Design

Abstract

Bio-enabled building technologies, that integrate living organisms into our building blocks, have enjoyed great attention in recent years in the architectural community. The integration of microalgae into building skins for example holds the potential to improve air quality, purify grey water, stabilize the thermal conditions in buildings, and contribute to the production of biomass as well as feed and food supplies. Concerns of a performance gap between the promised outcomes and the actually achieved benefits of these interventions are becoming more apparent.

This paper scrutinizes the benefits of testing and validation of these building blocks in their early development phase and explores the integration of research prototypes into the Internet of Things (IoT) in the context.

Introduction:

Concerns of energy consumption in buildings have played a significant role in the architectural decision making process in recent decades. The energy used in buildings, accounts for a third of the global energy consumption[1], which has a devastating effect on our natural environment. The associated carbon dioxide emissions can be directly linked to the "unequivocal"[2] warming of our average global temperatures, a fact that has been widely accepted by the scientific community[3].

In the United States, we spend a significant time of our days in indoor environments[4] that require more than a third of the energy used in buildings (see Figure 1), to maintain comfortable indoor conditions. Hence, the potential energy savings, that could contribute to the reduction of anthropogenic greenhouse gases, can be found by scrutinizing the way we maintain comfortable indoor temperatures and ensure adequate lighting.

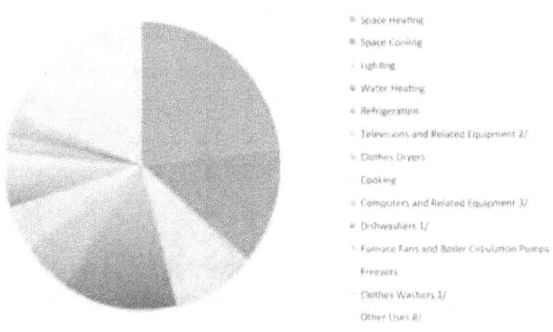

Fig. 1: Energy Used in Residential buildings 2014, data by U.S. Department of Energy

Another factor that has to be taken into account when we are studying our global energy balance, is the constant rise of the consuming class: compared to 1990, in 2025 three billion people are projected to join the consuming class[5], a point at which we will have a larger number of consuming class citizens than those that are living below this standard (see Figure 2).

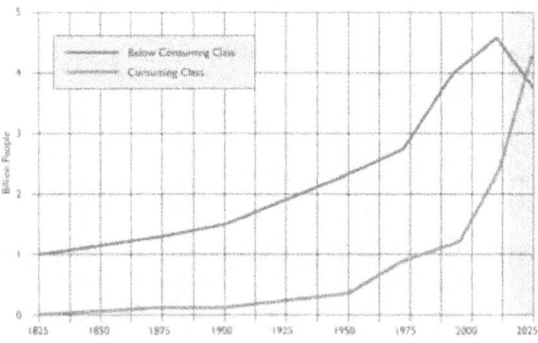

Fig.2: compared to 1990, in 2025 three billion people are set to join the consuming class. Data by McKinsey Global Institute, 2012

By an improved comfort and life style of the larger expected populous, the energy issues we are already facing in architecture will be amplified and continue to contribute to a considerable surge in architectural research concerning the optimization of energy and comfort management[6]. As new energy-conscious solutions are desperately sought after, the ever-increasing complexity[7] of environmental control systems of buildings raise concerns regarding their effectiveness. It is of great importance that these innovations don't fall into the so-called performance gap, that describes the significant discrepancy between the predicted performance of architectural environments and the actually measured outcomes[8]. To stay clear of this trajectory, it is important to scrutinize the causes of the performance gap that can be diverse, even within one building project, and that can be overcome by an integration of simulation, validation, verification and testing in the development process[9].

The availability of more affordable sensor systems will benefit the mission to overcome the energy performance gap, which is currently a main target in this research area. It might also help us in evaluating architectural designs concerning indoor air quality, daylighting, acoustic performance, thermal comfort[10] as well as active and reactive design elements, that respond to user inputs such as varying transparency of façade systems that can grant or deny the views to the outside[11].

This paper presents an approach for the development of active and reactive façade systems, through a case study that integrates the steps of validation, verification and testing into the early development phase.

Bio-Enabled Building Systems:

The previously mentioned tendency of architectural research to move towards systems of ever increasing complexity might be driven in part by a heightened interest in biomimetic or biologically inspired architectures[12]. Besides the adaptation of geometric or formal similarities for architectural elements, examples emerge that take inspiration from biological organisms to help design smart building systems[13]. While these research trajectories integrate behavioral aspects of living organisms into the building system

context; another line of investigation is directly striving to integrate living organisms into our buildings.

Green roofs or green walls are the most common examples of such a bio-enabled design approach and have been applied in buildings for centuries already. They have been praised to improve thermal qualities of buildings and counteract the urban heat island effect, aid in storm water management, provide oxygen and an urban wildlife habitat[14]. Researchers at the Center for Architecture Science and Ecology[15] are investigating green wall systems to improve indoor air quality by removing airborne contaminants. With this phytoremediation strategy, the potential of indoor plants is being studied for the removal of formaldehyde[16].

Another example in which biological organisms are completely merged with the constructed environment can be found in various projects that strive to integrate microalgae (see Figure 3) into façade systems[17]. The photosynthetic organisms have the potential to contribute to air quality by turning carbon dioxide into oxygen and they can further contribute to bioremediation by their ability to thrive on greywater. Their potential for biomass production and as a food or feed source have also intrigued many architects and designers.

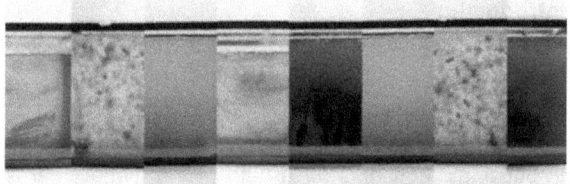

Fig.e Various examples of microalgae including: Nannochloropsis, Spirulina, Scenedesmus, and Callithamnion | Material Dynamics Lab.

When it comes to the implementation of bio-enabled systems in the constructed environment, the difference between predicted and actual outcomes are of concern, as it is with the energy performance gap. A detailed analysis of research outcomes, that can be found in the example of the bioremediation project conducted at the Center for Architecture Science and Ecology, are rare. A detailed study of these bio-enabled building components and the dissemination of the related research findings is necessary to allow for a timely implementation and a push towards an effective use in the constructed environment.

Microalgae Case Study:

In a series of research projects that are being conducted at the Material Dynamics Lab at the New Jersey Institute of Technology, team members from Architecture, Industrial Design as well as the Computer Sciences are testing the potential of integrating microalgae into the constructed environment. The early design experiments followed a highly iterative development process that integrated a series of interconnected steps (see Figure 4) and was enabled by the interdisciplinary explorations. It included the design of the system, its simulation, further development of the initial design, the production of prototypes and their testing as well as the evaluation of the test data.

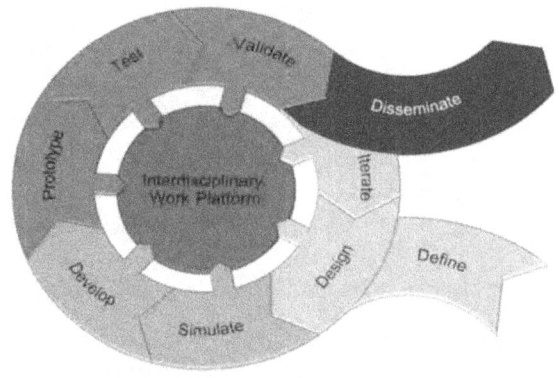

Fig.4 Interdisciplinary Work Platform |Material Dynamics Lab

The prototypes consisted of a series of photo-bioreactor panels, that could be integrated along an architectural façade. The panels were design to pivot in their setup through the integration of servomotors. On the one hand this allows the algae panels to be perfectly positioned for maximum light irrigation, and, on the other hand, it can facilitate views and access to light for human users.

For the purpose of initial data collection, the reactor panels were applied in a controlled test environment that allowed the study of light transmission as well as fluctuating transparency of the bioreactor panels (see figure 5). The data collection was greatly enhanced through the integration of the test environments into the Internet of Things (IoT). The IoT builds upon the pervasive proliferation of devices and things that have the capability to communicate and actuate in a network. In the IoT the virtual world of information technology blends with the physical objects of the real world around us.

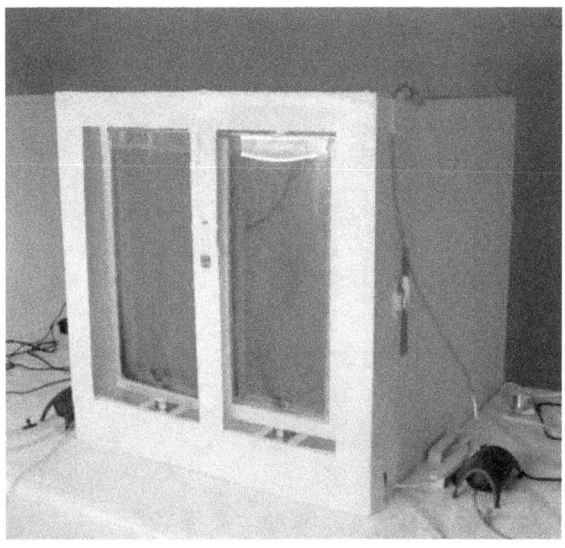

Fig.5 Algae Bioreactor in Test Environment | the Material Dynamics Lab

In the case of the prototype, the specific IoT setup, designed by George Hahn, allowed for the fine-grained data collection and data storage, to enhance the testing and validation phase of the study. The hub of the IoT platform (See Figure 6) consists of a Raspberry Pi SD-Card image, that boosts to a configured Linux system. It provides the essential services such as data storage and graphing, as well as a visual programming environment. For a detailed description of the IoT set up, including sensor and actuator integration, see Decker et al 2016[18].

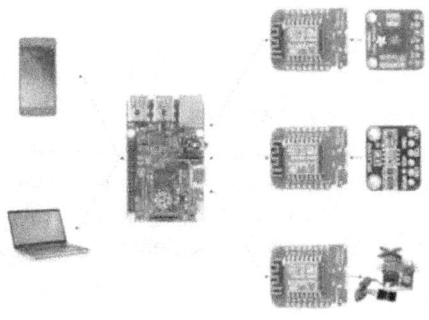

Fig. 6 IoT Platform by George Hahn

Preliminary Test Results:

The collected data showed that the positioning of the photo bioreactors to the light source influenced the growth rate of the micro algae colony. At the same time, it greatly impacted the light quality inside the test environments (see figure 7 and 8). In an architectural setting the findings would suggest a continuous conflict between the preservation of optimal living conditions for the microalgae and the maintenance of comfort levels of the human users.

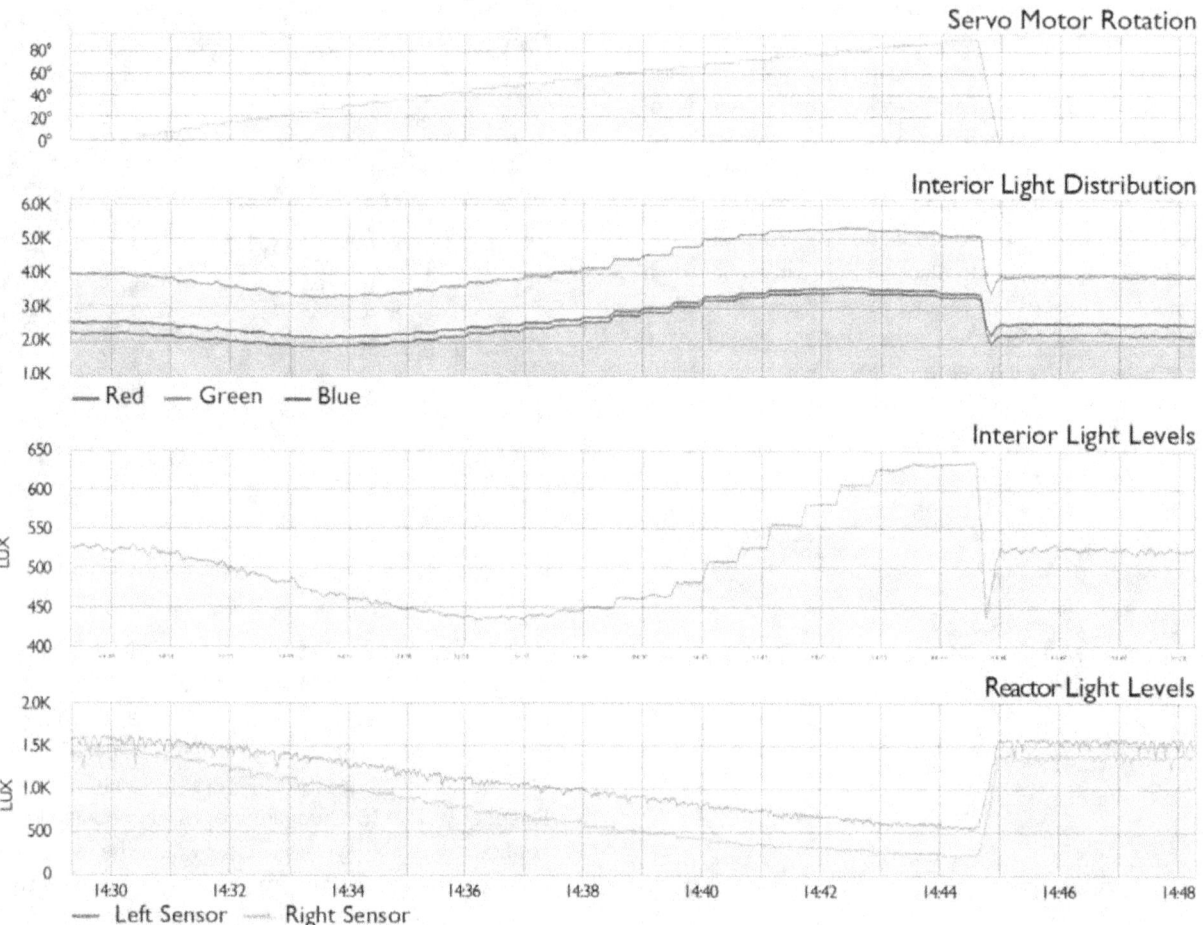

Fig. 7. Bioreactor Test Data | Material Dynamics Lab

Furthermore, the rapid growth of the algae colony, especially during the initial four to five days of the 14-day growth cycle, caused a significant drop in the transparency and translucency of the panels (see Figure 9). In an architectural environment, the lack of views during two thirds of the growth cycle, could indicate that this bio-enabled system would be best applied only to a carefully calibrated percentage of the façade's surface.

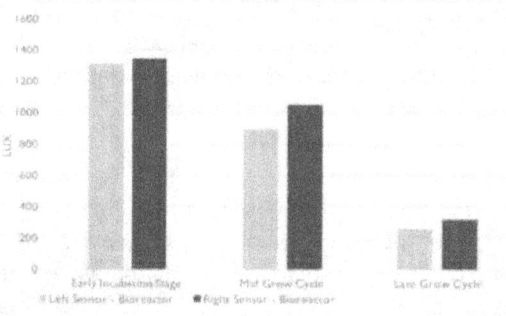

Fig.8 Light Condition in the Test Environment depending on Growth Cycle | Material Dynamics Lab.

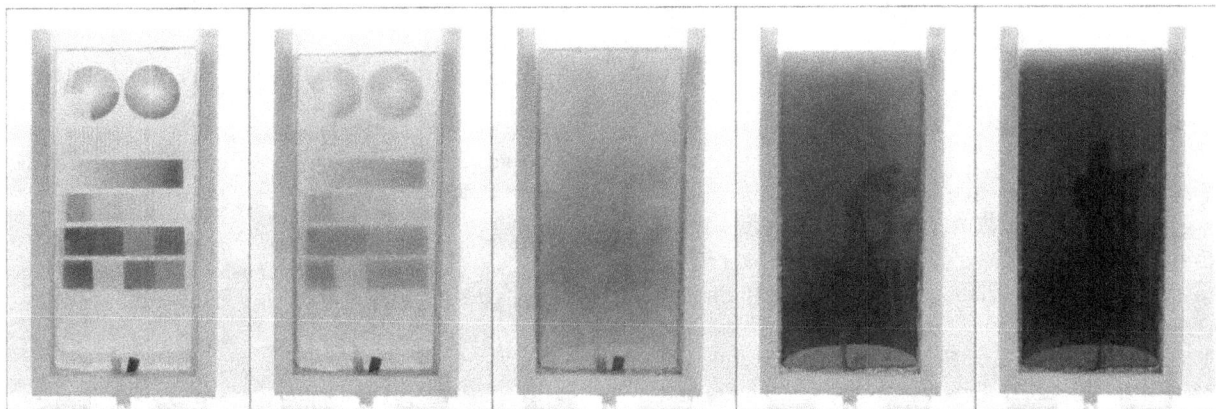

Fig. 9. Transparency documentation of bioreactor during different stages of the growth cycle | Material Dynamics Lab

The light distribution within the test environment also showed significant shift towards the green spectrum and has to be taken into account when designing for human comfort. A recent study conducted at Oxford University suggest for example that green light can play an important role in the regulation of our sleep patterns[xix].

Additionally, it has to be noted that the cleaning of the reactor panels in between the growth cycles is an important aspect for future designs that has to be contemplated. The removal of algal residue (see figure 10), depending on the bioreactor geometry, can be a cumbersome undertaking and has to be accounted for in the early design stages of the architectural application.

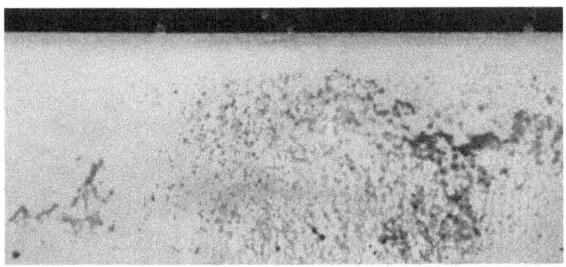

Fig.10 Algae residue in bioreactor panel | Material Dynamics Lab.

Conclusion:

The creation of an additional ecosystem along building skins and the integration of a biological organism can not only contribute positively to the building, it can also have negative impacts. This becomes especially concerning when the biological organism and the human inhabitants are competing for the same resources, such as sun light. The complexity of the environmental control system increases significantly considering that it constantly has to negotiate between the various constituencies as well as the seasonal or diurnal climatic fluctuations.

The integration of prototyping, testing, verification, and validation into the development of architectural innovations can only be beneficial. The empirical evidence, acquired by observation and experimentation, gives us the opportunity to evaluate if we are designing the right intervention for a given architectural application (validation). It also allows us to question, if the designs of the specific building blocks are indeed adequate for their intended use (verification). Even if the validation of isolated building components and subsystems seem like a small step towards an improvement of the constructed environment, it could present us with the opportunity to improve current simulation models used in architecture.

The utilization of the IoT in this study has been proven to be an effective tool to streamline the data collection process. It also enhanced the collaboration between the various team members, since it allows for the access of sensor data and the actuating features of the prototype even from remote locations.

By integrating the IoT into early investigation stages of new technologies, this strategy might even allow for the development of pioneering building blocks for smart buildings and a move towards smart cities.

ACKNOWLEDGEMENTS

The research presented in this paper has been supported by a NJIT URI grant as well as the NJIT Center of Building Knowledge. The author would like to thank Dr. Wen Zhang and Likun Hua from the Department of Civil and Environmental Engineering at NJIT, as well as Dr. Eric Fortune from the Department of Biology at NJIT, for their support, insights and advise throughout the research. Special thanks also go to Lauren Harris, George Hahn, Andrew Biron for their dedication to this project during the prototyping stage.

Notes:

1 "Tracking Clean Energy Progress 2015." Tracking Clean Energy Progress 2015. Accessed February 28, 2017. https://www.iea.org/etp/tracking2015/.

2 Anderegg, William RL, James W. Prall, Jacob Harold, and Stephen H. Schneider. "Expert credibility in climate change." Proceedings of the National Academy of Sciences 107, no. 27 (2010): 12107-12109.

3 Anderegg, William RL, James W. Prall, Jacob Harold, and Stephen H. Schneider. "Expert credibility in climate change." Proceedings of the National Academy of Sciences 107, no. 27 (2010): 12107-12109.

4 Klepeis, Neil E., William C. Nelson, Wayne R. Ott, John P. Robinson, Andy M. Tsang, Paul Switzer, Joseph V. Behar, Stephen C. Hern, and William H. Engelmann. "The National Human Activity Pattern Survey (NHAPS): a resource for assessing exposure to environmental pollutants." Journal of Exposure Science and Environmental Epidemiology 11, no. 3 (2001): 231.

5 Dobbs, Richard, Jaana Remes, James Manyika, Charles Roxburgh, Sven Smit, and Fabian Schaer. Urban world: Cities and the rise of the consuming class. McKinsey Global Institute, 2012.

6 Shaikh, Pervez Hameed, Nursyarizal Bin Mohd Nor, Perumal Nallagownden, Irraivan Elamvazuthi, and Taib Ibrahim. "A review on optimized control systems for building energy and comfort management of smart sustainable buildings." Renewable and Sustainable Energy Reviews 34 (2014): 409-429.

7 ibid.

8 de Wilde, P., and Alba Fuertes. "The gap between simulated and measured energy performance: A case study across six identical new-build flats in the UK." (2015).

9 De Wilde, Pieter. "The gap between predicted and measured energy performance of buildings: A framework for investigation." Automation in Construction 41 (2014): 40-49.

10 ibid.

11 Krietemeyer, Bess, and Kurt Rogler. "Real-time multi-zone building performance impacts of occupant interaction with dynamic facade systems." (2015).

12 Brownell, Blaine Erickson, and Marc Swackhamer. Hypernatural: Architecture's New Relationship with Nature. 2015.

13 Park, Daekwon, and Martin Bechthold. "Designing Biologically-inspired Smart Building Systems: Processes and Guidelines." International Journal of Architectural Computing 11, no. 4 (2013): 437-463.

14 Oberndorfer, Erica, Jeremy Lundholm, Brad Bass, Reid R. Coffman, Hitesh Doshi, Nigel Dunnett, Stuart Gaffin, Manfred Köhler, Karen KY Liu, and Bradley Rowe. "Green roofs as urban ecosystems: ecological structures, functions, and services." BioScience 57, no. 10 (2007): 823-833.

15 "Active Bioremediation Systems." CASE. Accessed March 10, 2017. http://www.case.rpi.edu/page/project.php?pageid=3.

16 Aydogan, Ahu, and Lupita D. Montoya. "Formaldehyde removal by common indoor plant species and various growing media." Atmospheric environment 45, no. 16 (2011): 2675-2682.

17 Henrikson, Robert, and Mark Edwards. "Imagine Our Algae Future." Visionary Algae Architecture and Landscape Designs (2012).

18 Decker, Martina, George Hahn, and Libertad M. Harris. "Bio-Enabled Façade Systems-Managing Complexity of Life through Emergent Technologies." (2016).

xix Pilorz, Violetta, Shu KE Tam, Steven Hughes, Carina A. Pothecary, Aarti Jagannath, Mark W. Hankins, David M. Bannerman et al. "Melanopsin regulates both sleep-promoting and arousal-promoting responses to light." PLoS Biol 14, no. 6 (2016): e1002482.

www.ingramcontent.com/pod-product-compliance
Lightning Source LLC
Chambersburg PA
CBHW080903170526

45158CB00008B/1976